Lecture Notes in Computer Science 9193

Commenced Publication in 1973
Founding and Former Series Editors:
Gerhard Goos, Juris Hartmanis, and Jan van Leeuwen

More information about this series at http://www.springer.com/series/7409

Jia Zhou · Gavriel Salvendy (Eds.)

Human Aspects of IT for the Aged Population

Design for Aging

First International Conference, ITAP 2015
Held as Part of HCI International 2015
Los Angeles, CA, USA, August 2–7, 2015
Proceedings, Part I

 Springer

Editors
Jia Zhou
Chongqing University
Chongqing
P.R. China

Gavriel Salvendy
Purdue University
West Lafayette, IN
USA

and

Tsinghua University
Beijing
P.R. China

ISSN 0302-9743   ISSN 1611-3349   (electronic)
Lecture Notes in Computer Science
ISBN 978-3-319-20891-6   ISBN 978-3-319-20892-3   (eBook)
DOI 10.1007/978-3-319-20892-3

Library of Congress Control Number: 2015942475

LNCS Sublibrary: SL3 – Information Systems and Applications, incl. Internet/Web, and HCI

Springer Cham Heidelberg New York Dordrecht London

Printed on acid-free paper

Springer International Publishing AG Switzerland is part of Springer Science+Business Media
(www.springer.com)

Foreword

The 17th International Conference on Human-Computer Interaction, HCI International 2015, was held in Los Angeles, CA, USA, during 2–7 August 2015. The event incorporated the 15 conferences/thematic areas listed on the following page.

A total of 4843 individuals from academia, research institutes, industry, and governmental agencies from 73 countries submitted contributions, and 1462 papers and 246 posters have been included in the proceedings. These papers address the latest research and development efforts and highlight the human aspects of design and use of computing systems. The papers thoroughly cover the entire field of Human-Computer Interaction, addressing major advances in knowledge and effective use of computers in a variety of application areas. The volumes constituting the full 28-volume set of the conference proceedings are listed on pages VII and VIII.

I would like to thank the Program Board Chairs and the members of the Program Boards of all thematic areas and affiliated conferences for their contribution to the highest scientific quality and the overall success of the HCI International 2015 conference.

This conference could not have been possible without the continuous and unwavering support and advice of the founder, Conference General Chair Emeritus and Conference Scientific Advisor, Prof. Gavriel Salvendy. For their outstanding efforts, I would like to express my appreciation to the Communications Chair and Editor of HCI International News, Dr. Abbas Moallem, and the Student Volunteer Chair, Prof. Kim-Phuong L. Vu. Finally, for their dedicated contribution towards the smooth organization of HCI International 2015, I would like to express my gratitude to Maria Pitsoulaki and George Paparoulis, General Chair Assistants.

May 2015

Constantine Stephanidis
General Chair, HCI International 2015

HCI International 2015 Thematic Areas and Affiliated Conferences

Thematic areas:

- Human-Computer Interaction (HCI 2015)
- Human Interface and the Management of Information (HIMI 2015)

Affiliated conferences:

- 12th International Conference on Engineering Psychology and Cognitive Ergonomics (EPCE 2015)
- 9th International Conference on Universal Access in Human-Computer Interaction (UAHCI 2015)
- 7th International Conference on Virtual, Augmented and Mixed Reality (VAMR 2015)
- 7th International Conference on Cross-Cultural Design (CCD 2015)
- 7th International Conference on Social Computing and Social Media (SCSM 2015)
- 9th International Conference on Augmented Cognition (AC 2015)
- 6th International Conference on Digital Human Modeling and Applications in Health, Safety, Ergonomics and Risk Management (DHM 2015)
- 4th International Conference on Design, User Experience and Usability (DUXU 2015)
- 3rd International Conference on Distributed, Ambient and Pervasive Interactions (DAPI 2015)
- 3rd International Conference on Human Aspects of Information Security, Privacy and Trust (HAS 2015)
- 2nd International Conference on HCI in Business (HCIB 2015)
- 2nd International Conference on Learning and Collaboration Technologies (LCT 2015)
- 1st International Conference on Human Aspects of IT for the Aged Population (ITAP 2015)

Conference Proceedings Volumes Full List

1. LNCS 9169, Human-Computer Interaction: Design and Evaluation (Part I), edited by Masaaki Kurosu
2. LNCS 9170, Human-Computer Interaction: Interaction Technologies (Part II), edited by Masaaki Kurosu
3. LNCS 9171, Human-Computer Interaction: Users and Contexts (Part III), edited by Masaaki Kurosu
4. LNCS 9172, Human Interface and the Management of Information: Information and Knowledge Design (Part I), edited by Sakae Yamamoto
5. LNCS 9173, Human Interface and the Management of Information: Information and Knowledge in Context (Part II), edited by Sakae Yamamoto
6. LNAI 9174, Engineering Psychology and Cognitive Ergonomics, edited by Don Harris
7. LNCS 9175, Universal Access in Human-Computer Interaction: Access to Today's Technologies (Part I), edited by Margherita Antona and Constantine Stephanidis
8. LNCS 9176, Universal Access in Human-Computer Interaction: Access to Interaction (Part II), edited by Margherita Antona and Constantine Stephanidis
9. LNCS 9177, Universal Access in Human-Computer Interaction: Access to Learning, Health and Well-Being (Part III), edited by Margherita Antona and Constantine Stephanidis
10. LNCS 9178, Universal Access in Human-Computer Interaction: Access to the Human Environment and Culture (Part IV), edited by Margherita Antona and Constantine Stephanidis
11. LNCS 9179, Virtual, Augmented and Mixed Reality, edited by Randall Shumaker and Stephanie Lackey
12. LNCS 9180, Cross-Cultural Design: Methods, Practice and Impact (Part I), edited by P.L. Patrick Rau
13. LNCS 9181, Cross-Cultural Design: Applications in Mobile Interaction, Education, Health, Transport and Cultural Heritage (Part II), edited by P.L. Patrick Rau
14. LNCS 9182, Social Computing and Social Media, edited by Gabriele Meiselwitz
15. LNAI 9183, Foundations of Augmented Cognition, edited by Dylan D. Schmorrow and Cali M. Fidopiastis
16. LNCS 9184, Digital Human Modeling and Applications in Health, Safety, Ergonomics and Risk Management: Human Modeling (Part I), edited by Vincent G. Duffy
17. LNCS 9185, Digital Human Modeling and Applications in Health, Safety, Ergonomics and Risk Management: Ergonomics and Health (Part II), edited by Vincent G. Duffy
18. LNCS 9186, Design, User Experience, and Usability: Design Discourse (Part I), edited by Aaron Marcus
19. LNCS 9187, Design, User Experience, and Usability: Users and Interactions (Part II), edited by Aaron Marcus
20. LNCS 9188, Design, User Experience, and Usability: Interactive Experience Design (Part III), edited by Aaron Marcus

Human Aspects of IT for the Aged Population

Program Board Chairs: Gavriel Salvendy, USA & P.R. China, and Jia Zhou, P.R. China

- Jenay Beer, USA
- Marc-Eric Bobillier Chaumon, France
- Alan H.S. Chan, Hong Kong
- Veena Chattaraman, USA
- George Demiris, USA
- Jesús Favela, Mexico
- Tova Gamliel, Israel
- Mohammad Anwar Hossain, Saudi Arabia
- Sri Kurniawan, USA
- Jiunn-Woei (Allen) Lian, Taiwan
- Eugene Loos, The Netherlands
- Jean-Claude Marquie, France
- Tracy L. Mitzner, USA
- Lisa J. Molnar, USA
- Karen Renaud, UK
- Marie Sjölinder, Sweden
- António J.S. Teixeira, Portugal
- Patrice Terrier, France
- Gregg Vanderheiden, USA
- Ying Wang, R.P. China
- Wan Chul Yoon, Korea
- Martina Ziefle, Germany

The full list with the Program Board Chairs and the members of the Program Boards of all thematic areas and affiliated conferences is available online at:

http://www.hci.international/2015/

HCI International 2016

The 18th International Conference on Human-Computer Interaction, HCI International 2016, will be held jointly with the affiliated conferences in Toronto, Canada, at the Westin Harbour Castle Hotel, 17–22 July 2016. It will cover a broad spectrum of themes related to Human-Computer Interaction, including theoretical issues, methods, tools, processes, and case studies in HCI design, as well as novel interaction techniques, interfaces, and applications. The proceedings will be published by Springer. More information will be available on the conference website: http://2016.hci.international/.

General Chair
Prof. Constantine Stephanidis
University of Crete and ICS-FORTH
Heraklion, Crete, Greece
Email: general_chair@hcii2016.org

http://2016.hci.international/

Contents – Part I

ICT Use and Acceptance

Aging, the Web and Social Media

Contents – Part II

Home and Work Support

Smart Environments and AAL

Communication, Games and Entertainment

HCI Design and Evaluation Methods for the Elderly

The Benefits of Involving Older People in the Design Process

Britt Östlund(✉)

Royal Institute of Technology, Stockholm, Sweden
brittost@kth.se

Abstract. The more experience we get of involving older people in innovation and design processes, the more we recognize the benefits of having to do with life experience as input to the development of digital products and services. Heterogeneity raises personalization as a key component in design. This paper argues that old people are an asset in innovation processes, which is illustrated by projects conducted in Sweden from 1992 to 2014. The aim is to present how older people contribute to the development and what hinders them. The goal of these projects was to promote participation of older people during the design process but to varying degrees depending on the question. Different degrees of participation and involvement are discussed based on the "participation ladder", on an idea of Arnstein from 1969 and on conclusions from innovation research.

Keywords: Life experiences · Participative design · Older innovators

1 Introduction

Aged, older, elderly – what do we call those who have reached old age? Depending on our understanding of old age it makes a difference when designing for and with old people. The problem is that aging and later life is still too little problematized compared with the technology being tested [1, 2]. While technologies has shifted over the years from easy-to-use interfaces, GPS support and alarms to robotics and systems for monitoring, the image of old people remains more or less the same. According to stereotypes, old people are socially isolated and lonely, and they experience physical and social losses that are to be compensated for by cleverly designed technologies.

The purpose of this paper is to add leverage why involvement of older users in design is beneficial. Not only do their contributions result in more accurate solutions and lead us faster towards the goal, they also make design more innovative and help preventing prejudices and stereotypes. I will present conclusions from innovation research to back up these arguments and illustrate various degrees of participation with examples from Swedish design projects.

1.1 Design for Whom

Looking back at funding schemes for research and development of technology for old people during the last thirty years, the expectation that technology is the driving force

© Springer International Publishing Switzerland 2015
J. Zhou and G. Salvendy (Eds.): ITAP 2015, Part I, LNCS 9193, pp. 3–14, 2015.
DOI: 10.1007/978-3-319-20892-3_1

for change is pretty obvious. The European Commission, for example, expect the framework programs to meet a range of presumed needs among the older population, and to manage the increased costs of health care and social services. Their argument for the IT society is evident from the beginning – older people have much to gain from an increase in communication and access to information [3]. Recently, the issue has taken a turn in the EC. 2012 was proclaimed as the Year for Active Ageing. The purpose was to highlight reforms for helping people to stay in charge of their own lives for as long as possible as they age and, where possible, to contribute to the economy and society [4]. The WHO report before World Health Day 2012 took another step when launching the call for "Adding life to years" by connecting a longer life with participation and attitudes [5]. These are steps which make a difference for designers, when trying to understand how to enhance later life for ageing populations. The step takes us away from the image of the elderly as a single homogeneous group, whose needs can be generalized to apply to all elderly people, to a more nuanced picture.

It is true that ageing populations increase. Between 2000 and 2050, the proportion of the world's population over 60 years will double from about 11 % to 22 %. The absolute number of people aged 60 years and over is expected to increase from 605 million to 2 billion over the same period [5]. It is also true that the total fertility rate 2006 was below its replacement level in all OECD countries except Mexico, Turkey, Iceland and the United States [6]. These numbers probably indicate that there will be an increase in needs for health care and social services as the consumption of health care services increase with age. But it does not reflect the fact that the majority of older populations continue their life course as independent citizens without incorporating the role of being a patient or a care receiver as a part of their identity. This is obvious at least when it comes to Swedish statistics. In Sweden, this group constitutes less than 20 % of the population over the age of 60. They encompass those receiving public health care and home help services provided by public or private enterprises (8.2 %) or those living in nursing homes (7.5 %) [7]. Relatives and friends also perform services, which in Sweden covers 75 % of the total caring needs [8]. The question of how to measure this is an ongoing discussion. Municipalities are obliged to give anyone who needs help. However, the fact that more than 80 % are not patients or care receivers seem to be a hidden secret. The dominating image of old people as a homogenous group with similar needs and demands has for a long time been the prevailing notion. The consequence is that older people become characterized in political documents as well as in media in terms of disease, incompetence, stagnation and decline [9]. Traditional images of aging based on perceptions of needs that have been institutionalized for a long time were partially obsolete already in the 1990s. Even today few players have been able to capture the demands of old people living a modern life [10]. The outcome is that even those in need of home help services or living in nursing homes are minorities – yet they still define the stereotype for the entire aging population. These stereotypes are limited because they focus on aging as a downhill process by physical and social loss and they frame older technology users as passive recipients of technology. Current design practices for older persons, therefore, imply a threefold risk. They are likely to generate technology which is unattractive for older consumers, which provides limited cues for meaningful activity, and which suppresses the co-creational inputs of older persons to innovation [11]. The good news is that we are now at the frontier between the old and new images of aging.

Today, more and more designers experience that these stereotypic images crack when old people themselves are let into projects as participants. When fictive older users are replaced by real older users, you quickly discover that this is about a diverse group of people characterized by heterogeneity. The categorization of older people as a homogeneous group is quickly replaced by a more individualized approach. In fact, longitudinal research shows that individual differences increase with age [12]. This means that forty year olds are more homogenous compared to eighty year olds. However, the heterogeneity among older people does not mean they do not have common features. It has been suggested that retirement may be one thing they have in common as it involves a new social arena with other expectations from themselves and society. Other common experiences may be that they are among the oldest in the community and thus have life experiences that younger lack, which has been shown to influence their priorities including when it comes to new technology. To be treated like old can also be a shared experience as well as generations of old people may have lived through the same historical events [13].

1.2 Design to Change Attitudes

Older people have a history of being invisible. Even though the images of old people are changing it is still relevant to state that they are neglected as users and consumers of new information and communication technologies [14]. Lay end users is a concept that was introduced to differentiate between those involved and not involved in the expert discourse as a part of the design process [31]. Implicated users is another concept, where users are defined as "those silent or not present but affected by the action" [15]. These implicated users consist either of those who are physically present but discursively constructed and targeted by others, or of those who are physically present but who are generally ignored or made invisible by those in power. Old people belong to both these groups. They are definitely present but often as a discursive construct, not as participants.

One reason why it is important to give the elderly more opportunities to express their own needs and desires is that this is strongly related to influence and visibility. Designers can thus affect significantly and accelerate the change in attitude to the elderly. A thought-provoking parallel could be drawn to women's struggle for power over the situation. The author Betty Friedan compares the view on women in the 1970s in the United States with the current view on older people [16]. She discovers that there are no images of aging she can identify with. When older people are described, it is always relative to others, especially to those who are active and productive. It's always someone else who defines the problems, not the aging man himself with his experience. This was also the situation for women, whose experiences long lacked a name or an expression. Friedan describes how experts' awareness and identification of older people's needs and problems are as invisible as when men previously identified women. The change came when women themselves began to articulate their own problems and experiences.

One challenge is to reinforce the view of older people as active, involved and experienced and broaden their roles beyond being patients and care receivers. The shift from considering users as passive objects of research to giving them a role as active and pro-active innovators include concepts such as "universal design" and "empowerment" [17]. These concepts were coined in the context of disability research that paved the way for a broader, non-discriminatory view but also a deeper understanding of how design contributes to improved quality of life. Eric von Hippel launched the concept "lead users" to show that the user is the carrier of the aspects necessary for the innovation process [18, 19]. This has now been replicated in a number of concepts related to the aging population and digital development. These include "personaliza-tion" [20], "social needs" [21], and "the innosumer" [11].

2 Method

Depending on whether one considers users as objects or as subjects, they get different roles in the design process. Using them as research objects, the designer is seeking generalizations to be applied in design. As a subject they participate themselves in design and development. Moreover the domestication of new technologies in people's life spaces is far from predictable. The fact is that it is when technology comes into the user's hands and is contextualized that its real value turns out [22, 23]. Including user's home or daily context takes us closer to reality, meaning discovering unpredictable aspects and innovative ideas. Depending on what we want to achieve, what steps users themselves are willing to take or are already taking, their participation will be high or low. The choice of method is determined by the question, and in turn, the extent to which we give users the opportunity to participate. Active citizens are in a sense a prerequisite for the development of society in general, but a conscious choice of methods provides greater opportunities to go further with projects. When users are involved in the development of technology, it means that they will be jointly responsible for the results, they will better understand the consequences and may for these reasons continue to contribute to improvements.

2.1 How to Make Them Participate

One way to illustrate the degrees of participation is the participation ladder [24]. This is a ladder developed in the context of housing planning in the US in the 1960s to illustrate the degree of participation of citizens in the planning process. Today, we can use this ladder both as a mirror to understand on what step we ourselves are collab-orating with users and as a framework for different options of participation. See Fig. 1.

The ladder can have many steps. Arnstein split the steps into three categories of participation. First, complete citizen participation and influence by the citizens perhaps on their own initiative. An example is if you belong to a group that has initiated a senior housing to be built. The second step, symbolic participation, includes consul-tation and information. This is probably the step where most design activities take place and where we invite people to test prototypes. The lowest level, non-participation,

Citizen participation
Citizen control
Delegated power
Partnership

Symbolic participation
Consultation
Information

Non-participation
Treatments
Manipulation

Fig. 1. The participation ladder on an idea by Arnstein (1969)

requires a pretty passive user. However, this should not be interpreted only in negative terms. General information to households, for example, is very important at certain stages. The term manipulation is however what we should avoid since it runs the risk of violating ethics and human rights.

3 Examples of Design for Various Degrees of Participation

This ladder will illustrate the degree of user participation in relation to the kind of results obtained in the Swedish design projects presented below. The projects were part of the Ageing and design program at the Department of Design sciences at Lund University 2005–2014, except for the project about Home shopping terminals that were part of the research at The Institute for Tema Research at Linköping University 1992–1995. The projects were different in their goals and nature but followed the leading principle to include older participants in every project. Here we worked with five steps to clarify the choice of methods. The lowest step will not be exemplified since we lack such project examples (Fig. 2).

3.1 How Can We Get Access to Products and Services We Need?

The first example illustrates older people as co-actors driving the changes they want to accomplish. In a project initiated by a group of fifteen women, 63–69 years old, the purpose was to investigate available services in the local neighbourhood directed

1.Older people are co-actors and are themselves driving the changes they want to accomplish.

2. Older people participate as the experts on their own life situation.

3. Older people contribute with their own views in consultation together with others.

4. Older people recieve information and/or being the subject todifferent types of operations.

5. Manipulation – people are objects for other's actions.

Fig. 2. Levels of participation distributed on the idea of the participation ladder (Arnstein 1969)

towards independent older people living at home in the city of Stockholm and the possibilities of organizing local networks in which they were involved themselves in the performance of services. The older women noted early on that they lacked access to adequate services and were particularly critical of the municipal elderly care service: They realized that it was not the old people's needs, but rather the service provider's priorities which governed the supply of help they could receive. Nor did the commercial market offer the services they wanted to purchase. They were in particular interested in the access to information and the potential of IT-development including both hardware and software.

The assessment ran from September 2007 to May 2008 and included working meetings, focus groups and a workshop on technical design. The workshop was organized with expertise in industrial design, electronics and construction of computer systems. Individual examples and ideas were discussed and requirements were specified. The most important requirement was to keep the power to interpret the needs and demands within the group.

In summary, the participants came to the conclusion that the services available today primarily address old people who are vulnerable, ill and chiefly require help with household matters. The study results suggest the need for the public care sector to re-evaluate their supply and better assess changes in demand. There is also room for the development of various forms of services and business models that better match the needs and demands of independent older people. Access to information was discussed as necessary to become an active consumer. However, none of these products existed at that time in the way the older people wished. The phone appeared to be a simple and accessible way to communicate but was no longer optimal for everything due to automated, key pressing systems for delivering information, a variety of interfaces and mobile phones. Access to the Internet was still troublesome for them and they felt marginalized when they heard on TV that, "The information is available at www. . . ." announced at television or in papers. The women responded specifically to the fact that their experience of using technology was not taken advantage of. Neither were they attracted to use 'phones for the elderly "because they found that this could be stigmatizing. They were also disappointed of how phones in general were designed. They concluded that these products had hardly been tested before they were labelled as being products for older people.

As a result, they organised a telephone based network to support each other in various ways in the local neighbourhood. Besides the network this endeavour show that there is a lack of services demanded by old people and that the nature of these demands can only be understood from their point of view.

3.2 Will New Technology Based on Existing Habits Increase Acceptance and Use?

The second example is about older people as experts of their own life situation. In another project with eleven older users, 57–80 years old, the purpose was to study the extent to which older people's lifelong experience of watching television reduced their uncertainty when faced with new TV-based applications. The project was initiated by a research group in collaboration with a company: In view AB (later ippi AB). In view AB provided the project with a patented system for asynchronous communication – "ippi" – used as a basis for a prototype communication device utilizing the participant's television as the primary interface. See Figs. 3 and 4.

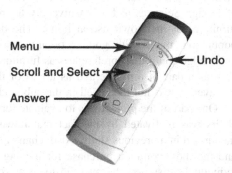

Menu

Scroll and Select

Answer

Undo

Fig. 3. ippi™

Fig. 4. The ippi remote control with wheel button

The implementation and testing of the system were structured as an iterative design process based on the necessity to get access to users' daily context and TV-habits to understand the potential of the prototype. The implementation included conceptual development, a six-month test period in the homes of eleven users with usability tests and interviews, monthly focus groups and information gathered by a backup function that also provided the users with immediate help with the technology if necessary.

The results show that while the use of TV as a metaphor or platform succeeded in getting the older users to try out and use the ippi prototype, it did not contribute primarily to using the ippi on a daily basis during the test period. Rather, participants' access to a social context or a social network determined the extent of usage. There was a difference between what was easy to use in terms of the interface, and what was easy and worth using in a social everyday context on the other hand. In order to be used, a new product of this type must add value and that value depends upon integration into daily communication [25]. This is the kind of "sticky information" that von Hippel ascribes to users and which can be obtained only in relation to the users themselves and their daily context [26]. The length of the tests at home also was of considerable importance to understand the role of technology in relation to established routines and habits.

The product is today used in about 25 local communities in Sweden. However, since the public market for these kinds of products is still quite undeveloped the company sold the product to Care Communications AB and we do not have information about its future.

3.3   What Are the Preferences for Furniture Among Older Consumers?

The third example describes older people contributing with their views in consultations. A sub study of the PLUS-furniture project conducted 2008–2010 was a laboratory test where thirty men and women, 57–87 years old, tried out furniture, more precisely to evaluate properties and characteristics of chairs [27]. The PLUS-furniture project including seven Swedish furniture design companies aimed at exploring the use of furniture and activities among the older population. The background was a common interest in The Swedish Wood and Furniture Industry Association and the Department of Design Sciences at Lund University to investigate older people's preferences for furniture for their own use at home. The demographic trend of a growing elderly population, many with good economy, was well known. However, there was no knowledge about their preferences as furniture consumers. The IT-aspect was stressed both as a part of furniture and as a part of the situation where the furniture is used, however, it was not discussed in the sub study presented here.

One part of the project was to evaluate furniture on the market. The choice to study chairs was motivated by the fact that it was the type of furniture most frequently mentioned in a previous study. Also, chairs are the most frequently used furniture type and the most common purchase for nursing homes [28]. However, it was the older individual consumers that were in focus as companies identified them as an unknown group of customers who do not just represent a growing percentage of the population but, above all, are more active, healthier and have greater purchasing power than previously and who do not want products that communicate aging and helplessness.

The study was conducted in a usability laboratory with chairs that the companies picked out themselves based on their assumptions of what older consumers prefer. A method for evaluating user satisfaction through structured interviews was used to highlight participants' interaction with furniture in a systematic sequence of human-product interaction. For example, the systematic sequence comprised items such as looking at, ingress into, sitting in, egress from and moving the chairs.

The results showed that the participants displayed different needs of and wishes for comfort. The participants shared an appreciation for chairs with properties and characteristics suiting their bodies, homes and desired identities.

The companies integrated part of these results in their design and marketing. To test a selection of chairs in a laboratory proved to be a relevant match, and answered questions about sitting, egress and moving the chair. The results however suggest that the designer should consider the experience of comfort and previous experience with similar furniture, data which requires access to user context outside the laboratory [27].

3.4   Trying to Impose the Visions of IT-Society on Older Care Receivers

The fourth example show older people being the object for new IT-systems. In a study conducted between 1992 and 1994, the first home shopping terminals to support elderly people in Sweden were evaluated with twenty older users, 80–102 years old, living at home and dependent on the public home help service for daily shopping of groceries. The purpose was to examine to what extent such a home shopping system could replace store shopping and how it intervened with the users' relations with the home help service. The adventure was initiated by the Municipality of Malmoe, the National Telecommunications Authority – Televerket and Samhall, a state-owned Swedish company assigned to provide meaningful work for people with disabilities. More than 800 home shopping terminals were tested among elderly persons dependent on help with the shopping of daily groceries. The purpose was that they should do the shopping from home, on their own or together with their personal caregiver from the home help service. In doing this, the caregiver was supposed to free up time which could be spent together with the care receiver. At the same time, the municipality would save money. The time spent and the costs saved were calculated in detail. To pick up the groceries at the store and delivering them to the homes was done by people employed at Samhall. On the first page of the main regional newspaper, there was a picture of four men representing actors involved in this venture assured that "*this is the future home helper for elderly people. The home help service is first out using computer shopping*". They proudly announced that the home help service were the first at launching "computer shopping" and thus were supposed to get a first glimpse into the future. Like the Bangemann report, this venture identified the needs of elderly people as a perfect fit into IT-development [3].

The result of this venture was described in a dissertation where the importance of technology in everyday life was studied from the perspective of older people (Östlund 1995). Very few terminals were actually used by the elderly or by their care givers. The resistance among the elderly people was misinterpreted, the efficiency of the relationship between the home help service and the elderly care receivers was misunderstood and the time needed to make the system work miscalculated. The majority of the elderly that were provided with home shopping terminals did not make use of them; neither did the home help services because of a range of technical failures. Being active users in charge of their own lives and with a lifelong experience of technological change they didn't find that the home shopping terminals had any comparative advantage to the existing shopping practice. Consequently, increased usability, meaning a more usable and appropriate interface would not change the situation.

The venture ended after two years trials. It was overthrown by another solution procured by the municipality: a car delivering groceries once or twice a week, picking up shopping lists and assisting the elderly with carrying in the packages. If this example will constitute a step towards home shopping on the Internet as we know it today, will show in a later historical perspective. Nevertheless, it is an example of a technically driven venture, typical of the early days of IT development. Elderly people were discovered as a potential target group, or at least as fictive users with, what seems to be, needs that met the technical possibilities of that time.

4 Conclusions

The projects above illustrate different degrees of user participation and demonstrate the importance of choosing appropriate methods for what you want to achieve. Obviously, older participants can contribute to design in various ways. The complete citizen participation on the upper steps of the ladder brings more options to sustainable changes compared to the lower steps, of which the designer is more in control. The advantages of involving older users are first, that they have lifelong experience of technology use. Second, their experiences include a wide range of technological changes and technological development. Hence, they are familiar with changes. Third, the effect of aging makes them more pragmatic compared to when they were younger. This is a consequence of that they now have to economize their time and energy. They are willing to learn to use new technology if it is worthwhile but not because it is new. This experience, combined with the ability to see the big picture is nearly unbeatable.

Some learning lessons from innovation research prove that life experienced people fit very well into what is needed for successful innovation processes. In this paper, the examples reflect both innovation processes i.e. driving changes where defining what kind of IT will be the best support is a part of the project as in the first example, and design processes where the technological support is already defined but needs to be designed as in the second and third examples.

Readings of Porter and von Hippel prove that some of their findings and theories should be worthwhile applying in this field, trying out the benefits of involving old people in design [18, 19, 29]. The readings of these authors make me draw the conclusion that the following factors are among those contributing to successful innovation processes: high demands and difficult problems that offer resistance but include users that are patient and experienced. Old people meet these demands since they are experienced, pragmatic, patient and trustworthy. The latter can of course change over time if values in society change. On the other hand, dependency and independency probably effect the relationship to project leaders as well as to care givers. The benefit of involving older users is, in terms of innovations, especially important when it comes to their participation on the higher steps of the ladder. They are not, as has been often referred to, laggards, they are also early adopters if they get the chance [30].

Acknowledgements. The author owe many thanks to Sabina Fabrizi for proof reading the manuscript.

References

1. Gerontechnology 9th World Conference in Taiwan, vol 13, no. 2 (2014)
2. Graafmans, J., Taipale, V., Charness, N. (eds.): Gerontechnology. A Sustainable Investment in the Future. IOS Press, Amsterdam (1998)
3. Bangemann, M.: Europé and the global information society. Recommendations to the European Council, European Union. High-Level Group on the Information Society. European Commission, Brussels (1994)
4. European Year for active Ageing (2012). http://ec.europa.eu/archives/ey2012/
5. WHO: Good health. Add life to years. Global brief for World Health Day 2012 (2012)
6. OECD Factbook 2009. Evolution of the population (2009)
7. Swedish National Board for Health and Welfare: Statistics – Social Welfare (2002)
8. Szebehely, M. (ed.): Hemhjälp i Norden - illustrationer och reflektioner, [Home help in the Nordic countries - illustrations and reflections]. Studentlitteratur, Lund (2003)
9. Nilsson, M.: Våra äldre. Om konstruktioner av äldre i offentligheten [Our older. If constructions of older people in public] Linköping Studies in Arts and Science No. 450, Linköpings universitet (2008)
10. Sawchuk, A.K.: From gloom to boom. Age, identity and target marketing. In: Featherstone, M., Wernick, A. (eds.) Images of Aging. Cultural representations of later life, pp. 173–187. Routledge, London (1995)
11. Peine, A., Rollwagen, I., Neven, L.: The rise of the innosumer. Rethinking older persons as users of technology. Accepted for Publication in JN for Technological Forecasting and Social Change (2013)
12. Eriksson, B.G.: Studying ageing: experiences, description, variation, prediction and explanation. Gothenburg Studies in Sociology, no. 41. University of Gothenburg, Göteborg (2010)
13. Östlund, B.: Design paradigmes and misunderstood technology. The case of older users. In: Jeager, B. (ed.) Young Technologies in Old Hands – An International View on Senior Citizen's Utilization of ICT. DJØF Publishing, Copenhagen (2005)
14. Oudshoorn, N., Pinch, T. (eds.): How Users Matter. The Co-construction of Users and Technology. MIT Press, Cambridge (2005)
15. Clarke, A.E., Olesen, V.L.: Revisioning Women, Health and Healing: Feminist Cultural and Technoscience Perspectives. Routledge, New York (1998)
16. Friedan, B.: The Fountain of Age. Simon and Schuster, New York (1993)
17. Melander Wikman, A.: Definitioner och modeller för e-hälsa. In: Gard, G., Melander Wikman, A. (red.) E-hälsainnovationer, Metoder, Interventioner och Perspektiv, ss. 17–31. Studentlitteratur AB, Lund (2012)
18. Von Hippel, E.: The Sources of Innovation. Oxford University Press, Oxford (1988)
19. Von Hippel, E.: Democratizing Innovation. MIT Press, Cambridge (2005)

20. Majumder, A., Shrivastava, N.: Know your personalization: learning topic level personalization in online services (Senast uppdaterad 2012-12-13) (2012). http://arxiv.org/pdf/1212.3390v1.pdf. Accessed 25 June 2013
21. Raboy, M., et al.: The dilemma of social demand: shaping media policy in new civic contexts'. Gazette **65**, 4–5 (2003)
22. Wyatt, S.: Non-users also matter: the construction of users and non-users of the internet. In: Oudshoorn, N., Pinch, T. (eds.) How Users Matter: The Co-construction of Users and Technology, pp. 67–79. MIT Press, Cambridge (2003)
23. Silverstone, R., Hirsch, E., Morely, D.: Information and communication technologies and the moral economy of the household. In: Silverstone, R., Hirsch, E. (eds.) Consuming Technologies. Media and Information in Domestic Spaces. Routledge, London (1992)
24. Arnstein, S.: A ladder of citizen participation. Am. Inst. Plan. J. **35**(4), 216–224 (1969)
25. Östlund, B., Lindén, K.: Turning old people's experiences into innovations: ippi, as the example of mobile services and TV viewing. Gerontechnology **10**(2), 103–109 (2011)
26. Von Hippel, E.: Horizontal innovation networks – by and for users. Ind. Corp. Change **16** (2), 293–315 (2007)
27. Jonsson, O.: Furniture for later life. Design based on older people's experiences of furniture in three housing forms. Dissertation, Division of Industrial Design, Department of Design Sciences, Lund University, Lund (2013)
28. Malone, E., Dellinger, B.A.: Letter to the editor. Healthc. Des. **11**(1), 11 (2011)
29. Porter, M.E.: The Competitive Advantage of Nations. Free Press, USA (1998)
30. Essén, A., Östlund, B.: Laggards as innovators? old users as designers of new services and service systems. Issue Int. J. Des. **5**(3), 89–98 (2011)
31. Saetnan, A., Oudshoorn, N., Kirejczyk, M. (eds.): Bodies of Technology: Womens Involvement with Reproductive Medicine. Ohio State University Press, Columbus (2000)

Emotions Identification to Measure User Experience Using Brain Biometric Signals

Ivan Carrillo(✉), Victoria Meza-Kubo, Alberto L. Morán,
Gilberto Galindo, and Eloisa García-Canseco

Universidad Autónoma de Baja California, Ensenada, Mexico
{ivan.carrillo,mmeza,alberto.moran,gilberto.galindo.
aldana,eloisa.garcia}@uabc.edu.mx

Abstract. There are different techniques (e.g. direct or indirect observation, questionnaires, etc.) with which it is possible to estimate user experience. Biometric data obtained with different devices (e.g. EEG, EMG) have been used as a source to infer user experience. In this work, as part of the construction of an evaluation model of user experience, we present a preliminary study that seeks to identify emotions using records of brain electrical activity through the visualisation of preset images that stimulate emotions known a priori. The results include identifying emotions of joy and displeasure through brain activity using the Emotive device in older adults.

Keywords: Electroencephalogram · Emotions · Elderly people · International affective image system

1 Introduction

The aging of population and increased incidences of diseases such as the Alzheimer's disease have moved researchers to look for alternative non-drug treatments, including technologies supporting cognition, that seek to maintain the cognitive status of the elderly through cognitive stimulation [1, 2]. To this end, diverse intelligent environment applications that seek to promote cognitive stimulation have been proposed [3]. However, due to the characteristics of this group of users, caused by their decline in their physical and cognitive skills, it is necessary to assess what is the elderly's perception regarding the use, acceptance and adoption of these applications.

In the literature various types of usability and user experience evaluations have been reported to assess the perception of the elderly regarding the use of technology [4], however, conducting this kind of assessments may be a difficult task due to the inherent limitations of the evaluation methods themselves. It is well known that in techniques based on self-report, participants tend to respond thinking about what the researcher wants to hear, or tend not to be sincere and "improve" their perception of the results because they feel assessed, or because they have forgotten the details of their experience [5]. Because of this, the results of these evaluations may not be very reliable. In addition there are additional elements that can affect user experience, including [6]: context of use, devices, cultural factors, social factors and the user features.

© Springer International Publishing Switzerland 2015
J. Zhou and G. Salvendy (Eds.): ITAP 2015, Part I, LNCS 9193, pp. 15–25, 2015.
DOI: 10.1007/978-3-319-20892-3_2

As an alternative to traditional user experience assessment techniques, we propose to record brain electrical activity of the participant by means of a low-cost electroencephalogram (EEG) device, to infer the user experience in an automated manner; and this through the design of a baseline EEG reference associated with two basic emotional states (pleasure-displeasure). The goal is to build a model with which we could identify emotions using biometrics brain data and based on these determine the user experience. In this work we present the first results of the process towards building this model.

2 Related Work

In recent years, biometric data have been used to assess the experience of users. For example, in [7], an assessment is made using the game Half-Life 2 by means of galvanic skin response, video, questionnaires and electromyography of users. Additionally, in [8] different physiological data such as galvanic skin response, electrocardiogram, electromyography of the jaw, and respiration rate are used to measure the user experience in entertainment technology, specifically using EA Sport video game NHL 2003.

Chai [9] evaluates three mobile phone applications using three self-report questionnaires to obtain subjective data as well as recording brain activity using EEG of participants. These data were used to determine the positive and negative states in the user experience of the applications used. Yao [10] evaluates the user experience of a cell phone application using the User Experience Questionnaire (UEQ) as well as physiological data such as brain activity (EEG), galvanic skin response, pulse, heart rate and respiration rate.

Hakvoort [11] evaluated the user experience of a brain-computer interface (BCI) game based on the expectation of users. For such assessment, a modified version of the SUXES method [12] was used. They used an evoked visual response as stimuli, and an EEG to register physiological data.

In a similar fashion, in this work we propose to design a model that uses brain biometric data to evaluate the user experience of the elderly during their use of computer applications, and compare these results with those of other more traditional assessment techniques.

3 The Brain and Emotions

The brain has approximately 100 million neurons and is responsible for processes such as reasoning and emotions, among others. The brain is divided into two hemispheres, the left and the right[1], which in turn are divided into four lobes[2]: frontal, parietal, occipital, and temporal [13] (see Fig. 1).

On the one hand, emotions can be positive or negative. At all times, no matter the context of the (private or public) situation people experience a range of emotions whether positive (e.g. joy, gratefulness, sympathy, happiness, love, etc.) or negative (e.g.

---

[1] http://neurocirugiacontemporanea.com.

[2] http://www.nlm.nih.gov.

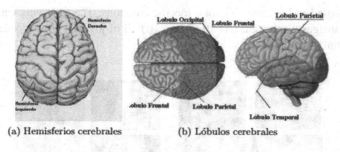

(a) Hemisferios cerebrales   (b) Lóbulos cerebrales

Fig. 1. Hemispheres and brain lobes

displeasure, irritability, disgust, anger, sadness, etc.) [14, 15]. Investigations concerning emotional state indicate that left prefrontal cerebral activity is associated with positive facial expressions while viewing joyful films, whereas right prefrontal cerebral activity is associated with negative facial expressions while viewing unpleasant films [16]. Positive emotions are associated with the activation of regions of the left hemisphere while negative emotions relate to the activation of regions of the right hemisphere [16–19].

On the other hand, asymmetry analysis of the power of the alpha wave, is recognized as a useful procedure for the study of emotional reactivity [20]; further, it is common to find the asymmetries in the frontal region of the brain, which may be perceived on a subject since childhood [18]. In a study conducted in [21] a spectral analysis of the electrical activity obtained through an EEG is conducted. In this analysis it is established that the power of the alpha wave varies depending on the emotion present (positive or negative emotion). Coan [22] mentions that frontal EEG asymmetry serves as a moderator in case of emotional activity and also functions as a mediator if there is an emotional response. Papusek [23], by means of brain activity EEG records and the Scalar Emotional Abilities Self-Report (SEAS), shows that people perceive the emotions of others and are able to regulate their own emotions, this by means of asymmetric changes in the prefrontal cortical regions during social interaction and emotional stimuli. Also in Papusek [23], other works on EEG and emotional states are presented, which show the asymmetrical changes that occur in the prefrontal cortical part of the brain during social emotional stimulations [23].

Taking this background into consideration, in the next section a controlled study is described that seeks (i) to analyze the biometric signals of an electroencephalogram (EEG) of the participants and (ii) identify patterns in the frequencies of signals and the activated brain areas according to known a priori stimuli.

4 Methodology

In order to build a model that interprets a set of user experience emotions, we conducted a preliminary study that presents selected images to stimulate known a priori emotions and registers the EEG response. For the study we used the International Affective Picture System (IAPS) [24], which establishes a set of standardized images that are used by researchers in the study of emotions and attention. A subset of the images proposed in [25], which evoke specific emotions. The following categories of emotion in images were used: (A) 10 of fear, (B) 10 of joy, (C) 10 of displeasure and (D) 29 neutral (see Fig. 2).

Fig. 2. Example of selected images from the IAPS catalog

The results of brain activity were studied using spectral analysis of power = $10*\log_{10}(\mu V^2/Hz)r^2$ in the alpha, betha and theta bands, including 15 min of trace clean of artifacts removed by visual analysis, in the frontal and occipital derivations: (1) AF3, (2) F7, (3) F3, (4) FC5, (7) O1, (14) AF4, (12) F4, (13) F8, (11) FC6 y (8) O2.

4.1   Participants

Participants were 8 seniors, 2 men and 6 women, aged 60 to 83 years (avg. = 72.3 years, s.d. = 8.46 years). Inclusion criteria were: aged over 60 years, not having suffered a head trauma, absence of moderate or severe cognitive problems and absence of visual problems (i.e. not being able to see well without glasses at a distance of 30–50 cm). All participants signed an informed consent, the procedures of this study did not represent any risk to them. To determine that participants did not have cognitive problems, we applied the Mini Mental State Examination (MMSE).

4.2   Materials

- Device: We used the Emotiv EEG device (See Fig. 3) with which is possible to obtain and record brain activity through 14 electrodes (AF3, F7, F3, FC5, T7, P7, O1, O2, P8, T8, FC6, F4, F8, AF4). The electrodes are placed according to the International 10–20 System, which sets the position of the electrodes on the craneal surface corresponding to cortical areas. The device also has a filter for frequencies from 0.2 to 45 Hz, which takes 128 samples per second for each channel.
- Software: We used Camtasia Studio to record the facial expressions of each participant; TestBench software, included with the Emotiv EEG device, to record data from brain activity with the 14 electrodes; EEGExProc, to display images; and EEGLAB to process the electroencephalography data [26].

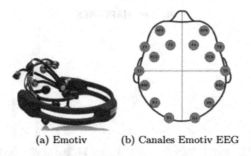

(a) Emotiv   (b) Canales Emotiv EEG

Fig. 3. Device and EEG channel positions

4.3 Reduction, Filtering and Data Analysis

To perform data analysis of the recorded brain activity using the EEGLAB software, we applied a finite response filter to the impulse for powers above ranges of electrical brain activity, in order to attenuate all signals with frequencies less than 0.2 Hz and eliminate various artifacts. Deleted artifacts are generated by eye blinking, lateral eye movements, muscle activity and others movements [27, 28]. This was corroborated by visual analysis. Once applied the filter and removed the unnecessary signals and artifacts, we proceeded to apply the Fast Fourier Transform, in order to obtain the powers of the different brain waves (alpha, betha, theta and delta) and to graphically identify the different brain areas activated depending on the analyzed brain wave.

4.4 Procedure

- Introduction to the study: Firstly, we explained to the elderly the purpose of the study and the characteristics of the Emotiv EEG device. They were also asked to sign a consent form.
- Device calibration: For best performance of the device, this was calibrated for each participant by recognizing facial gestures and the manipulation of a virtual 3D cube through brain interaction.
- Image presentation: In this stage, each participant was presented with a set of images according to the proposal in [24]. The images were presented in a sandwiched way: joy, fear, disgust and neutral for 6 s each, and immediately after, we asked the participant to indicate what was his/her impression upon seeing the image according to one of the following categories: joy, fear, disgust and neutral. During this phase, the brain activity of each participant was recorded by the TestBeanch software.

5 Results

According to the classification verbally reported by each participant, we obtained that the answers to the selected images to provoke emotions of joy fitted 92 % of the times (see Fig. 4). Additionally, responses to images of disgust agreed 84 % of the times (see Fig. 5). In both cases, the images converge to the categories of the established test.

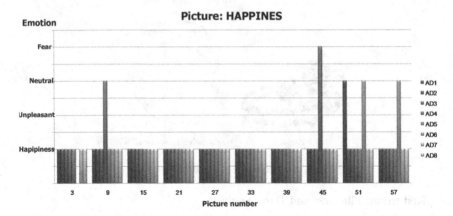

Fig. 4. Joy

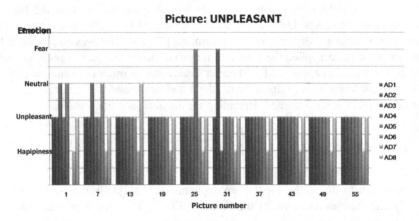

Fig. 5. Disgust

Responses to the images selected to evoke fear agreed 49 % (see Fig. 7) of the times, while for those selected as Neutral their responses corresponded 56 % of the times (see Fig. 6). As can be seen, the responses in these categories did not reported as expected.

Later, once brain activity data was processed by means of the methods described in section "Reduction, filtering and analysis", different EEG frequency spectra were obtained for each of the bands. The analysis of EEG data was corroborated by an expert in the area of neuroscience. The asymmetry in the alpha band of subject ADM1 indicates the possibility of observing through EEG patterns a relationship with the affective state during the observation of stimulus with emotional valence as a synchronization response caused in the limbic system and its relation to the frontal structures.

The power of the beta band was more prominent in the dorsolateral frontal of the left hemisphere, associated to cognitive analysis of observed information, which suggests an interpretation of disgust by the user, coinciding with the stimuli presented in the activity (see Fig. 9).

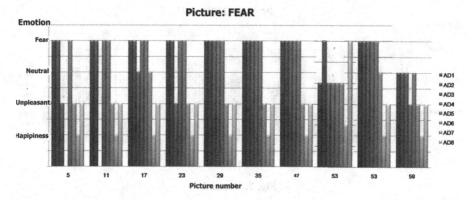

Fig. 6. Fear

In the same vein, regarding the analysis of power of the theta band, it is possible to observe an asymmetry whose greatest value is seen in the right frontal, consistent with the stimuli in the activity with emotional charge, besides indicating attention by the elderly in the activity (see Fig. 10).

6 Discussion

From the results obtained from verbal responses for the images in the joy category 92 % of the responses were reported as joy, 6 % as neutral and 2 % as fear (See Fig. 5). The image shows that participant AD4 expressed that image 45 caused fear to him/her; in this case the image corresponded to 3 girls smiling, so it could be a coding error by the participant; while for image 51, which corresponded to an older woman, it was classified as neutral by participants AD1 and AD6.

In Fig. 6, corresponding to the verbal responses for the images in the disgust category, it can be observed that over 80 % transmitted emotions of disgust to participants, while 10 % were reported as neutral, 3 % as fear and 2 % as joy. Participant AD3 indicated that image 31, which showed a hand surgery, brought joy to him/her as s/he was a medical doctor, so that it could be concluded that the activities being undertaken by participant AD3 as a professional affected his/her answer.

For images of the neutral category, we obtained that 56 % of these were classified as neutral, 40 % of them caused joy and 2 % were reported as disgusting (see Fig. 7). Participant AD2 consistently indicated the same disgust response for pictures 4, 24 and 44, in which the same fungus appeared, while participant AD5 responded as neutral for image 4, as disgust for image 24 and as neutral for image 44. These two participants were the only ones who gave responses of disgust for the images.

For the fear category, only 49 % of the responses indicated that the images provoked this emotion, 39 % of responses indicated disgust and 10 % of responses were classified as neutral (see Fig. 8). Of this group of images, image 59, which shows a skeleton, was the only one that did not caused fear; 40 % of participants responded with neutral and 30 % responded with disgust. It is important to highlight that participant

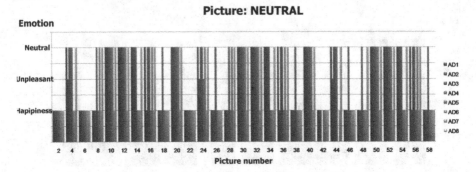

Fig. 7. Neutral

AD7 was a special case, as s/he responded that all images caused him/her joy. We observed that participant AD7 was greatly nervous during the test, which along with a possible misunderstanding during the explanation of the activity could caused that s/he always provided the same answer.

Fig. 8. Power spectrum of alpha wave

The analysis conducted of the EEG data is preliminary, as we only obtained power spectra for each band using the EEG registry of each elderly. This analysis allowed us to visually identify different brain regions where an activity related to the emotional stimuli were shown depending on the selected band (See Figs. 8, 9 and 10). These results can be related to those obtained by the categories of joy (positive emotion) and disgust (negative emotion). The analysis of EEG records stimulus in order to establish a better relationship between the categories of images with different power spectra and the brain areas involved remains pending. This type of analysis will reveal which elements have to be considered in the design of the model to assess the user experience.

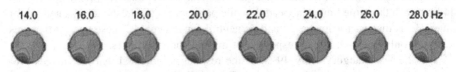

Fig. 9. Power spectrum of beta wave

Fig. 10. Power spectrum of theta wave

7 Conclusions and Future Work

This paper presents preliminary results of our proposal to determine a set of emotions through brain activity (EEG) records. The results of verbal responses of participants validated the emotional presence of joy and disgust, especially when the selected images to evoke these emotions were presented.

In the analysis of the spectra for each subject, asymmetries are seen in the frontal EEG recording of the elderly, this is related to changes in mood showing joy at left frontal activation and disgust at right frontal activation, allowing the detection of brain regions linked to these emotions [20, 29, 30]. The electrophysiological results of this study confirm the possibility of identifying changes in the affective state (displeasure vs. joy) during the activity through the biometric signals of the brain obtained with the eMotiv headset. Our future work includes processing the EEG records by type of stimulus to make a comparison between what is verbally said by the elderly and what is registered with the eMotive headset. Additionally, we will conduct an analysis of variance (ANOVA) to determine significant differences between the types of stimuli administered to subjects.

Acknowledgements. We acknowledge the support of UABC, specially that in the form of the Programa de Servicio Social 212, and CONACYT by scholarship number 538130 to first author. We also acknowledge the elderly participants from Ensenada, B.C., México for their support and participation in the study.

References

1. Buiza, C., Soldatos, J., Petsatodis, T., Geven, A., Etxaniz, A., Tscheligi, M.: HERMES: pervasive computing and cognitive training for ageing well. In: Omatu, S., Rocha, M.P., Bravo, J., Fernández, F., Corchado, E., Bustillo, A., Corchado, J.M. (eds.) IWANN 2009, Part II. LNCS, vol. 5518, pp. 756–763. Springer, Heidelberg (2009)
2. Meza-Kubo, V., Morán, A.L.: UCSA: a design framework for usable cognitive systems for the worried-well. Pers. Ubiquit. Comput. 1–11 (2012)
3. Augusto, J.C.: Ambient intelligence : basic concepts and applications. In: Filipe, J., Shishkov, B., Helfert, M. (eds.) ICSOFT 2006. CCIS, vol. 10, pp. 16–26. Springer, Heidelberg (2008)
4. Meza-kubo, V.: Guias para el diseno de aplicaciones de estimulacion cognitiva utilizables por el adulto mayor. Universidad Autonoma de Baja California (2012)

5. Arhippainen, L., Tähti, M.: Empirical evaluation of user experience in two adaptive mobile application prototypes. In: Proceedings of the 2nd International Conference on Mobile and Ubiquitous Multimedia (2003)
6. Arhippainen, L.: Capturing user experience for product design (2003)
7. Mandryk, R.L., Atkins, M.S., Inkpen, K.M.: A continuous and objective evaluation of emotional experience with interactive play environments. In: Proceedings SIGCHI Conference Human Factors Computing Systems - CHI 2006, p. 1027 (2006)
8. Mosquera, G., Daniel, S.: Adquisición de señales electroencefalográficas para el movimiento de un prototipo de silla de ruedas en un sistema BCI (2012)
9. Chai, J., Ge, Y., Liu, Y., Li, W., Zhou, L., Yao, L., Sun, X.: Application of frontal EEG asymmetry to user experience research. In: Harris, D. (ed.) EPCE 2014. LNCS, vol. 8532, pp. 234–243. Springer, Heidelberg (2014)
10. Yao, L., Liu, Y., Li, W., Zhou, L., Ge, Y., Chai, J., Sun, X.: Using physiological measures to evaluate user experience of mobile applications. In: Harris, D. (ed.) EPCE 2014. LNCS, vol. 8532, pp. 301–310. Springer, Heidelberg (2014)
11. Hakvoort, G., Poel, M., Gurkok, H.: Evaluating user experience with respect to user expectations in brain-computer interface games, pp. 1–4 (2011)
12. Turunen, M., Hakulinen, J., Melto, A., Heimonen, T., Laivo, T., Hella, J.: SUXES—user experience evaluation method for spoken and multimodal interaction, pp. 2567–2570 (2009)
13. Isotani, T., Lehmann, D., Pascual-Marqui, R.D., Fukushima, M., Saito, N., Yagyu, T., Kinoshita, T.: Source localization of brain electric activity during positive, neutral and negative emotional states. Int. Congr. Ser. 1232, 165–173 (2002)
14. Fredrickson, B.L., Losada, M.F.: Positive affect and the complex dynamics of human flourishing. Am. Psychol. 60(7), 678–686 (2005)
15. Piqueras Rodriguez, J.-A., Ramos Linares, V., Matínez Gonzalez, A.E., Oblitas Guadalupe, L.A.: Emociones negativas y su impacto en la salud mental y física. Suma Psicológica. 16, 85–112 (2009)
16. Harmon-Jones, E., Sigelman, J.: State anger and prefrontal brain activity: evidence that insult-related relative left-prefrontal activation is associated with experienced anger and aggression. J. Pers. Soc. Psychol. 80(5), 797–803 (2001)
17. Simón, V.: Mindfulness y neurobiología. Rev. Psicoter. 66, 5–30 (2007)
18. Navarro, F.S., Pedro, J., Lapuente, R.: Amígdala, corteza prefrontal y especialización hemisférica en la experiencia y expresión emocional. Serv. Publicaciones, Murcia Univ., Murcia (2004)
19. Winkler, I., Mark, J., Jager, M., Mihajlovic, V., Tsoneva, T., Winkler, I., Mark, J.: Frontal EEG asymmetry based classification of emotional valence using common spatial patterns. World Acad. Sci. Eng. Technol. 45, 373–378 (2010)
20. Bermúdez Cicchino, A.N.: Técnicas de procesamiento de EEG para detección de eventos (2014). Postgradofcm.Edu.Ar
21. Kostyunina, M.B., Kulikov, M.A.: Frequency characteristics of EEG spectra in the emotions. Neurosci. Behav. Physiol. 26(4), 340–343 (1996)
22. Coan, J.A., Allen, J.J.B.: Frontal EEG asymmetry as a moderator and mediator of emotion. Biol. Psychol. 67(1–2), 7–49 (2004)
23. Papousek, I., Freudenthaler, H.H., Schulter, G.: Typical performance measures of emotion regulation and emotion perception and frontal EEG asymmetry in an emotional contagion paradigm. Pers. Individ. Dif. 51(8), 1018–1022 (2011)
24. Bertron, A., Petry, M., Bruner, R., Mcmanis, M., Zabaldo, D., Martinet, S., Cuthbert, S., Ray, D., Koller, K., Kolchakian, M., Hayden, S.: International affective picture system (IAPS): technical manual and affective ratings (1997)

25. Bradley, M.M., Lang, P.J.: The international affective picture system (IAPS) in the study of emotion and attention. In: Coan, J.A., Allen, J.J.B. (eds.) Handbook of Emotion Elicitation and Assessment, pp. 29–46. Oxford University Press, Oxford (2007)

26. Delorme, A., Makeig, S.: EEGLAB: an open source toolbox for analysis of single-trial EEG dynamics including independent component analysis. J. Neurosci. Meth. **134**, 9–21 (2004). Elsevier

27. Vecchio, F., Babiloni, C., Buffo, P., Rossini, P.M., Bertini, M.: Inter-hemispherical functional coupling of EEG rhythms during the perception of facial emotional expressions. Clin. Neurophysiol. **124**(2), 263–272 (2013)

28. Mandryk, R.L., Inkpen, K.M., Calvert, T.W., Science, C., Canada, B.C.V.A.: Using psychophysiological techniques to measure user experience with entertainment technologies, vol. 2005 (2005)

29. Marcuse, L.V., Schneider, M., Mortati, K.A., Donnelly, K.M., Arnedo, V., Grant, A.C.: Quantitative analysis of the EEG posterior-dominant rhythm in healthy adolescents. Clin. Neurophysiol. **119**, 1778–1781 (2008)

30. Wheeler, R.E., Davidson, R.J., Tomarken, A.J.: Frontal brain asymmetry and emotional reactivity: a biological substrate of affective style. Psychophysiology **30**, 82–89 (1993)

Adopting Scenario-Based Design to Increase the Acceptance of Technology Innovations for Older People

Diego Compagna[1(✉)] and Florian Kohlbacher[2]

[1] University Duisburg-Essen, Duisburg, Germany
Diego.Compagna@uni-due.de
[2] Xi'an Jiaotong-Liverpool University, Suzhou, China
Florian.Kohlbacher@xjtlu.edu.cn

Abstract. This paper describes the strengths and weaknesses of the Scenario-based Design as a method to achieve a user-centered development of technology for the elderly. Our assumptions are based on findings from a three-year research project dedicated to the application of service robotics in a stationary nursing home. In summary, the increasingly specific nature of the phases during the design process afford a needs-based technical development, thus providing a good basis for participatory technical development. Nonetheless, some weak points were identified during the case study. They are related to the graphic nature of the scenarios as well as following the users' notions in each and every case. In consideration of the difficulties that arose during the use of Scenario-based Design, we conclude with some suggestion for future applications of this method.

Keywords: Scenario-based design · Participatory technology development · Assistive technology for elderly target groups

1 Introduction

Regarding the demographic shift, an increasing number of technological developments strictly related to the healthcare sector occurred over the past decade. Still an ongoing trend and a topic of great importance (e.g. the main ICT-Agenda of the European Union: Horizon 2020), research projects dedicated to the development of technology for the care-giving sector invited participation. In this regard, we describe the process of ICT developments for the healthcare sector as promising as well as problematic. Our assumptions are based on findings from a three-year research project, which was funded by the German Federal Ministry for Education and Research and was conducted in Germany primarily within the years 2009-2012. The research was dedicated to the application of service robotics in a stationary nursing home. Due to the sensitivity of the field with its morally charged context and its characterization as a highly human driven "relational" work sector, the development was guided in part by participatory methods - i.e. the development should have been driven completely and without any exception by user's needs. Even though the adopted method for mediating the users' needs and the technological feasibility were very helpful and delivered promising results, some weak points and misleading processes became apparent.

© Springer International Publishing Switzerland 2015
J. Zhou and G. Salvendy (Eds.): ITAP 2015, Part I, LNCS 9193, pp. 26–34, 2015.
DOI: 10.1007/978-3-319-20892-3_3

In the case study "Scenario-based Design" [1] was examined as a procedure for a participatory technology development [2, 3]. Scenario-Based Design (SBD) as an instrument for participatory technology development – according to the optimistic descriptions in the literature [4] – at first sight offers significant potential for early inclusion of future users. The obvious clarity along with the iterative process of coordination and implementing pilot applications ensure an ideal exchange among users and designers. Ultimately, this process should allow an optimal balance with regard to the social desideratum and the technical feasibility. In the course of the above-mentioned three-year research project, this process is almost complete.

Nonetheless, some weak points were identified during the case study. (A) One is related to the graphic nature of the scenarios. In some cases, the development follows an approximated interpretation of a drawing showing the new technology in action, while at the same time, the user follows an interpretation of the same drawing. As we show with clear empirical evidence from the case study, this might result in completely useless development simply because the two primary groups involved in the adjustment process have two very different ways of imagining the implementation of new technology in the social field in question. (B) Another main issue is related to the problem of always following the users' notions. As we also will prove with data from the case study, sometimes this could obviate the development of very innovative solutions due to lack of imagination on the part of the users, who are usually guided by the technologies they already know and use. (A) will be discussed in Sect. 3.1, (B) in Sect. 3.2.

2   Characteristics of Scenario Based Design

The basic idea behind SBD is to enable the developer of highly innovative technologies to imagine the needs and wishes of the target group at stake. The core process of the method consists in iterative adjustment-loops. The graphical and narrative scenarios become increasingly detailed, ensuring user-oriented development. SBD is a very useful method for the inclusion of elderly user target groups in the development of (very) innovative technologies because of the graphic nature of the scenarios (easy to understand) as well as the iterative adjustments between the involved groups of developer and user.

"Like other user-centered approaches, scenario-based design changes the focus of design work from defining system operations (i.e. functional specification) to describing how people will use a system to accomplish work tasks and other activities [...]. However, unlike approaches that consider human behavior and experience through formal analysis and modeling of well-specified tasks, scenario-based design is a relatively lightweight method for envisioning future use possibilities." [1: 1033].

As scenarios are generated in most cases anyway, it is only important to make them explicit and write them down. The advantage of scenarios lies in their dynamism and how easily they can be comprehended, which arise from their development in relationship to the user and, amongst all those involved in the developmental process, eases communication about the planned execution and/or implementation of a technological innovation [5].

2.1   Scenarios in Scenario Based Design

A scenario contains a sequence of actions and events that lead to a concrete result. The defining characteristic of a scenario consists in sketching a narrative description of activities that a user will typically employ in accomplishing a given task. The description should be detailed enough that design-relevant conclusions can be drawn and later discussed. Scenarios are usually graphically portrayed, and are accompanied by a series of individual drawings, each accompanied by short written commentaries which "narrate" the planned action, as in a comic strip or a storyboard [6].

Generally, scenarios are set from the perspective of the potential user and take into account the user's social and emotional background, as well as his or her personal motivations and goals. The scenarios themselves involve one or more participants interacting in the form of "personas" with the aid of various instruments in order to achieve a certain goal. Personas are fictitious participants and/or characters who incorporate the typical characteristics of a certain group of users, possess a concrete usage pattern, and should be representative of the majority of actual subsequent users. From the outset, personas should be designed to minimize the development of an end result that is not actually possible for a potential user. Therefore, a unique scenario should be developed for each persona and narrated in the third person [7].

The advantage of scenarios as opposed to use cases lies in how easy they are to comprehend, even for non-specialists. Moreover, use cases often proceed from a determined sequence of actions and reactions between users and a system whose characteristics are already relatively certain. While scenarios are concrete, they are nevertheless incomplete and painted in broad strokes, allowing new perspectives on design to emerge and preventing any assumed, fixed "best solution" from arising prematurely. Via a gradual and iterative adjustment of concept and detail, scenarios successfully model the entire phase of analysis and conception [8].

2.2   The Relevance of the Prototype and Evaluation Phase

It is a fundamental requirement of SBD to make an early evaluation of conceptual ideas, and to repeat this regularly throughout the design and developmental process. If, however, user orientation is significant in the application of SBD [5] and design-focused development is understood from the outset as a social process in which heterogeneous groups are brought together and come into dialogue via the scenarios [6], it is precisely the narrative character of the procedure that poses a significant risk:

"Part of the appeal of scenarios is that they are short, fun, and vivid. But when used uncritically, without proper attention given to data quality and representativeness, scenarios will be no more expressive of the needs of real users than the musings of engineers or researchers unaided by a representation of user experience. It is easy to feel that one has captured a user's experience because it is represented in a narrative or storyboard, but these accessible representations can easily be inflated into more than they really are. We should be careful to distinguish the form that the information is packaged in from the quality of the content therein. As we attempt to design for broader and broader classes of users who are less and less like designers themselves, it is critical that we find a way to pipe stimulating input to designers that faithfully captures users' needs and problems." [9: 397f].

An important method for avoiding blundering into this "scenario case" is intensive and repeated adjustment to users [8: 373]. Whether or not SBD is suitable as a procedure for participatory technological development is finally determined not by accommodating the desires of the user – and/or the developer determining the scenario's technological feasibility beforehand – in the version of the scenario as it appears "on paper." It is rather only trial runs that can provide evidence as to the efficacy of scenarios intended for participatory technological development [8: 371f].

3   Case Study: The Application of Scenario Based Designs for the Advancement of Service Robotics

The primary objective of our case study consisted of creating and optimizing a knowledge transfer between developers and users through the choice and application of suitable procedures. For these requirements, SBD presented itself as the method of choice: SBD's descriptive quality and relative openness were characteristics which not only permitted caregivers and inhabitants of stationary nursing facilities to evaluate planned usage ahead of time, but also allowed developers to identify technically feasible applications.

In each of the two, one-week pilot runs, the use scenarios developed and conceived on the basis of SBD were generated to provide a successful knowledge transfer between the users in the nursing facility and the team developing the two robots. A central result derives in this context from supplementing SBD with "rapid prototyping." From the experiences in the project serving as a case study (from which generalizations cannot yet be drawn), one would have to seriously consider the systematic implementation of rapid prototyping in the pilot phase for projects using SBD – at least with regards to certain applications that will be discussed in the next Sect. (3.1).

In the following Sect. (3.2), we will take a step back in the chronology of the project to discuss some important observations with regard to the application of SBD, which probably arise due to the particular characteristics of the field of deployment (caregivers and seniors in need of a stationary nursing facility).

3.1   Prototype and Evaluation Phase - Pilot Use

During the prototype and evaluation phase, it became evident that aside from further developments in the service robots and the design of the user interface, elaborations were also necessary with regards to the interaction concept, as well as the screen design for the respective control surfaces of the robots in use; these were often – as far as possible – carried out "on site." While the general conception and the basic screen design for the control surfaces were prepared during the design phase, this phase focused on specialization and detailed changes. It quickly became apparent that the work took on the characteristics of rapid prototyping during the pilot phases. Johnson et al. had addressed the importance of rapid prototyping within the context of using SBD early on [10].

Two examples from the case study here should confirm the importance of a systematic combination and/or integration of rapid prototyping with SBD. At the same time, they cast a helpful light on a problem related to SBD in a brief discussion following the examples. The examples concern two particular scenarios that were tested within the context of the pilot applications: The beverage scenario (conducted by a service robot provided with a manipulator including a three-finger gripper) and the transportation scenario (conducted by a less sophisticated service robot, a revised automated guided vehicle).

The beverage scenario refers to the typical tasks at stations intended to manage the residents' beverage supply, which in the case study were to be transferred by a service robot. Elderly seniors frequently tend to drink too little. Therefore, providing residents with a sufficient supply of fluids represents a crucial task in nursing facilities, and caregivers must make particular efforts to ensure that certain residents have enough to drink. In the case study, a service robot independently filled a glass at a beverage station, then offered it to the seniors in common rooms. The robot was to acquire the desired quantity of fluid, automatically document it, then add up fluids consumed by each inhabitant. Caregivers can thus quickly establish an overview of the conditions of the residents, and intervene if necessary. This way, at the end of their shift, caregivers only need to examine how much each resident has drunk, and then - if necessary - make their own, additional offers.

Within the context of the beverage scenario, it turned out that several of the residents in the common room did not notice the service robots because of how quietly they moved from place to place, so that the seniors were at times startled when a robot offered them something to drink. This undesired effect could be repaired on site by programming and activating an additional function which consisted of the robot announcing itself when it "entered" the room with simple phrases such as "Good Morning," "Hi, it's me again," etc. Of course, this effect was difficult to recognize in the SBD's visual aides, and accordingly was nearly impossible to predict and/or implement before the pilot study.

The second scenario that serves as an example of the problematic aspects of SBD is concerned with the transportation operations commonly used in nursing facilities. In nursing facilities such as senior homes, there are many transportation needs. From dirty laundry to meals to medication, heavy loads must be carried from A to B on a daily basis, often over long distances. Frequently, these tasks are carried out by experienced caregivers. The transportation scenario was developed in order to relieve these caregivers of this cumbersome routine and thus create more free time for care-giving activities. A driverless transport system could accomplish these tasks independently. Both regular transportation services as well as unique transportation tasks can be delegated to a driverless transport vehicle. The removal of dirty laundry and delivery of fresh laundry, for example, is a routine transportation activity that occurs daily, or several times daily. In addition, however, meal trays, beverage crates, mail, or medications could also be delivered by such a system from a central office to individual stations or floors, and/or collected from these stations. These tasks are generally perceived to be time-consuming and burdensome, as they prevent caregivers from spending more time on their key responsibilities to the residents.

This second example brings up a core element of the SBD, i.e. the visualization of the planned operation on the basis of drawn sketches. During the transportation scenario – which was adjusted several times between user and developer before the development and first pilot run, just as the beverage scenario was – it turned out that the containers for the dirty laundry presented a substantial stress to caregivers, since the opening of the container was too high. Laundry bags may contain wet clothing and can weigh up to 15 kg, which means that depending on their height, caregivers may have to lift this heavy load up to their chest in order to deposit it into the container. As was later discovered, an early sketch showing the revised automated guided vehicle with a laundry container was used for the scenario adjustment. For basic adjustment, this was completely sufficient.

With regards to the size of the container, the caregivers presumably regarded it symbolically, and did not note that the container was too small for practical use, nor indicate how big it could or – better yet – should be. For their part, the developers tacitly and naturally assumed that the container, in order to be functional, must be larger. Although in the long run the development of the transportation scenario was oriented by the rough guidelines of the scenario, in the end it obviously came to an addition of two opposing "deviations": During the design phase, the caregivers did not "look too carefully" at the size of the container in the drawings (Fig. 1(a)), and the actual container was (obviously) larger in its execution than it appeared in the sketches (Fig. 1(b)) – too large:

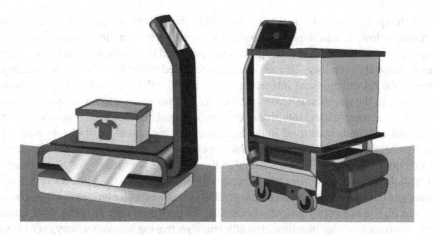

Fig. 1. (a) and (b) The picture on the left shows the sketch of the laundry transportation scenario used in the scenario adjustment, and on the right the dirty laundry containers which were used in the pilot run. Both pictures are accurate sketches of the original drawing or photograph, made by Annika Metze following the authors' instructions. The sketches were made to ensure the highest anonymity of the involved persons, firms, and organizations.

As is made clear by the example, the figures used in SBD are not "merely" designs with a symbolic character, but representations of a prospective reality that should be taken seriously [11]. If this fact is not considered, any desired positive effect resulting from an adjustment of planned operations before the development work actually begins disappears all at once. The "problem" of the laundry container could obviously not be solved quickly through the use of rapid prototyping (a procedure that derives from software development [10]), and had to be delayed to the next pilot run, as a container with new dimensions had to be produced.

Apart from the obviously important evaluation of the scenarios, which inhere in the procedure of SBD and must occur as early as possible within the pilot tests [8: 371f], these examples also point to another important factor: SBD was developed in the context of software development, and was initially applied and discussed only within this field. The examples reveal the limitations of and improvements necessary to the procedure in different regards: Firstly, it was clear that when using SBD for the development of complex robots designed for complex social environments, early pilot studies are particularly important, and also that SBD would be much more efficient if rapid prototyping formed an integral component. Moreover, the transfer of the procedure to the development of robots (in contrast to software) makes it much more susceptible to unforeseeable effects. Reversing the conclusion, this means that in such test scenarios rapid prototyping becomes all the more important (as far as possible), but also that – precisely because rapid prototyping is much more difficult to apply given the materiality of equipment development – considerably greater attention would have to be given to the mode of representation in the scenarios [11].

3.2 Generating Scenarios - the Design Phases

Two field-specific aspects that were noticeable during the design phase are briefly discussed below. It was apparent from the survey of the operational procedures that caregivers remained wedded to the procedures provided by the documentation software already in use at the facility. This tendency was revealed particularly clearly in situations in which the information and interaction scenarios with the user interface design were concerned. In the questionnaire on suggestions for improvement, the (on paper) theoretically more complex and intuitive operation of the robots and/or documentation (e.g. the quantity of fluids consumed in the beverage scenario) could hardly be determined. This was because it was nearly impossible for caregivers to deviate from the documentation routines of the EDP software used in the facility, even though this represented a substantial improvement from the viewpoint of its usability. The tenacity of a work routine and the deeply-embedded nature of EDP systems in such routines is evident from this, and may make improvements impossible. The question thus arises to what extent relying too much on user interface in an efficiency-increasing innovation may even prove an obstacle, if the imaginative power of the users is restricted by the "habit of practice."

A further aspect related specifically to the field of providing care is related to the seniors' ability to integrate. Different factors come in to play here, which, depending upon their field of deployment, can vary greatly. In the case study the field of application and accordingly the inclusion of user groups were restricted to stationary nursing facilities. The senior citizens at such facilities are often very close to death, which usually leads to a general lack of interest in future developments [12, 13].

Moreover, it seems justified to raise the question as to how the scenarios concern changes that exceed the imaginative power of this particular group of people, and consequently makes feedback regarding the planned employment of service robotics difficult if not impossible. Despite repeated interviews with a large number of residents at the nursing facility, the responses received from this user group were scant. Thus the question arises to what extent SBD is either too concrete or not concrete enough. On the other hand, these findings may under no circumstance be applied to seniors generally, since – as was already mentioned – the inhabitants in need of care at a stationary facility form a special "sub-group" [13].

A presumably more trivial circumstance – yet not insignificant for the iterative application of SBD – which puts the practicality of this procedure for this particular user group in doubt, is the fact that the group's mortality rate is very high, so that even before the conclusion of the design phase, and shortly before the beginning of the first pilot and evaluation phase, approximately half of the seniors involved in the coordination process and the generation of scenario had passed away.

4 Summary

In summary, the fundamental precept of SBD consists in aiding usually interdisciplinary product development teams and other stakeholders to imagine themselves in the position of the target group, use context, and product ideas via scenarios and personas. The increasingly specific nature of the phases during the design process afford a needs-based technical development, thus providing a good basis for participatory technical development. Moreover, an iterative procedure is supported via increasingly concrete and detailed scenarios, which provides sufficient freedom for experimentation in problem-solving and design, while also ensuring continuous workflow management that aids technological advancement. In consideration of the difficulties that arose during the use of SBD, the following conclusions for future applications of this method can be drawn:

Ad (3.1) With regards to scenario generation, their clarity should continually increase, so that the last version of the co-ordinated scenarios has achieved a very high level of detail; moreover pilot runs should be carried out as early as possible, in order to single out aspects that do not "graphically present themselves" as soon as possible.

Ad (3.2) In some cases it can be quite sensible to ignore user feedback, above all if the planned development represents an "obviously" better solution than the system currently in use; regarding the integration of certain user groups two things should be considered: Does the technology being developed lie beyond the intellectual horizon of this particular user group? Is the affected user group sufficiently motivated to aid in developing the technology?

References

1. Rosson, M.B., Carroll, J.M.: Scenario-based design. In: Jacko, J.A., Sears, A. (Hg.) The Human-Computer Interaction Handbook. Fundamentals, Evolving Technologies and Emerging Applications, (2. Aufl.), pp. 1032–1050. Erlbaum, Mahwah (2003)
2. Compagna, D.: Lost in translation? The dilemma of alignment within participatory technology developments. Poiesis Praxis 9(1–2), 125–143 (2012)

3. Compagna, D., Kohlbacher, F.: The limits of participatory technology development: the case of service robots in care facilities for older people. Technol. Forecast. Soc. Chang. 93(1), 19–31 (2015)
4. Carroll, J.M. (Hg.): Scenario-Based Design. Envisioning Work and Technology in Systems Development, (1. Aufl.). Wiley, New York (1995)
5. Carroll, J.M.: Introduction. The scenario perspective on system development. In: Ders. (Hg.) Scenario-Based Design. Envisioning Work and Technology in Systems Development, (1. Aufl.), pp. 1–17. Wiley, New York (1995)
6. Erickson, T.: Notes on design practice. Stories and prototypes as catalysts for communication. In: Carroll, J.M. (Hg.) Scenario-Based Design. Envisioning Work and Technology in Systems Development, (1. Aufl.), pp. 37–58. Wiley, New York (1995)
7. Pruitt, J., Adlin, T.: The Persona Lifecycle. Keeping People in Mind Throughout Product Design, (1. Aufl.). Elsevier, Amsterdam (2005)
8. Mack, R.L.: Discussion. Scenarios as engines of design. In: Carroll, J.M. (Hg.) Scenario-Based Design. Envisioning Work and Technology in Systems Development, (1. Aufl.), pp. 361–386. Wiley, New York (1995)
9. Nardi, B.A.: Some reflections on scenarios. In: Carroll, J.M. (Hg.) Scenario-Based Design. Envisioning Work and Technology in Systems Development, (1. Aufl.), pp. 387–399. Wiley, New York (1995)
10. Johnson, P., Johnson, H., Wilson, S.: Rapid prototyping of user interfaces driven by task models. In: Carroll, J.M. (Hg.) Scenario-Based Design. Envisioning Work and Technology in Systems Development, (1. Aufl.), pp. 209–246. Wiley, New York (1995)
11. Compagna, D.: Partizipative Technikentwicklung: Eine soziologische Betrachtung und Reflexion, (WPktS 03/2011). In: Compagna, D., Shire, K. (Hg.) Working Papers kultur- und techniksoziologische Studien, Universität Duisburg-Essen, Institut für Soziologie, Duisburg (2011). http://www.uni-due.de/soziologie/compagna_wpkts.php. letzter Abruf: 26 Sept 2011
12. Charles, S.T., Carstensen, L.L.: Social and emotional aging. Annu. Rev. Psychol. 61, 383–409 (2009)
13. Compagna, D., Derpmann, S., Helbig, T., Shire, K.A.: Partizipationsbereitschaft und -ermöglichung einer besonderen Nutzergruppe. Funktional-Partizipative Technikentwicklung im Pflegesektor. In: Bieber, D., Schwarz, K. (Hg.) Mit AAL-Dienstleistungen altern. Nutzerbedarfsanalysen im Kontext des Ambient Assisted Living, (1. Aufl.), pp. 161–176. Iso-Verl, Saarbrücken (2011)

Constructing Third Age eHealth Consumers by Using Personas from a Cultural Age Perspective

Maria Ekström[1] and Eugène Loos[2(✉)]

[1] Laurea University of Applied Sciences, Metsänpojankuja 3, FIN-02130 Espoo,
Finland
maria.ekstrom@laurea.fi
[2] University of Amsterdam, Nieuwe Achtergracht 166, 1018 WV Amsterdam,
The Netherlands
e.f.loos@uva.nl

Abstract. Society ages and our already extensive use of a host of different portable devices continues to expand. No leap of the imagination is needed to grasp that an exponential growth of the eHealth market is at hand. While the ageing of the baby boomers will have an impact on the global economy as a whole, of particular interest is the impact this will have within the context of eHealth market development. We wish to clarify and raise the level of awareness about how older age identity is constructed in the marketer-consumer dialectic within the eHealth context and how the *personas* method can be used from a *cultural age* perspective. Our focus is on the process of third agers becoming eHealth consumers. We present an analytical framework for future studies aiming to analyze eHealth offerings. This will allow us to gain insight into the process of constructing the third age eHealth consumer group's identity through multimodal communicative acts, as is the case in advertising, or in settings requiring interactivity, such as the service design process. It is through these multimodal acts that new eHealth offerings could be marketed to the third age eHealth consumer, focusing especially on both the written and visual language used. Our approach is meant to offer an alternative to studies in which ageing has mostly drawn upon the chronological age concept and where marketing has not been seen as a discursive practice shaping consumers' identities.

Keywords: eHealth · Services · Third age eHealth consumers · Personas · Cultural age

1 Introduction

Western societies today have more older people than ever before. The question is: how can these societies cope with the challenges of this growing number of people who are very likely also to require care and support? One answer is to create solutions for "aging in place" (Rodeschini [1, p. 521]), which refers to the ability of older people to remain living in their homes for as long as possible, through the use of various technologies. Rodeschini [1] makes a distinction between AT and ICT, drawing on research

© Springer International Publishing Switzerland 2015
J. Zhou and G. Salvendy (Eds.): ITAP 2015, Part I, LNCS 9193, pp. 35–43, 2015.
DOI: 10.1007/978-3-319-20892-3_4

by e.g. Blaschke et al. [2]. Whereas AT (Assistive Technologies) is mainly about health monitoring, ICT (Information and Communication Technologies) is more about communicating and informing [2, p. 523], e.g. the Whatsapp users who designed a quiz that demanded that users change their profile picture whenever they gave a wrong answer is a case in point - the technology was already there, but the users themselves designed the use. For this paper, we concentrate more on ICT than on AT; the focus of our analytical framework is on the encounter between third age consumers (see Sect. 5 for a clarification of this concept) and the eHealth providers and designers.

In our approach, we build on the personas method that was introduced by Cooper [3] in 1999 within the context of software design. The personas approach is usually aimed at finding a typical average user: "Creating personas involves identifying the critical behavior patterns and turning them into a set of useful characterizations" (Goodwin [4, p. 242]). According to Goodwin, personas can, but are not required, to be created with the help of demographics, unlike the use of segmentation techniques, which in most cases are based on demographic criteria. In our opinion, the personas method certainly has advantages, although the use of chronological age as an age variable is problematic, as this might invoke stereotyping effects (see e.g. Turner and Turner [5] who argue that stereotyping is highly prevalent). To avoid this risk of stereotyping, we use the concept of cultural age, which refers to the way a person experiences her or his age (in contrast to cognitive age, a concept introduced by Barak and Schiffman [6] in 1981 referring to a person's self-perceived age (feel-age, look-age, do-age, and interest-age).

Hence the cultural age concept addresses the issue of stereotyping and puts forward the dialectic that is always present when something is designed for or with a user group. The aim is also to find more viable, sustainable solutions in accordance with this (see also [7]). This is important because there will probably be an exponential growth of the eHealth market, where eHealth providers and designers, as well as older users, will meet to create new better solutions through the use of different, existing tools. Note that, although we refer here to a 'market', we are well aware that the size of any market is not easily measurable, but must necessarily be estimated by using various statistical data. Paul Sonnier, a famous social entrepreneur (http://storyofdigitalhealth.com/about/), addresses this issue by pointing out that the digital health market is not monolithic and has to be parsed with information from different sources (personal communication, September, 20, 2014).

The growth of this market is coupled with the ageing of our society, as well as the extensive use of different portable devices.[1] From an ICT-perspective, it is important to note that there is an average growth of 9.9 % in health-related use of the internet in, for example, Denmark, Germany, Greece, Latvia, Norway, Poland and Portugal (according to the results of an extensive survey conducted in 2005 and 2007 [8]). At the same time, something called mhealth has also emerged, which puts a different light on the consumer's role. Akter and Ray [9] emphasize how a consumer perspective on mhealth services could be an important factor in creating possible business growth through

---

[1] We will use eHealth throughout our paper to describe the new services that are relying on ICT even if we include portable devices.

scalability. Focusing on consumer needs is important in the process of empowerment and when creating sustainable solutions [9, p. 79]. Affordability, availability, awareness and acceptance are major concepts when creating mhealth services [9].

2 Awareness About Constructing Older Age Identity in the Marketer-Consumer Dialectic in an EHealth Setting

Whitten, Steinfield and Hellmich [10] have presented the "21st century health care consumers" as an important driving force in the development of eHealth. In this paper, we will scrutinize the role of the consumer [11, 12], and especially that of the ageing consumer, within this context. We use the definition of eHealth suggested by Eng [13]: "e-health is the use of emerging information and communications technology, especially the Internet, to improve or enable health and healthcare", but have expanded this to include a consumer perspective. We also wish to emphasize that we treat markets as scripts, i.e., eHealth markets do not exist as such, but are born in different encounters between providers and consumers (in other words, the market is socially constructed; see further Storbacka and Nenonen [14]. According to consumer culture theory (see e.g. Arnould and Thompson [15]), the various different kinds of consumers do not exist without the encounter, or as Caruana and Crane [16, p. 1498] phrased it: "Consumer culture theory assumes consumers do not (pre-) exist 'out there' as homogenous, a priori categories." Markets are in this sense a social construction, emerging through discursive practices. In these encounters the role of the older consumer and how she or he will be identified is important. One basic problem is that marketing practitioners often use the chronological age concept to identify consumers. The chronological age concept [17–19] easily gives a too static view of a consumer and her or his actions. Marketers often do not take into account the diversity in the older age group [20]. According to Rodeschi [1, p. 524], in the development of new technology with or for older people, the dynamics in the relationship between older people and technology should be more critically examined. Rodeschini also points out that it is important to focus on ageing.

With the following quote, we attempt to clarify our approach: "Consumer culture theorists have turned attention to the relationship between consumers' identity projects and the structuring influence of the marketplace, arguing that the market produces certain kinds of consumer positions that consumers can choose to inhabit. While individuals can and do pursue personally edifying goals through these consumer positions, they are enacting and personalizing cultural scripts that align their identities with the structural imperatives of a consumer-driven global economy" [21, p. 871].

In the following, we will discuss the chronological age concept that we see as problematic when designing eHealth services for and with older people, as well as in the use of personas.

3 Contesting the Chronological Age Concept

As mentioned above, we feel that the chronological age concept is a problematic one. Additionally, in our view, markets are born in specific encounters between, for example, consumers, eHealth providers and designers. To understand how the third age eHealth consumer (see Sect. 5) will be constructed in such encounters, we need another way of understanding these older people, in order to avoid being overly influenced by the chronological age concept as discussed in the previous section. So, on the one hand, a more dynamic view of ageing is important. But on the other hand, chronological age is an important concept for most of us. We define, categorize and position ourselves in relation to others on the basis of the magical numbers telling us how long we have been walking on earth. Chronological age is in fact as important a dimension of categorizing people as race and gender [22]. Knowledge of the chronological age provides information about the possibilities of accomplishing certain goals. The possibilities for becoming a world famous opera singer at the age of 50 are different from those at the age of 25. But what makes this age concept problematic is that it is often presented as a fact, or as an independent social category [23]. If consumers are defined on the basis of their chronological age alone, this gives rise to the notion that a person and her or his abilities are definable by her or his age. However, in everyday life, age is created and recreated when interacting and communicating with other people. In this we follow Nikander, who states: "(…) the focus in the current work is exclusively on the communicative and dialogic processes in and through which situational meanings of age and ageing emerge in interaction" [23, p. 13].

We also follow Mathur and Moschis [24], who emphasize processes where adults learn roles and norms connected to older age. To create more dynamic eHealth solutions, we suggest that these roles and norms be made visible. We also submit that the consumer's identity is created through discursive practices, which are materialized in advertising, for example. We do not want to see the older consumer as passive and the marketing practitioner as active, as presented by Bristor and Fischer [25]. We feel that marketing is a practice that shapes roles, identities and norms, a view that is similar to the thoughts of Hackley [26–28], Penaloza and Gilly [29], Hänninen [30] and Puustinen [31]. We want to ameliorate the communicative literacy [32] among older consumers as well as among eHealth providers and designers creating different eHealth services.

We define reality as socially constructed, and hence research in this field and our contribution to the discussion about older consumers in this field should be seen as a social construction. The much-used monolithic approach, in which consumers are described using the chronological age concept, has not been conducive to a dynamic discussion. Our aim is to create a more vivid discussion leading to a more dynamic way of seeing older people.

4 A Cultural Perspective on Age and Identity

Our contemporary society is increasingly defined by consumption. It has even been stated that we define ourselves through consumption of different products and services. Arnould and Thompson [15, p. 868] have analyzed so-called consumer identity projects and related these to consumption through which consumers both create and search for an identity. When identity is seen from this perspective, brands are mostly involved: people use certain brands to strengthen a desired identity. We wish to emphasize how the discursive practices of practitioners create frameworks of interpretation in which older people find their identity. Hence we are not talking about identity projects that use brands to underline a consumer's identity, but rather about how discursive practices shape the way consumers find their identity.

While Katz [21] talks about cultural ageing, we would like to introduce the concept of cultural age, as analogous to the concept of chronological age. The difference here is that we emphasize how age is constructed through representation and interaction. The concept is to gender what chronological age is to sex (see the discussion about the concepts in Rubin [33]). Gender is defined as the way the masculine or the feminine role is constructed in different discursive practices; sex has to do with the visual biological differences between a man and a woman. By analogy, we all have a chronological age, but also a cultural age by which our identities are shaped as old or young in interaction with each other.

5   The Combination of Older Age and Consumption

To illustrate our perspective on the role of older people in the design process of eHealth services, we provide an example taken from a consumption context. Until recently, older people were not regarded as an interesting consumer segment. One of the reasons for this was that they were seen as consumers with traditional consumption patterns (see e.g. Suokannas [19]). This situation has changed, mainly because marketers have begun to be convinced that this segment is valuable. The baby boomers who changed society in the past [34] are now having a similar effect in the marketing context. This has led to a wholly different idea of who the future older consumers will be: "The little old lady of 2025 won't have a spotless Ford Fairlane (that she drives once a week, to church) sitting in her garage, She'll be buzzing around town in an Alfa-Romeo (standard equipment with hydraulic lifts), dressed head to toe in the Nike "Silver" line, parking in the plentiful spaces reserved for people who are old but not impaired (as mandated by the 2009 Perky Aging Americans Act). Thanks to improved health care, nutrition, fitness and cosmetic surgery, at seventy she'll look and feel like her mother did at fifty" ([35], pp. 129–130).

This quote emphasizes the differences between the way older people of the future are expected to look and act, and the older people we have been used to. However, while this may hold true for third age [36], i.e., those who are healthy (and often rich enough) to be marketed as a valuable consumer segment to marketers, obviously this will not apply to the category of older people who are not as fortunate (see Loos [17] for two discourse coalitions related to these two kind of older people: the eternally youthful seniors and the frail needy seniors, and see Suokannas [19] and Loos and Ekström [20] on other possible categorizations of older people).

In this paper we focus on older people who are in their third age and on how their identity as active eHealth consumers is constructed (by themselves and others, such as eHealth providers and designers). In other words, we want to understand the process of becoming a third age eHealth consumer. We therefore present an analytical framework for future studies aiming to analyze eHealth offerings and to gain insight into the construction of the third age eHealth consumer group's identity through multimodal communicative acts as is the case in advertising or in settings requiring interactivity, such as the service design process. These multimodal acts could be the way new eHealth offerings are marketed to the third age eHealth consumer, focusing especially on both the textual and visual language in use. Our approach is meant to offer an alternative to studies in which ageing has mostly drawn upon the chronological age concept and where marketing has not been seen as a discursive practice shaping consumers' identities (see also Loos and Ekström [20]). As these markets develop, it is important to raise the awareness of age stereotypes, confront possible ageism in society and to develop communicative acts of high ethical standards. By using and elaborating on the Foucauldian "technologies of the self" (Foucault [37] - in other words, by making visible the ways older people are constrained or empowered in our society - we aim to find a means to reach our goal.

6 Towards the Use of Personas for the Design of EHealth Services for Third Age Consumers

Within the emerging field of eHealth services, it is important to find out how the dynamic dialectic between the ageing discourse and the eHealth discourse, as discussed in this paper, will construct the third age eHealth consumer. To that end, we proposed to use a specific method called personas creation [3, 38]. In the past, personas have largely been used to derive a more hands-on impression of users within product or service design. We propose to use personas for eliciting the various power relations and the dynamics of specific encounters in which the third age eHealth consumer is constructed. To our knowledge, this method has mainly been used to create fictive personas. The use of personas as a method may enable a better understanding among eHealth providers and designers of the third age eHealth consumer, although care should be taken to avoid the risk of creating stereotypes. This might occur if designers allow themselves to be led by the chronological age concept. We recommend scholars, marketers, eHealth providers and designers in this field to further develop this method by adopting our cultural age concept in order to avoid too much stereotyped categorization. As personas are archetypes and the aim is to develop these distinct types,

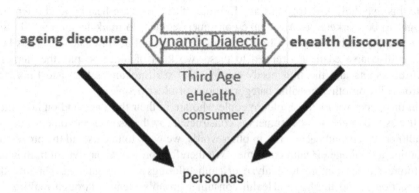

Fig. 1. Constructing the third age eHealth consumer

stereotyped categorization can easily occur (see Sect. 1 and [3, 38]). Although personas are used to create a deeper connection with the user by narratives, the hypothetical persona is described through the use of chronological age. In other words, eHealth providers and designers are creating offerings that are informed by this age concept. By focusing on how age is constructed and making use of the cultural age concept, personas can be created in a more realistic way.

In Fig. 1, we finally visualize how the third age eHealth consumer will be constructed in the dynamic dialectic between the ageing discourse and the eHealth discourse, in relation to the creation of personas. As explained in this paper, this process will take place in specific encounters between third age eHealth consumers, providers and designers.

References

1. Rodeschini, G.: Gerotechnology: a new kind of care for aging? An analysis of the relationship between older people and technology. Nurs. Health Sci. **13**(4), 521–528 (2011)
2. Blaschke, C.M., Freddolino, P.P., Mullen, E.E.: Ageing and technology: a review of the research literature. Brit. J. Soc. Work **39**(4), 641–656 (2009)
3. Cooper, A.: The Inmates are Running the Asylum: Why High-Tech Products Drive us Crazy and How to Restore the Sanity, vol. 261. Sams Publishing, Indianapolis (1999)
4. Goodwin, K.: Designing for the Digital Age: How to Create Human-Centered Products and Services. Wiley, New York (2011)
5. Turner, P., Turner, S.: Is stereotyping inevitable when designing with personas? Des. Stud. **32**(1), 30–44 (2011)
6. Barak, B., Schiffman, L.G.: Cognitive age: a nonchronological age variable. In: Monroe, K. B. (ed.) Advances in Consumer Research, vol. 9, pp. 602–606. Association for Consumer Research, Washington (1981)
7. LeRouge, C., Ma, J., Sneha, S., Tolle, K.: User profiles and personas in the design and development of consumer health technologies. Int. J. Med. Inf. **82**(11), e251–e268 (2013)
8. Kummervold, P.E., Chronaki, C.E., Lausen, B., Prokosch, H.-U., Rasmussen, J., Santana, S., Staniszewski, A., Wangberg, S.C.: eHealth trends in Europe 2005–2007: a population-based survey. J. Med. Internet Res. **10**(4), e42 (2008). doi:10.2196/jmir.1023
9. Akter, S., Ray, P.: mHealth-an ultimate platform to serve the unserved. Yearb Med. Inform. **2010**, 94–100 (2010)
10. Whitten, P., Steinfield, C., Hellmich, S.: eHealth: market potential and business strategies. J. Comput. Mediated Commun. **6**(4). http://onlinelibrary.wiley.com/doi/10.1111/j.1083-6101.2001.tb00129.x/fulln (2001). Accessed 21 Jan 2015
11. Keränen, N., Pulkkinen, P., Jämsä, T., Reponen, J.: Drivers of the eHealth transformation: beyond age and BMI. Finnish J. eHealth eWelfare **5**(4), 180–188 (2013)
12. Simon, F., Meurgey, F.M.: New strategies for digital health. http://www.marketing-trends-congress.com/archives/2014/pages/PDF/317.pdf. Accessed 21 Jan 2015
13. Eng, T.: The e-Health Landscape – A Terrain Map of Emerging Information and Communication Technologies in Health and Health Care. The Robert Wood Johnson Foundation, Princeton (2004)
14. Storbacka, K., Nenonen, S.: Markets as configurations. Eur. J. Mark. **45**(1/2), 241–258 (2011)

15. Arnould, E.J., Thompson, C.J.: Consumer culture theory (CCT): twenty years of research. J. Consum. Res. Gainesville **31**(4), 868–882 (2005)
16. Caruana, R., Crane, A.: Constructing consumer responsibility: exploring the role of corporate communications. Organ. Stud. **29**(12), 1495–1519 (2008)
17. Loos, E.F.: Senior citizens: digital immigrants in their own country? Observatorio (OBS*) J. **6**(1), 1–23 (2012)
18. Loos, E.F.: Designing for dynamic diversity: representing various senior citizens in digital information sources. Observatorio (OBS*) J. **7**(1), 21–45 (2013)
19. Suokannas, M.: Den anonyma seniorkomsumenten identifieras. Om identitetsskapande processer i en marknadsföringskontext [Identifying the anonymous senior consumer: The processes creating elderly identities within a marketing context]. Dissertation, Economics and Society, Swedish School of Economics and Business Administration Helsinki, Finland (2008)
20. Loos, E.F., Ekström, M.: Visually representing the generation of older consumers as a diverse audience: towards a multidimensional market segmentation typology. Participations **11**(2), 258–273 (2014)
21. Katz, S.: Cultural Aging, Life Course, Lifestyle, and Senior Worlds. Broadview Press, Peterborough (2005)
22. Kunda, Z.: Social Cognition: Making Sense of People. MIT Press, Cambridge (1999)
23. Nikander, P.: Age in Action Membership Work and Stage of Life Categories in Talk. The Finnish Academy of Science and Letters, Helsinki (2002)
24. Mathur, A., Moschis, G.P.: Socialization influences on preparation for later life. J. Mark. Pract. **5**(6/7/8), 163–176 (1999)
25. Bristor, J.M., Fischer, E.: Feminist thought: implications for consumer research. J. Consum. Res. Gainesville **19**(4), 518–536 (1993)
26. Hackley, C.E.: Social constructionism and research in marketing and advertising. Qual. Mark. Res. **1**(3), 125–131 (1998)
27. Hackley, C.E.: An epistemological odyssey: towards social construction of the advertising process. J. Mark. Commun. **5**(3), 157–168 (1999)
28. Hackley, C.E.: Marketing and Social Construction: Exploring the Rhetorics of Managed Consumption. Routledge, London (2001)
29. Penaloza, L., Gilly, M.C.: Marketer acculturation: the changer and the changed. J. Mark. **63** (3), 84–104 (1999)
30. Hänninen, S.: Sukupuoli laihdutustuotemainonnassa. In: Eriksson, P., et al. (eds.) Gender and Organisations in Flux?, pp. 229–240. Swedish School of Economics and Business Administration, Helsingfors (2004)
31. Puustinen, L.: Kuvitteellisen kohderyhmän metsästys: Miten kuluttajuutta rakennetaan mainonnan tuotannossa? In: Eriksson, P., et al. (eds.) Gender and Organisations in Flux?, pp. 203–215. Swedish School of Economics and Business Administration, Helsingfors (2004)
32. Firat, A.F., Dholakia, N.: Theortical and philosophical implications of postmodern debates: some challenges to modern marketing. Mark. Theor. **6**(2), 123–162 (2006)
33. Rubin, G.: The traffic in women: notes on the 'political economy' of sex. In: Reiter, R. (ed.) Toward an Anthropology of Women, pp. 157–210. Monthly Review Press, New York (1975)
34. Dychtwald, K.: Age Power How the 21st Century will be Ruled by the New Old. Tarcher/Putnam, New York (1999)
35. Underhill, P.: Why We Buy: The Science of Shopping. Simon and Schuster, New York (1999)

36. Laslett, P.: A Fresh Map of Life. The Emergence of the Third Age. Harvard University Press, Cambridge (1991)
37. Foucault, M.: Ethics: subjectivity and truth. Robert Hurley and others. In: Rabinow, P. (ed.) Essential Works of Foucault 1954–1984, vol. 1. Pinguin Press, London (1997)
38. Adlin, T., Pruitt, J.: The Essential Persona Lifecycle: Your Guide to Building and Using Personas. Morgan Kaufmann, Amsterdam (2010)

Capturing Older People's Cognitive Capability Data for Design

Shan Huang[1] and Hua Dong[2(✉)]

[1] College of Architecture and Urban Planning, Tongji University,
Shanghai, China
shan_huhu@aliyun.com
[2] College of Design and Innovation, Tongji University, Shanghai, China
donghua@tongji.edu.cn

Abstract. There is a lack of cognitive capability data in design. Existing capability databases lack consideration of older people who are suffering decline of cognitive capabilities. To explore older people's cognitive capability data for the design context, two pilot studies were conducted: a small-scale cognitive capability survey in China, and a study of a group of industrial designers' needs regarding user data. A Framework of user data were developed and key issues for cognitive capability data collection and application in design were identified and discussed.

Keywords: Cognitive capability · User data · Design for older people · Human factors and ergonomics

1 Introduction

In the context of design, capability refers to an individual's level of functioning, from very high ability to extreme impairments, which has implications for the extent to which they can interact with products [1]. However, the study on user cognitive capability data is relatively weak comparing to other functional capability data. For instance, the ongoing "Basic Chinese adults' ergonomics data collection" project by the China National Institute of Standardization (CNIS), has added the measurements on sensory capabilities, such as visual and hearing abilities [2]. But this project has not yet covered the measurement on cognitive capability. This is probably because it is more difficult in measuring cognitive capability [1]. A study named *Towards Better Design* [3] initiated by the University of Cambridge has incorporated cognitive capability measurement, but the tests were mainly adapted from cognitive psychology, thus having limited relevance to design.

Technology development pushes older people into the mobile-internet world, and there is a need to understand how they interact with information and communication technology. Cognitive capabilities play an important part in older people's interaction with these technologies.

1.1 User Capability Data

User capability data, derived from Human factors and ergonomics (HF&E), are widely recognized as a good resource that informs design in the early stages [4]; they are fundamental to the design of safe and usable products [5].

J. Zhou and G. Salvendy (Eds.): ITAP 2015, Part I, LNCS 9193, pp. 44–52, 2015.
DOI: 10.1007/978-3-319-20892-3_5

Categories. There are two categories of user capability data: (1) physical capability data, (2) functional capability data [6] (Fig. 1). Physical capability data refer to traditional human factor data such as height, grip strength and the reach of limbs, which are associated with physical attributes. Functional capability data relate to senses, cognition and motion; and there are more and more studies focusing on these fields [7, 8].

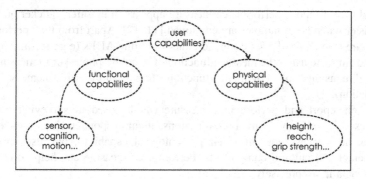

Fig. 1. Categories of user capability data (adapted from [6])

Functions. The benefits of involving user capability data in the design process are two folds. On one hand, it can serve as benchmarks that assist designers to make the design decisions and to estimate whether the design is accessible or not. And the metric that can serve as the benchmark is the significant element of design evaluation. By providing suitable metrics, designers should be able to measure the success of their designs and also identify accessibility shortcomings [6]. Apart from that, the range of capabilities is also an essential factor. Johnson et al. claims that tools for predicting difficulties need to be able to "give designers a picture of the full range of capabilities and also the ability to consider and understand the multi-dimensional nature of capability profiles" [1]. On the other hand, designers regard user capability data as resources that can inspire them. Design is a series of mental processes, manipulating intelligence to discover and solve problems, with moments of sudden illumination [9].

Capture Methods. Self-report and performance measure are methods commonly used to assess physical functions in health surveys of older people [10]. The method of self-report is based on a series of questions, which offers a fast, low-cost and easily executed path to users' information that can be gathered by questionnaires, face-to-face interviews or remote interviews (telephone or online interviews). Proxy response is a kind of self-report that can be conducted when an interviewee cannot answer by himself/herself. However, that should not be equivalent to self-report, because research has shown that a proxy report is not as accurate as self-report for the rating of ability to perform activities of daily living (ADLs) among older people [11]. Based on Fors and his colleagues' study [10], the limitation of self-report can be listed as follow:

- There is limited value in identifying clinically significant change.
- Lack of reliability: the subjective factor as individual expectations and aspirations may affect a person, especially an older one, to comparing to peers and level of functioning in earlier life.
- Be sensitive to the influence of cognitive impairments, culture, language and education.

Compared to self-report, performance measure appears to be safer, quicker and easier to administer when large samples are employed [11, 12]. Apart from that, performance measures are standardized tests designed either to mimic ADLs (e.g., reading message on cards to simulate using the message function of a mobile-phone) or to measure more specific dimensions of cognitive function (e.g., short-term memory, visual discrimination).

Both self-report and performance measure can be used in surveying cognitive capabilities [1]. Self-report involves questions about respondents' past experience, which can help access not only their physiological capability, but also attitudinal, environmental and cultural components. Performance measure can help collect some capability data more precisely.

1.2 Older People's Cognitive Capability

Cognition abilities are typically used in combination to perceive information, and the function of cognition can explain information processing [13]. But complex information processing contains much more than a cognition process. Figure 2 shows a model for the typical cycle of perceiving, thinking and acting that occurs in the interaction with a product [7], which suggests that the ability to successfully interact with computer terminals could be predicted according to the demands made on users' sensory, cognitive and motor abilities [14]. Information perceiving, memory and acting process compose a rounded cognitive process, and the cognitive capabilities involved in that process are considered in this study.

Individuals of all ages believe that memory undergoes a relatively precipitous decline after age 40 [15]. This cognitive retrogression makes it more challenging to design for older people. Older people's cognitive capabilities are mainly reflected in their visual perception, auditory perception, memory abilities and their sometimes attitudes. These factors are not isolated, but inter-related. Due to the decline of perception, older people's perception of time is intentionally longer than the other adults [16]. And due to their habitual thinking, acting and the decline of memory, their learning capacity falls sharply after age 45 [17], which often makes it more difficult for older people to learn to use products that they are not so familiar with (e.g. some mobile-internet products).

2 Pilot Studies

Many studies show that existing user capability databases are still lack of the consideration of older people [18]. Inclusive design as a design methodology emphasises on consciousness of the demands to design for a wider range of users, including the

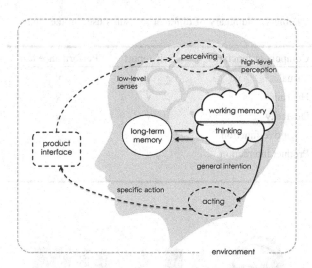

Fig. 2. A typical information-processing model for a product interaction (adapted from [14])

demands of older and disabled people. Studies also suggest that existing ergonomics database are lack of the consideration of designers [19].

An ideal user capability database need to be able to give designers a picture of the full range of capabilities and also the ability to consider and understand the multi-dimensional nature of capability profiles [1]. Therefore, two pilot studies were conducted to get insights into older people's cognitive capability data for design.

2.1 Pilot Study 1: A Small-Scale Cognitive Capability Survey in China

The first pilot study was a small-scale cognitive capability data collection, which was conducted by the Inclusive Design Research Group at Tongji University. It covered seven different cities and towns of China. The age range of respondents was from 50 to 80. Both self-report and performance measures were employed in the study. Self-assessed measures most likely draw on the participants' experiences from their everyday life whereas performance-based measures are more specific and standardized [10].

This pilot study was the cognition section of a multiple capability-related data survey conducted by the Tongji University. The survey questions were derived and adapted from *Towards Better Design* [3]. A variety of data were collected in this survey, including vision, hearing, dexterity, cognition, health condition, and contextual data collection. Table 1 summarises the methods employed in measuring different types of capabilities (i.e. component functions). As seen in Table 1, Cognitive function was measured through self-report.

A toolkit was designed for collecting multiple capability-related data. Figure 3 shows the tools included in the toolkit.

This paper focuses on the aspect of cognitive capability. The questions were directly derived and adapted from the field of psychology. For instance, to test short-term memory, the respondent was asked to recall the words that were prerecorded

Table 1. Summary of different measures used in the study

Component functions	Self-report	Performance test
Visual	√	√
Hearing	√	√
Dexterity	√	√
Cognitive function	√	
Product interaction	√	√
...		

Fig. 3. The toolkit for the pilot multiple capability survey in China

in an audio file; to test their comprehension, a made-up medicine prescription was given to the respondent, followed by a few questions to test whether the respondent has fully understood the prescription; to test numerical abilities, the respondent was asked questions relating to his/her use of numbers in everyday life.

Main Findings. The cognitive data collected from the study seem to have little direct relevance to design, and it is difficult to predict product interaction based on the data collected. In addition, many respondents tended to overestimate their abilities in self-reporting.

Discussion. As the cognitive questions are mainly derived from the fields of psychology and healthcare surveys [20], the results have limited use for design. In the design process, user capability data are applied to predict a solution of a specific design problem, aiming at making the product more accessible to target users. Therefore it is important to develop new, design-relevant cognitive measures. In addition, because self-report is subjective [8], it is necessary to introduce objective measures in cognitive capability test.

2.2   Pilot Study 2: A Study of Industrial Designers' Needs for User Data

In order to develop design-related user capability survey, it is important to understand designers' needs regarding user data, including users' cognitive capability data. Existing ergonomics data are not designer-friendly; a study carried out in the UK [7] shows that 'all the interviewed designer considered the existing anthropometric data out of date, and seven out of ten believed the data was irrelevant or not applicable to their specific field of design practice.' So what are the useful and usable user data for design? A study was conducted with industrial designers to identify their needs.

There were two steps in this study. In the first step, 12 in-house designers, 12 consultant designers and 12 freelance designers were invited to answer a questionnaire. The questions covered the time designers use in understanding user capabilities, the means designers usually adopt when they need user data, the data designers prefer, and how they use user data in the design process. Table 2 shows the profiles of the participants. In the second step, designers from each category in the step 1 were invited for a focus group discussion, and three designers were able to participate in the focus group.

Table 2. The profiles of the designers participating in the study

Categories of designer	Design field	Number	Total
In-house designer	Digital device	4	12
	Household appliance	4	
	Engineering product	4	
Consultant designer	Digital device	4	12
	Household appliance	4	
	Engineering product	4	
Freelance designer	Student major in design	6	12
	Other	6	
			36

Main Findings. The results showed that different categories of designers spent quite different time in understanding user capabilities. In-house designers (27 %) spent more time than the other two categories of designers, while freelance designers (7 %) spent least time. Apart from that, the proportions of time designers spend on user data differed for different types of designs. There is a consistent trend that designers spent more time on understanding users for digital device design than for household appliances, and for engineering product design, designers seem to spent less time in understanding user capabilities.

The designers most often searched the Internet for information about their target users. The designers in the field of engineering product design preferred ergonomics data. Small-scale user research was a crucial method for designers to get first hand data of users. Almost all of the designers who did not prefer ergonomics data claimed that current ergonomics database was hard to use and had little relevance to their specific design problems.

There was not much difference on the preference of data formats among the three types of designers. The respondents all preferred visualized data (e.g. photos and informational graphics) than text information (e.g. numerical data). Designers needed both qualitative data and quantitative data. Moreover, some designers considered descriptive words as a kind of qualitative data that could help them to quickly get the information of target users.

It was also found that designers needed user data throughout the whole design process. Designers usually used qualitative data to get conceptual inspiration, and quantitative data could help designers to explore references to support a specific design decision.

Discussion. The study of designers' needs for user data suggest that a new type of user data (probably differ significantly from existing ergonomics data) is needed by designers, which should contain both qualitative and quantitative data. These data should be developed to support design activities at different design stages.

3   A Conceptual User Data Framework

Based on literature review and pilot studies, a conceptual user data framework was developed to illustrate the landscape of user data for design (Fig. 4). On one hand, quantitative data are obtained from larges (population), which can be regarded as benchmarks in the design process. On the other hand, qualitative data are obtained from relatively small samples (i.e. individual users), which can help designers to get conceptual inspiration. Most of existing capability databases focus on data collection. In contrast, designers tend to focus on data application. Therefore, establishing the connection between data collection and data application is the key issue for a designer-oriented user capability database.

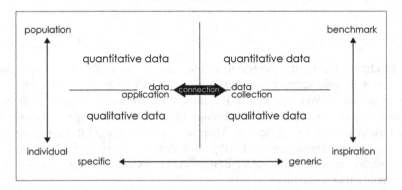

Fig. 4. The range of user capability data

In addition, it is also crucial to ingeniously combine quantitative data and qualitative data. Ergonomics data are often quantitative data, which cannot provide designers with contextual information of users. Particularly, in the concept generation phase, qualitative data are more helpful for gaining insights into target users.

4 Conclusions and Further Study

In a word, it is necessary to develop survey questions that can help collect older people's cognitive capability data for the purpose of improving design. Tests in the field of cognitive psychology can be used as a source of reference. Crucially, the test tasks (including self-report questions and performance measured tasks) should be related to product interaction.

The further study should aim to solve two critical questions:

(1) How to make cognitive capability data useful to designer?
(2) How to make the data easy to use?

In addition, more designers from different fields should be involved in the future study; this will help gain a deeper understanding of designers' needs and desires, so as to make the database useful and usable for the design community.

Acknowledgments. We thank all the people who participated in this study. Many members of the Inclusive Design Research Centre (China) helped data collection in the pilot study; our sincere thanks go to Ning weining, Zhou qian, Cui xiaochen, Jiang yingcheng, Zhang yingyu, Ma xuezi and Zhang wenyun.

References

1. Johnson, D., Clarkson, J., Huppert, F.: Capability measurement for inclusive design. J. Eng. Des. **21**(2–3), 275–288 (2010)
2. China National Institution of Standardization. http://www.cnis.gov.cn/. Accessed 5 Oct 14
3. Towards better design. http://www.esds.ac.uk/findingData/snDescription.asp?sn=6997. Accessed 12 Oct 14
4. Meister, D.: The History of Human Factors and Ergonomics. Lawrence Erlbaum Associates, Mahwah (1999)
5. Norris, B.J., Wilson, J.R.: CHILDATA—The Handbook of Child Measurements and Capabilities—Data for Design Safety. Department of Trade and Industry, London (1995)
6. Clarkson, P.J., et al.: Approaches to estimating user exclusion. Appl. Ergon. (2013). doi:10. 1016/j.apergo. Accessed 01 Mar 13
7. Waller, S.D., Langdon, P.M., Clarkson, P.J.: Using disability data to estimate design exclusion. Univ. Access Inf. Soc. **9**(3), 195–207 (2010)
8. Tenneti, R., Johnson, D., Goldenberg, L., et al.: Towards a capabilities database to inform inclusive design: Experimental investigation of effective survey-based predictors of human-product interaction. Appl. Ergon. **43**(4), 713–726 (2012)
9. Cross, N.: Designerly Ways of Knowing. Springer, London (2006)
10. Fors, Stefan, Thorslund, Mats, Parker, Marti G.: Do actions speak louder than words? Self-assessed and performance-based measures of physical and visual function among old people. Eur. J. Ageing **3**(1), 15–21 (2006)
11. Reuben, D., et al.: Refining the categorization of physical functional status: the added value of combining self-reported and performance-based measures. J. Gerontol. **59A**(10), 1056–1061 (2004)

12. Guralnik, J., et al.: A short physical performance battery assessing lower extremity function: association with self-reported disability and prediction of mortality and nursing home admission. J. Gerontol. **49**(2), M85–M94 (1994)
13. Solso, R.L., et al.: Cognitive Psychology, 7th edn. Pearson Education, Boston (2005)
14. Waugh, N.C., Norman, D.A.: Primary memory. Psych. **72**, 89–104 (1965)
15. Hertzog, C., Kramer, A.F., Wilson, R.S., et al.: Enrichment effects on adult cognitive development can the functional capacity of older adults be preserved and enhanced? Psychol. Sci. Publ. Interest **9**(1), 1–65 (2008)
16. Feifel, H.: Psychology and Death-Meaningful Rediscovery. AMER Psychological ASSOC, Washington (1957)
17. Cohen, G.: Language comprehension in old age. Cogn. Psychol. **11**(4), 412–429 (1979)
18. Langdon, P., Johnson, D., Huppert, F., et al.: A framework for collecting inclusive design data for the UK population. Appl. Ergon. **46**, 318–324 (2015)
19. Dong, H., McGinley, C., Nickpour, F., et al.: Designing for designers: insights into the knowledge users of inclusive design. Appl. Ergon. **46**, 284–291 (2015)
20. Iburg, K.M., Salomon, J.A., Tandon, A., et al.: Cross-population comparability of self-reported and physician-assessed mobility levels: evidence from the third national health and nutrition examination survey. In: Global Programme on Evidence for Health Policy Discussion Paper. World Health Organization, Geneva (2001)

Designing Tangible Interactions for Aged Users Though Interactive Technology Prototyping

Wei Liu[1](✉) and Yanrui Qu[2]

[1] Tongji University, Shanghai, China
liuwei.dk@gmail.com
[2] Beijing University of Technology, Beijing, China

Abstract. This research aims to explore how to bring the richness of tangible interaction designs into the everyday living and working contexts of the aged users. To do so, we introduced an interactive technology design at two Chinese Universities, for the first time interactive prototyping skills become important for their undergraduate and graduate students to learn and practice. In an interactive prototyping course, a number of prototypes designed for aged users were built and experienced. From these prototypes, experiences for regularly running interaction design education based on traditional industrial design education were discussed.

Keywords: Interaction design · Interaction qualities · User experience · Interactive design technology · Context of use · Aged users

1 Introduction

Being educated as industrial designers, the design students at the Tongji University and the Beijing University of Technology are used to and are good at crafting physical car models, designing graphical illustrations and making Chinese porcelains. However, interaction design, specifically interactive prototyping will play a crucial role in their educational curriculums in the coming years. In order to improve the fit, we organized an interactive technology design course with experts from practice. The goal was to help the students learn and practice interactive prototyping skills by developing interactive and working prototypes.

Key questions for students are: how does aged users experience and use a product? What is his understanding of that product? Is it the design of the product that determines or influences these responses, the needs and abilities of the user, or the environment in which it is used and its social context? Experience design [5, 9, 23] brings a broad perspective to the design of product interaction, encompassing such traditional activities as product styling and user-centered design but additionally requiring attention for all psychological effects elicited by interaction including stimulation of the senses, meaning and value attribution to the product and the feelings and emotions that are elicited. In the traditional product design process [12, 19, 30], there are insufficient provisions to consider the design of interactive products. Alternative approaches propose a highly

© Springer International Publishing Switzerland 2015
J. Zhou and G. Salvendy (Eds.): ITAP 2015, Part I, LNCS 9193, pp. 53–60, 2015.
DOI: 10.1007/978-3-319-20892-3_6

iterative design process that allow for concepts to grow by making experiential prototypes (also called sketches in the early stages of the design). Important roles of these prototypes are to allow the designer to communicate the concept to the design team and to give him insight on how well the designed features of the interactive product concept match the design brief.

2   Related Work

In aged user interaction design domain, Keller [10] designed cabinet that helps designers collect and organize their visual material for inspiration. The design makes interaction with digital material more physical by dragging digital images on a table as if they are real objects. It offers a fluent way to add physical material to the digital collection by digitizing and projecting any objects placed on the table. This type of study was followed by several other recent projects in the domain of computer supported collaborative work (CSCW), such as designing an intelligent robot worker that transports goods and samples in semi-public hospital context [13] and designing a shape-changing communication device that facilitates expressive 'knocking' communications [20]. Another example is the intelligent reading lamp, which aims to demonstrate ethics and esthetics in products and systems. By moving the hand over the lamp, a 'living light' can be directed onto an object such as a book.

3   Settings

The interactive technology design course aims to equip students with design theory while gaining practical experience in the development of interactive prototypes, which utilize potentials of embedded interactive technology in products in terms of enriching user experience [1, 6, 7, 22]. Max/MSP, Phidgets sensors and Arduino were selected as development environments. These tools make it possible to build experiential prototypes, even with students who have few electrical and programming skills [15–17]. Fifty students worked in teams of three on three design briefs concerning aged user group's styles of interaction in an office context. The concept and prototype development involved a total of five phases. The first two phases focused on exploring conceptual possibilities and building initial prototypes by hacking existing products. The third phase aimed to nut-crack the hardest technological problems and further develop the concept to a mature level. The fourth phase involved users, while the last phase targeted on integrating user comments to finalize the prototypes.

4   Approach

Our research objective has been to explore how to bring the richness of tangible interaction designs into the everyday living and working contexts of the aged users. This is an interesting challenge that presents itself to developers, designers and researchers. The course lasted for a total of seven calendar weeks. It run in parallel with others and it was supposed to take up one and half days per week. We developed a design brief together with the brief holder who contributed some money to partially cover prototyping material and expenses. After a kick-off presentation, the students were distributed into teams, and each team received the same brief. We made sure that each team had at least one technology-focused students, although the course does not assume any technology expertise. The course consists of five iterations of increasing length, each one producing a prototype with a different focus. The five iterations can be summarized under the form of assignments given to the students.

We envisage using interaction qualities [3, 14, 21] as design guidance and a new approach that can help researchers, designers and students to integrate functional design, experiential interactions and interactive technology. Some interaction qualities (e.g., playful, collaborative and expressive) were explored and used as design guidance. The students were asked to explore IT supported user-product interactions through learning the characteristics of different sensors and actuators, how to program them, and how to employ them in realizing engaging interactions [26, 28, 29]. They had to focus on the experiential interaction qualities instead of programming details. The primary goal for the students was that it had to be a working demo and to be engaging for aged users.

5   Interactive Technology Designs

From the beginning and throughout the whole research, digital and physical prototypes that are rich in aesthetic, expressive and experiential quality are built and tested in real living and working contexts. To ensure a high flow of thoughts, ideas and knowledge, a research through design approach is taken, in which the generation of knowledge and the development of applications go hand in hand. Research through design is used as a form of research to contribute to a design activity [2, 4]. It is recognized as a form of action research, defined as systematic investigation through practical action calculated to devise or test new information, ideas, forms or procedures and to produce communicable knowledge [8, 31]. Action research is an iterative process involving researchers and practitioners acting together in a particular cycle of activities [24, 25]. The research through design approach is highly iterative, integrating theory and practice from different fields into working experiential prototypes. These prototypes can be experienced as working artefacts and can be used as research means to demonstrate and explore these theories [11, 18]. Designing and building working prototypes that are rich in experiential quality therefore plays a key role in this approach. The reflection on the action (of designing and building) creates new knowledge. The designing act of creating prototypes is in itself a potential generator of knowledge [6, 17], leading to new design insights and refinement of research issues. Below are brief descriptions of three concept interactive designs for aged users, concerning their real living and working contexts.

5.1   Glasses

Glasses is an interactive installation designed for aged users with bad eyesight. They wear glasses to read newspapers and might always forget where the glasses are put. This design helps them to allocate the glasses and to form a good habit of putting the glasses in a box. A user swipes in the front of the box to open it. After reading, while the user folds the glasses, the box opens and lights from inside glows. This indicates the user to put back glasses in a good order. Infrared and bend sensors are embedded in the box and in the glasses. See Figs. 1 and 2 for an impression. A video scenario can be found at http://v.youku.com/v_show/id_XNTkxMDA5OTgw.html.

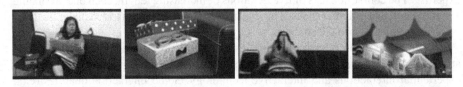

Fig. 1. The user interaction of glasses

Fig. 2. The design and development process of glasses

5.2 Toy

Toy is a pair of interactive devices designed for aged users and their family members to communicate with tangible inputs. A user touches and twists one device to trigger rotation and light effects on the other device. This indicates that a message is sent and attention is needed. Rotation and light sensors are embedded in the design. See Figs. 3 and 4 for an impression. A video scenario can be found at http://v.youku.com/v_show/id_XNTkxODEyMzI0.html.

Fig. 3. The user interaction of toy

Fig. 4. The design and development process of toy

5.3 Puppet

Puppet is an interactive device designed for aged bus drivers. This design helps them to exercise and get a quick massage after a long time driving. Every one hour, the device activates and asks the user to rest for a while. It starts vibrating and generates voice commands, which guides the user to tap and massage shoulder, arm, leg, etc. After completing the commands, the vibration stops. Vibration, touch and gravity sensors are embedded in the device. See Figs. 5 and 6 for an impression. A video scenario can be found at http://v.youku.com/v_show/id_XNTkzMjY3MTE2.html.

Fig. 5. The user interaction of puppet

Fig. 6. The design and development process of puppet

6   Discussion

All prototypes show promise by providing novel user interactions - that is the power of making experiential prototypes. From working on the design assignment, the students understand that aged users, context and action are the key elements of interaction design. They designed and tried out various ways of interacting. With skills, students can design and build more interactive prototypes in other domains.

We have mentioned that the objective of the course is to teach students how to create concepts in a group for interactive products manifested as interactive experiential prototypes. This objective places technology in a clear ancillary role. The course structure, based on group work, tends to obscure individual contributions and, in particular, makes it impossible to evaluate the degree to which students have learned prototyping technologies. Moreover, the number and complexity of the deliverables encourages the students to take on the project roles that we have already mentioned. In learning terms, the consequence is that a student may go through interactive technology design without ever writing a line of code or touching a soldering iron. While the course has a big space for techniques of all sorts, something that we personally delight in, it remains a design course in a faculty of Design.

The course was done in an educational setting but not in a practice setting of commercial product development, because in the educational setting we can take control, pay attention to design interactions and structure the course as an exercise, which does not have to have full complexity and pressures of commercial reality. The students in the course are also treated as designers.

The limitations of this course include the short amount of time, insufficient knowledge on interaction design from the students and lack of comprehensive user tests.

7 Conclusion

We have presented the model of interactive technology education. We have seen this aggressively prototyping oriented approach produce good designs that have resulted in publications and products. Our contribution to the existing body of knowledge is to draw attention to IT supported new ways of interacting that will have a great influence on aged users. Our findings have implications on the development of the future products, services and systems for aged users should utilize the power and advantages of modern, appropriate and innovative interactions and technologies. We believe that this same approach could be used for other adjacent domains that do not have a physical base like web application design or mobile application development. Designing and prototyping interactions successfully promoted the students to learn and practice interactive prototyping skills.

8 Future Work

In order to accumulate experience on interaction design education, the next step is to conduct more prototyping studies on the incoming research projects within the college, to run user tests and to set a curriculum syllabus. These prototypes will get evaluated based on how it functionally works, how its user interactions fit into context and how it can benefit future ways of living and working for the aged users.

Acknowledgements. We thank all students for their enthusiasm and hard work. We thank Aadjan van der Helm and Marco Rozendaal for their knowledge. We thank Microsoft Research Asia for their support.

References

1. Aprile, W., Van der Helm, A.: Interactive technology design at the delft university of technology - a course about how to design interactive products. In: Proceedings E&PDE 2011, London (2011)
2. Archer, B.: The nature of research. J. Codesign **2**, 6–13 (1995)
3. Arvola, M.: Interaction design qualities: theory and practice. In: Proceedings NordiCHI 2010, pp. 595–598. ACM Press (2010)
4. Avison, D.E., Lau, F., Myers, M.D., Nielsen, P.A.: Action research. Commun. ACM **42**(1), 94–97 (1999)

5. Buxton, W.: Sketching User Experience – Getting the Design Right and the Right Design. Morgan Kaufmann, San Francisco (2007)
6. Crowley, T., Milazzo, P., Baker, E., Forsdick, H., Tomlinson, R.: MMConf: an infrastructure for building shared multimedia applications. In: Proceedings of the 1990 ACM Conference on Computer-Supported Cooperative Work, pp. 329–342. ACM Press, New York, NY, USA (1990)
7. Greenberg, S., Marwood, D.: Real time groupware as a distributed system: concurrency control and its effect on the interface. In: Proceedings of the 1994 ACM Conference on Computer Supported Cooperative Work, pp. 207–217. ACM Press, New York, NY, USA (1994)
8. Hoeben, A., Stappers, P.J.: Taking clues from the world outside: navigating interactive panoramas. J. Pers. Ubiquit. Comput. **10**(2–3), 122–127 (2006)
9. Hughes, J.A., Randall, D., Shapiro, D.: Faltering from ethnography to design. In: Proceedings of the 1992 ACM Conference on Computer-Supported Cooperative Work, pp. 115–122. ACM Press, New York, NY, USA (1992)
10. Keller, A.I.: For inspiration only, designer interaction with informal collections of visual material. Doctoral dissertation, Delft University of Technology, Delft (2005)
11. Koskinen, I., Zimmerman, J., Binder, T., Redström, J., Wensveen, S.: Design Research Through Practice, 1st edn. Morgan Kaufmann, San Francisco (2011)
12. Kumar, R.: Research Methodology: A Step-by-Step Guide for Beginners, 2nd edn. Sage Publications, Thousand Oaks (2005)
13. Ljungblad, S., Kotrbova, J. Jacobsson, M., Cramer, H., Niechwiadowicz, K.: Hospital robot at work: something alien or an intelligent colleague? In: Proceedings of the ACM 2012 Conference on Computer Supported Cooperative Work (CSCW). ACM Press, New York (2012)
14. Löwgren, J.: Articulating the use qualities of digital designs. In: Aesthetic Computing, pp. 383–403 (2006)
15. Mellis, D.A., et al.: Arduino: an open electronics prototyping platform. In: CHI, CHI 2007, San Josè, USA (2007)
16. Nardi, B.A., Whittaker, S., Bradner, E.: Interaction and outeraction: instant messaging in action. In: Proceedings of the 2000 ACM Conference on Computer Supported Cooperative Work, pp. 79–88. ACM Press New York, NY, USA (2000)
17. Neuwirth, C.M., Kaufer, D.S., Chandhok, R., Morris, J.H.: Issues in the design of computer support for co-authoring and commenting. In: Proceedings of the 1990 ACM Conference on Computer-Supported Cooperative Work, pp. 183–195. ACM Press New York, NY, USA (1990)
18. Norman, D.A.: Emotion and design: attractive things work better. Interactions **9**(4), 36–42 (2002). ACM Press, New York
19. Paton, M.: Qualitative Research and Evaluation Methods, 3rd edn. Sage Publications, Thousand Oaks (2002)
20. Rasmussen, M.K., Lehoux, N., Ocnarescu, I., Krogh, P.G.: I'll knock you when I'm ready…: reflecting on media richness beyond bandwidth and imitation. In: Proceedings of the ACM 2012 Conference on Designing Interactive Systems (DIS), pp. 106–115 (2012)
21. Rullo, A.: The soft qualities of interaction. ACM Trans. Comput. Hum. Interact. **15**, 4 (2008)
22. Sanders, L., Stappers, P.J.: Convivial Toolbox: Generative Research for the Front End of Design, pp. 224–225. BIS Publishers, Amsterdam (2013)
23. Schifferstein, H.N.J., Hekkert, P.: Product Experience. Elsevier Science Ltd., Amsterdam (2007)

24. Visser, F.S., Stappers, P.J., Van der Lugt, R., Sanders, E.B.-N.: Contextmapping: experiences from practice. J. Codesign **1**(2), 119–149 (2005)
25. Stappers, P.J., Hekkert, P., et al.: Consolidating the user-centered design focus in industrial design engineering. In: Proceedings E&PDE 2007, London (2007)
26. Stappers, P., Hekkert, P., Keyson, D.: Design for interaction: consolidating the user-centered design focus in industrial design engineering. In: International Conference on Engineering and Product Design Education, Northhumbria University, Newcastle upon Tyne, United Kingdom, pp. 69–74 (2007)
27. Strong, R., Gaver, B.: Feather, scent and shaker: supporting simple intimacy. In: Proceedings CSCW 1996, ACM Press (1996)
28. Tang, J.C., Isaacs, E.A., Rua, M.: Supporting distributed groups with a Montage of lightweight interactions. In: Proceedings of the 1994 ACM Conference on Computer Supported Cooperative Work, pp. 23–34. ACM Press New York, NY, USA (1994)
29. Woolfolk, A., Winne, P.H., Perry, N.E.: Social cognitive and constructivist views of learning. In: Educational Psychology, pp. 329–370. Pearson Canada, Toronto (2009)
30. Whyte, W.: Advancing scientific knowledge through participatory action research. Sociol. Forum **4**(3), 367–385 (1989)
31. Zimmerman, J., Forlizzi, J., Evenson, S.: Research through design as a method for interaction design research in HCI. In: Proceedings of the SIGCHI Conference on Human Factors in Computing Systems. ACM Press, New York (2007)

Developing a Framework for Effective Communication with Older People

Ying Jiang, Hua Dong[⊠], and Shu Yuan

Tongji University, 1602 Zonghe Building, 1239 Siping Road,
Shanghai 200092, China
donghua@tongji.edu.cn

Abstract. Communicating with older people is more challenging because of age-related cognitive and sensory impairments. How to develop an approach to enable inexperienced and young designers to effectively communicate with older people? A new and pragmatic framework is developed which aims to identify key factors of communication techniques that designers need to learn. This framework can help designers to decide which techniques are most relevant for specific conversation situations. It can also be used to systematically collect communication knowledge and skills as a designer's personal communication guidance.

Keywords: Effective communication · Older people · Cognitive impairments · Sensory impairments

1 Introduction

Effective communication between designers and older people is perhaps one of the most critical elements of interview. Communication with older people can be made more challenging as a result of age-related impairments. These age-related changes in hearing, vision, cognitive and physical abilities make face-to-face communication even more demanding [1]. The results of numerous surveys indicate that age-related cognitive and sensory impairments highly affect communication. Many older people with a vision, hearing impairment experience frequent communication breakdowns [2]. Between 30–50 % of 70 year-olds have a hearing loss that is sufficient to interfere with conversations [3]. About 20 % of adults older than 65 years of age experience visual difficulties that can limit clarity of a person's face at a conversational distance [4]. About 6 % of adults older than 65 years of age exhibit combined hearing and vision impairments (dual sensory loss) [5].

Older people-related communication barriers have been reported in design literature. Communication with users having speech or hearing problems can be difficult [6]. Interaction with older users often presents particular communication challenges for designers. In many cases, designers are forced to rely on their own experience or intuition to guide their assumptions about user characteristics, which may have little relevance to the real situation [7].

© Springer International Publishing Switzerland 2015
J. Zhou and G. Salvendy (Eds.): ITAP 2015, Part I, LNCS 9193, pp. 61–72, 2015.
DOI: 10.1007/978-3-319-20892-3_7

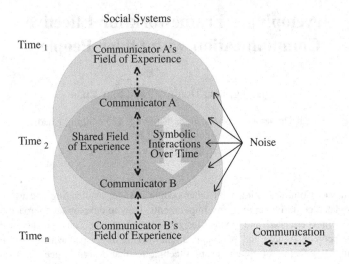

Fig. 1. The transactional model of communication (Source: Adapted from [8])

In addition, designers with young minds and attitudes are often fashion lovers: they pay more attention to trendy ideas, rather than the knowledge on older people. Very few designers have had training or education in communicating with older people.

This paper presents a first stage of study that seeks to develop a framework, which can help designers learn skills that will enhance their effectiveness in communicating with older people with cognitive and sensory impairments. This study is organized as follows: 1. To identify age-related cognitive and sensory impairments which are relevant to communication; 2. To categorise key aspects of communication that can help designers identify key factors for interacting with older people; 3. To develop a framework to aid communication.

This framework of effective communication was developed based on the transactional model of communication (Fig. 1). The model indicates each communicator is both "the sender" as well as "the receiver" simultaneously. It takes into account "noise" and the factors in communication. Noise is anything that interferes with the intended communication. Time shows that communication changes over time as a result of what happens between people. The outer lines of the model indicate that communication happens within systems that both communicators share their personal systems. It also considers changes that take place in the communicators' fields of personal and common experiences.

2   The Three Levels of Effective Communication

The most common deficiency in interviewing with older people remains a failure to demonstrate empathic listening and responding. Empathy is the ability to see things from the other person's perspective. Developing empathic listening is particularly necessary for understanding the deficits that impede communication with older people.

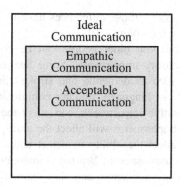

Fig. 2. The three levels of effective communication

Empathic listening, according to Stephen (1989), is listening with intent to understand. This kind of listening is not skill-based. It should not truncate from character and relationships. This means seeking first to understand, to really understand.

> "The essence of empathic listening is not that you agree with someone; it's that you fully, deeply, understand that person, emotionally as well as intellectually. Empathic listening involves much more than registering, reflecting, or even understanding the words that are said. Communications experts estimate, in fact, that only 10 % of our communication is represented by the words we say. Another 30 % is represented by our sounds, and 60 % by our body language. In empathic listening, you listen with your ears, but you also, and more importantly, listen with your eyes and with your heart" [9].

However, sometimes we thought we have fully understood what people said, but we did not. An ideal communication requires people to eliminate their personal prejudice. But it is rare and difficult, because we often cannot interact with people without our personal view all the time.

Some people have extraordinary talent in empathic communication, but everyone can learn to become a competent communicator. There are three levels of communication (Fig. 2): acceptable communication, empathic communication and ideal communication. It is possible to learn the skills to conduct acceptable communication and empathic communication (the gray parts in Fig. 2). The framework to be developed later also addresses these two levels of effective communication.

3 Age-Related Impairments with Communication

Aging process is not a simple process of declining [10]. It is important to consider that individual differences of communication skills do exist throughout the life span. But, we should be aware that much remains unchanged along the aging process. For example, there is no evidence of decline in most aspects of language abilities among older adults, including the use of language sounds, meaningful combination of words, and verbal comprehension [11]. When communicative differences between older and young adults have been observed, those differences have revealed that in some areas the older perform better than the young [10].

However, communication with older people can be challenging as a result of age-related cognitive and sensory impairments. Some age-related conditions such as hearing loss, and diseases such as dementia and stroke, directly affect individuals' ability to produce and process language, making communication itself problematic [12, 13]. For instance, cognitive impairments can affect the quality and quantity of linguistic capability; visual impairments will affect the ability to read, and to interpret lip movements. They also affect the ability to detect and interpret other non-verbal communications that accompany speech; hearing impairments can cause difficulties with understanding verbal communication, and also generating speech [14].

Effective communication with these older people requires designers to have a thorough understanding of older people's capabilities and communicative difficulties (Table 1). Designers may learn techniques to adapt to communication deficits of older people with cognitive and sensory impairments. Developing empathy is particularly necessary for understanding the physical deficits of older people that impede communication.

Cognitive changes in older adults are highly variable from one person to another [11]. Dementia adversely affects people's receptive and expressive communication. Older people with memory loss have some difficulty with recall of recent activities or events.

Vision is important for understanding non-verbal communication cues. Gestures, lip reading, contextual cues, facial expressions and eye gaze are important non-verbal elements to communication that may be missed by an older person with vision impairment [2].

Hearing loss makes it difficult for older adults to understand and remember speech in the presence of background noise, especially multiple competing conversations [11]. Older adults with age-related hearing loss often try to compensate by reading the speaker's lips. This is possible only if the older adult can see the speaker's lips, preferably at face level [11].

4   The Factors of Effective Communication with Older People

Effectiveness involves achieving the goals we have for specific interactions [8]. Effective communication is vital for the designer and the older people in obtaining a successful and positive relationship, and allow them to have a satisfied interaction. Here, within the design context, the term "communication" is narrowly defined, referring only to designer-user face to face interactions within a work setting.

Assumptions are often made that because someone has chosen to design for older people as a project, so they will have empathy when interacting with older people. Sometimes this is not the case. Some designers appear to have the innate ability to be empathetic; others may never have had these traits or with little respect and recognition of the needs of older people. Even though we speak to older people with empathy, sometimes even regarding older people as grandparents, we may recognize that we still

Table 1. Age-related cognitive and sensory capabilities and communication

	Capabilities	Communicative effects of impairments	Typical causes of communicative difficulties
Cognition	Cognition is the way we respond to sensory perceptions of the world, process them and choose our responses. Cognition capabilities include information on perception, working memory, long-term memory, attention, visual thinking and verbal thinking. At a higher level, the sensory, cognitive and motor functions of thinking are integrated together within the brain [15].	Cognitive impairments can affect the quality and quantity of linguistic capability [14]. As the Alzheimer's disease progresses, problems with visual perception and early difficulties with language can emerge [16]. Changes such as: using familiar words repeatedly; inventing new words to describe familiar objects; easily losing his or her train of thought; reverting back to a native language; having difficulty organizing words logically; speaking less often [19].	- Distance (reduced visual angle) - Visible distraction - Poor illumination of partner's face - Low contrast facial features - Unfamiliar words - Complex sentences - Partner's rapid speech rate - Partner's unclear articulation
Vision	Vision capabilities include visual acuity for perceiving fine details, contrast sensitivity for perceiving form, colour perception for detecting the range of color used, usable visual field for seeing extents and depth perception for judging distances in three dimensions [17].	Visual impairments (Cataract, Age-related maculopathy, Glaucoma, Diabetic retinopathy Hemianopia) will affect the ability to read, and to interpret lip movements. They also affect the ability to detect and interpret other non-verbal communications that accompany speech [14].	- Distance (reduced visual angle) - Visible distraction - Reflective glare - Poor illumination of partner's face - Low contrast facial features - Partner's rapid speech rate - Partner's unclear articulation [18]
Hearing	Hearing capabilities include the ability to detect sounds at different frequencies, speech discrimination and sound localisation.	Hearing impairments (Presbycusis, Cerumen occlusion, Noise induced hearing loss, Otosclerosis) can cause difficulties with understanding verbal communication, and also with generating speech [14].	- Distance (reduced sound level) - Background noise - Room echo - Partner's low voice level - Partner's rapid speech rate - Partner's soft/high-pitched voice [18] - Partner's unclear lip movements

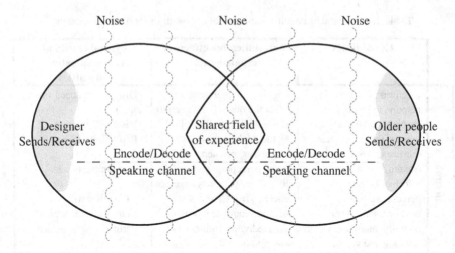

Fig. 3. The designer-older people transactional model of communication

need to combine specific techniques, especially with those older people who have cognitive and sensory impairments.

Therefore, designers need to learn how they transmit information and how to be sensitive to those messages expressed by older people. We have to look for an acceptable and efficient approach to achieve this goal by combining techniques and empathy. Meanwhile, we need to remember to eliminate our prejudice as much as possible. It should also be highlighted that listening is more important than speaking, although communication is a two-way process.

First, we need to understand the designer-older people communication system presented in Fig. 3, which is developed based on the transactional model of communication [8]. As we know, effective communication is an activity that depends on clear expression and full comprehension of both sides. But in the interview, it is often the designer who remains in control [20] because he/she collects data from the older respondent. Therefore, it is the designer's responsibility for choosing an appropriate means for communication which can work well for both sides.

Designers' interviewing older people is a conversation (speaking channel) that has a structure and a purpose determined by designers. It is a research professional interaction, which goes beyond the spontaneous exchange of views as in everyday conversations, and becomes a careful questioning and listening approach with the purpose of obtaining thoroughly tested knowledge about [21]. Ethical issues go through the entire process of an interview investigation, and potential ethical concern should be taken into consideration from the very start of an investigation and up to the final report [21].

A designer/an older person encodes messages (verbal/nonverbal), and then transmits the message via a speaking channel to the other side, and then decodes the message (verbal/nonverbal). The message may encounter noises, which interferes with the decoding of messages sent over a speaking channel by an encoder (e.g., any physical environment, psychological, physiological distraction or interference), which could prevent the message from being received or fully understood as the sender intended. The shared field of experience shows how communication becomes more difficult when designers and older people have less in common.

From the Fig. 3 we can see designers could achieve effective communications mainly through three means: i.e., 1. Increasing shared field experience; 2. Encoding/decoding messages correctly; 3. Decreasing "noises".

4.1 Increasing Shared Field Experience

Shared field experience is a common ground between a designer and an older person. To share a common experience is helpful to understand each other, and can create trust and security. Before interview, it is useful to gather preliminary data on user background; at the beginning of the interaction, engaging with older people in a brief dialogue may help the designer to understand the culture background, personal experience of the older person. They can also assess the level of sensory impairments of the older person.

4.2 Encoding/Decoding Messages Correctly

The designer encodes messages by using verbal/non-verbal ideas and thoughts to process the information. The purpose for decoding is for the designer to be able to comprehend the older person's messages to his/her best of understanding. To encode/decode messages correctly requires designers to be more attentive to both verbal (i.e., words spoken) and nonverbal cues (i.e., the ability to express and interpret facial expressions, body posture and movements, and vocal tones). This process should not be conceived as a one-size-fits-all sets of procedures. It requires the designer to take into account the diversities of older people. Every old person is special; designers need to listen and respond to each one on an individual basis.

4.3 Decreasing "Noise"

Noise can be anything that prevents effective communication from happening.

- To exclude the negative influences on context (physical environment and time)
  - Environment: eliminate visual and auditory distractions as much as possible. For example, provide adequate illumination; eliminate reflective glare; visual distractions; and reduce noise and echo in the room.
  - Time: to appoint an appropriate time and control the length of time. For example, hearing worsen later in the day, morning appointments are generally better for older people [22]; it is useful to consider their nap time and provide frequent washroom times if possible.
- To isolate physiological noise
  This requires an understanding of the capabilities of older people with cognitive and sensory impairments.

- To isolate psychological noise

  Real communication barriers exist beyond linguistic. Designers' attitudes and behaviors can make older people unwilling to listen and talk. One of the most important things to remember is to avoid ageism. Designers should regard each older person as a unique individual with valuable experiences and treat them respectfully. Designers need to express respect nonverbally and verbally as this is the most powerful way to build a relationship. Moreover, if one wants to have a really effective interpersonal communication, one cannot do it with techniques alone. One has to build the skills of empathic listening on a base of one's character that inspires openness and trust [9].

- To avoid semantic noise

  It exists when words themselves are not mutually understood. Sometimes the designer creates semantic noise by using jargon or unnecessary technical terms. It is better to use everyday language.

5   A Framework of Effective Communication

Any communication process can be divided into three stages: before, during, and after, the communication. In the Fig. 4, before the communication, the designer should collect the older person's personal information, including cultural background, personal experience and capabilities. The designer also needs to be aware of the communication context, to choose appropriate environments and arrange proper time, such as providing adequate illumination, eliminating reflective glare and visual distractions, reducing the environment noise and echo. During the process of the communication, designers need to reasonably use verbal and nonverbal communication skills. At the same time, empathic listening and responding should be applied from the beginning to the end. After the communication, designers should summarize the feedback which is provided by older person. It will tell the designer how well they have decoded the message.

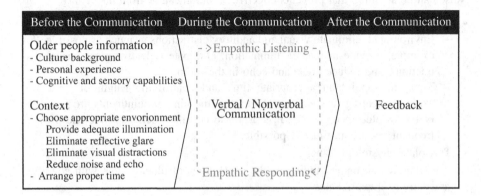

Fig. 4. A time process model of communication

The designer must know how to use verbal and nonverbal skills effectively when he/she interviews older people with cognitive and sensory impairments. In the framework (Table 2), the typical causes of older people's communication difficulties are listed in rows, and the verbal/nonverbal behaviors of designers are listed in columns.

Table 2. A framework of effective communication with older people

Empathic listening →

Older people's typical causes of communicative difficulties	The designer's nonverbal/verbal communication behaviors	Nonverbal behaviors						Verbal behaviors					
		Eye contact	Facial expressions	Body posture	Vocal tone	Touch	Images	Clarity of speech	Voice modulation	Pitch	Speed	Volume	Written materials
Cognitive impairment	Distance (reduced visual angle)												
	Visible distraction												
	Poor illumination of partner's face												
	Low contrast facial features												
	Unfamiliar words												
	Complex sentences												
	Partner's rapid speech rate												
	Partner's unclear articulation												
Vision impairment	Distance (reduced visual angle)												
	Visible distraction												
	Reflective glare												
	Poor illumination of partner's face												
	Low contrast facial features												
	Partner's rapid speech rate												
	Partner's unclear articulation												
Hearing impairment	Distance (reduced sound level)												
	Background noise												
	Room echo												
	Partner's low voice level												
	Partner's rapid speech rate												
	Partner's soft/high-pitched voice												
	Partner's unclear lip movements												

← Empathic responding

The framework can be used either as a checklist or as an information collection tool:

(1) A checklist: The framework as a checklist let designer consider what communication techniques should be focused on before an interview; If any communication barrier occur, designers can correct their behaviors immediately by checking the factor in the framework.

(2) An information collection tool: After the interview, designers sum up all their communication experiences, using the framework provided. After accumulating enough experiences, designers can create a personal communication guidance. As a common framework, it offers flexibility to all designers, which could be shared, augmented and personalized over time.

For example, in preparing for an interview with a visually impaired older person, the designer can identify the important areas by mapping the links between communicative difficulties of vision and verbal/nonverbal behaviors. And then write down appropriate communication techniques in each area. After a number of interview practices, the designer will enrich this framework as a systematic guidance full of communication tips.

Meanwhile, the designer needs to be more attentive to both verbal and nonverbal cues of the older person. Designers could ask questions and paraphrase what the older people said to clarify meaning. Furthermore, as we know, cognitive and sensory impairments have considerable impacts on self-image and confidence. Many older people are reluctant to disclose their cognitive, visual and hearing impairments. Designers need to be sensitive to the behaviors that indicate the older person's impairments. For example, if an older adult is turning his or her head to one side, it may be to adjust the visual distance or angle for improving vision to see you. If an older person often asks you to repeat what you have said, he/she may have a hearing impairment.

6 Conclusion

This paper is intended as a starting point for designers interested in understanding how age-related changes may influence communication and how to effectively communicate with older people with cognitive and sensory impairments. A framework provides an acceptable approach to help designers learn communication techniques. However it is not a panacea. Designers need to practice and find which strategies work best for them. Different older adults have different communication needs, which may require different techniques of communication. However, if we begin with this simple framework and if we train ourselves, we will find increased effectiveness and satisfaction, and will be able to communicate better with older people who have cognitive and sensory impairments.

The framework will be further developed with designers to ensure that the categorization is as useful as possible, and will be tested with designers to improve its usability and appropriateness.

References

1. World Health Organization: Ageing and life course. http://www.who.int/ageing/en
2. Heine, C., Browning, C.J.: Communication and psychosocial consequences of sensory loss in older adults: overview and rehabilitation directions. Disabil. Rehabil. **24**(15), 763–773 (2002)
3. Stephens, S.D.G.: People's complaints of hearing difficulties. In: Kyle, J.G. (ed.) Adjustment to Acquired Hearing Loss, pp. 37–47. University of Bristol, Centre for Deaf Studies, Bristol (1987)
4. Morse, A.R., Silberman, R., Trief, E.: Aging and visual impairment. J. Vis. Impairment Blindness **81**, 308–312 (1987)
5. Horowitz, A., Stuen, C.: The prevalence and correlates of concurrent vision and hearing impairments among the elderly. Paper presented at the 44th Annual Scientific Meeting of the Gerontological Society of America, San Francisco (1991)
6. Dong, H., Keates, S., Clarkson, P.J., Cassim, J.: Discounted user research for inclusive design, HEAT 2004. The Home and Electronic Assistive Technology (2004)
7. Newell, A., Monk, A.: Involving older people in design. In: Coleman, R., Clarkson, J., Dong, H., Cassim, J. (eds.) Design for Inclusivity: A Practical Guide to Accessible, Innovative and User-Centred Design, pp. 111–130. Gower Publishing Limited, Hampshire (2007)
8. Wood, J.T.: Interpersonal Communication: Everyday Encounters, 7th edn, pp. 17–30. Wadsworth, Boston (2013)
9. Covey, S.R.: The 7 Habits of Highly Effective People, pp. 239–241. Simon and Schuster, New York (1989)
10. Hummert, M.L., Wiemann, J., Nussbaum, J.F.: Interpersonal Communication in Older Adulthood: Interdisciplinary Theory and Research, p. 3. Sage Publications, Thousand Oaks (1994)
11. The Gerontological Society of America: Communicating with older adults: an evidence-based review of what really works, pp. 4–10. http://www.agingresources.com/cms/wp-content/uploads/2012/10/GSA_Communicating-with-Older-Adults-low-Final.pdf. Accessed 6 Feb 2015
12. Kemper, S.: Language and aging. In: Craik, F.I.M., Salthouse, T. (eds.) Handbook of Aging and Cognition, pp. 213–270. Lawrence Erlbaum Associates, Hillsdale (1992)
13. Ryan, E.B.: Language issues in normal aging. In: Lubinski, R. (ed.) Dementia and Communication: Clinical and Research Implications, pp. 84–97. B.C. Decker Publishing, Toronto (1991)
14. Cambridge Engineering Design Centre: Inclusive design toolkit. http://www.inclusivedesigntoolkit.com/betterdesign2/UCcomm/comm.html. Accessed 6 Feb 2015
15. Cambridge Engineering Design Centre: Inclusive design toolkit. http://www.inclusivedesigntoolkit.com/betterdesign2/usercapabilities/usercap.html. Accessed 6 Feb 2015
16. Gregor, T., Jiang, Y., Johanson, L.: www.bettercarehomes.org. Royal College of Art Helen Hamlyn Centre for Design. http://bettercarehomes.org/ability/dementia/ability-profile.php. Accessed 11 Feb 2015
17. Umesh, P., Langdon, P., Clarkson, P.J.: A framework for analytical inclusive design evaluation. In: International Conference on Engineering Design, ICED 2007 (2007)
18. Erber, N.P., Scherer, S.C.: Sensory loss and communication difficulties in the elderly. Aust. J. Ageing **18**(1), 4–9 (1999)
19. The Alzheimer's Association. http://www.alz.org/care/dementia-communication-tips.asp. Accessed 6 Feb 2015

20. Collins, H.: Creative Research: The Theory and Practice of Research for the Creative Industries, p. 134. Fairchild Books, New York (2010)
21. Kvale, S.: Doing Interviews: Qualitative Research Kit. SAGE, Thousand Oaks (2008)
22. Veras, R.P., Mattos, L.C.: Audiology and aging: literature review and current horizons. Braz. J. Otorhinolaryngol. **73**, 122–128 (2007)

Music in the Retiring Life: A Review of Evaluation Methods and Potential Factors

Mao Mao[1(✉)], Alan F. Blackwell[2], and David A. Good[1]

[1] Department of Psychology, University of Cambridge, Cambridge, UK
{mm992, dg25}@cam.ac.uk
[2] Computer Laboratory, University of Cambridge, Cambridge, UK
alan.blackwell@cl.cam.ac.uk

Abstract. People retiring now differ greatly in knowledge, motivation, attitudes towards and use of digital music-related technologies to younger generations or their predecessors. This paper reviews the methods that have been used to investigate why people use music-related technologies, how they use them and why. Using a lens provided by social cognitive theory it identifies future themes for research into music and ageing. Hopefully, these analyses will inform the design of future music related technologies for people at the transition to retirement, and the elderly.

Keywords: Retirement · Transition · Music · Social cognitive theory

1 Introduction

Life is full of transitions. Retirement is one such major transition, which results in major differences in patterns of activity, sense of self, and social relations. These changes are correlated with and often consequential for a person's physical and psychological well-being [1, 2]. The "individual's normative role as an elderly person" [1], may have an important impact on their attitudes and behaviours [3], at a time when adopting and adapting to new leisure, voluntary and other social activities is important for enjoyment and health. On such activity is community music, and many forms of engagement with or enjoyment of music have been greatly affected by new music-related technologies over the past decade and longer.

Even though older people are often stereotyped as being resistant to novelty, many actually "continue and even increase their use of technology" [4], because they tend to focus more on maintaining close relationship and personal life interests when they are getting older. We define music-related technologies as all types of digital or mass media technologies that are involved in music practices. For example, not only music streaming services and digital instruments are included, but also traditional media technologies such as TV, CD, and radio. Technology use by older adults has been extensively studied by researchers from multidisciplinary areas, and in this paper we will build on the work of Wagner et al., applying Social Cognitive Theory (SCT) as a lens to view and organise the literature related to music-related technology use behaviour of people at retiring.

© Springer International Publishing Switzerland 2015
J. Zhou and G. Salvendy (Eds.): ITAP 2015, Part I, LNCS 9193, pp. 73–83, 2015.
DOI: 10.1007/978-3-319-20892-3_8

Social Cognitive Theory (SCT), addresses "how people motivate and regulate their behaviour and create social systems that organise and structure their lives" [5]. According to Compeau and Higgins, SCT is "based on the premise that environmental influences such as social pressures or unique situational characteristics, cognitive and other personal factors including personality as well as demographic characteristics, and behaviour are reciprocally determined" [6]. In other words, there are important inter-dependencies between these three domains.

In this paper, we adopt the Wagner framework and define Person as people who actively engage in music activities at their transitions to retirement, Behaviour as using digital media technology for music-related activities, and Environment as the social context of group/individual music making and technological system.

1.1 Review Method and Definitions

For this review, we gathered articles from 2004 to 2014 by searching various databases for peer-reviewed journal articulate and conference proceedings on the subject of music and retirement. We used nine databases specifying gerontology and psychology (PubMed, PLoS ONE), computer science (ACM Digital Library, IEEE), and multi-disciplinary subject areas (Web of Knowledge, SpringerLink, ProQuest, Elsevier, JSTOR). Search keywords include reference to retirement and ageing (age or ageing or old or senior or elderly or retirement), music (music or music making or choir or singing), technology (technology or media or digital technology). The total size of this sample is 52 papers, covering the period 2004–2014. The following information was analysed: the sample studied, methods, variables or constructs studied, research questions, evaluation goals, evaluation measures, theory involved, and key findings.

Thus using Wagner's Social Cognitive Theory (SCT) to organise the literature from psychology, gerontology, as well as HCI and human factors, we first examine the methodologies used and then the factors affecting the interaction between people at the transition to retirement relevant to their use of music-related technologies. Thereby we focus on the three reciprocal determinants: person, behaviour and environment. The paper then concludes with a discussion of future themes of HCI studies concerning music and ageing.

2   Methods to Understand Technology and Community Music

A common feature of the methods used in reviewed studies is that they often use several different methods to "triangulate on a particular question" [7]. There are many reasons to recommend this approach as it ensures that a study is not vulnerable to the weaknesses of any single method. Nevertheless, we will consider the separate methods independently so as to identify their value across this domain of interest.

2.1 Qualitative Methods

27 of the 52 papers use qualitative methods, ranging from interviews, focus groups, qualitative survey, contextual observations, ethnographic studies, to diary journals and

cultural/technology probes. Interviews (40.7 %) and qualitative survey (29.6 %) are the most common used methods for understanding how people use technology to conduct their music-related practices.

Interviews. Interviews are among the most widely used method [7]. When engaging in a conversation with individual participants, interviewers have explored the interviewee's subjective opinion about the use of technology, and how they are influenced by the social or technological environment. Interviews are conducted either in the interviewee's own place (homes, workplace) or in the lab environment. Compared to lab environment, conducting contextual interviews at the participant's place allow researchers to better understand why certain technologies are used or barriers exist, and provide an opportunity to see how environmental factors might have an effect. For example, Vaisutis and colleagues explored the role of objects and social relations in place through contextual interviews, then identified objects with different functionalities and how people attribute emotional meanings to them [8]. The interview is a flexible and adaptable way of finding out the relationship between user, behaviour and the environment. However, interview findings can be subject to a variety of errors including participant recall [7], leading questions, and a desire to provide the answers the interviewee believes the interviewer wishes to hear. This entails that high quality interview data depends on the skill and experience of the interviewer [9].

Focus Groups. The focus group originated in market research in the 1920s, and is now widely used in many fields of applied social research [9]. Examples include examining exploring technology usage and attitudes among older adults [10], investigating older adults' motivation to adopt technological innovation [11], and how older people keep in touch with friends and relatives [12]. Even though the focus group method is efficient in obtaining the most important topics and flexible to conduct, it may produce a false consensus in attitudes [9] and may not elicit confidential issues. Hence, researchers who would like to use focus groups need to use other techniques to validate the information generated by the group.

Diary Study. Diary studies allow participants to record their experiences as and when they occur, and enable the capture of substantial amounts of data with much less effort on the part of the investigator [9]. A diary could also serve as a proxy for observation in situations which are hard to make direct observation [9], and might help to improve the accuracy of participant recall [7]. For example, Salovaara et al. used diary-aided interviews to investigate the interplay of technologies and transitions of people at the age of 55–65 [13]. The concrete diary data provides use practices and communication circles of participants within one week, and later serves as a means of generating specific questions of interviews. It was identified that life interests at the transition stage were always conflicting, forcing people to choose among "possible selves". There are two diary methods that are widely used in HCI. One of them is to keep the diary with "critical incident". This approach allows participants to record the "incidents that they perceive to be important or critical in obtaining a satisfactory outcome" [9]. Another diary method is known as "reflective journal", where participants are asked to provide an account of their experience in a particular situation, and a reflection on that experience.

Ethnographic Study. Ethnography is growing in popularity as the first step in any investigation. The virtues of ethnography in HCI are: (1) to make visible the context of system usage, social practice that might not be encountered, and (2) to provide exploratory frameworks for observed context to offer designers a view of interaction between people and technology. In the field of technology and music, examples using ethnographic study include how nightclub DJs mix tracks, collect music, prepare for performances, conduct promotion and networking with the help of music technologies [14], how older people understand their relationship with technology [15]. Ethnographic methods are beneficial in observing the naturally "accountable" ways [16] of the social context of use, real-life interactions and expectations [17]. However, the richness of ethnographic findings are often set against concerns as to their validity and reliability and depend greatly on the training and skills of the ethnographer. The latter should always be borne in mind when using the results of such work.

Probes. The concept of cultural probes was introduced by Gaver et al. [18], originally aiming at eliciting "inspirational material while avoiding the understood social roles of researchers and researched" in design-oriented research. Example includes Leonardi et al.'s work on investigating the functional and emotional geography of older adults' domestic space [19]. An example of X probe (or technology probes) is the study conducted by Rogers and colleagues on reframing the relationship in terms of wisdom, creativity and invention among retired people. They used a Makey MaKey inventor's toolkit to engage retired people in the design-oriented workshop, asking them to invent future technologies and suggest ideas for new technologies. Interestingly, the participants in this study were able to master the technology and collaborate in its use [20]. Probes provides open-ended, provocative, and oblique tasks which inspire design responses, but are surprisingly regarded as non-scientific [21] giving their rich idiosyncrasy. However, as Boehner et al. observe, the use of probes provides an alternative way to encourage participative engagement between individuals, which can reveal facets of an issue that traditional HCI methods have left unexplored [22].

Qualitative methods in our reviewed study typically follow either a data-driven or theory-driven logic. In data-driven logic, bottom-up coding is used to derive themes from the recorded transcripts, field notes, and verbal protocols. In theory-driven logic, top-down coding is used to "identify existing constructs in a particular dataset" [7]. The time-consuming process of qualitative data analysis can be assisted with computer aids, e.g., key-word-in-context (KWIC), and qualitative data can be subjected to quantitative analysis e.g., word frequency lists and category counts. However, whatever analysis techniques are used, most writers using these techniques stares that it is essential to return to the original text document to "validate the interpretation of themes derived from statistical results" [9].

2.2 Quantitative Methods

While qualitative methods are valuable in developing a rich description of our target population of retiring and retired people and how they vary in their use of technology, the richness and local validity comes at a cost to our ability to generalise away from the particular. This problem is addressed by methods that seek to deliver a broader if less rich understanding from larger samples, and which offer quantified parameters to aid our investigations.

Quantitative Surveys. Surveys are often used to capture user perception, their psychological status, behaviour patterns, attitudes, and motivations. Surveys are not typically suited to exploratory work; but often build on good qualitative work to deliver a focussed and substantial data set in a standardised form which facilitates comparisons [9]. In the literature under consideration here, 29 % of the studies adopted questionnaire-based survey as their primary research method. Two-thirds of them use surveys to assess participants' psychological status (e.g., quality of life, well-being measures, psychological needs, age-related symptoms), and just over half of them assess technology use and relevant motivation and attitudes. A small subset of these (4 papers) conducted cross-sectional or longitude surveys, in order to investigate the changes in participants' psychological status or behaviour over time. For instance, Tamplin et al. measured participants' mood, visual analogue mood, cognition and global functioning, as well as social functions at the 12th week and the 20th week after joining a community choir established to support music therapy for elderly patients recovering from a stroke [23]. This study reported that singing in a community choir has positive effect on mood and social engagement in such cases. Survey data collection is mostly done via self-completion questionnaires, face-to-face and telephone interviews, although more expensive to conduct permit the use of more complex item sequences and the possibility of unstructured follow up questions to explore specific answers. Thus, general considerations such as the questionnaire length, question complexity, close/open-ended questions should be taken into account when designing surveys for late mid-aged and older people.

Experimentation. Controlled laboratory experiment clearly provide the most informative way to evaluate if a certain intervention is successful [7], and it has been used widely to evaluate the effects of music (training, performing) on psychological status or the alleviation of symptoms. A fifth of studies in the papers under review here use controlled experiments to answer such research questions. The tasks used can be categorised into three groups: (1) behaviour tasks; (2) cognition and perception, (3) collaboration. The performance-oriented tasks, usually involved a new/unfamiliar technology/tool so as to test the possibilities of using the technology/tool freely and safely. Tasks include gambling, information searching and multitasking with different media. Time and accuracy were the most common measures used to assess performance, and, behavioural and physiological measures such as gaze durations and eye movement are also used in multitasking and searching tasks. Just over half the papers (55 %) used cognitive and perceptual tasks and measures [24–27], such as auditory Stroop task, Simon tasks, and [24, 28]. Outcome measures linked to psychological well-being focussed on anxiety, dysphonia severity, cardiac and respiratory patterns, mood states, and even immunological profile. A common focus for "community music" is collaboration tasks where synchronisation tasks such as the drumming experiment, body movement synchrony tasks, entrainment building, and resonance within instrument are among the most frequently used paradigms [26, 29–31]. A good example of this approach to the investigation of recreational music-making and the health of older adults is Koyama et al. which measured blood sample and mood state during a series of synchrony tasks, finding that creative music-making does have improvement effect in immunological profile and mood states in the older group [30].

Technology Logs. The recording of detailed logs from systems or applications that participants are using is an effective method to gain an extensive source of quantitative data. Technology logs reflect the a deeper analysis to actual use of technology [7], compared to limited scenarios and data in controlled laboratory experiments or trials. In the case of digital media technologies and music for late midage and older adults, commonly used logs include system visiting rate [32], text comments, as well as user-generated contents [33]. The log data can be further used in analysing psychological measures, such as psychological well-being [34], caregiver burden [7].

Experience Sampling Methods. A key issue for survey questionnaires that require the recall of past behaviour is the various biases that can affect recall. An *in situ* measure of behaviour, which avoids this problem, is the Experience Sampling Method (ESM). ESM collects self-report experience throughout certain moments of interest [7] or at random occasions during the day [35]. In the case of HCI and ageing, there are two ways of collecting experience through this kind of sampling: (1) participants have to either complete a questionnaire immediately after they interact with the system; or (2) behavioural parameters (e.g., limb positions, right hip positions) or physiological status (e.g., eye movement, mood status, heart rate, respiration, ECG, skin conductance) can be collected at key moments. Researchers tend to use ESM to assess user experience in context-aware situations often with the use of embedded sensors [36]. This method has benefits in gaining in situ "observation" results, which are hard to obtain outside lab settings; but they can be burdensome to some participants and necessarily might "miss important activities" [36]. There is no use of ESM in our surveyed studies. Taruffi & Koelsch's work on mood experience with sad music mentioned that the validity of their study could be potentially improvement if ESM were used [35]. Their use offers an important additional avenue for research in this area.

3   Key Influencing Factors

Together these studies focus on three different factors, the nature of the persons involved; their behaviour; and their environment.

3.1   Person

Given our focus on retirement the persons being considered are typically late middle age and older adults who engage in music activities (individual or community-based) with a focus on their physical, emotional and cognitive aspects of personal attributes. The musical background of those studied is extensively addressed.

Key dimensions of music background include musical expertise, length of music training (e.g., instrument, vocal), music practice style (e.g., long-term or short-term). Existing studies have identified the positive relationship between music background and psychological well-being, cognitive abilities, and quality of life [24, 28, 37]. There have been an increasing number of HCI studies focusing on the experience of amateur musicians, since this group of users are "serious about their leisure" and are "distinct from the professional as from the novice and hobbyist" [38]. The relationship between music background and wellbeing appear to combine with personality traits [39]. Researchers have investigated the relationship between trait empathy and the sadness perception of people who listen to music, with the finding that empathy contributes to the evocation of sadness via appraisal and nostalgia - which in turn are related to well-being factors [35].

Another bunch of factors affects engagement or adoption: perceived benefits, prior similar experience, and self-efficacy [10, 40–42], mono-chronicity [43], self-construal are among the most frequently mentioned factors. Three forms of self-efficacy - technology efficacy, information efficacy, and connective efficacy – may influence one's desire and confidence to engage in community music or accept related technologies [44].

3.2 Behaviour

Unsurprisingly, people at the transitions to retirement tend to use computer and the Internet to a less extent than the younger generation, but spend more time on face-to-face activities like community music making or connection to close relation ships (e.g., relatives and good friends). The most extensively studied technology use for older people is communication and social support [11, 45–48]. Different types of communication technologies include email, telephone, text messages, social network sites, and online forums or blogs, to provide specific support.

Individual music-related behaviours include music listening [35, 49], managing music crates (both physical and digital), self-promotion [14]. Social music-related behaviours include music-sharing [50, 51], community singing [23, 26, 27, 30, 37, 40, 52, 53], and collaborating with other musicians [14].

3.3 Environment

Environmental factors can be cast along two dimensions: artefacts and socio-musical environment. The artefacts dimension refers to the instruments, devices, hardware and software systems related to music that users are using. In our reviewed studies, artefacts include instruments, sheet music, lyric sheets, as well as MIDI files used for learning and archiving. Technology systems include media devices (e.g., MP3, radio, TV, computer), the Internet services (e.g., music streaming services, social network sites, personal websites, video gaming), computer-mediated communication technologies (e.g., telephone, email, video camera, smart phones, cell phones), as well as music-making applications (e.g., Sibelius, synchroniser, GarageBand, etc.) The socio-musical environment dimension especially applies when more than one person is involved (e.g., sharing music with friends, engaging in a choral life). Usability of the artefacts has been found to have a direct correlation with adoption and decreased cost, and further, engagement in the community [54] (Fig. 1).

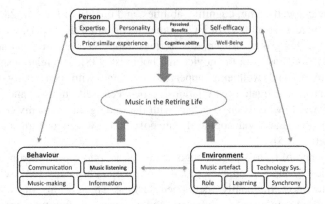

Fig. 1. Triadic reciprocal relationship of influencing factors on music and ageing

One important scenario in socio-musical interaction is group music-making. Such groups always develop shared social habits naturally, which is known as "chameleon effect" [55]. Firstly, the role (e.g., conductor, or chorister) that people undertake in group music-making impact their experience. As a chorister, the kinaesthetic relationship with the conductor will reinforce or undermine individual's habits for reaching the consensus condition. Second, learning style (e.g., singing by ear or sight reading) requires different memory modals (e.g., aural memory, kinaesthetic memory, factual memory), which in turn impacts experience in music-making and relevant technology use. Third, a strong group identity can lead to a greater number of member contributions and build stronger ties among members [44].

4 Conclusion

In this paper we have examined the literature on music-related technology use by people who are at the transitions to retirement through the lens of Social Cognitive Theory. Through this approach when can see that the personal characteristics at the retiring age, their use of music-related technologies, as well as the technologies and socio-musical environment exist in a triadic reciprocal relationship. Although there has been extensive research addressing the use of technologies among people during late middle age and older age, there are still many opportunities for further study in addressing this field through the lens of music and life transitions. We hope that this study will draw attention to this specific area of study and provide researchers with a foundation upon which future knowledge can be built.

References

1. Ryu, M.-H., Kim, S., Lee, E.: Understanding the factors affecting online elderly user's participation in video UCC services. Comput. Hum. Behav. **25**, 619–632 (2009)

2. Kralik, D., Visentin, K., Van Loon, A.: Transition: a literature review. J. Adv. Nurs. **55**, 320–329 (2006)
3. Lee, E., Moschis, G.P., Mathur, A.: A study of life events and changes in patronage preferences. J. Bus. Res. **54**, 25–38 (2001)
4. Lindley, S.E., Harper, R., Sellen, A.: Designing for elders: exploring the complexity of relationships in later life. In: Proceedings of the 22nd British HCI Group Annual Conference on People and Computers: Culture, Creativity, Interaction, vol. 1. pp. 77–86, British Computer Society (2008)
5. Lange, P.A.M.V., Kruglanski, A.W., Higgins, E.T.: Handbook of Theories of Social Psychology, vol. 1. SAGE Publications Ltd, London (2012)
6. Compeau, D.R., Higgins, C.A.: Computer self-efficacy: development of a measure and initial test. MIS Q. **19**(2), 189–211 (1995)
7. Connelly, K., Laghari, K.U.R., Mokhtari, M., Falk, T.H.: Approaches to understanding the impact of technologies for aging in place: a mini-review. Gerontology **60**, 282–288 (2014)
8. Vaisutis, K., Brereton, M., Robertson, T., Vetere, F., Durick, J., Nansen, B., Buys, L.: Invisible connections: investigating older people's emotions and social relations around objects. In: Proceedings of the SIGCHI Conference on Human Factors in Computing Systems, pp. 1937–1940. ACM, New York, NY, USA (2014)
9. Robson, C.: Real World Research: A Resource for Social Scientists and Practitioners-Researchers. Black Well Publ. Ltd., Oxford (1993)
10. Mitzner, T.L., Boron, J.B., Fausset, C.B., Adams, A.E., Charness, N., Czaja, S.J., Dijkstra, K., Fisk, A.D., Rogers, W.A., Sharit, J.: Older adults talk technology: technology usage and attitudes. Comput. Hum. Behav. **26**, 1710–1721 (2010)
11. Melenhorst, A.-S., Rogers, W.A., Bouwhuis, D.G.: Older adults' motivated choice for technological innovation: evidence for benefit-driven selectivity. Psychol. Aging **21**, 190–195 (2006)
12. Dickinson, A., Hill, R.L.: Keeping in touch: talking to older people about computers and communication. Educ. Gerontol. **33**, 613–630 (2007)
13. Salovaara, A., Lehmuskallio, A., Hedman, L., Valkonen, P., Näsänen, J.: Information technologies and transitions in the lives of 55–65-year-olds: the case of colliding life interests. Int. J. Hum. Comput. Stud. **68**, 803–821 (2010)
14. Ahmed, A., Benford, S., Crabtree, A.: Digging in the crates: an ethnographic study of DJS' work. In: Proceedings of the SIGCHI Conference on Human Factors in Computing Systems, pp. 1805–1814. ACM, New York, NY, USA (2012)
15. Talamo, A., Giorgi, S., Mellini, B.: Designing technologies for ageing: is simplicity always a leading criterion? In: Proceedings of the 9th ACM SIGCHI Italian Chapter International Conference on Computer-Human Interaction: Facing Complexity, pp. 33–36. ACM, New York, NY, USA (2011)
16. Benford, S., Tolmie, P., Ahmed, A.Y., Crabtree, A., Rodden, T.: Supporting traditional music-making: designing for situated discretion. In: Proceedings of the ACM 2012 Conference on Computer Supported Cooperative Work, pp. 127–136. ACM, New York, NY, USA (2012)
17. Sayago, S., Blat, J.: Telling the story of older people e-mailing: an ethnographical study. Int. J. Hum. Comput. Stud. **68**, 105–120 (2010)
18. Gaver, B., Dunne, T., Pacenti, E.: Design: cultural probes. Interactions **6**, 21–29 (1999)
19. Leonardi, C., Mennecozzi, C., Not, E., Pianesi, F., Zancanaro, M., Gennai, F., Cristoforetti, A.: Knocking on elders' door: investigating the functional and emotional geography of their domestic space. In: Proceedings of the SIGCHI Conference on Human Factors in Computing Systems, pp. 1703–1712. ACM, New York, NY, USA (2009)

20. Rogers, Y., Paay, J., Brereton, M., Vaisutis, K.L., Marsden, G., Vetere, F.: Never too old: engaging retired people inventing the future with MaKey MaKey. In: Proceedings of the SIGCHI Conference on Human Factors in Computing Systems, pp. 3913–3922. ACM, New York, NY, USA (2014)

21. Hemmings, T., Clarke, K., Rouncefield, M., Crabtree, A., Rodden, T.: Probing the probes. In: PDC, pp. 42–50 (2002)

22. Boehner, K., Vertesi, J., Sengers, P., Dourish, P.: How HCI interprets the probes. In: Proceedings of the SIGCHI Conference on Human Factors in Computing Systems, pp. 1077–1086. ACM, New York, NY, USA (2007)

23. Tamplin, J., Baker, F.A., Jones, B., Way, A., Lee, S.: Stroke a chord: the effect of singing in a community choir on mood and social engagement for people living with aphasia following a stroke. NeuroRehabilitation 32, 929–941 (2013)

24. Amer, T., Kalender, B., Hasher, L., Trehub, S.E., Wong, Y.: Do older professional musicians have cognitive advantages? PLoS ONE 8, e71630 (2013)

25. Berghs, G., Creylman, N., Avaux, M., Decoster, W., De Jong, F.: A lifetime of professional singing: voice parameters and age in the Netherlands radio choir. Logoped. Phoniatr. Vocol. 38, 59–63 (2013)

26. Müller, V., Lindenberger, U.: Cardiac and respiratory patterns synchronize between persons during choir singing. PLoS ONE 6, e24893 (2011)

27. Sung, H., Lee, W., Li, T., Watson, R.: A group music intervention using percussion instruments with familiar music to reduce anxiety and agitation of institutionalized older adults with dementia: group music intervention for older adults with dementia. Int. J. Geriatr. Psychiatry 27, 621–627 (2012)

28. White-Schwoch, T., Carr, K.W., Anderson, S., Strait, D.L., Kraus, N.: Older adults benefit from music training early in life: biological evidence for long-term training-driven plasticity. J. Neurosci. 33, 17667–17674 (2013)

29. Kokal, I., Engel, A., Kirschner, S., Keysers, C.: Synchronized drumming enhances activity in the caudate and facilitates prosocial commitment - if the rhythm comes easily. PLoS ONE 6, e27272 (2011)

30. Koyama, M., Wachi, M., Utsuyama, M., Bittman, B., Hirokawa, K., Kitagawa, M.: Recreational music-making modulates immunological responses and mood states in older adults. J. Med. Dent. Sci. 56(2), 79–90 (2009)

31. Moens, B., Muller, C., van Noorden, L., Franěk, M., Celie, B., Boone, J., Bourgois, J., Leman, M.: Encouraging spontaneous synchronisation with D-Jogger, an adaptive music player that aligns movement and music. PLoS ONE 9, e114234 (2014)

32. O'Neill, S.A., McClean, S.I., Donnelly, M.D., Nugent, C.D., Galway, L., Cleland, I., Zhang, S., Young, T., Scotney, B.W., Mason, S.C., Craig, D.: Development of a technology adoption and usage prediction tool for assistive technology for people with dementia. Interact. Comput. 26, 169–176 (2014)

33. Harley, D., Fitzpatrick, G.: Creating a conversational context through video blogging: a case study of geriatric 1927. Comput. Hum. Behav. 25, 679–689 (2009)

34. Shklovski, I., Kraut, R., Cummings, J.: Routine patterns of internet use & psychological well-being: coping with a residential move. In: Proceedings of the SIGCHI Conference on Human Factors in Computing Systems, pp. 969–978. ACM, New York, NY, USA (2006)

35. Taruffi, L., Koelsch, S.: The paradox of music-evoked sadness: an online survey. PLoS ONE 9, e110490 (2014)

36. Intille, S.S., Bao, L., Tapia, E.M., Rondoni, J.: Acquiring in situ training data for context-aware ubiquitous computing applications. In: Proceedings of the SIGCHI Conference on Human Factors in Computing Systems, pp. 1–8. ACM, New York, NY, USA (2004)

37. Kirsh, E.R., van Leer, E., Phero, H.J., Xie, C., Khosla, S.: Factors associated with singers' perceptions of choral singing well-being. J. Voice **27**, 786.e25–786.e32 (2013)
38. Hoare, M., Benford, S., Jones, R., Milic-Frayling, N.: Coming in from the margins: amateur musicians in the online age. In: Proceedings of the SIGCHI Conference on Human Factors in Computing Systems, pp. 1295–1304. ACM, New York, NY, USA (2014)
39. Seale, L.: The cambridge companion to choral music. Ref. Rev. **27**, 47–48 (2013)
40. Johnson, J.K., Louhivuori, J., Stewart, A.L., Tolvanen, A., Ross, L., Era, P.: Quality of life (QOL) of older adult community choral singers in Finland. Int. Psychogeriatr. **25**, 1055–1064 (2013)
41. Lee, B., Chen, Y., Hewitt, L.: Age differences in constraints encountered by seniors in their use of computers and the internet. Comput. Hum. Behav. **27**, 1231–1237 (2011)
42. Kurniawan, S.: Older people and mobile phones: a multi-method investigation. Int. J. Hum. Comput. Stud. **66**, 889–901 (2008)
43. Brasel, S.A., Gips, J.: Media multitasking behavior: concurrent television and computer usage. CyberPsychol. Behav. Soc. Netw. **14**, 527–534 (2011)
44. Tedjamulia, S.J., Dean, D.L., Olsen, D.R., Albrecht, C.C.: Motivating content contributions to online communities: toward a more comprehensive theory. In: Proceedings of the 38th Annual Hawaii International Conference on System Sciences, HICSS 2005, pp. 193b–193b, IEEE (2005)
45. Riley, P., Alm, N., Newell, A.: An interactive tool to promote musical creativity in people with dementia. Comput. Hum. Behav. **25**, 599–608 (2009)
46. Damodaran, L., Olphert, C.W., Sandhu, J.: Falling off the bandwagon? Exploring the challenges to sustained digital engagement by older people. Gerontology **60**, 163–173 (2014)
47. Vroman, K.G., Arthanat, S., Lysack, C.: Who over 65 is online? Older adults' dispositions toward information communication technology. Comput. Hum. Behav. **43**, 156–166 (2015)
48. Bobillier Chaumon, M.-E., Michel, C., Tarpin Bernard, F., Croisile, B.: Can ICT improve the quality of life of elderly adults living in residential home care units? From actual impacts to hidden artefacts. Behav. Inf. Technol. **33**(6), 574–590 (2014)
49. Travers, C., Bartlett, H.P.: Silver memories: implementation and evaluation of a unique radio program for older people. Aging Ment. Health. **15**, 169–177 (2011)
50. Hope, A., Schwaba, T., Piper, A.M.: Understanding digital and material social communications for older adults. In: Proceedings of the SIGCHI Conference on Human Factors in Computing Systems, pp. 3903–3912. ACM, New York, NY, USA (2014)
51. Lee, D., Park, J.Y., Kim, J., Kim, J., Moon, J.: Understanding music sharing behaviour on social network services. Online Inf. Rev. **35**, 716–733 (2011)
52. Creech, A., Hallam, S., Varvarigou, M., McQueen, H., Gaunt, H.: Active music making: a route to enhanced subjective well-being among older people. Perspect. Public Health. **133**, 36–43 (2013)
53. Settles, B., Dow, S.: Let's get together: the formation and success of online creative collaborations. In: Proceedings of the SIGCHI Conference on Human Factors in Computing Systems, pp. 2009–2018. ACM, New York, NY, USA (2013)
54. Jarvenpaa, S.L., Staples, D.S.: The use of collaborative electronic media for information sharing: an exploratory study of determinants. J. Strateg. Inf. Syst. **9**, 129–154 (2000)
55. Chartrand, T.L., Bargh, J.A.: The chameleon effect: the perception–behavior link and social interaction. J. Pers. Soc. Psychol. **76**, 893 (1999)

Collecting Old People's Data for More Accessible Design: A Pilot Study

Weining Ning[(⊠)] and Hua Dong

College of Design and Innovation, Tongji University, Shanghai, China
ningweining@sina.cn

Abstract. Good design should be equipped with the quality of being accessible to broad user groups, including older people. As the population becomes older, the needs and capabilities of people become ever more diverse. However, there exists limited effective data for designers to understand older people's capability condition. The lack of good data becomes a great barrier to make design accessible to older people. This paper introduces a pilot study of collecting older people's multiple capability data in China. It aims to explore principles and instructions to design the process, methods and testing tasks of such a study. The results show that in the pilot study, (1) there are discrepancies between users' self-assessment and performance measurement, (2) the selection of products should take into account the cultural context, and (3) ceiling effects exist and they greatly affect the validity and reliability of the data.

Keywords: Accessibility · Inclusive design · Multiple capability · Data collection

1 Introduction

Successful design with good accessibility to a wide range of people requires in-depth understanding of the user, from the designers' perspective, knowledge about (1) users' capabilities, needs, and aspirations, (2) different scenarios that people will use products, systems and services, and (3)other factors include psychological, social, economic and other considerations should be identified [1]. In the context of a rapidly-aging society, the philosophy of inclusive design is given accumulating consideration. As the population becomes older, the needs and capabilities of people become ever more diverse [2], Neerincx et al. classify users' abilities form a product-usage perspective [3]:

- Sensory abilities such as seeing, hearing, touch, taste, smell and balance.
- Physical abilities such as speech, dexterity, manipulation, mobility, strength and endurance.
- Cognitive abilities such as intellect, memory, language and literacy.
- Allergies can also be a significant factor in some products.

The necessity of user database, which contains users' capabilities and contextual data, is raised to help designers to understand the nature of this diversity. A person's multiple capabilities can reflect individual's ability to operate or interact with products and the breadth and multivariate nature of capabilities can be best captured and represented

© Springer International Publishing Switzerland 2015
J. Zhou and G. Salvendy (Eds.): ITAP 2015, Part I, LNCS 9193, pp. 84–93, 2015.
DOI: 10.1007/978-3-319-20892-3_9

through a database that covers multiple capability domains for a representative sample of the population [2]. Such databases that include users' multiple capabilities information are also expected to help designers in different design phases, e.g. to get conceptual inspiration, to better understand users or to explore references to the prototype.

The current sources of regulated databases that designers can reach are almost ergonomics data, especially anthropometric data. However, there are many 'gaps' in the ergonomics data available to designers. For instance, in a study conducted by Nickpour and Dong, the results show that 'all interviewed designers considered the existing anthropometric data out of date and seven out of ten believed the data was irrelevant or not applicable to their specific field of design practice. The data was also reported as being unreliable, not appealing and confusing' [4].

To plug the gaps between existing databases and designers' requirements, studies have been conducted to collect capability-related data, but varied shortcomings emerged [2]:

- Databases tend to focus on a specific domain of capability, and every single survey is based on a specific sample, a product interaction often covers more than one capability, thus it is unreasonable to refer to data from different samples.
- Some studies have captured multiple capabilities, but insufficient information was unable to be applied in supporting a practical use.
- In sampling, the sift criteria often exclude specific population groups and often cannot represent the whole population.
- Very few databases include data of older people.
- Most studies were collected from western countries [5].

Additionally, technologies develop rapidly, people are always adopting new products and services, so studies based on out-of-date scales or users' habits are no longer applicable to the new context of use. Stephanidis et al. [6] state that in the context of the emerging Information Society, we are meeting a global requirement of coping with diversity in the 'scope and nature of tasks' in using products.

This paper describes a pilot study that collects Chinese older people's capability data. The main methods of the survey were derived and adapted from *Towards Better Design* [7], which was initiated by the University of Cambridge. That study has gained good results in gathering information of the whole age range among UK population. As a pilot study, the main aim of our survey was to verify the feasibility of this foreign study in a new background (i.e. new context and a specific target respondents: older Chinese people), as well as to explore possible factors that affect the conduct of such a survey and to conclude principles or instructions for establishing an effective older people's database for designers in the future.

2 Methods

This pilot data collection study was conducted through a comprehensive questionnaire that contains questions as well as actual testing tasks. On one aspect, respondents were asked to verbally report some information, on the other aspect, actual performance tests were employed through three different granularities of measurements [8]:

- Component function (such as grip strength test).
- Activity (such as reading the LCD screen on a mobile phone).
- Task (a product interaction that integrates number of functions and activities).

The testing items of this study were derived from the technical report of *Towards Better Design* with adaptations after translating the report into a Chinese version to cater for the new context and to explore insights that may emerge when employing such a survey on Chinese older people. The main adaptations were: (1) the wording and expression of the statements were modified to make it more accessible to Chinese older people and to prevent ambiguous statements and questions. (2) Testing items that involve English language (letters, numbers and words) need to be listened, read or cognized by the respondents were all replaced with Chinese. (3) Some products in the tests were replaced with other products to suit Chinese older people.

The survey collects the following information from each respondent:

1. Age, gender and basic household information
2. Health condition
3. Vision
4. Hearing
5. Dexterity
6. Mobility
7. Reach and stretch
8. Cognitive function
9. Technology use and experience
10. Product use
11. Physiological resources
12. Interface style experience
13. Anthropometrics
14. Demographics

Pretests were conducted with three older persons to refine the questions and to evaluate the time of the whole process. Finally, the expected time was set 1.5–2 h. Seven interviewers received training and observed the pretests.

3   General Results

The respondents' age range from 50 to 80. Finally, 70 sets of valid data were collected from seven different towns and cities of China. The mean age of the samples was 64 (SD = 8.9). Basic information of the respondents is shown in Table 1.

As a face-to-face survey, it was well balanced in the quantity and quality of the inquiry. When applied in China, new issues and problems emerged in a totally new context. What should be emphasized is that the expected result of this study is not just data collected, but also the assessment of the methods and items setting applied in this survey.

After the collected data were converged, all the interviewers involved in the actual survey gathered together to assess the process and content of the survey, and the defects

Table 1. Basic information of the respondents

Age	51–60 (N = 3)	61–70 (N = 2)	71–80 (N = 18)	All (N = 70)
Gender				
Male	47 %	55 %	61 %	53 %
Female	53 %	45 %	39 %	47 %
Education				
No qualifications	None	None	6 %	1 %
Primary school	10 %	41 %	28 %	24 %
Junior middle school	30 %	32 %	33 %	31 %
High school	33 %	18 %	17 %	24 %
Secondary technique school	7 %	5 %	6 %	6 %
Junior college	10 %	5 %	None	6 %
Bachelor degree	10 %	None	11 %	7 %
Living arrangements				
Alone	None	None	6 %	1 %
With partner	80 %	64 %	66 %	71 %
With children	20 %	36 %	28 %	27 %
Rural/Urban				
Urban	60 %	46 %	61 %	56 %
Rural	40 %	55 %	39 %	44 %

were put forward. First, sample bias emerged in the process, i.e. specific population groups were excluded (e.g. illiteracies and people who were unable to speak mandarin or their regional dialects were too difficult for the interviewers to understand). Secondly, the options of the questions in the same nature are not unified, both in the amount and the way of presentation, which has negative impact on the respondents' comprehension to the questions. Thirdly, wording and expression of the statements still need to be refined, and fourthly, there are some problems regarding the items settings of the survey, which will be discussed in the next session.

4 Discussion

4.1 Self-Reporting vs. Performance Test

The methods applied in this pilot study were self-reporting and performance test. The correlations or discrepancies of the results were expected to give instructions to determine a more reasonable and effective way for the corresponding items in future research. This could lead to a new structure of a user's comprehensive data collection work in a large-scale survey, i.e. on the premise of quality assurance, a specific capability data could be obtained just through self-reporting or performance measures, or through a mixed methods, so that the cost of such a survey could be reduced. Additionally, such a comparison may also reveal some shortcomings of this study, so that some new data collection questionnaires, devices or methods could be explored.

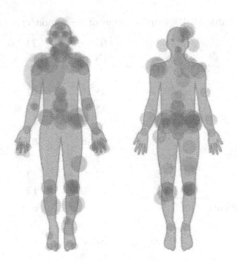

Fig. 1. Visualized general heath condition self-assessment (left: Male, right: Female)

In our study, we found some discrepancies between self-reporting and performance tests. Figure 1. depicts the stiffness, pains or other uncomfortable conditions of the respondents; they were asked to mark any problems specified on the diagram. After overlaying all the collected results, we can see that male respondents tend to report more problems on phalangeal joints and wrists, but the performance test shows that there is no significant difference between male and female respondents (right hand: Sig. = 0.886 > 0.05; left hand: Sig. = 0.585 > 0.05).

In the memory test, 25.7 % of the respondents reported that their daily lives were "not at all limited" by their memory, but 34.3 % of them had lower performance than the average in actual test.

Fors et al. summarized the advantages and disadvantages of self-reporting and performance test [9]. Self-reporting offers a more inexpensive and easily-executed means to obtain information, and it can be realized through flexible means, including face-to-face survey, telephone and email, additionally, proxy survey could be carried out if the respondent was not able to participate in some special situations. However, its shortcomings are obvious: the reliability of self-reporting is often questioned and the results are firmly correlated with social and cultural factors, and they are sensitive to the change of these factors. Milanović et al. suggested that the indirect estimation of old peoples' physical ability levels via questionnaire rather than actual measurement tend to lower the study's reliability [10].

Compared with self-assessed measures, standardized performance tests have clear face validity for the task being performed, better reproducibility and are less sensitive to cognitive impairments and sociocultural factors [9]. Nevertheless, results from our study imply that a respondent may perform a test very well, but he or she does face some actual difficulties in daily life, at the same time, the environment can also affect respondent's performance.

Related studies indicate that considerable discrepancies exist between self-reported limitations in function in independent activities of daily living and actual physical impairments. For instance, persons characterized by current joint pain or stiffness, using prescription medications, staying in urban dwelling, in depression, being female, lacking memory, having arthritis, and lack of exercise, were more likely to report higher levels of disability [11].

The reasons that lead to such discrepancies are complicated; significant portions of variance in self-reported disability can be explained by demographic, cultural, social and psychological variables such as gender, familiarity with testing activities, depression and helplessness [12–14].

It should be noticed that, form a designer's perspective, the differences existing in users' self-assessment and actual performance may offer some valuable insights for them to better understand the users or find a 'design chance'. These 'gaps' can also be 'opportunities' for both researchers and designers.

As a result of the limitation of the item setting, we do not acquire enough data to compare the correlations and discrepancies of every specific capability, but the principles of related research are clarified to some extent: some categories of users' capabilities can be obtained just through self-reporting, at the same time, capabilities that are correlated with users' sociocultural factors should be collected through integrating self-reporting and performance measurements to achieve the reliability and to offer insights to designers.

4.2 The Selection of Products

Users' capability of operating and interacting with products can provide direct reference for designers, in this pilot study, product-operating related testing items were both involved in questionnaire and actual performance tests.

One fundamental issue is what kind of products should be adopted in such a survey. Older people may be exposed to many specific products in their daily life. Chen et al. summarize comparatively intact product categories that are involved in the elderly's daily living, based on different technologies, the products are classified into five categories [15]:

- *Housing and daily living,* with the functions of convenience, safety, security, comfort and entertainment.
- *Communication technology,* with the functions of communication and transfer information.
- *Mobility and transport,* with the function of compensating or preventing physical limitations in personal mobility.
- *Health technology,* with the function of home healthcare and medical assistance.
- *Education and recreation,* with the functions of education and entertainment.

It is undoubtedly unrealistic to bring a detailed range of products that contains all the specific devices. But it may provide a clear structure and practical instructions to select representative products for a capability survey.

Two main categories of products were employed in our pilot study: (1) common housing products (chairs, bottles, keys, etc.), and (2) technology products (i.e. a smart phone with touch screen). The implications can be discussed from two aspects.

First, the selected products should ensure enough angles, the new trend and development of related technologies and their application on products are necessary to be taken into consideration. For instance, mobile phones are very commonly used among older people, in our study, 95.7 % of the respondents own at least one mobile phone, and 64.3 % of them use it "frequently". Previous studies on older people's use of mobile phone mainly based on a feature phone (normally with physical keypad and cannot download and run applications) rather than a smart phone. It is reported that China has been the biggest country smart phone assumption, and for the elderly, they are also in the context of the transition from feature phones to smart phones, especially for the 'future' older people, that means difficulties with smart phones that younger adults encounter now may be encountered by older adults in the future when using smart phones [16].

This big change profoundly affects the selection of products in such research; naturally, it may directly determine the detailed testing items of the survey. For example, existing research based on feature phones shows that older adults were more likely to get lost in the hierarchical menu of mobile phones than younger adults [17], however, the mainstream of smart phones now all adopt a flatting menu structure, in our survey, we have found that only 15.7 % of the respondents failed to executed the Interface Style Experience task (i.e. finding a specified menu icon).

Zhou et al. described the effects of this transition through three aspects: (1) what used to be important in feature phones (e.g., font size, icon size) is no longer so important in smart phones; (2) what used to be not so important in feature phones (e.g., connectivity) becomes important in smart phones; (3) what used to be important is still important, but it is in different embodiments (e.g., ease to find the desire functions, ease to get help, soft keys & multi-tap) [16].

Secondly, the gaps of products using between different subgroups of the elderly are reducing but still exists. We found that gender and rural-urban differences, additionally, the North and South differences, which are also addressed in most demographic-related research in China, do not have distinct effects on the purchasing, using and perceived difficulties of common housing and daily living products, but there are significant differences in communication technology products.

For instance, we raised a hypothesis that, because older people in urban and rural areas have different living habits and may conduct difference daily activities, they may show differences in product use. The statistical analysis results show that there is no significant difference (Sig. > 0.05) between these two groups in the using frequency of 'calling on a mobile phone' and 'operating TV remote control', but in 'taking photos' and 'sending text message' we can observe significant differences (Sig. < 0.05). The corresponding perceived difficulties of the products, however, had no significant differences (Table 2). The reasons behind this phenomenon are not clear, we believe that it could be partly explained by the difference of education situation: in our research, the urban respondents' educational levels are generally higher than the rural ones. This may imply that a standardized and unified setting of housing and daily living products in a capability survey is acceptable and reliable, while products that correlated to respondents' cognitive capabilities should be chosen carefully.

Table 2. Significant difference between urban and rural in frequency of use and perceived difficulties in product use.

Items	Call on a mobile phone	Send text message	Take photos using mobile phone or digital camera	Operate TV remote control
Frequency of use	0.13	0.05	0.01	0.47
Perceived difficulties	0.73	0.43	0.16	0.89

4.3 Ceiling Effects

The elderly's capabilities present great diversity, specifically, an old person's performance are affected by his or her health condition, background, experience, etc. Research has shown that the results of a physical function measurement study is limited by a ceiling effect, i.e., the majority of the sample, especially the younger groups, neither report nor exhibit disabilities. This, in turn, makes it difficult to attain statistical significance in the analyses [9].

In our study, ceiling effects obviously affect the test of technology products. More than half of the respondents have never or rarely used the products specified, and it results in a great data missing in the following perceived difficulty tests (Table 3).

To reduce the ceiling effects, older peoples' characteristics and preferences should

Table 3. The Proportion of respondents who never or rarely use the specified products

Items	Use internet	Listening to MP3 tracks on a portable device	Play games on PC or mobile phone	Use GPS
The proportion of "Never"	61.4 %	71.0 %	65.7 %	91.4 %
The proportion of "Rarely"	7.1 %	11.6 %	7.1 %	1.4 %

be addressed to adapt the current items and scales. For instance, Jones et al. find that older adults are more likely to seek health information, make purchases, and obtain religious information, but less likely to watch videos, download music, play games, and read blogs online [18]. That means applying some so activities or products that are common to general users in a survey focusing on the elderly is unreasonable.

5 Conclusions

Based on the results of this pilot study, some significant influencing factors in a multiple capability data collection survey are raised. First, there exists discrepancies between users' report and their actual capabilities; capabilities that correlated with users' sociocultural factors should be collected through integrating self-reporting and performance test to get the reliability and offer insights to designers. Secondly, products involved in this research should ensure multi angles, and address the gap of products using between different subgroups of older people. Thirdly, to reduce the ceiling effects, older peoples' characteristics and preferences should be addressed in the survey.

References

1. Langdon, P., Johnson, D., Huppert, F., Clarkson, P.J.: A framework for collecting inclusive design data for the UK population. Appl. Ergon. **46**, 318–324 (2013)
2. Johnson, D., Clarkson, J., Huppert, F.: Capability measurement for inclusive design. Eng. Des. **21**(2–3), 275–288 (2010)
3. Neerincx, M.A., Cremers, A.H., Kessens, J.M., van Leeuwen, D.A., Truong, K.P.: Attuning speech-enabled interfaces to user and context for inclusive design: technology, methodology and practice. Univ. Access Inf. Soc. **8**(2), 109–122 (2009)
4. Nickpour, F., Dong, H.: Designing anthropometrics! requirements capture for physical ergonomic data for designers. Des. J. **14**(1), 92–111 (2011)
5. Sharma, V.: Importance of anthropometric research in developing regional accessibility standards. Newsletter of Design for ALL Institute of India, pp. 69–81 (2008)
6. Stephanidis, C., Savidis, A.: Universal access in the information society: methods, tools, and interaction technologies. Univ. Access Inf. Soc. **1**(1), 40–55 (2001)
7. Towards Better Design (2010). http://www.esds.ac.uk/findingData/snDescription.asp?sn=6997
8. Tenneti, R., Johnson, D., Goldenberg, L., Parker, R.A., Huppert, F.A.: Towards a capabilities database to inform inclusive design: experimental investigation of effective survey-based predictors of human-product interaction. Appl. Ergon. **43**(4), 713–726 (2012)
9. Fors, S., Thorslund, M., Parker, M.G.: Do actions speak louder than words? self-assessed and performance-based measures of physical and visual function among old people. Eur. J. Ageing **3**(1), 15–21 (2006)
10. Milanović, Z., Pantelić, S., Trajković, N., Sporiš, G., Kostić, R., James, N.: Age-related decrease in physical activity and functional fitness among elderly men and women. Clin. Interv. Aging **8**, 549 (2013)
11. Daltroy, L.H., Larson, M.G., Eaton, H.M., Phillips, C.B., Liang, M.H.: Discrepancies between self-reported and observed physical function in the elderly: the influence of response shift and other factors. Soc. Sci. Med. **48**(11), 1549–1561 (1999)
12. Blalock, S.J., DeVellis, B.M., DeVellis, R.F., Sauter, S.V.H.: Self-evaluation processes and adjustment to rheumatoid arthritis. Arthritis Rheum. **31**(10), 1245–1251 (1988)
13. Lorish, C.D., Abraham, N., Austin, J., Bradley, L.A., Alarcon, G.S.: Disease and psychosocial factors related to physical functioning in rheumatoid arthritis. J. Rheumatol. **18**(8), 1150–1157 (1991)
14. McDowell, I., Newell, C.: Measuring Health: A Guide to Rating Scales and Questionnaires. Oxford University Press, New York (1996)
15. Chen, K., Chan, A.H.S.: The ageing population of China and a review of gerontechnology. Gerontechnology **10**(2), 63–71 (2011)

16. Zhou, J., Rau, P.L.P., Salvendy, G.: Age-related difference in the use of mobile phones. Univ. Access Inf. Soc. **13**(4), 401–413 (2014)
17. Arning, K., Ziefle, M.: Barriers of information access in small screen device applications: the relevance of user characteristics for a transgenerational design. In: Stephanidis, C., Pieper, M. (eds.) ERCIM Ws UI4ALL 2006. LNCS, vol. 4397, pp. 117–136. Springer, Heidelberg (2007)
18. Jones, S., Fox, S.: Generations Online in 2009. Pew Internet & American Life Project, New York (2009)

Time Reduction Design Method for Cognitive Assist Technology

Junji Ohyama[✉], Nana Itoh, Kenji Kurakata, and Ken Sagawa

National Institute of Advanced Industrial Science and Technology,
1-1-1, Higashi, Tsukuba City, Ibaraki 305-8566, Japan
{j.ohyama,nana.itoh,k-kurakata,ken.sagawa}@aist.go.jp

Abstract. Given the importance and abundance of current visual information, visual display designs should consider their accessibility to elderly people. However, adapting designs not only to young users but also to older users is difficult because the difference in perception and cognition between these age groups remains unclear. In order to solve this accessible design issue, we introduce three studies: a study on the effect of aging on visibility, the construction of a database containing the sensory characteristics of older persons and persons with disabilities, and experimental and conceptual studies of our proposed design method, the time reduction design. The time reduction design method can solve the cognitive problems of aging societies by improving both spatial visibility and recognition speed.

Keywords: Vision · Time design · Cognitive technology · Experimental psychology

1 Introduction

Important signs, user interfaces, and other visual information should be designed in a way that can be read and understood by all users. Designers can create user-friendly visual designs by drawing upon their experience and existing design methods. However, a substantial number of these designs are adapted only to young users. The United Nations reported that the percentage of elderly people in most industrialized countries will be 30 % or greater by the year 2050 [1]. Therefore, designers should consider the ways in which their designs will be read and understood by elderly people. However, adapting designs not only to young users but also to older users is difficult because the difference in perception and understanding between the young and old remains unclear. The goal of our study is to complete this data in order to obtain accessible designs.

Three studies are presented as solutions to the issue of accessible design. Part 1 discusses experimentation that was performed in order to study the effect of aging on visibility. Part 2 constructs a database that contains the sensory characteristics of older persons and persons with disabilities. Lastly, Part 3 analyzes the experimental and conceptual studies of our proposed design method: the time reduction design (TRD).

© Springer International Publishing Switzerland 2015
J. Zhou and G. Salvendy (Eds.): ITAP 2015, Part I, LNCS 9193, pp. 94–103, 2015.
DOI: 10.1007/978-3-319-20892-3_10

2 Part 1: The Effect of Aging on Visibility

In the introduction, we discussed the experimental studies conducted on the effect of aging on visibility. The elements of visual signs that enhance visibility are size, shape, color, and contrast. Therefore, we examined the effect these visibility factors have on both the young and elderly.

2.1 How to Examine the Effect of Aging on Visibility

In order to examine visual perception data, we primarily used general psychophysics and experimental psychology methods. However, some considerations are necessary in the study of aging, especially as they concern the measurement and analysis of aging data.

One of the elements that must be examined when studying the effects of aging is the age of the participants. The experiment must be designed in a way that examines the differences between age groups. The most conscientious way to do this includes recruiting participants from each decade, i.e., participant ages should range between 10 and 70. We used this method to study the effects of aging on basic visual functions, such as visual acuity and spectral sensitivity. The results showed two types of aging change, the linear and sigmoidal types, which had previously been observed in the aging change of other visual functions. Therefore, if the purpose of studying aging is to create accessible, user-friendly visual designs, only two age groups must be studied: the younger and the older. If the proposed design system applies to both younger and older users, the system's visual design will also apply to users between these two age groups. In our other studies, we compared two age groups (20s and 60s) and estimated each aging trend by complementing data between the two groups.

Another element that can be explored is the medical history of ophthalmological surgeries. In order to calculate the effect of aging on visibility, we can separate participants according to eye surgery experience, such as surgery for cataracts. In our studies, we recruited people who had not received eye surgery.

To calculate the effect of visual design features on visibility, the difference in individual basic visual acuity must be addressed. We measured the visual accommodative power of each participant using an auto refract meter and corrected individual vision to the topmost visual acuity for given test distances using an optometry lens.

When applying the results of vision studies to display design, we regarded not only the participants' average but also their distributions are meaningful. For example, in some cases, the acceptable visibility level of the 80 % of the 60s population was more practically meaningful than the average level (i.e., 50 % of the population). In order to enable this analysis, data must be collected from a substantial number of participants. In our research, we enlisted approximately 100 participants for each study. Table 1 lists our investigations concerning the effects of aging on visibility.

Using these results, we developed methods for evaluating and improving accessible visual design not only for the young users but also for older users. For example, we calculated the minimum legible font size and proposed a legibility estimation formula that depends on age. In order to obtain an elder-friendly accessible design, the visual

Table 1. Examples of the effect of aging on visual perception

Studied aging effects on visual characteristics	Participant age groups (Number of participants)	Relative examined conditions in addition to age
Legibility of font size	20–29, 60–79 (90)	Viewing distance, Environmental illumination, Font type, Letter complexity
Legibility of letter contrast	18–29, 60–83 (108)	Size, Viewing distance, Environmental illumination, Contrast polarity, Font type, Letter complexity
Spectral sensitivity	10s, 20s, 30s, 40s, 50s, 60s, 70s (91)	Target color, Background color, Luminance contrast
Useful field of view	20–29, 60–79 (98)	Target size, Target color, Target luminance, Target, direction, Background color, Environmental illumination
Contrast sensitivity	10s, 20s, 30s, 40s, 50s, 60s, 70s (110)	Environmental illumination, Duration of target presentation
Readability of text	20–29, 60–79 (36)	Kerning, Leading, Viewing distance, Font type, Font size
Ability of categorization of colors	20–29, 60–79 (89)	Target color, Environmental illumination

functions of older people must be considered when selecting color, contrast, and size. The data for these visual characteristics have been used to establish the international and Japanese standards [2, 3]. We are also preparing another proposal of the related guidelines to present to the international standards.

2.2 Legibility Data

A typical study on aging includes its effect on the minimum legible font size. We measured the effects of aging on the minimum legible font size under multiple conditions, including distance, luminance, font type, and characters, assuming that the characters were written in black on a white background. The results for one of these experiments are shown in Fig. 1.

Additionally, we used these results to estimate the minimum legible font size of one character for a person of a given age with a given viewing distance, luminance, font type, and characters. This estimation equation can be written as

$$P = a\,(D/V) + b \tag{1}$$

Here, D represents the viewing distance in meters, V is the visual acuity, P is the estimated minimum legible font size, and a and b are coefficients decided by the font type and letter complexity. For example, in order to estimate the minimum legible font size of Gothic font numerals, we have $a = 6.4$ and $b = 3.0$ (see [4, 5] for other conditions). Visual acuity is related to environmental illumination and age. Therefore, V is estimated using the target user's age and environmental luminance, and we can estimate the minimum legible font size and preferred legible font size using this formula or gathered data in order to improve legibility.

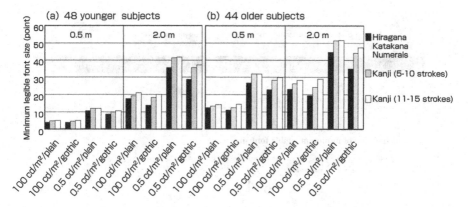

Fig. 1. Minimum font size required to read a single Japanese letter (hiragana/katakana/numerals, kanji 5–10 strokes, kanji 11–15 strokes) with viewing distances 0.5 and 2 m and luminance levels 100 and 0.5 cd/m2. (a) Results of 48 younger participants. (b) Results of 44 older participants. (Figure provided by [4].)

This estimation formula was used to establish the JIS S 0032: 2003 *Guidelines for the elderly and people with disabilities—Visual signs and displays—Estimation of minimum legible size for a Japanese single character* [3], which has been proposed to the International Standards Organization (ISO).

3   Part 2: Development of Interactive Database for Accessible Design Assistance

In Part 1, we suggested some practical considerations when examining aging effects on visual perception. We also explained how to apply the data in order to evaluate and improve design accessibility. These data and evaluation methods are useful to designers who are familiar with their technical terms and academic data; however, they remain difficult for most laypersons to comprehend. In addition, accessing reports and guides is difficult. Therefore, we developed an interactive online database, which has a simple graphical interface, using the visual characteristic data explained in Part 1. The database graphically describes various sensory characteristics using equations and tables, and it also presents preferred designs based on the target users' information and environmental settings, such as age, viewing distance, and luminance. A sample application of this database can be seen in Fig. 2.

Not only is the minimum legible font size calculated but also eight estimations concerning age-rerated visibility characteristics. Table 2 exhibits these database items and the corresponding effects of aging on vision. We also examined age-related changes in auditory characteristics (see [6, 7]). Moreover, we are cooperating with other researchers and institutes in order to link their reports and studies in our database, compiling a worldwide guide for accessible design. This constructed database has been released charge-free to the public on our institute's website [6].

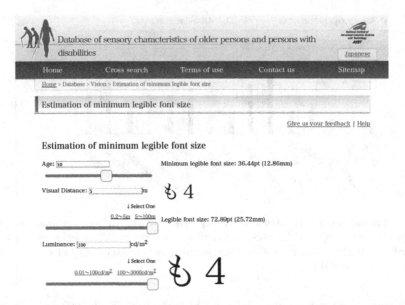

Fig. 2. Example from the database of sensory characteristics of older persons and persons with disabilities: input to the left; calculated results and corresponding examples to the right.

Table 2. Database items and supporting experimental data for the effects of aging

Design items	Supporting experimental data
Estimation of minimum legible font size	Legibility of font size
Size and contrast threshold for legibility	Legibility of letter contrast
Age-related relative luminance	Spectral sensitivity
Age-related changes of visual field size for detection: size of visual field & detection rate	Useful field of view
Contrast sensitivity function	Contrast sensitivity
Preferred kerning and leading of text and sentences	Readability of text
Color combinations based on fundamental colors	Ability of categorization of colors

4 Part 3: Time Reduction Design for Accessible Design and Future Cognitive Assist Technology

In the final part of this paper, we introduce the conceptual and experimental studies of our proposed design method: the time reduction design.

4.1 Time Reduction Design Concept

Previously, we discussed studies concerning the effects of aging on visual characteristics and a method for using this data in order to improve design. For example, the visibility of visual information and signs can be improved using the spatial characteristics of vision that change with age, such as shape and color, found in our database. However, the improvement of spatial visibility is not sufficient for the creation of useful visual signs because most signs dynamically change, and their everyday recognition has time constraints. Designs that enable fast, accurate recognition are necessary in an aging society that is flooded with information. Our time reduction design (TRD) method can solve the cognitive problems of aging societies by improving not only spatial visibility but also recognition speed [8–10].

Assisting Recognition Speed for Fast, Adaptive Control Using the TRD. Improvements made using the TRD method have the potential to save lives. Elderly people are often the victims or victimizers of accidents caused by a lack of available recognition time. For example, the number of careless car accidents perpetrated by elderly drivers is increasing in Japan [11]. Drivers must quickly and accurately recognize multiple signs while driving. However, the time required for older drivers to recognize visual information is not considered when signs are being designed or arranged. Some of these careless accidents could be related to the decrease in older drivers' recognition speed.

Assisting Recognition in Time-Pressured Situations Using the TRD. It has been argued that the evacuation delay of elderly people in Japan was one of the factors that increased the number of flood victims [12]. Emergency signs and evacuation maps do not take into account the recognition speed of elderly people. The TRD can transmit information quickly and accurately to all people—both young and old alike—in time-pressured situations.

Assisting the Personalization of Individual Cognitive Abilities Using the TRD. A substantial gap exists between the increase of available information due to technological progress and the decrease of sensory and cognitive ability due to aging. Our information technology society demands that people have access to and understand the dynamic up-to-date contents provided by smartphones, tablets, and digital signage. The TRD can adapt the interfaces of these informational devices to individual users.

In order to do this, we calculated the relation between the display duration and recognition accuracy of signs and letters. We then estimated the time required for visual design recognition. We also introduced some examples of ongoing studies and discussed the proposed method's effectiveness.

4.2 Time Reduction Design Experimental Results

As part of our experimental evaluation, we calculated the relation between the display duration and recognition accuracy of signs and letters, and we estimated the time required for visual design recognition. The experimental settings and method were similar to previous visibility studies. The exception to this concerns the timing control. We constructed a computer program that can precisely fix stimulus display time to 10 ms per frame (100 Hz). This technique for producing stable high-frequency displays was previously used in the fields of computer information and gaming but has rarely been used in experimental psychology and accessibility studies. We applied the time control technique to the TRD experiments in order to calculate the time required for visual design recognition.

TRD Studies on Visual Elements. As was previously mentioned, visual signs must be understood within a short time period. We examined the amount of time required to recognize visual signs and the ways in which spatio-temporal abilities change with aging. Table 3 displays the amount of time required to recognize the basic elements of visual signs.

These studies supported multiple observations. First, the required recognition time for a 5.62-degree letter was approximately half of that for a 1.69-degree letter. Letter luminance affected only small letters. Letter color affected letter recognition for letters with an approximate size of 1.69 degrees but did not affect smaller or larger letters. Word recognition speed was strongly influenced by its familiarity value but was not influenced by its ease of utterance. Four-digit numbers required a duration that was about 1.6 times longer than that needed for three-digit numbers. Pictograms were recognized faster than road signs, and the simultaneous recognition of three road signs required 736.2 ms for older persons. If a vehicle were traveling 60 km/h, it would travel 12.2 m in this duration. To recognize three road signs in 50 % of accuracy, older drivers need to pay attention to the sign during 12.2 m travel. Therefore, our results imply that demand for the accurate recognition of triple road signs would be difficult and dangerous for older drivers in most cases.

TRD Study of Caption and Subtitle Design. Movie captions and subtitles are examples of displays that require a TRD. These texts must have a duration that considers recognition speed. Moreover, captions are useful alternative methods for communicating auditory information for deaf and hard of hearing people. Although a substantial percentage of hearing-impaired people are elderly, the effect of aging on recognition speed is not addressed during the caption design and creation process.

Figure 3 shows one example from our experimental studies concerning the required duration of caption presentation. The graph displays the mean required duration for both young (twenties) and old (60 and older) participants. In the preliminary study, we found that captions containing 25 to 30 letters most frequently appeared in Japanese National Broadcasting news programs. Therefore, we sampled captions having 25 to 30 letters from the news to use in the study. Results suggested that both the threshold and preferred levels of required display time for captions are approximately twice as long for elderly people than for young people. The average number of words in each caption was approximately 18 words. Therefore, the minimum duration required for recognition was approximately 44.9 ms per word for young

Table 3. Time required to recognize basic visual elements. Young signifies people in their twenties, and Elder represents people between the ages of 60 and 80. The estimated durations, measured in milliseconds, were 50 % and 80 % of the correct duration.

			Young		Elder	
Design for	Stimulus conditions		50 % correct	80 % correct	50 % correct	80 % correct
A letter	Size: 0.63 degree	Color: White	31.44	39.12	38.40	47.49
		Color: Gray	30.79	38.28	51.47	60.41
		Color: Lime	32.50	38.95		
		Color: Aqua	33.15	41.07		
		Color: Yellow	30.80	38.62		
		Color: Fuchsia	38.05	48.54		
	Size: 1.69 degrees	Color: White	22.76	32.64	27.13	37.00
		Color: Gray	22.17	31.66	34.95	50.01
		Color: Lime	21.89	35.12		
		Color: Aqua	21.02	33.36		
		Color: Yellow	22.46	32.36		
		Color: Fuchsia	24.03	35.35		
	Size: 5.62 degrees	Color: White	5.11	11.14	19.06	30.35
		Color: Gray	6.25	14.20	18.24	33.06
		Color: Lime	5.79	10.73		
		Color: Aqua	4.66	11.06		
		Color: Yellow	6.18	11.25		
		Color: Fuchsia	4.95	10.15		
A word (Size: 1.69 degrees)	3 letters	Familiar	36.97		96.22	
		Unfamiliar	40.83		109.35	
	4 letters	Easy utterance	36.40		97.39	
		Difficult utterance	69.05		238.16	
Number	3 digits (Size: 1.69 degrees)		49.78		105.68	
	4 digits (Size: 1.69 degrees)		75.37		173.83	
Sign	Pictogram		2.82		20.16	
	Road sign	One	9.63		31.48	
		Triplet	35.77		736.2	

people and 85.2 ms per word for elderly people. These results are consistent with the TRD studies of visual elements.

We are preparing to propose our guide for the accessible visual presentation of captions and subtitles to the international standard, ISO/IEC/JTC1.

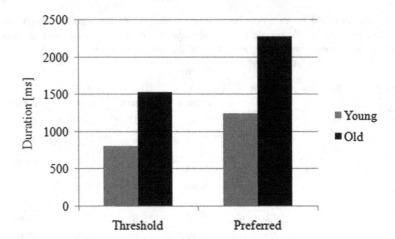

Fig. 3. Age-related difference for caption recognition time requirements. The threshold is the mean minimum duration needed to recognize captions, as determined by the participants. The preferred level is the mean duration in which caption evaluation is considered easy.

5   Conclusion

In this paper, we discussed multiple aspects of visibility and its age-related changes, and we demonstrated a method for applying experimental data to the improvement of everyday designs. We also introduced the long-term accessible visual design research performed in our laboratory. An interactive database and standard guidelines were provided as examples. In addition, we introduced the concept of our spatio-temporal design, the time reduction design, and analyzed experimental results concerning the time required for visual element recognition. Moreover, our study on caption recognition speed and its relation to aging was presented as an application of our method. The TRD clarifies the dynamic process of visual recognition for older persons and can be applied to the estimation and evaluation system of visual designs and user interfaces. Furthermore, the TRD calculates and evaluates personal abilities of perception and cognition. Therefore, it can be applied to personalized cognitive assist tools in the near future.

References

1. United Nations: World Population Ageing 2009, United Nations Publications, New York (2010)
2. ISO 24502:2010 Ergonomics—Accessible design—Specification of age-related luminance contrast for coloured light (2010)
3. Japan Industrial Standard Committee: JIS S 0032 Guidelines for the elderly and people with disabilities—Visual signs and displays—Estimation of minimum legible size for a Japanese single character (2003)

4. Sagawa, K., Kurakata, K.: Estimation of legible font size for elderly people. Synthesiology **6** (1), 24–33 (2013)
5. Sagawa, K., Ujike, H., Sasaki, T.: Legibility of Japanese characters and sentences as a function of age. In: Proceedings of the IEA 2003, vol. 7, pp. 496–499 (2003)
6. Database of sensory characteristics of older persons and persons with disabilities. http://scdb.db.aist.go.jp/?lng=en
7. Kurakata, K., Itoh, N., Ohyama, J., Sato, H., Sagawa, K.: Database of sensory characteristics of older persons and persons with disabilities. Gerontechnology **13**(2), 126–127 (2014)
8. Ohyama, J., Itoh, N.: A study of the effect of font color on minimum legible duration of a character for the time reduction design. In: Proceedings of the 11th Conference of the Japanese Society for Cognitive Psychology, pp. 3–34 (2013)
9. Ohyama, J.: Time reduction design: maximize communication efficiency of visual information by shortest presentation duration. In: Proceedings of 12th Conference of LS-BT, p. 62 (2013)
10. Ohyama J.: Essential studies of visual cognition for time reduction design. In: Proceedings of 13th Conference of LS-BT, p. 126 (2014)
11. Cabinet Office of Japan: Summary of the Eighth Fundamental Traffic Safety Program (2006)
12. Tamura, K., Hayashi, H., Kimura, R.: Clarifying Suffering of the elderly in the 2004 Niigata flood and the 2004 Mid-Niigata prefecture earthquake. J. Nat. Disaster Sci. **27**(2), 67–84 (2005)

A Robot of My Own: Participatory Design of Socially Assistive Robots for Independently Living Older Adults Diagnosed with Depression

Selma Šabanović[1(✉)], Wan-Ling Chang[1], Casey C. Bennett[1,2], Jennifer A. Piatt[3], and David Hakken[1]

[1] School of Informatics and Computing, Indiana University, Bloomington, USA
{selmas,wanlchan,dhakken}@indiana.edu
[2] Centerstone Research Institute, Bloomington, USA
[3] School of Public Health, Indiana University, Bloomington, USA
jenpiatt@indiana.edu

Abstract. This paper presents an ongoing project using participatory design methods to develop design concepts for socially assistive robots (SARs) with older adults diagnosed with depression and co-occurring physical illness. We frame SARs development in the context of preventive patient-centered healthcare, which empowers patients as the primary drivers of health and aims to delay the onset of disease rather than focusing on treatment. After describing how SARs can be of benefit in this form of healthcare, we detail our participatory design study with older adults and therapists aimed at developing preventive SARs applications for this population. We found therapists and older adults to be willing and able to participate in assistive robot design, though hands-on participation was a challenge. Our findings suggest that important areas of concern for older adults with depression are social interaction and companionship, as well as technologies that are easy to use and require minimal intervention.

Keywords: Assistive robotics · Social robots · Participatory design · Elderly · Depression · Patient-centered healthcare

1 Introduction

Recent years have seen the proliferation of socially assistive robots (SARs) developed to improve the functioning and quality-of-life (QOL) of people who experience chronic and age-related health issues [1, 2]. Much of the research and evaluation related to these emerging technologies is performed in laboratories and institutionalized care settings (e.g. nursing homes) and focuses on treatment and rehabilitation. The growing focus on patient- and community-centered care, however, emphasizes that health is a daily and lifelong concern, not just an issue that becomes relevant when someone is diagnosed with a medical condition. Impacting health in daily life – prior to the development of illness or the need for institutionalized care (i.e. preventative healthcare) – therefore represents a novel opportunity for exploring applications of assistive robotics. This, in

© Springer International Publishing Switzerland 2015
J. Zhou and G. Salvendy (Eds.): ITAP 2015, Part I, LNCS 9193, pp. 104–114, 2015.
DOI: 10.1007/978-3-319-20892-3_11

turn, brings up the need to understand how robots may fit into peoples' everyday lives and caregiving communities.

A noteworthy example of a space in which socially assistive robots might be used is clinical depression in the elderly. Depression is the second leading cause of disability in the United States [3]; clinical depression affects 15–20 % of older adults in the US [4]. One particular area in which SARs stand to be beneficial is in addressing loneliness, which is a key component of depression in the elderly and a risk factor for physical/cognitive decline in this population [5]. Research with SARs in institutionalized settings has shown that robots can help alleviate feelings of loneliness in older adults [6], suggesting they could provide therapeutic benefits that reduce symptoms of clinical depression in older adults living independently as well.

The project presented here explores how SARs could be designed for and used in the homes of older adults before they become institutionalized, with the aim of preventing or delaying the need for institutionalization. To address the social and ethical challenges of developing and deploying assistive robotic technologies in domestic settings, and in accordance with the paradigm of patient-centered care, we use a participatory design (PD) approach. This method actively involves relevant stakeholders – older adults with depression, therapists, and case workers – in deciding on the issues that need to be addressed by research, as well developing ideas for and evaluating new technologies. The long-term aim of our project is to provide a better understanding of appropriate designs, deployment methods, and uses of SARs that can lead to more successful technical and social outcomes. We also explore which PD methodologies are appropriate for co-designing assistive robots with older adults and staff. We describe the motivation for our work in more detail below, followed by a description of our participatory design methodology and initial results from stakeholder interviews and two participatory workshops held in the Summer and Fall of 2014. We conclude with a summary of lessons learned so far, and directions for future work.

2 Background and Motivation

2.1 Socially Assistive Robots in Eldercare

Socially assistive robots are expected not only to help people accomplish certain tasks, but also to have measurable behavioral, cognitive, or therapeutic effects [1]. Researchers have shown that the therapeutic effects of SARs on the elderly can include positive health impacts, decreased stress and improved mood, decreased loneliness and better communication with others [2]. One projected use for socially assistive robots is to complement therapists in the course of rehabilitation (e.g. [7]), as well as play both functional and affective roles in the lives of older adults. Care-O-bot, for example, supports independently living older adults by delivering meals and drinks [8]. The seal-like robot PARO [9, 10] is used as a social companion. Robots can also act as communication devices between older adults and remote caregivers (e.g. [11]).

SARs development has so far focused on two main contexts of use: the home, where robots can provide aid to independently living individuals, and institutions such as nursing homes and hospitals, where robots assist caregivers as well as older adults.

The development of SARs for these environments raises significant social concerns beyond the technical issues involved. Field studies of interactions between people and robots in hospitals (e.g. [12]), nursing homes (e.g. [13, 14]), and private homes (e.g. [15]) have brought attention to the effects of emergent social factors (e.g. workflow, user values and life histories, the physical environment) on the success and consequences of robots in healthcare. This suggests that developing SARs for everyday use requires research, design, and evaluation sensitive to the social context.

2.2 Healthcare-Related Challenges and Opportunities

A patient-centered, long-term view of health emphasizes the importance of preventive care for improving a person's quality-of-life over their lifespan [16]. This is particularly true in chronic illnesses, where a cure is often not available [17]; with issues like dementia, for example, delaying onset is a key strategy [18]. A preventive approach to health can also reduce costs and better aligns with patient preferences to minimize time spent in institutionalized settings [19].

SARs hold significant potential in supporting preventive healthcare, especially among the elderly. A majority of older adults (70 % of the broader population from which we draw our participants) have multiple co-occurring chronic health conditions and/or are at risk of several others. Development of mental illness in older adults (e.g. clinical depression) often precipitates a significant decline in physical health, which in turn often leads to the need for institutionalized care [20], and the incidence of co-occurring disorders only increases with age [21]. SARs can be used to directly intervene in this cycle, using the abovementioned benefits of SARs to assist users in their homes, before they become institutionalized.

2.3 Participatory Design and Healthcare

In concordance with patient-centered care and prevention, our approach is also informed by the use of participatory design methods to develop healthcare solutions. Over forty years of practice and research in participatory design (PD) for information technology has shown that negotiation of the social meanings, uses, and effects of technologies by various groups that stand to be affected throughout the design process can lead to more successful technical and social outcomes.

Applications of PD methodologies to robotics, though few to date, suggest that active participation in the design of robotic technologies can empower users with knowledge about technology, allowing them to take part in critical discussions of the potential social consequences and meanings of robots [22]. PD has been used to work with community members to build robotic sensing devices [23]; older adults have also evaluated assistive robot mock-ups in their homes to explore the potential uses and appearance of assistive robots [24]. Ezer et al. [25] found that technological experience, rather than age, was the main predictor of people's expectations from robots, suggesting that making older adults more aware of the technical possibilities of robots through PD could increase acceptance [26]. We can therefore expect stakeholders active in system development to be invested in and scaffold its deployment and use.

3   Method

3.1   Participants

Our participants were recruited among older adults (>55) experiencing co-occurring chronic mental (major clinical depression) and physical illness (mainly hypertension, diabetes, chronic pain, and cardiovascular disease), who receive treatment services from a large outpatient healthcare provider in rural Indiana, and care staff at the institution. The providers see over 80,000 distinct patients a year across 150 outpatient clinical sites in multiple states (e.g. Tennessee, Indiana, Kentucky, and Illinois). The director of one of the provider's facilities helped us identify appropriate staff members and older adults for the study. With their help, we recruited five staff members and five older adults. The staff members included two therapists, two rehabilitation specialists, and one care coordinator. The five older adult participants included two women and three men, with ages ranging from 58 to 71. One of the five older adults was currently employed and all lived independently on their own.

3.2   Study Procedure

We conducted in-home interviews with individual participants to understand their daily living context, and then two group workshops to study how participants make sense of existing SARs, which everyday life issues they find important for their quality of life, and which design characteristics they desire to be part of future SAR technologies. Interviews and workshops were transcribed and thematically analyzed by researchers to describe how older adults thought about and evaluated robots, the challenges they faced on a daily basis, and how robots might be used to help them.

Interviews. Five *staff members* were interviewed about their experiences working with independently living older adults with depression to better understand their practices and needs. We showed staff videos of existing assistive robotic technologies and asked them to critique the robots, letting us know whether they thought they would be useful in their work and what kinds of attributes they thought assistive robotic technologies should have so they could use them successfully. The videos presented three different types of robots that were either already available on the market, or under development for everyday use by older adults in their homes: the seal-like robot PARO[1], an assistive home robot Care-O-Bot[2], and the assistive telepresence platform Giraff Plus[3]. The videos showed people in nursing homes interacting with PARO in a group activity, while Care-O-Bot and Giraff Plus were filmed in a user's home. Care-O-Bot reminded a user to take her pills, and Giraff Plus was used by a physician to remotely check in on and examine an older adult at home.

Initial semi-structured interviews were also performed with five *older adults in their homes*. We first collected demographic information about participants, and then asked

---

[1]   https://www.youtube.com/watch?v=3npV-npZkxI.

[2]   https://www.youtube.com/watch?v=3tTKiVuyem4 (showed approximately first 3 min).

[3]   https://www.youtube.com/watch?v=Pjgf3Yi81ao.

them to tell us about their current life situation and experiences, the social relationships they were involved in (e.g. partners, family, friends), specific issues they faced in their daily lives (e.g. mental and physical health, social interaction), and the types and uses of technology in their daily life. The interviews ended with a walk-through of the participant's house, documented through field notes and photos.

Participatory Design Workshops. We held two participatory design workshops with older adults to give them opportunities to more actively contribute to the development of SARs.

The *first workshop* lasted approximately two hours. Four participants (3 male and 1 female) and four researchers were in attendance. One participant could not attend due to health reasons. For the first hour, participants watched and critiqued the same videos showing assistive robotic technologies that the therapists saw (PARO, Care-O-Bot, Giraff Plus), with one additional robot (Papero[4]). The Papero robot was added as an example of a robot used for multimedia communication and social interaction, since the initial interview suggested these topics were of particular interest to participants. Papero was described in the video as a robot that could recognize individual participants and help them use email and communicate with others. In the second hour, participants saw live demonstrations of robots, including the robotic seal PARO, MugBot, Keepon, and Roomba (see Fig. 1). The live demonstrations consisted of researchers giving a brief description of each robot's functions (e.g. "Roomba can vacuum the floor by itself"; "Keepon can dance to music") as the robot performed them (e.g. PARO moved and made seal-like sounds, Keepon danced, and we showed how to program Mugbot using a simple Scratch-based interface). During the demo, participants could touch and explore the robots as they liked. Our main aim for this workshop, and the focus of questions to participants, was to learn what participants think of existing technologies, how they relate these technologies to their experiences and concerns, whether they can see themselves using such technologies, and what they would want such technologies to do for them in the future. We also noted successes and challenges in getting participants to actively participate in the workshop to help us further develop PD methodologies for older adults.

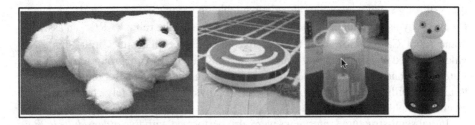

Fig. 1. Participants experienced live demos of PARO, the Roomba, MugBot (a programmable social robot), and Keepon, during which they could freely interact with the robots.

---

[4] https://www.youtube.com/watch?v=s7MqCNgFAzY.

The *second workshop* lasted approximately 3 h. Three participants (1 female and 2 male) and five researchers were in attendance. This time two participants could not attend due to health reasons. The aim of the workshop was for researchers to work together with participants to design assistive robots that could fit into their daily lives. We started the workshop by asking participants to tell us about specific challenges they faced the last time they were feeling sad or lonely. We also explored PD methods to help participants engage in creative thinking regarding assistive technologies. Researchers assisted participants in materializing their visions of robots by sketching them out during the workshop. We ended the workshop with a general discussion of the potential uses of assistive technologies, how they can be used to address issues related to aging and depression, and comments on the workshops themselves.

4   Findings

4.1   Interviews

Staff members showed a lively interest in integrating more digital technologies, including robots, into their therapeutic practice. After viewing videos of four different assistive robots, the staff was unanimous in choosing PARO as the one they would be most likely to use with their clients. They particularly commented that the robot was low maintenance, and could provide companionship for the older adults they worked with– something they can care for like a pet, without overwhelming them. The interviews with older adults, carried out in their homes, showed this population is interested and able to take part in participatory research related to SARs. In the course of the interviews, one of the main challenges older adults emphasized was loneliness, along with physical health problems. They all mentioned social interaction with friends, family members, and pets as a factor that can make them feel better when they are depressed. Two of the five older adults had pets, but both mentioned they may not be able to take care of them for much longer due to their condition. All the participants used computers and cell-phones, but only two used it regularly for email and online purchasing, and only one enjoyed using the computer. These interviews also provided researchers with a sense of participants' home arrangements, which included one house, three apartments, and a trailer home.

4.2   Workshop 1

Four older adults participated in the first workshop, led by the first author. In contrast to expectations that older adults might be wary of robots, the participants had no hesitation about discussing them and considering their usability at home. All participants described several ways they might use the robots and commented which devices they would like to buy, defining themselves as potential consumers of robots.

The most positive responses were to PARO, both after watching the video and while interacting with the robot. One participant, who had previously worked in a nursing home, was impressed at the level of interactivity older adults in the video showed toward the robot. Participants liked that PARO was easy to take care of and did not require cleanup. One participant remarked that the robot's presence created a "happy attitude about life" in users. The only downside to PARO that participants mentioned when prompted was that it was "not alive". When asked where they might use PARO, participants mentioned it could be helpful after surgery or at home, particularly during "gloomy days."

Participants were also positive about the Giraff Plus telepresence robot they viewed. They liked the idea of having someone track their activities, and the ability to communicate with medical staff, family and friends in a more physically embodied way. Participants liked the idea of having a robot present in case of a fall, mentioning that it could notice the problem more quickly than they could call for help, and be able to assist them and keep them company while they wait for humans to arrive. They commented on the robot's ease of use. One additional design request was for portability, so they could take the robot outside while doing yard work or walking.

The Care-O-Bot, a mobile domestic robot, was seen as good for reminding participants about their medications (a function shown in the video), and possibly warning them against eating too many sweets or doing other unhealthy things (ideas from participants). Participants commented positively on the robot's ability to support communication and staying in touch with loved ones. They described the early version of the Care-O-Bot shown as not aesthetically pleasing, too big to fit in their homes, and not appropriate for children and pets, who might harm or get hurt by the robot.

NEC's communication robot Papero also inspired many positive comments. Participants found it easy to use and fun, and appreciated its communication and social capabilities, particularly the ability to recognize people and adjust to their needs for personalized interaction. One participant also mentioned that Papero might be able to help him get out of his gloomy moods by talking to him and keeping him company.

In addition to responses to robot videos, the robot demonstrations allowed us to see how participants might actually interact with robots. As mentioned above, participants started interacting with PARO as soon as it was brought out and did not hesitate to touch and talk to it. They also easily approached Keepon, which they anthropomorphized readily (one participant said the robot "didn't like him," another mentioned it was "checking everyone out"). One participant mentioned Keepon would be good for their grandkids to play with when they visited, another said it might inspire him to get up and dance. Participants liked the appearance of MugBot, a minimalist social robot, but were quite negative about the possibility of developing programs for the robot with the Scratch-based[5] interface we showed them. They commented that working with the computer seemed difficult, and one participant mentioned that he preferred not to be on the computer, though he had one at home. Two out of four participants said they would like to use the Roomba, and one chose it as the robot they would most like to have in their house.

Overall, the ability to support companionship and sociability, whether with the robot itself or with others through telepresence, emerged as the most compelling use of SARs for this group. The unanimous interest in PARO seemed due to the possibility of having a close, tactile interaction with it. One participant described it as "inviting... almost like

---

[5] http://wiki.scratch.mit.edu/wiki/Scratch_User_Interface.

a real animal that can relate to you." Another said he found it "comforting" and "motivating" to be more active. Papero was appreciated for its ability to recognize individual users and its communication skills. In contrast, the most machine-like robot seen on video, and the programmable robot we demonstrated, were quickly dismissed as unattractive, difficult to use, and not fitting into the home.

4.3   Workshop 2

The negative responses participants gave to the mechanical appearance of the Care-O-Bot and the idea of programming MugBot suggested they were not ready for hands-on work with robots, so we decided to design and critique robots with them by visualizing their ideas on paper. We first prompted participants to tell us about the day-to-day challenges they face in their homes, then reminded them of the various capabilities robots have to provide social and physical assistance, and finally asked them which functions and capabilities they would want robots to have to help them with the daily issues they had identified. In order to make the process iterative, two researchers produced drawings of the robots as participants described their appearance, capabilities, and uses. The three participants then critiqued the drawings, pointing out things they liked or did not like, and leading to further iterations of their desired robot designs.

When asked to remember a time when they were feeling sad or lonely in the last month, and to tell us something they would have liked help with during those times, one participant mentioned physical challenges: difficulties in lifting things around the house and cleaning. Another pointed to his anger issues, and the desire to have some help in curbing them. A third participant mentioned that his big challenge were the upcoming Thanksgiving and Christmas holidays, with which the other two then agreed. The participants went on to discuss not being able to spend the holidays with family, friends and loved ones for various reasons. They also mentioned not having money, or the health for holiday preparations. Most of all, participants discussed wanting someone to talk to and spend the holidays with, even pets. Two participants mentioned they had been able to work as volunteers before their illness; they now missed the feeling of helping others and being useful. All participants described the lack of companionship as a trigger for their depression, mentioning that days when they do not have doctor visits of other activities planned (such as the weekend) were the most difficult, "the longest days."

After discussing their everyday challenges, participants and researchers collaborated to design robots that might be able to help them. The first suggestions from participants were to make a talking version of the robotic seal PARO, which might say "Good morning to you" or "It is now time for this [activity]," or that it could be used as a medicine or event reminder. Participants then said that what they really want is a something or someone that will keep them company, read and discuss the news and television shows with them, play games and eat with them. The participant who had mentioned anger issues pointed out that such a robot could help him deal with his anger by asking him to "Get your act together." Another participant said the robot could know the weather and tell her how to dress, and help her control her diet.

To realize these ideas about robots, two researchers drew up their interpretations of the participants' ideas as the conversation proceeded. The first suggested embodiment was a robotic coffee pot (See Fig. 2), which participants unanimously evaluated as not being humanlike enough. One participant mentioned that he would like his robot to be like the singer Mariah Carey, more humanlike in size and appearance. The need for portability, and wanting to take the robot along on walks, to the park, to the doctor's office, was brought up. Finally, participants agreed that the robot would have to be low maintenance, not something they would need to fix or attend to in any way.

Fig. 2. Workshop 2 produced designs for robotic appliances, small robotic assistants, and humanlike robots that could provide a companionship role for participants.

As in the prior workshop, the need for companionship and social interaction was discussed at length and became a focal point of participants' designs. Along with social interaction, however, participants also pointed out a variety of health-related functions that robots could perform, including providing reminders and suggesting appropriate things to eat, wear and do during the day. The use of visualizations during the second workshop allowed participants to critique and develop more specific ideas of robots that would be appropriate for their daily lives. In future work, we are interested in inspiring more in-depth discussions of specific interaction scenarios between robots and people, so that we can further hone our understanding of participant needs and perceptions of domestic SARs designs.

5   Conclusion

Socially assistive robots are a promising technology for preventive, patient-centered care. The ongoing project described here uses participatory design to explore appropriate ways of implementing SARs to aid older adults with co-occurring depression and chronic physical illness in order to delay the need for institutionalized care. The participatory design activities we performed provided us with concrete evidence of interest and support from both staff and older adults for the introduction of SARs technologies into their therapeutic services. These experiences also demonstrated that there is clearly a place to explore the therapeutic value of these technologies in the home and gave us confidence, based upon our developed understanding of these specific home environments, that it will be possible to integrate them into therapeutic practice and the daily life of their clients. We identified companionship as a central unmet need in the lives of our older adult population, and started discussing with them how this need might be met through the application of robotic technology. Finally, we showed that older adults are willing and able to participate in design projects for SARs (admittedly their participation is partially motivated by the desire to get social interaction), and identified the need for developing methods for actively engaging older adults in SARs design. Our future work will focus on further understanding how older adults might interact with SARs in their homes, and on increasing the level of hands-on participation of our participants and their self-identification not only as consumers, but as creators of assistive robotic technologies.

References

1. Tapus, A., Matarić, M.J., Scassellati, B.: The grand challenges in socially assistive robotics. IEEE RAM **14**, 35–42 (2007)
2. Broekens, J., Heerink, M., Rosendal, H.: Assistive social robots in elderly care: a review. Gerontechnology **8**(2), 94–103 (2009)
3. González, H.M., Tarraf, W., Whitfield, K.E., Vega, W.A.: The epidemiology of major depression and ethnicity in the United States. J. Psychiatr. Res. **44**(15), 1043–1051 (2010)
4. Ciechanowski, P., Wagner, E., Schmaling, K., Schwartz, S., Williams, B., Diehr, P., Kulzer, J., Gray, S., Collier, C., LoGerfo, J.: Community-integrated home-based depression treatment in older adults. JAMA **291**(13), 1569–1577 (2004)
5. Adams, K.B., Sanders, S., Auth, E.A.: Loneliness and depression in independent living retirement communities: risk and resilience factors. Aging Ment. Health **8**(6), 475–485 (2004)
6. Robinson, H., MacDonald, B., Kerse, N., Broadbent, E.: The psychosocial effects of a companion robot: a randomized controlled trial. J. Am. Med. Directors Assoc. **14**, 661–667 (2004)
7. Kang, K.I., Freedman, S., Matarić, M., Cunningham, M.J., Lopez, B.: A hands-off physical therapy assistance robot for cardiac patients. In: Proceedings of ICORR 2004, pp. 337–340 (2005)
8. Graf, B., Reiser, U., Hagele, M., Mauz, K., Klein, P.: Robotic home assistant Care-O-bot 3-Product vision and innovation platform. In: Proceedings of ARSO 2005, pp. 139–144 (2005)
9. Šabanović, S., Bennett, C.C., Chang, W.L., Huber, L.: PARO robot affects diverse interaction modalities in group sensory therapy for older adults with dementia. In: Proceedings of ICORR 2013, pp. 1–6 (2013)
10. Shibata, T., Wada, K.: Robot therapy: A new approach for mental healthcare of the elderly - a mini-review. Gerontology **57**(4), 378–386 (2011)
11. Ogawa, K., Nishio, S., Koda, K., Balistreri, G., Watanabe, T., Ishiguro, H.: Exploring the natural reaction of young and aged person with Telenoid in a real world. J Advanced Computational Intelligence and Intelligent Informatics. **15**(5), 592–597 (2011)
12. Mutlu, B., Forlizzi, J.: Robots in organizations: the role of workflow, social, and environmental factors in human-robot interaction. In: Proceedings of HRI 2008, pp. 287–294 (2008)
13. Chang, W.-L., Šabanović, S., Huber, L.: Situated analysis of interactions between cognitively impaired older adults and the therapeutic robot PARO. In: Herrmann, G., Pearson, M.J., Lenz, A., Bremner, P., Spiers, A., Leonards, U. (eds.) ICSR 2013. LNCS, vol. 8239, pp. 371–380. Springer, Heidelberg (2013)
14. Chang, W., Šabanović, S.: Interaction expands function: social shaping of the therapeutic robot PARO in a nursing home. In: Proceedings of HRI 2015 (2015, in press)

15. Forlizzi, J.: How robotic products become social products: an ethnographic study of cleaning in the home. In: Proceedings of HRI 2007, pp. 129–136 (2007)
16. Wilson, I.B., Cleary, P.D.: Linking clinical variables with health-related quality of life: a conceptual model of patient outcomes. JAMA **273**(1), 59–65 (1995)
17. World Health Organization: Constitution of the World Health Organization Basic Documents, Forty-fifth edition, Supplement (2006). http://www.who.int/governance/eb/who_constitution_en.pdf. Accessed 26 June 2014
18. Bennett, C.C., Doub, T.W.: Expert systems in mental healthcare: AI applications in decision making and consultation, In: Luxton, D. (ed.) Artificial Intelligence in Mental Healthcare. Elsevier Press (2015, In Press)
19. Fratiglioni, L., Qiu, C.: Prevention of cognitive decline in ageing: dementia as the target, delayed onset as the goal. Lancet Neurol. **10**(9), 778–779 (2011)
20. Kane, R.L., Kane, R.A.: What older people want from long-term care, and how they can get it. Health Aff. **20**(6), 114–127 (2001)
21. Lee, Y.: The predictive value of self assessed general, physical, and mental health on functional decline and mortality in older adults. J. Epidemiol. Community Health **54**(2), 123–129 (2000)
22. van Oostrom, S.H., Picavet, H.S.J., van Gelder, B.M.: Multimorbidity and comorbidity in the Dutch population–data from general practices. BMC Public Health **12**(1), 715 (2012)
23. DiSalvo, C., Nourbakhsh, I., Holstius, D., Akin, A., Louw, M.: The Neighborhood Networks project: A case study of critical engagement and creative expression through participatory design. In: Proceedings of Conference on Participatory Design, pp. 41–50 (2008)
24. Frennert, S., Eftring, H., Östlund, B.: What older people expect of robots: a mixed methods approach. In: Herrmann, G., Pearson, M.J., Lenz, A., Bremner, P., Spiers, A., Leonards, U. (eds.) ICSR 2013. LNCS, vol. 8239, pp. 19–29. Springer, Heidelberg (2013)
25. Ezer, N., Fisk, A.D., Rogers, W.A.: Attitudinal and intentional acceptance of domestic robots by younger and older adults. In: Stephanidis, C. (ed.) UAHCI 2009, Part II. LNCS, vol. 5615, pp. 39–48. Springer, Heidelberg (2009)
26. Flandorfer, P.: Population ageing and socially assistive robots for elderly persons: the importance of sociodemographic factors for user acceptance. Int. J. Popul. Research, Article ID 829835, 13 pp. (2012). doi:10.1155/2012/829835

Universal Design as an Approach to Technology Intervention for Seniors

Jon A. Sanford[✉]

Center for Assistive Technology and Environmental Access, Georgia Institute of Technology, Atlanta, GA, USA
jon.sanford@coa.gatech.edu

Abstract. Typical design approaches for technology interventions for seniors tends to focus on specialized design to accommodate functional limitations associated with either disability or aging. This paper will propose universal design as an alternative approach that focuses on design for all users, regardless of age or ability. Moreover, while specialized design is based on prescriptive requirements that often dictate what to design, universal design is an approach to technology intervention that is guided by a set of performance principles and guidelines that provide a rationale for how to design technologies. As such, universal design as extends the usability of everyday design to seniors, without the need for special adaptations or devices.

Keywords: Universal design · Design for aging · Specialized design · Technology for seniors

1 Introduction

Much has been written about the design of assistive and other types of technology interventions as a rehabilitation strategy to facilitate health, activity and participation of individuals with a variety of impairments and disabilities. Similarly, much has been written about the design of technology interventions as a strategy to promote aging in place by seniors undergoing the normal aging process. However, little consideration has been given to universal design as an approach for technology intervention for seniors who are experiencing both disability and age-related declines in function. The reason is simple, universal design is typically viewed as incompatible with the fundamental goals of rehabilitation and design for aging technologies (Nichols et al. 2006). Whereas these approaches are specialized designs tailored to needs of individuals or groups of individuals with either impairments or age-related deficits, or both, universal design is not intended specifically for older adults or those with impaired function. Rather, it is design that is usable by all people to the greatest extent possible without the need for adaptation or specialized design (Mace et al. 1991). As Steinfeld (1994) pointed out, these differences are not simply semantic. Specialized design typically results in separate designs for people with functional limitations, while universal design provides one design solution that can accommodate people with disabilities and limitations as well as everyone else.

© Springer International Publishing Switzerland 2015
J. Zhou and G. Salvendy (Eds.): ITAP 2015, Part I, LNCS 9193, pp. 115–122, 2015.
DOI: 10.1007/978-3-319-20892-3_12

Although universal design may be conceptually appealing, this paper recognizes that it is a utopian design philosophy that is not technically achievable in the design of hardware, which has a fixed form, although more likely achievable with software, which has a more fluid form. Nonetheless, universal design imagines what a world should be, not necessarily what the world will be. As a result, the contribution of this paper is in providing technology designers with a new way of thinking about interventions for seniors.

2   Types of Interventions

Technology can be, at the same time, prosthetic and therapeutic, compensating for limitations in functional abilities and enabling health maintenance and management. As a prosthetic, technology interventions for seniors can facilitate basic activities associated with safe and independent living, participation in social roles and provision of personal assistance from caregivers as needed. Therapeutically, it can facilitate health promoting behaviors and provision of healthcare services.

2.1   Specialized Technology as a Prosthetic Intervention

To remove or overcome barriers to performance of routine tasks and activities by people with disabilities and age-related limitations specialized "accessibility" technologies have traditionally been added to (e.g., voice over and high contrast screens) or replaced (e.g., devices with large simplified, large font keypads or augmentative communication devices) everyday designs. Acting as facilitators that address barriers created by the design of everyday technologies, specialized designs serve as prosthetic supports that facilitate the performance of everyday activities by compensating for disability and other limitations in ability. With the assistance of specialized designs individuals with a variety of limitations are able to carry out basic activities associated with daily living safely and independently and receive personal assistance from caregivers that would otherwise not be possible.

Nonetheless, specialized technologies are solely intended to enhance the performance of individuals with functional limitations, not of the general population (Sanford 2012). They are, by nature, reactive approaches that are added on to everyday designs or are specialized designs only for those who need it. Thus, despite their role in enabling activity by people with functional limitations, they are often associated with the stigma of disability, and as such are not used by seniors who do not see themselves as being "disabled."

However, people are growing older and a larger number of individuals are living longer with disabilities. Not surprisingly, a considerable amount of research over the past three decades has shown that the traditional specialized design approach does not adequately compensate for the range of age-related comorbidities and secondary conditions, including limitations in strength, stamina, reach, dexterity and fine motor control, lifting legs and sit-to-stand, loss of contrast sensitivity and visual acuity, memory loss and diminished cognitive functioning, and hearing loss that are common among seniors. As a result, specialized design, which is intended to promote accessibility, neither ensures usability, but may do more to promote excess disability among older people than to ameliorate it (Sanford et al. 1999; Sanford and Megrew 1995). Similarly, specialized design, which is intended to promote independent functioning, may not be adequate for seniors who are often dependent in one or more basic activities of daily living; or for their spousal (i.e., also aging) caregivers, for whom accessible design is not intended. These suggest that a more universal approach based on the needs and capabilities of a wider range of individuals is warranted.

2.2 Health Technology as a Therapeutic Intervention

By 2015 an estimated 150 million Americans will have at least one chronic condition due to a variety of causes such as congestive heart failure, cardio pulmonary diseases, deterioration in musculoskeletal system and connective tissue, and injury (Wu and Green 2000). With the increase in chronic health conditions there has been a dramatic increase in the level of care requirements including the need to engage teams of multiple physicians, specialists and formal and informal caregivers. As a result, chronic diseases account for 75 % of all U.S. healthcare costs (Scheschareg 2005).

As the intensity and cost of chronic care has increased, the use of personal health technologies, particularly in the home environment has played an ever-expanding role in health management and prevention. With the dramatic increase in home care services provided by Medicare in the past two decades, the boundary between hospital and home has become blurred (Binstock and Cluff 2000). This growth has not only been fueled by a desire for reduced lengths of stay and controlling cost, but also by a variety of new home-based therapeutic products and technologies that support aging in place through more active care management and passive monitoring of safety and activity.

By placing a greater emphasis on prevention and wellness than on acute care, home-based technologies are changing the way health care is provided to seniros and the way in which the home environment is utilized and conceptualized. Such technologies enable family members and health care providers to manage and promote health by: (1) actively monitoring health status (e.g., vital signs, weight, and oxygen saturation) that requires engagement of individuals to manage own their care; (2) passively monitoring activity (e.g., bathing, toileting, eating, medication adherence, and physical movement), and potential safety hazards (e.g., turn off stove burners, maintain water temperature to prevent scalding, adjust lighting levels to prevent falls risks, detect smoke and lock doors to prevent wandering of individuals with dementia) through sensors, transmitters, and receivers embedded in the environment (e.g., woven into carpet); and (3) promoting interactive communication with social networks and clinicians via cell phones, videophones, internet, television, camcorders, and communications software to enhance both psychological and physical health.

Like specialized designs, medical devices and technologies can have a large impact on the home environment and on the individuals living there. Many healthcare devices and technologies were developed for institutional settings, which are very different in size and appearance than residential settings. Moreover, they these devices and technologies were designed to be used by trained healthcare professionals not lay consumers. As a result, technologies often exceed the skills and abilities of seniors. Of equal importance in residential environments is aesthetics. Devices that look institutional are neither compatible with residential settings, nor do they consider the personal needs and tastes of the residents. This not only creates stigma, but leads to disuse and abandonment.

3 Universal Design as a Technology Intervention Strategy

Conceptually, universal design does not view disability as a single point requiring specialized technology intervention, but a segment of the continuum of ability that benefits from usability and inclusivity to promote positive activity and participation outcomes, respectively (Sanford 2012). Rather than focus on limitations in ability, the appropriate focus of universal design is on the range of human performance characteristics that are shared by all and experienced across our lifespans. Thus, universal design not only facilitates performance for an individual at any point in time, but also at any point across an individual's lifespan.

Universal design of technology for seniors is radically different from specialized technology design both conceptually and in physical form. Conceptually, specialized design is an add-on component or special "senior" design to remove the barriers created by the misfit between everyday design and seniors with functional limitations. In contrast, universal design is an integral component of everyday design that addresses barriers from the very beginning of the design process. As such, universal design supports the broadest range of types and levels of all abilities for all individuals, regardless of age, stature or physical function. These qualities are captured by and articulated in the Principles of Universal Design (Connell and Sanford 1997).

4 The Principles of Universal Design

With support from the National Institute on Disability and Rehabilitation Research, ten leading proponents of universal design, including architects; industrial, landscape, and graphic designers; and engineers developed the 7 Principles of Universal Design (Table 1) to define the general performance goals and guidelines for universal design. Although the Principles have never been validated and are too generic to apply as design criteria, in less than a decade they had been translated into a number of different languages and reprinted on hundreds of websites around the globe. Despite their shortcomings, the Principles are useful for guiding and evaluating the usability and inclusivity of technology interventions for seniors.

4.1 Equitable Use

Design of technology should be equally usable by and marketable to everyone. It should avoid segregating and stigmatizing users, and it should provide the same means of use for everyone. When possible means of use should be identical (e.g., the same

Table 1. Principles of Universal Design (Connell 1997)

Principle 1. Equitable Use: The design is useful and marketable to people with diverse abilities.
1a. Provide the same means of use for all users: identical whenever possible, equivalent when not.
1b. Avoid segregating or stigmatizing any users.
1c. Provisions for privacy, security, and safety should be equally available to all users.
1d. Make the design appealing to all users.
Principle Two: Flexibility in Use: The design accommodates a wide range of individual preferences and abilities.
2a. Provide choice in methods of use.
2b. Accommodate right- or left-handed access and use.
2c. Facilitate the user's accuracy and precision.
2d. Provide adaptability to the user's pace.
Principle Three: Simple and Intuitive Use: Use of the design is easy to understand, regardless of the user's experience, knowledge, language skills, or current concentration level.
3a. Eliminate unnecessary complexity.
3b. Be consistent with user expectations and intuition.
3c. Accommodate a wide range of literacy and language skills.
3d. Arrange information consistent with its importance.
3e. Provide effective prompting and feedback during and after task completion.
Principle Four: Perceptible Information: The design communicates necessary information effectively to the user, regardless of ambient conditions or the user's sensory abilities.
4a. Use different modes (pictorial, verbal, tactile) for redundant presentation of essential information.
4b. Provide adequate contrast between essential information and its surroundings.
4c. Maximize "legibility" of essential information.
4d. Differentiate elements in ways that can be described (i.e., make it easy to give instructions or directions).
4e. Provide compatibility with a variety of techniques or devices used by people with sensory limitations.
Principle Five: Tolerance for Error: The design minimizes hazards and the adverse consequences of accidental or unintended actions.
5a. Arrange elements to minimize hazards and errors: most used elements, most accessible; hazardous elements eliminated, isolated, or shielded.
5b. Provide warnings of hazards and errors.
5c. Provide fail-safe features.
5d. Discourage unconscious action in tasks that require vigilance.
Principle Six: Low Physical Effort: The design can be used efficiently and comfortably and with a minimum of fatigue.
6a. Allow user to maintain a neutral body position.
6b. Use reasonable operating forces.
6c. Minimize repetitive actions.
6d. Minimize sustained physical effort.
Principle Seven: Size and Space for Approach and Use: Appropriate size and space is provided for approach, reach, manipulation, and use regardless of user's body size, posture, or mobility.
7a. Provide a clear line of sight to important elements for any seated or standing user.
7b. Make reach to all components comfortable for any seated or standing user.
7c. Accommodate variations in hand and grip size.
7d. Provide adequate space for the use of assistive devices or personal assistance.

hardware and software), when not possible, equivalent means should be available (e.g. the same hardware, with different or customizable interfaces). Universal design features should be integrative and inclusive. In this way, universal design is everyday design, appealing to everyone, not just people who need special design features.

4.2   Flexibility in Use

Technology design should accommodate a wide range of individual preferences and abilities. It should also be forgiving, providing choices in methods of use. At the scale of interface control, use of multimodal input/output (I/Os) (e.g., touch, voice, physical buttons) and navigation (e.g., touch buttons, scroll, and swipe gestures) methods enable an individual to choose according to need and ability. Similarly, interfaces should also be tolerant and forgiving of different abilities by adapting to a user's levels of precision, accuracy and pace, such as physical inputs that minimize exactitude (e.g., large touch buttons separated by sufficient space), visual information that requires little acuity (e.g., large text size, high color contrast) and audio information that has variable speed and volume. At the level of flexibility of interfaces, software enables the design of multiple or customizable interfaces with choices of I/Os to be used with the same hardware.

4.3   Simple and Intuitive Use

Regardless of the user's experience, knowledge, language skills, or level of concentration, interfaces should be easily understood. In addition, the information should be intuitive, obvious and spontaneous, even if an individual has never encountered that design before (e.g., yes/no responses, widely recognized icons for text size, audio speed, contrast, up and down arrows). To accomplish this, interfaces should eliminate unnecessary complexity (e.g., multiple screens or dropdown menus to control visual clutter), present information in a manner that is consistent throughout the application (e.g., the same input controls in the same place on each screen) and with its importance (e.g., on/off button on top) and provide prompting (e.g., visual and verbal queries) and feedback (e.g., auditory response or visual acknowledgement) to respond to inputs.

4.4   Perceptible Information

To effectively communicate information to users who have different abilities to see, hear and understand, interface design should use as many different modes (e.g., pictorial, text, verbal, tactile) as possible. Devices should integrate simultaneous visual and audio output as a default, rather than using separate outputs that require that the audio be turned on. In addition, touch screen buttons should provide redundant visual cues through color, icons, and text.

Regardless of the mode used, design should maximize "legibility" of the essential information by providing large/adjustable font sizes, adequate (e.g., visual, auditory, cognitive) contrast between the essential information and the background, differentiating elements in ways that can be described (i.e., make it easy to give instructions or directions, such as "push the red button first") and enabling users to use any assistive devices, such as low vision or hearing aids, that they might require to obtain information. Finally, tactile information should be integrated into the hardware to help locate inputs on non-tactile digital interfaces.

4.5 Tolerance for Error

Errors can result in both a risk to personal safety (e.g., communicating wrong medical information or not pushing the right button in an emergency) as well as inadvertent mistakes that can lead to loss of time and frustration (e.g., hitting the delete button). As a result, technology design should minimize hazards and unintended actions that could have adverse outcomes. To do so, unconscious actions in tasks that require undivided attention (e.g., communicating medical information) should be discouraged by using of fail-safe features, such as locating contradictory input buttons (e.g., yes/no, accept/delete) far apart; providing warnings and verification queries to confirm a selection or identify mistakes; and arranging elements so that those that are most important are most accessible and those that are least important are omitted or protected (e.g., menus and help buttons) at the top and forward/back buttons at the bottom. Finally, page sub-review and final review options should be provided to ensure that all inputs are as intended.

4.6 Low Physical Effort

Ease of use is perhaps the one quality that is most commonly associated with usability. However, Principle 6 goes beyond simple ease/difficulty to include performing tasks efficiently, comfortably and with minimal fatigue. To accomplish these outcomes, the design should locate the primary input buttons and use gestures that will enable the user to maintain a neutral body position; minimize strength and stamina by enabling use of low (or no) operating forces, such as using digital touch vs. physical buttons; minimizing the need to apply sustained force (e.g., voice input); and minimizing repetitive and simultaneous actions without resting, such using a single tap vs. a double tap.

4.7 Size and Space for Approach and Use

Size and space for interface design includes the visibility (both visual and tactile), location and size of targets on the screen to permit use by individuals with a range of visual and dexterity abilities. For example, placing large buttons in the corners or the edges of the screen enhance visibility for blind or visually-impaired users. In addition, large targets can enable components to be reached comfortably by users with limited reach or dexterity.

5 Discussion

Adopting universal design as a viable technology intervention strategy for seniors requires discarding current, yet outdated 20th Century paradigms that favor specialized interventions for identified groups over those that promote functionality for everyone. Despite the technical success of traditional specialized technology intervention strategies in increasing function for individuals, they have, on the one hand, promulgated the proposition that being able to perform an activity would enable seniors to successfully age in the community, while creating stigmatizing and segregating devices, on the other. In contrast, universal design is rooted in a more integrative paradigm that makes function and functionality (i.e., usability and inclusivity) the design norm rather than the exception. By integrating specialized design into everyday technology, universal design is not just hard to see, it is invisible.

This idea of intervention invisibility is clearly not an outcome with which rehabilitation and design for aging practices are familiar. It clearly requires a paradigm shift from one that is emboldened by a set of *prescriptive rules* of *what to do* to a set of *performance guidelines* (i.e., Principles of Universal Design) that define *why it should be done*.

References

Binstock, R.H., Cluff, L.E.: Home Care Advances: Essential Research and Policy Issues. Springer, New York (2000)

Connell, B.R., Sanford, J.A.: Research implications of universal design. In: Steinfeld, E., Danford, S. (eds.) Measuring Enabling Environments, pp. 35–57. Springer, New York (1999)

Mace, R., Hardie, G., Place, J.: Accessible environments: toward universal design. In: Steinfeld, E., Danford, S. (eds.) Innovation by Design, pp. 155–175. Van Nostrand Reinhold Publishers, New York (1991)

Nichols, T.A., Rogers, W.A., Fisk, A.D.: Design for aging. In: Salvendy, G. (ed.) Handbook of Human Factors and Ergonomics, 3rd edn, pp. 1418–1445. Wiley, Hooboken (2006)

Sanford, J.A.: Design for the Ages: Universal Design as a Rehabilitation Strategy. Springer, New York (2012)

Sanford, J.A., Echt, K., Malassigné, P.: An E for ADAAG: the case for accessibility guidelines for the elderly based on three studies of toilet transfer. J. Phys.Occup. Ther. Geriatr. **16**(3/4), 39–58 (1999)

Sanford, J.A., Megrew, M.B.: Using environmental simulation to measure accessibility for older people. In: Steinfeld, E., Danford, S. (eds.) Measuring Enabling Environments, pp. 183–206. Plenum Press, New York (1999)

Steinfeld, E.: The concept of universal design. Paper presented at the Sixth IberoAmerican Conference on Accessibility, Centre for Independent Living, Rio De Janiero (1994)

Scheschareg, R.: Gaining Access To The$300 Billion + Consumer Out-of-Pocket Spending Market, Advanced Home Healthcare Products and Services 2005. Intuitive care advisors (2005)

Wu, S., Green A.: Projection of Chronic Illness Prevalence and Cost Inflation. RAND Corporation, Santa Monica, October 2000

A Living Lab Method for Innovations to Increase Quality of Life for Elderly - A Pilot Case

Isabella Scandurra[1(✉)], Madeleine Blusi[2], and Rolf Dalin[2]

[1] School of Business, Department of Informatics, Örebro University, Örebro,
Sweden
Isabella.Scandurra@oru.se
[2] R&D Department, The Association of Local Authorities in Västernorrland
County, Härnösand, Sweden
{madeleine.blusi,rolf.dalin}@kfvn.se

Abstract. A Swedish Living Lab has recently been established offering care organizations a test and evaluation method as an activity in their intrinsic development process. Using the method, innovations for an aging population are assessed, guided by quality criteria as well-being, dignity, value for the elderly and usability.

This paper describes the method through a pilot test, carried out in November 2014 by the elderly themselves and health and social care staff at a nursing home together with different academic parts in a multidisciplinary test process. The method allows for interaction between innovators and stakeholders as well as potential end-users in the elderly care sector. Simultaneously, the users' quality aspects are kept in focus when innovations for the aging society are tested.

Keywords: Aging society · Elderly care · Innovation · Living lab · Usability · User participation · Health/welfare development · Test · Evaluation · User-centricity

1 Introduction

Many countries with ageing populations need to work on how to incorporate innovations of different forms into the ongoing process of change in social service, support and care of the elderly. Future care provision for the elderly is facing multiple challenges. There is an ongoing change in demographic structure, where proportions as well as numbers of older people with care needs are rapidly increasing, bringing an increased demand for long-term care services [1, 2]. Current supply is considered as insufficient and inadequate in terms of meeting future needs for long-term care [1]. Yet another challenge is difficulties recruiting new work force to health professions [3]. In Sweden the prognosis is a deficit of 100 000 healthcare professionals by 2030 [4]. Including technology in long term care of elderly is an opportunity not only to increase quality of care, but also to maintain care in the future [5]. Some established examples are Internet-based support services that can contribute to elderly people living in their own homes to live their lives with higher levels of independence and electronic devices

J. Zhou and G. Salvendy (Eds.): ITAP 2015, Part I, LNCS 9193, pp. 123–133, 2015.
DOI: 10.1007/978-3-319-20892-3_13

that increase social inclusion of elderly [6–8]. Another technology useful in care of the elderly, at home or in nursing homes, is sensor technology. Sensor technology retrieves essential information about the individual which can be used by e.g. nursing staff to supplement their own observations, thereby helping them to better understand and tend to the needs of the elderly person [9]. The pilot case that exemplifies the method in this paper tested an innovation based on sensor technology.

A Test Arena Initiative. In society there is an ongoing trend to bring in new methods, systems or tools to aid the renewal of life situations and work processes as well as to realize the usage and dissemination of those new ideas, methods and techniques. In Sweden, a national initiative to innovate elderly care is taken based on the firm belief that test and demonstration arenas can help companies and organizations to increase their competitiveness, efficiency and quality [10].

Test and demonstration arenas are promising as they create new knowledge that cannot be captured using simulations or small-scale experiments; new partnerships can be developed and complex tests that an individual actor could have difficulties to afford can be realized by cost-sharing and joint learning and developing. The assembly and management of a realistic test arena both related to e.g. technology and real-life observations is costly and therefore impossible for small innovative companies to carry out, especially when testing their first product. To enable relevant and qualitative testing, it is of outmost importance that test facilities are available and functions on a per usage cost [11]. Further, it is sometimes crucial to create an understanding and visibility of potential social benefits thanks to technical innovations in order to develop and spread certain products and services.

Test arenas can move from the very delimited to the extremely wide, from an area which actually has a different main objective, such as a neighborhood, to specifics and details like lab tests of research equipment. A mapping study performed by the Swedish Innovation Agency VINNOVA showed a great mix of research and innovation infrastructure with many different denominations, e.g. test bed, living lab, prototype workshops, pre-incubator and pilot plants to name a few [10].

Moreover, innovations or new ideas may arrive from different actors; e.g. from well-experienced care personnel, from research, as well as from technical innovators. An important matter is that the innovations need to be tested in real-life situations before implemented in elderly care practice, to date an activity hard to achieve.

Norrlandicus is an open innovation and test environment formed as a Living Lab, established in 2013 in Sweden. In Norrlandicus actors aiming to develop health and social care for elderly through innovation, are offered a test and evaluation method as an activity in their intrinsic development process. The method intends to suit tests of not only products, but also services and processes. The objective of the test method is to show whether the innovation adds increased value in a health and social care process for the elderly, and to measure to what extent the innovation is perceived useful by the end-users.

The purpose of this paper is to present the novel test method that is the basis for the test process used in the Living Lab Norrlandicus. The method is exemplified by a pilot case that tested an innovation for an aging population by guidance of quality criteria as well-being, dignity, value for the elderly and usability of the innovation.

The Norrlandicus Living Lab. As a Living Lab, Norrlandicus consists of a number of test persons in a number of test arenas. A test arena can for example be a nursing home, a sheltered housing or the private homes of older persons living in their own houses. For each innovation to test a specific living lab is created, where the purpose and goal criteria of the innovation are mapped to a suitable setting in the municipality elderly care, i.e. an ad hoc-setting. In the living labs, innovations are tested based on a triangular approach [12] where the elderly, their next of kin and health- and social care staff are not only involved, but are the real test persons and drivers of the test of the innovation. As an aid in the assessment, experts from academia and industry with many years of experience in evaluating usability, health and social care quality, innovation, business models, functionality and health economics are provided within Norrlandicus [13]. Norrlandicus is an ongoing research and development project, partly financed by The Swedish Agency of Innovation Systems, VINNOVA, and the County Administrative Board in Västernorrland. Norrlandicus is owned by a partnership constellation that works to create an environment where industry, academia and expertise in health and social care can meet to develop innovations for future care.

2 Method and Materials

Each innovation in Norrlandicus is assessed via quality measures from the users' perspectives and for validation purposes. Validation in this context means to examine to which extent the innovation contributes with intended effects to a health and social care process for elderly. The foundation of the novel test method is described along with an example providing more detailed information from a pilot case that tested an innovative tool for investigation of urine incontinence.

Norrlandicus Test Method. Innovations are tested in Living Labs. For each test an ad hoc environment is selected in an appropriate care facility within the elderly care sector, e.g. a nursing home or a home care district. The authors of the test method work on-site in a multidisciplinary team, with expertise from the domains of caring science, statistics, health informatics and human-computer interaction. The test method as such builds on the "National Values for Social Care of Elderly", here translated as "Dignity of Life" [14]. Addressing basic health and functional needs is important; a salutogenic approach to health, considering participation and independence, promoting good health and rehabilitation [15], has been a core value in developing the test method. Along with salutogenic values the test method strives to enlighten dignity and well-being as dimensions of Dignity of Life. There is a lack of evaluations following such quality measures in the care sector in general, and a method that measures dignity of life related to innovations in elderly care was until now completely absent. Therefore, this test method is unique as it is based on concepts from Dignity of Life and relates those to a (technical) innovation in elderly care. The evaluation is further guided by a third dimension, quality criteria of the international usability standard, highlighting the usage as a function of the innovation and its defined end-users [16], (Fig. 1).

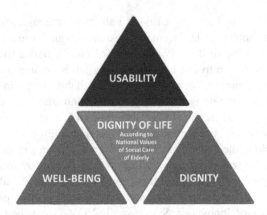

Fig. 1. Three dimensions of the test method with the core value Dignity of Life

Based on the concepts of values a few factors were derived, for which the research team developed a number of issues (sets of "items") with scales for the factors. On a policy level, the questions are general. On the level of details, tests are based on the purpose and potential usability of the specific innovation in its real context, according to the international usability standard [16].

The target audience is older people (65+) with age-related needs. Innovations will affect the elderly, either directly or indirectly. The Norrlandicus method investigates whether the introduction of an innovation in older people's immediate environment or nursing situation alters the experience of having a dignified life. The aim is to highlight the impact and how the innovation affects the elderly and their closest stakeholders, next of kin and care staff.

The measurements are carried out by the elderly themselves, health and social care staff and/or next of kin together with different academic parts in a multidisciplinary test process. Products and services can be evaluated from three perspectives; the "care customers" (elderly or seniors), their next of kin and health and social care professionals. For evaluation a mixed method is used, to capture quantitative as well as qualitative measures.

Depending on the character of the tested innovation and its purpose, in the pilot case two of the perspectives stated above were considered relevant, namely care customers and professionals.

Quantitative Method - Questionnaires Regarding Usability. The efficiency and effectiveness can be measured along with user satisfaction of the innovation to demonstrate potential benefit for current care organization, the elderly sector as a whole or for personal use [16]. Structured (statistical) data were collected from a number of the involved staff. The instrument used for this was the System Usability Scale [17, 18] that measures perceived ease of use. Originally created in 1986, it has become an industry standard, with references in over 1300 articles and publications. SUS measurement is intended to cover the products'

- effectiveness (how well a user can complete a task and achieve their goals),
- efficiency (how easy/difficult a user fulfills its goal using the product),
- satisfaction (the level of comfort the user experiences in achieving those goals).

In practical, the SUS measurement consists of 10 statements rated on a 5-point scale according to how much the user agrees or disagrees with the statement. The result can be between 0 and 100, higher scores indicates higher perceived ease of use.

Ten persons among the staff who worked with the elderly test persons during the test period filled out the SUS questionnaire.

Qualitative Method. A qualitative evaluation was made after the test period. Semi-structured group interviews were conducted with staff that during the test period had used and worked with the innovation [19]. Interviews were made with groups as it was more convenient for the staff and easier for them to fit into their busy schedule than individual interviews. A topic guide was used [19] covering the following three areas: (1) Information about the respondents (occupation, role in the test, how often you have used the innovation), (2) Experiences from using the innovation (usability of the innovation, benefits and problems from the perspectives of staff, the elderly and next of kin) and (3) Comparison with "practice as usual" (daily routines, effects on the working environment, advantages and disadvantages).

Data from interviews were analyzed using qualitative content analysis with a summative approach, where analysis goes beyond mere word counts and also include a latent content analysis [20].

Pilot Case - Setting and Current Practice. Living lab for the pilot case was a nursing home for elderly, located in rural areas of north Sweden. The nursing home had 40 residents, all with extensive long term care needs. Nursing services were provided 24/7, mostly by assistant nurses and care staff with lower education. In addition, there were three registered nurses with overall nursing- and medical responsibility. Nearly all residents used absorbent products for protection against urine leakage. This nursing home already had good routines for investigation of urine incontinence and subsequent follow-up work, but when the manager and registered nurse were offered to test an innovative tool they accepted immediately.

Nursing home routines for determining the most suitable protective product for each individual included a 72-hour measuring period. For each individual the 72 h measuring period demanded that the staff manually weighted each incontinence product after use. Weight and time of weighing were documented. After 72 h data was analyzed in order to figure out voiding patterns and volumes, which were then used as guidelines when determining which product to choose for each individual.

Pilot Case - The Innovation. The innovation tested as a pilot case in the Living Lab during November 2014 was a tool for incontinence investigation. The protection product electronically tracked voiding patterns as they occurred over time, in this case 72 h to compare with standard routines.

The product used sensor technology, where data was transmitted wirelessly to a computer. Data was then graphically converted into actionable reports, where nurses in charge of prescribing incontinence products were able to see the exact time and volume of the individuals' urination. The disposable protective product was shaped like a diaper and had a logger device attached to the front. Upon change of product the logger was disinfected, then attached to a new product (Fig. 2). The purpose of the innovation was to increase accuracy in incontinence investigations. The purpose of the product was to facilitate the process of the 72 h test and optimize the outcome of products to match the needs of each individual.

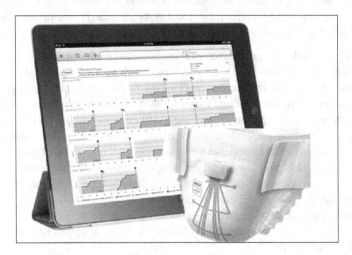

Fig. 2. Illustration showing the idea of the innovation tested: a disposable protective product with sensors and logger along with an example of graphic report of data. Picture courtesy of © Copyright 2015 Svenska Cellulosa Aktiebolaget SCA.

3   Results

Quantitative Results - Questionnaires Regarding Usability. Ten of the staff at the nursing home, one registered nurse and nine assistant nurses, who participated in the practical use of the innovation, completed the usability questionnaire. Three were between 41–50 years and the rest over 50 years, 9/10 had more than 20 years of professional experience. They were positive or very positive to innovations in care and very supportive of this innovation. Besides these answers, the SUS questionnaire revealed their opinions of the usability of the innovation.

The SUS usability score scale ranges from 0 to 100 and the measurement results for the ten nurses who answered these questions about perceived ease of use of the innovation were 87.5, 100, 100, 100, 100, 65, 60, 72.5, 97.5 and 87.5 in assessing usefulness of the innovation (Fig. 3). The result of the ten evaluators was well above the average value calculated on long term use of the scale in situations where the perceived ease of use has been assessed. That mean is 68. The median of this evaluation was 92.5.

Qualitative Findings. Interviews were conducted with seven persons, representing the different professions involved with the test. Assistant nurses were mostly involved in changing the disposable protective product and changing the logger device. The main

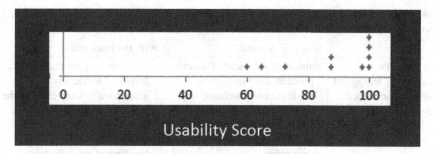

Usability Score

Fig. 3. Result of the usability scores of the 10 evaluators

role of registered nurses was to analyze the graphic information. Determining which protection product that was the most suitable for each person was a team effort including all professions. In the process of analyses of the measurements a representative from the company supported the nursing staff and guided them through the graphical data. Several of the residents participating in this test had dementia and were not able to give verbal input. Therefore, in this pilot case, the staff acted as proxy for the elderly in giving information.

Experiences from Using the Innovation. The Innovation was Considered Reliable and Useful. Handling it was neither technically advanced nor stressful. Removing the disposable product from the individual was easy, however fastening the product on the individual was somewhat challenging. To ensure correct fastening it was preferable to be two persons working together. Changing the logger was not difficult. Graphic reports were detailed in measuring time and volume for urinating. The staff discovered that in order to optimize use of data, it was necessary to add specific information about each individual, such as cognitive status, mobility, medication etc. Data reports were easy to understand and gave detailed information. The staff appreciated the possibility to follow leakage activity in real time. By being able to put leakage into a context gave even further assistance in choosing the right protection for the individual, and even more valuable in optimizing toilet routines. According to the staff, the residents did not experience wearing the sensor product as different from wearing their ordinary product. Staff felt the innovation contributed to improved quality of life for the residents, as it improved the knowledge about their situation, which was helpful in providing for the needs of the residents. Next of kin did not participate in this test.

Regarding the perceived usability of the web-based tool, the staff created a detailed list of potential improvements of the interface and the interaction. The list was fed back to the responsible of the innovation at the company. Staff from the company also participated during the evaluation of the test, gathering direct information from the test participants.

Comparison with "Practice as Usual". According to the Staff, the Major Difference Was that They Went from Guessing to Using Facts. Through exact knowledge about individuals' leakage they were able to optimize product selection as well as toilet routines. Some differences between working with 'practice as usual' and using the innovation are displayed in Table 1.

Table 1. Examples of main differences between practice as usual and using the innovation, as experienced by nursing staff in the living lab.

	"Practice as usual"	With the innovation
Procedure for measuring leakage of urine incontinence during 72 h	Manually by the staff. Protective products are carried to a washroom and weighed on a scale. Weight is documented on paper. Staff exposed to and handling urine. Time consuming	Continuous and automatic. Data regarding leakage is automatically transferred to the system, which graphically shows when and how much leakage has occurred. No handling of urine in the procedure
Precision in data and measurements	Absence of precision. Shows total amount of urine since last measure	High precision. Shows exact time and amount of leakage
Documentation	Extensive, time consuming	Simple, mostly automatic
Analysis of data	Gathering and structuring of data is handled manually for each person. Overview of measurement is lacking	Gathering and structuring of data is handled automatically for each person. Easy to compare registered information of a person to new information as graphically displayed
Knowledge about the needs of the resident	Data forms the basis for assumptions about needs	A decision support tool. Precise data gives knowledge about the needs of residents. Facilitates the transparency of taken decisions

The analysis of gathered data led to the following changes for the five test participants: change of the routines occurred in four occasions and change of product occurred in three occasions, all of them to a thinner product.

4   Discussion

Norrlandicus' test environment and method are based on the conceptual idea that staff and the elderly in each living lab are the ones providing measures regarding an innovation's success in enhancing quality of life for the elderly. Each innovation (product, service or process) needs to be assessed using quality measures from the users' point of view. In the pilot case described above the authors wanted to test the method and see if it was possible for the elderly and their care staff to conduct the tests in their natural environment, the Living Lab. We found that the participants were able to provide relevant measures of the innovation. Initially we had anticipated a higher level of information input from the elderly themselves. We may need to re-think how to capture the experiences from the elderly. Using staff or next of kin as proxy may be one way to go, although another study by one of the authors [7] points out the need to allow end-users to participate in the evaluation of the innovation based on their own capacity. This dilemma will be further research and future work within the Norrlandicus Living Lab. This also brings some ethical considerations. Conducting research in settings involving vulnerable subjects is an ethically complex issue. In nursing homes and other forms of elderly care, where the Living Labs are situated, there are several individuals with dementia in the test population. As an actor in close cooperation with nursing- and social sciences, Norrlandicus follows common ethical guidelines [21]. Participation in tests was voluntary. Prior to inclusion in the tests, all participants gave written consent. For participants with dementia, next of kin gave written consent. Another ethical issue to consider was the heavy work load at nursing homes. For Norrlandicus it was essential to minimize disturbance for the staff as well as the residents. Organizing the test, with meetings and research activities in adjustment with staff and resident schedules, shift work and a rather high staff turnover was a time consuming challenge.

Further, healthcare to date has been focused on service for illnesses rather than addressing citizens' holistic health needs, including e.g. social services, prevention and support for informal care givers [22]. In recent publication, researchers call for the inclusion of social care informatics as an essential part of holistic healthcare, stressing the importance of this emerging field of research [23]. In order to strengthen the role of patients and next of kin, this method focuses on patient-centric provision of care, following the ongoing shift from organization to citizen-centered care [24]. The usability of the intended innovation is another quality measure, a key to failure or success of a product [25].

The expected result from an academic point of view was that Norrlandicus test method as such was validated. The aim is to measure the contribution of the innovation in terms of "Dignity of Life" for the elderly as well as the degree of usability of the innovation. The "Dignity of Life" criteria need to be measured a while after the changes of routines and products have been made and is hence part of the work that lies ahead of us.

Although there is a national initiative supporting deployment of test arenas, it is still not common that test arenas use qualitative values to evaluate the benefit of the tested innovations as is the case of our test method. This method has already attracted interest; however it is yet to experience whether other test arenas will seize the opportunity and start using the Norrlandicus test method.

Expected results from the innovators and the aging society may vary depending on type of innovation. As this method focuses on the quality of life of the elderly and allows for interaction between industry, health and social care and academia there is some ground to claim that the Norrlandicus Living Lab can support in providing real health and social care improvements via technical innovations.

5 Conclusion

Norrlandicus is an open innovation and test arena aiming to meet tomorrow's needs and contribute to increased quality in healthcare and care for the elderly. In the Living Lab private and public stakeholders are invited to evaluate innovations (products, services and processes) using the Norrlandicus method to determine if they add increased value in a health and social care process for the elderly and to measure to what extent the innovation is perceived useful by the end-users. The success factor lies in the joint testing work between the elderly, the nursing staff and the research team with different specialties. In short, the test method examines the introduction of an innovation in the local environment of the elderly and whether this intervention alters their experience of having/getting a dignified life, while at the same time the method also assesses the usability of the innovation. Future work is to continue refining the test method by conducting pilots and field studies to gather knowledge and experiences from different stakeholders in the aging society.

Acknowledgements. We would like to thank all participants at the nursing home Vikto-riagården in Kramfors, Sweden, for their work and engagement. We would also like to thank the representatives of SCA Hygiene Products AB for good teamwork and for providing the inno-vation TENA *Identifi*™ for pilot testing as well as Pär Näslund and Katarina Palmgren for their field work. Finally we thank the Swedish agency for innovation systems, VINNOVA and the County Administrative Board in Västernorrland for financing the research and development project Norrlandicus.

References

1. European Commission: The 2009 Ageing Report: Economic and budgetary projections for the EU-27 Member States 2008-2060. European Commission - DG for Economic and Social Affairs, Economic Policy Committee, Brussels (2009)
2. Hoffmann, F., Rodrigues, R.: 'Informal Carers – Who takes care of them?' Policy Brief, April 2010. European Centre for Social Welfare Policy and Research, Vienna (2010)
3. Keating, N.: Rural Ageing: A Good Place to Grow Old? The Policy Press, Bristol (2008)
4. Håfström, D., Fransson, E.: eHealth in Swedish Municipalities 2013-2015- For Better Services, Independence and Autonomy. SKL, Stockholm (2013). (In Swedish)
5. Blusi, M.: E-health and information- and communication technology (ICT) as support systems for older family caregivers in rural areas. Mid Sweden University doctoral thesis: 203, Sundsvall (2014)
6. Blusi, M., Asplund, K., Jong, M.: Older family carers in rural areas: experiences from using caregiver support services based on Information and Communication Technology (ICT). Eur. J. Ageing **10**(3), 191–199 (2013). doi:10.1007/s10433-013-0260-1
7. Sjölinder, M., Scandurra, I.: Effects of using care professionals in the development of social technology for elderly. In: Proceedings of Human Computer Interaction International 2015, HCII 2015, 2–7 August 2015, Los Angeles, USA (2015)
8. Blusi, M., Kristiansen, L., Jong, M.: Exploring the influence of Internet-based caregiver support on experiences of isolation for older spouse caregivers in rural areas: a qualitative interview study. Int. J. Older People Nurs. (2014). doi:10.1111/opn.12074
9. Sävenstedt, S., Florin, J.: Information- and communication technology. In: Edberg, A.K., Ehrenberg, A., Friberg, F., Wallin, L., Wijk, H., Öhlén, J. (eds.) Nursing at Advanced Level – Core Competences Within Specialist Nursing. pp. 217–258, Lund (2013). (In Swedish)
10. Walldén, M.: Test beds – to test for the future. In: Cory, A., Wandrell, K. (eds.) Vinnova-nytt 1: 2013 (2013). ISSN 1653-2759 (In Swedish)

11. eHealth Projects: Research and Innovation in the field of ICT for Health and Wellbeing: an overview, September 2014. https://ec.europa.eu/digital-agenda/en/news/ehealth-projects-research-and-innovation-field-ict-health-and-wellbeing-overview. Accessed 14 Feb 2015
12. Flick, U.: Triangulation. In: Flick, U., von Kardorff, E., Steinke, I. (eds.) Qualitative Research – Paradigms, Theories, Methods, Practice and Contexts. Sage, London (2004)
13. Norrlandicus. http://www.norrlandicus.se
14. SOSFS Swedish National Board of Health and Welfare: National Advice on values in eldercare. In Swedish: Socialstyrelsens allmänna råd (SOSFS 2012:3) om värdegrunden i socialtjänstens omsorg om äldre (2012). http://www.socialstyrelsen.se/publikationer2012/2012-3-3 (In Swedish)
15. Antonowsky, A.: Unraveling the Mystery of Health: How People Manage Stress and Stay Well. Jossey-Bass Publishers, San Francisco (1987)
16. ISO 9241-11:1998: Ergonomic requirements for office work. Part 11: Guidance on usability. http://www.iso.org/iso/home/store/catalogue_tc/catalogue_detail.htm?csnumber=16883
17. Brooke, J.: SUS: a retrospective. J. Usability Stud. 8(2), 29–40 (2013). http://uxpajournal.org/wp-content/uploads/pdf/JUS_Brooke_February_2013.pdf
18. Sauro, J.: Measuring Usability with the System Usability Scale (SUS) (2011). http://www.measuringu.com/sus.php
19. Polit, D.F., Beck, C.T.: Nursing Research: Generating and Assessing Evidens for Nursing Practice, 9th edn. Lippincott Williams & Wilkins, Philadelphia (2011)
20. Hsieh, H.F., Shannon, S.E.: Three approaches to qualitative content analysis. Qual. Health Res. **15**, 1277–1288 (2005)
21. World Medical Association: World Medical Association Declaration of Helsinki Ethical Principles for Medical Research Involving Human Subjects. http://www.wma.net/en/30publications/10policies/b3/
22. Hägglund, M., Scandurra, I., Koch, S.: Supporting citizen-centred care for seniors – experiences from two Swedish research projects. In: Proceedings of 25th International Symposium on Computer-Based Medical Systems, CBMS (2012)
23. Rigby, M., Koch, S., Keeling, D., Hill, P., Alonso, A., Maeckelberghe, E.: Developing a new understanding of enabling health and wellbeing in Europe – harmonising health and social care delivery and informatics support to ensure holistic care. ESF SCSS Science Position Paper (2013). ISBN: 978-2-918428-92-3
24. Wagner, E.H., Bennett, S.M., Austin, B.T., Green, S.M., Schaefer, J.K., Vonkorff, M.: Finding common ground: patient-centeredness and evidence-based Chronic Illness Care. J Altern. Complement Med. **11 (Suppl.)**, S7–S25 (2005)
25. Kaplan, B., Shaw, N.: People, organizational, and social issues: evaluation as an exemplar. In: Haux, R. (ed.) Yearbook of Medical Informatics, pp. 71–88. Schattauer, Stuttgart (2002)

Talking Faces in Lab and Field Trials

A View on Evaluation Settings and User Involvement Results of Avatar Based User Interaction Techniques in Three Ambient Assisted Living Projects

Miroslav Sili[1(✉)], Jan Bobeth[2], Emanuel Sandner[1], Sten Hanke[1], Stephanie Schwarz[2], and Christopher Mayer[1]

[1] Health and Environment Department, Biomedical Systems, AIT Austrian Institute of Technology GmbH, Vienna, Austria
miroslav.sili@ait.ac.at
[2] Innovation Systems, Technology Experience, AIT Austrian Institute of Technology GmbH, Vienna, Austria

Abstract. In recent years, there has been an increasing interest in Ambient Assisted Living technology to support older adults. Research and industry are working jointly on reliable and suitable solutions to help older adults to remain healthy and safe while living independently. Appropriate interaction methods play an important role for the acceptance of such supporting systems. Today, solutions mainly rely on common and well-evaluated interaction techniques such as TV remotes or touch screens to enhance the usability. Projects presented in this work are based on the same interaction techniques, but additionally enrich the interaction experience with a real-time, empathic virtual assistance avatar. In this paper, we present evaluation settings and user involvement results acquired from three different Ambient Assisted Living projects focusing on avatar-based user interaction. Our results show that avatar-based interaction in the Ambient Assisted Living context is very well applicable, especially when combined with speech recognition.

Keywords: Avatar · User interaction · Ambient assisted living · Multimodality

1 Introduction

This work summarizes evaluation results of prototypes developed in the projects AALuis[1], ibi[2] and Miraculous-Life[3] with special focus on avatar aspects. We present lab and field trial outcomes from the accomplished projects AALuis and ibi as well as interim lab trial results from the still ongoing project Miraculous-Life. All three

---

[1] http://www.aaluis.eu.
[2] http://www.ibi.or.at.
[3] http://www.miraculous-life.eu.

© Springer International Publishing Switzerland 2015
J. Zhou and G. Salvendy (Eds.): ITAP 2015, Part I, LNCS 9193, pp. 134–144, 2015.
DOI: 10.1007/978-3-319-20892-3_14

projects use avatar-based output in order to support the end user during the interaction with the system. Prototypes developed within the ibi and Miraculous-Life projects also include speech recognition, thus allow a smooth user-system interaction.

The prototypical outcome of AALuis is an open middleware layer that can be used to connect various AAL services to a variety of devices with the help of automatically generated user interfaces [1–4].

The overall goal of the ibi prototype is to provide a tailored communication platform which is easy to understand and which can easily be used by three target groups, namely older adults, their relatives and professional caregivers.

The aim of the Miraculous-Life project is to design, develop and evaluate a Virtual Support Partner (VSP) assisting older adults throughout their daily activities and safety needs [5].

2 Methodology

To guarantee high usability and user acceptance we followed a user-centered approach in all three projects [6]. User involvement took place in the concept phase as well as in the two prototype evaluation phases. This section gives an overview about the evaluation settings, the involved user groups and the evaluation methods.

2.1 Phase One: Evaluation Settings During the Concept Phase

Before the first phase, user wishes, needs and requirements were collected with the help of cultural probing. Results were discussed in several workshops to identify the needed functional requirements for the planned prototypes. Afterwards, we involved different user groups into the design process by discussing scenarios and conducting usability studies (e.g., thinking aloud [7, 8]) with early mock-ups. Additionally, service developers and providers, user interface designers as well as experts from care organization helped to classify requirements and to identify usability problems in the early development stage. Table 1 shows a comparison of the evaluation settings from the projects.

2.2 Phase Two: Evaluation Settings for the Lab Trials

The second phase was conducted in a similar way as the first phase. Different user groups evaluated the first running prototypes which already covered most of the previously defined user requirements. A limitation on functionality and offered services during the lab trials allowed us to rather focus on general system characteristics like usability, performance, complexity and efficiency. Table 2 summarizes the evaluation settings during the lab trials.

2.3 Phase Three: Evaluation Settings for the Field Trials

In this phase, final versions of the prototypes were tested during a period of 2 to 6 weeks. Since Miraculous-Life is still an ongoing project, we evaluated only two of the

Table 1. Comparison of evaluation settings during the concept phase

	AALuis	ibi	Miraculous-Life
Period	Dec. 2012 – Jan. 2013	Nov. 2012 – Feb. 2013	Mar. 2014 – Sep. 2014
Participants	12	26	41
Sex F/M	7/5	16/10	25/16
Average age	74.5	70[a]	79.7; 50.2[b]; 32.5[c]
User groups	Older adults, younger & active seniors	Older adults, informal caregivers	Older adults, formal and informal caregivers, experts
Methods	Structured interview, task-based empirical investigation, System Usability Scale SUS[9]	Structured interview, task-based empirical investigation, questionnaire	Structured interview, questionnaire, expert walkthrough [10], heuristic analysis [11]
Devices	Smartphone, PC, tablet, TV	Smartphone, tablet, TV	PC, tablet, kinect

[a] Age calculated based on the average value of the estimated participants age
[b] Formal and informal care givers
[c] Experts

Table 2. Comparison of the evaluation settings for the lab trials

	AALuis	ibi	Miraculous-Life
Period	Apr. 2013	Feb. 2014	Sep. 2014
Participants	9	17[a]	18
Sex F/M	3/6	4/3[b]	13/5
Average age	71.2	72.1[b]	81.71; 45.6[b]
User groups	Older adults, younger & active seniors	Older adults, informal and formal caregivers	Active older adults, formal caregivers
Methods	Task-based empirical investigation, SUS	Task-based empirical investigation, post-interviews, questionnaires	Task-based empirical investigation, think aloud method, questionnaire (SUS)
Devices	Smartphone, PC, tablet, TV	Smartphone, tablet, TV	PC, tablet, Kinect

[a] Sex and age of users in the user group older adults have not been elaborated
[b] Formal and informal care givers

Table 3. Comparison of the evaluation settings for the field trials

	AALuis	ibi	Miraculous-Life
Period	Apr. 2014 – Aug. 2014	Jul. 2014 – Aug. 2014	Jan. 2016 – Jul. 2016
Participants	46	8	/
Sex F/M	33/13	4/4	/
Average age	82.8	68.9	/
User groups	Older adults, younger & active seniors	Older adults	/
Methods	living lab setting	Log files, media diary, interview	/
Devices	Smartphone, PC, tablet, TV	Smartphone, tablet, PC, TV	/

three projects in a natural setting. Table 3 presents the evaluation settings of the AALuis and ibi project during the field trials.

3 Evaluation Results

Although all three prototypes use avatar based interaction technology, the main goal of each project is different. However, the presented projects also share various numbers of comparable aspects. The following section focuses on theses comparable aspects but also on project specific findings.

3.1 Evaluation Results from the Concept Phase

Project Specific Findings

AALuis. The group of healthy and active seniors assessed early mock-ups of the AALuis communication service using a laptop and a smartphone. In general, participants reported that the usage of the service was easy for them. One person noticed that it would be interesting if appointments would synchronize automatically with the calendar on their smartphone or PC. There was also the fear to get too dependent on a mobile device in terms of being available all the time.

Older adults evaluated mock-ups of the AALuis reminder service using a tablet and a TV in an assisted living center where we set up a mobile usability lab. For both versions, we could hardly detect any clear usability issue. Nevertheless, some participants had problems interacting with the prototypes. One reason was that the participants were not familiar with the used remote control. The buttons were too small and it was perceived as too complex. Furthermore, participants were hesitant to touch the tablet and had problems to activate a button. They were too hastily or pressed too hard. Sometimes the system did not recognize these touches and the supervisor guided their fingers by hand. It was not possible to test the avatar in this early stage because the development of this module was still ongoing.

ibi. In this early phase, the ibi system was represented by two functional mock-ups implemented on the tablet and on the TV. Users liked the simple designed GUI containing three areas (avatar area on the top, textual representation of the spoken dialog in the middle and the interaction area with maximal three buttons on the bottom). Participants emphasized that it was very helpful to see the textual representation of the spoken dialog. These users preferred to read the presented contend instead of listening to the avatar. The interaction using the four colored buttons on the TV remote control was easy and intuitive enough for almost all participants.

The used speech recognition model, which was originally designed for seniors using the Styrian dialect, was also appropriate enough for the testing group of Viennese citizens. Participants perceived the vocal interaction with the system as something natural. Users emphasized that they liked the speech recognition because they would not need to put their glasses on to be able to read a message from their relatives.

Investigation on the avatar appearance showed that participants prefer a human like middle-aged female avatar which is dressed in everyday clothes and which interacts in a private surrounding like a living room.

Miraculous-Life. Older adults as well as formal and informal caregivers assessed the basic functionalities and avatar mock-ups early on in the project. Based on the evaluation results, a first prototype with reduced functionality was tested by experts on a tablet. Avatar mock-ups in conjunction with a questionnaire revealed that the avatar should act as a friendly personal assistant. Furthermore, most users preferred a human like avatar with a young woman's appearance. The avatar should indicate different interaction modes like waiting, listening and talking.

The expert group analyzed the avatar interaction and the available services. It was found that the dialogues used with the avatar should be more friendly and natural when addressing the older adults. The avatar was considered to have a clearly understandable speech output. Some issues were reported on behalf of wrong pronunciation and intonation of certain words and letters, especially when using the French language. Furthermore, strange system behavior was observed where the avatar was arbitrarily giving commands to himself. This happened because the speech recognition module recognized certain commands given by the avatar while presenting new information.

Apart from the avatar analysis, the experts noticed some inconsistencies in the service workflows, especially regarding the navigation. Additionally, experts found that sometimes the system response time after issuing a command was too long.

Summary of the Evaluation Results

Table 4 provides a comparison of the evaluation results during the concept phase using rating scales. Ratings were performed by project experts based on the empirical findings from the user involvements.

Implications for the First Prototype

AALuis. At the smartphone version targeting the healthy older adults, some interaction elements like radio buttons and tabs were too close together and the navigation area should be visible all the time. Some older adults struggled with using the tablet because they used a touch screen for the first time and did not dare to really touch the screen.

Table 4. Overview of evaluation results from the concept phase. Rating scale interpretation: Entries on the left side of the vertical line indicate usability or understanding problems, entries on the right side indicate better usability and understanding.

	AALuis	ibi	Miraculous-Life
GUI usability	--- | -x-	--- | -x-	--x | ---
Service understanding	--- | x--	--x | ---	--- | x--
Interaction on the smartphone	--- | x--	not tested	not applicable
Interaction on the tablet	--- | -x-	---x---	--- | -x-
Interaction on the TV	--- | x--	--- | -x-	not applicable
Speech recognition	not applicable	--- | -x-	--- | x--
Avatar appearance	not tested	x-- | ---	--- | --x

Therefore, a training period for this target group had to be considered. The standard remote control for the TV version confused some participants due to the high amount of unnecessary buttons, thus later on a simplified version was used.

Ibi. Intended services for the first prototype needed to be reconsidered based on the questionnaire results performed in this phase. Not all users were familiar with the touch based interaction so they required a training period. The presented avatar also had to be redesigned, because users preferred rather a female, middle-aged avatar.

Miraculous-Life. The avatars text pronunciation and intonation had to be improved so that the older adults do not have problems understanding the avatar. Moreover, the speech recognition had to be disabled during the avatar playback in order to prevent the avatar from activating actions through spoken commands. The service workflow needed also improvements to yield a consistent flow of information and navigation.

3.2   Evaluation Results from the Lab Trials

Project Specific Findings

AALuis. The group of healthy and active seniors evaluated the first functional prototype of the AALuis communication service using a PC and a smartphone. In the beginning, 4 of 5 participants felt more comfortable using the application on the PC, but 3 of 5 participants got used to operate the smartphone rather quickly. Nevertheless, when the participants were asked which device they would prefer to use, 4 of 5 favored the PC. Despite some usability problems, participants gave positive feedback to the well-structured and similar layout of the application on both devices.

The participants in need of care assessed the AALuis reminder service on TV and a tablet. In general, usability of the AALuis reminder service was restricted since all participants had general problems with the TV navigation and were not familiar using a touch-based device. Since participants had no experience with touch screens and mostly refused to use them, 3of 4 participants preferred using the TV compared to the tablet.

ibi. Although the speech recognition was not implemented into the first prototype, some of the users intuitively tried to respond vocally on questions asked by the avatar. After a short clarification and some hints about interaction possibilities, most of the users were able to confirm the presented dialogs by using the TV remote control. Two users felt a little bit uncomfortable and insecure, hence they refused the interaction with the remote control.

Care receivers had problems to confirm messages on the tablet. They were not used to tablets and were not familiar with the concept of touchable buttons. The device was also not sensible enough and users had to click buttons multiple times in order to trigger an action. Informal and formal caregivers had troubles with the smartphone, trying to activate the on-screen keyboard. Additionally, typing on the small screen was perceived to be a difficult task.

Miraculous-Life. The overall impression of the system was positive and the end users found the provided services useful. Two users suggested that the Miraculous-Life system could be an interesting solution for older adults who live alone at home. On the contrary, other end users suggested that the VSP is a "tricky solution", since it could potentially encourage social isolation.

While the avatars speed of speech was adjustable, a similar feature for adjusting the volume was missed by the end users. Furthermore, the end users missed the possibility to skip an avatar video. Many participants did not know when the system accepted the next command and wondered why the system would not react on their behalf. Additionally, the users found that the speech recognition was not always accurate, which lead to an unexpected system behavior.

Two older adults experienced difficulties hearing and understanding the avatar. Furthermore, the gestures of the avatar were perceived to be fluent and fit to the spoken words but the repertoire was too limited to simulate a natural interaction.

Regarding the user interface, older adults stated that the buttons and labels were too small to read. Additionally, the avatar was considered to be too small in the service view and too big in the main view.

Summary of the Evaluation Results

Table 5 presents an overview of the evaluation results from the lab trials using rating scales.

Implications for the Second Prototype

AALuis. Evaluation results from the second phase indicated that the mock-ups were easier to use by the participants than the prototypes. Thus, for the final prototypes the automatically generated user interfaces needed to be closer to the mock-ups taking the findings of both reported evaluations into account. While some aspects of the prototypes should be solved with better user interface templates (e.g., better highlighting of the focused UI element), other aspects required updates within the underlying

Table 5. Overview of evaluation results from the lab phase

	AALuis	ibi	Miraculous-Life
GUI usability	-x- | ---	--- | -x-	-x- | ---
Service understanding	--x | ---	--x | ---	--- | x--
Interaction on the smartphone	-x- | ---	-x- | ---	not applicable
Interaction on the tablet	--x | ---	x-- | ---	--- | x--
Interaction on the TV	x-- | ---	-x- | ---	not applicable
Interaction on the laptop	-x- | ---	not tested	not applicable
Speech recognition	not applicable	not tested	---x---

middleware layer (e.g., the differentiation between headline and normal text). The creation of a UI template for each device was considered to be a solution to reduce some of the device-specific usability issues.

ibi. The usage of a remote control beyond the TV context was for some users unnatural. They needed time to get familiar with this interaction type. Additionally, the remote control had to be simple and clearly designed in order to increase user acceptance. High quality and more sensible tablets were required. The application for the informal caregivers had to be redesigned. Predefined text blocks should help to eliminate the need for typing and to speed up the message generation process.

Miraculous-Life. Since the Miraculous-Life project is currently under development, the following improvements have to be implemented in the final prototype. The UI has to be redesigned by means of avatar size, element contrast and coloring to meet the user requirements and suggestions. The usage of external speakers to better understand the avatar rather than using the built-in ones needs to be assessed further. The current interaction mode of the avatar must be clearly visible and perceivable. Furthermore, a possibility to skip an avatar video is desired. The speech volume must be adjustable directly from the UI by spoken commands. Finally, the system latency has to be reduced significantly.

3.3   Evaluation Results from the Field Trials

Project Specific Findings

AALuis. We found that many participants of both user groups appreciated the idea and the services offered by AALuis. However, using the prototype was inferred from time to time by technical problems. Accordingly, the user experience results did not reflect the positive attitude towards AALuis. While the healthy and active older adults got first of all frustrated, the persons in need of care became more insecure and sometimes did not dare to use the service anymore. Nevertheless, many participants uttered their regrets that they could not use the services more often to benefit from their offers. Positive experiences of users which faced only a few technical problems suggest that a fully functional product offering these services might be interesting for the two involved user groups.

ibi. In general, all participants were satisfied with the functionality and the benefits of the offered services. In some cases the internet connection was not as stable as expected, therefore some messages were delivered with an evident delay.

Users appreciated the possibility to interact with the system using multiple devices. Hence, many users combined these devices, e.g., by starting the dialog on the tablet and continuing the interaction by using the avatar-based TV output and the speech recognition. The overall impression of the speech recognition was quite positive. Unfortunately, a few numbers of dialogs were automatically confirmed by the continuous activated speech recognition. Sources of noise, like the radio speech, triggered commands on the system without explicit intention from the users.

Informal and formal caregivers reported that it was sometimes difficult to use the smartphone because of the small screen size. Furthermore, the problem with the insensitive tablet devices remained. It was not possible to purchase new devices for the field trials so the lab trial devices had to be reused. Informal caregiver remarked that it would be practical to have an automatic synchronization between the ibi calendar and a private calendar, e.g., on the smartphone.

Summary of the Evaluation Results

Table 6 summarizes the evaluation results during the field phase using rating scales.

Implications for Further Improvements

AALuis. Developers have to make sure that the technical setup and the system performance can be guaranteed in terms of stability of the integrated system, functionality of all components, and suitability of the external conditions such as sufficient network

Table 6. Overview of evaluation results from the field trials

	AALuis	ibi	Miraculous-Life[a]
Overall usability	--- | -x-	--- | -x-	/
Service satisfaction	--- | -x-	--- | -x-	/
System reliability	--- | x--	--- | -x-	/
Interaction on the smartphone	--x | ---	--x | ---	/
Interaction on the tablet	--- | -x-	-x- | ---	/
Interaction on the TV	--- | x--	--- | -x-	/
Interaction on the laptop	--- | x--	---x---	/
Speech recognition	not applicable	--- | -x-	/

[a] The Miraculous-Life project has not been evaluated in the field so far.

coverage. Apart from these technical issues, the avatar was well appreciated, especially by the older adults. It would be good to offer more control possibilities to the users in terms of replaying, pausing or stopping the avatar. Other AALuis UI elements would benefit from a more visually appealing graphic design which also requires adjustments in the middleware layer.

ibi. The speech recognition must not be activated all the time but just by special activation commands, e.g., by the name of the used avatar. Formal caregivers, who mainly used the smartphone, need a smarter solution to announce a delay of the home-care visit. Neither the typing of a delay message, nor the selection of a predefined text-message are appropriate options for this task on small smartphone screens. As an improvement one can, e.g., use location based services and a scheduler to automatically pre select the user and the message for a delay announcement. Older adults require devices with an acceptable touch sensibility. Therefore, touchable devices have to be pretested before the deployment. For the informal caregivers, automatic calendar synchronization could be a practical feature.

4   Conclusion

In this paper, we present evaluation results of avatar-based supporting systems developed in three different Ambient Assisted Living projects. Prototypes developed in the projects AALuis and ibi generally use an avatar but the focus is rather on a versatile interaction with different modalities on different devices. In contrast, Miraculous-Life strongly focuses on the avatar as a virtual interaction partner and not on modality and device diversity. However, results from all three projects showed that avatar-based interaction in the Ambient Assisted Living context is very well applicable. This kind of interaction, especially when combined with speech recognition, offers big advantages for the target group.

Acknowledgments. The project AALuis was co-funded by the AAL Joint Programme (REF. AAL-2010-3-070) and the following National Authorities and R&D programs in Austria, Germany and The Netherlands: BMVIT, program benefit, FFG (AT), BMBF (DE) and ZonMw (NL).

The ibi project was co-funded by the benefit programme of the Federal Ministry for Transport, Innovation and Technology (BMVIT) of Austria.

The Miraculous-Life project is co-funded by the European Commission under the 7th Framework Programme (Grant Agreement No 611421).

References

1. Mayer, C., Morandell, M., Gira, M., Sili, M., Petzold, M., Fagel, S., Schüler, C., Bobeth, J., Schmehl, S.: User interfaces for older adults. In: Stephanidis, C., Antona, M. (eds.) UAHCI 2013, Part II. LNCS, vol. 8010, pp. 142–150. Springer, Heidelberg (2013)
2. Sili, M., Mayer, C., Morandell, M., Gira, M., Petzold, M.: A practical solution for the automatic generation of user interfaces – what are the benefits of a practical solution for the automatic generation of user interfaces? In: Kurosu, M. (ed.) HCI 2014, Part I. LNCS, vol. 8510, pp. 445–456. Springer, Heidelberg (2014)

3. Mayer, C., Zimmermann, G., Grguric, A., Alexandersson, J., Sili, M., Strobbe, C.: A comparative study of systems for the design of flexible user interfaces. J. Ambient Intell. Smart Environ. (2014, in press)
4. Mayer, C., Morandell, M., Gira, M., Hackbarth, K., Petzold, M., Fagel, S.: AALuis, a user interface layer that brings device independence to users of AAL systems. In: Miesenberger, K., Karshmer, A., Penaz, P., Zagler, W. (eds.) ICCHP 2012, Part I. LNCS, vol. 7382, pp. 650–657. Springer, Heidelberg (2012)
5. Hanke, S., Sandner, E., Sili, M., Hochgatterer, A., Ben Moussa, M., Christodoulou, E., Trindadem, P., Samara, G., Andreou, P., Wingskölgen, C., Van Der Aa, N., Stockloew, C.: Virtual support partner: a real-time, emphatic elder care system that attends to the daily activity and safety needs of the elder at home, during his normal daily life. In: Broader, Bigger, Better – AAL solutions for Europe - Proceedings of the AAL Forum 2014 Bucharest (in press)
6. Preece, J., Rogers, Y., Sharp, H.: Interaction Design: Beyond Human-Computer Interaction. Wiley, New York (2011)
7. Nielsen, J, Clemmensen, T, Yssing, C.: Getting access to what goes on in people's heads? - reflections on the think-aloud technique. In: NordiCHI 2002 (2002)
8. Lewis, C., Rieman, J.: Task-Centered User Interface Design: A Practical Introduction. University of Colorado, Boulder (1993)
9. Brooke, J.: SUS: a quick and dirty usability scale. In: Jordan, P.W., Weerdmeester, B., Thomas, A., Mclelland, I.L. (eds.) Usability Evaluation in Industry. Taylor & Francis, London (1996)
10. Wharton, C., Rieman, J., Lewis, C., Polson, P.: The cognitive walkthrough method: a practitioner's guide. In: Nielsen, J., Mack, R.L. (eds.) Usability Inspection Methods, pp. 105–140. Wiley, New York (1994)
11. Nielsen, J., Molich, R.: Heuristic evaluation of user interfaces. In: Proceedings of the SIGCHI Conference on Human Factors in Computing Systems: Empowering people. ACM (1990)

Gamification and Accessibility

Andreas Stiegler[✉] and Gottfried Zimmermann

Responsive User Interface Experience Research Group, Stuttgart Media
University, Stuttgart, Germany
mail@andreasstiegler.com, gzimmermann@acm.org

Abstract. There are many software requirements for the development of
accessible applications, in particular for elderly people or people with disabilities. In particular, user interfaces have to be sufficiently abstract to cover
required adaptations. In this paper, we introduce a gamification approach for
teaching, connecting and engaging developers on accessible design of applications. A particular challenge hereby is combining gamification patters with the
requirements of accessibility. As many gamification patters build on visual
representation or usage metaphors, they are not suited for adaptation. Instead,
we derive a representation-agnostic set of gamification patters from actual game
design of commercial games. We identify and illustrate five categories of
representation-agnostic gamification patterns, based on a games survey: action
space, reward, challenge, progress, and discovery.

Keywords: Human computer interaction · Gamification · Accessibility ·
Elderly · Game development · Serious games · Game design · Game
mechanics · Game theory

1 Introduction

A particular challenge for computing and aging is supplying applications that are
adaptable and configurable enough to support simplified or modified user interfaces or
usage metaphors. Adaptations can be quite simple, for example coloring or size, but
can also be very complex modifications on content, such as simpler text or altered
usage metaphors and timeouts [15].

There are various technical approaches to adapt an existing application, either
through the application directly or through interface abstraction layers as supplied by
the operation system or window manager. Yet, adaptations regarding usage metaphors
or deeper adaptions regarding the visual representation can usually not be covered by
those approaches, as they require an application to have a sufficient API to inject new
interface models.

The Prosperity4All project [11] therefore aims at software developers, supplying
them with resources, documentation and online help texts to integrate such approaches
into their software project. An important piece of the Prosperity4All approach is the
community server, which serves as a platform for developers interested in providing the
necessary adaptations for their application. The community server uses gamification to
increase acceptance. The challenge herein is to combine gamification techniques and

© Springer International Publishing Switzerland 2015
J. Zhou and G. Salvendy (Eds.): ITAP 2015, Part I, LNCS 9193, pp. 145–154, 2015.
DOI: 10.1007/978-3-319-20892-3_15

accessibility constraints. As most common approaches of gamification focus on visual representation, those are unsuited for an accessible platform. Our approach is derived from analyzing gameplay and game mechanics patterns of popular games, deriving representation-independent gamification models.

2 Gamification

Gamification has been described as using elements of game design in non-game contexts [1]. The core idea is to identify the mechanics that make people enjoy a certain process [2]. It has been shown that people enjoying a process are either more productive in executing said process, or more careful in maintaining external constraints [3]. As such, gamification is not a single, precisely defined method, but rather a methodology to transfer knowledge from the games industry and utilize it to optimize and enrich non-game processes [1].

Both physical and computer games offer patterns that are supposed to make player actions enjoyable [5]. Some patterns, such as clearly defined rules, are often shared between both categories of games. Some are unique to either environment. As our research is focused on creating a purely virtual platform for software developers and combining this virtual platform with accessibility for virtual devices, we will focus on computer games and the metaphors used for gamification in virtual worlds.

Since first research in the 1980s, such as [4], gamification became a powerful and popular tool for both academia and industry. Nowadays, gamification is often introduced as a method to add additional benefit to a business process without actually altering the business process itself [8]. Following this logic, it is important to note that gamification should always be optional [7]. As soon as a user is forced to participate in a gamification system, the gamification system becomes part of the actual process gamification is trying to improve. For most applications, however, the business process should remain as fast and efficient as possible, without taking gamification elements into account. Gamification aims at the user, not at the underlying process. Yet, deploying gamification to a business process can lead to the discovery of shortcomings and ineffective sections of the respective business process and should then lead to alterations and improvements.

Our research focuses on three aspects of gamification: gamification used for teaching, gamification in complex application interfaces and gamification used for self-organization and coordination. We will illustrate the problems of combining gamification used for teaching and accessibility in this paper.

2.1 Gamification for Teaching

Gamification can be used to improve the process of learning, resulting in faster or more reliable knowledge consumption [5, 6]. This is of particular interest to us, as many developers have to be familiarized with the problems and issues of accessible software design. The GPII [11], for example, requires a software developer to express their application settings in a certain way, or to integrate interfaces to GPII components for runtime adaption.

Particularly for learning, gamification and serious games blend [9], and there is no clearly defined, sharp line between them. Many learning systems or games build on reward messages (for example by using success messages, such as used by Anki [10]) or extrinsic motivation via measurable reward points (such as school grades). The process of learning is very individual and not tied to specific software or patterns. Reward in learning applications often comes in the form of high-scores, badges, unlockable achievements or other features like customizable avatars. Reward-based gamification approaches – or serious games – have to face various problems when combined with accessibility, as described in the following chapters.

3 Gamification and Accessibility

One of the core requirements of gamification is to be optional and not distracting from the gamified core task [7]. In graphical user interfaces, this is often achieved by placing the visual representation of reward in a sidebar where it is not visually distracting. Further visual techniques can be used, such as color-coding or visual styles to clearly mark the gamification part of the user interface. As argued in [13], this can work well for two-dimensional user interfaces. Yet, it is obviously tied to a specific form of representation. Even simple modifications, such as zooming, can cause the sidebars to consume a more significant portion of the screen space; altering the color settings, such as contrast, can render color coding ineffective; icons and symbol graphics can be meaningless to some audiences. For more complex modifications, such as using a screen reader, the drawbacks of gamification relying on visual representation become obvious. A screen render uses a one-dimensional representation of a document, such as a web page, to read it to the user. In contrast to a two-dimensional user interface, there is no simple way of arranging a user interface element in a way so that it is present, but not distracting. A gamification interface previously placed on a sidebar will end up at the beginning, the end, or somewhere else in the one-dimensional stream of representation. This will force a user to either skip those parts when reading a document, clearly violating the prerequisite of optional gamification.

One approach to overcome those limitations is to create explicit gamification alternatives for each possible interface modification. Taking the vast amount of possible interface modifications into account, such an approach becomes impractical. Yet, there are gamification approaches that work without relying on their visual representation. These representation-agnostic elements of gamification are typically of a more abstract nature and are harder to identify.

3.1 Identifying Representation-Agnostic Gamification Patterns

In order to derive gamification patterns that do not rely on their visual representation, we analyzed a collection of 21 commercial PC games for their game play and game design. The analysis was conducted through interviews of a variable number (2–6) of experienced players per game. The findings were further categorized into gameplay patterns. Game design and game mechanics considerations were taken into account where feedback from the game developers was present. An interesting finding was that similar or even identical patterns can occur in variable contexts for different effects. Instead of forming a fixed set of gamification patterns, we therefore assembled a pool of patterns that can be applied to different scenarios. The following chapter will highlight some of them with a respective game example.

4 Gamification Patterns

The representation-agnostic gamification patterns derived from the games survey can be grouped into five major categories: action space, reward, challenge, progress, and discovery. This chapter will illustrate each of them with an example from the survey.

Fig. 1. Tetris on the Nintendo Game Boy (1989)

4.1   Action Space: "Tetris"

Tetris is popular puzzle game dating back to 1984. As such, it formed the foundation of gameplay mechanisms for many generations of puzzle games to come. Both the gameplay and rules of the game are very simple but addictive. Due to the simplistic game design, the mechanisms that make Tetris fun to play are clearer to identify. One category in which Tetris shines is a fully observable and small action space (Fig. 1).

The action space of a problem is the number of options per decision a user can select from. There are multiple aspects to the action space that are relevant to making a game enjoyable. First off, the action space of Tetris is fully observable: The player is aware of all possible actions they can do at a given point of time: rotating blocks clockwise or counterclockwise, moving blocks left and right or accelerating their descent. More importantly: A player knows that they know the complete action space. This is a sharp contrast compared to many business tasks, where the action space is typically vast (filling out documents has a giant action space, but even the average document processing software offers dozens of options just to style the text). In our survey, users enjoyed selecting from a small collection of options. In many office applications, one can observe a trend of shifting programming problems into the action space of a user. A typical example are dialogues like "You are performing an action that you cannot undo, are you sure?". Instead of implementing a reliable undo function, the problem was moved to the user, unnecessarily expanding their action space.

The other interesting aspect of the action space of Tetris is that users not only know the complete action space, but they are also aware that they know the complete action space. There are no advanced or hidden commands in Tetris that allow any other interaction, besides going to the menu and ending the game. In many applications, on the other hand, user actions are grouped into actions a user often wants to do, and advanced settings only used for specialized tasks. Yet, this seems to reduce the joy in performing those actions, probably as users are uncertain if they actually picked the best possible action, or if there would have been a smoother way to solve a problem hidden in some advanced menu. Applications should therefore be designed in a way to require as few actions as possible, so that all can be presented to a user. This is unrealistic for complex software, like an image editing program, but interface structures could be arranged in a way, so that for a certain problem – like applying a blur-effect to an image region – all possible actions are presented.

A small and fully observable action space, with the knowledge of being fully observable, is a base principle in all the games mentioned in this paper.

4.2   Reward: "Diablo III"

Diablo III is a hack'n'slay game where a player ventures through a dark fantasy world and slays demons and other creatures and solves challenges. As with many examples of this genre, one of the most important gameplay concepts is acquiring new equipment to defeat stronger foes. Many games use specific reward models to distribute and handle rewards for players. Reward in games fulfills a few important characteristics different from real-life: being immediate, measurable and expectable (Fig. 2).

Fig. 2. Diablo III from Blizzard Entertainment (2012)

In games, reward is usually given right after the action that caused it, unlike real-life examples, where rewards – or penalties – are often distributed a long time after the action that triggered it. That makes it hard for users to associate the reward with the actual action and therefore decreases the probability to trigger a positive feedback cycle. Defeating a difficult enemy in Diablo III will immediately reward new equipment, similar to the lines in Tetris immediately disappearing once they are filled.

Similarly, reward in games is usually measurable and comparable. Reward is sometimes just awarded in non-measurable form, like a "Congratulations" message, but in most games, players gain score – as in Tetris – or measurable improvements to character attributes – as in Diablo III. This is important to compare different rewards between alternative actions. These metaphors are already used by gamification a lot, as high scores and reward points are a very commonly used gamification pattern.

Also, reward in games is often expectable. That means, that the rules that may yield a reward are clearly communicated to the players. This goes along with the fully observable and known action space discussed above.

4.3   Challenge: "Portal 2"

Portal 2 is a first-person puzzle game where the player has to solve a wide variety of physics puzzles, utilizing the conservation of momentum, gravity and fluid mechanics. The puzzles become more challenging throughout the game and are very challenging, if compared to other puzzle games (Fig. 3).

Fig. 3. Portal 2 from Valve Corporation (2011)

The design and dramaturgy of designing challenge is an essential part in game design. A common approach is game flow [14]. Game flow is a concept of keeping challenges offered by the game in check with the skill progression of the player. From a more abstract perspective, game flow is dealing with learning effects of the user. One example of applying flow to gamification for elderly was demonstrated by Korn [16].

Challenge in games and in gamification is very different. In games, challenge can be designed and planned, as the underlying game mechanics, story, and gameplay can be altered. A boss encountered deemed to be too difficult can be made easier by offering assistance to a user or reducing the capabilities of the other non-player characters. When dealing with challenge in gamification, the challenge is often implied by the business process being gamified. In that case, challenge cannot be designed freely. Yet, gamification approaches might introduce their own challenges, for example by adding mini-games, such as a puzzle where each solved work-task allows performing an action in the puzzle. In that case, the mini-game can be considered a full-fletched game, with all possibilities of game design, with the only difference that the action space of the mini-game is bound to a real-life business task.

If utilizing challenge in gamification, it goes along with action space and reward, as described above. A challenge in a game has to be solvable with a fully observable action space and should offer some kind of reward.

4.4   Development: "World of Warcraft"

The core principle behind Massively Multiplayer Online Role-Playing Games (MMORPGs), such as World of Warcraft, is the ongoing development of a character. This is very similar to many real-life scenarios, where most actions come with persistent, ongoing consequences (Fig. 4).

Fig. 4. World of Warcraft from Blizzard Entertainment (2004)

According to the survey, an important requirement for players to perceive a persistent development of a character as enjoyable is, that such a development is clearly measurable. This seems to be a consequence of measurable progress as described earlier. Persistent development shares most of its requirements and aspects with progress, but does not require reward to be enjoyable. In a sense, the persistent development itself can be sufficient reward for players to continue playing, as they see constant improvements. Many MMORPGs exploit that to an extreme extend, as those games typically don't offer any kind of ultimate goal in the game. You can never win an MMORPG. Instead, the developer supplies new options to improve your character, and it is only possible to achieve a perfect setup by investing a lot of time (or money).

Persistent development is related to progress and challenge and can serve as a form of intrinsic reward.

4.5   Discovery: "Elite: Dangerous"

Curiosity and – associated with it – discovery can be very powerful and driving reasons to perform an action. Many open world games offer very fast virtual environments, which allow players to explore. In Elite: Dangerous, a player can discover our whole Milky Way galaxy with countless solar systems and planets, some of them inhabited (Fig. 5).

Fig. 5. Elite: dangerous from frontier developments (2014)

In order to be enjoyable, the survey showed that virtual worlds to be discovered have to be consistent both in regards to the rules they imply (such as gravity or the laws of magic) but also – and more importantly – in regards to their story. This can either be an overall story of the game universe, or just small stories originating from character interaction. Tailoring a vast consistent game world is a challenge.

While discovery can be very motivating, the underlying requirements of discovery – a vast virtual world – are usually not fit for gamification. Some serious games utilize this technique, but for the average gamification task developing a while virtual world is not an efficient approach.

5 Conclusion

In this paper, we have discussed the five primary gamification aspects that the game survey revealed: reward, action space, progress, development, and discovery. All of them are rather abstract concepts of game design and don't rely on a certain visual representation. One could, for example, think of an action space represented in a 2D visual display, or explained through a screen reader. Such representation-agnostic metaphors are the fundamental building blocks when setting up a gamification framework supporting accessibility.

Future work will focus on deriving discrete representations for the patterns we discovered. They will be utilized in a community server platform for the GPII helping developers finding and coordinating accessibility efforts, and also for teaching developers on how to implement basic accessibility guidelines into their work or using gamification themselves. As such, we will focus on action space representations, reward and progress.

Congrats for reading this far! You gain 100 points!

Acknowledgments. The research leading to these results has received funding from the European Union Seventh Framework Programme (FP7/2007-2011) under grant agreement n° 610510, Prosperity4All ("Ecosystem infrastructure for smart and personalised inclusion and PROSPERITY for ALL stakeholders"). This publication reflects only the authors' views and the European Union is not liable for any use that may be made of the information contained herein.

References

1. Deterding, S., Dixon, D., Khaled, R., Nacke, L.: From game design elements to gamefulness: defining gamification. In: Proceedings of the 15th International Academic MindTrek Conference: Envisioning Future Media Environments, pp. 9–15. ACM, September 2011
2. Hamari, J., Koivisto, J., Sarsa, H.: Does gamification work?–a literature review of empirical studies on gamification. In: 2014 47th Hawaii International Conference on System Sciences (HICSS). IEEE, 2014
3. Mekler, E.D., et al.: Disassembling gamification: the effects of points and meaning on user motivation and performance. In: CHI 2013 Extended Abstracts on Human Factors in Computing Systems. ACM (2013)
4. Malone, T.W.: Heuristics for designing enjoyable user interfaces: Lessons from computer games. In: Proceedings of the 1982 Conference on Human Factors in Computing Systems, pp. 63–68. ACM, March 1982
5. Balkin, J.M., Noveck, B.S.: State of Play: Law, Games, and Virtual Worlds. Law, Games, and Virtual Worlds (Ex Machina: Law, Technology, and Society). NYU Press, New York (2006)
6. Kapp, K.M.: The Gamification of Learning and Instruction: Game-Based Methods and Strategies for Training And Education. Wiley, San Francisco (2012)
7. Glover, I.: Play as you learn: gamification as a technique for motivating learners. In: Proceedings of World Conference on Educational Multimedia, Hypermedia and Telecommunications 2013, pp. 1999–2008. AACE, Chesapeake, VA (2013)

8. Barata, G., et al.: Engaging engineering students with gamification. In: 2013 5th International Conference on Games and Virtual Worlds for Serious Applications (VS-GAMES). IEEE (2013)
9. Landers, R.N., Callan, R.C.: Casual social games as serious games: the psychology of gamification in undergraduate education and employee training. In: Ma, M., Oikonomou, M., Jain, L.C. (eds.) Serious Games and Edutainment Applications, pp. 399–423. Springer, London (2011)
10. Anki. http://ankisrs.net/
11. Global Public Inclusive Infrastructure. http://gpii.net/
12. Wouters, P., Van der Spek, E.D., Van Oostendorp, H.: Current practices in serious game research: a review from a learning outcomes perspective. In: Connolly, T.M., Stansfield, M., Boyle, L. (eds.) Games-based Learning Advancements for Multisensory Human Computer Interfaces: Techniques and Effective Practices, pp. 232–255. IGI Global, Hershey (2009)
13. Stiegler, A., Zimmermann, G.: Gamification in the development of accessible software. In: Stephanidis, C., Antona, M. (eds.) UAHCI 2014, Part I. LNCS, vol. 8513, pp. 171–180. Springer, Heidelberg (2014)
14. Jegers, K.: Pervasive game flow: understanding player enjoyment in pervasive gaming. Comput. Entertainment (CIE) 5(1), 9 (2007)
15. Zimmermann, G., Vanderheiden, G.C., Strobbe, C.: Towards deep adaptivity – a framework for the development of fully context-sensitive user interfaces. In: Stephanidis, C., Antona, M. (eds.) UAHCI 2014, Part I. LNCS, vol. 8513, pp. 299–310. Springer, Heidelberg (2014)
16. Korn, O.: Industrial playgrounds: how gamification helps to enrich work for elderly or impaired persons in production. In: Proceedings of the 4th ACM SIGCHI Symposium on Engineering Interactive Computing Systems. ACM (2012)

ICT Use and Acceptance

Evaluating All-Inclusive ICT with Developers, End Users and Stakeholders

Eleni Chalkia[1]([⊠]), Evangelos Bekiaris[1], and R. Ignacio Madrid[2]

[1] Hellenic Institute of Transport, Center for Research and Technology Hellas,
57100 Thessaloniki, Greece
{hchalkia, abek}@certh.gr
[2] Accessibility, Studies and R&D, ILUNION Consultoría, C/Albacete 3, 28027
Madrid, Spain
NMadrid@consultoria.ilunion.com

Abstract. ICT have been moving rapidly into people's lives nowadays. Even if living without access to ICT would be a barrier in the past, today access to ICT is required for most education, employment, and commerce, and is increasingly required for travel, health, safety, daily living and participation in most of our society. In this paper we present the evaluation of an all-inclusive ICT infrastructure from the perspective of different type of users that use it for different purposes based on their abilities, needs and preferences.

Keywords: Evaluation · All inclusive ICT · Accessibility · People with disabilities · Developers · Stakeholders

1 Introduction

Over 2 billion people worldwide have different types, degrees, or combinations of disability, literacy, digital literacy or aging related barriers that impede or prevent them from using ICT [1]. Society cannot afford to have this cumulatively large percentage of people offline, yet there is no way to reach them with the current model. Thus all-inclusive ICT that can be used from all different users is an urgent need.

To address this need, a new model is under preparation, and is called Global Public Inclusive Infrastructure (GPII) [1]. GPII is an infrastructure that will be able to support the usage of ICT by all, including end users, developers and stakeholders. GPII is an umbrella under which many different projects are running to compile its vision. In this paper we will focus on the evaluation of the all-inclusive ICT infrastructure GPII is building in Cloud4all EU project [3].

Cloud4all focuses on creating instant and ubiquitous auto-personalization of interfaces and materials based on user needs and preferences (N&Ps), so as to deliver accessibility to every individual where they need it, when they need it and in a way that matches their unique requirements.

© Springer International Publishing Switzerland 2015
J. Zhou and G. Salvendy (Eds.): ITAP 2015, Part I, LNCS 9193, pp. 157–165, 2015.
DOI: 10.1007/978-3-319-20892-3_16

2 Methodology

2.1 Cloud4all Methodology at a Glance

Cloud4all evaluates its all-inclusive ICT using the user centered design (UCD) approach of ISO 13407, with continuative evaluation phases, where users test specific Cloud4all prototypes. The results of the tests return to the developers who use them in order to evolve their tools/solutions. Then, the updated tools/solutions are tested again and the results return to the developers, and so on. This loop targets on creating tools/solutions that fit the needs of their user, whoever these are; end-users, developers or stakeholders.

The evaluation of Cloud4all is realized in three iterative phases. Each iteration phase has different objectives which depend upon the tools' functionalities, available at the time of the iteration, as well as, the general needs of the project. In addition, in some cases, tools that have been tested at one phase may be tested also at the next phase/s, since additional functionalities will be added to them or the objective of the evaluation phase may vary and new conclusions (additional to the ones of the previous phase) may derive for the respective tools.

In each evaluation phase, the scope of the testing has been based on assessing the usability and the user experience of the whole system, as well as its components separately. In each evaluation phase though, the way which the features will be used and tested is going to be different, depending on the maturity of the different components that participate in the developed scenarios. Thus, across the iterative phases, different solutions will be tested with users (end-users, developer, stakeholders) in different scenarios, at different level of maturity (Mock-up, LoFi, MeFi and HiFi prototypes). Thus, complexity and diversity of the tested tools/solutions will characterize all steps of the development work and this will be reflected in the evaluation framework.

2.2 Methodology for Piloting the Evaluation

Piloting the evaluation testing gives research programs an opportunity to make revisions to instruments and data collection procedures to ensure that appropriate questions are asked, the correct data will be collected and the data collection methods will work [6]. Additionally, this has the potential to help researchers identify ways to improve how an instrument is administered. For example, if participants show fatigue while interacting with the solutions, then the researcher should look for ways to shorten the solution or change the device, or even the experimental planning. If respondents are confused about how to perform a task, then the solution needs to clarify the possible interaction and simplify this process.

Thus, in Cloud4all, in all 3 evaluation phases, the testing involves conducting a preliminary test of data collection tools and procedures to identify and eliminate problems, allowing researchers to make corrective changes or adjustments before actually collecting data from the target population. In Cloud4all pilot tests, 15 participants are asked to go through the whole study, so that we can learn about the process and correct any problems [3].

A typical pilot test involves administering instruments to a small group of individuals that has similar characteristics to the target population, and in a manner that simulates how data will be collected when the instruments are administered to the target population.

3 Evaluation with End Users

3.1 Problem Statement

There are a number of key problems affecting the access of certain user groups to assistive technologies and specialised accessibility features that are being addressed by the Global Public Inclusive Infrastructure (GPII) [7]. Cloud4all works directly in two of these problems:

1. Solutions are too complicated, being difficult to find, set up and adjust, especially when the systems should be used by different users.
2. Solutions don't work across all of the devices and platforms that users encounter in education, employment, travel, and daily life.

Thus, the evaluation of Cloud4all focuses on assessing the greater picture of Cloud4all and trying to evaluate the whole procedure of Cloud4all system and the auto-configuration of preferences. The aim is to find weak points to fix before the finalization of the project, as well as to define issues for future developments in order to create a seamless and flawless interaction process for the user.

Thus, the problem statement for which Cloud4all is providing a solution could be summarized in the following scenario:

> "A user is trying to use a device that is not configured based on their Needs and Preferences. Then the user is trying to use a device which is configured based on their Needs and Preferences. The user cannot use the device which is not configured based on their Needs and Preferences, but they can use the device which is already configured before, based on their Needs and Preferences.
>
> The user cannot configure the device to fit their Needs and Preferences, either because they cannot (due to their disability) or because he/she does not know how to. It would be easier for the user if there was an automatic mechanism, which he/she could understand, with which they could easily login to the device they want to use and it would be automatically configured. It would also be easier for the user if there was a tool that would allow them to create an account and set their own Needs and Preferences than visiting the settings of each solution they want to use and tweak them manually.
>
> Users with disabilities are pledged to the environment in which they use the different solutions/devices. The users cannot use the devices they want under specific contexts. A mechanism that would allow the solution/device to automatically change based on the user's Needs and Preferences would enhance the user's interaction."

Thus the users' problem is twofold. On the one hand they cannot use solutions that are not configured based on their needs and preferences and on the other hand most of the users cannot configure these solutions at all, either because they are not aware of their needs and preferences or because they are not aware how to change the solution settings to match them.

3.2   Evaluation with End Users Objectives

Each of the three evaluation phases of Cloud4all had different objectives based on the maturity of the tools and the information the developers needed to extract from the users to evolve their developments. Below, the objectives of each evaluation phase are presented. Going through the following objectives of each iteration phase, the evolvement of Cloud4all evaluation tests is conspicuous.

- **1st evaluation phase of Cloud4all**
  - Introducing the concept of Cloud4all to users and getting their general reaction and early input.
  - Presenting the ability of the basic infrastructure to automatically launch and set up access solutions for users according to their preferences.
  - Realizing very early preliminary testing of matchmaker technologies for products that the user has not specified any preferences yet, in Windows and in Linux environment.
  - Compare the results of the rule-based matchmaker with the results of the statistical matchmaker. The matchmakers are the features that provide the intelligence of the Cloud4all system, by matching with each other all the different components that participate in the procedure.
  - Compare the results of the rule-based matchmaker and the results of the statistic matchmaker with experts.
- **2nd evaluation phase of Cloud4all**
  - Identify how Cloud4all will foster digital inclusion by improving user experience, in comparison to the current way of performing a common task in different, familiar or not, non-personalized solutions.
- **3rd evaluation phase of Cloud4all**
  - Evaluate the user experience with the Cloud4all auto-configuration procedure.
  - Evaluate the improved use of different devices and solutions.
  - Evaluate the acceptance of the context-related changes functionality.
  - Evaluate the management of Needs and Preferences with the PMT.

3.3   Evaluation with End Users Scenarios

As the objectives of each evaluation phase evolve, the scenarios the users test are evolving too. Thus in the 1st evaluation phase a guided scenario was realized by the users where they had to set their preferences using a simplified tool. The preferences were captured in the form of application specific settings, which means that the facilitator noted the value that each specific setting of the specific application under evaluation had, after explaining it to the user and defining the effect of this setting to the entire solution interface. The scenario was that the user would identify his/her preferences first in Windows and then go to Linux and evaluate how the settings were inferred in that OS. Then the user would have to do the procedure vice versa, identify the preferences in Linux and then go to Windows and evaluate how the settings were inferred in that OS. Thus we had two different set of settings to compare. One set of settings the user defined in Windows (Token A) and compare them with the inferred settings from Linux to Windows (Log A). And a second set of settings the user defined in Linux (Token B) and compare them with the inferred settings from Windows to Linux (Log B). The aforementioned procedure is depicted at the figure that follows (Fig. 1).

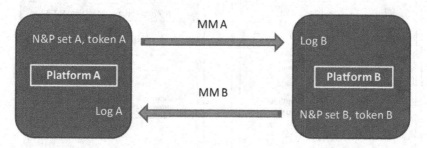

Fig. 1. Cloud4all 1st evaluation phase. Auto-configuration scenario

Moving forward in the second evaluation phase, the developments evolved and so did the procedure. The users no longer used application specific settings to define their N&Ps, but used the Cloud4all Preferences Management Tool (PMT), which uses common terms. Common terms are terms that harmonize the application specific settings and values throughout all the applications used in Cloud4all. Thus, the users now had a more user friendly tool to use in order to define and explore their N&Ps which were now captured in the needs and preferences server and retrieved from there. Additionally the users in the 2nd evaluation phase had the possibility to navigated between different devices and not only Window and Linux. Thus, android OS, Java mobile phones and other Cloud4all applications were made available to them. The procedure, which is depicted in the following figure, asks the user to use the PMT in Platform A to define their N&Ps and create a token and use this token to login to Platform B and evaluate the inferred settings (Fig. 2).

Finally at the 3rd evaluation phase, which is the last evaluation phase, more naturalistic scenarios will be evaluated. The users will be given a set of devices and applications and also a token which will be set by the pilot facilitator based on their disability profile. The users will be asked to navigate to these different devices and applications as if they were in their own environment and validate the auto-configuration procedure and results. The applications used will be close to ones the users use in their everyday life, including TV, laptop, desktop, tablet, ticket vending machine and the evaluation will be realized in controlled, close to reality environments like domotic labs or user own environments.

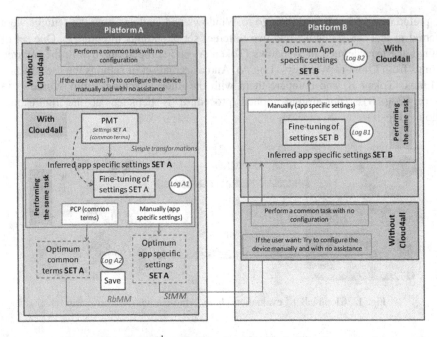

Fig. 2. Cloud4all 2nd evaluation phase. Auto-configuration scenario

4 Evaluation with Developers

4.1 Problem Statement

Apart from the tools for the end users, Cloud4all also develops tools to be used by different types of developers who may benefit from the use of Cloud4all. These developers are mainly AT developers who can add additional accessibility features to their solutions only by incorporating them in Cloud4all and GPII framework.

One of the main objectives of GPII is "*to provide the tools and infrastructure needed to allow diverse developers and vendors to create new solutions for these different users and platforms and to easily and cost effectively move them to market and to users internationally*" [7].

The Cloud4all project has been trying to assist the developers throughout the whole process of integrating their solution to Cloud4all/GPII infrastructure. The greatest existing problem is that there is no automatic way for the developers to include their settings to the Cloud4all/GPII unified listing that has been created in Cloud4all.

4.2 Evaluation with Developers Objectives

Cloud4all provides various channels that can be used by developers in order to work with Cloud4all and GPII. A key solution for developers provided by the Cloud4all project, which was ready from very early stages of the project, is the Semantic Alignment Tool (SAT), a software module for the syntactic and semantic analysis of solutions, by taking into account the different adaptation dimensions of the offered Cloud applications, services and tools.

An early prototype of the SAT was tested during the 1st iteration, showing that its usability was below the project expectations and that additional efforts should be allocated for its improvement. Therefore one of the objectives of evaluation during the 2nd evaluation phase was to test that the usability of the solution has been improved, fostering the acceptance of the Cloud4all concept and GPII framework by developers.

The results of the 2nd evaluation phase appeared to be quite positive for the SAT, thus in the final evaluation phase the objectives have been broadened and the objective of the evaluation is more high level, assessing all the material that has been created for developers within Cloud4all including the developers' kit which encompasses the following:

- Guidelines about the installation of Cloud4all.
- Guidelines about testing the Cloud4all/GPII architecture.
- Guidelines about the integration of a new solution to Cloud4all/GPII
  - When the solution runs on a specific platform.
  - When the solution is web-based.
- Additional information like
  - GPII source code
  - Blog for the developers
  - Cloud4all wiki
  - Cloud4all/GPII issue tracker.

5 Evaluation with Stakeholders

5.1 Problem Statement

The Stakeholders' profiles in Clou4all range from governments to service providers, caregivers or end users' experts, encompassing financing organizations, AT ICT industry organizations, technology oriented organizations, governmental and legal organizations, service providers and end-users organizations. This heterogeneous group has different points of view and face different problems when dealing with ICT accessibility delivery.

The main problem with the various stakeholders groups is that most of the time even if they are totally aware of the needs and preferences of individuals with disabilities, they are not aware on how to accommodate them. Stakeholder involvement in Cloud4all has allowed us to gather ample material and knowledge about user needs and preferences, as well as to pinpoint some challenges that we face throughout the lifecycle of the project, such as the need to make simpler configuration processes and/or to make users aware of the built-in accessibility features of different products and services.

5.2 Evaluation with Stakeholders – Objectives and Plan

Since the stakeholders group in Cloud4all is such a broad one the need of the identification of the needs of each subgroup was revealed early in the project. In each step of the evaluation different subgroups have been participating providing different, but in a lot of cases similar results.

At the first evaluation iteration only end-users organizations participated. Participants with different profiles of disability have been involved in the evaluation; however, as the end-users provided a personal view of their problems and preferences, it was important to involve also expert representatives from end-users organizations in order to gather as well a wider overview and experience over the needs and preferences of the different groups of disabilities. To that end, expert representatives from organizations of elderly people, visual impaired users, people with learning difficulties and cognitive impairments, low literacy and people with dyslexia formed the panel of stakeholders in the 1st evaluation iteration of Cloud4all.

As the project evolved in the 2nd evaluation phase, stakeholders with different profiles (governments, service providers, caregivers, end users' experts) have been involved in qualitative data gathering, to complement the end users' and developers' evaluations.

The goal of the stakeholders' participation in the 2nd evaluation phase was to gather their impressions and qualitative feedback on the concepts, tools and the whole Cloud4all process from a different perspective. Therefore, the evaluation with the different stakeholders was explorative and not guided by a specific research question. This has been achieved mainly by the participation of stakeholders in structured focus groups organized around concrete research topics like the Cloud4all/GPII concept and auto-configuration scenario, the context-related changes scenario, the optimum N&P gathering scenario, the GPII marketplace and recommendation system scenario, etc.

Finally, during the 3rd evaluation phase a more focused feedback is needed from the stakeholders. For this reason, stakeholders participating in this evaluation sessions will be selected among experts related with end user organizations as well as AT providers and caregivers. Stakeholders with a more industrial vision, such as ICT vendors and software industry, policy makers, etc. will be involved in Cloud4all through the Open Days that will be planed and realized later on in the project, where Cloud4all will be demonstrated and existing applications and tools may be experienced.

Thus, the goal of the stakeholders' evaluation in the 3rd evaluation iteration is to gather their impressions and qualitative feedback on the concepts, tools and the whole Cloud4all process (including installation) from two different perspectives:

- Which is the usefulness for users? (from stakeholders' point of view), and
- Which is the usefulness for stakeholders? (Being the stakeholders as mediators/supporters of end-users organizations or AT providers).

Stakeholders will be involved in structured focus groups where the whole Cloud4all concept (from installation to use on different devices) will be presented. Based on this, stakeholders will participate on discussions around the following concrete research topics.

6 Conclusions

In this paper, we presented the evaluation framework developed for all 3 evaluation iterations of all-inclusive ICT with end users, developers and stakeholders in the scope of Cloud4all/GPII. Each user group has been treated as a different part of the evaluation, being all though under the general umbrella of the evaluation and evolvement of the all-inclusive ICT infrastructure of Cloud4all and GPII.

In each evaluation phase different objectives and research questions have been sketched in order to serve the needs of the project in each stage. These have been evaluated using different scenarios for each user group and for each evaluation iteration going from more simplistic to more mature and complex ones.

Starting from the 1st evaluation iteration where the participants had in their hands mainly mock-ups and only some low fidelity (Lo-Fi) prototypes and were able to assess only basic functionalities of restricted Cloud4all tools being fully guided from the facilitators, we moved to the 2nd evaluation iteration where the participants had a full range of medium fidelity (Me-Fi) Cloud4all functional prototypes and were able to go through the whole Cloud4all experience from setting their own preferences to viewing who these preferences are inferred to a specific set of devices. And finally being on the 3rd iteration where the users can transfer their set of needs and preferences throughout a vast number of solutions in a very close to reality, unguided scenario and environment.

Acknowledgements. This research was funded by the European Union's Seventh Framework Programme (FP7/2007-2013) grant agreement n° 289016, by the National Institute on Disability and Rehabilitation Research, US Dept of Education under Grant H133E130028 (UIITA-RERC), the Ontario Ministry of Research and Innovation, and the Canadian Foundation for Innovation. The opinions and results herein are those of the authors and not necessarily those of the funding agencies environment.

References

1. Prosperity4all project. http://www.prosperity4all.eu/
2. Global Public Inclusive Infrastructure (GPII). http://gpii.net/
3. Cloud4all EU project. http://www.cloud4all.info/
4. Dix, A., Finlay, J., Abowd, G., Beale, R.: Human-Computer Interaction. Prentice Hall, New York (1997)
5. Preece, J., Rogers, Y., Sharp, H., Benyon, D., Holland, S., Carey, T.: Human-Computer Interaction. Addison-Wesley Longman Limited, Harlow (1994)
6. Tullis, T., Albert, W.: Measuring the User Experience: Collecting, Analyzing and Presenting Usability Metrics. Morgan Kaufmann Publishers, Inc., San Francisco (2008)
7. Vanderheiden, G.C., Treviranus, J., Markus, K., Clarck, C., Basman, A.: The Global Public Inclusive Infrastructure Cloud4all and Prosperity4all. In: Encarnação, P., Azevedo, L., Gelderblom, G.J., Newell, A., Mathiassen, N.-E. (eds.) Assistive Technology: From Research to Practice. IOS press, Amsterdam (2013)

Access and Use of ICTs Among the Italian Young Elderly: A Field Study

Fausto Colombo and Simone Carlo[✉]

Università Cattolica del Sacro Cuore, Largo Gemelli, 1, 20121, Milan, Italy
{fausto.colombo,simone.carlo}@unicatt.it

Abstract. Our research aims to investigate the relationship between the young elderly (65–74 years old) and use of technologies [1], and to explore active ageing and the role played by media and ICTs in building a friendly and positively domestic environment for the elderly in their everyday life [2]. Hence the use of ICTs by the elderly takes into account two different perspectives: (1) Generational approach: the young elderly are here considered by looking at the role played by their generational identity in shaping their media use [3]. (2) Domestication and Leisure: Media consumption is spatially and temporally located and media uses and routines are shared within the household and are enabled by processes of domestication [4]. The project is based on an theoretical study about ageing, a preliminary survey with a representative sample of the Italian "young elderlies" regarding ICTs equipment and usage (N = 900), (3) 20 family in-depth interviews in Milan area.

Keywords: Elderly · ICTs · Active ageing · Domestication · Generations

1 Introduction

The role of media and communication technologies in helping the quality of life, health [5] and care [6] of the elderly is today a key issue in the academic and political debate. Studies have been mainly focused on the use of the ICTs as tools replacing physical or cognitive deficits of the elderly [7]. Political institutions have regarded digital technologies as a way to avoid a new kind of divide among the elderly of today and tomorrow, hence promoting policies designed to build technological literacy among them elderly. These policies are often utopian and deterministic. The ICTs would allow the elderly to solve some problems related to their age such as disability, loss of mental faculties, diseases and loneliness.

If it is true that ICTs are a useful resource for the elderly to improve their health, their care and their social life [1], it is equally true that they are used by the elderly for their entertainment [8]. The usefulness of ICTs is accompanied and often is exceeded by their role as pastime, in a stage of life with a lot of spare time.

Taking into account these assumptions, a quantitative and qualitative study was conducted with the aim to understand social contexts, positive and negative attitudes related to the use of ICTs in the daily life of the elderly.

This study aimed to question the possible benefits and risks related to the use of new technologies for the elderly users, by taking into account the issue of domestication of

© Springer International Publishing Switzerland 2015
J. Zhou and G. Salvendy (Eds.): ITAP 2015, Part I, LNCS 9193, pp. 166–176, 2015.
DOI: 10.1007/978-3-319-20892-3_17

the ICTs in today complex social context [18], and by considering the third age as part of a particular generation. The paper here presented shows the main results of this research and is structured as follows: in the next section the research background and the theoretical approach used will be discussed; in the following sections the results of the study will be presented; and finally some implications for the potential orientation of policy-making will be formulated.

2 Context, Theoretical Framework and Research Methodology

2.1 National and European Context

The over 65 years elderly people are in Italy generally less online comparing to the average European population. There are significant developments but the Italian population is less digitized than the European one: with 16.3 % of Italian young elderly users (65–74 years old) comparing to the European average which sees 34.4 % of regular Internet users in the same age group (Source: European Commission).

Digital media are used by a very small niche of young Italian elderly [3]. 21.3 % of the Italian elderly own or use a computer: only 17.5 % a laptop and only 16.7 % a desktop computer. Data become more relevant if related to specific age groups (distinguishing between two age groups: 65–69 and 70–74) and gender.

Moreover 45 % of the young elderly using the computers today started using it before being 50 years old, 28.2 % between 50 and 59 years, 19.1 % between 60 and 64 years old. Only 9.1 % of users are "new" ICTs users (starting to use the computer after the age of 64), with a significant difference between males and females: respectively with 6.8 % of men compared to 12.8 % of women. When looking at the spaces of the ICTs, home is regarded as the best place for Internet access, with 98.8 % of domestic connections and, in second place, 15.3 % of connections at work (among our sample with Internet access). The young elderly access to the Internet alone. However there is a significant amount of young elderly users accessing with the partner (19.2 %), with their children (17.6 %), with their grandchildren (4.7 %). As regards the frequency of use: 71 % of the young elderly accessing the Internet do so almost every day. Moreover 58.8 % of the young elderly argue that they access to the Internet any time of the day, when it is probably useful to do so.

2.2 The Digital Elderly: Beyond a Biological Approach

The biological age seems to represent, for many theoretical approaches, a key element to explain the aforementioned gaps and to determine the use of ICTs by the young elderly [9]. Biological age is regarded as a such crucial element in making the elderly "laggards" digital users by definition when compared to younger subjects [5].

This point has led to the birth of a series of comparative analyses between young and old Internet users, taking into account the theoretical metaphor by Prensky [10] between digital immigrants and digital natives. This metaphor has strongly influenced the following academic debate, coming to describe the increasingly digital world as a world naturally more suitable for young people than the elderly. As regards to use of the ICTs, this approach has also often pointed out how young people use the ICTs for the leisure time, and conversely adults, in their general strangeness to the digital world, use ICTs only in few limited occasions and for specific tasks.

To overcome this limiting approach focused upon biological age, two theoretical perspectives are here considered: one is the generational theory, the other the theory of domestication [4, 18] and the importance given to the household as a (physical and symbolic) space to use technology in everyday life of the elderly [2]:

- Generational Approach and (Digital)Media Consumption: The generation of the young elders of the here presented research is enjoying the benefits of a progressive lengthening of life expectancy: this lengthening has created a new third age, which is distinct from the fourth, characterized by double emancipation from the family and work constraints [11] with a considerable amount of free time [12], money and status [13]. The adoption and use of ICTs fit in stories/biographies of the older generations [14], in their spare time and economic resources hence influencing their media consumption [15, 16];
- Leisure, Domestication, Everyday Life: The theoretical approach of domestication [4, 17] seems extremely helpful to take into account both the growing importance of digital media in the (spatial and temporal) contexts of the young elderly and the relationship between symbolic consumption and consumption of devices [18].

As regards to a "new generation" of digital users, domestication can be a very useful model to understand the ways in which the young elderly get used to digital media and to the use of new devices in their everyday lives, but also the role played by social and family networks in the process of incorporation to the ICTs [19].

In particular, daily family relations (with grandchildren, children, peers) are a key element in the dynamics of adoption of the ICTs in general and in the definition of a media consumption that is daily organized [20].

2.3 Objectives and Methodology

The main research objective was to understand the role played by the ICTs in the daily life of the elderly and the spatial and temporal organization of their lives. A crucial importance was given to the role played by the intergenerational relations in shaping media use and learning style of the elderly.

The research wanted even to investigate the possible relationships in place between the elderly and young people, with the aim of understanding the dynamics of intergenerational exchange, family use and domestication of ICTs [21].

The research project is based on a survey conducted between December 2013 and January 2014 through a face-to-face questionnaire administered to a statistically representative national sample of 900 young elderly Italians aged between 65 and 74 years of age (selected according to a random, proportional, stratified division defined by region and by the size of the place of residence, divided into two sampling stages).

Taking into account the preliminary results of the questionnaire, in May of 2014, 20 in-depth and unstructured interviews to young elderly aged between 65 and 74 years old and ICTs users were conducted. Interviewees was selected according to age (divided in two subsamples: 65–69 and 70–74 years old), household composition (with or without cohabitants) and geographical location (large or small city in Milan area).

3   The Young Elderly and the Adoption of Digital Media

In the following pages some of the main results of ethnography will be discussed, postponing the release of the in-depth survey analysis for other publications [13]. Starting from a grassroots approach, we describe here the main results using 4 categories that help us to frame the role of ICTs in biography, everyday life and domestic contexts of elderly.

3.1   Use of the ICTs and (Spare) Time

Use of the ICTs by the respondents is strongly influenced by their employment status: almost all of interviewees are not working (as retirees or housewives). This condition allows them to have a considerable amount (but variable from subject to subject) of non-working time which is managed differently among them:

- For some respondents, non-working time is regarded as "free" time: these respondents (i.e. housewives or those being retired from a long time) have now a consolidated management of their spare time. For these people, the time off from work - that exceeds the time spent on activities such as sleeping, bathing, dressing, cooking, tidying the house, grocery shopping and so forth - it is now an central part of their daily routine. For these subjects, their timing seems to be more standardized, more stable, less problematized, more time-spending.

- For other respondents, those being retired more recently, the perception of free time is mostly understood as a new time to spend off from work: these people perceive more than others the sharp divide between "before" ("when they used to work") and "after" ("now that they are not working anymore"). For some people this changing situation is handled in a problematic way: the time freed from work is considered a time of "forced laziness" for the loss of any productive role. These people are therefore living with the urgent need of making their time useful, meaningful, creative and productive rather than time-spending. Spare time therefore, conceived as time off from work, is likely to be considered as an empty time, and as a significant time for all older people, but especially for recent retirees who consider this time strongly linked their new life and identity as retirees. In this context, the use of ICTs is strongly influenced by the spare time of these respondents and is part of their effort to "shape" and/or "give value" to their time: the value given to (digital and otherwise) media consumption is strongly connected to the value given to their spare time.

3.2 Biography of Appropriation

Apart from any specific individual and personal story, three major trends or biographical paths of appropriation and incorporation can be identified. Contexts, family stories of the respondents strongly influence their expectations, motivations, anxieties and enthusiasm over the use of the ICTs.

(a) New Digital Elderly in an Old Digital Home. These are the young elderly who even though having never used the ICTs, they had at home computers and laptops of their children, but they have approached recently the world of the ICTs. These young elders decided to approach the ICTs once being retirees, hence once having a lot of free time. For these people, family relations (children, partly the partner and grandchildren) play a crucial role in their approach to the digital world. Processes of intergenerational learning are here in place. As regards their skills these people have recently had to learn to write with a keyboard and to use the mouse. Learning process takes place through a constant and everyday use: the use of the computer is perceived as a tiring but rewarding "commitment", which makes their time significant.

(b) New Digital Elderly in a new Digital Home. These are the elderly who have never used the ICTs, have bought recently the first computer of their household and have started using them only late in life, as part of leisure activities. These people are usually housewives, workers, those retired from late '80s, mid-90s, who have never used the computer at work. In some cases, these individuals had careers in management and business and did not need to know how to use the computer, the use of which was intended to more operational roles. They are generally people without children, or with children who have never owned and used a computer. Therefore they recently own a computer and if not very recent, when the children were already out from home. These respondents decided to have and use a computer not a any specific need but because they wanted to keep themselves update.

(c) The Digital Experienced Elderly. These are the young elderly who already used the ICTs at work since the 90s and have continued to do so even after the retirement. These people worked until the early 2000s and fully experienced the digitization of administrative procedures occurred in the late '80s and '90s with word processing, data entry, office suite, accounting and management software. Since the early '90s, thanks to the lowering costs of PCs these young elderly had a PC at home and decided to deepen their skills in the use of PCs and the Internet within the household. PC is not the only digital device for the household: some PCs (IBM compatible with Windows operating systems) have replaced or have been joined to the previous computers provided for the children (Commodore 64), however, used only for entertainment. Owning and using the computer was a largely established and domesticated practices in the family history of these respondents. PCs became available to the whole family and used by both parents (often solely and exclusively by the already digitized parents in charge of the buying decision) and by their children. At this early stage, parents were teaching the use of computer and the Internet, because of educational needs of their children (in the '90s some of them were students). As regards the issue of digital literacy, these young elders prove to have a strong independence. Users show advanced computer skills, developed over years of daily computer use. To summarize, for these subjects the domestication of the computer is rooted in a long family history. The retirement has radically changed computer use from being useful to being entertaining.

3.3 Spaces of the ICTs

The analysis of the spatial arrangement of the ICTs makes clear the processes of acquisition, the biographies of use, the history of the adoption of technologies, but also the moral economies, routines, methods of use of the technologies.

As regards this issue, a great difference can be found between those buying PCs only in recent times and those owning and using computers from a long time.

- The first type of young elderly recently buying a computer at home usually do not have a room for the PC and have adapted the space of the house to make room for the computer. That is why that these people (most of the respondents) usually have laptops with some of them having or not a fixed workstation. Those not having a fixed workstation do not necessarily have a less intense use of the computer of those having a fixed workstation. In some cases, the arrangement of the workstation (laptop, mouse, printer) is a daily routine, a sort of "ritual" to start to use the computer. The main difference between those households having workstation and those without concerns the sharing of skills: the arrangement of the station is a further barrier to the use of the ICTs for a couple who is in need of help at the beginning. In many cases, the organization of the space for the computer thus becomes an additional element in the gap and difficulty of access for some less digitized subjects. Moreover, in some cases, the advent of the computer causes tension between the partners, with respect to the possible mess caused by the computer, from the wires and the various devices connected to the computer (printer and modem). In this case, the choice of the location can be a further matter of argument in the couple, especially between digital and not digital spouses.
- The second type of family has a computer at home from a long time and has left the computer in the same location, usually the room of their children which has been changed into a study room. Hence this room is used primarily by one of the partners (usually the more digitized, who has more control and availability of the computer) and not equally by both of them, hence, in some families, increasing isolation and separation between the couple. These couples have also usually more than a TV, hence avoiding any possible negotiation about what to watch on TV. More than that, the asymmetric digitization has radicalized the differences between partners: digital knowledge and skills are not usually shared between the partners. Digital divides hence increase between those who "know and use the ICTs" and those who rather leave the use of the computer to the partner.

3.4 Incorporation and Timing of Use

The role given to computer and the Internet by the subjects under study has a strong impact on the timing of use of the ICTs for the respondents.

- On the one hand, some respondents have a strongly focused use aimed at doing something specific, at carrying on a task (i.e. at finding out, at looking at, at buying something), and at saving time for a task which would have required more efforts (one above all: home banking). Internet is meant to be time saving. In this case the use of computer and the Internet takes place once needed.
- On the other hand, other respondents have a more time spending use with the computer and the Internet being time spending. In this case the use of computer and the Internet happens without any specific purpose and often in specific day times (after waking up in the morning, after lunch, before dinner, before going to bed, etc.).

However many respondents tend to have a dual use, combining time spending attitudes to more focused sessions of use. They finally have, in terms of time, a very intense use of the computer and the Internet, spending a long time during the day at the computer and turning on the computer as the first activity of the day.

The majority of elderly people who have access to the Internet are therefore heavy users. The Internet is a world that is rooted in the everyday life of the sample: once crossed the threshold of access to the ICTs the elderly become not occasional users.

For some people, browsing sessions are mostly time spending, hence transforming the use of the ICTs that despite being typically time saving or functional in a time spending activity (e.g.: to open new mail account without real utility, to download many apps without using them, to enroll in many forums with no real participation in the discussion).

The extended and excessive use of the Internet is in some cases regarded as an issue hindering family life, previous routines, and the potential activities not carried out in favor of the Internet use.

Respondents are therefore particularly heavy users of the computer and the Internet. Such use, however, is not equally distributed during the day or the week. It clearly emerges that the computer and the Internet are predominantly used during the day and the week days, because these are the time mostly spent alone (children or partner might be away to work) with the chance of not being disturbed. The use of the computer during "office hours" thus seems to recreate working routines recently overcome because of retirement.

The values attributed to the time of use of the ICTs is also affected by biographies of appropriation:

(a) New Digital Elderly in an Old Digital Home. For these subjects, to be in the digital world means also to have the chance to get in touch with their children, relatives and friends and to an already digitized networks of relationships. Activities, such as spending time learning to use the Internet and the computer, asking for help to their children or relatives, but also online chatting or emailing, are considered rewarding because they strengthen and increase the relations among their family network. Being offline would also mean to lose these relational opportunities: their digital literacy encompasses a continuous exchange of information with their children or relatives already on Internet. For the respondents, the (long) time spent at the computer, with the goal of learning something radically new, it is perceived as well spent time because it enables them to be constantly connected to their social network.

(b) New Digital Elderly in a New Digital Home. For these subjects, the very recent use of the computer and the Internet makes them feel "active" to learn and to explore a new digital world and fits firmly in everyday life and in their time off from work. The use of the computer is often part of other time spending activities, as a new and exciting hobby. They are not necessarily fans of technology, but they rather see in learning something "new" a way to overcome a repetitive routine. The computer becomes for these subjects a key element to enrich their everyday life and to give value and meaning to too much free time.

(c) The Digital Experienced Elderly. For the digital experienced elderly, the use of the computer was meant to be, once they were still working, limited to certain times of the day (in the evening after work, after dinner and on weekends) and task-oriented. In recent years, because of retirement, something have changed in their timing of use from being task-oriented to being very time spending and entertaining.

Those who retired recently feel the time they spent at the computer as a time off from work, as a free time to fill up: for these digital elderly the ICTs are perceived to be essential but mostly entertaining and as filling their time, which is perceived (because of the retirement) too much.

Moreover it generally emerges a loss of time spent watching TV in favor of surfing the Internet. However this replacement is limited to specific times of the day, mainly morning and afternoon, when television programming is perceived to be low quality.

From this point of view, surfing the Internet during the morning or afternoon seems to be a viable alternative, being more involving, interesting and entertaining than watching TV. It is also interesting to notice that watching TV can be more frustrating than surfing the Internet, as if watching TV as a time spending activity is likely to be less appreciated that wasting time surfing the Internet. If the young elderly seem to watch less TV in the morning and afternoon, during the prime time, television seems to still be central in the media diet of the young elders: on the one hand because they have established routines with certain TV programs, on the other hand watching TV is still considered a family moment, and despite the passing years, it is still perceived as crucial.

4 Conclusions: ICTs, Domestication and Risks

The here presented study has aimed to investigate the role played by the ICTs in the daily life of the young elderly. These first research results allow us to draw some conclusions and make some inferences.

Our research show that (1) ICTs and the Internet have a significant impact on young elderly everyday life and their spatial - temporal domestic routines; (2) processes of ICTs domestication are basically influenced by personal and generational biography of the young elderly (previous job, intra- and inter-generational relationship, familiar contexts) and not only by age or other socio-demographic characteristics (gender, income, education) (3) ICTs and the Internet seem to be a good opportunity for a better and active ageing (e.g. in terms of improvement of social relations, information, entertainment), but even a risk in terms of social isolation inside and outside family.

1. First, the age group under research (65–74 years old) is characterized by an high percentage of non-workers (housewives and retirees) [22]. These people have a significant amount of free time, off from work that they mainly spend at home [23] where practices of media consumption and processes of adoption of new technologies take place. Media consumption involves processes of domestication and routines which are shared within the household and the family. The use of the ICTs is mostly happening in the household, with a significant resistance to mobile use. Second, although a relatively low ICTs diffusion among the elderly is confirmed by the study, it clearly emerges a trend among the young-older users: the ICTs are central for their daily lives and for their time at home. For the minority of those who are digitized, the ICTs have a major impact in shaping their free time (quite significant in terms of amount): Internet is used by elderly basically for entertainment and leisure as a time spending activity.

2. It significantly emerges that the biographies of adoption allows us to understand the different approaches to the ICTs: beyond the biological age, the personal, working, family, generational dimensions influence the paths of domestication to technology. The retirement, the relationships with family members, but also the spatial organization of the household, are all elements strongly influencing access and use of the ICTs, confirming the usefulness of domestication approach to understand these phenomena. In particular, our study shows that the domestication of the ICTs (as objects and symbols) is a slow process that has its roots in the history of the young elderly as digital "users", able to (more or less enthusiastically) domesticate previous technologies (televisions, video games consoles, computers, digital TVs, mobile phones, etc.). The domestication allows us to understand the adoption of technology by the elderly as an evolutionary process, as an *everyday social practice*, as the outcome of a biography of media consumption enabled by domestications and re-domestications to technologies as an outcome of processes of remediation [24]. As regards the generation, the category of multi-dimensional generation appears to be particularly useful to study the elderly, who are hardly describable by looking at their socio-demographic traits (age, gender, education, employment position) but rather at several elements - as social position, social contexts and changes that these contexts have had over the years and relationships, shared values with their own generation, biographies of media consumption, and social networks. All these elements work as environment to the experience of media consumption. The present young elders – first of all - belong to a specific generation: the Baby Boomers generation. The study shows how this generation is related to learning process developed since the 90s (intra-generational dimension) thanks to the digitization of their job and workplace, and learning mediated by children and grandchildren (intergenerational dimension). The subjects under study belong to a generation that experienced, primarily in the workplace, the birth of computer science and that had the chance to learn and get updated by the younger and strongly digitized generations. The today 65–74 years old Italians seem to belong to a "in the middle" generation with several features depending on their past (of partly digitized workers) and present (healthy, wealthy and generally with a lot of free time retirees): in the future, with the gradual spread of digital skills, with the increase in the retirement age, with changes in the welfare system, those aged 65–74

years old will probably have other practices of domestication and use of the ICTs, associated with a reasonable different time management between work and leisure, different family relationships, and a likely different level of wealth and health.

3. Finally the dual role of the ICTs in daily life of the young elderly is the last issue of interest. Literature and research around the use of the ICTs among young people has long urged the potential for (personal and social) empowerment arising from the use of the Internet but also the risks arising from an unaware and irresponsible use of communication technologies [25]. This focus given to the complex and dual relationship between ICTs and risks/benefits for users appears to be a marginal part of the debate regarding silver users. ICTs are more often regarded as tools able "deterministically" to positively impact the lives of the elderly. However it is necessary to, especially when discussing about policies aimed to promote active ageing, carefully consider the complex nature of media and the ICTs. For example, it clearly appears in the research that ICTs can help the young elderly to broad their relational network (inside and outside the family) but also to close themselves in the household sharpening isolation between the partners. ICTs are both promoting active ageing (enabling update, the relationships and brain activity), but also new risks of loneliness, because in some cases the overuse (with online time-consuming *brainless* activity) do not encourage the young elderly to spend their free time outside from home and to live their relations with the partner fully.

In terms of policies, these results seem therefore to be a recommendation to develop inclusive policies that take into account the dual role played by the ICTs: the processes of inclusion should aim to promote active ageing and not simply the diffusion of ICTs. In line with the recent sociological debate [25], active ageing should not be understood solely in terms of health and lengthening of life expectancy but also as owning and using technologies [7]. Active ageing means quality of life and being able to experience a sense of subjectively and socially rewarding ageing: quality and gratification that also depends on (conscious, careful, thoughtful, moderate, in relational contexts) "good use" of the ICTs.

References

1. Selwyn, N.: The information aged: a qualitative study of older adults' use of information and communications technology. J. Ageing Stud. **18**, 369–384 (2004)
2. Loos, E., Haddon, H., Mante-Meijer, E. (eds.): Generational Use of New Media. Ashgate, Farnham (2012)
3. Aroldi, P., Carlo, S., Colombo, F.: "Stay Tuned": the role of icts in elderly life. In: Riva, G., Ajmone-Marsan, P., Grassi, C. (eds.) Active Ageing and Healthy Living: A Human Centered Approach in Research and Innovation as Source of Quality of Life. IOS Press, Amsterdam (2014)
4. Silverstone, R., Hirsch, E. (eds.): Consuming Technologies: Media and Information in Domestic Space. Routledge, London (1992)

5. European Commission: Ageing well in the Information Society - an i2010 Initiative - Action Plan on Information and Communication Technologies and Ageing. EU publishing, Bruxelles (2010)

6. Olve, G.N., Vimarlund, V.: Elderly Healthcare, Collaboration and ICT - enabling the Benefits of an enabling Technology. VINNOVA - Swedish Governmental Agency for Innovation Systems Publishing, Stockholm (2006)

7. Dickinson, A., Gregor, P.: Computer use has no demonstrated impact on the well-being of older adults. Int. J. Hum.-Comput. Stud. 64(8), 744–753 (2006)

8. Nimrod, G.: The internet as a resource in older adult leisure. Int. J. Disabil. Hum. Dev. 8(3), 207–214 (2008)

9. Cabrera, M., Malanowski, N. (eds.): Information and Communication Technologies for Active Ageing. IOS Press, Amsterdam (2009)

10. Prensky, M.: Digital natives, digital immigrants. Horiz. 9(5), 1–6 (2001)

11. Gauchet, M.: La redéfinition des âges de la vie. La Débat 132, 27–44 (2004)

12. Nimrod, G.: Retirees' leisure: activities, benefits, and their contribution to life satisfaction. Leisure Stud. 26(1), 65–80 (2007)

13. Censis, Gli anziani, una risorsa per il paese, Dossier Censis, Report on-line (2013). http://www.censis.it/7?shadow_comunicato_stampa=120933

14. Edmunds, J., Turner, B.S.: Generations. Culture and Society. Open University Press, Buckingham and Philadelphia (2002)

15. Aroldi, P.: Generational belonging between media audiences and ICT user. In: Colombo, F., Fortunati, L. (eds.) Broadband Society and Generational Changes, pp. 51–67. Peter Lang, Frankfurt am Main (2011)

16. Becker, H.E., Hermkens, P.L.J. (eds.): Solidarity of generations: Demographic, economic and social change and its consequences, vol. II. Thesis Publishers, Amsterdam (1993)

17. Bakardjieva, M.: Internet Society: The Internet in the Everyday Life. Sage, London (2005)

18. Silverstone, R., Haddon, L.: Design and the domestication of ICTs: technical change and everyday life. In: Silverstone, R., Mansell, R. (eds.) Communication by Design: The Politics of Information and Communication Technologies, pp. 44–74. Oxford University Press, Oxford (1996)

19. Pasquali, F., Scifo, B., Vittadini N.: Media e culture digitali tra innovazione e senso comune: un'introduzione. In: Pasquali, F., Scifo, B., Vittadini N. (eds.) Crossmedia cultures. Giovani e pratiche di consumo digitali, pp. XV–XXXIX. Vita e Pensiero, Milano (2010)

20. Aroldi, P., Colombo, F.: La terra di mezzo delle generazioni. Media digitali, dialogo intergenerazionale e coesione sociale. Studi di Sociologia 3–4, 285–294 (2013)

21. Mandy, T.: Think Community: An Exploration of the Links Between Intergenerational Practice and Informal Adult Learning Research Report. NIACE Publishing, Leicester (2009)

22. Zenini, M.: Invecchiamento della popolazione, crescita, occupazione. Studi e Note di Economia XIV(3), 431–468 (2009)

23. ISTAT Cambiamenti nei tempi di vita e attività del tempo libero. Report on-line (2009). http://www.istat.it/it/archivio/47442

24. Bolter, D., Grusin, R.: Remediation: Understanding New Media. MIT Press, London (1999)

25. Livingstone, S., Haddon, L., Görzig, A. (eds.): Children, Risk and Safety Online: Research and Policy Challenges in Comparative Perspective. The Policy Press, Bristol (2012)

26. Rossi, G., Boccacin, L., Bramanti, D., Meda, S.: Active ageing: intergenerational relationships and social generativity. In: Riva, G., Ajmone-Marsan, P., Grassi, C. (eds.) Active Ageing and Healthy Living: A Human Centered Approach in Research and Innovation as Source of Quality of Life, pp. 57–69. IOS Press, Amsterdam (2014)

Patterns of ICT Use among "Senior Technology Experts": The Role of Demographic Variables, Subjective Beliefs and Attitudes

Michael Doh[⊠], Laura I. Schmidt, Florian Herbolsheimer,
Mario Jokisch, and Hans-Werner Wahl

Department of Psychological Aging Research, Institute of Psychology,
Heidelberg University, Bergheimer Str. 20, 69115 Heidelberg, Germany
{michael.doh,laura.schmidt,
florian.herbolsheimer,mario.jokisch,
hans-werner.wahl}@psychologie.uni-heidelberg.de

Abstract. Information and communication technologies (ICT) play a substantial role for enhancing participation and autonomy in old age. In Germany, as in most modern industrialized societies, huge diffusion gaps between younger and older age groups exist regarding the use of the internet and ICT devices. Very few studies address the differential role of older "frontrunners" in terms of modern ICT. In this project, we address patterns of ICT use and competence beliefs among "senior technology experts" (N = 108; aged 51–81, M = 68.37), who took part in a German initiative to help older novice users with ICT, and explore the associations with psychological constructs such as self-efficacy and obsolescence. Findings suggest a strong relationship of two self-efficacy measures and perceived obsolescence with usage patterns and competence ratings. Insights on usage patterns, perceived competence and associations with psychological constructs are discussed, as they may help improve the understanding of early technology adopters among older adults with implications for research and practice.

Keywords: Technology Use · Diffusion · Self-efficacy · Obsolescence · Aging

1 Introduction: Ageing Societies and Mediatization

Modern societies undergo a fundamental transformation that can be characterized by two developments: On the one hand, there is the global trend of aging populations with a higher number of individuals reaching increasingly higher ages, and with continuously decreasing numbers of younger individuals at the same time. On the other hand, due to dynamic technological innovations and intensified diffusion of information and communications technology (ICT), nearly all areas of modern life are increasingly affected by media und technologies [1–3].

There is evidence that those two trends are strongly interconnected. For instance, innovations in the field of medical technology and engineering have been playing a

© Springer International Publishing Switzerland 2015
J. Zhou and G. Salvendy (Eds.): ITAP 2015, Part I, LNCS 9193, pp. 177–188, 2015.
DOI: 10.1007/978-3-319-20892-3_18

substantial role for life expectancy, particularly among individuals in their later stages of life. Furthermore, the societal and economic importance of older persons as consumers and recipients of medial and technological devices is growing.

Following Baltes [4] these cultural-historical developments can be integrated into his concept of an "incomplete architecture of the human ontogenesis": With higher age and with age-associated vulnerability and declining abilities and resources, culture-based resources are required at increasing levels. However, because of age-related losses in biological plasticity, the efficiency of culture is reduced in advanced age. Gerontechnological devices and services represent an application of these assumptions, as technology in general can be incorporated to the umbrella of "culture". (Mobile) information and communication technology hold the potential, especially for older individuals, to facilitate everyday activities and foster independence, for instance in the domains of information, communication, participation, autonomy, mobility, education and health. But, referring to the assumption of reduced efficiency, technological innovations also imply environmental pressure [5], and autonomy or participation in the later years could also be impeded by devices that are difficult to manipulate [6, 7]. This is particularly the case for older generations and inexperienced individuals, who consider the access to the digital world itself as a major challenge and may face various barriers related to new ICT devices.

At this point, an interaction of barriers related to the environment, to the technological device and to the person can be assumed. In Germany, for instance, learning opportunities for older people living in rural and structurally underdeveloped regions are scarce and, moreover, there is often a lack of fast broadband or WLAN connection [8]. Additionally to the environmental perspective, many devices lack usability or intuitive design and have a short half-life. Due to a highly dynamic innovation process, acquired knowledge is rapidly becoming outdated. Further hindrances, located at the intersection of the person and the device, may be imposed by unnecessary use of jargon or complicated language and uncertainty regarding privacy issues. Person-related aspects with relevance for technology ownership, use and performance include socio-demographic variables (age, sex, education, and income), personality, health and cognitive abilities, but also attitudes towards and experience with technology, self-efficacy and obsolescence [9, 10].

Therefore, both society and the aging individual are challenged to make use of the potentials of technological innovations. According to the commission of the "5th report on ageing" of the German Federal Government lifelong learning is both a right and a duty [11].

2   Cohort Effects in Internet Diffusion

In order to better understand the background of the current study, the German diffusion rates regarding the internet are shortly summarized. In 2014, 79% of persons aged 14+ were using the internet, representing the largest community in Europe with 55 million internet users. With respect to persons aged 60+, the diffusion rate is 45%, with 9 million users [12]. A decade ago in 2004, the general diffusion rate among 14+ was 55% and among 60+ 15%, and in 1998, only 10% and 1% respectively. However, this

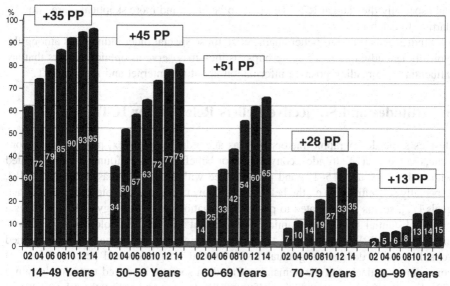

Source: Own analysis from the (N)Onliner-Atlas, 2002-2014 (n = 30.000 – 50.000)

Fig. 1. Internet diffusion in Germany 2002–2014

huge development reached a phase of stagnation in the last years. In a European comparison, Germany only reaches a rank 11, far behind Iceland or Scandinavian countries [13]. Furthermore, when comparing older age groups, large differences emerge as well. Own analyses reveal a diffusion rate of 65% in the group of persons aged 60–69, but only 35% among persons aged 70–79 and 15% among those aged 80–89 years (see Fig. 1).

The growth rates in Fig. 1 are mostly due to younger internet users that are growing into the age segment, which is supported by cohort analyses indicating relatively low or stagnating increases in diffusion rates for those born 1949 and earlier.

Alongside age, other socio-demographic factors such as sex, education and income are related to technology and internet use, with a cumulative effect in older ages (sometimes labeled as "singularization" and "feminization" of old age). For instance, among men aged 60+ with high socio-economic status living in a multi-person household in western Germany, the internet diffusion rate is 88%. For comparison, among women in the same age group with low socio-economic status living in a single-person household in eastern Germany, the corresponding rate is 6%, and those differences between groups have been found to have increased since 2002 (own analysis based on data of the (N) Onliner-Atlas).

Rogers' diffusion theory [14] can be drawn on to explain those differences, stating that technological innovation are adopted first by groups with high social status, financial liquidity, advanced education and social forwardness ("innovators" and "early adopters"). Later on, when the larger group of "early majority" has decided to adopt a technology and the earlier groups have reached a point of saturation, the "late majority" and especially the "laggards" – who tend to be older and more skeptical – are (slowly) starting to catch up.

Studies are needed to better characterize those special older individuals among the typically late adopting older age groups, as they may serve as opinion leaders that are influential in spreading positive information about the internet and modern ICT.

3   Attitudes and Subjective Beliefs Relevant for ICT Use

Besides socio-demographic factors such as age, education or sex, psychological constructs in the area of attitudes, convictions, or beliefs have been found to be associated with technology use [15–17] and performance with technology-based tasks [12, 18]. Especially self-efficacy, i.e., the belief in one's own ability to complete tasks and reach goals [17], seems to be related to positive evaluations of technology [20], and plays a more substantial role in explaining involvement in new technologies than demographics [21, 22]. Furthermore, there are first indications that a construct named "obsolescence", defined as gradual loss of social integration and perceived lack of competence to deal with the demands of modern society, is related to technology use [23]: Findings indicate a mediation effect of obsolescence regarding the relationship of technological experience and loneliness. Furthermore, persons with higher feelings of obsolescence (for instance: "being antiquated") revealed a higher numbers of errors and needed more time for tasks with technologies such as a mobile phone or an eBook reader and reported more concerns regarding usability issues [10]. Typically, feelings of obsolescence increase with age [24].

With respect to our intention to focus on those older "frontrunners", who belong to the early adopting individuals within the older age groups, specific self-efficacy beliefs are more promising than global or general attitudes towards technology in order to explore relations with technology competence and usage patterns. As self-efficacy can be improved by mastery or vicarious experience [19], self-efficacy might also imply a starting point for interventions.

Furthermore, very few studies address the concept of obsolescence, which might help to understand differences in competence and breadth of modern ICT use, even among this special group.

4   Aim of Current Project and Research Questions

Summarizing existing research gaps, there is the need for studies addressing psychological factors, environmental-structural issues and technology specific aspects for the adoption and successful handling of ICT in older adults, and further, a need to link those concepts to internationally renowned theories such as Roger's diffusion theory [14] or Bandura's social learning theory [19]. Therefore, our study combines media research and behavioral gerontology approaches.

The study builds on the German initiative "Senior Technology Experts – Transfer of ICT knowledge from older adults to older adults" launched by the German Federal Ministry of Education and Research (BMBF). Within this initiative, 18 regional projects in ten federal states of Germany received funding in order to promote and facilitate the use of modern ICT (i.e. tablet, smartphone, and laptop) and Ambient Assisted Living (AAL) applications among older adults. Target groups also included novice users with little access to technology such as persons with a migration background, women, inhabitants of rural areas, or even blind persons. The projects offered low-threshold educational programs such as courses in small groups, information meetings, consultations or home visits.

Project FUTA (Factors for the Use of New Information and Communication Technologies in Old Age) has the aim to gather data on resources and barriers that explain variance in usage patterns and perceived competence in managing mobile ICT and AAL applications among two groups of older individuals that differ in terms of technology experience: (a) so called "senior technology experts" and (b) novice users with limited prior technology experience or knowledge.

As the data collection with respect to AAL and among novice users is still ongoing, the current paper is focused on 12 projects on mobile ICT and on the group (a) of "senior technology experts". These older frontrunners are empowered – to some extent even trained – to explain the use of modern ICT to novices. In this initial paper, we aim to better understand usage patterns and associations among those senior experts, as they are meant to serve as successful role-models for novices later on. Furthermore, we aim to overcome the lack of differentiation with regard to psychological variables.

Research questions are as follows:

(1) How can the biographical development of ICT adoption help to better characterize the senior technology experts?
(2) How is the relationship of specific psychological constructs (obsolescence and two measures of self-efficacy) and breadth of ICT use and competence?

As modern ICT are increasingly becoming an integral part of daily life among older adults, but relatively little is known about the characteristics of older "frontrunners", we thereby aim to contribute to this upcoming area of research. The study of those "early adopters" might be the key to better understand the process of diffusion among older users, as they may serve as opinion leaders and role models for non-users of the same age-group.

5   Method

We used data from the online-questionnaire of the FUTA project that was carried out between October 2014 and January 2015. A convenience sample was drawn from all participants within the initiative "Senior Technology Experts". The study collected information on individuals' attitudes towards new technology, media use, and social and economic circumstances. In total, 108 participants, all representing senior technology experts who provided courses or information sessions with mobile ICT (laptop, tablet and smartphone), completed the whole online questionnaire (mean overall time = 43.11, SD = 14.06). A prior feasibility study has estimated that over the period of the whole initiative (October 2013 until September 2014) about 240 experts were engaged in one of twelve projects dealing with mobile technology. That implies a response rate of 45%.

Out of the full range of assessed constructs, we have selected seven concepts for the current paper: Internet self-efficacy, Web 2.0 self-efficacy, obsolescence, breadth of web use, digital media setting, computer/laptop competence, and smartphone/tablet competence. In addition, demographic variables concerning age, sex, education, partner status, and income were included.

To measure the digital media setting in one's household, participants completed a list of 11 digital devices (computer, smartphone, laptop, tablet, smart-tv, dvd-player, cd-player, mp3-player, automobile GPS, digital camera, e-book-reader) to indicate the degree of mediatization. Additionally, data were collected on the utilization of 17 online applications to indicate the breadth of web use [12]. The breadth of web use index included widely used applications like E-Mail to applications that are more difficult to use like social networks. For each item, respondents indicated the frequency of use (daily, weekly, rarely, never). All answers of either "daily" or "weekly" were added up which resulted in a breadth of web use index ranging from 0 to 17.

For the assessment of specific psychological constructs, we used a three-item internet self-efficacy scale from Schenk and Scheiko (2011) [25], which is a short version from Eastin and LaRose [26] with eight items (for example: "I feel confident to use blogs and make own contributions"). Participants responded on a scale from 1 (not at all true) to 5 (definitely true). Three items were averaged to form an index of internet self-efficacy (Cronbach's $\alpha = .84$). The same metric was applied for the three items measuring Web 2.0 self-efficacy that was also adopted from Schenk and Scheiko [25]. Three of the originally five items were selected (for example: "I feel confident trouble shooting Internet problems"). The internal consistency of the scale was good (Cronbach's $\alpha = .82$). Obsolescence was a five item measure (Cronbach's $\alpha = .82$) developed by Brandstädter and Wentura [24]. It measures problems of orientation and alienation in the rapid change of modern societies ("More and more, I have the feeling that I have been passed over by the times") and was originally part of a lager assessment of the "Future Time Perspectives and Future Meaning Scale". Obsolescence consists of five Likert-type items rated from 1 (not at all true) to 5 (definitely true). In addition, respondents were asked to rate their device-specific media competence: "How would you estimate your abilities/ skills in dealing with the following devices?" These self-rated competence scores for computer, laptop, smartphone, and tablet were rated on a scale ranging scale from 1 (no competence) to 5 (a lot) and summarized for computer/ laptop and smartphone/ tablet.

Differences in characteristics between persons aged 51 to 69 and persons aged 70 to 81 were tested using one-way ANOVA for normally distributed variables, the Kruskal-Wallis tests for skewed variables, and Pearson Chi^2 tests for categorical variables. Pearson product moment correlation coefficients were calculated using pairwise deletion. The data were analyzed using STATA 10.1 software (StataCorp LP, Texas, USA).

6 Results

Table 1 provides information on descriptive statistics and group comparisons for all variables used in this study. Sample age range from 51 to 81 years with an average of 68.37 years (SD = 6.51). They are highly educated (61.76% university degree), predominantly male (67.59%), and revealed high levels of self-rated computer competence (67.59%). As may be expected, high interest in technology and a wide breadth of online applications and well equipped digital media devices was observed.

We found clear differences among media utilization and personality-related characteristics when we classified our sample in two age groups (51 to 69 years, n = 58; 70 to 81 years, n = 50). The older age group appears to be even more selective in terms of higher education levels (p < .05), a higher rate of university degrees, a tendency to larger incomes and a higher proportion of men. The majority of all participants had longstanding experience with the internet of over ten years. Compared to the younger age group, older participants showed lower values in both competence measures and

Table 1. Descriptive sample data

Variable	51 – 69 yrs.			70 – 81 yrs.			
	n	M	SD	n	M	SD	p
Age	58	63.45	(4.10)	50	74.08	(3.32)	–
Sex (%, female)	58	41.38		50	22.00		<.05
Income (%, low)	4	10.81		0	0.00		–
middle	8	21.62		10	27.78		–
high	25	67.57		26	72.22		ns
Education (%, low)	9	16.36		7	14.00		–
middle	19	34.55		6	12.00		–
high	27	49.09		37	74.00		<.05
University degree (%)	55	52.73		47	72.34		ns
Married/living with a partner (%)	58	82.76		50	82.00		ns
Computer/Laptop competence[a]	56	4.28	(0.67)	48	3.89	(0.88)	<.05
Smartphone/Tablet competence[a]	53	3.70	(0.89)	43	3.23	(0.77)	<.01
Internet use (>10 years) (%)	57	73.68		50	64.00		ns
Digital media setting[b]	58	8.03	(2.00)	50	6.72	(2.12)	<.01
Breadth of web use[c]	58	8.47	(3.22)	50	6.54	(2.78)	<.01
Obsolescence[d]	58	9.76	(3.31)	50	11.78	(3.90)	<.01
Internet Self-efficacy[e]	58	13.19	(1.91)	50	12.18	(2.58)	<.05
Web 2.0 Self-efficacy[e]	58	10.43	(3.34)	50	7.23	(3.71)	<.001

Note. Higher scores indicating higher ratings of the corresponding scale; ns = not significant. [a] Two-item measure ranging from 1 to 5; [b] Possible score 0 to 11; [c] Possible score 0 to 17; [d] Possible score 5 to 25; [e] Possible score from 3 to 15

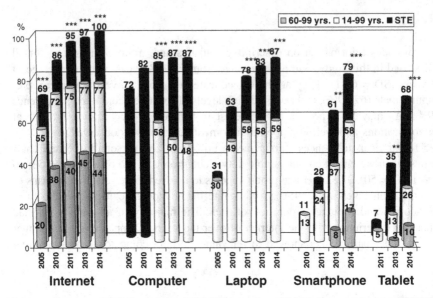

Sources: Internet: (N)Onliner-Atlas 2004-2014, each n=30.000 (own analysis); . HUAWEI-Study: Computer, Smartphone, Tablet 2012-2014, each n=1.000; ARD/ZDF-Study „Massenkommunikation": Laptop 2005, 2010, each n=4.500 (own analysis). Test of significance with chi^2 comparing participants aged 14 -99 years and STE.

Fig. 2. Trends in diffusion of ICT: Comparison of "Senior Technology Experts" (STE) and representative population data of Germany

self-efficacy scores. The breadth of internet usage as well as the number of digital media devices was significantly below the values of the younger experts.

In the last decade, senior technology experts have continuously shown higher diffusion rates compared to the whole German population regarding all ICTs (Fig. 2). For instance, 67.60% of the experts used tablets in 2014 compared to 26.00% in the general population (14 – 99 years).

As shown before, age did correlate significantly with all media-related measurements but history of internet usage. In Table 2, a wide variety of digital devices and usage of online applications was accompanied with higher self-efficacy scores. Those who scored high on web 2.0 self-efficacy also showed the widest spectrum of internet applications (r = .57; p < .001). Contrary association were found between obsolescence and breadth of internet use (r = .24; p < .05). Sex was only associated with a later start using the internet and a tendency for lower self-rated computer/laptop competence. Beside demographic variables, the three person-related factors internet/web2.0 self-efficacy and obsolescence explained a significant part (δ adj. R^2 = .19) of the variation of the number of used internet applications.

Table 2. Relationship of socio-demographic and psychological variables with media-related measures

	Competence Computer/ Laptop[a]	Competence Smartphone/ Tablet[a]	Digital media setting[b]	Internet use >10 years	Breadth of web use[c]
n	104	96	108	107	108
Age[a]	−.26 **	−.24 *	−.37 ***	−.06	−.25 **
Female[a]	−.16	.06	−.09	−.30 **	.04
Internet Self-efficacy[a]	.65 ***	.51 ***	.37 ***	.35 ***	.37 ***
Web 2.0 Self-efficacy[a]	.42 ***	.37 ***	.46 ***	.28 **	.57 ***
Obsolescence[a]	−.06	−.24 *	−.17	−.06	−.24 *

Notes [a] n = 108

7 Discussion

In order to better understand patterns of ICT use in older technology experts, this paper addresses associations between psychological variables, competence ratings and differentiated measures of usage characteristics. Findings demonstrate the special role of the senior technology experts with regard to their high social-economic and media psychological resources. Despite the trend of feminization in old age, a marked male predominance among the senior experts was expected and found, which is related to low acceptance and diffusion rates among women (see Sect. 2). In the framework of Rogers' diffusion theory [14], these senior frontrunners belong to the innovators and early adopters, not only with respect to the older population but also in comparison to the general adoption across all age groups. Alongside early adoption, a wide spectrum of application use and high competence was found. Following Schubert and Büser [27], this can be framed as "media-related capital" that can be used to enhance participation and autonomy in everyday life.

As higher scores in self-efficacy measures and low perceived obsolescence were related to a wider breadth of use and explained a substantial proportion of variance in regression analyses, our study points to the vital role of those psychological constructs. With respect to obsolescence, an increase with age was theoretically derived [24] and found between the two age groups. Especially the link between feelings of obsolescence and competence in smartphones and tablets, but not in computers, is remarkable and might indicate the sensitivity of this construct to technological and societal chance. Going further, according to Kaspar, obsolescence was found to mediate the impact of low technological competence on loneliness [23].

Associations between self-efficacy measures and competence as well as breadth of use were even stronger, which can be partly due to the technology-specific framing of items in contrast to the general wording of obsolescence which does not explicitly address technology but a gradual loss of social integration as well as a perceived lack of competence to cope with modern society. As earlier studies also found a relationship of self-efficacy and usage patterns [15, 21, 22], our results replicate those findings among older technology experts.

Several limitations should be noted for this study. First, the study population was based on a convenience sample. For this paper 12 projects on mobile ICT affiliated to the German initiative were contacted several times to ensure high diffusion of the online questionnaire, but as the response rate was about 45% a selection bias cannot be ruled out. Second, our cross-sectional findings should not be interpreted in terms of causality. For instance, further longitudinal studies are needed to determine if higher feelings of obsolescence and lower self-efficacy are consequence or cause of low competence and low adoption. Furthermore, as our sample population is highly specific in terms of socio-demographic variables, findings are not generalizable to the wider population.

Nevertheless, our study is the first to explore both psychological constructs and differentiated measures of usage and modern ICT adoption among older expert users of modern ICT. Ongoing longitudinal analyses concerning these experts, as well as a comparison with their inexperienced counterparts within the German initiative, will further explore processes and patterns of ICT use and relationships with psychological variables. In terms of "successful aging" in a technology-driven world, those front-runners are meant to serve as role-models for inexperienced novices within the initiative. As self-efficacy can be improved by mastery or vicarious experience [19, 28] this is a means to help older users to achieve success by providing challenging yet attainable tasks and by exposure to the expert role model who belongs to the same age group and conquers the challenge of modern ICT successfully. First hints of small-scale or case studies [29] indicate that self-efficacy might be a starting point for interventions in the context of older adults and ICT.

Furthermore, in the ongoing project FUTA, we aim to explore factors facilitating and hindering the use of new technologies of older adults, for instance usability issues and the role of social support. In addition, our quantitative findings will be enriched and complemented with qualitative data generated in focus groups.

Acknowledgements. This ongoing research is supported by the German Federal Ministry of Education and Research (BMBF). For providing media data we thank TNS Deutschland GmbH, and the ARD-Werbung SALES & SERVICES GmbH. We thank the Association for Electrical, Electronic & Information Technologies (VDI/VDE) for valuable comments in earlier stages of the project FUTA.

References

1. Hepp, A., Krotz, F. (eds.): Mediatized Worlds: Culture and Society in a Media Age. Palgrave Macmillan, Basingstoke (2014)
2. Loos, E.F., Haddon, H., Mante-Meijer, E.A. (eds) The Social Dynamics of Information and Communication Technology. Ashgate, Aldershot

3. Loos, E.F., Haddon, L., Mante-Meijer, E.A. (eds.) Generational Use of New Media. Ashgate, Farnham

4. Baltes, P.B.: On the incomplete architecture of human ontogeny: selection, optimization, and compensation as foundation of developmental theory. In: Staudinger, U.M., Lindenberger, U. (eds.) Understanding Human Development. Dialogues with Lifespan Psychology (pp. 17–44). Kluwer Academic, Dordrecht (NL) (2003)

5. Lawton, M.P.: Future society and technology. In: Graafmans, J., Taipale, V., Charness, N. (eds.) Gerontechnology. A Sustainable Investment in the Future, pp. 12–22. IOS Press, Amsterdam (1998)

6. Claßen, K., Oswald, F., Doh, M., Kleinemas, U., Wahl, H.-W.: Umwelten des Alterns: Wohnen, Mobilität, Technik und Medien. (Environments of aging: housing, mobility, technology and media). Kohlhammer, Stuttgart (2014)

7. Schmidt, L.I., Wahl, H.-W., Plischke, H.: Older adults performance in technology-based tasks: cognitive ability and beyond. J. Gerontological Nurs. 40, 18–24 (2014)

8. Peacock, S.E., Künemund, H.: Senior citizens and internet technology: Reasons and correlates of access versus non-access in a European comparative perspective. Eur. J. Ageing 4, 191–200 (2007)

9. Doh, M.: Der ältere Mensch auf dem Weg zur Informationsgesellschaft – Entwicklungslinien, Potenziale und Barrieren am Beispiel von Internet und Mobiltelefon. (The older persons on his way to the information society - lines of development potentials and barriers on the example of the Internet and mobile phone). In: Plechaty, M., Plischke, H. (Hrsg.) Ältere Menschen und die Nutzung Neuer Medien (Older persons and the use of new media), pp. 38–76. Peter-Schilffarth-Edition, Bad Tölz (2011)

10. Claßen, K., Schmidt, L.I., Wahl, H.-W.: Technology and aging: potential for European societies. In: Phellas, C.N. (ed.) Aging in European Societies. Springer, New York (2012)

11. Bundesministerium für Familie, Senioren, Frauen und Jugend (BFSFJ) (eds.): Fünfter Bericht zur Lage der älteren Generation in der Bundesrepublik Deutschland. Potenziale des Alters in Wirtschaft und Gesellschaft. (Fifth Report on the situation of the older generation in the Federal Republic of Germany. Potentials of age in the economy and society), Berlin (BFSFJ) (2006)

12. Van Eimeren, B., Frees, B.: 79 Prozent der Deutschen online – Zuwachs bei mobiler Internetnutzung und Bewegtbild. Ergebnisse der ARD/ZDF-Onlinestudie 2014. (79 percent of the Germans are online – Increase in mobile Internet usage and moving pictures. Results of the ARD/ZDF-Online-Study 2014), Media Perspektiven, 7-8, 378–96 (2014)

13. European Commission (ed.).: Eurostat – your key to European statistics (2014). http://ec.europa.eu/eurostat/web/information-society/data/database

14. Rogers, E.M.: Diffusion of Innovations, 5th edn. The Free Press, New York (2003)

15. Czaja, S.J., Charness, N., Fisk, A.D., Hertzog, C., Nair, S.N., Rogers, W.A., Sharit, J.: Factors predicting the use of technology: findings from the center for research and education on aging and technology enhancement (CREATE). Psychol. Aging 21, 333–352 (2006)

16. Mitzner, T.L., Boron, J.B., Fausset, C.B., Adams, A.E., Charness, N., Czaja, S.J., Sharit, J.: Older adults talk technology: technology usage and attitudes. Comput. Hum. Behav. 26, 1710–1721 (2010)

17. Neyer, F.J., Felber, J., Gebhardt, C.: Entwicklung und Validierung einer Kurzskala zur Erfassung von Technikbereitschaft. (Development and validation of a brief measure of technology commitment). Diagnostica 58, 87–99 (2012)

18. Wagner, N., Hassanein, K., Head, M.: Computer use by older adults: a multidisciplinary review. Comput. Hum. Behav. 26, 870–882 (2010)

19. Bandura, A.: Self-Efficacy: The Exercise of Control. Freeman, New York (1997)

20. Arning, K., Ziefle, M.: Understanding differences in PDA acceptance and performance. Comput. Hum. Behav. **23**, 2904–2927 (2007)
21. Sun, S.: An examination of disposition, motivation, and involvement in the new technology context computers in human behavior. Comput. Hum. Behav. **24**, 2723–2740 (2008)
22. Erickson, J., Johnson, G.M.: Internet use and psychological wellness during late adulthood. Can. J. Aging **30**, 197–209 (2011)
23. Kaspar, R.: Technology and loneliness in old age. Gerontechnology **3**, 42–48 (2004)
24. Brandtstädter, J., Wentura, D., Schmitz, U.: Veränderungen der Zeit- und Zukunfts-perspektive im Übergang zum höheren Alter: Quer- und längsschnittliche Befunde (Changes in time and Future perspective in the transition to old age: cross-sectional and longitudinal findings). Zeitschrift für Psychologie mit Zeitschrift für angewandte Psychologie **205**, 377–395 (1997)
25. Schenk, M., Scheiko, L.: Meinungsführer als Innovatoren und Frühe Übernehmer des Web 2.0. (Opinion leaders as innovators and early adopters of Web 2.0), Media Perspektiven 9/2011, 423–431 (2011)
26. Eastin, M.S., LaRose, R.: Internet self-efficacy and the psychology of the digital divide. J. Comput. Mediated Commun. **6**, 1 (2000)
27. Schubert, C., Büser, T.: Medienhandeln als generationenspezifisches Phänomen (Media behavior as a generation-specific phenomenon). Medien Alter **5**, 83–89 (2014)
28. Usher, L.E., Pajares, F.: Sources of self-efficacy in school: critical review of the literature and future directions. Rev. Educ. Res. **78**, 751–796 (2008)
29. Xie, B.: Information technology education for older adults as a continuing Peer-learning process: a Chinese case study. Educational Gerontology **33**(5), 429–450 (2007)

Why Age Is Not that Important? An Ageing Perspective on Computer Anxiety

Mireia Fernández-Ardèvol[1]([⊠]) and Loredana Ivan[1,2]

[1] IN3, Open University of Catalonia, Av. Carl Friedrich Gauss,
5 - Parc Mediterrani de la Tecnologia, 08860 Castelldefels, Catalonia, Spain
mfernandezar@uoc.edu
[2] Communication Department, National School of Political Studies and Public
Administration (SNSPA), B-dul Expozitiei, 30A, 012104 Bucharest, Romania
loredana.ivan@comunicare.ro

Abstract. We analyze the influence of age on mobile computer anxiety in a sample of 158 individuals 55+ by means of path analysis modeling. Taking as the endogenous variable a mobile computer anxiety scale (MCAS, Wang 2007), models include demographic and socioeconomic variables and a computer experience scale – based on the familiarity and frequency of use of different information and communication technologies. Results confirm a positive influence of age on mobile computer anxiety which is mediated by both socio-economic variables and computer experience. The influence of age on mobile computer anxiety is comparatively low. Age is not the relevant dimension to explain computer anxiety, as socio-economic background and computer experience have higher explanatory capacity. This result may explain the inconsistent results regarding the direct relationship between age and computer anxiety available in the literature.

Keywords: Older people · Computer anxiety · Romania · Survey · Path analysis · MCMC bayesian estimation

1 Introduction

"Some people hesitate in using computers for fear of making mistakes. Some people think they may break the machines if they do not operate them correctly" [1, p. 4].

The pervasiveness of information and communication technologies (ICT) seems to bring the assumption that individuals are comfortable when using them. Therefore, research interests on ICT-related problems are currently looking into technology anxiety that appears when it is not possible for users to check in with ICT as often as the individual would like (social network sites – SNS, e-mail, voice mail, text messages or cell phone calls) and which can be related to Internet dependence [2]. But there are other users who struggle with computers and other (mobile) ICT. Rejection and negative experiences of ICT use are approached by looking at computer anxiety, as the negative emotional tendency of an individual towards using computers [3, 4]. Even though precise and consistent definitions are lacking [5], computer anxiety is often defined as an individual's fear or apprehension of working directly with a computer or the anticipation of having to work with computers [6, p. 2338]. A person may feel

© Springer International Publishing Switzerland 2015
J. Zhou and G. Salvendy (Eds.): ITAP 2015, Part I, LNCS 9193, pp. 189–200, 2015.
DOI: 10.1007/978-3-319-20892-3_19

intimidated, hostile, or worried about social embarrassment or just looking stupid in current or future use of computers, causing rejection or impacting performance. With the proliferation of mobile computers, authors (e.g. [7]) have begun discussing individual anxiety towards mobile computers, overcoming the limitations of traditional computer anxiety measures, which look at desktop computers or at wire-based Internet (see for example Computer Anxiety Rating Scale – CARS, [8]).

Nevertheless, ICT devices have become everyday tools for communication, a process that affects not only all spheres of life, for instance [9], but different generations [10] - among others, the younger elderly [11]. As (mobile) ICT are everyday tools, one may think they are well-appropriated devices which do not generate stress. However, available evidence shows that (mobile) computer anxiety is not a disappearing phenomenon. For instance, advanced users also face computer anxiety [4] and low self-efficacy [12]. Contrastingly, a common assumption is that older individuals would be among the most technology-averse [4] and experience higher computer anxiety.

In this paper we analyze the influence of age on mobile computer anxiety on a group of adults 55+ by taking into account both computer experience and socio-economic factors. Research studies on computer anxiety in the case of older people are limited [6], with [13–15] being exceptions. In addition, there are no studies on mobile computer anxiety that focus on the older segments of the population. For these reasons, this is relevant, timely research.

2   Analytical Framework

In what follows we develop the concepts that are the focus of our analysis: Firstly, (mobile) computer anxiety in relation to age; secondly, in relation to computer experience. The aim of our empirical approach is to analyze the determinants, or predictors, of mobile computer anxiety (see [6]). As mobile computer anxiety is a concept evolved from the discussions around computer anxiety, and given the current proliferation of mobile computers [7], in the subsequent sections we refer to the main concept - computer anxiety - and its correlates, with an emphasis on contextual factors.

2.1   (Mobile) Computer Anxiety and Socio-Economic Background

Computer anxiety is more commonly associated with older, less educated adults who tend to be reluctant to technology in general. Still the evidence of age predicting computer anxiety is inconsistent [16]. By means of a narrative analysis of the academic literature on older people and new communication technologies Richardson et al. [17] argue that computer anxiety reinforces the discourse that considers computers as potential dividers that marginalize seniors, as the literature sees it as a barrier to computer use. Kim [18] also develops a critical review on older people and computer learning and use: Even though older adults are found to be less confident in their computer knowledge than younger adults, for instance [19], it is not age that is the explanatory variable of these difference, but the fact that older adults have less opportunities to use computers. The way a person approaches computer mediated communication, at any life stage, is not necessarily determined by age but by a large number of socio-economic factors, such as status, income and education, that create different opportunities for individuals [20].

Still, we find a limited number of papers analyzing the relationship between computer anxiety and the social context of individuals. Bozionelos [12], for example, conducted empirical research that analyzes the mechanism to explain the relationship between socio-economic background and computer use, which considers two intervening variables, computer anxiety and computer experience. He concluded that "individuals from more privileged socio-economic backgrounds are expected to demonstrate lower computer anxiety than their less socio-economically privileged counterparts" [12] p. 727. The author claims that this is the first paper connecting socio-economic background with computer anxiety. An extensive meta-analysis of the research on computer anxiety comparing the literature in the 1990 s and in the 2000 s confirms the lack of interest in this area [6]. The author identified 269 empirical articles and analyzed the issues that accounted for at least 10 hits in the corpus. She distinguished computer anxiety antecedents, correlates and outcomes. First, antecedents include personal characteristics (gender, age, other anxieties, education, personality and profession) and human-computer interaction dimensions (experience/use, training and ownership). Second, correlates correspond to self-efficacy, attitude, and perceived ease of use, usefulness and satisfaction. Finally, outcomes refer to performance and intent of use. None of these categories refer to the socio-economic background (SES) with regards to computer anxiety. In the current research, we argue that the inconsistent results regarding the relationship between age and computer anxiety can be explained by the assumed direct relation between the two concepts and the undervalued role of socio-economic variables (SES) that could play a moderating role.

With this approach, we formulate

Hypothesis 1: *The relation between age and mobile computer anxiety, for older individuals, is mediated by socio-economic variables (SES): work status, level of education, and household income.*

2.2 Computer Experience and Age

Particularly in the case of older people, experience in using computers plays an important role in individuals' attitudes towards computers [15]. Chien [1], for example, highlights lower levels of computer experience among older adults, compared to younger adults. In addition, Kim [18] explains that younger adults' computer experience may cause them higher confidence levels on their abilities to handle computers, a self-efficacy feeling that would impact their willingness to use a particular technology. Yet, social aspects should be considered to understand computer experience. Particularly, knowledge acquisition might be shaped by social dynamics, as suggested by the technology appropriation [21] and technology domestication [22] frameworks. Social dynamics, conversely, would also shape computer experience and willingness to use ICT devices.

Although most studies [23–25] found that prior experience in using the computer is associated with lower computer anxiety, some research studies (e.g. [26]) found an opposite relation between the two variables: when working with computers increases, people can become more anxious or develop negative attitudes towards computer. Certainly the way we operationalize "experience in using computers" could have some influence on the type of results we get when analyzing the impact on computer anxiety. We have noticed that most of the cross-sectional research recorded time length of computer use or self-reported measures of familiarity with different types of applications – see also [27]. Still a consistent relationship between computer experience and computer anxiety seems to be recorded in studies when experience has been operationalized as frequency of use [25, 28]. In this paper we consider the role of computer experience in mediating the relationship between age and computer anxiety. We measure computer experience by a composite measurement of self-reported measures of familiarity and frequency of use.

With this approach, we formulate

Hypothesis 2: The relation between age and mobile computer anxiety, for older individuals, is mediated by computer experience.

Hypothesis 3: The relation between age and computer experience, for older individuals, is mediated by socio-economic variables (SES): work status, level of education, and household income.

3 Method

In what follows we describe, first, the process of data collection and the sample characteristics; and second, the building of the two constructs that are part of the path analysis models.

3.1 Data Collection and Sample Characteristics

We employed a face to face questionnaire among a convenience sample (N = 158) of people 55+ living in urban and rural areas in Romania. Students enrolled in a Research Methods course voluntarily subscribed to be field operators and obtained informal consent from the participants. The second author designed and supervised the collection of data. With ages ranging from 55 to 84 years, we targeted two subgroups of participants, 55 to 64 years of age (n = 91) – most probably active on the labor market, and 65 years and above (n = 67) – at retirement age. The questionnaire included questions about the familiarity and frequency of use of different technology devices, the purposes of using specific technologies (work related/spare time activities), mobile computer use and access to internet, computer anxiety and socio-demographic characteristics: gender, residence (rural/urban), level of education, income and marital status.

With an average age of 63.9 years (SD = 7.5), there were more women (66.5 %) than men (33.5 %) among respondents (see Table 2 in the Appendix). Most respondents reported secondary level of education (49.5 %), with 28.4 % of the participants having primary level of education (8 years of school or less) and 21.5 % graduated from college. The structure of the sample on education level is consistent with the educational structure for people in Romania having 55 years of age and above [29]. Regarding the working status, most of our respondents were retired with pensions (68.4 %), whereas 26 % were full time or part time employees. Compared to the structure of the Romanian population aged 55+, our sample is overrepresented by urban areas (76 %), reproducing the socio-demographic characteristics of older people living in large urban communities.

3.2 Constructs

Computer Anxiety Measurement. Computer anxiety was assessed by Wang's [7] *Mobile Computer Anxiety Scale* (MCAS). Participants answer using a 7 point scale, from 1 - not anxious at all - to 7 - very anxious, about how they would feel when a series of mobile computer interactions would happen in the following days. MCAS comprises 38 items divided on seven subscales: (1) anxiety about *learning* activities (i.e. "taking a class about the use of mobile computer"; identified as FL in what follows); (2) anxiety about *internet use* (i.e. "browsing web pages using a mobile computer"; FI); (3) anxiety about *the equipment limitation* (i.e. "using a mobile computer with a limited memory"; FE); (4) anxiety about *job replacement* (i.e. "mobile computers would replace someone's job"; FJ); (5) anxiety about computer use (i.e. "working on mobile computer"; FU); (6) anxiety about *computer configuration* (i.e. "disassembling hardware components, such as memory card, battery"; FC); and (7) anxiety about *Internet stability* (i.e. "using a mobile computer in the context of less stable wireless network"; FS). A Romanian back-translated version of MCAS (38 items instrument) was used in the current research study. The overall internal consistency was high (Cronbach's $\alpha = .97$) and reliability was good for all seven components (Cronbach's α ranging from .81 to .96). We conducted a CPA (Component Principal Analysis) for each subscale, all of them loading a unique factor with eigenvalue over 1 that explained between 62 % and 84 % of the corresponding dependent variance.

Computer Experience Measurement. We assess participants' experience with information and communication technologies using an *ICT experience index* that comprises: (a) familiarity with ICT - measured by the years of using a given communication technology; and (b) frequency of use, measured by the number of hours spent in using the device. We conducted a CPA with the 12 variables that gathered this information, obtaining 5 factors that explained 86.2 % of the variance. While this construct could be improved (for instance, by adding information on the kind of use of the device) it proved to have an acceptable internal consistency in the context of the current research (Cronbach's $\alpha = .79$) and the reduction of the dimension was appropriate.

First factor, ICT1, gathered information of experience in using smart phones and other mobile devices that go online; second, ICT2, experience with laptops; Third,

ICT3, experience with desktop computers and Internet ownership at home; fourth, ICT4, experience with tablet pc; and fifth, ICT5, experience with mobile phones. These factors will serve as observed indicators of the construct 'ICT experience' in the model.

4 Results

We analyzed the relationship age has with MCAS and ICT experience. On the one hand, age positively correlates with six of the seven factors that summarize the MCAS subscales. In the case of not significant correlation (Internet stability or FS) the parameter is also positive.[1] On the other hand, age shows a negative relationship with the factors that summarize ICT experience.[2] We question whether this relationship is mediated by individual characteristics and computer experience; thus we took a path analysis approach. Model specification followed the literature review. Figure 1 gathers the main characteristics of the initial model (Model 1) after adjusting its specification. Particularly, the model includes direct effects from Age to ICT experience and to MCAS. The illustration does not include covariances or error terms while for dichotomous variables the category under analysis is depicted. For statistical methodology aspects we follow [30–32].

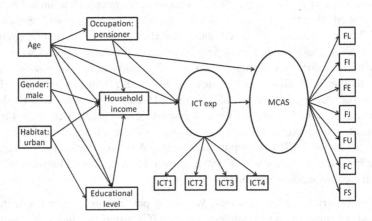

Fig. 1 Model 1, specification.

We distinguish between observed and unobserved variables. Among the observed variables in the model (see Table 2, Appendix) there are three exogenous variables of the model (Age, Sex and Habitat: urban); and three intermediate variables (Occupation: pensioner, Household income in the last month, and Educational level). The model

---

[1] Pearson's correlation with Age: FL, .369*; FI, .363*; FE, 0.178**; FJ, .257*; FU, .253*; FC, .242*; and FS, .088 (* significant at least at 99% level, ** significant at 95%).

[2] Pearson's correlation with Age: ICT_1, −.223*; ICT_2, −.321*; ICT_3, −.334*; ICT_4, .010; ICT_5, −.212* (* significant at least at 99% level, ** significant at 95%).

includes two unobserved variables: ICT experience and MCAS. The observed indi-cators of the ICT experience construct are all the obtained PCA factors except one.[3] The observed indicators of MCAS are the unique PCA factors obtained for each of the 7 subscales.

We conducted Markov Chain Monte Carlo (MCMC) Bayesian estimations because the model includes qualitative variables as intermediate variables. In MCMC Bayesian estimations, goodness of fit is assessed by means of two elements: First, CS or con-vergence statistic – which must take a value of 1.002 or lower in all the estimated parameters of the model; second, the posterior predictive p-value (PPP) – which must reach a value around .50. Model 1 did not achieve convergence. Even though PPP equaled .50, we discarded Model 1 for not meeting the goodness of fit criteria.

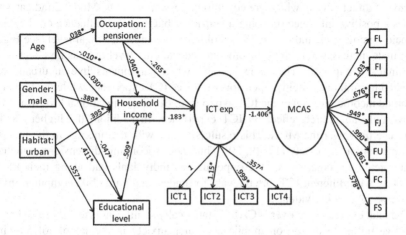

Fig. 2 Model 2, specification and estimated parameters

Model 2 includes a direct path connecting Age and ICT experience but no path connecting Age and MCAS. It converged in less than 500,000 iterations and PPP equaled to .50, thus goodness of fit is acceptable. As shown in Fig. 2, all the regression weights have the expected sign. While most parameters are significant at a 95 % level, the direct path from Age to ICT experience is significant at a 90 % level. There is one non-significant parameter, but we decided to keep it because it is one indicator of ICT experience (ICT4) and its deletion did not impact other elements of the model.

Total effects are the addition of direct effects - represented by arrows directly connecting two variables - and indirect effects - represented by arrows connecting two variables through other variables. Table 1 shows that total effects keep the same sign as direct effects in all cases.

---

[3] We arbitrarily excluded the last one, as PCA returns orthogonal factors.

Table 1. Total effects over intermediate and endogenous variables. Model 2

	Age	Habitat: urban	Gender: man	Occupation: pensioner	Household income	Educational level	ICT exp
Pensioner	.038[a]	0	0	0	0	0	0
Income	−.069[a]	.679[a]	.598[a]	−.400[b]	0	.509[a]	0
Education	−0.47[a]	.557[a]	.411[a]	0	0	0	0
ICTexp	−.033[a]	.124[a]	.109[a]	−.338[a]	.183[a]	.093[a]	0
MCAS	.044[a]	−.167[a]	−.147[a]	.450[a]	−.246[a]	−.125[a]	−1.406[a]

Total effects of variables in columns over those in rows. Significance level: [a]95%; [b]90%.

5   Discussion and Conclusion

In terms of direct effects, which are equal to regression weights, Model 2 indicates that age has a positive influence on being a pensioner but negative influence on the rest of the socio-demographic indicators: household income and educational level (see Fig. 2). Being male increases household income and educational level but has no effect on the individual's occupation. The same is valid when participants live in urban areas, compared to rural ones. Being a pensioner reduces ICT experience while the higher the household income, the higher the ICT experience; Besides, educational level was found to have only an indirect effect on ICT experience. In addition, the higher the ICT experience the lower the MCA. This result is in line with the findings in the literature regarding computer anxiety [12, 19, 20]. Thus, socio-economic dimensions, which can be interpreted as indicators of the opportunities individuals had along their life for interacting with different ICT, are relevant for understanding mobile computer anxiety in the case of 55+ individuals.

The total effect of Age over MCAS is statistically significant (see Table 1), showing a positive influence of age on mobile computer anxiety in the sample of 55+ individuals under study. Yet, this influence is not direct, as the goodness of fit of Model 1 was not acceptable. Variables acting as intermediaries are occupational status, pensioner; household income; educational level; and ICT experience. The magnitude of the total effect of Age over MCAS is the smallest one in the model (.044). Similarly, it is neither the most important factor explaining ICT experience, as Age total effect (.033) is the lowest one. These results reinforce the idea that age should not be considered the main explanatory variable of mobile computer anxiety.

In fact, the individual characteristic with the greatest impact on MCAS is occupational status, pensioner (total effect = .450), followed by household income (−.246). In addition, being a pensioner increases mobile computer anxiety, while higher household incomes reduce it. The role of ICT experience is key to explain this relationship, as these are precisely the two variables with higher total effects on ICT experience (−.338 and .183 respectively).

Therefore, the three hypotheses are accepted.

Hypothesis 1. The relation between age and *mobile* computer anxiety, among older individuals, is mediated by socio-economic variables (SES): work status, level of education, and household income.

Hypothesis 2. The relation between age and *mobile* computer anxiety, among older individuals, is mediated by computer experience.

We confirmed the mediated relationship of SES and computer experience. Particularly, we found a positive influence of age on mobile computer anxiety but it was the predictor with the lowest explanatory capacity.

Hypothesis 3. The relation between age and computer experience, for older individuals, is mediated by socio-economic variables (SES): work status, level of education, and household income.

We found a negative relationship between age and computer experience. In this case it was partly direct and partly indirect, showing that socio-economic background could better explain this relationship than age. This evidence supports the idea that inconsistent results regarding the relationship between age and computer anxiety can be explained by the assumed direct relation between the two concepts and the undervalued role of socio-economic variables (SES) that could play a moderating role.

Yet, the empirical analysis could be improved by incorporating other variables that go beyond the narrow scenario in which computer experience is the only aspect that directly impacts mobile computer anxiety. Aspects related to learning processes or to perceived computer self-efficacy would be relevant. In addition, a comparison between the mobile computer anxiety scale [7] we use here and more traditional computer anxiety scales (as [33]) would bring nuances of the specific characteristics of the fast-evolving landscape of mobile ICT devices. Finally, it would be of most interest to validate the hypotheses from a broader perspective, to replicate the study in other countries, as cultural differences might play a role.

All in all, our empirical analysis individuals 55+ living in Romania validates that the influence of age on mobile computer anxiety happens through two different intermediate channels. One corresponds to social and economic personal context, and the other corresponds to familiarity and frequency of ICT use. The influence of age is positive but comparatively low. Other factors, as socio-economic background, have higher explanatory capacity. Our analysis also confirms that the influence of age on computer experience is mediated by socio-economic variables and, again, is the predictor with the lower influence on computer experience in the sample under study. We can conclude that while age could be used as a proxy of other individual characteristics in the study of the relationship of (older) individuals with ICT, it should not be considered the main explanatory variable. That is, age is not that important for explaining mobile computer anxiety.

Appendix: Characteristics of the Sample

Table 2. Characteristics of the sample (N = 158)

Age			Education	
	Mean	63.91	Primary school (4 classes) (4 years)	10.2%
	St. Dev.	7.51		
	Median	63,5	Secondary School (8 years)	18.5%
	Min - Max.	55 - 84		
	N	158	High school/ professional high school	49.7%
Gender				
	Female	66.5%	Faculty/master/PhD	21.7%
	Male	33.5%	N	157
	N	158		
Habitat			**Household monthly income**	
	Urban	75.9%	Up to 700 lei	10.8%
	Rural	24.1%	701 - 1500 lei	37.3%
	N	158	1501 - 2500 lei	27.8%
Occupation			2501-3500 lei	11.4%
	Pensioner	68.4%	3501 - 4500 lei	3.8%
	Other	31.6%	More than 4500 lei	7.0%
	N	157	N	155

References

1. Chien, T.-C.: Factors influencing computer anxiety and its impact on E-Learning effectiveness: a review of literature. Presented at the Academy of Human Resource Development International Research Conference in the Americas (Panama City, FL, Feb 20–24, 2008), 20 February 2008
2. Rosen, L.D., Whaling, K., Carrier, L.M., Cheever, N.A., Rokkum, J.: The media and technology usage and attitudes scale: an empirical investigation. Comput. Hum. Behav. **29**, 2501–2511 (2013)
3. O'Driscoll, M.P., Brough, P., Timms, C., Sawang, S.: Engagement with information and communication technology and psychological well-being. Res. Occup. Stress Well-being **8**, 269–316 (2010)
4. Beckers, J.J., Schmidt, H.G., Wicherts, J.: Computer anxiety in daily life: old history? In: Loos, E., Mante-Meijer, E., Haddon, L. (eds.) The Social Dynamics of Information and Communication Technology, pp. 13–23. Ashgate, Aldershot (2008)
5. Kay, R.H., Loverock, S.: Assessing emotions related to learning new software: The computer emotion scale. Comput. Hum. Behav. **24**, 1605–1623 (2008)
6. Powell, A.L.: Computer anxiety: Comparison of research from the 1990 s and 2000s. Comput. Hum. Behav. **29**, 2337–2381 (2013)
7. Wang, Y.-S.: Development and validation of a mobile computer anxiety scale. Brit. J. Educ. Technol. **38**, 990–1009 (2007)

8. Heinssen Jr., R.K., Glass, C.R., Knight, L.A.: Assessing computer anxiety: development and validation of the computer anxiety rating scale. Comput. Hum. Behav. **3**, 49–59 (1987)
9. Loos, E., Mante-Meijer, E., Haddon, L. (eds.): The Social Dynamics of Information and Communication Technology. Ashgate, Aldershot (2008)
10. Loos, E., Haddon, L., Mante-Meijer, E. (eds.): Generational Use of New Media. Ashgate, Farnham (2012)
11. Haddon, L., Silverstone, R.: University of Sussex., Centre for Information and Communication Technologies., University of Sussex., science policy research unit.: Information and communication technologies and the young elderly: a report of the ESRC/PICT study of the household and information and communication technologies. Science Policy Research Unit, University of Sussex, Brighton (1996)
12. Bozionelos, N.: Socio-economic background and computer use: the role of computer anxiety and computer experience in their relationship. Int. J. Hum.-Comput. Stud. **61**, 725–746 (2004)
13. Dyck, J.L., Smither, J.A.-A.: Older adults' acquisition of word processing: the contribution of cognitive abilities and computer anxiety. Comput. Hum. Behav. **12**, 107–119 (1996)
14. Laguna, K., Babcock, R.L.: Computer anxiety in young and older adults: Implications for human-computer interactions in older populations. Comput. Hum. Behav. **13**, 317–326 (1997)
15. Wild, K.V., Mattek, N.C., Maxwell, S.A., Dodge, H.H., Jimison, H.B., Kaye, J.A.: Computer-related self-efficacy and anxiety in older adults with and without mild cognitive impairment. Alzheimer's Dementia **8**, 544–552 (2012)
16. Fuller, R.M., Vician, C., Brown, S.A.: E-learning and individual characteristics: the role of computer anxiety and communication apprehension. J. Comput. Inf. Syst. **46**, 103–115 (2006)
17. Richardson, M., Zorn, T.E., Weaver, C.K.: Older people and new communication technologies. Narratives from the literature. In: Salmon, C.T. (ed.) Communication Yearbook 35, pp. 121–154. Taylor and Francis, London (2011)
18. Kim, Y.S.: Reviewing and critiquing computer learning and usage among older adults. Educ. Gerontol. **34**, 709–735 (2008)
19. Marquié, J.C., Jourdan-Boddaert, L., Huet, N.: Do older adults underestimate their actual computer knowledge? Behav. Inf. Technol. **21**, 273–280 (2002)
20. Bennett, J.: Online communities and the activation, motivation and integration of persons aged 60 and older. A literature review. Version 1.1 (2011)
21. Oudshoorn, N., Pinch, T.J. (eds.): How Users Matter: The Co-construction of Users and Technologies. The MIT Press, Cambridge (Mass.) (2003)
22. Silverstone, R., Hirsch, E. (eds.): Consuming Technologies, Media and Information in Domestic Spaces. Routledge, London (1992)
23. Chang, S.E.: Computer anxiety and perception of task complexity in learning programming-related skills. Comput. Hum. Behav. **21**, 713–728 (2005)
24. Fagan, M., Neill, S., Wooldridge, B.: An empirical investigation into the relationship between computer self-efficacy, anxiety, experience, support and usage. J. Comput. Inf. Syst. **44**, 95–104 (2003)
25. Tekinarslan, E.: Computer anxiety: a cross-cultural comparative study of Dutch and Turkish university students. Comput. Hum. Behav. **24**, 1572–1584 (2008)
26. King, J., Bond, T., Blandford, S.: An investigation of computer anxiety by gender and grade. Comput. Hum. Behav. **18**, 69–84 (2002)
27. Bozionelos, N.: Computer anxiety: relationship with computer experience and prevalence. Comput. Hum. Behav. **17**, 213–224 (2001)

28. Chua, S.L., Chen, D.-T., Wong, A.F.L.: Computer anxiety and its correlates: a meta-analysis. Comput. Hum. Behav. **15**, 609–623 (1999)
29. Institutul National de Statistica: Romania in Cifre 2012. Sinteze (2012). http://www.insse.ro/cms/files/publicatii/Romania%20in%20cifre_%202012.pdf
30. Bollen, K.A.: Structural Equation Models with Latent Variables. Wiley-Interscience, New York (1989)
31. Kline, R.B.: Principles and Practice of Structural Equation Modeling. Guilford Press, New York (2005)
32. Lee, S.-Y.: Structural Equation Modeling: A Bayesian Approach. Wiley, Chichester (2007)
33. Marcoulides, G.A.: Measuring computer anxiety: the computer anxiety scale. Educ. Psychol. Measur. **49**, 733–739 (1989)

Values and Ethics in Making Emerging Technologies Work for Older People

Caroline Holland[(⊠)]

The Open University, Milton Keynes, UK
caroline.holland@open.ac.uk

Abstract. Since the early 20th century, population ageing and technological developments have developed apace. Many social changes took place, including the development of digital technologies and the ageing of populations worldwide. The purpose of this paper is to explore the implications of these two phenomena and to think about how certain values and may be drawn upon to help make technologies work better for older people as both technology markets and world-wide demographic profiles continue to evolve.

Keyword: Ageing Technology Values Ethics

1 Introduction

The twentieth century saw many highly significant and accelerating social changes, of which just two were the development of digital technologies [1, 2], and the ageing of populations worldwide [3]. The purpose of this paper is to explore the implications of these two phenomena when considered together, and to think about how certain kinds of values and ethics may be drawn upon to help make technologies work better for older people as both technology markets and worldwide demographic profiles continue to evolve. 'Values' are those personal (or collective, within a group) principles or judgments about what is important in life, contributing to approved standards of behavior: so for example in balancing freedom of speech against offending religious sensibilities, different people may value one more highly than the other. 'Ethics' describes a more codified and systematized description of concepts of right and wrong conduct: so for example most professions identify ethical standards required of their members in particular circumstances. The paper draws specifically on the Capabilities Approach, as conceptualized and developed by Amartya Sen [4, 5] and Martha Nussbaum [6, 7] which focuses on individuals' capability of achieving the kind of life they value.

© Springer International Publishing Switzerland 2015
J. Zhou and G. Salvendy (Eds.): ITAP 2015, Part I, LNCS 9193, pp. 201–209, 2015.
DOI: 10.1007/978-3-319-20892-3_20

2   Global Ageing

Global Age Watch data [8] shows that by the early 2010s it was already the case that marginally more older people lived in developing[1] countries compared to developed ones, and it is projected that by 2050 over three-quarters of older people worldwide will live in those countries that are currently regarded as developing. At the same time number of countries where the relative proportion of older people is expected to exceed 30 % will expand, especially in the northern hemisphere, to include most developed countries. So, by that point, numerically most older people will live in the developing countries, but with higher densities of older people in developed ones. Hence globally, the technology landscape of ageing ranges from the very rural and remote to the very dense and urban, and from areas of great wealth through to those of deprivation. This global ageing is itself taking place within the wider global context of interconnected changes. The concept of globalization, originally used in economics, is now often used to describe other aspects of global interaction including issues relating to the environment, culture, media, and technologies. In an interconnected world, and one where corporate power and influence can equal or indeed exceed that of nation states, is it possible for an ethical approach based on shared values be brought to bear on the development and use of technologies where older people, by design or not, are potential end users?

3   Values and Ethics in ICT Development

ICT for ageing is a field in which much has already been written about older people's use of technologies, often either to understand their attitudes to using/not using technologies, and in particular to explore the efficacy of specific of assistive technologies in the growing telehealth and telecare markets. In contrast relatively little attention has been paid to the fundamental values that underpin the whole ICT ecology, and the nature and location of the decision-making that embeds specific values within technological environments that we all share. Tim Berners Lee [9] acknowledged that the world wide web represented humanity connected, involving both the "wonderful" and the "ghastly". He commented that it is now time for big communal decisions: "In front of us are two roads - which way are we going to go? ... Are we going to continue on the road and just allow the governments to do more and more and more control - more and more surveillance? Or are we going to set up a bunch of values? Are we going to set up something like a Magna Carta for the world wide web and say, actually, now it's so important, so much part of our lives, that it becomes on a level with human rights?" This begs the question as to which values can and should and could be incorporated into such an agreement, as well as how those values would then be accounted for in professional ethical frameworks.

---

[1] Both the concept and the definition of 'developing' countries are contested, but for the purposes of economic differentiation and development aid a (varying) number of nations are so identified. GDP per capita compared to other nations is a key indicator.

Much of the thinking behind this paper stems from Value Ageing [10], a Marie Curie *Industry-Academia Partnerships and Pathways Action* (2010–2014) with nine European partners from a range of sectors and disciplines: the Centre for Science Society and Citizenship (CSSC) in Rome; The Austrian Academy of sciences, Institute for technology assessment; Technalia, Spain; the Free University of Brussels; Frontida Zois Ltd, Greece; INNOVA SPA, Italy; the Netwell Centre, Ireland; Queen's University Belfast, UK and Vegan Solutions SRL, Italy. The goal was to foster co-operation between noncommercial and commercial organizations on a joint research project aimed at examining, through policy documents and examples of practice, the Fundamental Values of the European Union in Info-Communication Technology (ICT) for Ageing were evident. These EU values are set out in Articles 1–2 of the union, and are a requirement for membership [11]. They are based on concepts of respect for human dignity, liberty, democracy, equality, the rule of law and respect for human rights, including the rights of persons belonging to minorities. Societies of the Member States are to be characterized by pluralism, non-discrimination, tolerance, justice, solidarity and equality between women and men. Hence for the purposes of the Value Ageing analysis, the concepts of non-discrimination, dignity and inclusion are described as values.

Value Ageing also looked at statements of Corporate Social Responsibility within ICT companies in Europe and found that they rarely paid much attention to ageing. Of those that did, several were working with health monitoring technologies rather than social, gaming or more general use technologies. Many companies recognize the strategic importance of universal design solutions, and increasingly, the need to involve end-users in the design process, but the notion that older people are conservative, brand-loyal consumers reluctant to get involved with cutting-edge technology has affected corporate decision-making.

3.1 Non-discrimination

Age has its own salience, reflected both in bodily change (physical and mental) and in social position, but nobody is just old. Other factors, for example gender and sexuality, wealth, education and culture have an impact on how a person experiences both ageing and technologies. The impact of individual's life experiences and their lifetime exposure to technologies do affect (thought they do not entirely define) how, in later life, individuals respond to new technologies. This leads to the first of our 'bunch of values' when it comes to ageing: no discrimination on the grounds of age. Value Ageing suggests that ICT developments can produce conditions that risk discrimination for older people, but they can also provide solutions to those risks: 'it is generally not ICT developments per se that threaten dignity and inclusion, but the ways that specific ICTs and services are conceived, designed, promoted, introduced, used, supported, and monitored' [12]. Crucially, this includes simultaneously taking on board that there are age-related conditions, such as compromised hearing or visual impairments, that must be considered: and that older people are not all the same with respect to any of those conditions.

3.2 Dignity

This leads to consideration of another fundamental value: dignity. The Value Ageing definition of dignity built upon Nora Jacobson's notion of dignity encounters, i.e. the value that belongs to every human being simply by virtue of being human. [13]. She argues that the actors, the setting, and the wider social/political context where encounters take place can all either promote or violate dignity. Value Ageing researchers used this notion of dignity encounters as one of the ways to understand the impact of uses of technologies with older people. Risks of indignity arise when people's different needs are ignored ('batch treatment') and when older people are not in control or in a position to make informed choices. Issues of the affordability of technologies, and local access and cultural practices are highly significant - especially when thinking about the range of places where older people live.

One of the key mechanisms for preventing discrimination and dignity violations is the inclusion of older people is the development process for new technologies, from concept to marketing. For many of those commentating on the Value Ageing findings, the direct participation of older people in design was essential to impart age-friendly/all-age-friendly values. The main caveat here was the position of people living with middle and late stage dementia without the cognitive capacity to participate directly. Here commentators talked about the role of relationships: *'In dementia, concepts of autonomy, choice and participation don't necessarily apply the same way and become less useful – the route to dignity is in relationships and behavior'* [14]. In this approach, it is how ICTs are used and the awareness of others of the ethical issues involved in the use of technologies with people with dementia that matters: *'dignity requires a step-by-step approach that can take on board everyone's viewpoint'* [14].

3.3 Inclusion

This brings us to the next value: inclusion – where the corollary is exclusion. Older people are relatively at risk of social exclusion for a number of reasons. While old age does not of itself cause loneliness or social isolation, there is an important relationship between the two, not least because reduced income and mobility can reduce opportunities for social interactions. Phillipson and Scharf [15] pointed to some other key causes including the cumulative effects of disadvantage across the life course; the effects of age discrimination; the vulnerability of older people as a group to local changes such as population turnover or general economic decline; and particular age-related characteristics such as disability and widowhood. Older people in any case tend to spend more time alone in the home or immediate home environment compared to younger adults: and those who live alone are more vulnerable to exclusion from civic and cultural activities. Technologies and ICTs in particular have the potential for a huge beneficial impact on the loneliness that can often accompany old age. Digital communication has the power to ameliorate physical problems of mobility or face-to-face communication and allow older people to remain engaged socially and with the life of the city. One obvious social space where people might go when physical space gets difficult is the social media. Older people have initially been slower to get engaged in numbers in social platforms but the popularity, where they can be accessed, of touch screen tablets (by-passing PCs) and visual communications with family are groundbreaking for both online and physical inclusion of older people [16].

4   Capabilities

As one of the mechanisms for exploring values in ICT, Value Ageing used the idea of Capabilities, a human rights-based concept developed by the philosopher Amataya Sen [17] and subsequently developed by others including Martha Nussbaum [18]. Sen stated that the importance of 'real' freedoms, meaning that for each person the ability to transform available resources into activities of value to them personally was an individual process. Nussbaum elaborated on this concept to describe ten categories of personal and social circumstances that she argued were fundamental to democracies. Value Ageing considered that technologies have the potential to enhance people's lives across most of her categories, stating that:

> 'However a consequence of the Information Society is that for full engagement in almost all aspects of contemporary life in Europe (and increasingly, world-wide) ICTs are an essential component of how people can control their environments. For this reason we suggest that to Nussbaum's tenth category, 'Control over one's environment' should be added (C) Technological: Being able to access, on an equal basis, the essential technologies of civic and social engagement and personal support' [19].

According to Value Ageing, ICTs can support older people's independence and safety, including the physical, cognitive, emotional, social and cultural aspects of their daily lives. They can support social inclusion by opening up avenues to physical and online communities, support dignity, and encourage self-fulfillment by allowing older people to continue longer with chosen activities. But they also have the potential to damage well being if used inappropriately: or if not used - for example on the grounds of age - when they could be of benefit. The work of Value Ageing included examples of good practice where efforts had been made to produce beneficial dignity encounters between older people and technologies, and to support their capabilities. One of the characteristics of these examples was that thought had been given to ageing as an issue, for example through co-design and the involvement of older people at pilot stages of development. Another was that when it came to introducing a technology to individuals, assumptions were not made about their needs and receptiveness. However

5   Emerging Technologies

However the general principles of this kind of rights-based approach to values and ethics requires further consideration for emergent technologies. Any consideration of how in recent years high-tech companies have chosen to absorb emergent ones indicates a lot about where the locus of decision-making lies. Whereas companies that became large and affluent might have started out with one idea for a technological innovation, the drive in most cases has been for large corporates to expand into the future by bringing in and integrating, developing, or in some cases sitting on emerging and early stage concepts. It could be argued that this is just business, but in the case of technologies that can impact profoundly on the personal lives of older people, Berners Lees' call for a values in the world wide web applies equally here because ICTs have the potential to support people as they age, including supporting independence and perhaps more importantly, social connectedness. They can also be harmful if used inappropriately, but perhaps the lager risk at present is that of potentially beneficial technologies bypassing older people because of faulty assumptions about their needs and preferences. Three examples of emergent technologies illustrate this argument for integrating values and ethics in development - implants, robotics, and big data.

5.1 Implants

The idea of having foreign objects inserted into the body is not immediately appealing to most people but tooth implants, piercings for jewelry, and contact lenses, all demonstrate that in context such practices can become accepted and commonplace. Implants for the medical mitigation of physical deficit or injuries are also familiar: for example fully implantable pacemakers have been around since 1958 and are becoming increasingly fine-tunable. Brain-Computer Interaction research and development has tended to be focused primarily on neuroprosthetics applications aimed at restoring damaged hearing, sight and movement, with the first neuroprosthetic devices implanted in humans in the mid-1990s. As the group most at risk from these conditions, older people need to be involved in these developments. The medical implications of most of these procedures means that legitimate practitioners will be bound by professional ethical standards, but it is important that values also come in to play because values may drive or influence decisions about the direction or pace of developments, or indeed attitudes to who 'deserves' or 'can benefit from' such interventions.

5.2 Robotics

Despite the industrial application of most current robots, the popular picture of a robot is of a humanoid assistant. In the case of older people, suggested uses for robotics have included companionship, service, and lifting and handling [20]. Following the 2011 earthquake and tsunami in Japan, recognition was given of the usefulness of some older survivors of the Paro baby seal robot for emotional comfort [21]. At another scale, exoskeletons, emerging from military, industrial, and rehabilitation research, can harness the motions of the human body and the intentionality of the human brain within an engineered framework to enhance power, reach and durability, or they could supplement or replace human assistants. Developments like these might also become the new mobility scooter, able to go up and down stairs like an advanced Darlek. In spite of a relative lack of convincing empirical studies, age-related uses of robotics is on the radar of developers. Middle aged and older people need to be more involved in discussions about future prospects, and consulted about their effectiveness and acceptability in everyday life to ensure their inclusion among the beneficiaries of developments in robotics.

A further aspect of the relationship between robotics and ageing was exemplified by work from Accenture showing the correlation between the incidence of industrial robots, aging populations, and GDP per capita. Hence Japan and Germany have been leading in this area, with younger, poorer economies such as the Philippines, South Africa, India, Malaysia lagging behind. The Accenture argument is that moving to low-wage economies for manufacturing is no longer the only or best way to control costs in labour-intensive manufacture and indeed automation and robotics technologies have been quietly developing in capability and affordability. They showed that countries with ageing populations have also been the most active in adopting technology (measured as robotics), as well as maintaining high GDP per capita levels, to stay competitive: 'Indeed, countries like Germany, Japan and South Korea excel in quality automotive manufacturing, the benchmark of industrial production' [22] – this is an example of population ageing interacting with commerce in a context that is not directly about older people as consumers.

5.3   Big Data

Technologically what has counted as big data has changed along with computing capacities: for non-technologists it is generally regarded as data produced at a volume which humans cannot process. This means that most people must rely on experts to interpret data being generated at volume. At this scale the idea of dignity vested in consent becomes ill-fitting: for example it is not possible to opt out of outdoor surveillance by municipal or private CCTV cameras.

The relative recentness of issues of big data means that, as with the general population, older people are often unaware of the implications for them personally of the handling of their personal data. Uses such as health informatics; ICTs in public places – for example through public information installations; ICTs to monitor people in public places and gather information about them; and the collection of data about people as they go about their business, for example using payment, swipe or access cards, are generally unfamiliar to most people, including older people [23]. This presents a real risk of discrimination and dignity affronts, giving rise to concern for the kind of human values-led ethical framework suggested by Berners Lee. Big systems such as e-health, e-government and e-transport, and systems talking to systems in the internet of things, place personal consent in a different context. That is, while in some circumstances a person can opt out – for example by declining to allow their personal health data to be included in a database – they can't opt out of the higher level changes to how systems conduct business and run services - and these systems are very rarely designed with ageing in mind. In this kind of situation an opted-out person might in effect become an excluded person. The position that older people very often find themselves in now, is one of being exceptionalised by digital systems. By this I mean that there may well be the possibility to opt out of using a digital default mode – for example by completing a form in hard copy rather than online - but that may well be seen by the organization as creating work and something of a nuisance, and singling out the older person as someone incapable of doing a simple online task. Hence very often an older person who is not comfortable with digital systems will compromise by getting help from someone who is: potentially surrendering privacy and dignity in the process. Yet as with social media many of these barriers could be reduced by paying better attention to ageing and creating systems that work better for people with low technical skills.

6 Summary

This paper has considered some of the issues of use and non-use of technologies that are emerging within a globally ageing population, looking through the lens of values and ethics. It argues that non-discrimination, dignity, social inclusion and respect for individual capabilities cannot be ignored if our increasingly technologically infused environments are going to work better for older people – and indeed for everyone. Because age is only one of many aspects that make up a person, an individuals' capacity to respond to technologies should not be defined in terms of age, even though the effects of human ageing often need to be taken into account in everything from design to the implementation of services and marketing of products. Focusing on respect for the individual and their capabilities will make it more likely that new technologies are introduced in a responsible, effective and non-discriminatory way, but in a globalized commercial ICT environment there is no guarantee that these values will be key considerations. As new technologies emerge, so will new ethical dilemmas: for example identifying who will be responsible for accidents caused by driverless vehicles. In large part these will be resolved eventually by codification in law and professional standards. However it is less likely that the core values described in EU Articles 1 and 2 will coincide exactly with the core values of all of the transnational corporations and other entities working in emerging technologies. For those who highly value respect for human dignity and rights, liberty, democracy, equality, and the rule of law, there is a continuing need for vigilance and information sharing about the effects of new technologies on individuals and communities. For developers, practitioners and users of technologies, paying attention to the experiences of older people is one of the ways of recognizing potential challenges and opportunities in making technologies work for people as well as organizations.

References

1. Beniger, J.: The Control Revolution: Technological and Economic Origins of the Information Society. Harvard University Press, Cambridge (1989)
2. Cerruzi, P.: A History of Modern Computing. MIT Press, Cambridge (2003)
3. Mc Daniel, S.A., Zimmer, Z.: Global Ageing in the Twenty-First Century. Ashgate, Farnham (2013)
4. Sen, A.: Equality of What?. Tanner Lectures on Human Values, Stanford University, Stanford (1979)
5. Sen, A.: Commodities and Capabilities, North-Holland (1985)
6. Nussbaum, M.: Nature, function, and capability: Aristotle on political distribution. In: Oxford Studies in Ancient Philosophy. Oxford University Press, Oxford (1988)
7. Nussbaum, M.: Women and Human Development. Cambridge University Press, Cambridge (2001)

8. Global Age Watch. http://www.helpage.org/global-agewatch/. Accessed 18 Feb 2015
9. Berners-Lee, T.:http://www.independent.co.uk/life-style/gadgets-and-tech/news/web-at-25-sir-tim-bernerslee-calls-for-online-bill-of-rights-to-protect-internet-users-9186346.html. Accessed 18 Feb 2015
10. Value Ageing. http://www.value-ageing.eu/
11. Consolidated articles of the European Union 26.10.2012, Articles 1–2. In: Official EN Journal of the European Union C 326/13
12. Value Ageing Final Report of Work Package 1, p. v (2014)
13. Jacobson, N.: A Taxonomy of dignity: a grounded theory study. BMC Int. Health Hum. Rights **9**, 3 (2009)
14. Value Ageing Final Report of Work Package 1, pp 79–80 (2014)
15. Scharf, T., Phillipson, C., Smith, A.E.: Social exclusion of older people in deprived urban communities of England. Eur. J. Ageing **2**(2), 76–87 (2005)
16. Ofcom: Media Use and Attitudes Report 2014. Ofcom, London (2014)
17. Sen, A.: Human Rights and Capabilities. J. Hum. Dev. 6(2), 151–166
18. Nussbaum, M.: Creating capabilities: the human development approach. Harvard University, Cambridge (2012)
19. Value Ageing Final Report of Work Package 1, p. 32 (2014)
20. Mordoch, E., Osterreicher, A., Guse, L., Roger, K., Thompson, G.: Use of social commitment robots in the care of elderly people with dementia: a literature review. Maturitas **74**(1), 14–20 (2013)
21. Techcitement. http://techcitement.com/hardware/robot-pets-help-elderly-japanese-cope-in-tsunami-aftermath/. Accessed 19 Feb 15
22. Oxford Economics. The CIA World Factbook; "World Robotics, 2013", International Federation of Robots
23. Graeff, T.R., Harmon, S.: Collecting and using personal data: consumers' awareness and concerns. J. Consum. Mark. **19**(4), 302–318 (2002)

Accessing InterACTion: Ageing with Technologies and the Place of Access

Constance Lafontaine[(✉)] and Kim Sawchuk

Department of Communication Studies, Concordia University, Montreal, Canada
{constance.lafontaine,kim.sawchuk}@concordia.ca

Abstract. In this paper, we reflect upon our participation in a pilot digital literacy project titled InterACTion currently being deployed in low-income housing for seniors the city of Montreal. To assess the complexities of access with respect to ageing in this real world setting, we draw upon Clement and Shade's 'Access Rainbow Model.' We use the InterACTion project as a case study and formulate seven lessons that we have gleaned in the carrying out of the project, each of them working to display intricacies of access within a context of precarious ageing and situated engagements with technologies. Our interest in drawing from the model lies in our understanding of access a multi-layered concept that relies both on the establishment of technical requirements and on a host of entangled conditions that are crucial in determining an individual's ability to use digital technologies.

Keywords: Access rainbow · Access · Digital literacy · Place · Ageing

1 Introduction

This paper focuses on the relationship between ageing and digital technologies, with a particular emphasis on devices such as laptops, tablet computers and other hand-held portables. These are the devices that promise users wireless telecommunication or networked services anywhere and at anytime. Within North American society, the wireless industry is burgeoning. However, if one looks at data on adoption rates, one notices that the demographic groups with one of the lowest rates of use are older adults.[1] However, is age itself the only relevant "variable"? What other factors determine or predict access to mobile networked devices and services?

To understand barriers to access in relation to older adults, we reflect upon our participation in a digital literacy project titled InterACTion currently being deployed in the city of Montreal in Québec, Canada. InterACTion is conducted with a community-based group of social service providers, Groupe Harmonie, an organization that works with older

---

[1] For instance, we can draw here from data gathered by the *Centre facilitant la recherche et l'innovation dans les organisations, à l'aide des technologies de l'information et de la communication (TIC)* (CEFRIO) for the province of Québec in 2010. Though their report noted the high uptake of technology by seniors, it further affirmed that ICT use by older Québécois lagged substantially behind that of younger cohorts. Some 54 % of adults over 55 regularly use the Internet (more specifically this corresponds to 68 % of those 55 to 64 and 40 % of those over 65). Some 75 % of the general population uses Internet while 94 % of those 18 to 24 use it) [1].

© Springer International Publishing Switzerland 2015
J. Zhou and G. Salvendy (Eds.): ITAP 2015, Part I, LNCS 9193, pp. 210–220, 2015.
DOI: 10.1007/978-3-319-20892-3_21

adults living in social housing in the downtown core of the city. InterACTion began in April 2014 and is on-going as of the writing of this paper. InterACTion is not only a pilot project, but it is a unique case study, for it highlights the desires, needs and barriers to access faced by groups of seniors living in poverty and requiring social assistance in an urban centre. While perhaps not the ideal target market from an industry standpoint, the case of InterACTion draws attention to real-world challenges for understanding the experience of access faced by many older adults in a moment where there is increasing pressure to go digital and greater gaps between rich and poor across the globe.

To assess the complexities of access with respect to ageing in this real world setting, we draw upon Andrew Clement and Leslie Shade's 'Access Rainbow Model.' The Access Rainbow Model is a heuristic tool that identifies seven interrelated layers that pose a challenge to access provision including: carriage facilities, devices, software tools, content/services, services/access providers, literacy/social facilitation and finally governance as an integrated socio-technical architecture [2]. For Clement and Shade, layers are stacked and ordered yet overlapping, and all of them are necessary for a model that "forms the basis of a workable definition of 'universal access'" [2, p. 1]. Lower layers of the rainbow point to the technical dimensions of access, upper ones refer to social aspects while "the main constitutive element is the service/content layer in the middle, since this is where the actual utility is most direct" [2, p. 4].

In using the Access Rainbow Model we reflect upon our engagement with the InterACTion project tin their intertwined complexity, by this particular population. As Clement and Shade argue, communications infrastructures are already less accessible to certain individuals in society, often to those who continually experience systematic disadvantages connected to age, gender, income, language, ethnicity, disability and so on [2, p. 5]. Our interest in the model lies in its definition of access as a multi-layered concept that relies technical requirements and a host of conditions that determine an individual's ability to use digital technologies at different moments in the life course. While we agree that the model offers an important set of guidelines we also contend that in a real world setting, the image of a layered rainbow is not so easily applied. The strands not only overlap, but they are interwoven at each and every moment.

To unravel this interweaving, we offer seven lessons gleaned in the carrying out of the project. The lessons we articulate display the intricacies of access within an overall context of precarious living, and also emphasize the emplacement and contextuality of access. What does it mean for this particular group of people to age in a digital world full of promises of unfettered connectivity and technological abundance? How do we understand access within this context, and from their points of view? What lessons can be learned from the project?

2   Situating InterACTion: The Context

The non-profit community organization Groupe Harmonie[2] was created in 1983. Groupe Harmonie works with seniors (55 and over) in Montreal who are dealing with addictions, including alcohol, drugs and gambling. Groupe Harmonie reached out to

---

[2] www.groupeharmonie.org.

our research team *Ageing, Communication, Technologies* (ACT)[3] to jointly put in place the InterACTion digital literacy workshops in two social housing buildings (*habitations à loyer modique* or HLM) located in the downtown core of Montreal. The two buildings are meant to house adults 60 and over who are living later life in a state of poverty (generally understood to be living with less than $27,500 CAD annually) [3].

The initial task consisted in installing routers in the common rooms of each building to provide an Internet connection in the shared spaces to all residents without cost or password requirements. The InterACTion project intended to provide a physical, material connection, what Clement and Shade identify as the availability of an adequate carrier mechanism that is fundamental to the provision of services online. As it soon became obvious, enabling this physical infrastructure is far from being tantamount to access. To introduce the new infrastructure, a router with a connection, we organized welcome parties in the common rooms in April 2014 in the hopes of meeting residents, sharing food with them, explaining the project, asking them about their interests, showing them laptop and tablet computers, and instigating them into participating in future workshops. We initiated a door-to-door survey: some thirty residents responded to a simple bilingual questionnaire. With our initial impressions and feedback obtained from the welcome party and the survey, we purchased equipment (four laptops and six tablets), and we launched monthly workshops in each of the building (thus organizing two workshops per month). The workshops last two hours and consist in matching an elder with a device and a tech mentor. The one-on-one tutorial demands of the project, though an effective way to teach technology use and to share knowledge and to engage with elders, are labor and resource-intensive. We have had to mobilize a sufficient number of bilingual tech mentors (often student volunteers) and equipment for each session. At times, the demand has been so high that we have had to turn away elders from the workshops.

To date, we have given eleven monthly workshops in each building, for a total of twenty-two workshops and, at time of writing, the workshops are still ongoing. Since the beginning of the project, over fifty elders have partaken. There are about five residents who regularly attend and there are an average of six residents per workshop. Thus far, ten students and postdoctoral researchers have been involved from Concordia University and Université de Montréal, four members of Groupe Harmonie, a number of volunteers affiliated with Groupe Harmonie, as well as an administrator from Concordia University. During this time we have taken field notes and engaged in informal discussions with the participants.

As the name suggests, the overarching goal of InterACTion is to create a convivial, intergenerational environment for elders to learn how to use digital technologies, identified by Clement and Shade as fundamental to access through social facilitation. But also, and in no small part, an important goal was to find a way for Groupe Harmonie to promote positive human interactions among the building residents (whereas interactions can be fraught and conflictual at times), and to put to good use the common rooms that often go unfrequented by building residents. Here, situating the workshop within the often difficult milieu of shared spaces of low-income housing is

---

[3] www.actproject.ca.

key to understanding learning as situated in particular spaces and places: in the HLMs, people 60 and over are living together in small individual apartment units out of necessity, and not necessarily out of choice.

3 Lessons

3.1 Lesson 1: Situated Methodologies—Accessing Information on Access

One of the key ways of determining access, and constructing meaningful interaction, is to have information on the needs of the population with which one is working. One way to access information is through participant observation. When we organized 'WIFI welcome parties' in the common rooms of both buildings in April of 2014, we quickly noticed that seniors seemed more excited about using the tablets and exhibited less curiosity about the laptops at this event. The tablets were initially objects of desire. They captured the interest of residents in the particular setting of the WIFI welcome parties, where the use of the equipment was more cursory, often done while standing up, and thus differed from the longer-length one-on-one workshop setting that would later be adopted. This initial reaction, combined with the societal enthusiasm towards the adoption of mobile tablet computers, and other research that points to the potentially high acceptance and satisfaction rate of seniors learning with tablets [4, 5] led us to speculate that they would serve as a preferred means of technological engagement in the workshops. This was not to be the case.

A second means of accessing information about access is through more formal mechanisms. As a follow-up to this initial encounter, we fashioned a short bilingual ten-question survey to learn more about the interests, desires, and current computer-related skills of the residents who would be our potential workshop participants. We asked what technologies they had on hand. Given the low level of access to both devices and networked services, an online survey would have been impossible: a door-to-door approach throughout both buildings was the only option. Yet even this proved to be a challenge. In a situation of social housing where people rely on government subsidies and are often under the scrutiny of governmental agents and agencies looking to cut benefits, people are suspicious and mistrustful. Residents most often did not want to open the door to talk about computer and mobile computing workshops. When people did answer the door and agreed to the survey, the desire for interpersonal contact meant that a short survey that would normally call for about five minutes often took over forty minutes and we often had to fill it out with them.

What did we learn from those who allowed us access to their homes and who were willing to share information through our survey? The thirty people who did answer indicated that there was a high level of interest in free Internet workshops and that if the community rooms could be opened for this purpose they would be used. The survey further outlined future challenges: the majority of respondents were self-assessed beginners or had "average" level of skills. When we asked what they would like to learn they suggested the some of the basics of Internet searches as well as email, Skype, photo scanning, Facebook and YouTube. But we also noted that "What would you like to learn?" had been the question that was most skipped. This query was frequently met with uncertainty, and nearly a third of the respondents opted not to answer, unable to point exactly to what they wanted.

A large majority, 84 %, thought that learning more about digital technologies would have an impact on their lives with some 44 % indicating that they thought that this impact could be "big". Yet this assessment of potential impact was speculative, for the majority of our participants cannot afford to keep up with technology, had never used a digital device for a sustained period of time in their working or personal lives and could not pay to ensure steady, in-home access to an Internet service provider or for a cell phone. As we learned from these first two forays into making contact, methodological inquiries are situated in place and are related to questions of access. Even the ways that one would find out about access is related to access to current technologies.

3.2   Lesson 2: Physical Affordances and Human Encounters

Clement and Shade point out that devices come with particular affordances, which, as other researchers in HCI have indicated, are often seen as some of most important and significant barriers for older adults [6]. Indeed access is often, from this perspective, tantamount to the design of the device and software. While for Clement and Shade, the main issue of access is the high cost of the devices, they also point to usability as a key issue. This intermingling of cost and design affordance became evident in our inter-actions with seniors partaking in InterACTion, yet even here there are important lessons about what can be learned from working with a group of people over time.

Given our observations at the WIFI welcome party, we initially expected tablets to be more popular. Yet within the first few workshops, it became clear that many of the seniors found it easier to work with laptops. The swiping motion needed for tablet-use was foreign to many residents and, for some, impaired hearing, vision and trouble with fine motor skills became important factors in selecting specific devices. For these participants, the keyboard and screen of the laptops provided them with better affordances. In fact, many of the women, in particular, commented that they were more comfortable with keyboards because of their previously acquired typing skills, which they had developed through a gender-based formal education and work experience. This skillset served as an entry-point, bolstering confidence in their ability to use the technologies. In this instance, while it may have initially seemed as if the design of the tablets offered better affordances, for some of our participants their histories of prior computer use and their embodied subjectivity influenced their choice of device, a point on the importance of embodiment in computer learning supported by the research of Christina Buse [7].

3.3   Lesson 3: Affordances: Financial Considerations

Ironically, although laptops were preferred by the majority of our participants, when making the decision about what they might buy most did not chose this option. Despite the participants' discomfort and reluctance in using tablets, and their preferred use of laptop computers at the workshops, those planning to purchase equipment decided to buy android tablets because of their relatively lower cost. These devices have been primarily devised for mobile use and networked connectivity, immediately articulating them to our regulatory context of pricing and contracts in Canada [8]. More affordable and potentially networked, the tablets were not used in the workshop setting, but later purchased anyway: the cost associated with services that is key.

Most residents do not have Internet access in their own units and cannot afford it seeing as the average cost in Canada is extremely high—approximately $75 a month— and it goes up incrementally every year and often requires a credit card or a credit check. Without either a credit card or a sustained connection in their own apartments, the participants cannot partake in being systematically networked, and therefore see little reason to own either a laptop or tablet. Yet the desire to be a part of a networked society they cannot necessarily afford is present. In one instance, a participant who is using the workshops to write her memoirs on a laptop computer does not need Internet access for the purposes of her project. Yet she still wants connectivity explaining this is "because I am missing out on so much." Likewise, because of limited funds, she has decided a tablet is a better option for her because of cost, despite the fact she prefers typing on a laptop.

Through this and other conversations with these elders, participants have openly talked about their desires: they imagine themselves wandering the city with tablets surfing the Internet in a park or going to a coffee shop to be a part of a larger cultural scenario of anywhere, anytime connectivity. However, for most of these residents the reality of ownership and unfettered connectivity is quite different: it is mitigated not only by the affordances of the device, but by their ability to quite literally afford to stay connected [9].

3.4 Lesson 4: Language and Literacies

There are other factors of exclusions linked to socio-economic class that influence the ability of our participants to interact with these devices- and to engage in digital learning. While Clement and Shade emphasize the need to enable digital literacy and of the requirement of a "broad range" of knowledge and skills required to engage with network society, *general* literacy is not included in their figuration of access. Lower levels of literacy (along with lower levels education and income) have elsewhere been identified as correlated with non-use of ICTs [10], a consideration that needs to be foreground in an examination of the conditions of access of an older and impoverished population. Canadian data from the International Adult Literacy and Skills Survey reveals that only 18 % of respondents over 65 are situated at a literacy level of 3 or above—level 3 being "the desired threshold for coping well in a complex knowledge society" [11]. A large majority (82 %) of Canadian elders have been deemed to have general literacy challenges. Surprisingly, Canada has significant gaps between levels of general literacy, and has a notably "higher proportion of its population at the highest and lowest levels" [12] thus emphasizing the need to consider general literacy as an important marker of social inequality in the country.

A number of the residents who participate in our workshops have variable levels of literacy that impact their ability to use the Internet, and especially to conduct keyword-based searches. Although this was not an intended part of our project, those least able to read and write are excluded from the workshops either through their reluctance to engage in a public setting that would put their lack of literacy on display or through an exclusion fostered by our reliance on flyers and posters to promote workshops.

As Clement and Shade suggest "[k]nowledge includes an understanding of the various types, sources and uses of a global networked information; the role of information in research and problem solving; and systems whereby information is stored, managed and transmitted" [7, p. 11]. Such information and network literacy assumes an array of knowledge related to information retrieval. With years of Internet use, one builds a verbal and visual lexicon to facilitate software use. Even simple web searches rely on decoding expressions like "quick search," "I'm feeling lucky" and icons like drop-down arrows, hour and magnifying glasses and spinning beach balls all have a symbolic value that is learned progressively by users and comes to be taken for granted as it is incorporated into what Bourdieu would call one's "habitus" [13]. The perceived work required to acquire this lexicon can feel like a daunting task for beginners as we found in our workshops. Everything needs to be explained and sometimes translated. Here again, the term literacy is even connected to an ability to operate in several languages in a context like Québec, a province that primarily comprises Francophone speakers who are living in a digital world dominated by English.

Most of our participants are Francophone and they immediately found themselves with the need to customize language settings, as many are ill at ease with the default English configuration of software. This was also the case for several seniors who had visual impairments, and who were burdened by dim screens and unable to read the small characters. In these cases, device and software settings needed to be altered. Customization and the use of optional accessible interfaces require a level of proficiency beyond those afforded by a beginner, presenting a further accumulation of barriers and challenges to be confronted and overcome.

3.5   Lesson 5: Interpersonal Barriers and the Need for "Warm Experts"

As a way of promoting universal access, Shade and Clement emphasize the need for community centers and libraries to provide free internet access, and to be located in proximity to the dwellings of people who would need them the most [2, p. 11]. Ironically, there are libraries and community centers near the two HLMs providing WIFI access, public computers, and affordable workshops on a regular basis. Although we found that these seniors were aware of these devices and publicly available services, our participants remained reluctant to make use of them. They are trapped in a double bind. On one hand they were unprepared to use the technologies alone, did not have access to them in their rooms, nor did they have anyone to turn to in their immediate environment. On the other, they were unwilling to reveal their precarity, alienation and isolation in a public setting. Conversely, the one-on-one setting of the InterACTion workshops for these participants broke through the barrier of personal reluctance by favoring an approach based on establishing a rapport between participants. Clement and Shade point to the importance of "the social aspects of learning" and the importance of "informal learning environments" where "local experts" can engage in casually mentoring future users, on the job and on the fly, in situations with little pressure. In such contexts, the acquisition of skills occurs in informal settings.

By emphasizing a bi-directional sharing of knowledge and stories our students and other tech-mentors became surrogates for what Maria Bakardjieva [14, 15] calls 'warm experts,' or "a close friend or relative who possesses relatively advanced knowledge of computer networks and personal familiarity with the novice user's situation and interests" (15, p. 74). Warm experts, for Bakardjieva, are uniquely enabled to find potential uses and relevance of the Internet for the learner because they have established relations of trust over time. In this respect, understanding "human practices" not only as a set of skills, but as a part of a set of affective and emotional approaches that can facilitate learning in a particular place, are essential and entangled factors that are typically associated with the macro-level.

3.6   Lesson 6: Spaces of Access

Clement and Shade note that "[g]overnance is about the ways in which decisions are made concerning the development and operation of the information/communication infrastructure" [2, p. 12]. In their discussion of governance, they make specific and explicit reference to a policymaking perspective, which they tie to the actions and abilities of actors from the public and private sectors who play a politically prominent role in affording access to individuals through the imposition of particular legislative choices.

Our case study brings us to consider that governance, regulation and communication infrastructure operates in smaller and more precise, but still immensely powerful ways at local levels- in place. For instance, the structural specificities of the HLM have had an impact on the ways seniors can engage with technologies on site. Despite the fact that WIFI had been made available in the common room, what we imagined as their potential digital commons, the daily realities of the residents have an impact on the uses of this common space, which in turn influence their ability to practice their newly acquired skills to reinforce their learning between our monthly sessions.

While there may be technical connectivity in the common rooms, taking care of the issue of "carriage" identified as essential within the Access Rainbow Model, there were in fact few opportunities for the residents to frequent the space and to use this Internet access to reinforce their learning. Over the years, the use of the common room has been an instigator of conflict among the residents, some of whom are grasping with physical and psychological impairments, and who are not all co-habiting *by choice*. The common space is kept locked by the governing body that controls this residency. Unless Groupe Harmonie is physically present in the building to prevent both conflict and theft, access is restricted for residents who might want to avail themselves of this common connectivity. In addition, because of the lack of funding to the maintenance of the building, no one is currently employed to clean the common room, which deters its use. Keeping the room locked has become a cost-efficient alternative to finding adequate staff or volunteers to do rudimentary maintenance. Because of these circumstances, a bench located outside of the locked common room has become an important and impromptu point of access in one of the buildings, as the WIFI network is still accessible from there and the bench itself has no history of contestation.

3.7   Lesson 7: Meaning, Purpose and Intermittent Access

Clement and Shade identify content as a principal constitutive element, explaining that "this is where the actual utility is most direct" [2, p. 4]. Yet what does this mean for users living in conditions where there is an accumulation of barriers to access? One of the key elements that determined *return* participation for our residents was finding a *reason* to use the internet, a sense of purpose—what Jean-Paul Sartre [16] identifies as a 'project'—that actually imbue the sessions with meaning. Likewise, Clement and Shade suggest that content and services "must include the ability for users to interact in a creative and participative fashion as well as simply to receive stimuli" [2, p. 10]. These reasons expressed for wanting access to content were often very personal in nature. For instance, one woman who intermittently attends found exercises that could improve her back pain and learned to look them up on YouTube videos. As she doesn't own a computer, she used the sessions to write down notes on paper that she then could carry up back up to her unit. Even without owning a computer, motivated by her own discomfort and desire for information on her pain management, she nevertheless found a way to make our sessions and even the most intermittent of access work to her advantage.

Information management in the context of intermittent access became key. Because they lacked ownership of a device, participants tended to forgo an interest in learning that would require sustained use or daily management (such as email) or use that demanded privacy (such as Skype). As such, the workshops became focused on acquiring information and viewing online materials that would not conflict with these concerns. As they perceptively pointed out to us "why would I get an email address, if I can only look up my emails once a month?" This situation of lack of sustained access, and temporal breaks between sessions, also indicates the ability of residents to find resilient and creative workarounds. Some began to carefully think about topics they wanted to look up and learn in the intervals between workshops. Others began conversations amongst themselves in the preceding weeks in preparation for the workshop. Many, in fact, now come with a list (written or otherwise) of things they specifically want to do or ask during sessions.

For example, two participants are working together to make lists of old buildings in the Montreal downtown area that have been important places in their lives, such as hospitals, schools, churches, parks and restaurants. They began using the monthly sessions as dedicated time to work on what they termed as "their project" of searching through city archives to find information and photos. During the workshop, they used these Internet results as prompts to tell stories about their childhood and how their lives in Montreal have overlapped indicating the juncture of finding meaningful content with "the social aspects of learning" taking place in "supportive" and non-censorious environments, which as Clement and Shade argue "are often overlooked" [2, p. 12].

4 Conclusion

From the momentary ephemerality of the WIFI welcome party, to the door-to-door survey through our sustained and on-going encounters with the participants in the InterACTion project, it is evident: first that when dealing with human computer inter-action, it is vital to consider the question of place and its important as a mediating variable that influences digital learning of those who are older. Second, we can see how uneven access to wealth has its tributary effect differential experiences with ICTs. It creates precarious and often difficult living situations for our InterACTion participants; it entails a host of interconnected material and other barriers to the uses and learning of technol-ogies that require troubleshooting and innovative workarounds. Industry documents are often geared towards exploiting the untapped seniors market and promote a language of innovation that makes it seems that all have unfettered access to perpetual connectivity in a networked society. This focus does not take into account the large percentage of elders in 'developed worlds,' such as those living in Montreal HLMs, who are not living in the top 20 percentile. In this context, the realities of poorer seniors are neglected experiences from the purview of a pure marketing mentality towards ICTs, which is typically interested in the lives of affluent seniors who have 'successfully aged.'

By reflecting on the lessons presented above, we want to inform the development of future learning activities and indeed inclusive design approaches. But mainly, we intend to emphasize that learning to use technologies always occurs within the spec-ificity of context—in the dynamics of a place and at a particular time. In this con-sideration of place, the age and generation of the users are vitally important to consider. However, they are not the only consideration. Any thinking about digital technologies and elders cannot be done apart of an understanding of variegated ageing experiences and the realities of precarious ageing, where socio-economic factors of exclusion such as class, education, and language (and also culture, race, ethnicity and gender) are compounded when it comes to interacting with technologies.

As we have seen, the Access Rainbow Model usefully pinpoints the multi-faceted and complex ways that access to digital technologies and learning are connected in specific places. In their discussion of access, Clement and Shade make use of the rainbow as a visual metaphor for the plural barriers to access, yet the assemblage of layers cannot aptly reflect the entangled nature of the ways access is lived by the elder participants of the InterACTion workshop. Barriers to access are plural, certainly, but they merge, overlap and crisscross persistently: they are closer, perhaps, to a ball of string or a bowl of rainbow-colored spaghetti than a neat rainbow.

References

1. CEFRIO. http://www.cefrio.qc.ca/media/uploader/Rapport_complet.pdf
2. Clement, A., Shade, L.R.: The access rainbow: conceptualizing universal access to the information/communications infrastructure. In: Gurstein, M. (ed.) Community Informatics: Enabling Communities with Information and Communications Technologies, pp. 1–20. Idea Group, Hershey (2000)

3. OMHM. http://www.omhm.qc.ca/en/are-you-eligible
4. Werner, F., Werner, K.: Tablets for seniors: bridging the digital divide. Gerontechnology **11**, 208–226 (2012)
5. Burkhard, M., Koch, M.: Evaluating touchscreen interfaces of tablet computers for elderly people. In: Reiterer, H., Deussen, O. (eds.) Mensch and Computer 2012, pp. 53–59. Oldenbourg Verlag, München (2012)
6. Kurniawan, S.: Older people and mobile phones: a multi-method investigation. Int. J. Hum. Comput. Stud. **66**, 889–901 (2008)
7. Buse, C.E.: E-scaping the ageing body? Computer technologies and embodiment in later life. Ageing Soc. **30**, 987–1009 (2010)
8. Middleton, C., Shepherd, T., Shade, L.R., Sawchuk, K., Crow, B.: Intervention regarding the consultation on proceeding to establish a mandatory code for mobile wireless services (2012, 2013)
9. Sawchuk, K., Crow, B.: I'm G-Mom on the phone: remote grandmothering, cell phones and inter/generational dis/connections. Feminist Media Stud. **12**, 475–489 (2012)
10. Statistics Canada. http://www.statcan.gc.ca/pub/56f0004m/56f0004m2005012-eng.htm
11. Statistics Canada. http://publications.gc.ca/Collection/Statcan/89-617-X/89-617-XIE2005001.pdf
12. Statistics Canada. http://www.statcan.gc.ca/daily-quotidien/131028/dq131028a-eng.htm
13. Bourdieu, P.: Distinction: A Social Critique of the Judgement of Taste. Harvard University Press, Cambridge (1984)
14. Bakardjieva, M.: Internet Society: The Internet in Everyday Life. Sage, London, Thousand Oaks, New Delhi (2005)
15. Bakardjieva, M.: The internet in everyday life: exploring the tenets and contributions of diverse approaches. In: Consalvo, M., Ess, C. (eds.) The Handbook of Internet Studies, pp. 59–82. Wiley-Blackwell, Malden, Oxford (2011)
16. Sartre, J.: Being and Nothingness. Washington Square Press, New York (1984)

Review of Empirical Research in Recent Decade About the Use of IT for Older Adults

Yi-Chang Li[⊠]

School of Health Policy and Management, Chung Shan Medical University,
Taichung, Taiwan
yclil970@csmu.edu.tw

Abstract. This study reviews the research articles about the use of IT for older adults' from 2009–2015. As result, fourteen articles published in peer reviewed journals are reviewed.

Keywords: Older adults · IT usage · Review

1 Introduction

The ability to use Computer and information technologies (CIT) is now assumed by most commentators to be a prerequisite to living in the information age. Access to CIT is a major public policy concern as technology has become a significant aspect of economic, social and health equity. Recent data suggest that although CIT use is lower among older, as compared to younger adults access is increasing among older people. Wagner et al. (2010) reviewed 151 existing articles covering the period 1990–2008 and provides a holistic view of the field. They concluded that "although there has been significant research dedicated to the use of computers by older adults, there is certainly still a plethora of opportunities for further study in this increasingly relevant field." Therefore, the purpose of this study is to review the articles that published after 2009 (the end of year in Wagner et al. (2010)'s review). We focus on the papers that reported empirical research findings in order to realize the research progress in these years.

2 Material and Method

The articles for this review were gathered by searching various databases for peer reviewed journal articles on the subject of CIT use by older adults. However, only papers with empirical research (such as survey, experiment, focus group, interview, and secondary data) are included. Search strings included reference to aging (age or aging or old or older or senior or older adults) as well as reference to computer use (computer or Internet or web or interface or mobile phone). Two research assistants and the author are responsible for categorizing the select papers according to their journal discipline, theoretical basis, IT related activities, and variables. Inter-rater reliability was calculated using a variant of Cohen's kappa as 0.72 which is above the recommended minimum of 0.70 (Straub, et al., 2004).

© Springer International Publishing Switzerland 2015
J. Zhou and G. Salvendy (Eds.): ITAP 2015, Part I, LNCS 9193, pp. 221–229, 2015.
DOI: 10.1007/978-3-319-20892-3_22

3 Results

As in Table 1, most journals we found were in HCI discipline, followed by healthcare journals. Table 2 revealed that half of the papers did not outline their theoretical basis. TAM was the most frequently used theory in the study of older adult's CIT usage. In Table 3, survey was the most frequently used data collection strategies, followed by secondary data (such as government or industrial investigation). Table 4 revealed that older adults use ICT for general use, contact people or relatives and health-related activities.

Table 1. Journal dicipline and number of empirical research published

Journal discipline	Number of empirical research published
HCI	6
Healthcare	5
Psychology	1
Gerontology	1
Education	1

Table 2. Theoreitcal basis

Theory	Number of empirical research published
TAM	5
UTAUT	1
TPB	1
No obvious theory mentioned	7

Table 3. Data collection strategies

Strategies	Number of empirical research published
Survey	8
Secondary data	4
Experiment	1
Focus group and interview	1

Table 4. ICT used for older adults

ICT used	Reference
General ICT	Mitzner et al. 2010
	Pan and Jordan-Marsh 2010
	Cotten et al. 2012
	Choi and DiNitto. 2013
	Ramón-Jerónimo et al. 2013
	Elliot et al. 2014
Mobile phone	Kurniawan, 2008
	Conci et al. 2009
Social network ICT	Chung et al. 2010
	Hogeboom et al. 2010

(*Continued*)

Table 4. (*Continued*)

ICT used	Reference
health-related ICT	Chu et al. 2009
	Choi, 2011 Or et al. 2011
	Heart and Kalderon, 2013

4 Conclusion

CIT was found to be promising in increasing the quality of life for older adults. However, successful use of CIT by older adults is predicated on systems that are designed to accommodate the needs and preferences of this user group. As Chen and Chang (2011) concluded that "Technology has been shown to be beneficial to older people, but a digital divide remains".

Appendix

Paper	Data collection and sample	Major findings	Note (the kind of IT, theoretical basis, journal discipline)
Kurniawan, 2008	Online survey of 100 people	1. Older people are passive users of mobile phones 2. Gender differences in preferred design features were observed, with women focusing on haptic aids and men on perceptual aids.	• Mobile phone • No obvious theoretical basis • HCI *this paper might be neglected by Wagner et al. 2010 because it was published in Dec. 2008.
Chu et al. 2009	Experiment 137 adults aged 65+	Reduction in computer anxiety and increases in computer confidence and computer self-efficacy in retrieving and evaluating online health information if older adults receiving computer training	• Internet health information resources • No obvious theoretical basis • Healthcare

(*Continued*)

		in appropriate situation	
Conci et al. 2009	Survey 740 questionnaires from people over 65 years old	1. Intrinsic motivations play an important role albeit always mediated by utilitarian motives. 2. A strong influence of the reference social group (children and relatives) in increasing the utilitarian values of the use of mobile phones.	• Mobile phone • TAM • HCI
Chung et al. 2010	Survey 989 (11.1 %) out of 8935	1. Perceived usefulness positively affects behavioral intention, yet it was determined that perceived ease of use was not a significant predictor of perceived usefulness. 2. Negative relationships between age and Internet self-efficacy and the perceived quality of online community websites. 3. Moderating role of age was not found (the relationships among perceived ease of use, perceived usefulness, and intention to participate in online communities do	• Online community participation • TAM • HCI

(Continued)

		not change with age.)	
Hogeboom et al. 2010	Secondary data A sample (n = 2284) from the 2004 wave of the Health and Retirement Survey was used. (adult age > 50)	Frequency of contact with friends, frequency of contact with family, and attendance at organizational meetings (not including religious services) were found to have a significant positive association with Internet use for adults over 50.	• Internet use for social networking • No obvious theoretical basis • Education
Mitzner et al. 2010	Focus group Older adults (n = 113)	1. Older adults perceive the benefits of technology use to outweigh the costs of such use. 2. Perceived benefits of use and ease of use have positive influence on computer use	• Computer technologies • TAM • HCI
Pan and Jordan-Marsh 2010	Survey 374 (age 50 +) Beijing, China	Perceived useful (+) Perceived ease use (+) Social norm (+) Internet adoption intention: Perceived useful (+) Social norm (+)	• Internet adoption behavior • Extended TAM • HCI

(Continued)

(*Continued*)

		Facilitating condition (+) Perceived ease use: Older (+)	
Choi, 2011	Secondary data derived from US National Health Interview Survey (NHIS) 2009 aged 65 or older (n = 5294)	Older-adult users of general health services were more likely to use HIT than nonusers of general health services, while older-adult users of specialized health services were not different from nonusers of specialized health services in their odds of HIT use.	• HIT usage • No obvious theoretical basis • Healthcare
Or et al. 2011	Survey 101 participants of home care nursing practice with adults with chronic cardiac disease	Perceived usefulness, perceived ease of use, subjective norm, and healthcare knowledge together predict most of the variance in patients' acceptance and self-reported use of the web-based self-management technology.	• Web-based interactive self-management technology • Unified Theory of Acceptance and Use of Technology (UTAUT) • Healthcare
Cotten et al. 2012	Secondary data Retired Americans age 50 years or older using data from the Health and Retirement Survey	A positive contribution of Internet use to mental well-being of retired older adults reducing	• Internet use and depression • No obvious theoretical basis • HCI

(*Continued*)

(*Continued*)

		depression categorization by approximately 20–28 %.	
Choi and DiNitto. 2013	Face-to-face or telephone surveys 980 recipients of home-delivered meals in central Texas (78 % were age 60 years and older and 22 % under age 60).	Due to lack of exposure to computer/internet technology; lack of financial resources to obtain computers and technology; or medical conditions, disabilities, and associated pain that restrict use.	• Low-income disabled and homebound adults' and older adults' Internet use. • No obvious theoretical basis • Healthcare
Heart and Kalderon, 2013	Survey 123 respondents(63 from the US and 60 from Israel.)	• ICT use was determined by accessibility of computers and support and by age, marital status, education, and health. • Health was found to moderate the effect of age, healthier older people being far more likely to use computers than their unhealthy coevals. • Only perceived behavioral control (PBC) emerged as significantly affecting intention to use a computer	• Readiness to adopt health-related ICT • Theory of planned behavior (TPB) • Healthcare
Ramón-Jerónimo et al. 2013	Survey 492 individuals over 50 years old in Spain	• Male elders seem to perceive more usefulness due to higher levels of ease of use than woman.	• Internet use • TAM and gender differences for older adults • Gerontology

(*Continued*)

(Continued)

		• Ease of use is also better explained by the level of enjoyment for males.	
Elliot et al. 2014	Secondary data a sample of community-dwelling older adults from the National Health and Aging Trends Study (N = 6,443).	• Socioeconomic status (SES), age, and cognitive function accounted for approximately 60 % of the variance in ICT use. • SES was a stronger predictor for Blacks/African Americans, whereas cognitive function was a stronger predictor for Whites. • ICT use was unrelated to depressive symptoms or well-being. However, it acted as a moderator, such that limitations in activities of daily living (ADLs) was a stronger predictor of depressive symptoms for high ICT users, whereas ill-health was a stronger predictor for non/limited users.	• ICT use • IT and depressive • Psychology

References

Choi, N.: Relationship between health service use and health information technology use among older adults: analysis of the US national health interview survey. J. Med. Internet Res. **13**(2), e33 (2011)

Choi, N.G., DiNitto, D.M.: The digital divide among low-income homebound older adults: internet use patterns, eHealth literacy, and attitudes toward computer/internet use. J. Med. Internet Res. **15**(5), e93 (2013)

Chu, A., Huber, J., Mastel-Smith, B., Cesario, S.: Partnering with seniors for better health: computer use and internet health information retrieval among older adults in a low socioeconomic community. J. Med. Libr. Assoc. **97**(1), 12–20 (2009)

Chung, J.E., Park, N., Wang, H., Fulk, J., McLaughlin, M.: Age differences in perceptions of online community participation among non-users: an extension of the technology acceptance model. Comput. Hum. Behav. **26**(6), 1674–1684 (2010)

Conci, M., Pianesi, F., Zancanaro, M.: Useful, social and enjoyable: mobile phone adoption by older people. In: Gross, T., Gulliksen, J., Kotzé, P., Oestreicher, L., Palanque, P., Prates, R.O., Winckler, M. (eds.) INTERACT 2009. LNCS, vol. 5726, pp. 63–76. Springer, Heidelberg (2009)

Cotten, S.R., Ford, G., Ford, S., Hale, T.M.: Internet use and depression among older adults. Comput. Hum. Behav. **28**(2), 496–499 (2012)

Chen, K., Chan, A.H.S.: A review of technology acceptance by older adults. Gerontechnology **10**(1), 1–12 (2011)

Elliot, A.J., Mooney, C.J., Douthit, K.Z., Lynch, M.F.: Predictors of older adults' technology use and its relationship to depressive symptoms and well-being. J. Gerontol. Ser. B Psychol. Sci. Soc. Sci. **69**(5), 667–677 (2014)

Hanson, V.L.: Influencing technology adoption by older adults. Interact. Comput. **22**(6), 502–509 (2010)

Heart, T., Kalderon, E.: Older adults: are they ready to adopt health-related ICT? Int. J. Med. Inform. **82**(11), e209–e231 (2013)

Hogeboom, D.L., McDermott, R.J., Perrin, K.M., Osman, H., Bell-Ellison, B.A.: Internet use and social networking among middle aged and older adults. Educ. Gerontol. **36**(2), 93–111 (2010)

Kurniawan, S.: Older people and mobile phones: a multi-method investigation. Int. J. Hum. Comput. Stud. **66**(12), 889–901 (2008)

Mitzner, T.L., Boron, J.B., Fausset, C.B., Adams, A.E., Charness, N., Czaja, S.J., Sharit, J.: Older adults talk technology: technology usage and attitudes. Comput. Hum. Behav. **26**(6), 1710–1721 (2010)

Or, C.K., Karsh, B.T., Severtson, D.J., Burke, L.J., Brown, R.L., Brennan, P.F.: Factors affecting home care patients' acceptance of a web-based interactive self-management technology. J. Am. Med. Inform. Assoc. **18**(1), 51–59 (2011)

Pan, S., Jordan-Marsh, M.: Internet use intention and adoption among Chinese older adults: from the expanded technology acceptance model perspective. Comput. Hum. Behav. **26**(5), 1111–1119 (2010)

Ramón-Jerónimo, M.A., Peral-Peral, B., Arenas-Gaitán, J.: Elderly persons and internet use. Soc. Sci. Comput. Rev. **31**(4), 389–403 (2013)

Straub, D., Boudreau, M.-C., Gefen, D.: Validation guidelines for IS positivist research. Commun. AIS **13**, 380–427 (2004)

Wagner, N., Hassanein, K., Head, M.: Computer use by older adults: a multi-disciplinary review. Comput. Hum. Behav. **26**(5), 870–882 (2010)

Zickuhr, K., Madden, M.: Older adults and internet use. Pew Internet and American Life Project, 6 (2012)

Exploring the Impacts of Age and Usage Experience of e-Service on User Perceived Web Quality

Chien Hsiang Liao[✉]

Department of Information Management, Fu Jen Catholic University,
New Taipei City, Taiwan
jeffen@gmail.com

Abstract. Prior studies have shown that while older adults use web or e-service, they tend to rely on user accessibility guidelines or friendly web appearance. For instance, older people have difficulty reading text presentations more than younger readers. Inappropriate design decisions might create barriers for older people. However, this causality might not be entirely resulting from age. This study found that the usage experience of e-service is also strongly associated with the requirements of web quality for users as well. The empirical study was conducted on a sample of 318 users of using web services. The results reveal that the requirements of web quality (including web appearance, context quality, and technical adequacy) between older and younger adults are not significantly different. Instead, users with low usage experience require greater web quality than experienced users.

Keywords: Web quality · Age · Usage experience · Satisfaction · Trust

1 Introduction

With the development of information technology, the Internet or web-based environment has become an important service channel for users. More specifically, providing services via electronic channel are available all day long for users and will lead to lower service cost for enterprises. Therefore, both users and enterprises increasingly use e-service to interact with each other. However, not all users are adept at using e-service or self-service technology at the website. Prior studies have shown that while older adults use web or e-service, they tend to rely on user accessibility guidelines or friendly web appearance (Hart et al., 2008). For instance, older people have difficulty reading text presentations more than younger readers. Inappropriate design decisions might create barriers for older people (Curran et al., 2007). That is, the requirement of web contents and appearances for older adults is higher than younger adults. However, as the Internet becomes popular, more and more elderly people have begun to use e-service. This study proposes that age may no longer be the key determinant affecting their requirements of using e-service. Perhaps some latent factors need to be explored and discussed. For example, usage experience has been proven to be associated with user behavior, intention, and performance (Taylor and Todd, 1995; Venkatesh and

© Springer International Publishing Switzerland 2015
J. Zhou and G. Salvendy (Eds.): ITAP 2015, Part I, LNCS 9193, pp. 230–238, 2015.
DOI: 10.1007/978-3-319-20892-3_23

Davis, 1996; Venkatesh et al., 2012). Specifically, because experience makes knowledge more accessible in memory, it will help users to shape intention (Taylor and Todd, 1995). Accordingly, the purpose of this study is to compare the impacts of age and usage experience of e-service on the associations between e-service quality, satisfaction, and trust (see Fig. 1). The results will help us determine which factor will be the main moderator affecting the user perceptions. The discussions of research constructs are mentioned as follows.

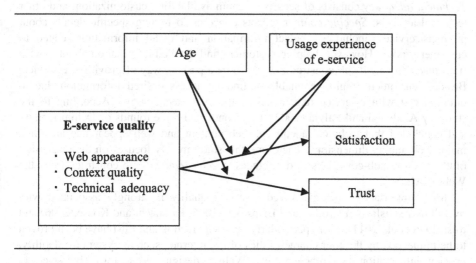

Fig. 1. Research model

2 Literature Review and Hypotheses Development

2.1 The Linkages Between e-Service Quality, Satisfaction, and Trust

As mentioned, the Internet is an important service channel for users. User perceived quality on the Internet has been measured and operationalized by many studies. First of all, perceived e-service quality is defined as the pure information component of a customer's service experience provided in an automated fashion and without human intervention (Sousa and Voss, 2006). With most virtual channels encompassing more than the Internet, many instruments have been developed to assess the quality of Internet portals, such as web quality. In this vein, this study also anchors discussion on the Internet as the primary e-service channel of service delivery.

e-service quality has been operationalized by several instruments, such as e-service quality (E-S-QUAL) by Zeithaml et al. (2000; 2002), Website quality (SiteQUAL) by Yoo and Donthu (2001), Web quality (WebQUAL) by Aladwani and Palvia (2002), and Quality of e-service (QES) by Fassnacht and Koese (2006). However, most of these instruments have been developed primarily for online shopping context (e.g., E-S-QUAL and SiteQUAL), with the exception of WebQUAL (Gummerus et al., 2004).

More specifically, WebQUAL is established to measure perceived web quality from the perspective of Internet users (Aladwani and Palvia, 2002). This instrument is suitable for general context of web-based applications, whether website is concerned with online shopping or not. Therefore, this study uses WebQUAL to measure the e-service quality.

WebQUAL measures four sub-constructs of web quality: *content quality*, *appearance, technical adequacy*, and *specific content*. *Content quality* consists of information usefulness, completeness, accuracy, and conciseness. *Appearance* means the proper use of fonts, colors, multimedia, and other website attractive factors. *Technical adequacy* consists of security, system availability, customization, and other technical abilities. *Specific content* reflects concerns to finding specific details about products/services, including contact information and detail information related to customer service. However, helping customers find detailed information about service (i.e., *specific content* sub-construct) seems to be a passive way of providing e-service. Besides, customers might be unable to find or access desired information due to unfamiliarity with e-service (e.g. a new self-service technology). According to the study by Aladwani and Palvia (2002), they conducted three rounds of Delphi method and concluded that technical adequacy, web content and web appearance are three major web quality dimensions. Therefore, this study merely focuses on the discussion of these three sub-constructs and excludes *specific content* sub-construct from the WebQUAL.

Most importantly, user perceived e-service quality is strongly associated with overall user satisfaction (Collier and Bienstock, 2006; Fassnacht and Koese, 2006) and trust (Liao et al., 2011). More particularly, user satisfaction and trust have been proven to be influenced by the four characteristics of the Internet, such as system availability, privacy, information comprehensiveness, Website design, and so forth (Bauer et al., 2002; Muylle et al., 2004; Wolfinbarger and Gilly, 2003). These characteristics will attract users to stick Internet or use e-service, and thereby influence their satisfaction and trust after they visited the website (Muylle et al., 2004). Therefore this study proposes that the causal associations are positively supported *no matter what user's age and past experience*.

H1. Perceived e-service quality is positively related to satisfaction.
- **H1a.** Web appearance is positively related to satisfaction.
- **H1b.** Context quality is positively related to satisfaction.
- **H1c.** Technical adequacy is positively related to satisfaction.

H2. Perceived e-service quality is positively related to trust.
- **H2a.** Web appearance is positively related to trust.
- **H2b.** Context quality is positively related to trust.
- **H2c.** Technical adequacy is positively related to trust.

2.2 The Moderating Effects of Age and Usage Experience

This study expects the impact of e-service quality on satisfaction and trust to be moderated by age and usage experience. Firstly, older adults tend to face more diffi-culty in operating complex information, thus influencing their learning performance of new technology (Morris et al., 2005; Venkatesh et al., 2012). Computer-based information requires several cognitive skills that may result in age differences in the website task performance (Priest et al., 2007). Therefore, compared with younger adults, older adults require higher e-service quality helping them familiar with e-service functions. In this vein, this study predicts that age has positive moderating effect on the relationship between e-service quality and user satisfaction and trust. That is to say, user with higher age will lead to more significant relationship between e-service quality and user satisfaction and trust.

H3a. The impact of e-service quality on user satisfaction is positively moderated by age.

H3b. The impact of e-service quality on trust is positively moderated by age.

Prior experience of using a technology is typically defined as the passage of time from the initial use by an individual (Venkatesh et al., 2012). Ajzen and Fishbein (1980) suggest that feedback from past experiences will influence various beliefs and future behavioral performance. For instance, the strength of the relationship between information usefulness and intention to use is stronger for users with higher experience (Saeed and Abdinnour-Helm, 2008). Also, information technology usage may be more effectively modeled by experienced users (Taylor and Todd, 1995). Accordingly, before inexperienced users use a new e-service, they may require higher e-service quality than experienced users. In this vein, this study proposes that past experience has negative moderating effect on the relationship between e-service quality and user satisfaction and trust.

H4a. The impact of e-service quality on user satisfaction is negatively moderated by past experience.

H4b. The impact of e-service quality on trust is negatively moderated by past experience.

3 Methodology

3.1 Data Source

Data are collected from a university in Taiwan. This university has been established for more than 50 years and establishes an e-service website for alumni in 2003. The Public Affairs Office (PAO) of this university is an institution responsible for alumni e-services, including helping the alumni to seek lost-contact alumni, apply for diplomas of graduation online and so on. Totally, 318 respondents are selected from a web survey at the PAO website. Of the sample, 53 % are male and 65 % graduate more than 5 years ago.

3.2 Measures

E-service Quality. This study uses the WebQUAL instrument (Aladwani and Palvia, 2002) to measure user perceived e-service quality because it is suitable for non-profit web-based context. A total of 15 items are used to measure WebQUAL (see Table 1); specifically, 3 items for *technical adequacy*, 3 items for *content quality*, and 5 items for *web appearance*.

Satisfaction and Trust. User satisfaction is the result of a process of evaluation and is benefit for relationship development (Bauer et al., 2002). Trust reflects a willingness to rely on an exchange partner in whom one has confidence (Morgan and Hunt, 1994). Both satisfaction and trust are usually measured as the relationship with the service provider based on all the service experiences (Garbarino and Johnson, 1999; Roberts et al., 2003). Thus, this study uses 3 items and 2 items to measure the overall satisfaction and trust with website.

Table 1. The questionnaire items of research constructs

e-Service Quality
- **Technical adequacy** (Aladwani and Palvia, 2002)
TA1. This website looks secure for providing service functions.
TA2. Web pages load fast on this website.
TA3. This website is always up and available.
- *Content quality* (Aladwani and Palvia, 2002)
CON1. The content of this website is accurate.
CON2. The content of this website is complete.
CON3. The content of this website is clear.
- *Appearance* (Aladwani and Palvia, 2002)
APP1. This website looks organized.
APP2. This website uses multimedia features properly.
APP3. This website uses fonts properly.
APP4. This website uses colors properly.
- *Satisfaction* (Garbarino and Johnson, 1999)
SAT1. I am satisfied with using this website.
SAT2. I am satisfied with services from this website.
SAT3. The website strengthens my relationship with the university.
- *Trust* (Roberts et al., 2003)
TRU1. This website is trustworthy.
TRU2. This website has high integrity.

Age and Past Experience. The respondents are asked to answer to their age and past experience of using e-service. According to distribution of age, research respondents are divided into three groups. The first group (A1) is the young adults less than 30 years old. The second group (A2) is between 31–40 ages, and the third group (A3) is older adults more than 41 years old. Likewise, the respondents are divided into three groups based on their past experience. The first group (P1) is the inexperienced users whose usage experience less than 1 time, and the second group (P2) is the users who have had e-service experiences 2 or 3 times. The third group (P3) is experienced users who have had more than 4 times e-service experiences before.

4 Results and Discussions

The hypothesized associations are tested by using regression analyses. As expected, web appearance, content quality, and technical adequacy are positively related to satisfaction. The beta coefficients (β) of these three sub-constructs are .236 ($p <= .001$), .224 ($p <= .001$), and .360 ($p <= .001$), respectively. The H1 is supported. Similarly, trust is positively influenced by web appearance ($\beta = .174$; $p <= .01$), content quality ($\beta = .121$; $p = .063$), and technical adequacy ($\beta = .437$; $p <= .001$). The H2 is supported as well. The results are corresponded with the findings by prior studies (Cristobal et al., 2007;

Table 2. The results of regression analysis on different age groups

Dependent variable	Satisfaction		
Age groups	A1 (young adults)	A2 (middle-aged adults)	A3 (older adults)
Web appearance	.239**	.175	.348+
Technical adequacy	.407***	.267*	.252
Content quality	.176*	.361**	.338+
F value	76.000***	25.107***	14.673***
Adjust R^2	.526	.472	.570
Dependent variable	Trust		
Age groups	A1 (young adults)	A2 (middle-aged adults)	A3 (older adults)
Web appearance	.124	.157	.454*
Technical adequacy	.427***	.479***	.442*
Content quality	.210**	.032	-.187
F value	56.815***	15.048***	8.897***
Adjust R^2	.452	.342	.433

+: $p < .1$; *: $p < .05$; **: $p < .01$; ***: $p < .001$

Yang et al., 2005), suggesting greater web quality will lead to higher user satisfaction and trust. But this study duplicates the study and suggests that the causal association is supported without interference from user's age and past experience.

To test the H3, the results are analyzed based on different age groups (i.e., A1, A2 and A3 groups). Table 2 shows that web quality is positively related to user satisfaction for young adults. But, for older adults, the effects of web appearance and content quality merely approached significance (p value ranges from .05 to .1). The causality from web quality to user satisfaction is not more significant for older adults, showing that the H3a is not supported. Similarly, due to lack of obvious evidences, the H3b is not supported. A possible explanation is that because the Internet is becoming increasingly popular, most of older adults are used to use e-service and thereby do not pursue higher demands for web quality.

For the H4, Table 3 shows that web quality is strongly associated with user satisfaction for users with low usage experience, but this association is not significant for users with high usage experience. The result suggests that the causality from web quality to user satisfaction is much more significant for people who seldom use e-service. Corresponded with the expectation, the H4a is supported. The finding reveals that the requirement of web quality is determined by user's usage experience rather than user's age. The enterprise managers could spend more efforts on catching users' past experience and develop appropriate strategy to serve them. For instance, managers can use cookie or system log at the website to analyze users' usage experience. If they are inexperienced users or did not use the e-service before, the website will pop up a message inquiring the users about the needs of user guideline or friendly web appearance.

Furthermore, there is no enough evidence to show the H4b is supported. According to the results of the H3b and H4b, only technical adequacy positively and significantly affects trust in any groups. A plausible explanation is that trust represents a much deeper relationship with user (Corritore et al., 2003). Compared with web appearance and context, providing better technical adequacy (e.g., system security) has a more direct impact on trustworthy relationship. The finding reveals that if enterprise managers aim to establish trustworthy relationships with users, they should be thinking about how to enhance website technology, such as customization, privacy, security and so on.

Table 3. The results of regression analysis on different usage experience groups

Dependent variable	Satisfaction		
Usage experience groups	P1 (low)	P2 (middle)	P3 (high)
Web appearance	$.195^*$	$.256^*$	.293
Technical adequacy	$.388^{***}$	$.340^{***}$	.231
Content quality	$.227^{**}$	$.212^*$	.290
F value	57.138^{***}	32.236^{***}	14.644^{***}
Adjust R^2	.498	.460	.539
Dependent variable	Trust		
Usage experience groups	P1 (low)	P2 (middle)	P3 (high)
Web appearance	$.174^+$	.152	.231
Technical adequacy	$.417^{***}$	$.448^{***}$	$.505^*$
Content quality	.126	.112	.079
F value	38.122^{***}	22.911^{***}	15.358^{***}
Adjust R^2	.396	.374	.552

$^+$: $p < .1$; *: $p < .05$; **: $p < .01$; ***: $p < .001$

5 Conclusions

The aim of this study is to compare the impacts of age and usage experience on the relationship between perceived web quality and user satisfaction and trust. This study found that older adults do not necessarily require greater web quality to serve them because the Internet is becoming popular and they are used to use e-service. In contrast, inexperienced users (or users with low usage experience) require greater web quality than experienced users. Therefore, regarding to website design pursuing higher user satisfaction, the importance of usage experience is higher than user's age.

References

Ajzen, I., Fishbein, M.: Understanding Attitudes and Predicting Social Behavior. Prentice Hall, Englewood Cliffs (1980)

Aladwani, A.M., Palvia, P.C.: Developing and validating an instrument for measuring user-perceived web quality. Inf. Manag. **39**(6), 467–476 (2002)

Bauer, H.H., Mark, G., Leach, M.: Building customer relations over the internet. Ind. Mark. Manag. **31**(2), 155–163 (2002)

Collier, J.E., Bienstock, C.C.: Measuring service quality in e-retailing. J. Serv. Res. **8**(3), 260–275 (2006)

Corritore, C.L., Kracher, B., Wiedenbeck, S.: Online trust: concepts, evolving themes, a model. Int. J. Hum. Comput. Stud. **58**(6), 737–758 (2003)

Cristobal, E., Flavián, C., Guinalíu, M.: Perceived e-service quality (PeSQ): measurement validation and effects on consumer satisfaction and web site loyalty. Manag. Serv. Qual. Int. J. **17**(3), 317–340 (2007)

Curran, K., Walters, N., Robinson, D.: Investigating the problems faced by older adults and people with disabilities in online environments. Behav. Inf. Technol. **26**(6), 447–453 (2007)

Fassnacht, M., Koese, I.: Quality of electronic services conceptualizing and testing a hierarchical model. J. Serv. Res. **9**(1), 19–37 (2006)

Garbarino, E., Johnson, M.S.: The different roles of satisfaction, trust, and commitment in customer relationships. J. Mark. **63**(2), 70–87 (1999)

Gummerus, J., Veronica, L., Pura, M., Allard, R.: Customer loyalty to content-based websites: the case of an online health-care service. J. Serv. Mark. **18**(3), 175–186 (2004)

Hart, T.A., Chaparro, B.S., Halcomb, C.G.: Evaluating websites for older adults: adherence to 'senior-friendly' guidelines and end-user performance. Behav. Inf. Technol. **27**(3), 191–199 (2008)

Liao, C.H., Yen, H.R., Li, E.Y.: The effect of channel quality inconsistency on the association between e-service quality and customer relationships. Internet Res. **21**(4), 458–478 (2011)

Morgan, R.M., Hunt, S.D.: The commitment-trust theory of relationship marketing. J. Mark. **58** (3), 20–38 (1994)

Morris, M.G., Venkatesh, V., Ackerman, P.L.: Gender and age differences in employee decisions about new technology: an extension to the theory of planned behavior. IEEE Trans. Eng. Manag. **52**(1), 69–84 (2005)

Muylle, S., Moenaert, R., Despontin, M.: The conceptualization and empirical validation of web site user satisfaction. Inf. Manag. **41**(5), 543–560 (2004)

Priest, L., Nayak, L., Stuart-Hamilton, I.: Website task performance by older adults. Behav. Inf. Technol. **26**(3), 189–195 (2007)

Roberts, K., Varki, S., Brodie, R.: Measuring the quality of relationships in consumer services: an empirical study. Eur. J. Mark. **37**(1/2), 169–196 (2003)

Saeed, K.A., Abdinnour-Helm, S.: Examining the effects of information system characteristics and perceived usefulness on post adoption usage of information systems. Inf. Manag. **45**(6), 376–386 (2008)

Sousa, R., Voss, C.A.: Service quality in multichannel services employing virtual channels. J. Serv. Res. **8**(4), 356–371 (2006)

Taylor, S., Todd, P.: Assessing IT usage: the role of prior experience. MIS Q. **19**(4), 561–570 (1995)

Venkatesh, V., Davis, F.D.: A model of the antecedents of perceived ease of use: development and test. Decis. Sci. **27**(3), 451–481 (1996)

Venkatesh, V., Thong, J.Y.L., Xu, X.: Consumer acceptance and use of information technology: extending the unified theory of acceptance and use of technology. MIS Q. **36**(1), 157–178 (2012)

Wolfinbarger, M., Gilly, M.C.: eTailQ: dimensionalizing, measuring, and predicting e-tail quality. J. Retail. **79**(3), 183–198 (2003)

Yang, Z., Cai, S., Zhou, Z., Zhou, N.: Development and validation of an instrument to measure user perceived service quality of information presenting web portals. Inf. Manag. **42**(4), 575–589 (2005)

Yoo, B., Donthu, N.: Developing a scale to measure the perceived quality of internet shopping sites (SITEQUAL). Q. J. Electron. Commer. **2**(1), 31–47 (2001)

Zeithaml, V., Parusuraman, A., Malhotra, A.: A Conceptual Framework for Understanding e-Service Quality: Implications for Future Research and Managerial Practice, pp. 1–115. Marketing Science Institute, Cambridge (2000)

Zeithaml, V.A., Parasuraman, A., Malhotra, A.: Service quality delivery through web sites: a critical review of extant knowledge. J. Acad. Mark. Sci. **30**(4), 362–375 (2002)

Acceptance of ICTs by Older Adults: A Review of Recent Studies

Qi Ma[1]([⊠]), Ke Chen[1], Alan Hoi Shou Chan[1], and Pei-Lee Teh[2]

[1] Department of Systems Engineering and Engineering Management,
City University of Hong Kong,
Kowloon Tong, Hong Kong
qima22-c@my.cityu.edu.hk
[2] School of Business, Monash University,
Selangor Darul Ehsan, Malaysia

Abstract. Objectives: Issues surrounding aging and information communication technologies (ICTs) are of critical importance. This study aims to identify the determinants of the acceptance of ICTs innovations by older adults, and discuss the research gap in the gerontechnology literature.

Methods: Research articles were selected from four multi-disciplinary databases (SCOPUS, ProQuest, EBSCOHOST, Science Direct) from 2004 to 2015. Articles were filtered by "Older than 55", "healthy", "acceptance", "ICTs", etc. Finally, a total of 29 papers including qualitative, quantitative and mixed-method research are used in this study.

Results: The majority of these studies indicated that older adults have a positive attitude towards using ICTs. The findings summarized ICTs-related technologies in five basic domains: Intelligent monitoring, Health care delivery, Online services, Social communication, and Internet & Computer. The review gathered and classified important acceptance factors into six themes: Perceived Benefits of Use, Subjective Norm, Perceived Behavior Control, Perceived Usability, Affections, and Socio-demographic Mediators.

Keywords: Review · Older adults · Information communication technologies (ICTs) · Technology acceptance

1 Introduction

Information and communications technologies (ICTs) is often used as an extended synonym for information technology (IT), but is a more specific term that stresses the role of unified communications and the integration of telecommunications (telephone lines and wireless signals), computers as well as necessary enterprise software, middleware, storage, and audio-visual systems, which enable users to access, store, transmit, and manipulate information. The increasing permeation of information communication technologies (ICTs) in our society leads to the challenge that everybody needs to interact with ICTs in daily life. Populations in many countries are aging at the same time, and the current cohort of older adults has experienced ICTs for a

© Springer International Publishing Switzerland 2015
J. Zhou and G. Salvendy (Eds.): ITAP 2015, Part I, LNCS 9193, pp. 239–249, 2015.
DOI: 10.1007/978-3-319-20892-3_24

relatively short period in their late lives [1]. Older adults differ considerably from young users in Human Computer Interaction (HCI) and they often meet difficulties while trying to accept and use new technology products and services. There remains an age-related digital divide that older adults lag behind in using and benefiting from information and communication technologies [2]. Venkatesh concluded that older adults, like anyone else, accept and adopt technology when it meets their needs and expectations [3, 4]. However, Verdegem and De Marez [5] reported that technology innovations often fail to be fully utilized since less attention is given to user acceptance. Thus, to ensure that older adults are able to adapt to the new information environment, there were some studies that explore from different perspectives the factors that influence the acceptance of information and communication technologies among older adults. Increasing attention on the acceptance of ICTs-related innovations by older adults makes a review of the recent studies on this topic timely and meaningful.

This study reviewed the existing research from a multi-disciplinary and holistic view to identify the predictors and areas concerned in the acceptance and usage of ICTs by older adults, and attempted to provide directions for further technology acceptance research within this specific group. A systematic review of qualitative, quantitative, and mixed methods studies examined the following research questions: What is the relevance of ICTs to the daily lives of older adults? What are the common ICTs applications in older adults' lives? Which factors influence the acceptance of different types of ICTs for aging in place by older adults with normal health status? What are older adults concerned with when using different innovations of ICTs? This review will try to shed light on all these issues.

2 Methods

2.1 Literature Search Strategy

Four multi-disciplinary databases (Scopus, ProQuest, EBSCOHOST, Science Direct) were searched using a combination of three groups of key-words regarding age, acceptance and ICTs respectively: (1) 'older adults' OR 'older people' OR 'elderly' OR 'aging', subjected to 'Title'; (2) 'acceptance' OR 'adoption', subjected to 'Title/Abstract/Keywords'; (3) 'information technology' OR 'ICTs' OR 'digital' OR 'electronics' OR 'computer' OR 'mobile phone' OR 'internet' OR 'e-health care' OR 'online service' OR 'home monitoring', subjected to 'Title/Abstract/Keywords'. Since technologies and social life changed so fast in recent years, this review will only focus on the batch of relatively new studies in recent ten years from 2004–2014/2015. A scientific selection process was developed by different kinds of exclusive and inclusive principles as shown in Fig. 1.

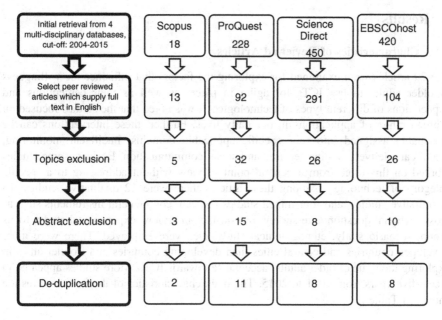

Fig. 1. Flow diagram of articles selection process

2.2 Article Extraction

In order to extract the appropriate and valid articles in this review, a set of inclusion principles regarding 'Topic exclusion' and 'Abstract exclusion' were developed as shown in Table 1.

Table 1. Criteria for inclusion in review

Criteria
1. The topic of an article should be within the range of 'ICTs acceptance', those topics on 'disease', 'cognitive/physical rehabilitation', 'child', 'women', 'social capital', etc. were excluded
2. After reading abstracts, review articles and narrative articles were excluded. Moreover, only those exploring or confirming acceptance factors and concerns were retained
3. Target technologies should be within the range of ICTs-related computerized or internet-based devices or systems which will generate data transmission
4. Participants in an empirical study should be older than 55 and with a normal health status physically and mentally

Finally, 29 valid papers were retained in total including qualitative methods (e.g. interviews, focus groups, contextual observations, diaries), quantitative methods (e.g. surveys, experiments) and mixed method.

3 Results

3.1 Characteristics of Reviewed Articles

The 29 articles were examined for exploring the factors that influence the willingness of older adults to use ICTs for aging in place, as well as their perceptions and expectations of different types of technologies. It was noted that the studies focused on a broad range of applications in our daily lives. Further, these interventions can be reasonably assigned into four specific applicable domains: intelligent monitoring, health care delivery, online services and social communication. Besides, some studies worked on this topic from a general point of view without addressing to a specific category of technology. Among these articles there were 12 qualitative studies, 13 quantitative studies, and four mixed studies respectively. General instruments such as cross-sectional questionnaire survey, face-to-face interview, experimental study, focus group, scenario study, ethnographical study, etc. were employed. There were more developed countries and central cities than developing countries and frontier areas in exploring the issue of older adults' acceptance towards ICTs. More studies appeared in recent five years from 2011 to 2015. The main characteristics of the 29 literatures are shown in Table 2.

3.2 Usage of ICTs by Older Adults

Older adults reported using a wide range of technology in their everyday lives and cited efficiency, making life easier, and communication as reasons for the use of technology. General ICT devices and services that are adopted by older users include mobile phone, desktop computer, Internet, electronic commerce, portable computer or mini-computer, and various kinds of computer/smartphone applications and internet applications. Apart from communicating with family members, friends, and health care providers, and dealing with daily routines, ICTs can be applied in various innovative fields in people's daily life, such as e-services, smart-home, tele-medicine, ambient intelligence monitoring, robots, etc. Literatures in this review covered majority of ICTs innovations which were classified into intelligent monitoring, health care delivery, online services and social communications, as shown in Table 2. ICTs are now highly relevant with older adults' daily life at home, work and health care environment [33]. Since work life is extending, to remain active, competitive, and useful in the workforce, older adults must use and learn to use basic digital technologies in the information era. Many older adults prefer to remain in their own home, the majority of their activities occur within the home environment. ICTs can support many home-based tasks, e.g., gathering information, safety and security monitoring of older adults at home, etc. More ICT applications will be brought into older adults' home environment and it is a positive trend for older adults to use ICTs in home. Besides, ICTs have the potential to assist in monitoring and maintaining health as well as managing health conditions and diseases, especially in facilitating cost-effective care [34].

Table 2. Characteristics of reviewed articles

ICTs domains	Ref.	Application	Study design			
			Method	Measurement	Sample	Country
Intelligent monitoring	[6]	Ambient intelligence technologies	Qualitative	Individual interview	18	USA
	[7]	Wireless sensor network (WSN)	Qualitative	Focus group	13	Australia
	[8]	Communication and monitoring technology	Qualitative	Scenario study	9	USA
	[9]	Medical monitoring	Quantitative	Questionnaire	127	USA
	[10]	Home-based monitoring	Qualitative	Focus group	64	USA
	[11]	Smart home information-based technologies	Qualitative	Focus group	14	USA
	[12]	Remote patient monitoring	Quantitative	Questionnaire	14	USA
Health care delivery	[13]	Medical assistive technologies	Mixed	Focus group, Questionnaire	104	Germany
	[14]	Health-related ICTs	Mixed	Questionnaire	123	USA Israel
	[15]	Electronic health record (her) systems	Qualitative	Questionnaire	372	USA
	[16]	Telehealth kiosk	Qualitative	Focus group	12	USA
	[17]	Mobile health service	Quantitative	Questionnaire	204	China
Online services	[18]	E-Government	Quantitative	Questionnaire In-depth interview	146	Gambia
	[19]	Online shopping	Quantitative	Questionnaire	574	Taiwan
Social communication	[1]	E-mail	Qualitative	Ethnographical study	200	Spain
	[20]	E-mail	Quantitative	Questionnaire	460	USA
	[21]	Mobile data services (MDS)	Quantitative	Questionnaire	266	Hong Kong
	[22]	Telephone voice menu systems	Mixed	Questionnaire, Experimental study	27	USA
Internet & Computer	[2]	Internet	Quantitative	Questionnaire	150	Germany
	[23]	Internet	Quantitative	Questionnaire	374	China
	[24]	Internet	Quantitative	Questionnaire	592	UK
	[25]	Computer	Quantitative	Questionnaire	52	Germany
General technology	[26]	Technology	Mixed	Socioeconomic survey, Questionnaire	100	Brazil
	[27]	Technology in home, work and healthcare	Qualitative	Focus group	113	USA
	[28]	Technology	Qualitative	Daily workbook questions	6	USA
	[29]	ICTs	Qualitative	Focus group, Individual interview	81	Ireland
	[30]	Information technology	Quantitative	Questionnaire	233	China
	[31]	Gerontechnology	Quantitative	Questionnaire, Face-to-face interview	1012	Hong Kong
	[32]	ICTs	Qualitative	Focus group, Questionnaire	7	Spain

3.3   Determinants of ICTs Acceptance

Research around technology acceptance and usage among older adults has now received increasing attention over time, especially in the developed countries such as the United States, Japan, and The Netherlands. Majority of the studies towards technology acceptance factors for aging in place were in the pre-implementation stage. Various factors were explored by prior researchers in different contexts. These factors can be basically categorized into Perceived Benefits of Use (i.e., perceived impact on life, perceived usefulness, needs satisfaction, perceived benefits, perceived convenience), Subjective Norm (i.e., children/family's influence, caregivers' influence, social influence), Perceived Behavior Control (i.e., self-efficacy, anxiety, facilitating condition, support availability), Perceived Usability (i.e., perceived ease of use, age-centered interface, system reliability), Affections, and Socio-demographic mediators (i.e., gender, age, education, income, health and post experience), as shown in Table 3.

Different structural models based on Technology Acceptance Model (TAM) [35], Unified Theory of Acceptance and Use of Technology (UTAUT) [3], and the Theory of Planned Behavior (TPB) [36]) were built according to the causal dependencies among the potential factors. Chen and Chan [31] built a gerontechnology acceptance model called "STAM" among older Hong Kong Chinese. The results showed that individual attributes including age, gender, education, self-efficacy and anxiety, and health and ability characteristics, as well as facilitating conditions explicitly and directly affected technology acceptance. Besides, Heart & Kalderon [14] explored older adults' adoption of health-related ICTs through examination of TPB in the context of computer use. The result indicated that perceived behavioral control could significantly affect intention to use information and communication technology. Whether older adults determine to use technology also depends on their perceived needs or benefits, it is the most frequently mentioned factor overall [16]. Non-use of computers can be attributed to their low relevance and 'relative advantage' to older adults [37] as older adults like to adopt and use technologies only if the value and personal relevance is clear [28]. Generally, older adults report that they care much more about the benefits they gain from ICTs than the costs on ICTs [22].

Furthermore, more external factors such as family and social influence and product usability were identified as important determinants towards various kinds of technology acceptance. Older adults' children, friends and professional caregivers may positively or negatively influence their acceptance [10, 11, 28]. The longer older adults have used the technology, the more they perceived those people who are important to them would want them to use it [12]. From a human factors and ergonomics view, most studies presented evidences for the common suggested physiological and psychological reasons behind older adults' lower levels of use of ICTs (e.g., poorer vision, memory, and dexterity) [38]. Older adults seemed to tolerate some complexity, but it should not be more than they could handle after learning [39], perceived usability was found to be important to the adoption and long-term use of the technology- the technology should be reliable, controllable, simple to use and tailored to users [7, 16]. Other than those modeling-based determinants, another determinant that can be extracted from the emotional dimensions of older adults is affections. Anxious or emotional reactions are expressed by older adults when they use computers or money-related technological services. Moreover, it was found that there was generally a negative prejudice or some discrimination attached to the use of assistive health technology like emergency alarm services [40]. Socio-demographics were shown as better predictors of gerontechnology usage behavior than the conventionally used attitudinal factors (usefulness and ease of use) [31]. Key socio-demographic variables in technology adoption were extracted as gender, age, income, and education [2]. Socio-demographic variables can further increase the power of technology acceptance model to determine whether older adults ultimately adopt the ICTs and to what extent.

Table 3. Summary of acceptance factors regarding ICTs

Themes of determinants	Items	References
Perceived benefits of use (PBoU)	Perceived impact on life	[7]
	Perceived usefulness	[10, 22–24]
	Needs satisfaction	[11, 30]
	Perceived benefits	[27]
	Perceived convenience	[27]
Subjective Norm (SN)	Children's/families' influence	[12, 28]
	Social influence	[8, 12, 15, 19]
	Subjective norm	[21, 23]
Perceived Behavior Control (PBC)	Self-efficacy	[14, 31]
	Facilitating condition	[14, 20, 25, 31]
	Anxiety	[7, 17, 31]
	Support availability	[30, 32]
Perceived Usability (PU)	Perceived ease of use	[17, 21, 23]
	Age-centered interface	[1, 15, 16]
	Perceived usability	[30]
	System reliability	[7, 27]
Socio-demographic mediators	Gender	[2, 9, 24, 26, 31]
	Age	[2, 9, 31]
	Education	[2, 31]
	Income	[2]
	Marital status	[14]
	Health	[1, 9, 14, 31]
	Experience	[8, 29]

4 Discussions

4.1 Usefulness and Findings

This review's strength lies in its literature set which includes most recent studies on older adults' acceptance of ICTs innovations, and it is more holistic since it gathered articles from four different multi-disciplinary databases (Scopus, ProQuest, Science Direct, EBSCOhost databases), involving studies from fields of ergonomics, sociology,

246   Q. Ma et al.

psychology, gerontology, health, etc. Besides, the review classified ICTs innovations adopted in older adults' lives (home/work/health care) into several groups, thereby highlighted that the development of recent ICTs innovations for older adults is clearly focused on intelligent monitoring or assistive products/services/systems, and indicated that the trend of adopting home-based information technology innovations is inevitable among older adults. Acceptance determinants (including mediators) were clearly distinguished in this review. Since determinants may promote users' acceptance, the identified determinants may contribute more on later academic studies.

From the review, word strings like 'needs', 'benefits', and 'relevance' were frequently referred in most literatures. It revealed that older adults cares most about the benefits they can gain from ICTs innovations instead of extended features. Besides, 'cost' or 'finance' were mentioned as concerns in most literatures, older adults do report a heavy concern on the monthly service cost of ICTs and they hope that someone or government can afford a part of the expense. However, several studies also indicated that older adults choose to adopt the technology product/service as long as they need it or the benefits they get are worth the costs. Another significant aspect is on the usability; older adults reported many complaints on the obstacles when learning to use technologies due to health and ability impairments compared with younger people. Finally, older adults reported that they need human assistance or some other kinds of facilitations when using ICTs innovations.

4.2 Limitations and Future Work

However, this review should be used under the premise that it has three critical limitations. First, the extraction criteria of literatures do not include some important personal attributes of participants such as older person's past experiences and their living arrangements, the influences of these attributes should not be ignored sometimes. Second, the review has now classified several groups of ICTs innovations, it would be better if the study continued to review acceptance factors and concerns specific to each type of ICTs application respectively rather than just gave a general idea on all ICTs innovations. Third, as technology and people's living style developed quickly, there should be a holistic comparison on the acceptance situation towards ICTs of older adults in recent ten years and past decades, it will be a promising way to enlighten researchers and practitioners studying this topic, and even predictions of the acceptance towards ICTs by older adults in future can be seen in advance.

Meanwhile, some gaps were identified for future research in this review. Most of prior studies identified various factors that influence the acceptance of information technology. However, few studies identified the interrelationship of these factors and few of them adapted these factors into established models such as TAM, UTAUT and TPB to measure the acceptance of ICTs (or one kind of ICT device or service) by older adults. Another important gap is that there are few studies focusing on the longitudinal usage or acceptance of ICTs innovations. From a quantitative view, the ICTs acceptance model of older adults should be a dynamic one instead of a static one along with usage period. More and more research attention is appealed to the understanding of reasons of non-use of ICT by older adults. Now, it is time to explore promising tools to facilitate older adults to adopt ICT devices and services more effectively. In addition to aging-centered design, both the traditional and computer training programs need further studies.

References

1. Sayago, S., Blat, J.: Telling the story of older people e-mailing: an ethnographical study. Int. J. Hum. Comput. Stud. **68**(1–2), 105–120 (2010)
2. Niehaves, B., Plattfaut, R.: Internet adoption by the elderly: employing IS technology acceptance theories for understanding the age-related digital divide. Eur. J. Inf. Syst. **23**(6), 708–726 (2013)
3. Venkatesh, V., Morris, M.G., Davis, G.B., Davis, F.D.: User acceptance of information technology: toward a unified view. MIS Q. Manag. Inf. Syst. **27**(3), 425–478 (2003)
4. Verdegem, P., De Marez, L.: Rethinking determinants of ICT acceptance: towards an integrated and comprehensive overview. Technovation **31**(8), 411–423 (2011)
5. Conci, M., Pianesi, F., Zancanaro, M.: Useful, social and enjoyable: mobile phone adoption by older people. In: Gross, T., Gulliksen, J., Kotzé, P., Oestreicher, L., Palanque, P., Prates, R.O., Winckler, M. (eds.) INTERACT 2009. LNCS, vol. 5726, pp. 63–76. Springer, Heidelberg (2009)
6. van Hoof, J., Kort, H.S., Rutten, P.G., Duijnstee, M.S.: Ageing-in-place with the use of ambient intelligence technology: perspectives of older users. Int. J. Med. Inform. **80**(5), 310–331 (2011)
7. Steele, R., Lo, A., Secombe, C., Wong, Y.K.: Elderly persons' perception and acceptance of using wireless sensor networks to assist healthcare. Int. J. Med. Inform. **78**(12), 788–801 (2009)
8. Mahmood, A., Yamamoto, T., Lee, M., Steggell, C.: Perceptions and use of gerotechnology: implications for aging in place. J. Hous. Elderly **22**(1–2), 104–126 (2008)
9. Himmel, S., Ziefle, M., Arning, K.: From living space to urban quarter: acceptance of ICT monitoring solutions in an ageing society. In: Kurosu, M. (ed.) HCII/HCI 2013, Part III. LNCS, vol. 8006, pp. 49–58. Springer, Heidelberg (2013)
10. Lorenzen-Huber, L., Boutain, M., Camp, L.J., Shankar, K., Connelly, K.H.: Privacy, technology, and aging: a proposed framework. Ageing Int. **36**(2), 232–252 (2010)
11. Courtney, K.L., Demiris, G., Rantz, M., Skubic, M.: Needing smart home technologies the perspectives of older adults. Inform. Prim. Care **16**, 195–201 (2008)
12. Giger, J.T., Pope, N.D., Vogt, H.B., Gutierrez, C., Newland, L.A., Lemke, J., Lawler, M.J.: Remote patient monitoring acceptance trends among older adults residing in a frontier state. Comput. Hum. Behav. **44**, 174–182 (2015)
13. Wilkowska, W., & Ziefle, M.: Perception of privacy and security for acceptance of E-health technologies: exploratory analysis for diverse user groups. User-Centred-Design of Pervasive Health Applications (UCD-PH 2011), held in conjunction with the 5th ICST/IEEE Conference on Pervasive Computing Technologies for Healthcare 2011, pp. 593–600 (2011)
14. Heart, T., Kalderon, E.: Older adults: are they ready to adopt health-related ICT? Int. J. Med. Inform. **82**(11), e209–e231 (2013)
15. Lam, R., Lin, V.S., Senelick, W.S., Tran, H.P., Moore, A.A., Koretz, B.: Older adult consumers' attitudes and preferences on electronic patient-physician messaging. Am. J. Managed Care (special issue) **19**, eSP7–eSP11 (2013)

16. Demiris, G., Thompson, H., Boquet, J., Le, T., Chaudhuri, S., Chung, J.: Older adults' acceptance of a community-based telehealth wellness system. Inform. Health. Soc. Care **38** (1), 27–36 (2013)

17. Guo, X., Sun, Y., Wang, N., Peng, Z., Yan, Z.: The dark side of elderly acceptance of preventive mobile health services in China. Electron. Mark. **23**(1), 49–61 (2012)

18. Lin, F., Fofanah, S.S., Liang, D.: Assessing citizen adoption of e-Government initiatives in Gambia: a validation of the technology acceptance model in information systems success. Gov. Inf. Q. **28**(2), 271–279 (2011)

19. Lian, J.-W., Yen, D.C.: Online shopping drivers and barriers for older adults: age and gender differences. Comput. Human. Behav. **37**, 133–143 (2014)

20. Werner, J.M., Carlson, M., Jordan-Marsh, M., Clark, F.: Predictors of computer use in community-dwelling, ethnically diverse older adults. Hum. Factors J. Hum. Factors Ergon. Soc. **53**(5), 431–447 (2011)

21. Hong, S.-J., Lui, C.S.M., Hahn, J., Moon, J.Y., Kim, T.G.: How old are you really? cognitive age in technology acceptance. Decis. Support Syst. **56**, 122–130 (2013)

22. Sharit, J., Czaja, S.J., Perdomo, D., Lee, C.C.: A cost-benefit analysis methodology for assessing product adoption by older user populations. Appl. Ergon. **35**(2), 81–92 (2004)

23. Pan, S., Jordan-Marsh, M.: Internet use intention and adoption among Chinese older adults: from the expanded technology acceptance model perspective. Comput. Hum. Behav. **26**(5), 1111–1119 (2010)

24. Nayak, L.U.S., Priest, L., White, A.P.: An application of the technology acceptance model to the level of Internet usage by older adults. Univ. Access Inf. Soc. **9**(4), 367–374 (2010)

25. Nagle, S., Schmidt, L.: Computer acceptance of older adults. Work **41**(Suppl 1), 3541–3548 (2012)

26. Raymundo, T.M., Santana, C.S.: Factors influencing the acceptance of technology by older people: how the elderly in Brazil feel about using electronics. IEEE Consum. Electron. Mag. **3**, 63–68 (2014)

27. Mitzner, T.L., Boron, J.B., Fausset, C.B., Adams, A.E., Charness, N., Czaja, S.J., Dijkstra, K., Fisk, A.D., Rogers, W.A., Sharit, J.: Older adults talk technology: technology usage and attitudes. Comput. Hum. Behav. **26**(6), 1710–1721 (2010)

28. Fausset, C.B., Harley, L., Farmer, S., Fain, B.: Older adults' perceptions and use of technology: a novel approach. In: Stephanidis, C., Antona, M. (eds.) UAHCI 2013, Part II. LNCS, vol. 8010, pp. 51–58. Springer, Heidelberg (2013)

29. Walsh, K., Callan, A.: Perceptions, preferences, and acceptance of information and communication technologies in older-adult community care settings in Ireland: a case-study and ranked-care program analysis. Ageing Int. **36**(1), 102–122 (2010)

30. Wang, L., Rau, P.-L.P., Salvendy, G.: Older adults' acceptance of information technology. Educ. Gerontol. **37**(12), 1081–1099 (2011)

31. Chen, K., Chan, A.H.: Gerontechnology acceptance by elderly Hong Kong Chinese: a senior technology acceptance model (STAM). Ergonomics **57**(5), 635–652 (2014)

32. Hernández-Encuentra, E., Pousada, M., Gómez-Zúñiga, B.: ICT and older people: beyond usability. Educ. Gerontology **35**(3), 226–245 (2009)

33. Czaja, S.J., Lee, C.C.: Information technology and older adults. In: Sears, A., Jacko, J.A. (eds.) Human Computer Interaction, Designing for Diverse Users and Domains, pp. 17–32. CRC Press, Boca Raton (2009)

34. Marschollek, M., Mix, S., Wolf, K.-H., Effertz, B., Haux, R., Steinhagen-Thiessen, E.: ICT-based health information services for elderly people: past experiences, current trends, and future strategies. Med. Inf. Internet Med. **32**(4), 251–261 (2009)

35. Davis, F.D.: Perceived usefulness, perceived ease of use and user acceptance of information technology. MIS Q. **13**(3), 319–340 (1989)

36. Ajzen, I.: The theory of planned behavior. Organ. Behav. Hum. Decis. Process **50**, 179–211 (1991)
37. Selwyn, N., Gorard, S., Furlong, J., Madden, L.: Older adults' use of information and communications technology in everyday life. Ageing Soc. **23**(5), 561–582 (2003)
38. Charness, N.: Aging and communication: human factors issues. In: Charness, N., Parks, D. C., Sabel, B.A. (eds.) Communication Technology and Aging, pp. 3–29. Springer, New York (2001)
39. Zhou, J., Rau, P.-L.P., Salvendy, G.: A qualitative study of older adults' acceptance of new functions on smart phones and tablets. In: Rau, P. (ed.) HCII 2013 and CCD 2013, Part I. LNCS, vol. 8023, pp. 525–534. Springer, Heidelberg (2013)
40. Chen, K., Chan, A.H.: Use or non-use of gerontechnology–a qualitative study. Int. J. Environ. Res. Public Health **10**(10), 4645–4666 (2013)

An Appraisal-Based Approach to the Stigma
of Walker-Use

Andrew McNeill[⊠] and Lynne Coventry

PaCT Lab, Department of Psychology, Northumbria University,
Newcastle upon Tyne NE1 8ST, UK
{andrew.mcneill,lynne.coventry}@northumbria.ac.uk

Abstract. Walker-use among older adults is often avoided because of the stigma of using one. Drawing on the appraisal theory of stress, we argue that stigma associated with walker-use is subject to various cognitive appraisals that affect whether the user sees the walker as stigmatizing and the extent to which they can cope with that stigma. We followed a participatory design approach to involve older adults in the design of an intelligent walker. One of the activities was to conduct focus groups to explore the role of the aesthetic design of the product in acceptance and use of such walkers. Qualitative analysis of these focus groups provides data explaining the ways in which potential users assess stigma and coping resources. We emphasise that while better design of walkers is important, tackling the self-stigma of users and increasing their ability to cope with using one is equally important.

Keywords: Psychology and cognition · User acceptance · Design

1 Introduction

One reason why some older adults do not use assistive technology such as walkers is stigma [1]: a "devalued identity" associated with their use [2]. When an older adult considers using assistive technology such as walkers, they have to deal with the potential of stigma from others who see the walker as a sign that they are old and disabled. People might talk down to them, treat them as being less mentally capable and exclude them from certain activities. The identity of being an "old person" is widely perceived as undesirable and this affects many of the ways in which older adults behave [3, 4]. Sometimes older adults will even avoid the use of blankets [3] or avoid reporting falls [4] because they fear being identified as "old". Others avoid using assistive walking aids like canes because of stigma [5, 6]. Devices like walkers are signs that a person is old and these can convey a stigmatised identity. For this reason, older adults sometimes utilise compensatory strategies to avoid stigma such as using umbrellas [7] or shopping trolleys [8, 9] as covert walking support. Such devices provide support for the user but do not evoke the stigma of being an "old person".

While stigma is a key reason why older adults may avoid using assistive technology, it is not always the case that older people are treated negatively. Sometimes attitudes towards older people can be described as "benevolent ageism" [10] which is a tendency to "over-help" older adults. Stigma associated with aging is also internal as

© Springer International Publishing Switzerland 2015
J. Zhou and G. Salvendy (Eds.): ITAP 2015, Part I, LNCS 9193, pp. 250–261, 2015.
DOI: 10.1007/978-3-319-20892-3_25

we are prejudiced not merely against others, but also our future selves [11]. Older adults may fear their future self who uses assistive devices and thus avoid such technology. Rather than simply targeting the wider population to decrease stigma, older adults must confront their own negative attitudes.

When older adults face stigma due to using a walker, whether external or internal, this stigma can be considered as a potential "stressor" [12]. They may fear using the walker because it gives them a negative self-image [13] or because they fear what other people will do or say to them [5]. This fear can lead to stress. However, the effect of this stressor is not the same for all people; different people react to stress differently via different coping mechanisms. According to the appraisal theory of stress [14], a stressful encounter is managed by ascertaining the meaning of the encounter (primary appraisal) and the availability of coping mechanisms (secondary appraisal). The coping strategies can either be problem-focused where the stressor is removed through altering the situation or emotion-focused where the stressor is reduced through regulating emotions. In the case of walkers, primary appraisal will evaluate whether using a walker is stressful and secondary appraisal will provide coping mechanisms if it is perceived as stressful. Those coping mechanisms could take the form of a problem-focused strategy (avoiding using the walker) or an emotion-focused strategy (choosing to focus on the benefits of use). These different coping strategies are apparent when users of assistive technologies negotiate their reliance on them by employing various strategies such as resignation, but limiting use or focusing on the benefits of using it [15].

Multiple strategies can be used to cope with the stigma-stress of using the device and this means that even when stigma does exist, it can be coped with and overcome. One possible way to decrease the stigmatizing effect of assistive technology is to increase our use of universal design principles. One of the key principles of universal design is the principle of equitable use which states that the design should be "useful and marketable to people with diverse abilities" [16]. This suggests that the service should be provided in the same way for all users wherever possible and should avoid segregating and potentially stigmatising users. This principle also emphasises the role of designs which are appealing to everyone. The most quoted example of this is the OXO good grips kitchen equipment, originally designed to be easier to grip by people with arthritis, but the design is sought after by many.

A key concept of universal design, is to provide accessibility without requiring an adaptation or assistive technology, by integrating assistive features unnoticed into the design. By its very nature, it should remove any stigma associated as the same design is used by everyone. Figure 1 illustrates how as abilities lessen, inclusive design has a role to play in increasing the number of people who still can use a product, by increasing the depth of the bottom layer of the pyramid. For instance, e-books with backlights can be seen as an inclusive design, providing greater contrast and font size without having to request an adapted version of a book. More advanced versions can even provide access to audio books, again not only something visually impaired people would want, but with celebrity narrators they are desirable to a wider audience. An alternative approach is to create adaptations which are not perceived as assistive, therefore not impacting self-efficacy, or stigma. As with the example of using a shopping trolley as a walking support, the alternative role of carrying shopping is emphasized. The final approach is to explore if the design of adapted environments and assistive technologies can be done in such a way that they are evaluated as socially acceptable – even desirable. We have seen such a shift in the design of eyeglasses, from undesirable, stigmatizing and medical to designer-led and aspirational.

Fig. 1. Changing Abilities and Inclusive Design

Alternatively, a kettle may be too heavy for a frail, older adult to lift and be dangerous. We could suggest that the older adult requires assistance and design an assistive aid that will support them in the lifting task but this clearly highlights their declining abilities and may lead to self-stigmatising. An alternative would be to suggest a smaller kettle and emphasize the positive effect on the environment and fuel bills rather than the lack of lifting ability. This may inadvertently trigger feelings of loneliness. Alternatively we could suggest the newer designs that remove the need to lift the kettle altogether by pouring the hot water directly into the cup without lifting. These designs again are more environmentally friendly, only heating water as it is poured, allow multiple cups and remove lifting of more than a cupful altogether (Fig. 2).

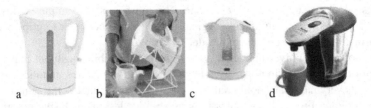

Fig. 2. Presenting adapted technology as aspirational technology

The question is whether or not it possible to make mobility aids more desirable? How can we design walking aids that everyone would be happy to use? An example is the design of Nordic Ski poles, which are widely viewed as more acceptable than a standard medical issue walking stick. They are promoted as an exercise aid rather than as an assistive technology. We also see more elaborate designs of walking sticks, turning them into desirable objects.

Exploring different forms of appraisal allows us to understand individual differences in response to the use of walkers and why not all older adults find using a walker stigmatising. By understanding why some people do not find walker-use stigmatising and how others successfully use coping mechanisms, suggestions can be made for how to assist other older adults to be more willing to use walkers. We conducted this study as part of our work on DALi (Devices for Assisted Living) [9, 17] where we are working with technology partners to design an intelligent walker which supports older adults in large unfamiliar public spaces such as shopping centres and hospitals. Our ultimate goal is to create a robotic support that is both functional and desirable. For people who require assistance, it will operate as a walking and navigation aid and help them to physically carry their shopping. Others will simply use it as a type of desirable "personal assistance". Consequently, we were eager to explore how to make such a product less stigmatizing and more appealing. Being able to achieve this is important because the development of acceptable walkers and ways to encourage older adults to accept and use walkers will encourage users who may fear going outdoors [18] to become more active. Becoming more mobile is associated with a range of physical, psychological and social benefits which will enhance users' lives [19].

2   Method

2.1   Data Collection

Five focus groups were held with groups recruited via a database of older participants. Each group contained 4–7 participants. These focus groups took the form of tea parties [17] which are less formal focus groups that include a time for tea and cakes. The less formal nature of these groups has been found to aid more open discussion.

Semi-structured questioning was used, supplemented by use of images of walkers to elicit views. While it can be difficult for participants to talk about what exactly makes a walker's appearance stigmatizing, discussing photographs provides opportunities for specific designs to be critiqued. We specifically used images that were not created within the project and emphasized to participants that these were not our designs and to feel free to critique them honestly. We felt it was essential for participants to not be "nice to the designers", a situation we have encountered in other projects. The sessions were recorded by both audio and video recorders.

2.2   Analytic Approach

The transcripts were coded using "template analysis" [20] which stresses the importance of developing an hierarchical structure of themes. The approach allows for a priori categories to be used (e.g. primary and secondary appraisal). The transcripts were read and coded to answer the research question, "What factors influence stigma associated with walker use?" These codes were then grouped into two categories: primary appraisal and secondary appraisal.

3 Analysis

Table 1 provides an overview of the two forms of appraisal. Primary appraisal relates to whether the experience is perceived as stressful/stigmatizing and secondary appraisal relates to the coping strategies that can be used if it is perceived as stressful/stigmatizing. Occasionally themes overlapped both forms of appraisal.

Table 1. Table of main themes from qualitative analysis

Primary appraisal	Secondary appraisal
Appearance of walker → Walker as extension of self → Perception of function and identity → Attention-drawing → Attractive design Social acceptability Self-esteem	Problem focussed → Ability to customize → Social support Cognition focused → Cognitive emphasis on benefits → Necessity → Age-related apathy → Time reduces stigma

3.1 Primary Appraisal

Appearance of Walker

Walker as Extension of Self. The appearance of the walker is important as it is linked to the person using it, - if it looks bad, the user looks bad. One participant compared the use of a walker to clothing and accessories: *"It's almost an extension of your dress really, it's an extension of your external appearance, it's another appendage, like a watch ..."*

If a walker is unattractive, this causes the user to look bad. On the other hand, an attractively designed walker can offer a user the same positive benefits as an attractive watch or attractive clothing. For this reason, some users also talked about the need to have gender-relevant designs. Walkers would be a positive benefit only if their appearance matched the gender of the user.

Perception of Function and Identity. A device that is designed for people with disabilities confers on the user the identity of "disabled". On the other hand, when participants discussed various devices, the devices that were associated with positive functions (i.e. those that stressed the *ability* of the user) often led them to confer a positive identity on the user. One participant noted that the use of racing wheelchairs is not associated with a negative identity: *"If you look at somebody in a racing wheelchair, particularly a young person in a racing wheelchair, people don't look at them with pity do they?"*

This fear of being "pitied" is interesting insofar as the user is not necessarily concerned about being maltreated as much as being perceived as less able than others. This is the essence of stigma which can be described as a "devalued social identity" [21]. Nevertheless, it is important to note that the wheelchair per se is not stigmatizing and that when it is constructed in a way to display the *ability* of the user, it avoids giving the user a devalued social identity. When participants were shown a range of designs, they preferred the designs that stressed positive attributes of the user: *"It's got impact you see hasn't it? It gets away from the idea of disability, it gets away from... It's got more of the idea of being "with it".*

In the design mentioned here (Fig. 3) the participant perceives that the design avoids connoting disability and instead confers upon the user the positive attribute of being "with it". However, we should not assume that all users react in the same way and for some, the same walker was perceived as bulky and unattractive. The notion of primary appraisal makes sense of this because some users find the same product identity-enhancing while others find it stigmatizing.

The participants often mentioned the idea that the design of walker communicates a "message" to others. Some designs say negative things: *"It says to me, very disabled that one"* (Fig. 4). Other designs, on the other hand, say positive things:

"It doesn't shout disability it says, "I'm out shopping"" (Fig. 5).

Fig. 3. A design described as being "with it".

Fig. 4. Device perceived as "disabled";

Fig. 5. Shopper-walker hybrid

While the message conveyed is a functional one (shopping), this is inextricably linked to identity because the activities performed often point to the identity of the person performing them. Being a "shopper" is perceived as positive while being "disabled" is negative.

People often arrive at their perception of function and identity by comparing the device with pre-existing products. Thus, when a design looks like a "baby bouncer" it is deemed inappropriate but when it looks like a golf cart it may be deemed suitable:

"A: In this form, it looks like a golf trolley; B: Or a wheelie bin! C: have your golf clubs in it! A: Yea, I quite like that" (Fig. 5).

As the quote above demonstrates, different people may have quite different reactions to the same device. For one the design is like a golf trolley whereas the other sees it like a bin. One design that was particularly liked by participants was likened to a scooter and participants said that they could pretend they were on a "Vespa or

Lambretta or something" (Fig. 7). The kind of comparisons people make therefore, form the basis of whether they find the device stigmatizing.

Attention-Drawing. Generally, most participants preferred walkers which did not draw attention to themselves. This attention can either be visual attention or attention caused by the size of the walker. One participant talked about how he noticed a woman on his bus struggling with the walker which was obstructing others and how it was embarrassing. Everyday incidents like this caused concern to participants about stigma. In the more extreme examples of walking aids, the idea of attention is prominent:

> "A: To be outside in that would be horrible! I mean, ...B: you couldn't miss it! C: no no! D: you'd get people lining up to watch" (Fig. 6).

The idea of having people deliberately watching causes the participants discomfort. Nevertheless, some participants feel at ease with being watched as long as it is for the right reasons: *"You are the one people are going to stare at. If they stare at you because it's funky, it's different."*

In this context, the participant anticipates being stared at but would accept it if it were because the walker is *"funky"*. While not all participants are comfortable with attention, for some it is acceptable if it is positive.

Fig. 6. Hanging walking aid;

Fig. 7. A popular design;

Fig. 8. Walker with model

Attractive Design. Designs which are unattractive can make the user feel stigmatized or embarrassed:

> "You could walk with it but you'd to have a bag over your head wouldn't you."

Even though this is a humorous quote, it belies a serious point. Users want to have designs which do not draw unnecessary attention and make the user feel proud of their walker. Not only do participants seek to have a product that is attractive for them, but they want something that other people would like.

> "It looks as though everybody would want one" (Fig. 7).

They also talk about being proud of the device if they took it outside and joked about having brand names like "MacLaren" or "Ferrari" on it – labels typically associated with prestigious and desirable products. A minor theme related to this was the idea that the apparent cheapness of a device was something that created stigma. Devices that appear to be more expensive are deemed more desirable and attractive.

Social Acceptability

Quite frequently, participants talked about how walkers would be more acceptable if used by others including prominent individuals. One person said that if the Queen used one, it would go a long way towards making their use more acceptable: *"If the Queen started to use a walker ... it would become more acceptable"*.

But it is not just prominent individuals that people look for when thinking about walker-use. The way ordinary people use their walkers contributes to their assessment of the walker. This became apparent when participants began discussing the models using the walkers in the images. In some images, the models were perceived as enhancing their impression of the walker: *"The one that I got, which has a positive outdoor looking lady on the top, influenced my opinion a lot"* (Fig. 8).

Because the model in this instance was perceived as being "positive", this contributed to the participant's sense that the walker was a positive thing. On the other hand, when the model is associated with negative characteristics, this negatively impacts their assessment of the walker: *"See that image of somebody bent over with their shoulders, it just ruins it."*

This means that the relationship between the walker and the person using it is not a one-way relationship (i.e. the walker can make the user look good or bad by virtue of its appearance) but a two-way one in which the user can also influence others' perceptions of the walker. People look to others who use walkers to make their appraisal of whether the walker is a stigmatizing device.

Self-Esteem

By making the user feel old or dependent, the walker can be a source of stigma. Nevertheless, being treated as an "old person" by others is something which some participants enjoy while others dislike:

> *"[People] ask questions over your head or shout at you because they think you're deaf. I think it's lovely! I love it [...] you know, it doesn't bother me one iota."*

This person apparently enjoys being treated as an older adult because many of the ways in which this can occur are benevolent rather than malicious. She explained, for example, that she enjoyed being allowed to join the front of the queue because she was perceived as older. However, while this experience of "benevolent ageism" is perceived as positive by some participants, others react against it. They talk about the "danger that you will be treated as an old person" and link this to avoidance of walking aids. One participant referred to her use of a wheeled shopping bag to carry her groceries and even linked this to stigma:

> *"I used to have one of those [a shopper] before I had a car, and I must admit I did feel a bit stigmatised because it felt like an old lady's trolley".*

The participants felt that shoppers and walkers both have a similar appearance sometimes. This is why the participant above refers to feeling "stigmatized" because she felt her trolley attributed the identity of "old lady" to her. This devalued identity is something that participants seek to avoid and while some people appreciate the benevolent aspects of ageism, others prefer not to be perceived as "old" in any way.

3.2   Secondary Appraisal

If walker-use is stigmatizing in some way, this does not mean that it will necessarily be avoided. Perceived stigma will be moderated by users' coping strategies. These coping strategies can be more problem focused or more cognition focused.

Problem-Focused

Ability to Customize. Some participants liked the idea of customizing their own walker to reflect their personalities. By doing so, this offsets some stigma associated with using a walker: *"One with flowers on it? Perhaps like the walking sticks? You could personalise them because that seems to be, people are much more creative now, and that might appeal to people to be able to put different motifs on them, different coloured seat covers or whatever you've got."* In this extract, participants suggest that customizing walkers would help to make them more acceptable.

Social Support. Social support can be both a primary and secondary appraisal strategy. If walker-use is common, this can encourage people to see them as devoid of stigma (primary). And if people use the walker with others, this can diffuse the stigma (secondary). One design of a walking aid was quite robotic and eye-catching. Participants talked about taking it into the city centre: *"A: The first time you did it, you might get some funny reactions; B: But if we were together...A: ... If you took it out a few times then people would get used to seeing it."*

The idea that being together would reduce the stigma associated with using it may stem from a diffusion of the stigma. Alternatively, the collective use of the walker may reflect identity dynamics whereby being associated with a social group provides a coping mechanism to reduce stress/stigma [22].

Cognition/Emotion-Focused

Cognitive Emphasis on Benefits. While the use of a walker may seem stigmatizing, users can use a coping strategy which stresses the benefits of using a walker. Participants talked about the benefits of being perceived as old at airports, in shops and on public transport. For these participants, the walker functions as a sign to other people that the user is elderly and implicitly invites benevolent age discrimination: *"People are very considerate of them, they do make room for them and they do help them onto buses and they do, you know, it's a sign to other people"*.

This use of the device as a signal to other people is both a good thing and a bad thing. For some users, the signaling that the user is old and dependent is limiting and stigmatizing whereas for others, it provides the help they desire. While participants recognize why some people do not like using walkers, they believe that persuading others of the benefits can encourage their use: *"I don't know, well I do know why people don't want to use them, I do understand that but, if you could just persuade them of the benefits of using them"*.

The walker may be stigmatizing in some ways, but users can cognitively reappraise what the reaction of other people means. Rather than perceiving it as a negative thing (pity or patronization), they can frame it as something positive (help and support).

Necessity. Another cognitive strategy that people use is to see the use of the device as a necessity. By being convinced of the need to use it, participants can outweigh the stigma of even the most unattractive of devices. One device that was particularly unattractive and conspicuous (Fig. 6) received unfavourable comments from many participants. Nevertheless, many also stressed that they would use it if it enabled them to perform tasks that they could not otherwise perform. Again, another lady who remembered her time when she could not walk and was bedridden said: *"If it had been offered to me, if it was pink with green spots and had feathers sticking out of it and it jangled like a tambourine, and they'd said, "P, this will help you get on your feet", I would have done it."* As she describes the walker, she deliberately emphasizes the extent to which it could be stigmatizing (*"pink with green spots"* with *"feathers"*) and stresses that in spite of this, necessity would outweigh stigma. This coping strategy focuses on the need to use the walker and thus reduces perception of the stigma (or concern with it).

Age-related apathy. On several occasions it was mentioned that in old-age there is less concern about what other people think. There is an acknowledgement that stigma may still be there, but it becomes irrelevant: *"But do you find that as you get older, one of the advantages is that you don't give a damn what anyone else thinks?"* This construction of the self as someone who does not care about what other people think allows the participants to ignore any stigma that may be present.

Time Reduces Stigma. Sometimes when participants saw images of walkers, they acknowledged that the walker may be initially stigmatizing but also believed that over time, the stigma would decrease. This was not used to argue that the participant would only use one when the stigma had decreased in the future, but the belief that the stigma would decrease in the future gave them reason to consider using it in the present:

> "A: I think it's an amazing piece of equipment [(Fig. 6)...] but if we're talking about walking round Eldon Square [shopping centre]; B: Of course people would get used to seeing them; A: There's that point!; B: The first time you saw it you would think, "What on earth's that?" But if you kept seeing it you would get used to it."

Participants acknowledge that there may be initial negative reactions but offset this with the belief that this type of reaction will fade over time. Beliefs about what the future will be like can provide a coping mechanism for enduring stigma in the present.

4 Discussion

Stigma associated with walker use is a subjective issue and influenced by appraisal of various issues. Seeing stigma through the eyes of the stress appraisal literature [21] allows us to argue that walkers are not stigmatizing per se but must be appraised as such by the potential users. While this may mean that they avoid using them, this study also argues that even the perception of stigma is not sufficient to discourage use if the user can mobilise coping strategies. This study has explored a range of ways in which people evaluate the use of walkers as stressful or not and if so, how they anticipate coping with using one.

This has relevance insofar as much research emphasizes developing more aesthetically pleasing devices or targeting problem attitudes in wider society [1]. We concur with this but argue that insufficient attention has been paid to helping the users come to terms with technology use. The range of strategies that can be used to either perceive a device as lacking in stigma or cope with stigma provide insight into encouraging the uptake of walkers. Older adults need help to see the benefits of using a walker. Furthermore, if the problem that many older adults face is that of self-stigma, their own stigmatization of walker-users, then changing older adult's appraisal of walkers is essential.

Our work suggests that more attractive designs, more gender relevance, hidden assistance and more positive societal attitudes are not important but equally we emphasise the importance of seeing stigma as an appraisal issue and then helping potential walker-users come to see their walker in a positive light.

5 Conclusion

We believe that this study addresses some important questions about psychosocial influences on mobility and well-being in older adults. These new results also have important clinical implications, highlighting the need to develop intervention strategies that deal with potential psychosocial barriers to mobility, such as fear of stigmatisation. This will help to ensure that mobility interventions, like the provision of mobility aids, do not fail at the outset as a result of user avoidance, but enable aging adults to have the best possible quality of life. It also highlights the need to carefully consider how design might influence older adults' perceptions of themselves and their abilities. Our work emphasizes the importance of using project independent stimuli to evoke genuine evaluation from participants – good and bad. The ultimate goal is to design assistive technology that is aspirational not stigmatizing.

Acknowledgements. This research was funded by EC Grant Agreement No 288917.

References

1. Parette, P., Scherer, M.: Assistive technology use and stigma. Educ. Train. Dev. Disabil. **39**, 217–226 (2004)
2. Link, B., Phelan, J.: Conceptualizing stigma. Annu. Rev. Sociol. **27**, 363–385 (2001)
3. Day, R., Hitchings, R.: 'Only old ladies would do that': age stigma and older people's strategies for dealing with winter cold. Health Place **17**, 885–894 (2011)
4. Hanson, H.M., Salmoni, A.W., Doyle, P.C.: Broadening our understanding: approaching falls as a stigmatizing topic for older adults. Disabil. Health J. **2**, 36–44 (2009)
5. Aminzadeh, F., Edwards, N.: Exploring seniors' views on the use of assistive devices in fall prevention. Public Health Nurs. **15**, 297–304 (1998)

6. Resnik, L., Allen, S., Isenstadt, D., Wasserman, M., Iezzoni, L.: Perspectives on use of mobility aids in a diverse population of seniors : implications for intervention. Disabil. Health J. **2**, 77–85 (2009)
7. Gooberman-Hill, R., Ebrahim, S.: Making decisions about simple interventions: older people's use of walking aids. Age Ageing **36**, 569–573 (2007)
8. Bright, A.K., Coventry, L., Toth, N.: Life Space Mobility, Quality of Life and Fear of Stigmatisation in Older Adults (2013)
9. Bright, A.K., Coventry, L.: Assistive technology for older adults. In: Proceedings of the 6th International Conference on PErvasive Technologies Related to Assistive Environments - PETRA 2013. pp. 1–4. ACM Press, New York, USA (2013)
10. Bugental, D.B., Hehman, J.A.: Ageism: a review of research and policy implications. Soc. Issues Policy Rev. **1**, 173–216 (2007)
11. Nelson, T.D.: Ageism: prejudice against our feared future self. J. Soc. Issues **61**, 207–221 (2005)
12. Miller, C.T., Kaiser, C.R.: A theoretical perspective on coping with stigma. J. Soc. Issues **57**, 73–92 (2001)
13. Pape, T.L.-B., Kim, J., Weiner, B.: The shaping of individual meanings assigned to assistive technology: a review of personal factors. Disabil. Rehabil. **24**, 5–20 (2002)
14. Folkman, S., Lazarus, R.S., Dunkel-Schetter, C., DeLongis, A., Gruen, R.J.: Dynamics of a stressful encounter: cognitive appraisal, coping, and encounter outcomes. J. Pers. Soc. Psychol. **50**, 992–1003 (1986)
15. Porter, E.J., Benson, J.J., Matsuda, S.: Older homebound women: negotiating reliance on a cane or walker. Qual. Health Res. **21**, 534–548 (2011)
16. The Center for Universal Design: The Principles of Universal Design, Version 2.0. North Carolina State University, Raleigh, NC (1997)
17. Coventry, L., Jones, E.: The role of tea parties to elicit technology requirements to support the mobility of older adults. In: Proceedings of 5th International Conference Pervasive Technology Related to Assistive Enviroment - PETRA 2012, p. 1 (2012)
18. Rantakokko, M., Mänty, M., Iwarsson, S., Törmäkangas, T., Leinonen, R., Heikkinen, E., Rantanen, T.: Fear of moving outdoors and development of outdoor walking difficulty in older people. J. Am. Geriatr. Soc. **57**, 634–640 (2009)
19. Metz, D.: Mobility of older people and their quality of life. Transp. Policy **7**, 149–152 (2000)
20. King, N., Cassell, C., Symon, G.: Using templates in the thematic analysis of texts. In: Cassell, C., Symon, G. (eds.) Essential Guide to Qualitative Methods in Organizational Research, pp. 256–270. Sage, London (2004)
21. Major, B., O'Brien, L.T.: The social psychology of stigma. Annu. Rev. Psychol. **56**, 393–421 (2005)
22. Jetten, J., Haslam, C., Haslam, S.A., Branscombe, N.R.: The social cure. Sci. Am. Mind. **20**, 26–33 (2009)

Perceptions of Computer System Usefulness: Insights for Design from Experienced Older Users

Tracy L. Mitzner[1(✉)], Neil Charness[2], and Wendy A. Rogers[1]

[1] Georgia Institute of Technology,
Atlanta, GA, USA
tracy@gatech.edu
[2] Florida State University,
Tallahassee, FL, USA

Abstract. Computer systems have the potential to assist older adults by supporting independence, enhancing social communication, and enabling healthcare activities. Yet older adults' adoption rates continue to lag behind younger and middle-aged adults. We report data from 249 older adult computer users (65–93 years of age) that identify the details of their perceptions of computer usefulness for a range of everyday activities. Participants rated the importance of activities to their quality of life and the usefulness of current computer systems for supporting those activities. These experienced computer users indicated that computers were meeting their needs for some activities (e.g., social communication, games) but not for other activities (e.g., calendaring, healthcare, recreation and learning). Our data provide guidance for (a) introducing the potential of computer systems to current non-users and (b) designing systems targeted to meet the needs of older adults and enhancing computing functionality for them.

Keywords: Technology · Older adults · Adoption · Perceived usefulness · Perceived ease of use

1 Introduction

Computers systems, from desktop computers to tablets and smart phones, can assist with many tasks of daily life and provide users with the ability to connect with people, information, and resources in the world without having to leave their home. Particularly for older adults, there is much potential for computer systems to benefit their lives in tangible ways such as social communication [1], access to health and other information [2], and support for hobbies and leisure activities [3].

The potential for computer systems to support older adults is particularly compelling in light of current demographic trends. Across the globe, the number of people 60 years or over is expected to more than double, from 841 million people in 2013 to more than 2 billion in 2050 [4]. Such changing demographic distributions must be considered in the context of computer technology development. Helping older adults remain independent as long as possible could minimize use of costly long-term care resources. Older adults also value being independent rather than relying on others for

© Springer International Publishing Switzerland 2015
J. Zhou and G. Salvendy (Eds.): ITAP 2015, Part I, LNCS 9193, pp. 262–272, 2015.
DOI: 10.1007/978-3-319-20892-3_26

daily life tasks [5]. Computer systems that meet older adults needs could facilitate their independence and, in doing so, reduce their need to depend on others.

Despite the potential of computer systems, older adults (e.g., 65+) continue to underutilize them relative to other age groups. The latest findings from the Pew Research Center show that 97 % of those 18–29 years of age and 93 % of those 30–49 years of age report using the Internet, compared 88 % of those 50–64 years of age, but only 57 % of those 65 and older [6]. Although the Pew data reflect U.S. trends, similar trends have been noted in other industrialized countries [7].

Research has pointed to characteristics of the user, as well as of the interface of the technology to explain older adults' underutilization of computer systems. Older adults are less likely to have the prerequisite skills, attitudes, and experience as compared to younger adults. In a sample of 1,204 adults (18–91 years of age) Czaja, Charness, Fisk, and colleagues (2006) found that age, cognitive ability (i.e., fluid intelligence), ethnicity, computer anxiety, and education predicted *computer experience*. Gender, education, cognitive ability (i.e., fluid and crystallized intelligence), computer anxiety, and age predicted breadth of *computer use* [8]. Education, ethnicity, cognitive ability (i.e., fluid and crystallized intelligence), computer anxiety, and age predicted *Internet experience*. Furthermore, older adults typically have less general technology experience compared to younger adults [1], and that general technology experience is predictive of computer and Internet attitudinal acceptance [9]. Moreover, interface design issues have been noted as potential barriers for older users [10], especially those with limited technology experience [1].

Beyond experience and usability issues, it is possible that older adult non-users do not perceive computer systems as useful for supporting the tasks and activities that are important to them. Indeed, an AARP poll of adults 50 years of age and older found that 71 % of non-Internet users were not interested in learning to use the internet; 47 % of those respondents did not want to learn how to use the Internet because they were not interested in the Internet all together [11]. Perception of usefulness is a strong predictor of older adults' technology use in a variety of contexts [3, 12]. In fact, the absence of benefits may be a stronger influence than the presence of costs when predicting the non-acceptance of a new technology. That is, if older adults perceive a technology to provide many benefits they may accept a new technology despite associated costs such as effort, expenses, or lack of skills [13]. Older adult non-users may not recognize the potential benefits of computer systems for their lives and this perception cannot be assessed from prior research that focused on usage patterns.

A goal for the present study was to assess perceptions of Internet usefulness of older adults who are experienced computer users. These data provide guidance for introduction, deployment, and training of non-users who represent nearly half of the older adult population in developed countries and a much higher percentage elsewhere. Knowing what other older adults find useful about the Internet might motivate non-user older adults to learn themselves. Alternatively, understanding what older adult users do not find useful can provide direction for design and instruction to computer developers, and provide insights about lack of awareness or understanding of utility. These findings have relevance to a wide range of current computer systems and software, including tablet, smart phone, and wearable applications, and also provide insight into the potential for future technologies, in terms of content and functionality.

2   Overview of Study

The Pew Research Center assessment of Internet use [14] is based on respondents saying yes to at least one of the following three questions: "Do you use the Internet, at least occasionally?", "Do you send or receive email, at least occasionally?" or "Do you access the Internet on a cell phone, tablet or other mobile handheld device, at least occasionally?" The Pew data provide a valuable broad assessment of Internet use but much less depth regarding specific activities and preferences. Our goal was to garner in-depth information about the perception of usefulness for using the computer for a wide range of activities. We queried a large sample of older adult computer users about the importance of a range of activities to their quality of life (i.e., personal relevance), and assessed whether computers were useful to them in accomplishing these activities. The activities where there was a match between importance and usefulness represent target areas wherein non-users might find computers to be useful to them (and hence be more motivated to learn). The activities where there was a mismatch between importance and usefulness represent opportunities for designers: the activity is important but yet the older adults did not find the computer to be helpful to them.

3   Method

3.1   Participants

We mailed questionnaires to 662 older adults who were part of the databases maintained by the Human Factors and Aging Laboratory at the Georgia Institute of Technology (Atlanta, Georgia) and the Laboratory of Dr. Neil Charness at Florida State University (Tallahassee, Florida). A total of 321 completed questionnaires were returned (15 were returned as undeliverable) which translates to a return rate of 50 %. Of the questionnaires returned, 249 were completed by older adults (65 and older) who reported themselves to be computer users. In this report we have only included these 249 respondents. The age range of these respondents who were computer users was 65–93 (M = 75, SD = 5.79). Note that the sample was generally healthy (84 % reported good to excellent health), well-educated (81 % reported completing at least some college), and living independently (89 % reported living in a house/apartment).

3.2   Materials

We developed the 381-item Computer Preference & Usage Questionnaire (CPU-Q); additional details are also provided in Mitzner et al. (2010) [3]. The CPU-Q includes:

1. Background & Health Information - gender, age, education, marital status, race, ethnicity, housing, income, occupation, general health, health satisfaction, vision, hearing, and limitations related to sitting, using hands, and reading.
2. General Importance of Activities - perceptions of the importance of various tasks in daily life using a five point Likert-type scale with a neutral point (not at all important to very important). The tasks and activities this paper focuses on are

social communication (e.g., communicating with family and friends; sending or receiving photos), health-related (e.g., communicating with health care professionals; researching symptoms and illnesses), calendar tasks (e.g., creating appointment reminders, tracking events with a calendar), and recreation and learning (e.g., travel directions, learning new information), and games (e.g., solitaire, bridge).

3. Technology Experience - 17 items assessing frequency of use for a wide range of technologies (answering machine, ATM, electronic book reader, cell phone) and 3 items assessing computer/Internet use, including frequency and duration.

4. Potential for Computers/Internet to Support General Activities - perceptions of usefulness of computers in assisting with the same tasks and activities included in the General Importance of Activities section, also using a six point Likert-type scale with a neutral point (not at all useful to very useful).

5. Attitudes towards a Computer System Designed for Older Adults - perceptions of the importance for an ideal system to support different activities. Participants were instructed to imagine that they had been given a computer system developed specifically for use by older adults, along with the appropriate personalized training for its use. The description was based on a system used in a randomized clinical trial designed to assess the impact of a computer intervention on the well-being of seniors with minimal computer experience (ClinicalTrials.gov Identifier: NCT01497613) [15, 16].

3.3 Procedure

Questionnaires were mailed to participants, along with a postage-paid envelope to return it once it was completed. This was a lengthy survey (47 pages) – participants were instructed as follows: "We expect this questionnaire to take 45 to 60 min to complete. At your convenience, please find a quiet area and time when you will have about an hour free from interruption to complete this questionnaire."

4 Results

For the goals of the current paper, the questionnaire responses were reviewed with the following goals in mind: (a) assess computer and Internet experience of the older adult computer users, and (b) identify activities that were important to them for which they found the computer to be useful as well as activities that were important but they did not find the computer to be useful. The data are descriptive but they represent a large sample and provide guidance for deployment, training, and design.

4.1 Computer and Internet Experience

Participants were included if they answered yes to the question "Do you ever use a computer and/or the Internet?" Most respondents (72 %) reported using the computer and/or Internet at least 5 h per week and most (89 %) reported having used it for at least 5 years. Thus, this sample represents a group of experienced older adult computer users.

4.2 Importance of Activities and Perceptions about the Usefulness of Perceptions of Current Computers

We queried participants about two aspects of a variety of tasks and activities. We asked, "For each task and activities listed in the table below, please indicate how important they are to your quality of life." Then, in a later section of the questionnaire we had the same list of tasks but the question was: "How useful are computers and the Internet for supporting the following tasks and activities?"

When participants were asked to indicate how important a wide range of activities were for their quality of life, on average they rated calendar, social communication, healthcare, and recreation and learning activities as important to very important. These contrasting sets of data for the categories of social communication, games, calendar healthcare, recreation and learning, and are presented in Table 1. In terms of the usefulness of current computer systems to support these activities, only the mean for social communication and recreation and learning approached a "useful" rating. We conducted a paired-sample t-test for each category to determine if the importance and usefulness responses were significantly different (see Table 1). The alpha level for significant effects was set at .001 to control for multiple tests.

Table 1. Importance and usefulness ratings

Activity categories	Importance mean (SD)		Usefulness mean (SD)		Df	t	p
Social communication	4.03	(.61)	3.97	(.90)	245	1.17	.243
Games	3.21	(1.17)	2.95	(1.41)	208	2.81	.006
Calendar	4.14	(.78)	2.49	(1.31)	230	17.26	<.001 (significant at .001)
Healthcare	4.02	(.73)	3.05	(1.08)	240	15.58	<.001 (significant at .001)
Recreation and learning	3.99	(.64)	3.77	(.93)	244	3.89	<.001 (significant at .001)

Note. Ratings were provided in the context of quality of life for importance (1 = not at all important to 5 = very important) and the usefulness of computers and the Internet for supporting tasks and activities (1 = not at all useful to 5 = very useful).

For social communication and games the ratings were not significantly different suggesting that computers were perceived to be successful in meeting older adults' needs for these categories. Yet, for recreation and learning, health, and calendar activities the ratings of computer usefulness were significantly lower than the importance ratings. To understand these patterns, we explored the data on an item level to gain insights about perceptions of usefulness for different tasks in the same categories.

Social Communication. We queried participants about six different social communication tasks; they were all deemed important to the older adults' quality of life (mean ratings > 3). Overall, the usefulness ratings were high with 3 of the tasks having a mean rating above a 4. The older adults were especially likely to perceive the usefulness of computers for communicating with family and friends and for staying in touch with people over long distance.

Games. We asked participants about both individual games (e.g., Solitaire, Dominos, Sudoku, puzzles) and group games (e.g., Bridge, Bingo, board games). Participants rated both types as important (mean ratings > 3), however the computer was only rated as useful for individual games, not group games (M = 3.37 and M = 2.33, respectively). Considering both individual and group games and with an alpha set at .001, perceptions of usefulness were not significantly different than those of importance for games.

Calendar. We queried about four different calendaring activities, including scheduling events and setting reminders. Although calendaring activities were rated as important to participants' quality of life (mean rating > 4), computers were rated as not useful for putting reminders on a calendar, creating appointment reminders, and tracking events with a calendar. The only calendaring activity for which computers were perceived as being useful was creating medication reminders. These findings indicate a mismatch (and thus a potential opportunity) between activities older adults consider important for their quality of live and the ability of computers to support them.

Healthcare. We queried participants about six different healthcare activities, all of which were rated as important to the quality of life of the older adults (mean rating > 3). Overall, the participants did not find the computer to be very useful for supporting the health-related tasks, with the exception of most research tasks. Researching general health issues, symptoms/illnesses, and medications were all above 3.0, suggesting that the older adults perceived the usefulness of computers for research tasks.

There were three health tasks that were rated quite low in usefulness (i.e., communicating with doctors or other healthcare professionals, researching health insurance, managing illnesses) but quite high in importance. These represent another mismatch between the older adults' needs and their perceptions of usefulness. Certainly computing technology has the potential to assist with these tasks but the older adult computer users in our sample did not perceive that usefulness.

In sum, clearly the older adults perceived healthcare activities as important to their quality of life, most notably communicating with doctors or other healthcare professionals, managing illness and researching general illness, medications, and symptoms. But there was a disconnect between the activities important to the respondents and their perceptions that computers and the Internet can be useful for these tasks. The notable exception to this pattern was for research.

Recreation and Learning. We asked participants about seven learning and recreation activities, all of which were rated as important to their quality of life (mean ratings > 3).

Nevertheless, ratings of computer usefulness to support these activities were significantly lower. The largest disconnect between importance and usefulness ratings were for following the news, acquiring new skills, learning new information, and accessing community resources. Although computers have the potential to be quite useful for these types of learning and recreation activities, these older adults did not perceive current computers as useful for such activities.

5 Discussion

The purpose of this study was to understand what types of activities are important to older adults and whether computers are perceived as useful for providing support for those activities. We explored the attitudes of experienced older adult computer users about current computer usefulness for different activities because we wanted to understand perceptions that were based at least partly on usage rather than primarily on expectations and assumptions. We sampled an older adult population who became users at a time when they were a minority user group in the older population (i.e., early adopters [17]). Although these participants are not representative of the total population of older adults, they are representative of older adult computer users, as reflected by large-scale survey data (e.g., mostly white/Caucasian, highly educated, and in good health) [18–20]. These experienced computer users showed a disconnect between what activities were important to them and how useful they found computers for supporting those activities, a finding contrary to what might be expected from technology-savvy people. That is, even having considerable computer experience may not prevent an individual from encountering barriers when trying to use computers for certain activities.

Previous research has provided insight into the types of computer and Internet activities older adults are engaged in. The Pew Research Center, in particular, has provided much data about what activities older adults engage in using the Internet, such as using email, search engines, hobby or interest, maps or directions [21]. Another large-scale study also collected data on activity engagement and found almost 86 % of Internet users 65 and older sent emails/text messages, 51 % shopped, paid bills, and/or did banking, and 45 % conducted health-related tasks on the Internet. However, 9 % of the users used the Internet only for sending emails/text messages and these users were more likely to be socially and economically disadvantaged [22]. These findings provide insights into Internet usage patterns of seniors and the findings presented here complement those data showing also how important different activities are to older adults' quality of life and how useful they perceive computers to be for providing support.

Our findings indicate that computers are meeting older adults' needs for some activities (e.g., social communication, games) more so than others (e.g., calendaring, healthcare, recreation and learning), an insight that has significant implications for training and design. For example, the finding that computers are meeting older adults' needs for social communication and games is a point that should be highlighted for their non-user peers during technology introduction and training. That is, if non-users can see how their peers benefit from using computers, they may be more likely to see those potential benefits for themselves.

Social communication was an activity our participants rated as important and that the computer was useful for providing support. Indeed, the Pew Research Center showed that email is a common computer activity of older adults [6]; 86 % of internet users ages 65 and older use email and 48 % do so on a typical day [23]. Nevertheless, there may be design opportunities for chat and social networking software. People are living longer and therefore more likely to have mobility losses. The majority of older adults are also choosing to stay in their homes. These factors may contribute to increased social isolation for older adults, which may be particularly severe for their age group [24, 25]. Consequently, there may be more of a need for social communication technologies in the future and the needs of older adults should be specifically considered.

Playing games was another activity for which participants seemed to feel the computer was meeting their needs. This finding suggests that computer games may be a ripe entry activity to show non-computer users potential benefits of using computers. Furthermore, games to support cognitive health by providing cognitive exercise are becoming popular and are being marketed toward older adults. Although challenges have been documented regarding the benefits of games for cognitive exercise [26], there is promising evidence and increasing interest in computer games designed to provide cognitive exercise [27]. However, the participants did not find the computer useful for group games and this represents a missed opportunity for increasing social interaction.

The older adults we surveyed did not view the computer as meeting their needs for calendaring, healthcare, and recreation and learning activities. Calendaring activities had the highest mean ratings for importance to quality of life and the largest mean difference between importance to quality of life and usefulness of computers for providing support. The high value placed on the importance of calendaring is consistent with the widely accepted finding that aspects of prospective memory declines with age [28] and that older adults are aware of this decrement [29, 30]. Nevertheless, these experienced computer users did not rate current computers as useful for supporting calendaring activities. This is a prime domain for which computer software has the potential to make a significant impact on the lives of older adults, yet our findings show that more work is needed to develop systems that are useable and useful to older adults.

Healthcare is another domain for which computer systems may be particularly useful for older adults [31], especially given that the percentage of adults with multiple chronic conditions increases with age [32]. Nearly 90 % of older adults have at least one chronic disorder [33]. In fact, in another large-scale survey, 53 % of adults who were Internet users and had chronic conditions reported using information found on the Internet in their decision-making about their own health or someone they care for [34]. However, with respect to design, the healthcare results presented here provided evidence that current computer options are not meeting the needs of older adults. Even experienced computer users did not perceive the usefulness of computers for a range of important healthcare tasks such as managing illness, scheduling appointments, and creating reminders for appointments or medications. These activities influence quality of life and potentially health care costs and safety as well. This finding suggests an opportunity for designers to capitalize on computing power to support these activities of older adults.

Computers were also not seen as meeting participants' needs for supporting recreation and learning activities. These types of activities can be thought of as enhanced activities of daily living [35] and are important for providing social opportunities and cognitive exercise [36]. Future computer systems and software should be designed to better support these activities, particularly in light of the relationship between social isolation and mortality [37] and cognitive exercise and cognitive functioning [38].

Our findings provide guidance for (a) introducing the potential of computers to current non-users and (b) design targeted to meet the needs of older adults and enhance computing functionality for them. First, consider older adults who are currently non-users. There are of course many reasons why people choose not to use computers, some of which may relate to financial cost or lack of training opportunity. However, perceived usefulness, attitudes, and anxiety are also predictive of computer and technology use [8, 9]. In fact, the most frequently stated reason for not using the Internet was 'not interested' (31 %) [21]. It is likely that many of the respondents who indicated they were not interested do not perceive the Internet as being useful. The present findings illustrate the value of computers for older adults performing activities that are important to their quality of life. Communication with family and friends in particular was important to life quality and computers were perceived as useful for these activities. Therefore, these activities are likely to be a good point of introduction for motivating and engaging older adults to use computers.

Acknowledgements. This research was supported in part by a grant from the National Institutes of Health (National Institute on Aging) Grant P01 AG17211 under the auspices of the Center for Research and Education on Aging and Technology Enhancement (CREATE; www.create-center. org). Data from this general questionnaire were presented at Human Factors & Ergonomics Society (Burnett et al., 2011), FICCDAT (Mitzner et al., 2011), GSA (Mitzner et al., 2011), and at the Cognitive Aging Conference (Burnett et al., 2012).

References

1. Olson, K.E., O-Brien, M.A., Rogers, W.A., Fisk, A.D.: Understanding age and technology experience differences in use of prior knowledge for everyday technology interactions. ACM Trans. Access. Comput. 4(2), Article No. 9 (2012)
2. Charness, N., Demiris, G., Krupinsky, E.A.: Designing Telehealth for an Aging Population: A Human Factors Perspective. CRC Press, Boca Raton (2012)
3. Mitzner, T.L., Boron, J.B., Fausset, C.B., Adams, A.E., Charness, N., Czaja, S.J., Dijkstra, K., Fisk, A.D., Rogers, W.A., Sharit, J.: Older adults talk technology: technology usage and attitudes. Comput. Hum. Behav. 26(6), 1710–1721 (2010)
4. United Nations DoEaSA, Population Division. World Population Ageing 2013 (2013)
5. Wiles, J.L., Leibing, A., Guberman, N., Reeve, J., Allen, R.E.: The meaning of "aging in place" to older people. Gerontologist 52(3), 357–366 (2012)
6. Internet user demographics. http://www.pewinternet.org/data-trend/internet-use/latest-stats/ (2014). Accessed 3 Jul 2014
7. Eurostat: Individuals frequently using the internet. Eurostat. http://epp.eurostat.ec.europa.eu/ tgm/refreshTableAction.do?tab=table&plugin=1&pcode=tin00092&language=en (2011). Accessed 31 Jul 2014

8. Czaja, S.J., Charness, N., Fisk, A., Hertzog, C., Nair, S., Rogers, W., Sharit, J.: Factors predicting the use of technology: findings from the center for research and education on aging and technology enhancement (CREATE). Psychol. Aging **21**(2), 333–352 (2006)
9. Mitzner, T.L., Rogers, W.A., Fisk, A.D., Boot, W.R., Charness, N., Czaja, S.J., Sharit, J.: Predicting older adults' perceptions about a computer system designed for seniors. Univ. Access Inf. Soc. (2014, in press)
10. Pak, R., McLaughlin, A.: Designing Displays for Older Adults. CRC Press, Boca Raton (2010)
11. Keenan, T.A.: Internet use among midlife and older adults: an AARP bulletin poll. AARP Bulletin (2009)
12. Caine, K.E., O'Brien, M.A., Park, S., Rogers, W.A., Fisk, A.D., Van Ittersum, K., Capar, M., Parsons, L.J.: Understanding acceptance of high technology products: 50 years of research. In: Proceedings of the Human Factors and Ergonomics Society 50th Annual Meeting, San Francisco, California, Human Factors and Ergonomics Society (2006)
13. Melenhorst, A.S., Rogers, W.A., Bouwhuis, D.G.: Older adults' motivated choice for technological innovation: evidence for benefit-driven selectivity. Psychol. Aging **21**, 190–195 (2006)
14. Rainie, L.: Changes to the Way We Identify Internet Users. Pew Research Center, Washington (2012)
15. Boot, W.R., Charness, N., Czaja, S.J., Sharit, J., Rogers, W.A., Fisk, A.D., Mitzner, T.L., Lee, C.C., Nair, S.: The computer proficiency questionnaire (CPQ): assessing low and high computer proficient seniors. The Gerontologist (Advance online publication) (2013)
16. Czaja, S.J., Boot, W.R., Charness, N., Rogers, W.A., Sharit, J., Fisk, A.D., Lee, C.C., Nair, S.N.: The personalized reminder information and social management system (PRISM) trial: rationale, methods and baseline characteristics. (1559–2030 (Electronic)). doi:D-NLM: NIHMS645340. Accessed 01 Jan 16, D - NLM: PMC4314316. Accessed 01 Jan 16, OTO - NOTNLM
17. Smith, A.: Older Adults and Technology Use. Pew Research Center, Washington (2014)
18. Choi, N.: Relationship between health service use and health information technology use among older adults: analysis of the US national health interview survey. J. Med. Internet Res. **15**(5), e33 (2011)
19. Neter, E., Brainin, E.: eHealth literacy: extending the digital divide to the realm of health information. J. Med. Internet Res. **14**(1), e19 (2012)
20. Werner, J.M., Carlson, M., Jordan-Marsh, M., Clark, F.: Predictors of computer use in community-dwelling, ethnically diverse older adults. Hum. Factors **53**, 431–447 (2011)
21. Zickuhr, K., Smith, A.: Digital Differences. Pew Research Center, Washington (2012)
22. Choi, N.G., DiNitto, D.M.: The digital divide among low-income homebound older adults: internet use patterns, eHealth literacy, and attitudes toward computer/internet use. J. Med. Internet Res. **15**(5), e93 (2013)
23. Zickuhr, K., Madden, M.: Older adults and internet use (2012)
24. Cacioppo, J.T., Hawkley, L.C.: Social isolation and health, with an emphasis on underlying mechanisms. Perspect. Biol. Med. **46**, S39–S52 (2003)
25. Tomaka, J., Thompson, S., Palacios, R.: The relation of social isolation, loneliness, and social support to disease outcomes among the elderly. J. Aging Health **18**, 359–384 (2006)
26. Green, C.S.B.D.: Exercising your brain: a review of human brain plasticity and training-induced learning. Psychol. Aging **23**(4), 692–701 (2008)
27. Boot, W.R., Blakely, D.P., Simons, D.J.: Do action video games improve perception and cognition? Front. Psychol. **2**, 226 (2011)

28. Hubbert, F.A., Johnson, T., Nickson, J.: High prevalence of prospective memory impairment in the elderly and in early-stage demen-tia: findings from a population-based study. Appl. Cogn. Psychol. **14**, S63–S81 (2000)

29. Gilewski, M.J., Zelinski, E.M., Schaie, K.W.: The memory functioning questionnaire for assessment of memory complaints in adulthood and old age. Psychol. Aging **5**, 482–490 (1990)

30. Zeintl, M., Kliegel, M., Rast, P., Zimprich, D.: Prospective memory complaints can be predicted by prospective memory performance in older adults. Dement. Geriatr. Cogn. Disord. **22**, 209–215 (2006)

31. Taha, J., Sharit, J., Czaja, S.: Use of and satisfaction with sources of health information among older internet users and nonusers. Gerontologist **49**(5), 663–673 (2009)

32. Ward, B.W., Schiller, J.S., Goodman, R.A.: Multiple chronic conditions among US adults: a 2012 update. Prev. Chron. Dis. **11**, E62 (2014). doi:10.5888/pcd11.130389

33. Prevention CfDCa: The state of aging and health in America 2013. Centers for Disease Control and Prevention, US Dept of Health and Human Services, Atlanta, GA (2013)

34. Fox, S.: E-patients with a Disability or Chronic Disease. Pew Research Center, Washington (2007)

35. Rogers, W.A., Meyer, B., Walker, N., Fisk, A.D.: Functional limitations to daily living tasks in the aged: a focus group analysis. Hum. Factors **40**, 111–125 (1998)

36. Williams, K., Kemper, S.: Exploring interventions to reduce cognitive decline in aging. J. Psychosoc. Nurs. Ment. Health Serv. **48**(5), 42–51 (2010)

37. Pantell, M., Rehkopf, D., Jutte, D., Syme, S.L., Balmes, J., Alder, N.: Social isolation: a predictor of mortality comparable to traditional clinical risk factors. Am. J. Pub. Health **103** (11), 2056–2062 (2013)

38. Valenzuela, M., Sachdev, P.: Can cognitive exercise prevent the onset of dementia? Systematic review of randomized clin-ical trials with longitudinal follow-up. Am. J. Geriatr. Psychiatry **17**(3), 179–187 (2009)

Useful or Easy-to-Use? Knowing What Older People Like about Near Field Communication Technology

Pei-Lee Teh[1]([⊠]), Pervaiz K. Ahmed[1], Alan H.S. Chan[2],
Soon-Nyean Cheong[3], and Wen-Jiun Yap[3]

[1] School of Business, Monash University, Bandar Sunway,
Selangor Darul Ehsan, Malaysia
{teh.pei.lee,pervaiz.ahmed}@monash.edu
[2] Department of Systems Engineering and Engineering Management,
City University of Hong Kong, Kowloon, Hong Kong
alan.chan@cityu.edu.hk
[3] Faculty of Engineering, Multimedia University, Cyberjaya, Malaysia
{sncheong,wjyap}@mmu.edu.my

Abstract. The goals of this study are two-fold: (1) To develop a novel concept of a light system with the use of Near Field Communication (NFC)-enabled technology, Bluetooth and Raspberry-PI. This new system is known as NFC Light System (NLS). (2) To set up an experimental design to examine the influence of perceived usefulness and perceived ease of use on older adults' behavioral intention to use the NLS. Our proposed system was empirically tested with 33 older adults in Malaysia. Our findings show that perceived ease of use appears to be the primary factor for the older adults to use the NLS. Interestingly, perceived usefulness was not a significant predictor of older adults' behavioral intention to use the NLS. From the practical viewpoint, this study offers a new insight for gerontechnology manufacturer and developers to focus their design efforts on easy-to-use attribute that are desired by older adults.

Keywords: Technology acceptance model · Experimental design · Gerontechnology · Near field communication · Malaysia

1 Introduction

The demographic profile of the world population has undergone significant transformation over the recent years, with one of the main demographic shifts is population ageing. The proportion of older adults (aged 65 year-old and above) has been increasing and the number is projected to raise from 841 million in 2013 to more than 2 billion in 2050 [24]. It was also reported that 40 percent of the older adults aged 60 years or above live independently [24], and projections indicate that the number of older adults living alone will rise considerably into the future. Given that older adults spend more time in and around their house, duty for care of this older population involves providing them with a safe and healthy home environment, in which they are

© Springer International Publishing Switzerland 2015
J. Zhou and G. Salvendy (Eds.): ITAP 2015, Part I, LNCS 9193, pp. 273–281, 2015.
DOI: 10.1007/978-3-319-20892-3_27

able to function independently. In this vein, gerontechnology is becoming an increasingly important means to support the older adults' vitality and independence.

According to Fozard et al. [10], gerontechnology is a word bearing gerontology (scientific study of aging) and technology (the development and implementation of technological products, services and physical environments). Gerontechnology relates to the use of technology for the benefit of both aging and aged people [5, 9, 25]. Within the scope of gerontechnology, technology is not an end in itself but a means to support the aging people for a better life [2]. Hence, both gerontological and technological studies are closely connected.

The core of gerontechnology focuses on the impact of different technologies within five domains of human activity [9, 25]. The five domains of human activity include: (1) Health and self-esteem (technology supporting physical, cognitive and emotional functioning of older people); (2) Housing and daily living (technology supporting independence, convenience and safety of daily activities among the older people); (3) Mobility and transport (technology supporting personal mobility of older people); (4) Communication and governance (technology supporting societal cohesion, the use of TV, Internet, mobile phone, etc., and remote monitoring of functional status of older people); and (5) Work and leisure (technology supporting older people to continue their work and perform educational and recreational activities). An example of housing and daily living domain includes developing smart technology for controlling lighting and heating that can help to address the limitations in physical function of older adults [10].

The 21st century has witnessed an unprecedented change in the way how technology affects people's daily lives. Today, numerous products and services are available, particularly with the proliferation of near-field communication (NFC)-enabled technology. This study focuses on NFC-enabled assistive technology in the home environment. As light/lamp is an everyday product that older adults use it in their daily lives, interest in NFC-enabled light system is timely and relevant.

In most instances, new technologies have great potential usage in ageing population, but successful implementation of the technology is highly dependent on the user's technology acceptance. Regardless of the extant gerontechnology studies published on electronic government services [19], health-related technology [11], smartphones [28], telecare services [21], there is still room for research that furthers the understanding of factors affecting technology adoption among the older adults. In this study, we draw on Technology Acceptance Model (TAM) to examine the older adults' technology decision.

Taken together, the goals of this study are two-fold: (1) To design an assistive technology for the home environment, we develop a light system with the use of NFC-enabled technology, Bluetooth and Raspberry-PI. This new system is known as NFC Light System (NLS). (2) Building from the lens of TAM, we examine the influence of perceived usefulness and perceived ease of use on older adults' behavioral intention to use the NLS.

In the following sections, we first discuss the design and development of NLS. Thereafter, we draw from TAM to develop our research hypotheses. This is followed by a description of the research method and results. We finally conclude this paper by discussing the findings, research implications, limitations and directions for future research.

2 Literature Review and Research Hypotheses

2.1 NFC Light System (NLS)

In technical research, NFC is known as a wireless technology for data transfer within short-range distance [27]. NFC technology supports two-way data exchange in digital devices [18]. For example, an NFC device can act as a smart key to interact with other NFC-enabled tag/device [18]. Technically, NFC-enabled devices can manage three operation modes, viz., read/write, peer-to-peer and card emulation mode [14].

In this study, we applied the NFC read operation to design and develop the NLS. The design of the NLS uses a set-top-box as a convergence platform, enabling the users to interact with the lamp using a NFC card. In other words, NLS uses the concept of tap-to-connect mechanism where operations are triggered by touching NFC card with a set-top-box. Furthermore, NLS does not require Internet connection for operations. With the use of Bluetooth Low Energy-enabled Raspberry-PI, users are only required to connect NLS with power source to activate the operation. Given that NLS is an assistive technology where users do not need to reach the light switch/lamp to switch on/off the light, our proposed NLS provides a fast and convenient home experience for older adults. The features of NLS include portable, easy-to-use and very low power consumption, thereby augmenting an independence experience for older adults.

2.2 Tam

The theoretical framework for this paper is drawn from TAM, a revised version of Theory of Reasoned Action (TRA) [7]. TAM was introduced in 1986 and has been the robust model to study users' technology acceptance [13, 22]. In the gerontechnology literature, several studies (e.g., [1, 3, 6, 17, 19, 20]) have applied TAM in understanding older adults' technology adoption decision. Within the TAM framework, Davis [7] posits that technology usage is predicted by behavioral intention that is affected by two key variables, namely, perceived ease of use and perceived usefulness.

According to Karahanna et al. [12:788], perceived usefulness is defined as the "instrumental value derived from use of a technology." For example, users are not keen to use the service application if it is not beneficial [15]. Past gerontechnology research has reported that perceived usefulness had a positive effect on older people's Internet use intention [17], intention to use social networking websites [3], and intention to use the electronic governance services [19]. In the context of NLS, we expect a positive usefulness-intention relationship among the older adults. Therefore, we propose:

H1: Perceived usefulness will have a significant positive influence on older adults' behavioral intention to use the NLS.

Davis [7:320] defines perceived ease of use as "the degree to which a person believes that using a particular system would be free of effort." Davis [7] postulates that a user will accept a system that is regarded to be easy-to-use. There have been strong empirical results that support that perceived ease of use has a positive relationship with behavioral intention (see: [17, 19]). In application to our study, perceived ease of use will have a positive impact on older people's behavioral intention to use the NLS. Therefore, we propose:

H2: Perceived ease of use will have a significant positive influence on older people's behavioral intention to use the NLS.

3 Research Methodology

3.1 Measures

In this study, the survey instrument used to operationalize the three variables were adapted from well-established literature and modified for use in the NLS context. Survey questions of perceived ease of use were adapted from [4, 7, 26]. Three new survey items were developed to measure perceived usefulness. Behavior intention to use the NLS was measured using items adapted from [4, 7, 23, 26]. Respondents were asked to indicate the degree to which they agreed or disagreed with each survey item, on a seven-point Likert scale from 1 (strongly disagree) to 7 (strongly agree).

3.2 Sample

The target sample was older adults in Malaysia. The current sample consists of 33 participants, who are part of a larger on-going study. Voluntary consent was sought and obtained from each participant. All research procedures were performed with the

Table 1. Profile of participants

Variable	Classification	Frequency (n = 33)	Percent (%)
Gender	Male	12	36.4
	Female	21	63.6
Age	55–64	10	30.3
	65–74	12	36.4
	75–84	8	24.2
	Above 85	3	9.1
Highest Education Completed	Informal *(no schooling or self-learning)*	8	24.2
	Primary School *(completed primary 1 to 6 education)*	4	12.1
	High school *(completed form 1 to form 5 education)*	10	30.3
	Diploma	4	12.1
	Bachelor degree/ professional qualification	4	12.1
	Master degree	1	3.0
	PhD degree	2	6.1

approval of university's human ethics review board, and informed consent of all participants.

Our participants included 12 males and 21 females. Table 1 shows our sample demographic profile including gender, age, and the education level.

4 Data Collection

Our experiential product was an in-house developed NLS. There were three components in this system, namely the NFC-enabled card, set-top-box and the lamp. Each participant was requested to switch on/off the lamp by tapping the NFC card on the set-top-box. After the practice session, participants were asked to complete a survey questionnaire about the experiment.

5 Results

5.1 Reliability, Validity and Factor Analyses

IBM SPSS software was used to check the psychometric properties of the survey instrument, and to test our hypothesized model. Reliability of the scales was tested using Cronbach Alpha. As shown in Table 2, all scales were reliable as the values of Cronbach Alpha were greater than 0.70, and met the desirable values suggested by [16]. Both convergent and discriminant validity were assessed using Average Variance Extracted (AVE). As presented in Table 2, convergent validity was confirmed as AVE of all constructs were at least 0.50, meeting the cutoff value suggested by Fornell and Larcker [8]. Discriminant validity was tested through the comparison of square roots of the AVE of construct pairs to the correlation between construct pairs. As shown in Table 2, all the square roots of AVE values were greater than the off-diagonal coefficients of construct pairs, providing an evidence of discriminant validity.

Principal component factor analysis was conducted to check the construct validity. The factor loadings, Kaiser-Meyer-Olkin (KMO), Bartlett test of sphericity, and eigenvalues of our model are shown in Table 3. All variables exhibited good construct validity.

Multiple regression analysis was performed to test the model. Table 4 and Fig. 1 show the results of multiple regression analysis. The predictors explained 52.1 percent of behavioral intention's variance in hypothesized model. Perceived ease of use ($\beta = 0.646$; p-value < 0.001) was the dominant factor predicting older people's behavioral intention. Our results showed non-significant perceived usefulness-intention relationships ($\beta = 0.131$; p-value > 0.05). These results lend support to hypothesis H2 but not H1.

Table 2. Results of reliability and validity

	Perceived usefulness	Perceived ease of use	Behavior intention
Perceived usefulness	*0.893*		
Perceived ease of use	0.512**	*0.829*	
Behavior intention	0.462**	0.713**	*0.943*
Average variance extracted	0.797	0.688	0.889
Cronbach's alpha	0.848	0.844	0.930
Standard deviation	1.275	0.596	1.378
Mean	5.647	6.152	5.434

Note: ** All correlations are significant at the 0.01 level (2-tailed); Italicized values in the diagonal row are square roots of the AVE.

Table 3. Results of factor analysis

Variable	No. of Item	KMO	BTS	EV	Factor Loadings			
					Item 1	Item 2	Item 3	Item 4
PU	3	0.728	46.843***	2.390	0.863	0.907	0.907	Nil
PE	4	0.658	62.472***	2.751	0.872	0.852	0.695	0.885
BI	3	0.758	81.191***	2.669	0.926	0.949	0.954	Nil

Note: *** $p < 0.001$; KMO = Kaiser-Meyer-Olkin; BTS = Barlett's Test of Sphericity; EV = Eigen-values; PU = Perceived usefulness; PE = Perceived ease of use; BI = Behavioral intention

Table 4. Results of Regression Analysis

	Beta Coefficient	Standard Error
(Constant)		
Perceived Usefulness	0.131	0.159
Perceived Ease of Use	0.646***	0.340
R^2	0.722	
Adj. R^2	0.521	
F	16.338	
Sig.	0.000***	

Note: Dependent Variable = Behavioral Intention; *** $p < 0.001$

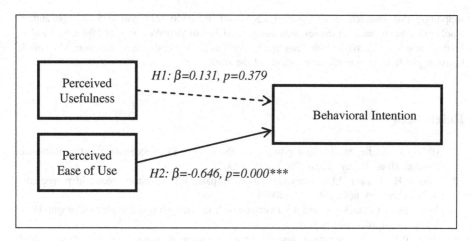

Fig. 1. Results of regression analysis

6 Discussion and Conclusion

Our findings show that perceived ease of use appears to be the primary factor for the older people to use the NLS. This finding is consistent with Pan and Jordan-Marsh [17], where they found a strong effect of perceived ease of use on Internet use intention for older adults. Our result indicates the importance of an easy-to-use technology design in encouraging technology adoption among the older adults. Interestingly, perceived usefulness was not a significant predictor of older people's behavioral intention to use the NLS. One possible explanation for this finding is that older adults do not necessarily adopt new technology even though the technology is a useful practical tool for them. Perception of usefulness/benefits was not the motivational factor for using a new assistive technology for older adults.

From the practical viewpoint, this study offers a new insight for gerontechnology manufacturer and developers to focus their design efforts on easy-to-use attribute that are desired by the older people. In addition, the NLS contributes in itself as a novel gerontechnology design. The proposed NLS is an effective assistive technology for older adults in maintaining their vitality and independence.

This study has two research limitations that should be acknowledged. First, data was collected from Malaysia and future research should be conducted in other countries to improve the generalizability of our findings. Second, we applied TAM as the theoretical basis in this study. Future studies should examine others variables and their relationships by drawing from different theoretical frameworks such as Innovation Diffusion Theory and Unified Theory of Acceptance and Use of Technology (UTAUT).

Acknowledgements. The authors thank the Ministry of Science, Technology and Innovation (MOSTI), Government of Malaysia, and Monash University Malaysia campus for financially supporting this research under contract ES-1-14/06-02-10-SF0211 and B-5-14. The authors would also like to thank all the research assistants (Cherish Voo Wen Yee, Natalie Ong Xi Men, Jayden Liew Yee Jin, Wong Poh Teng and Esther Tan En Yi) in the data collection. Most of all, heartfelt gratitude goes to the respondents of the study.

References

1. Arning, K., Ziefle, M.: Understanding age differences in PDA acceptance and performance. Comput. Hum. Behav. **23**(6), 2904–2927 (2007)
2. Bouma, H., Fozard, J.L., Bouwhuis, D.G., Taipale, V.: Gerontechnology in perspective. Gerontechnology **6**(4), 190–216 (2007)
3. Braun, M.T.: Obstacles to social networking website use among older adults. Comput. Hum. Behav. **29**(3), 673–680 (2003)
4. Chau, P.Y.K.: An empirical assessment of a modified technology acceptance model. J. Manag. Inf. Syst. **13**(2), 185–204 (1996)
5. Chen, K., Chan, A.H.S.: The ageing population of China and a review of gerontechnology. Gerontechnology **10**(2), 63–71 (2011)
6. Chen, K., Chan, A.H.S.: Predictors of gerontechnology acceptance by older Hong Kong Chinese. Technovation **34**(2), 126–135 (2014)
7. Davis, F.D.: Perceived usefulness, perceived ease of use, and user acceptance of information technology. MIS Q. **13**(3), 319–340 (1989)
8. Fornell, C., Larcker, D.F.: Evaluating structural equation models with unobservable variables and measurement error. J. Mark. Res. **18**(1), 39–50 (1981)
9. Fozard, J.L.: Impacts of technology interventions on health and self-esteem. Gerontechnology **4**(2), 63–76 (2005)
10. Fozard, J.L., Rietsema, J., Bouma, H., Graafmans, J.A.M.: Gerontechnology: creating enabling environments for the challenges and opportunities of aging. Educ. Gerontechnology **26**(4), 331–344 (2000)
11. Heart, T., Kalderon, E.: Older adults: are they ready to adopt health-related ICT? Int. J Med. Inform. **82**(11), e209–e231 (2013)
12. Karahanna, E., Agarwal, R., Angst, C.M.: Reconceptualizing compatibility beliefs in technology acceptance research. MIS Q. **30**(4), 781–804 (2006)
13. Lee, M.K.O., Cheung, C.M.K., Chen, Z.: Acceptance of internet-based learning medium: the role of extrinsic and intrinsic motivation. Inf. Manag. **42**(8), 1095–1104 (2005)
14. Leong, L.Y., Hew, T.S., Tan, G.W.H., Ooi, K.B.: Predicting the determinants of the NFC-enabled mobile credit card acceptance: a neural networks approach. Expert Syst. Appl. **40**(14), 5604–5620 (2013)
15. McKenna, B., Tuunanen, T., Gardner, L.: Consumers' adoption of information services. Inf. Manag. **50**(5), 248–257 (2013)
16. Nunnally, J.C., Bernstein, I.H.: Psychometric Theory, 3rd edn. McGraw-Hill Inc, New York (1994)
17. Pan, S., Jordan-Marsh, M.: Internet Use intention and adoption among chinese older adults: from the expanded technology acceptance model perspective. Comput. Hum. Behav. **26**(5), 1111–1119 (2010)
18. Pesonen, J., Horster, E.: Near field communication technology in tourism. Tourism Manag. Perspect. **4**, 11–18 (2012)

19. Phang, C.W., Sutanto, J., Kankanhalli, A., Li, Y., Tan, B.C.Y., Teo, H.H.: Senior citizens' acceptance of information systems: a study in the context of e-Government services. IEEE Trans. Eng. Manag. **53**(4), 555–569 (2006)
20. Ryu, M.H., Kim, S., Lee, E.: Understanding the factors affecting online elderly user's participation in video UCC services. Comput. Hum. Behav. **25**(3), 619–632 (2009)
21. Sintonen, S., Immonen, M.: Telecare services for aging people: assessment of critical factors influencing the adoption intention. Comput. Hum. Behav. **29**(4), 1307–1317 (2013)
22. Straub, D., Limayem, M., Karahanna-Evaristo, E.: measuring system usage: implications for IS theory testing. Manag. Sci. **41**(8), 1328–1342 (1995)
23. Teh, P.L., Ahmed, P.K., Cheong, S.N., Yap, W.J.: Age-group differences in near field communication smartphone. Ind. Manag. Data Syst. **114**(3), 484–502 (2014)
24. United Nations, Department of Economic and Social Affairs, Population Division: World Population Ageing 2013. ST/ESA/SER.A/348 (2013)
25. van Bronswijk, J.E.M.H., Bouma, H., Fozard, J.L.: Technology for quality of life: an enriched taxonomy. Gerontechnology **2**(2), 169–172 (2002)
26. Venkatesh, V.: Determinants of Perceived Ease of Use: Integrating Control, Intrinsic Motivation, and Emotion into the Technology Acceptance Model. Inf. Syst. Res. **11**(4), 342–365 (2000)
27. Volland, D., Noyen, K., Kayikci, O., Ackermann, L., Michahelles, F.: Switching the role of NFC tag and reader for the implementation of smart posters. In: 2012 fourth International Workshop on Near Field Communication, pp. 63–68, Helsinki (2012)
28. Zhou, J., Rau, P.L.P., Salvendy, G.: Older adults' use of smart phones: an investigation of the factors influencing the acceptance of new functions. Behav. Inf. Technol. **33**(6), 552–560 (2014)

Pitfalls when Placing Electricity Pylons - The Influence of Age on Acceptance

Barbara S. Zaunbrecher[1](✉), Katrin Arning[1], Baris Özalay[2],
Hendrik Natemeyer[2], and Martina Ziefle[1]

[1] Human-Computer Interaction Center, RWTH Aachen University,
Aachen, Germany
{Zaunbrecher,Arning,Ziefle}@comm.rwth-aachen.de
[2] Institute for High Voltage Technology (IFHT), RWTH Aachen University,
Aachen, Germany
{Oezalay,Natemeyer}@ifht.rwth-aachen.de

Abstract. The increasing penetration of renewable energies influences and changes the transmission task of electricity in Germany. However, the planning and construction of new lines is met with resistance from the public. To address public concerns adequately, a tailored information and communication concept is needed, for which knowledge about acceptance-relevant factors for different user groups is indispensable. In this paper we explore acceptance-relevant attributes in the context of electricity pylons contrasting attitudes of older and younger persons. Results of a conjoint study indicate that both age groups basically have comparable acceptance levels, but younger persons were found to be more sensitive with regard to distance of the pylon and possible health effects. Additionally, acceptance patterns similar to those for cell tower location were found, which implies that the analyzed attributes are not only stable across demographic groups but also across technologies.

Keywords: Energy infrastructure · Technology acceptance · Electricity pylons · User diversity · Renewable energies · Conjoint analysis

1 Introduction

The future high proportion of feature-dependent power generation as a consequence of the increasing penetration of renewable energies influences and changes the transmission task of electricity. Especially the high wind power capacity in the north of Germany requires an electricity transport from the north to the south of Germany. This is why the need for new transmission lines is a vital topic for the achievement of the ambitious aims of the energy transition.

But, the planning and construction of new lines is often met with resistance from the public, as they fear e.g. health problems due to radiation [1, 2] or criticize the visual impact on the landscape [3, 4]. Ignoring this criticism may lead to citizens' protests, which can cause delays and even cancelling of entire projects [5, 6]. Thus, public acceptance is a critical factor not only for the successful but also for the sustainable

© Springer International Publishing Switzerland 2015
J. Zhou and G. Salvendy (Eds.): ITAP 2015, Part I, LNCS 9193, pp. 282–293, 2015.
DOI: 10.1007/978-3-319-20892-3_28

implementation of novel technologies. Often it is assumed that any novel technology naturally evokes concerns and criticism in the very beginning and that those concerns fade as the public gets attuned to it over time [7]. Nonetheless, there are some major arguments to actively address the concerns, for two reasons: First, technology acceptance is a complex phenomenon [8, 9] which needs a specific evaluation methodology [10]. Different from former studies on acceptance, in which a more or less static single factor evaluation was done, it is increasingly understood that reliable acceptance decisions include several factors at a time. Characteristically, negative factors and positive factors are weighed, related to each other and then built to a final decision. This is especially the case in large-scale technologies, in which many, some times contradictory motives on different (time)scales have to be considered. Thus, contemporary acceptance research must be directed to identifying the relevant factors, understand the nature of the weighing and factors compensating each other and learn which of the factors might be scalable. Second, public acceptance should be implemented as early as possible within the technology development in order to adapt technology decisions in line with public opinions. Understanding the fears and wishes of the citizens is the grounding to react adequately and to specifically tailor communication and information policies. A prerequisite for such a concept to be successful is the knowledge about which acceptance-relevant factors are important to which user groups [7]. Understanding aged persons seems to be an especially crucial cornerstone in the context of technology acceptance, as many European countries face a demographic change with an increasing penetration of life with technology. Multiple studies have therefore addressed the attitude towards technology of older adults [8, 11–13]. For renewable energies, age was found to also influence attitudes towards green energy, nuclear energy and micro-scale technologies [14]. In particular, it was for example found that older persons were less positive towards wind power [15] and were less willing to pay for renewable energy and energy efficiency [16].

As the grid expansion is a topic closely related to the turn towards more renewable energy sources, it is reasonable to assume that age also plays a role for the acceptance and preferences concerning pylon placement. Therefore, we focused on an age contrast with regard to acceptance-relevant factors of electricity pylon siting. Two research questions on this topic will be addressed in this study:

1. How do different acceptance-relevant attributes in the context of electricity pylons siting (health concerns, compensation payment, distance to housing, location of installment) relate to each other?
2. Can age-effects be found for the weighing of these factors?

To answer the research questions, we conducted an empirical study (conjoint analysis) which was designed as an online study. Our research contributes to the existing literature on acceptance of energy infrastructure, as well as the influence of user factors on acceptance patterns. It provides useful insights for energy providers, urban planners and energy policy makers into social acceptance patterns and possible pitfalls for the siting of power lines.

2 Grid Expansion in Germany and Specifications for Placements of Electricity Pylons

The transformation to a sustainable energy supply without the use of nuclear power and with low carbon emission in Germany leads to changing geographical electricity generation patterns and thus to changing electricity transmission needs. The transport of electrical energy over long distances is usually performed by voltage levels of 220 kV and especially 400 kV. Most lines at those voltages are built as overhead line as underground cabling as option is still lacking technical long-term experience at those voltage levels and is much more expensive.

To avoid unnecessary extension, the NOVA-principle[1] is applied in Germany. It implies that *prior* to the construction of new lines, the optimization as well as the reinforcement of the existing infrastructure (i.e. by mounting additional circuits on exiting poles) has to be carefully analyzed.

The need for reinforcement is usually identified on a point-to-point basis, which means that the concrete routing of the lines is not or only to a limited extent considered. Once the need for the new connection is determined by the system operator and confirmed by the national authority[2], it finds its way into the Federal Requirement Plan – still on a point-to-point basis. In the next steps the transmission system operator elaborates a first suggestion and possible alternatives for the routing of the line, initially in terms of an up to 1000 m wide corridor and later with precise positions for the pylons. In each case, the following process is led by the federal state authority or by the national authority, in case more than one federal state is concerned. Every citizen or organization is invited to get involved in the process which targets to identify a routing that considers technical, economic, environmental and social aspects. As a result, the system operator can be committed to analyze additional alternatives and obtain expert advice. The responsible authority eventually decides on the final routing.

With regard to technical aspects, it has to be considered that the length of a line determines its technical parameters. The isolation distance needs to be kept, so that vegetation in the closer surrounding of the line is only possible to a limited extent and the underground has to be suitable for the foundation of the pylons. The complexity of the construction of a line is also higher, if the route is twisty as the direction of the line has to chance often and more or different pylons have to be built. On the voltage level of 220 kV and above, no special need for closeness to residential areas exists as the supply of the consumers is performed with lower voltages. Nevertheless, at some points the closeness to residential areas cannot be avoided. In these cases, the knowledge

---

[1] NOVA means "Netzoptimierung vor Verstärkung vor Ausbau," in English: "network optimization before reinforcement before extension".

[2] Bundesnetzagentur.

about public preferences for siting scenarios is crucial at this point in order to timely react on possible concerns and to develop a solution that suits both, developers and citizens.

3 Methodology

A Choice-Based Conjoint (CBC) study was designed with Sawtooth Software as an online survey. Originating in market research, conjoint analysis is a measurement approach that allows for the determination of relative preferences and closely mimics decision processes of respondents. In conjoint analyses, participants are presented with a set of attributes that make up a product, or, in this case, a scenario. Participants compare different scenarios against each other, which are defined by the same attributes, but by different manifestations (or levels) of the attributes. This way, participants are forced to take into account bundles of characteristics for their choice rather than comparing isolated characteristics of scenarios. Because of this, the choice task models real-life decisions in a more realistic way than other types of questionnaire techniques. By analyzing the choice behavior of the participants, it is possible to calculate the importance of one attribute for the decision relative to the other attributes (relative importance), and furthermore, to calculate the value of a level of an attribute for the choice of a scenario relative to the others levels of an attribute (part-worth utility).

Questionnaire Design. The questionnaire included items on demographic information, living area, proximity to electricity pylons and the use of "green electricity". Because earlier studies have shown that technical self-efficacy (TSE) [17] has an effect on technology acceptance and attitude towards energy related infrastructures, TSE was measured using eight selected items from Beier's TSE-questionnaire [17] for which reliability had been previously tested [9]. All questions, with the exception of the demographic information, were answered on a six-point-Likert scale ("1 = do not agree at all" to "6 = fully agree"). Finally, participants were invited to leave comments on the topic.

Experimental Design/Selection of Attributes. For the conjoint task, the four attributes "location", "distance to home", "health effects" and "compensation payment" were chosen and were assigned appropriate levels (Table 1). Participants were presented with different infrastructure scenarios that differed concerning the frequency of health concerns, distance of the pylon to housing, location of pylon and amount of compensation payment. The attributes were chosen based on prior research on acceptance of technology infrastructure (mobile phone masts [10]) and the consultations of experts. They were adapted to the context of electricity pylons when necessary. This methodology additionally provides the opportunity to compare the same acceptance-relevant attribute across different technologies (mobile phone masts and electricity pylons) and identify possible generic fears and perceived threats that are stable across technologies. Levels were illustrated by pictures to enhance understanding (Table 1).

Table 1. Attributes and levels used in the conjoint study

Location	Distance to home	Frequency of health effects	Compensation payment
near existing infrastructure	400m	never	0€
on an open field	800m	rarely	250€
in a forest	1200m	sometimes	500€
		often	1000€

In an introduction before the conjoint tasks, the attributes, levels and mode of the survey were explained to the participants. For location, the levels "near existing infrastructure", "on an open field" and "in a forest" were chosen. These locations represent possible locations according to current policies for pylon siting in Germany. It is assumed that they are accepted differently, as they present a different degree of fit in a landscape: while the pylon on an open field is highly visible, a location in a forest disguises the lines, however, it comes at the cost of cutting down trees. Placing pylons near existing infrastructure has been favored in other studies on the subject, as it minimizes additional interferences with the environment. The "distance from home" is set at 400 m, 800 m and 1200 m. It was communicated to the participants in the introductory part of the study that even the nearest location (400 m) was in line with current regulations and fulfilled the security standard. Finally, possible subjective health risks such as dizziness, headaches etc. which are associated with EMF emitted from transmission lines were introduced at frequency levels ("never", "rarely", "sometimes" "often") [10]. The levels of the different attributes were combined into scenarios from which the participants had to chose the one they preferred most. For each choice task, the respondent was presented with three scenarios (Fig. 1). Because a full-factorial design would have yielded 144 ($3 \times 3 \times 4 \times 4$) possible scenarios to judge, the amount of stimuli was reduced, so each participant only answered nine choice tasks, which were randomized across participants. To ensure design efficiency, a test for efficiency was applied (provided by Sawtooth Software). Taking into account 184 participants, the design was reported to have an efficiency of 100 % compared to the fully orthogonal design.

Data Collection. Data were collected in an online survey in Germany by distributing

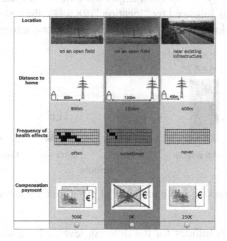

Fig. 1. Example of an original choice task from the conjoint study

the survey in social networks and online discussion forums. Citizen groups affected by the building of new power lines were especially invited to take part in the survey. The survey took approximately 15 min to complete.

3.1   Sample

231 participants took part in the survey. Because Sawtooth Software requires complete datasets for the conjoint analysis, all datasets with missing answers were excluded, so that 184 datasets remained for analysis. 44 % of the sample was female, 56 % male and the average age was 36.2 years (SD = 14.3). More than half of the participants (56.5 %) reported to hold a university degree, which shows that the sample was highly educated. The majority of the sample lived in the city center (41.3 %), followed by people living in the outskirts of a city (34.8 %), and the smallest group lived on the countryside (23.9 %). Most participants lived in an apartment house (60.9 %), further 26.1 % lived in a detached house.

On a scale of 1 (lowest) to 6 (highest), the average score for TSE was M = 4.6 (SD = 0.9). The self-reported knowledge about the grid expansion was low (M = 2.8, SD = 1.2). To control for effects of familiarity, participants were asked whether they lived within view of an electricity pylon (yes: 27.2 %, no: 72.8 %).

4   Results

The results of the conjoint analysis, average importances and part-worth utilities will be presented first for the whole sample and then contrasted for the two age groups.

Looking at the sample as a whole, an analysis of the average importances showed that health effects were by far the most important attribute for the choice of a scenario (Fig. 2) (54.8 %). It was followed by "location" (28.3 %), then by "distance" (11.0 %). A one-time compensation payment was the least important attribute (5.9 %).

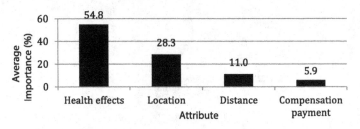

Fig. 2. Mean importances for attributes of pylon location scenarios (n = 184)

Next, the part-worth utilities for the different levels of the attributes are described (Fig. 3).

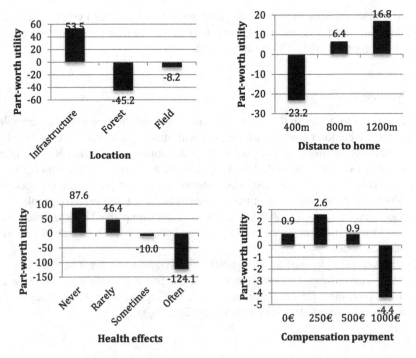

Fig. 3. Part-worth utilities for attributes location, distance to home, frequency of health effects, compensation payment (n = 184)

It was found that a pylon location near existing infrastructure was most accepted (53.5), while the location in a forest was the least accepted (–45.2). The location on an open field was less accepted than the placement near existing infrastructure, but more than the location "forest" (–8.2). Concerning the distance to home, the distances were accepted in descending order: the furthest away the pylon (1200 m), the more accepted the distance was (16.8). Next, the most important attribute "health effects" is examined. Participants accepted the most frequent health effects the least ("often": –124.1), and the least frequent health effects ("never": 87.6) the most. The opposition and acceptance were particularly strong for this attribute, as the large difference in utility values for the most and least accepted level showed (211.7), which is also reflected in the overall high average importance of this attribute. The compensation payment had almost no effect on the choice of the pylon placement scenario, which is illustrated by the very small differences in the part-worth utility values (difference between most and least accepted level: 7.0). Interestingly, the highest compensation payment of 1000€ was strongly rejected (–4.4), whereas 0€ and 500€ received the same, slightly positive rating (0.9). The most preferred compensation payment value was 250€ (2.6).

In the following, age effects were addressed. Participants were split into two age groups ("younger" group (<50 years), "older" group (50+ years)). The groups did not differ significantly in terms of gender distribution, however, the "older" group had a lower overall educational level (p ≤ 0.01), lived on the countryside and in the outskirts of a city rather than in the city center (p ≤ 0.01), and had a (slightly) lower TSE (p ≤ 0.01). They did not differ in other possible influential factors on acceptance such as familiarity (living within view of pylons) or knowledge about grid expansion.

In a first step, the average importances for the young and old were compared (Fig. 4). It is evident that the groups did not differ greatly with regard to the most important attributes for the choice of the pylon-placement scenario. For both groups, possible health effects were the most important attribute when choosing a scenario, however, this was slightly less so for the older group (46.5 compared to 55.8). In contrast to this, the location was less important for the younger age group (26.6) than for the older participants (31.4). The distance had equally low importance for both groups (11.4 and 11.5). Compensation payment had an overall low importance, but its effect on the choice of a scenario was stronger for the old (10.5) than for the young group (6.2) (Fig. 4).

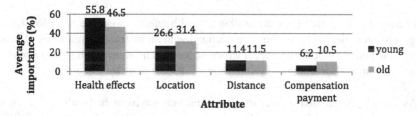

Fig. 4. Average importances for attributes of pylon location scenarios (younger: n = 141, older: n = 43)

Analyzing the attribute "location" for the two groups revealed that younger and older participants did not differ to a great extent in their preferences for the pylon setting. Both groups preferred a siting scenario in which the pylon is placed next to already existing infrastructure, followed by the placement on a field. The placement in a forest is most strongly rejected by both groups (Fig. 5).

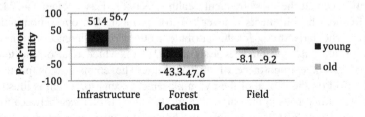

Fig. 5. Part-worth utilities for attribute "location" for age groups (young: n = 141, old: n = 43)

The preferences for the distance from the current place of living were more distinct between the two groups than for the location. The older and younger participants agreed in the fact that the closest location (400 m) was the least accepted. However, the young group preferred 1200 m over 800 m, while it was the other way around for the older participants. It is also noteworthy that the preference for 1200 m over 800 m by the young group was clearer (difference between the two levels: 15.9) than the preference of 800 m over 1200 m by the old group (difference: 7.0), indicated by the greater difference between the part-worth utility scores for the young group (Fig. 6).

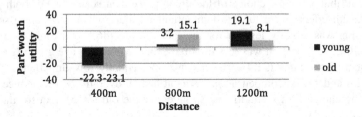

Fig. 6. Part-worth utilities for attribute "distance" for age groups (younger: n = 141, older: n = 43)

The preference patterns for the attribute "health effects" were the same for the two age groups: in both groups, acceptance declined with an increasing frequency of health effects. It is notable that health effects which occur "often" were much stronger rejected in comparison to "sometimes" by the young (−128.6) than by the old group (−92.7) (Fig. 7).

As already mentioned above, the compensation payment had only a very small effect on the choice of the pylon placement scenario, which is illustrated by the very small differences in the part-worth utility values. Differences between the groups exist, but they should not be overestimated because of the overall low effect on the choice of

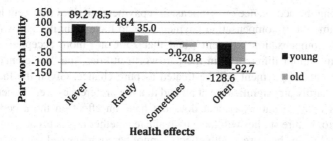

Fig. 7. Part-worth utilities for attribute "health effects" for age groups (younger: n = 141, older: n = 43)

the scenario. It is remarkable, however, that the highest compensation payment is not the best-accepted solution for either of the two groups (Fig. 8).

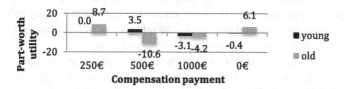

Fig. 8. Part-worth utilities for attribute "compensation payment" for age groups (younger: n = 141, older: n = 43)

Concluding, the best accepted scenario for the young participants would be a pylon placement near existing infrastructure, 1200 m away from their residential location, causing no health issues, with 500€ compensation payment. The scenario for the old participants looks similar: near existing infrastructure, with no health effects, but only 800 m away from their home with 250€ compensatory payment.

5 Discussion

Overall, the study was based on two different research questions. One was directed to the question if age of persons has an influence on the preference for a pylon placement scenario and the way the acceptance relevant criteria were evaluated. The results indicate that this is only partly true. It was found that the overall importance of the presented attributes was the same for young and old participants. The only noteworthy difference was found for the preference of the distance to home and frequency of health effects. Young participants presented themselves more sensitive than the older group: They favored a pylon location that was further away and were also more critical about possible health effects. A possible explanation could be that young people are generally in a better state of health than elders, and are thus more critical towards any impairment that could be caused. The overall more pronounced criticism of the young in combination with a higher technical self-efficacy compared to the older group could be an effect of them being better informed and thus also more informed about possible negative consequences.

Concerning the acceptance of compensation payments, it does not seem logical that the highest amount of compensation payment should have a similar part-worth utility value to "no compensation payment", and that 250€ are more accepted than 500€. Because of the minor differences in the part-worth utilities, the "preferences" for the different amounts of payment will be treated as pure chance. Given the fact that this attribute had hardly any significance at all and that the preferences were rather arbitrary, it seems that compensation payment does not have an effect on the acceptance of a siting scenario. Future studies will have to evaluate whether this is because the payment offered is too low, or because health effects cannot be compensated with money or if a compensation payment is rejected altogether in this context.

Another interesting finding is the striking parallel to the study with similar attributes on cell tower placement by Arning et al. [10]. In both studies, health effects were found to be the most important attribute for the choice of a scenario. Compensation payments, in contrast, were among the least important attributes. This suggests that these preference patterns are stable not only across different groups of people, but also across different technology contexts. With regard to the planning of any infrastructure, which could cause concerns related to health, this means that planners of such infrastructures should be aware of the power of these concerns.

There are of course further factors influencing acceptance of transmission lines which have not been treated in this study because of the special methodology chosen, for example fairness of the decision process and the influence of the sources of information, as mentioned by one participant in a comment:

"(Acceptance of the new transmission line) depends on the objective necessity for the local electricity supply, which has not been proven by independent sources. (...) As long as we feel cheated by the economy and politics, there will be no acceptance of the new transmission lines." (female, member of citizen protest group)

Regardless of the results found in this study, the possibility remains that differences between groups based on user characteristics also exist in the case of pylon placement, bearing in mind that the sample was very well educated. It would be insightful to extend the research onto other target groups for communication and information concepts, also taking into account the role opinion leaders play for citizen protest against power line siting.

Acknowledgements. Thanks to Clara Erner, Lino Kolb and Chantal Lidynia for research support. This work was funded by the Excellence Initiative of German federal and state government (Project "Urban Future Outline").

References

1. Poortinga, W., Cox, P., Pidgeon, N.F.: The perceived health risks of indoor radon gas and overhead powerlines: a comparative multilevel approach. Risk Anal. **28**, 235–248 (2008)
2. Jay, S.: Pylons in the back yard: local planning and perceived risks to health. Environ. Plan. C Gov. Policy **25**, 423–438 (2007)

3. Atkinson, G., Day, B., Mourato, S., Palmer, C.: Amenity or eyesore? negative willingness to pay for options to replace electricity transmission towers. Appl. Econ. Lett. **11**, 203–208 (2004)
4. Devine-Wright, P., Batel, S.: Explaining public preferences for high voltage pylon designs: an empirical study of perceived fit in a rural landscape. Land Use Policy **31**, 640–649 (2013)
5. Neukirch, M.: Konflikte um den Ausbau der Stromnetze [Conflicts about the grid expansion]. Stuttgarter Beiträge zur Organisations- und Innovationsforschung (SOI) [Contributions to Organization and Innovation Research from Stuttgart]. Discussion Paper 2014-01 (1/2014),   ISSN 2191-4990 (2014)
6. Cotton, M., Devine-Wright, P.: Putting pylons into place: a UK case study of public perspectives on the impacts of high voltage overhead transmission lines. J. Environ. Plan. Manag. **56**, 1225–1245 (2012)
7. Ziefle, M., Schaar, A.K.: Technical expertise and its influence on the acceptance of future medical technologies: what is influencing what to which extent? In: Leitner, G., Hitz, M., Holzinger, A. (eds.) USAB 2010. LNCS, vol. 6389, pp. 513–529. Springer, Heidelberg (2010)
8. Arning, K., Ziefle, M.: Different perspectives on technology acceptance: the role of technology type and age. In: Holzinger, A., Miesenberger, K. (eds.) USAB 2009. LNCS, vol. 5889, pp. 20–41. Springer, Heidelberg (2009)
9. Zaunbrecher, B.S., Kowalewski, S., Ziefle, M.: The willingness to adopt technologies: a cross-sectional study on the influence of technical self-efficacy on acceptance. In: Kurosu, M. (ed.) HCI 2014, Part III. LNCS, vol. 8512, pp. 764–775. Springer, Heidelberg (2014)
10. Arning, K., Kowalewski, S., Ziefle, M.: Health concerns vs. mobile data needs: conjoint measurement of preferences for mobile communication network scenarios. Int. J Hum. Ecol. Risk Assess. **20**(5), 1359–1384 (2013)
11. Arning, K., Ziefle, M.: Understanding age differences in PDA acceptance and performance. Comput. Hum. Behav. **23**, 2904–2927 (2007)
12. Mitzner, T.L., Boron, J.B., Fausset, C.B., Adams, A.E., Charness, N., Czaja, S.J., Dijkstra, K., Fisk, A.D., Rogers, W.A., Sharit, J.: Older adults talk technology: technology usage and attitudes. Comput. Hum. Behav. **26**, 1710–1721 (2010)
13. Wilkowska, W., Ziefle, M.: Which factors form older adults' acceptance of mobile information and communication technologies? In: Holzinger, A., Miesenberger, K. (eds.) USAB 2009. LNCS, vol. 5889, pp. 81–101. Springer, Heidelberg (2009)
14. Devine-Wright, P.: Reconsidering public attitudes and public acceptance of renewable energy technologies: a critical review. Manch. Sch. Environ. Dev. Univ. Manch (2007). http://geography.exeter.ac.uk/beyond_nimbyism/deliverables/bn_wp1_4.pdf
15. Ek, K.: Public and private attitudes towards green electricity: the case of Swedish wind power. Energy Policy **33**, 1677–1689 (2005)
16. Zarnikau, J.: Consumer demand for green power and energy efficiency. Energy Policy **31**, 1661–1672 (2003)
17. Beier, G.: Kontrollüberzeugungen im Umgang mit Technik [Locus of control when interacting with technology]. Rep. Psychol. **24**, 684–693 (1999)

Aging, the Web and Social Media

Usability Evaluation of a Social Networking Site Prototype for the Elderly

Jessica Arfaa$^{(\boxtimes)}$ and Yuanqiong (Kathy) Wang

Department of Computer and Information Sciences,
Towson University, Towson, MD 21252, USA
{jessicaarfaa,ywangtu}@gmail.com

Abstract. Social networking sites offer a number of benefits; however a large amount of elder adults still do not engage in these types of sites due to usability issues and a lack of understanding of Web 2.0 concepts. To alleviate these issues, a social networking site interface was redesigned to accommodate elders so that they can reap the benefits of social media. Following a three phased usability study, 22 elder adults utilized a redesigned website incorporating web standards and additional usability and accessibility considerations. With the use of the redesigned prototype, does it improve accessibility and usability for elder adults? What tasks improved in terms of success rates and task performance? How do the elders perceive the newly redesigned prototype? The preliminary findings of this study show that usability and accessibility for elder adults improved when utilizing the redesigned social networking site. In addition, elder adults had a more positive perception of these types of sites after using the redesigned prototype.

Keywords: Social media · Social networking · Elder adults · Usability study

1 Introduction

Social networking sites such as Facebook [6], Google+ [7], and LinkedIn [9], offer a number of benefits. They allow users to learn, share resources, collaborate, and build relationships with friends, families, co-workers, and people with similar interests [11]. For example, users are able to read posts and obtain quick feedback from others by communicating on related pages. Ideas, stories, and media can be easily shared in an organized fashion through commenting, tagging, trending, etc. The nature of these sites also allows for relationship building despite users' physical location or time constraints.

As people age, there is an increased likelihood of health impairments and logistical issues which may present barriers for the elderly connecting to the outside world. With the capability of social media, there is potential to break such barriers and make it possible for the elderly to live a more independent life. However, out of the 40 million elder adults aged 65 years and older, a little more than half (53 %) engage in online activities, such as checking email and searching the internet. Of these online elders, only a small percentage (32 %) use social media (such as social networking sites) [4]. Therefore, only a small portion of elder adults are currently taking advantage of the potential benefits offered by the social networking sites.

© Springer International Publishing Switzerland 2015
J. Zhou and G. Salvendy (Eds.): ITAP 2015, Part I, LNCS 9193, pp. 297–306, 2015.
DOI: 10.1007/978-3-319-20892-3_29

To investigate the possible reasons that led to the low social networking adoption of the elderly, Arfaa and Wang [3] conducted a study with adults aged 65 and older using a social networking site. The study showed that despite the low amount of users, elder adults do have an interest in utilizing social networking site. Many elders expressed wanting to view family photos and learn about current events through these types of sites. However, the study also showed that unreadable text and image attributes and a non-intuitive layout hindered the elders from these types of sites especially for those who have little computer experience. In addition, Arfaa and Wang [2] evaluated the usability and accessibility of a group of social media sites using both automatic tool as well as manual verification. The result of this study concluded that many social networking sites do not adhere to known web accessibility and usability guidelines such as Section 508 Compliance [10], WCAG 1.0 and 2.0 [13], Usability.gov [12], and the National Institute of Aging [8]. This result further confirmed the barriers identified earlier.

In addition to usability and accessibility issues, when faced with a social networking site without human support, many elders did not know where to start, were not aware of the functionality offered on these sites, nor did they understand web 2.0 concepts. They indicated that they would engage in more social media if it was easier to use [3].

Based on the results from the above studies, a redesign was undertaken to improve the usability and accessibility of social networking sites for the elderly. This was achieved by incorporating known guidelines and implementing additional considerations focused on elder computer illiteracy and misconceptions [1]. Elder adults were invited to utilize the redesigned website prototype and the results were compared to their performance of a mock-up of a current social networking site.

This study investigates the following research questions: (1) Does the redesigned prototype improve accessibility and usability for elder adults? (2) What tasks significantly improved in terms of success rates and task performance? (3) How do the elders perceive the newly redesigned site? Following this introduction the research methodology is described. Next, a brief overview of the newly designed networking site prototype is presented. The results of the usability study are then discussed and compared to previous phases of the study. The final sections discuss the findings and future research areas that can be extracted by this study.

2 Methodology

Twenty-two elder adults aged 65 years and older participated in two usability study sessions, one with the original design, another with the redesigned prototype. The participants were recruited from personal connections and community centers and chosen based on their age and computer experience. Elder adults were put into one of two groups based on their self-reported level of computer experience: none-to-basic experience group (group 1), intermediate to advanced experience group (group 2).

A baseline study was conducted before the design of the prototype to collect initial data. The introduction of the study included its purpose and why the users were chosen. Participants were asked to sign a consent form before the session began. The elder adults performed a number of social media-related subtasks categorized into six main tasks on a mock-up of the popular social networking site, Facebook. This site was chosen based on its popularity and usage. Associated tasks included logging into an account, understanding the homepage and profile, navigating and comprehending information on a profile, and commenting on profiles. After completing all the tasks, participants were asked to fill out a post-test questionnaire to comment on their experience. After the design and implementation of the two versions of the prototype, a final usability study session was conducted.

The same participants from the baseline study completed the similar set of tasks and subtasks utilizing the redesigned prototype during the final usability study sessions. To reduce bias from a learning effect by using both versions, the participants were randomly assigned to start with version 1 or 2. Since a new social media learning component was added in the prototype, a task regarding the learning of social media was added to the original task list. Participants were asked to fill out a similar post-test questionnaire which included questions regarding their experiences regarding the new prototype. In addition, questions around social media learning were added to the questionnaire.

During both study sessions, the researcher recorded observation notes including task performance (success or failure in task completion), task completion time, and additional observations while the participants performed the tasks. In addition, the participant's interaction with the system was captured using Camtasia [5]. Each usability study session ran for about an hour for each participant.

3 Prototype Design Overview

The newly designed prototype took both the feedback gathered from the baseline study and general usability and accessibility guidelines into consideration. This included adjusting the contrast between background color and text, adjusting the font and its size, and providing an intuitive layout that is easy to navigate. In addition, to accommodate different website layout preferences (especially in the scenario that a sub-navigation is required), elders were given two versions for the sub-navigation placement. Version 1 consisted of the sub-links placed at the top and the second version consisted of sub-links on the left-side of the page. Figure 1 is an example of the two versions of sub-navigation for the Read Previous and Next buttons.

For both versions, the main content of the page was found at the center of the screen.

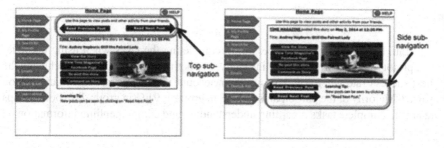

Fig. 1. Top and side sub-navigation for read previous and next post arrows

4 Results

This section presents the data analysis conducted during the final usability study with the newly designed social networking site interface prototype. The results in terms of task performance success rates, completion time, and participants' perception of their experiences are discussed next.

4.1 Comparison of Task Success Rates

The following table shows the results of the baseline study compared to the final usability study, categorized by computer experience groups: none-to-basic and advanced-to-intermediate. The number of success attempts (success rates) for each session and version are presented below (Table 1):

Table 1. Results of task performance based on previous computer experience

Task	Frequency and success rate Baseline		Frequency and success rate Final Version 1[+]		Frequency and success rate Final Version 2[++]	
	Group		Group		Group	
	1*	2**	1*	2**	1*	2**
Task 1: Logging into your account	1 (9 %)	3 (27 %)	11 (100 %)	11 (100 %)	11 (100 %)	11(100 %)
Task 2: Understanding the homepage	1 (9 %)	3 (27 %)	8 (73 %)	11 (100 %)	8 (73 %)	9 (82 %)
Task 3: Understanding your profile	0 (0 %)	2 (18 %)	2 (18 %)	8 (73 %)	4 (36 %)	3 (27 %)
Task 4: Navigating through the site	1 (9 %)	1 (9 %)	8 (73 %)	10 (91 %)	8 (73 %)	9 (82 %)
Task 5: Information on a profile	4 (36 %)	6 (55 %)	11 (100 %)	10 (91)%	9 (82 %)	8 (73 %)
Task 6: Commenting on other profiles	1 (9 %)	3 (27 %)	7 (64 %)	7 (64 %)	6 (54 %)	8 (73 %)
Task 7: Learning about social media	(N/A)	(N/A)	8 (73 %)	10 (91 %)	9 (82 %)	11 (100 %)

* Group1: none to basic computer experience group
* Group 2: intermediate to advanced computer experience group
+ Version 1: sub-navigation on top
++ Version 2: sub-navigation on the side

Overall, both groups were successful in completing the tasks when using the redesigned prototype comparing to baseline study. For both groups, participants achieved the highest success rate when logging into their account (task 1) no matter which version they used. Majority of the participants (100 % in group 1, 91 % in group 2) in both groups were able to complete tasks regarding understanding and comprehending information on a profile (task 5) especially when they were using version 1. For group 2, all (11, 100 %) participants were able to complete task 2, understanding the homepage, when using version 1. In addition, when utilizing version 2, all participants from group 2 were able to complete learning about social media. Conversely, task 3, understanding your profile, had the lowest success rate for both group 1 when using both versions and group 2 when using version 2. Both groups did have improvement in the performance on completing these tasks compared to the baseline study.

4.2 Comparison of Final Group's Completion Times

Each group's average time to complete a task and standard deviation are discussed next. Overall, both groups were successful in completing the tasks. Group 1 seemed to have slightly higher performance than group 2 in only a few tasks (Table 2). When using version 1 to complete tasks such as understanding the homepage (task 2), navigating (task 4), and commenting on other profiles (task 6), participants in group 1 were slightly faster on average than group 2. For version 2 group 1, logging into your account (task 1) and understanding information on a profile (task 5) were also completed slightly faster on average than group 2. The faster times could be attributed to the easy to understand layout. For example, a participant from group 1 noted during the post-test questionnaire that "information was presented clearly and did not require [me] to search" after using the newly designed interface prototype. Another elder stated that buttons were in the general areas she expected to see them.

Table 2. Final usability study's average completion time (Version 1 and Version 2)

Task	Final Version 1 Average Time for Completion in Seconds (Standard Deviation)		Final Version 2 Average Time for Completion in Seconds (Standard Deviation)	
	Group 1	Group 2	Group 1	Group 2
Task 1: Logging into your account	1(0.0)	1 (0.00)	2 (3.39)	4 (4.79)
Task 2: Understanding the homepage	2 (1.30)	3 (3.85)	5 (5.57)	5 (5.39)
Task 3: Understanding your profile	3 (2.45)	2 (1.45)	6 (6.88)	4 (3.88)
Task 4: Navigating	1 (0.85)	2 (1.05)	4 (3.65)	2 (1.81)
Task 5: Understanding information on a profile	2 (1.25)	2 (1.37)	3 (4.02)	4 (3.88)
Task 6: Commenting on other profiles	3 (3.34)	5 (5.17)	5 (6.02)	3 (2.60)
Task 7: Learning about social media	2 (0.96)	2 (3.02)	4 (4.04)	3 (3.59)

4.3 Comparison of the Baseline and Final Version's Task Completion Times

In order to compare the impact of the different versions towards participant's task performance, each individual task was further extracted into subtasks. The Wilcoxon test was used to find any significant difference between the performance data (subtasks) in the baseline study and the two versions of the prototype used in the final usability study. p values less than or equal to .05 were considered significant. Some significant differences were found when comparing the baseline and final usability studies.

For example, when completing task 1, the subtasks of entering a username, password, and clicking the submit button improved when utilizing either version of the redesigned prototype (Table 3). This could be attributed to separating the "sign-up" and "login" links, larger header, and instructions added per the design considerations.

Table 3. Wilcoxon test: Comparing task 1 performance among three versions

Task 1: Logging into your account		
Final V1/ Baseline	Final V1/ Final V2	Final V2/ Baseline
Enter username		
Z	−2.402	.000	−2.402
p	.016	1.000	.016
Enter password		
Z	−2.699	−1.342	−2.699
p	.007	.180	.007
Click submit button		
Z	−3.053	−1.000	−2.836
p	.002	.317	.005

Another example of a significant difference was when asking the participant to read a post in the newsfeed (Table 4). Previously, during the baseline study many participants did not know they had to scroll to view additional posts. Many were not sure where they could click to open the post. However, both versions of the final usability study redesign implemented an intuitive "next" button shaped like an arrow. In addition, labeled buttons also let the participants know how to open a post.

Table 4. Wilcoxon test: Comparing task 2 performance among three versions

Task 2: Understanding your homepage		
Final V1/ Baseline	Final V1/ Final V2	Final V2/ Baseline
Read out loud the title of another post in your newsfeed		
Z	−3.124	−.851	−3.317
p	.002	.395	.001

Table 5. Wilcoxon test: Comparing task 6 performance among three versions

Task 6: Commenting on other profiles			
	Final V1/Baseline	Final V1/Final V2	Final V2/Baseline
Click on your friend Ann Jones to go to her profile page			
Z	−2.825	.000	−3.222
P	.005	1.000	.001
Click where you would leave a comment on Ann Jones' wall			
Z	−2.19	−.687	−2.505
P	.028	.492	.012

The most significant changes based on completion times were the subtasks associated with web 2.0 concepts, such as navigating to a profile page and leaving a comment on one's wall (Table 5). This is a major improvement, as the baseline study elders could not locate the field to enter a comment. However, the redesign added instructions and headings that clearly facilitated learning when the elders were interacting with the redesigned prototypes.

4.4 Post-Test Questionnaire

After completion of the final usability study, participants answered a number of post-test questionnaires regarding their experience using the newly redesigned social networking site prototype.

Overall, the results were positive, with ten (91 %) participants from group 1 and all participants (11,100 %) from group 2 stating the overall ease of use of the prototype was easy to very easy (Fig. 2).

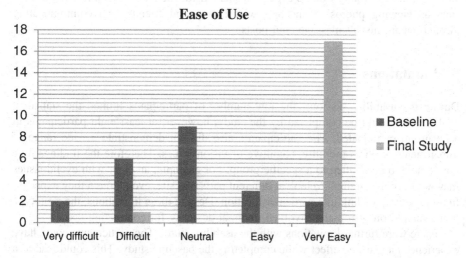

Fig. 2. Questionnaire results: ease of use

64 % of the less experienced computer users and 55 % of the more experienced computer users reported that they feel the text on the site was easy to read. In addition, 82 % of the less experienced computer group 1 and 100 % of the more experienced computer group felt the site was intuitive.

5 Discussion

The objective of this study was to improve the usability and accessibility of social networking sites for the elderly by redesigning the interfaces to accommodate this aging demographic. Improving interfaces allows for increased accessibility and usability for elder adults utilizing sites with Web 2.0 characteristics. Elder adults are more inclined to utilize a site that has an easy-to-use interface that allows for learning and support. This could lead to a more independent life for elders that are bound logistically due to physical impairments. In addition, having social media incorporated in their lives provides a medium to communicate with family, friends, and peers as well as the ability to access a number of resources and stories.

In terms of the sub-navigation, the preference between the groups was different. The participants in less experienced group preferred the side menu for sub-navigation while majority of the participants with more computer experience preferred the sub-navigation menu to be placed on the top of the screen. However, no conclusion on the specific preference in terms of the placement of the sub-navigation menus could be made, nor was a significant difference on the task performance between the final versions found.

The tested prototype was implemented using current website design research, existing guidelines, and additional social media usage feedback from the usability studies [2, 3]. Elders were not left confused by interfaces or web 2.0 concepts and felt comfortable completing tasks without assistance and intervention. A majority of the participants enjoyed this study because they are interested in learning about computers and social media. Many want to engage in social media activities to build relationships, such as viewing photos, connecting with family and friends, and communicating through email, instant message, and posts.

6 Limitations

During the usability sessions, the low number of participants limited the statistical analysis that could be completed by the study; however, at least eight participants in each group participated. The participant's also did not demonstrate a wide range of impairments, such as mobility, cognitive or vision issues. Therefore the findings may not be able to be applied to a specific group. For example, an elder with eyelid issues may not have the strength to look at different parts of a site, even though they expect to find the activity or link in a particular location. Despite these limitations, the prototype relied mainly on vision and involved minimal dexterity for completing tasks.

There were further limitations with the usability study. The participants could have experienced a learning effect while completing the baseline study. This could lead to a biased result as many of the elder's participation was motivated by gaining exposure to social media. Although this factor cannot be eliminated, the effect could have been reduced as the two sessions took place three months apart.

7 Conclusion

The final usability session showed that the redesigned prototype improved the usability and accessibility for elder adults. On almost every task, the times decreased for both the novice and experienced computer group in comparison to the baseline session. In addition, the results showed that 100 % of the elders preferred the newly designed prototype versus the current social networking site.

Even though the more advanced group did perform better than the less experienced group in general, their perception on the ease of use of the site was not significantly different. This indicated that users' previous computer experience and their performance on the system did not influence their perception regarding social networking site usage. Therefore, the interface design and features provided may not be the only factors that can contribute to the actual use of a system. Instead, user's attitude toward the system may lead to their positive or negative perception of the system as well.

8 Future Work

Utilizing the newly designed prototypes, continued research with a larger and more diverse sample is suggested. Diversity could include involving participants with more diverse background. For example, recruit participants from a broader location, with a larger and more categorized look of multiple elder age groups and physical impairments. In addition, this research strictly focused on social networking site usage on a laptop/desktop computer; however, many elder adults expressed their desire in using tablets and other mobile technologies. Therefore, future studies could involve the trend of social media websites and applications on mobile devices. In addition, a longitudinal study could be conducted to look at the change in participant's social media usage.

References

1. Arfaa, J., Wang, Y.: An improved website design for elders utilizing social media. J. Technol. Persons Disabil. **51**(6), 1173–1182 (2015)
2. Arfaa, J., Wang, Y.: An accessibility evaluation of social media websites for elder adults. In: Meiselwitz, G. (ed.) SCSM 2014. LNCS, vol. 8531, pp. 13–24. Springer, Heidelberg (2014)
3. Arfaa, J., Wang, Y.: A usability study on elder adults utilizing social networking sites. In: Marcus, A. (ed.) DUXU 2014, Part II. LNCS, vol. 8518, pp. 50–61. Springer, Heidelberg (2014)
4. Brenner, J.: http://pewinternet.org/Commentary/2012/March/Pew-Internet-Social-Networking-full-detail.aspx
5. Camtasia: http://www.techsmith.com/camtasia.html

6. Facebook. https://www.facebook.com/
7. Google+. https://plus.google.com/
8. HHS. http://www.hhs.gov/web/508/contracting/hhs508policy.html
9. LinkedIn. http://www.linkedin.com/
10. Section 508.gov. http://www.section508.gov/index.cfm?fuseAction=stdsSum
11. Susanta, M., Bagchi, I., Bandyupadhyay, A.: Design of a data model for social network applications. J. Database Manage. **18**(4), 51–79 (2007)
12. Usability.gov, Guidelines (2012). http://www.usability.gov/guidelines/index.html. Accessed 13 Dec 2012
13. Web Content Accessibility Guidelines (W3C). http://www.w3.org/WAI/intro/wcag

ICT Access in Libraries for Elders

Amrish Chourasia[1]([⊠]), Jim Tobias[2], Steve Githens[3], Yao Ding[1],
and Gregg Vanderheiden[1]

[1] Trace R&D Center, University of Wisconsin-Madison, Madison, USA
aochourasia@wisc.edu, ding@trace.wisc.edu,
gregg@raisingthefloor.org
[2] Inclusive Technologies, Matawan, NJ, USA
tobias@inclusive.com
[3] Raising the Floor, Washington, DC, USA
swgithen@mtu.edu

Abstract. The ability to use information and communication technologies (ICT) is becoming a necessity. Older users are one of the fastest growing segment of ICT users but many still face barriers in ICT use. Libraries are one of the first places that individuals turn to when looking for information or assistance with ICT. Libraries also serve as an important resource for individuals to access the Internet. However, libraries face several problems in providing services to elders. Lack of funding and trained staff, insufficient knowledge about accessibility prevents them from successfully serving their patrons. We present the Library-GPII-System, a cloud based auto-personalization system that will enable libraries to successfully serve their older patrons. Results from our library stakeholder needs analyses are also presented.

Keywords: Libraries · Auto-personalization · Cloud infrastructure · Assistive technology · Access features

1 Introduction

The ability to use information and communication technologies (ICT) is considered a pre-requisite to living in the information age [1]. Older users are a group that has shown impressive growth in Internet adaption but several barriers still exists for older users. Public libraries have recognized the need for providing better ICT services to older adults and guidelines have been developed for this purpose. However, numerous challenges exist for libraries to serve older adults successfully. We present an approach to reinvent accessibility in libraries to promote use of ICT by older users.

There have been numerous and continuous efforts by governments to promote widespread Internet use [2, 3]. However, there still exists a digital divide, a gap between those who have access to ICTs and those who do not. Determinants of the lack of access to ICTs include: income, disability, race, gender, and age [4, 5].

Although a lower percentage of older adults use the Internet than younger adults, older adults are the fastest growing segment of Internet users [6]. Some of the barriers to Internet use by older adults are: perceived lack of benefit, lack of interest or motivation, lack of knowledge, lack of access, cost, fear of hardware being outdated

© Springer International Publishing Switzerland 2015
J. Zhou and G. Salvendy (Eds.): ITAP 2015, Part I, LNCS 9193, pp. 307–316, 2015.
DOI: 10.1007/978-3-319-20892-3_30

quickly, and perceived barriers due to physical limitations [7]. The aging process results in physical and cognitive changes that have implications for ICT use by some older adults [7]. Some of the physical changes include declines in vision, hearing, and motor control [7, 8]. Cognitive changes include general slowing of cognitive processes, decreased memory capacity, decreased attentional control, and difficulty in goal maintenance [9]. Strategies such as larger targets, longer timeouts, and less complex interfaces have been recommended [8].

Public libraries play an important role in providing various services to the elderly [10]. Since 1970 the American Library Association (ALA) has issued guidelines on providing services to older adults. These guidelines encourage collecting data about the older population and including the needs and interests of the older adults in library programming [11]. Libraries are also the home of many digital literacy programs that are aimed at seniors.

The transition to electronic library resources necessitates that electronic accommodations for older adults are available. However, providing such accessibility services is outside the scope of many libraries due to a combination of factors such as reduced budgets, lack of expertise in providing electronic accessibility services, lack of control over IT environment, and expensive assistive technology (AT). Libraries that intend to serve whomever comes through the door cannot know in advance what those needs might be, nor how frequently the needs will arise.

What is needed is a solution that: (1) makes access to library materials and equipment much easier (for staff and patrons) to set-up and use; (2) meets the needs of patrons with very diverse needs and abilities in an affordable manner for libraries large and small; (3) makes materials and services accessible on demand so that any material/service that a person needs can be made accessible on demand; (4) sets up a workstation instantly not just with the type of AT a person needs, but with that user's AT settings, each time they come in; (5) enables diverse AT to work integrally with the ICT systems in libraries, in a stable and secure manner; and (6) allows libraries to keep up with the rapid change of assistive technologies and access features in their mainstream technologies without excessive investments in time or money.

2   The Library-GPII-System

The Library-GPII-System (LGS) aims to provide the above capabilities to libraries. The LGS will represent the first real-world application of the Global Public Inclusive Infrastructure (GPII). The GPII (http://www.gpii.net) is an initiative of the Raising the Floor Consortium and aims to utilize cloud computing to create the infrastructure to enable AT, mainstream and other service providers to provide affordable assistive services whenever and wherever a user demands them. The GPII will enable people to

- learn about and determine what solutions will assist them
- store that information in a common, portable, private and secure manner;
- use the stored preferences to invoke and configure needed accessibility and usability features, assistive technologies on any device they encounter; and
- provide tools and infrastructure to developers and vendors to create new solutions for different users in a cost effective and efficient manner.

The European Union funded projects, Cloud4all and Prosperity4all are currently underway helping build the GPII along with the Fluid and Floe projects and UIITA-RERC.

The LGS is a five-year project that is part of the GPII work being done by the Rehabilitation and Engineering Research Center at the Trace Research and Development Center at the University of Wisconsin-Madison. The LGS will be developed, implemented and evaluated in three phases:

1. Needs Analysis – work with stakeholders to define the needs, constraints and specifications for the LGS (2013-2014).
2. LGS Development and User Testing (2014-2016).
3. Empirical Field Testing of the LGS in Libraries (2017-2018).

We have results from the first phase and these inputs are currently being used to create prototypes of the LGS.

3 Needs Analysis Results

3.1 Public Library Services and Their Needs

Public libraries perform a wide range of services, not all of which are relevant to this study. The four that are most relevant are access to materials, Internet access, e-books, and technology training.

Access to Materials. Finding and getting books and other resources is still the primary service of public libraries. There are two parts to this function, both of which are still undergoing their transitions to digital technologies through what are typically called integrated library systems (ILS): catalog operations and check-out/check-in. Library searches are no longer restricted to items found within the walls; this applies to virtual resources as well as inter-library loan. To follow this trend, catalog systems are being re-envisioned as discovery systems, allowing patrons to search for all kinds of resources. On the administrative side, ILSs allow librarians to add items to their collections, track usage, notify patrons of due dates, etc. A larger percentage of transactions are being performed electronically, including holds, renewals, and in-person check-in and check-out at kiosks. The usual form of identification is the barcode on a library card. Off-site, libraries use both the library card ID number (often with a default PIN of its last 4 digits) and login/password pairs created by the patrons themselves. All libraries offer access to online databases, often through regional or state contracts [12]. These include periodicals, language learning, and other educational resources.

Internet Access. Virtually all public libraries offer Internet access on library machines; 98 % also offer WiFi to patrons bringing their own devices [12]. 62 % of public libraries provide the only free access to the Internet in their communities.

Libraries average about 20 computers per location, with city libraries double that and rural about half [12]. 65 % of libraries report having an insufficient number of public computers to meet demand; this increases to 87 % in urban libraries. 36 % report that they have waiting periods every day. In order to manage this problem, libraries use software to create waiting lists and limit time on workstations. About one-third of library computers are 4 years old or more [12].

E-books. E-book usage is growing rapidly. 90 % of libraries now offer access to e-books [12], 92 % of urban libraries, compared to 65 % of rural libraries. 39 % of libraries provide e-readers for checkout by patrons; other libraries load e-books onto patron-owned devices or provide readers for on-site usage only. 97 % of libraries use Overdrive to manage their e-book collection.

Technology Training. Public libraries appear to be the community technology training resource of first and last resort; 98 % offer technology training, though not always formal training [12]. This includes, but is not limited to, digital literacy. Libraries report that training usage continues to grow. A surprisingly small number (28 %) offer online training materials, this in the face of well-funded national campaigns to develop and distribute such materials. 44 % offer their own in–person training. Most notable is the role of one-on-one instruction. More than a third of all libraries offer such personal attention, by appointment. In addition, more than 80 % offer informal point-of-use assistance.

3.2 Accessibility in Public Libraries

To understand the current state of accessibility services in public libraries, we conducted a survey with a convenience sample of 18 public libraries. Questions in the survey were divided in two categories. The first set of questions was related to the information technology network in the libraries and their user account management and policies. The second set included questions about the AT software and hardware, accessibility of library media, website and outreach efforts. The results from the second set of questions are included below (Tables 1, 2 and 3).

Table 1. Survey results about availability of AT software in public libraries

No.	Question	Response
	At software	
1	Do you have screen readers for users who are blind?	Yes = 4
		No = 14
2	Do you have screen readers or highlighters for users with other reading disabilities?	Yes = 4
		No = 14
3	Do you have screen magnifier software?	Yes = 11
		No = 7
4	Do you have on-screen keyboard or other input software?	Yes = 3
		No = 15
5	Do you have speech recognition software?	Yes = 0
		No = 18
6	Do you have software for text relay or video relay service?	Yes = 1
		No = 17

(Continued)

Table 1. (*Continued*)

No.	Question	Response
	At software	
7	Do you have any tools for people with cognitive or learning disabilities?	Yes = 1 No = 17
8	Do you have alternative communication software for people who do not speak?	Yes = 1 No = 17
9	Are these packages available on only a subset of workstations, or on all workstations?	All = 1 Subset = 1 N/A = 15
10	How do you currently license these packages? [single user, site license]	Single user = 6 Site license = 0 Mixed = 1 N/A = 11
11	Do you permit patrons with disabilities to use their own AT (e.g., portable AT software, typically on a thumb drive)?	Yes = 5 No = 7 Undecided = 2 Don't know = 4

Table 2. Survey results about availability of AT Hardware in public libraries

No.	Question	Response
	At hardware	
1	Do you have special keyboard, trackball, switches, or other input device?	Yes = 6 No = 12
2	Do you have a camera for sign language communication?	Yes = 0 No = 18
3	Do you have any CCTV or other electronic magnifier device?	Yes = 7 No = 11
4	Do you have any scanner/optical character recognizer?	Yes = 6 No = 12
5	Do you have a Braille printer or electronic braille device?	Yes = 0 No = 17 Don't know = 1
6	Do you have assistive listening devices?	Yes = 5 No = 13

Table 3. Survey results about accessibility of media materials in public libraries

No.	Question	Response
	Media	
1	Are any videos in your collection captioned?	Yes = 18
		No = 0
2	About what percentage of your collection (rough estimate)?	<=50 % = 1
		> 50 % = 6
		Don't know = 9
3	Are any videos in your collection audio described?	Yes = 3
		No = 10
		Don't know = 5
4	About what percentage of your collection (rough estimate)?	<=50 % = 1
		Don't know = 4
		NA = 13
5	Do you have videos in your collection for people with cognitive disabilities, such as life skills videos?	Yes = 3
		No = 14
		Don't know = 1
6	About what.% of your collection (rough estimate)	5 % = 1
		NA = 14
		Don't know = 3
7	For all: are they indexed so patrons can search for them in your catalogue system?	Yes = 11
		No = 5
		Don't know = 2

Results of our library survey reinforce that there is a shortage of assistive technologies and media in public libraries and a solution that addresses accessibility on different levels is needed.

4 LGS Development

The development phase of the LGS project is currently underway and will last through the end of 2016. For the development process, we have recruited six different library partners (four public libraries and two university libraries). The first version of the LGS will allow users to activate Windows access features and the NVDA screen reader using near field communication (NFC) tags. Subsequent versions of the LGS will allow users to create their own needs and preferences for the supported access features and assistive technologies. Through 2015, Read&Write Gold, JAWS, and other AT requested by our development partners will be integrated with the LGS. Other AT is also being integrated through the Cloud4all project and will also be included in the future versions of the LGS. Software developers are invited to integrate the applications with the GPII.

4.1   Integrating Applications in the LGS

Developers can easily integrate their applications with the GPII. To integrate applications in the GPII it is necessary to understand the overall GPII architecture (see Fig. 1). A detailed description of the architecture can be found here: http://wiki.gpii.net/w/A_Detailed_Tour_of_the_Cloud4all_Architecture.

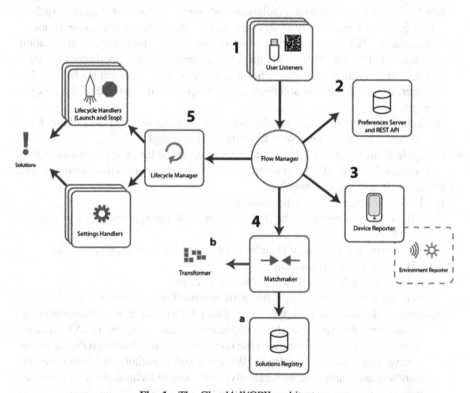

Fig. 1. The Cloud4all/GPII architecture

The different components of the GPII architecture are [13]:

1. Flow Manager: The Flow Manager is a event-driven, asynchronous orchestrator of the personalization workflow. Currently, it is implemented as a very small web server that runs on the local device and is responsible for bringing together the various components in the system and invoking them at the appropriate points in the

process. In the future, some of the Flow Manager's responsibilities will be distributed between both the local device and the cloud.

2. User Listener: The User Listener kicks-off the process of customizing a device or application to the user's needs and preferences. The user shares their key with the listener, which then starts the personalization process. The key can be a unique, random key or a personal ID based on user preference. Currently, a RFID and a USB user listener are available.

3. Preferences Server: The Preferences Server is a web-based service that provides a REST API for accessing preferences in a JSON format. Preferences will be represented according to a new version of the AccessForAll ISO 24751 standard.

4. Device Reporter: The Device Characteristics Reporter provides information about the user's device. This includes operating system, versions, and the list of applications currently installed. It will also provide information about the device's capabilities, such as screen resolution and size, support for features such as HTML5, and the availability of devices such as microphones and cameras, etc.

5. Matchmaker: The matchmaker considers the user's preferences, applications available on the user device and the environmental context to determine which solutions and settings best meet the user's needs. Upon invocation by the flow manager, it returns a list of solutions and settings, which is passed to the lifecycle manager.

   (a) Solutions Registry: The matchmaker gets the list of local and cloud based solutions available for a user from the solutions registry.

6. Lifecycle Manager: The Lifecycle Manager receives the list of appropriate solutions and settings from the Matchmaker and manages the process of setting them up using the lifecycle and settings handlers.

   (b) Lifecycle handler: It is a function that
       (i) Take a snapshot of the device's current settings, so they can be restored later
       (ii) Invokes the Settings Handler appropriate for each solution
       (iii) Launches each solution
       (iv) Stops each solution when the user is done
       (v) Restores the previous settings (if required) once the user is finished.

   (c) Settings handler: It is a type of a lifecycle handler that is responsible for configuring the settings of an application, access feature or AT. Settings Handlers typically interface with the operating system's built in APIs for storing settings (such as the Registry on Windows and GSettings on Linux). Settings Handlers are configured declaratively, and assistive technology developers will typically use the ones that are built in to the system. If the default settings handlers are not sufficient, developers can create their own. The follow settings handlers are available in Cloud4all/GPII by default.
       (i) XML files
       (ii) JSON Files
       (iii) Linux GSettings
       (iv) Linux DBus
       (v) Windows Registry.
       (vi) Windows SystemParametersInfo.

In order to register their software that runs on a platform like Windows or Linux, with the Solutions Reporter, developers need simply to create a standard JSON file called a Solutions Description, which will contain [14]:

- name (string): The name of the application/solution in a human readable format.
- id (string): A unique ID for the application. The general format used is the Reverse-DNS notation (e.g. "com.microsoft.win7.magnifier")
- contexts (object): Describes the context required for this solution to be applicable. (e.g. which platforms are supported)
- lifecycleManager (object): Instructions for the Lifecycle Manager describing what should happen to launch or quite an application or when a user logs in and logs out.
- settingsHandlers (array): An array of settings handlers (and their settings) that should used to configure this solution (If the product stores its preferences in a standard way for the platform, then these handlers will already exist in the GPII.)
- Ensure that all preferences are registered in the GPII Preference Terms Dictionary/Registry. (The GPII team will help with this.)

After creating the solutions description, developers write an acceptance test. In this context, an acceptance test involves testing the entire real-time "auto-personalization from preferences" framework end to end. The test starts with the user using a Key-Token to invoke their preferences from the preference server, and then checking that each possible preference is set appropriately in the target product under test. The they user is keys-out and again a check is made to ensure that all the settings on the target product are returned to their original state. This means that the actual system will be configured (and restored) when running the acceptance tests.

Examples of how to integrate native and web based applications with the GPII can be found at and http://blogs.cloud4all.info/developers/.

5 Next Steps

The development of the LGS will be completed in 2016. Subsequently the LGS will be deployed in at least four libraries that are not development partners, some of which will not have any previous connection to accessibility, in the effort to assess the impact of the LGS on library accessibility practices. A certain number of additional libraries will also be allowed to implement the LGS as possible. Feedback from these libraries will also help us develop guidelines for implementation of the LGS in other libraries.

6 Conclusion

Libraries face a number of problems in providing services to the elderly and those with disabilities. The problem is becoming more acute with continued lack of funding for expensive solutions and accessibility training. The LGS represents a solution that can help libraries address the problems on multiple fronts. The development of the LGS is currently underway and software developers are invited to integrate their solutions with the LGS.

Acknowledgement. Different components of the body of work described in this paper was, and/or is being, funded by the European Union's Seventh Framework Programme (FP7/2007-2013) grant agreement n° 289016 (Cloud4all) and 610510 (Prosperity4All), by the National Institute on Disability, Independent Living, and Rehabilitation Research, US Dept of Education and the Administration for Community Living under Grants H133E080022 (RERC-IT) and H133E130028 (UIITA-RERC) and contract ED-OSE-12-D-0013 (Preferences for Global Access), by the Flora Hewlett Foundation, the Ontario Ministry of Research and Innovation, and the Canadian Foundation for Innovation. The opinions and results herein are those of the authors and not necessarily those of the funding agencies.

References

1. Selwyn, N.: The information aged: a qualitative study of older adults' use of information and communications technology. J. Aging Stud. **18**(4), 369–384 (2004)
2. Federal Communications Commission, Connecting America: The national broadband plan (2010)
3. British Department for Culture, Media and Sport, Broadband Delivery, UK (2013)
4. Jackson, L.A., et al.: Race, gender, and information technology use: the new digital divide. Cyber Psychol. Behav. **11**(4), 437–442 (2008)
5. Selwyn, N., et al.: Older adults' use of information and communications technology in everyday life. Ageing Soc. **23**(05), 561–582 (2003)
6. Hart, T., Chaparro, B.S., Halcomb, C.G.: Evaluating websites for older adults: adherence to senior-friendly guidelines and end-user performance. Behav. Inf. Technol. **27**(3), 191–199 (2008)
7. Wagner, N., Hassanein, K., Head, M.: Computer use by older adults: a multi-disciplinary review. Comput. Hum. Behav. **26**(5), 870–882 (2010)
8. Hawthorn, D.: Possible implications of aging for interface designers. Interact. Comput. **12** (5), 507–528 (2000)
9. Charness, N., Boot, W.R.: Aging and information technology use potential and barriers. Curr. Dir. Psychol. Sci. **18**(5), 253–258 (2009)
10. Xie, B., Bugg, J.M.: Public library computer training for older adults to access high-quality Internet health information. Libr. Inf. Sci. Res. **31**(3), 155–162 (2009)
11. American Library Association: Guidelines for Library and Information Services to Older Adults (2008). http://www.ala.org/rusa/resources/guidelines/libraryservices. Accessed 22 Nov 2104
12. Bertot, J.C., et al.: 2013 Digital inclusion survey: survey findings and results (2014)
13. Architecture Overview. http://wiki.gpii.net/w/Architecture_Overview
14. Integrating a native solution. http://blogs.cloud4all.info/developers/information-about-your-solution/integrating-a-native-solution/

Examining the Validity of the Banner Recommendation System

Rong-Fuh Day[⊠] and Chien-Ying Chou

Department of Information Management, National Chi-Nan University, Nantou, Taiwan, ROC
{rfday, s101213511}@ncnu.edu.tw

Abstract. The phenomenon of banner blindness has concerned researchers, advertisers and website publishers during these years. In order to alleviate the phenomenon, this study attempted to develop a banner recommendation system which could arrange banners according the relative salience of keywords on a webpage viewed by a user. The prototypical system are being developed, however, we have made an initial examination on the effectiveness of its banner recommendation functionality. It was found that two recommendation accuracies for the system calculated with two different criteria both were significantly higher than the probability by chance.

Keywords: Banner blindness · Recommendation system · Eye tracking approach

1 Introduction

Currently, the Internet is one of the key channels for advertisements. However, researchers, advertisers and website publishers have observed that web users would intentionally ignore web advertisements and even some of editorial components that resemble online advertisement in shape, without determining the editorial component's content. This phenomenon is referred to as "banner blindness" [1–4]. Researchers and relevant practitioners are generally concerned that the long-term continuation of the status quo would substantially reduce the effectiveness of Internet advertisement communication and hinder efficient market operations. In recent years, numerous studies have examined the causes of banner blindness to identify an effective advertising method for communicating with consumers.

Previous studies have reported that Internet advertisements are ignored because Internet users demonstrate high goal- and task-oriented characteristics. In contrast to traditional media, Internet users often employ the Internet media for completing a specific task. In these circumstances, Internet advertisements frequently interfere with the ongoing work of the users, causing advertising irritation and avoidance [5–8]. Internet users eventually develop a habit of simply ignoring online advertisements. These findings further solidify the importance of personalized advertisements. We assert that if advertisements are arranged based on the current objective or needs of web users, advertisements are likely to provide users with a utility that yields additional benefits. Long-term application of this strategy may gradually reverse the banner

© Springer International Publishing Switzerland 2015
J. Zhou and G. Salvendy (Eds.): ITAP 2015, Part I, LNCS 9193, pp. 317–324, 2015.
DOI: 10.1007/978-3-319-20892-3_31

blindness phenomenon and entice users to pay attention to and understand the messages conveyed in the advertisements.

Personalized advertising has been an attractive concept; however, developing such a system is extremely complex [9]. The first challenge is determining how to automatically detect the purpose, needs, and preferences of browsers and use these data as a basis for advertisement arrangements. This study proposed a solution approach by employing an eye tracker for observing browser's viewing behavior on webpages, and thereby enabling the system to analyze the preferences of browsers as well as to recommend relevant advertisements to be presented to them based on the results of the analyses. The reason for applying the eye tracker is that the eye-tracker has been considered a precision apparatus which can provide real-time and fine-grained eye movement data for investigating underlying cognitive processes [10–16].

In this study, we developed an advertisement recommendation system based on the concept described previously. Furthermore, we conducted an experiment for verifying the accuracy of the advertisements recommended by the system. In the subsequent sections, we discuss our theoretical basis, experimental procedures, and experimental findings.

2   Literature

2.1   Personalization

Personalization has been an important and appealing idea in the development of information systems. Personalization emphasizes that the information systems is capable of adjusting its functionality, screen layout, and content...etc. According users' needs and preferences [17, 18]. Based on the idea, researchers and practitioners have developed various kinds of personalized services on the Internet. For example, Liu etc. [19] developed a news recommendation system, which could recommend readers the news which they might be interested in. Davidson etc. [20] developed a video recommendation system on YouTube, which could suggest users videos that are worth watching. The production recommendation system, which can suggest the productions buyers might like, has been common on todays' shopping sites, such as Amazon and e-bay. However, one general challenge such recommendation systems face is that how to infer users' needs and preferences. Therefore, efforts many researchers have been devoted are to find out potential meanings from traces which users leave when they browse websites.

One general method for inferring user's interests is through analyzing the characteristics of the content of webpages which an user has viewed. The approach is termed the content-based prediction, assuming that the content itself can manifest the interests of users. The approach has been further developed to a collaborative method, which takes into consideration the content which other people have viewed [17, 21].

Another approach for inferring user's interests is through analyzing users' behaviors of using webpages. When viewing webpages, users' explicit and implicit activities can be logged. The explicit activities are users' responses to a questionnaire about "like" or "unlike". The implicit activities includes the duration of viewing a webpage, scrolling down, zoom in and out, click, etc. [18, 21–25]. Although the explicit activities can be the most immediate relevant to users' interests, they could put much loading on users, thus making it unfeasible. In practice, the usage of the implicit response is more feasible. In this study, the eye tracking technology is applied to capture users' ocular activities, which can be considered as a kind of implicit activity.

2.2 Eye-Tracking Technology

During recent years, the eye-tracking technology has become feasible in our daily life, for example, Semsung S4 smart mobile phone has been equipped the eye-tracking technology using the camera embedded on the mobile phone. This provides several interesting applications, such as detect whether a user is looking at the screen in order to decide whether to continue playing a movie. Similar low-cost and effective eye tracking technologies have been developed with the webcam mounted on the desktop and laptop.

In general, the eye-tracking technology can provide real-time data about a variety of eye-movements, such as the location of eye fixation, the duration of eye fixation, and the pupil size of eye fixation. For the development of personalization system, the eye movement data is valuable in two ways. Firstly, the eye fixation can infer what an individual is processing in his/her working memory. According to the eye-mind assumption of Just and Carpenter [14, 26], what an individual is looking at is what s/he is processing. Their assumption has been supported by following research particularly in the field of reading [15, 16, 27]. In a broader sense, the location of fixation also manifests where an individual gets interested in. In addition, the fluctuation of pupil size is an immediate sensitive index about the arousal state of individuals and reflects individual's preference [28, 29]. Secondly, when viewing a webpage, the eyes generally keep capturing the information on the webpage, even when mouse and keyboard activities are stopped. Therefore, this study considers that the eye movement has a great potential to become an important implicit behavioral cue other than click to improve the prediction of users' needs and preferences. This study contributes to lead a better personalization.

3 Experiment

3.1 Participants

We recruited 56 college and graduate students at National Chi-Nan University, Taiwan, aged between 18 and 25, who voluntarily agreed to participate in this study as our formal study participants. After the experiments were completed, each participant received NT$150 as a reward. In addition, prior to the formal experiments, additional eight participants participated in a pilot test to determine necessary improvements for the system and the experiment process.

3.2   Stimulus

The experimental stimulus was an article that introduces the functions of three brands of digital cameras: Apple, Nokia, and Canon. In this article, the number of times that the three brand names appeared in the article is identical. We presented the contents of this article on six linked subsequent web pages. Regarding the design of web page layout, except for the first Web page that comprised only the main editorial area, web pages 2 to 6 contained an advertisement banner above the main editorial area (Fig. 1).

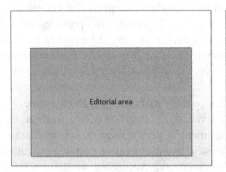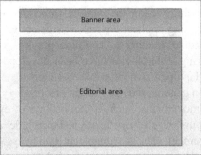

Fig. 1. The left picture illustrates the layout of the webpage first viewed by the participant, and the right illustrates the layout of the remaining experimental webpages.

3.3   Experimental System and Eye Tracker

We integrated the experimental system with the EyeLink II eye tracker function. The system features a web browsing function and can simultaneously analyze the number of fixations on the three brand names on the web pages. Second, when the participants want to browse the next web page, the experimental system identifies the brand name that received the most fixation points and places the advertisement banner corresponding to this brand on the next web page. Finally, the system records the advertisements that were recommended to each participant.

The EyeLink II is manufactured by SR Research and has an eye sampling rate of 5000 Hz/s. This system has high accuracy, an average gaze position error of $< 0.5°$, and can provide real-time sampling data at a data latency of only 3 ms.

3.4   Questionnaire

In order to estimate the accuracy rates of advertisement recommendation for the experimental system, we designed the following two questions as comparison criteria and asked the participants to answer them after the experiment. Question 1 pertains to subjective experience with the allocation of fixations: "When you were browsing the web pages, the Apple, Nokia, and Canon brands appeared in the pages. Which of these brands did you pay more attention to?" Question 2 pertains to prior brand preferences:

"Among the Apple, Nokia, and Canon brands, which on were you more interested in before you browsed the web pages?"

3.5 Experimental Procedure

Only one participant engaged in the experiment at a time. Before the experiment commenced, a brief description of the purpose and procedure of the experiment was presented to the participants and their questions about the experiment were answered. First, the laboratory assistant placed the headband of the eye tracker on the head of the participant and calibrated the eye tracker accordingly. The entire 5–10 min. The laboratory assistant then give the task instruction to the participant as follows: "Imagine that you wish to purchase a digital camera on the Internet and found an online article that introduces the functions for three brands of cameras. You are about to begin reading the Web pages that you found." The experiment program was then activated, and the participant began reading the Web pages and had to click the "next page" link to read the next page. After all of the Web pages were read, the laboratory assistant assisted the participant with removing the headband of the eye tracker and asked the participant to answer the questionnaire. Subsequently, the reward was given and the purpose of the study was explained to the participant.

4 Data Analyses

Data were collected from a total of 56 participants after the experiment. First, we examined the eye movement data for each participant. If the eye movement data deviation was exceedingly large and could not be calibrated, we deleted the data of this participant. After this process was completed, data from a total of 44 participants were valid for subsequent analyses.

Next, we calculated the system advertisement recommendation hit ratio based on the participants' responses to the questions regarding subjective experience with the allocation of fixations and prior brand preferences. The attained hit ratios was used as an accuracy indicator. The method by which hit ratio was calculated is explained as follows using the prior brand preferences as an example. During the experiment process, the experimental system recommended five advertisements to each participant. If a participant answered "Apple" on the prior brand preferences question, the recommendation correctness was defined as 1, 0.5, and 0 if the system recommended the Apple advertisement three times or more, two times, and one or zero times, respectively. Eventually, we derived the average accuracy for the 44 valid experiments to represent the accuracy of the advertisement recommendation for the experimental system. This method is similar to using a confusion matrix for calculating the hit ratio [30, 31].

The final results obtained are as follows: (a) The recommendation accuracy for the experimental system was 0.488 according to the participants' response to the questionnaire about subjective experience with the allocation of fixations. (b) The recommendation accuracy for the experimental system was 0.443 according to the participants' response to the questionnaire about prior brand preferences. Both of the accuracy were significantly higher than the probability of (1/3) * 1.25 = 0.41 by chance.

5 Discussion and Conclusion

Based on the rationale that people's preference can be manifested in their viewing, this study analyzed participant's fixation on the brand keywords on the web pages to infer participant's current brand preference while viewing the web pages, and used this inference as a basis for recommending web advertisement in a real-time manner. The results of this study indicated that the advertisement recommendation accuracy of the experimental system was significantly higher than that by chance. Therefore, we suggest that this method can serve as a basis for further developing an advertisement personalization system in the future. Several directions are suggested for future research. First, future studies can attempt using other machine-learning methods, such as the neural network, for analyzing the viewing behavior of web page to gain better prediction to user's preference. Second, an instant feedback mechanism can be developed for determining whether recommended advertisements satisfy user's current preference, and the results can serve as a reference for tuning the recommendation system.

This study has several limitations that must be addressed: First, this study only used one scenario (purchasing a camera) to validate the performance of the recommendation system. Second, we did not examine whether the recommended advertisements attract user's attention. Future research can address with the issue on the effectiveness of the recommended advertisements.

5.1 Limitation and Future Research

When interpreting the results, the reader should be aware of certain limitations. First, the layout of the experiment follows the typical webpage design, however, it has a little limitation in ecological validity. Second, in order to increase the ecological validity of our experiment, the brands used in this study, such as, Apple, Nokia, and Canon, are real in our daily life. The reader should be aware of that the manipulation would introduce some unexpected confounding factors into our findings. Thirdly, in the experiment, the eyetracker was mounted on the head of the participants. The participants would have some uncomfortable sensations in their head especially when they took a longer time to finish the experiment. This fatigue factor might confound the experiment results. In future research, we suggest the researchers to replace the mounted tracker with the remote eyetracker, which can be mounted under the screen, in order to decrease the loading of experimental participants. Finally, future research might develop other index on ocular behavior to validate the effectiveness of the recommendation system. In addition, the triangular validation can be applied to examine the developed ocular index with other traditional advertising measurements.

Acknowledgements. This research is sponsored by the NSC of Taiwan, grant no. 102-2410-H-260-038- and 103-2410-H-260-038 -.

References

1. Benway, J.P., Lane, D.M.: Banner Blindness: Web Searchers Often Miss 'Obvious' Links. Internetworking 3 (1998)
2. Hervet, G., Guérard, K., Tremblay, S., Chtourou, M.S.: Is banner blindness genuine? eye tracking internet text advertising. Appl. Cogn. Psychol. **25**, 708–716 (2011)
3. Dreze, X., Hussherr, F.-X.: Internet advertising: is anybody watching? J. Interact. Mark. **17**, 8–23 (2003)
4. Chatterjee, P.: Are unclicked ads wasted? enduring effects of banner and pop-up ad exposures on brand memory and attitudes. J. Electron. Commer. Res. **9**, 51–61 (2008)
5. Li, H., Edwards, S.M., Lee, J.-H.: Measuring the intrusiveness of advertisements: scale development and validation. J. Advertising **31**, 37–47 (2002)
6. Cho, C.-H., Cheon, H.J.: Why do people avoid advertising on the internet? J. Advertising **33**, 89–97 (2004)
7. Duff, B.R.L., Faber, R.J.: Missing the mark. J. Advertising **40**, 51–62 (2011)
8. Baek, T.H., Morimoto, M.: Stay away from me. J. Advertising **41**, 59–76 (2012)
9. Kazienko, P., Adamski, M.: AdROSA—Adaptive personalization of web advertising. Inf. Sci. **177**, 2269–2295 (2007)
10. Todd, P., Benbasat, I.: Process tracing method in decision support systems research: exploring the black box. MISQ **11**, 493–512 (1987)
11. Dimoka, A., Banker, R.D., Benbasat, I., Davis, F.D., Dennis, A.R., Gefen, D., Gupta, A., Ischebeck, A., Kenning, P., Pavlou, P.A., Müller-Putz, G.R., Riedl, R., Brocke, J.V., Weber, B.: On the use of neurophysiological tools in IS research: developing a research agenda for NeuroIS. MIS Q. **36**, 679–702 (2012)
12. Lohse, G.L., Johnson, E.J.: A comparison of two process tracing methods for choice tasks. Organ. Behav. Hum. Decis. Process. **68**, 28–43 (1996)
13. Payne, J.W., Bettman, J.R., Johnson, E.J.: The Adaptive Decision Maker. Cambridge University Press, New York (1993)
14. Just, M.A., Carpenter, P.A.: Eye fixations and cognitive processes. Cogn. Psychol. **8**, 441–480 (1976)
15. Rayner, K.: Eye movements in reading and information processing: 20 years of research. Psychol. Bull. **124**, 372–422 (1998)
16. Rayner, K., Rotello, C.M., Stewart, A.J., Keir, J., Duffy, S.A.: Integrating text and pictorial Information: Eye movement when looking at print advertisement. J. Exp. Psychol. Appl. **7**, 219–226 (2001)
17. Hirsh, H., Basu, C., Davison, B.D.: Learning to personalize. Commun. ACM **43**, 102–106 (2000)
18. Liang, T.-P., Lai, H.-J.: Discovering user interests from web browsing behavior: an application to internet news services. In: Proceedings of the 35th Annual Hawaii International Conference on System Sciences, HICSS 2002, pp. 2718–2727. IEEE (2002)

19. Liu, J., Dolan, P., Pedersen, E.R.: Personalized news recommendation based on click behavior. In: Proceedings of the 15th International Conference on Intelligent User Interfaces, pp. 31–40. ACM (2010)
20. Davidson, J., Liebald, B., Liu, J., Nandy, P., Vleet, T.V., Gargi, U., Gupta, S., He, Y., Lambert, M., Livingston, B., Sampath, D.: The YouTube video recommendation system. In: Proceedings of the Fourth ACM Conference on Recommender Systems, pp. 293–296. ACM, Barcelona (2010)
21. Pazzani, M.J., Billsus, D.: Content-Based recommendation systems. In: Brusilovsky, P., Kobsa, A., Nejdl, W. (eds.) Adaptive Web 2007. LNCS, vol. 4321, pp. 325–341. Springer, Heidelberg (2007)
22. Sakagami, H., Kamba, T.: Learning personal preferences on online newspaper articles from user behaviors. Comput. Netw. ISDN Syst. **29**, 1447–1455 (1997)
23. Billsus, D., Pazzani, M.J.: A hybrid user model for news story classification. In: Proceedings of the Seventh International Conference on User Modeling, pp. 99–108. Springer-Verlag New York, Inc., Banff (1999)
24. Joachims, T., Granka, L., Pan, B., Hembrooke, H., Gay, G.: Accurately interpreting clickthrough data as implicit feedback. In: Proceedings of the 28th Annual International ACM SIGIR Conference on Research and Development in Information Retrieval, pp. 154–161. ACM, Salvador (2005)
25. Joachims, T., Granka, L., Pan, B., Hembrooke, H., Radlinski, F., Gay, G.: Evaluating the accuracy of implicit feedback from clicks and query reformulations in web search. ACM Trans. Inf. Syst. **25**, 7 (2007)
26. Just, M.A., Carpenter, P.A.: A theory of reading: from eye fixations to comprehension. Psychol. Rev. **87**, 329–354 (1980)
27. Rayner, K.: Eye movements in reading and information processing. Psychol. Bull. **85**, 618–660 (1978)
28. Beatty, J.: Task-evoked pupillary responses, processing load, and the structure of processing resources. Psychol. Bull. **91**, 276–292 (1982)
29. Beatty, J., Lucero-Wagoner, B.: The Pupillary System. In: Cacioppo, J.T., Tassinary, L.G., Berntson, G. (eds.) Handbook of Psychophysiology, 2nd edn, pp. 142–162. Cambridge University, Cambridge (2000)
30. Stehman, S.V.: Selecting and interpreting measures of thematic classification accuracy. Remote Sens. Environ. **62**, 77–89 (1997)
31. Hair, J.F., Tatham, R.L., Anderson, R.E., Black, W.: Multivariate Data Analysis. Pearson Prentice Hall, Upper Saddle River (2006)

Conducting Acceptance Tests for Elderly People on the Web

Using the GPII Preference Set for a Personalized Evaluation

Alexander Henka[1(✉)], Andreas Stiegler[1], Gottfried Zimmermann[1],
and Thomas Ertl[2]

[1] Stuttgart Media University, Stuttgart, Germany
{henka, stiegler, gzimmermann}@hdm-stuttgart.de
[2] Institute for Visualization and Interactive Systems (VIS),
University of Stuttgart, Stuttgart, Germany
thomas.ertl@vis.uni-stuttgart.de

Abstract. Due to the overlapping requirements with people with disabilities, elders can benefit from accessible web design and the use of assistive technologies. But elderlies face also semantic problems that are derived from different perception models or the mere anxiety of using new technologies, which can't be evaluated by accessibility guideline conformance only. Tackling those semantic issues calls for more user-centered evaluation. The Global Public Inclusive Infrastructure (GPII) provides user interface adaptation based on peoples individual needs and preferences. These preferences are stored in so-called preference sets and can also contain sematic settings. In this paper, we propose an accessibility evaluation method, using the preference sets of the GPII to derive authentic accessibility requirements. Hereby, we're able to carry out tests according to guideline conformance and semantic requirements. In this context, we propose a personalized accessibility evaluation approach based on original user preferences that addresses the need for a user-centered evaluation.

Keywords: Human computer interaction · Accessibility · Elderlies · Acceptance tests · Web accessibility guidelines · GPII · User-preference set · User-centered accessibility evaluation · Technical accessibility · Semantical accessibility

1 Introduction

The accessibility requirements of web applications for elderly people are similar to the requirements of people with disabilities. Typical issues are related to vision, cognition or motor coordination constraints [1–3]. Therefore, accessibility guidelines (e.g., WCAG 2.0 [18]) can be used as one approach to evaluate the accessibility of a web application for elderly people, as it was indicated in [2, 4, 5], but are not sufficient, as suggested by Affonso et al. [2]. They advocate an extension to the WCAG 2.0 to meet specific accessibility requirements of elderly people. Based on their research, Pernice, Estes and Nielsen [19] have generated a set of guidelines that is specifically tailored to "senior citizens" on the Web.

© Springer International Publishing Switzerland 2015
J. Zhou and G. Salvendy (Eds.): ITAP 2015, Part I, LNCS 9193, pp. 325–336, 2015.
DOI: 10.1007/978-3-319-20892-3_32

Elderly users however, are frequently confronted with issues that cannot be identified by merely checking the conformance of an application to guidelines. These issues result from mental models that differ between designers and users, and from differences in strategies for the meaning making and problem solving process [6]. Those difficulties are not considered accessibility related issues in the general understanding of accessibility evaluation, according to guideline conformance, but need to be tackled in the application's design [2, 4]. Age-related disability issues also tend to change over time and new or additional impairments can arise [4, 7]. This calls for a constant tracking and adaptation of accessibility requirements for ICT products.

Studies [8–11] advocate for a strong User Centered Design approach, in which testing for web accessibility can benefit from existing work in usability evaluation. Furthermore, they suggest that accessibility in general is strongly user-centered. Barriers occur when there is a mismatch between a user and a web application in terms of interaction characteristics. Brajnik [8] characterizes accessibility in a user-centered context: *"[Accessibility is, when] specific users with specific disabilities can use it [the software] to achieve specific goals with the same effectiveness, safety and security as non-disabled people"*. According to this understanding, a barrier is a condition, which prevents a specific user, who has specific traits and is using specific assistive technologies, from achieving their specific goals.

Hence, a barrier is an attribute of the interaction between the user and the system, and the occurrence depends therefore on the user, the situation and the system. A barrier is defined by: The user and their specific traits, the assistive technologies being used, the goal(s) of the user and the properties (defects) of the web application, which, taken together, prevent the accomplishment of the goals. In consequence, conformance tests are not sufficient to fully clarify the accessibility of a web application, as discussed in [12, 13]. The conformance to accessibility guidelines is a technical property of the website and does not take the specific traits of the user, their devices and assistive technologies into account. Hence, when checking the accessibility of a web application, it is important to take the perspective of the end user, i.e. in a way that reflects how an end user would interact with the system [10].

It was stated that especially the elderly often encounter barriers on the web, which can't be determined by guideline conformance [2, 4, 6]. These issues originate mostly from the field of bad application design or usability flaws [2, 4]. To achieve accessibility, especially for elderly people, one must not only guarantee guideline conformance, but also the usability and understandability of a web application; therefore, we have to consider technical and semantical accessibility.

Technical Accessibility. Describes the conformance of an ICT product to accessibility guidelines. Even if guideline conformance is accomplished, there is no guarantee that this will result in an accessible product. Accordingly, accessibility-testing tools, which rely on guideline conformance only, can't ensure the accessibility of a product, if web applications are just designed to pass the conformance test [22, 23].

As the Web Accessibility Initiative (WAI) phrases it: *"[...] Web accessibility evaluation tools can not determine the accessibility of Web sites, they can only assist in doing so."* [21]. It is relatively easy for an automatic tool to determine if an "alt" attribute is present for an image, but hard to tell if the alternative text conveys any meaning to a specific user. But nevertheless, technical accessibility is a requirement, since the occurrence of a barrier is also connected with defects in the web application [8].

Semantical Accessibility. Characterizes that the content must be understandable and usable for the user. A web application could be perfectly accessible according to guideline conformance, but can still be inaccessible to some users. If one doesn't understand how to proceed at a certain stage of "purchasing a product" in an online shop, it is a barrier [8]. Strategies to overcome those issues are widely known in the school of usability design. On prominent example is the concept of personas, as introduced by Cooper in [24]. Personas are illustrations of hypothetical users. They are composed by an aggregation of stories, requirements, needs, goals and preferences of the product's end users. Personas are used to clarify features or the workflow of an application by rising questions like: *"Would Anna know what to do at this point of the purchasing process?"* or *"Is it clear for Anna what to enter in this web form?"* (Where *Anna* is the name of a persona) [25].

According to [19] elderlies often have anxieties in using systems, which they are not familiar with. Keeping the interaction paradigm consistent across application of the same kind empowers users to apply their learned interaction patterns they are familiar with. It is crucial to know who the products audience is, what their motivations, skills, goals, and preferences are, in order to meet the semantic accessibility.

The remainder of this paper is structured as follows: Sect. 2 introduces the general concept of our approach. Section 3 provides an introduction to the preference set of the *Global Public Inclusive Infrastructure* (GPII) [31] and how we envision deriving accessibility requirements. Section 4 provides a discussion on our work and an outlook on the current status and the next steps.

2 Concept of Persona-Based Accessibility Testing

Testing the accessibility is of special importance for *Rich Internet Applications* (RIAs) [26]. Typically those web applications have a complex behavior and generate large parts of their user interface components at runtime. Therefore, the accessibility of a RIA cannot be fully clarified by looking at the HTML code only, since lots of user interface elements are generated at runtime due to user interaction. This demands the conduction of acceptance tests [17], and involves testing the application as rendered in the browser, with dynamic code (e.g., JavaScript) being executed, and the user interacting with the application.

We are proposing an accessibility evaluation method for RIAs, focusing on technical and semantic accessibility. We understand conducting acceptance tests as testing a web application in the same way an end user would interact with. Our evaluation method is semi-automatic, which means that we are testing for technical accessibility, based on the WCAG 2.0 conformance, but also for semantic accessibility, by pointing the tester to potential problems derived from the end users' requirements and preferences. To control and simulate user interaction in a browser we use *Selenium* [32], an open source framework that is capable of simulating user interaction (e.g., interacting with buttons or filling in web forms) in the browser.

To provide a user-centered evaluation approach, we adapt the *persona* concept and use it as a vehicle to aggregate information about what and how a certain web application should be tested [14]. The typical domain of a *persona* is the actor's role in a scenario. This consists of a setting, the initial situation, and a storyline, the plot. The exact process of how a scenario evolves depends on the actor, their decisions, and traits. If the actor is exchanged, the scenario can have complete different outcome, despite the same initial situation and plot [27]. In order to use personas to conduct accessibility tests, we have to work in their domain.

So, rather than walking a list of technical problems that has been generated by a conformance-testing tool, the developer evaluates an application's accessibility based on the application-specific *use cases* and *user scenarios*. We define a user scenario as an instance of a *use case*, but with concrete usage data. For each use case of a web application, a user scenario with concrete usage data can be produced, by describing an interaction pattern for a dedicated use case. To underline its reusable character, we call this a *Blueprint* - since the role of the actor is exchangeable. This Blueprint consists of real usage data and an interaction pattern.

Each user scenario has an actor, typically represented by a *persona*. A persona consists of stories to illustrate the success criteria of accessible guidelines. Therefore, development teams can empathize with their target audience and use techniques like the barrier walkthrough to question features and functions.

Personas also provide a machine-readable representation, which consists of a persona-specific interaction pattern, such as keyboard-only navigation, and a set of relevant WCAG 2.0 [18] success criteria. The Blueprints and the personas provide the input for the acceptance tests. They tell the test system what and how to test and which interaction patterns to use, e.g., "check only for specific success criteria (e.g., WCAG 2.0) that are relevant for a particular preference set (persona), and consider navigation by keyboard or screen reader".

These tests are executed in the web browser of the client, as a simulation of how end users interact with the application. The basic principle of the system is to follow the navigation pattern, according to the Blueprint, but with the accessibility constraints imposed by the persona. Thus, the test system can automatically perform end-user acceptance tests, as introduced in a similar approach [17].

In extension to [14], we now use the GPII preference set [20] as a foundation to derive the user-specific interaction patterns and accessibility constraints for our machine-readable personas. Since a user can adjust their settings any time, and for any application, to fit their current needs, we are able to track the changing accessibility requirements of age-related disability issues, as discussed in [4]. The concept of this approach is illustrated in Fig. 1.

2.1 Blueprint Description

We designed a domain-specific language to describe the nature of a Blueprint, based on the work of Watanabe, Fortes and Dias [17]. They introduce a language to describe the interaction of people with disabilities in acceptance tests. They use explicit statements to express a specific navigation pattern, e.g.; use tab navigation. In contrast to

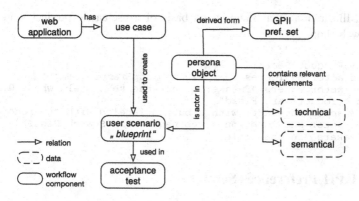

Fig. 1. Overview of the concept and the accessibility evaluation process

Watanabe, Fortes and Dias, a Blueprint doesn't include any specific interaction or navigation instructions. It defines only the interaction intention with certain elements, but not how this interaction, e.g., by mouse or keyboard, is performed, since the interaction is specific to a dedicated actor; just like the individual accessibility requirements. As the name implies, a Blueprint is an interaction draft, including only the setting and the plot. The outcome, also known as the level of accessibility relating to an application's use case, depends on the derived accessibility requirements and could be different amongst actors. Listing 1 shows an example of a Blueprint description.

The test system performs live interaction in the web browser. For every step in the Blueprint, the system performs an accessibility check, which is done automatically for those cases that can be clearly judged programmatically. For the cases where human judgment is required, e.g., verification for an image's alternative text, the system should hold the execution of the Blueprint and present the potential issues to the human tester. The tester can directly inspect the issues and decide about its validity. The same process applies for issues that fall under semantic requirements. By using GPII preference sets that are specific to an application, we can provide an evaluation method that is specific for this application, based on the application's end user requirements.

Since the test runs semi-automatically, the tester is part of the interaction and can empathize with the accessibility requirements more directly. Ignelzi [28] illustrated it nicely by using the metaphor of a farm for describing our knowledge and awareness for a certain problem domain. Everybody lives on their own farm and our knowledge and experience to a particular problem domain is limited to what we know and experienced on our own farm. By visiting other people's farms and seeing the same situation trough their eyes, our understanding and awareness for a specific problem domain increases. This implies that if one experiences the interaction, issues, and problems others stumble upon; one can get a better understanding for accessibility requirements. Changing the point of view can be an asset for web authors to make accessibility guidelines more comprehensible [15, 16]. Furthermore, the use of personas is a nice way to organize such trips to farms of other people [24, 25, 29, 30].

Listing 1. Illustration of a Blueprint on basis of a use-case: "product search" in a fictitious web shop.

```
Scenario: Product Search
Given  The actor navigates to: "www.WebShopExample.com"
When   The actor enters "Sneakers" into the text field whose @id
       is "productSearchField"
And    The actor interacts with a button labeled with "Search"
Then   The actor should be on a web page with "Search Result -
       Sneakers" in the title
```

3   The GPII Preferences Set

The GPII [31] is a generic system to transfer user needs and preferences between devices and contexts. One of the core artifacts within the GPII process flow is the needs and preference set. Such a set is specific per user and stores preferences and settings for applications used in the past. When new devices or contexts are encountered, the GPII tries to reconstruct the way known applications were set up for new, unknown applications. The following example scenario illustrates this auto-adaptation process.

Auto Adaptation Example Scenario: Martha. Martha has a notebook for surfing the internet and writing emails. At work, she has a personal computer and writes product reviews and uses an office suite for writing texts, both at home and at work. She is glad to have managed to use this application, and does not know much about other software. When she works with her office suite, she uses the computer mouse in the office and the touchpad on her notebook at home. For other features, such as text formatting, she uses the toolbar of the application. At work she received an assignment to write a report, together with her colleagues. They have agreed to use a new internet-based tool that allows them to work in parallel on the same text. It also promises to adapt automatically to the user's needs and preferences. Yet, the tool is different from the office application Martha is familiar with and she has never used a similar tool before.

Martha goes to the website and registers for the new tool. Before she can start using it, she has to fill out a questionnaire that asks a few questions about her preferences for different applications, such as what software she uses, whether she uses keyboard shortcuts and, if so, what kind of shortcuts.

In fact, the user interface of the web application looks very similar to her desktop program. She can start working immediately without learning the new interface. There are a few functions she does not know; however, the program informs her about the new functionality and tells her that other users (who have a similar set of preferences) have rated these functions as very practical. Martha reads the descriptions and decides that two of the four functions might be useful for her and disables the other two functions. Internally, the system recognizes the user adaptations and stores them in the user preference set, so the functions will no longer appear.

Over the time, Martha starts to use other Web applications and is very pleased about how well the user interfaces adapt to her behavior and needs. In particular, changes she makes in one application are also reflected in the other applications. Meanwhile, she wants this functionality for all of her applications.

A GPII preference set stores settings for an application for various contexts. Such a representation is sufficient for many use cases that cover a wide array of accessibility adaptations, for example increased font size, zoom factor, screen-reader settings etc. In the GPII, a context is a set of environmental information, such as lighting conditions, screen size or available software stacks. The functionalities of a needs and preference set and their adaptation is illustrated by transferring settings from one application to another, either in a direct relation manner, e.g., a setting is semantically equal in both applications, or in a subset or superset relation manner, e.g., if a setting in one application can be semantically represented by multiple settings of the other application. These relations are sufficient to represent many relations, but there are large families of adaptations for which this approach is not sufficient.

One example of an adaptation that cannot be expressed sufficiently is content adaptation. While a setting can express that the user requires alternative texts for images, it does not help an application actually to produce an alternative text. Or, if a setting expresses the user's desire of having always a search field to look up content, which is important for the elderly [19], won't empower a web application to generate a corresponding form element. This can result in inaccessible applications being unable to meet the desired preferences, not because they are not programmed to do so, but because they did not provide the relevant content to perform the adaptation.

3.1   Deriving Accessibility Requirements

Instead of transferring preferences to adapt a specific target application, we derive accessibility requirements and transfer the user preferences into a format to be used in accessibility acceptance tests.

Preferences, like language settings or a specific contrast ratio that can be mapped to WCAG criteria, are transferred in a direct relation manner and checked by guideline conformance. Generally, one can distinguish between different types of success criteria: Success criteria that can be evaluated programmatically, success criteria that can be detected automatically but need human verification, and success criteria that cannot be detected automatically and so need human verification in any case. Therefore, the test system should point the tester to issues where human verification is required. Since we are conducting live interaction, we are able to expand the space of success criteria that can be tested automatically. An example is the navigation pattern of a user, e.g., navigation by keyboard. We can hereby test the conformance to WCAG guideline 2.1 Keyboard Accessible.

Usually semantic requirements come in the form of textual descriptions [19] or wrapped in stories, if personas are used [24, 25]; therefore, we propose to use *textual requirement-statements*, which are presented to the tester during the Blueprint execution. An example: If the use-case *"searching for a product"* is evaluated for its accessibility, the system would show a semantic requirement, e.g., *"Make sure that the search button is labeled with "Search" or an equivalent text so that it is clear where to click"*, before the Blueprint step, where the actor should interact with a button to initiate the search, is executed; cf. Listing 1.

By approving the statement, the tester confirms that the corresponding semantic requirement is met. Single properties, or combination of properties, in a preference set, can be used to aggregate requirements for semantic accessibility. The study in [19] lists semantic requirements for elderly people, which can serve as a foundation for textual requirement statements. Another approach would be that textual requirement statements are stored in the user preference sets; therefore, a user can define their preferences directly.

Listing 2. Illustration of the envisioned format in JSON syntax, derived from the GPII preference set and used to create the accessibility requirements of an actor. The text content is partially from [19]. This showcase refers to a use case that is characterized by the Blueprint: "product-search", in Listing 1.

```
"product-search":{•
    "technical":{•
            "WCAG":{•
                "automatic":[•
                    "Guideline3_1.3_1_1",
                    "Guideline4_1.4_1_2"•]•,
                "manual":[•"Guideline1_2.1_2_3"]•
            }
        "selenium":{"navigation_pattern"  :  "keyboard"}
        },
    "semantic":{
            "text_field":["Display search as an open, visible
                field on all pages (I found it usually in
                the upper right corner) with a Search button
                to its right"],
            "button":["Make sure to label the search button with
                „Search" or an equivalent text so that it
                is clear where to click"
                ,"Make sure to describe in which format the
                search query should be entered"]
    }
}•
```

3.2 Benefits of Storing Accessibility Requirements as GPII Preferences

Part of the GPII process of transferring settings from one context to another is clustering. The GPII exploits similarity between users [33]. Similarity is derived from clustering. This clustering can be utilized to allow automatically derive matching accessibility requirements for users. For example: Given, we have 100 user preference sets, which were found to be similar, and some of them have associated accessibility requirements, similar to listing 2. Depending on the similarity-distance between those preference sets, the accessibility requirements can be propagated and even automatically altered to match the respective users.

Sometimes people can be uncertain what settings they need to accommodate their needs or from which setting or assistive technology they could also benefit from. Therefore, the GPII can make suggestions based on clustering and the preference set similarity, as illustrated in the GPII adaptation scenario in Chap. 3. Hereby, we're able to derive accessibility requirements that are essential for users sharing similar preferences, but which does an individual user not necessarily considered as a requirement in first place; yet, users can benefit from the compliance with these additional requirements.

As expressed by its name, a preference set reflects the needs and desires of a user. Besides requirements for technical accessibility, preferences can also include semantic requirements. By using the information derived from the preference set, we're able to work with personal accessibility requirements and won't relay on accessibility guidelines only; therefore, addressing the need for a more user centered and personalized accessibility evaluation [8–11].

The preference set is refined every time the user states new preferences or alters exiting ones. Hereby, the GPII learns more about a particular user and can provide better adaptations. Due to this process, preference sets are always up-to-date, which enables a constant tracking of accessibility requirements. This is of special interest for elderlies where accessibility demands can change over time and new or addition disabilities can accrue [4, 7].

4 Discussion and Next Steps

When using the GPII to transfer settings from one application to another, mismatches can also occur, e.g., if the target application doesn't provide suitable settings for properties in the preference set or applications can have settings that share some of their semantics, but also involve side effects or constraints that are not present in both applications. When transferring preferences into accessibility requirements we will most likely run into similar mismatches.

As a potential improvement, we propose to decouple the users' needs and preference sets from its usage fashion in the GPII and define a preference set format, which contains dedicated accessibility preferences and usability needs. Therefore, minimizing the potential mismatches when transferring preference sets into use-case specific accessibility requirements. The GPII preference set allows storing preferences for specific applications, so called application-specific preferences. In a first attempt, we can adopt this concept by storing use-case specific preferences for accessibility tests, as application-specific. Hereby, we would still be able to transfer preferences into accessibility requirements, but would define a distinct preference set format within the structure of GPII.

As described in [24, 25], personas are vehicles for shipping requirements, preferences and goals of a product's target audience. On this account they are highly specific to a certain product or product domain and cannot be properly used for other products. Since we use machine-readable personas to express accessibly requirements for defined uses cases of a product, they cannot be reused for accessibility tests in different products as well, especially if different requirements apply. The more specific the requirements for certain use cases are, the more precise we can state the accessibility of those use cases and the application. This restricts the application scope of our system, to test the use cases of one defined application with the preferences of the target audience.

In the usage scenario, our approach is integrated in the development process, where a web author provides Blueprints and user preferences (of the target audience) are used to generate machine-readable personas; however, we don't advocate substituting the usage of personas or accessibility evaluation techniques. We see our approach as an addition to established workflows and as a support for a more user centered accessibility evaluation.

This project is work in progress. So far, we have developed a prototype, which is capable of conducting accessibility evaluations on a technical level. Currently, we are enhancing our prototype to provide guidance for semantic accessibility. In a next step, we will use this prototype to conduct user tests, with web authors and students from the field of computer science, to validate the workflow and the concept for its usability among web authors and analyze the effectiveness of our approach in comparison with other accessibility evaluation methods.

Acknowledgments. Part of the research leading to these results has been researched within the Cloud4all project. Cloud4all is an R&D project that receives funding from the European Commission under the Seventh Framework Programme (FP7/2007-2013) under grant agreement n° 289016. This publication reflects only the authors' views and the European Union is not liable for any use that may be made of the information contained herein.

References

1. Becker, S.A.: A study of web usability for older adults seeking online health resources. ACM Trans. Comput.-Hum. Interact. **11**(4), 387–406 (2004)
2. Affonso de Lara, S.M., Watanabe, W.M., dos Santos, E.P.B., Fortes, R.P.M.: Improving WCAG for elderly web accessibility. In: Proceedings of the 28th ACM International Conference on Design of Communication, New York, NY, USA, pp. 175–182 (2010)
3. Dickinson, A., Arnott, J., Prior, S.: Methods for human–computer interaction research with older people. Behav. Inf. Technol. **26**(4), 343–352 (2007)
4. Abou-Zahra, S., Brewer, J., Arch, A.: Towards bridging the accessibility needs of people with disabilities and the ageing community. In: Proceedings of the 2008 International Cross-Disciplinary Conference on Web Accessibility (W4A), New York, NY, USA, pp. 83–86 (2008)
5. Arch, A.: Web accessibility for older users: successes and opportunities (keynote). In: Proceedings of the 2009 International Cross-Disciplinary Conference on Web Accessibility (W4A), New York, NY, USA, pp. 1–6 (2009)
6. Leitner, M., Subasi, Ö., Höller, N., Geven, A., Tscheligi, M.: User requirement analysis for a railway ticketing portal with emphasis on semantic accessibility for older users. In: Proceedings of the International Cross-Disciplinary Conference on Web Accessibility (W4A), New York, NY, USA, pp. 114–122 (2009)
7. Sloan, D., Atkinson, M.T., Machin, C., Li, Y.: The potential of adaptive interfaces as an accessibility aid for older web users. In: Proceedings of the International Cross Disciplinary Conference on Web Accessibility (W4A), New York, NY, USA, pp. 35:1–35:10 (2010)
8. Brajnik, G.: Beyond conformance: the role of accessibility evaluation methods. In: Hartmann, S., Zhou, X., Kirchberg, M. (eds.) WISE 2008. LNCS, vol. 5176, pp. 63–80. Springer, Heidelberg (2008)

9. Cooper, M., Sloan, D., Kelly, B., Lewthwaite, S.: A challenge to web accessibility metrics and guidelines: putting people and processes first. In: Proceedings of the International Cross-Disciplinary Conference on Web Accessibility, New York, NY, USA, pp. 20:1–20:4 (2012)

10. Petrie, H., Kheir, O.: The relationship between accessibility and usability of websites. In: Proceedings of the SIGCHI Conference on Human Factors in Computing Systems, New York, NY, USA, pp. 397–40 (2007)

11. Kelly, B., Sloan, D., Brown, S., Seale, J., Petrie, H., Lauke, P., Ball, S.: Accessibility 2.0: people, policies and processes. In: Proceedings of the International Cross-Disciplinary Conference on Web Accessibility (W4A), pp. 138–147. ACM, New York (2007). doi:10. 1145/1243441.1243471

12. Brajnik, G.: Web accessibility testing: when the method is the culprit. In: Miesenberger, K., Klaus, J., Zagler, W.L., Karshmer, A.I. (eds.) ICCHP 2006. LNCS, vol. 4061, pp. 156–163. Springer, Heidelberg (2006)

13. Kelly, B., Sloan, D., Phipps, L., Petrie, H., Hamilton, F.: Forcing standardization or Ac-commodating diversity? a framework for applying the WCAG in the real world. In: Proceedings of the 2005 International Cross-Disciplinary Workshop on Web Accessibility (W4A), New York, NY, USA, pp. 46–54 (2005)

14. Henka, A., Zimmermann, G.: Persona based accessibility testing. In: Stephanidis, C. (ed.) HCI 2014, Part II. CCIS, vol. 435, pp. 226–231. Springer, Heidelberg (2014)

15. Freire, A.P., Russo, C.M., Fortes, R.P.M.: A survey on the accessibility awareness of people involved in web development projects in Brazil. In: Proceedings of the 2008 international cross-disciplinary conference on Web accessibility (W4A), New York, NY, USA, pp. 87–96 (2008)

16. Greeff, M., Kotzé, P.: A lightweight methodology to improve web accessibility. In: Proceedings of the 2009 Annual Research Conference of the South African Institute of Computer Scientists and Information Technologists, New York, NY, USA, pp. 30–39 (2009)

17. Watanabe, W.M., Fortes, R.P.M., Dias, A.L.: Using acceptance tests to validate accessibility requirements in RIA. In: Proceedings of the International Cross-Disciplinary Conference on Web Accessibility, New York, NY, USA, pp. 15:1–15 (2012)

18. W3C: Web Content Accessibility Guidelines (WCAG) 2.0, 11 December 2008. http://www.w3.org/TR/2008/REC-WCAG20-20081211/

19. Pernice, K., Estes, J., Nielsen, J.: Senior Citizens on the Web, 2nd edn. Nielsen Norman Group, Fremont (2013). Research Report by Nielsen Norman Group

20. Iglesias-Pérez, A., Loitsch, C., Kaklanis, N., Votis, K., Stiegler, A., Kalogirou, K., Serra-Autonell, G., Tzovaras, D., Weber, G.: Accessibility through preferences: context-aware recommender of settings. In: Stephanidis, C., Antona, M. (eds.) UAHCI 2014, Part I. LNCS, vol. 8513, pp. 224–235. Springer, Heidelberg (2014)

21. Web Accessibility Initiative: Selecting Web Accessibility Evaluation Tools (2005). http://www.w3.org/WAI/eval/selectingtools.html

22. Brajnik, G., Lomuscio, R.: SAMBA: a semi-automatic method for measuring barriers of accessibility. In: Proceedings of the 9th International ACM SIGACCESS Conference on Computers and Accessibility, New York, NY, USA, pp. 43–50 (2007)

23. Vigo, M., Brown, J., Conway, V.: Benchmarking web accessibility evaluation tools: measuring the harm of sole reliance on automated tests. In: Proceedings of the 10th International Cross-Disciplinary Conference on Web Accessibility, New York, NY, USA, pp. 1:1–1:10 (2013)

24. Cooper, A.: The Inmates are Running the Asylum. SAMS, Indiana (2004)

25. Adlin, T., Pruitt, J.: The Persona Lifecycle. Morgan Kaufmann, San Francisco (2006)

26. Fernandes, N., Batista, A.S., Costa, D., Duarte, C., Carricco, L.: Three web accessibility evaluation perspectives for RIA. In: Proceedings of the 10th International Cross-Disciplinary Conference on Web Accessibility, p. 12 (2013)
27. Carroll, J.M.: Making Use, Scenario Based Design of Human Computer Interactions. The MIT Press, Cambridge (2000)
28. Ignelzi, M.: Meaning-making in the learning and teaching process. New Dir. Teach. Learn. **2000**, 5–14 (2000). doi:10.1002/tl.8201
29. Schulz, T., Skeide Fuglerud, K.: Creating personas with disabilities. In: Miesenberger, K., Karshmer, A., Penaz, P., Zagler, W. (eds.) ICCHP 2012, Part II. LNCS, vol. 7383, pp. 145–152. Springer, Heidelberg (2012)
30. Bailey, C., Pearson E.: Development and trial of an educational tool to support the accessibility evaluation process. In: Proceedings of the International Cross-Disciplinary Conference on Web Accessibility, New York, NY, USA, pp. 2:1–2:10 (2011)
31. Global Public Inclusive Infrastructure, January 2015. http://gpii.net/
32. Selenium browser automation framework, January 2015. https://code.google.com/p/selenium/
33. Loitsch, C., Stiegler, A., Strobbe, C., Tzovaras, D., Votis, K., Weber, G., Zimmerman, G.: Improving. In: Assistive Technology: From Research to Practice, Vilamoura, Portugal, pp. 1357–1365 (2013)

Older Adults' Usage of Web Pages: Investigating Effects of Information Structure on Performance

Jincheng Huang[(⊠)], Jia Zhou, and Huilin Wang

Department of Industrial Engineering, Chongqing University,
Chongqing 40044, China
cquhcijc@cqu.edu.cn, {zhoujia07,azerrman}@gmail.com

Abstract. This study focuses on older adults' usage of web pages. An experiment consisted of three information structures (the net structure, the tree structure, and the linear structure) was conducted to investigate effects of information structure (IS) on older adult's performance. Three findings were found. First, the number of clicks was the fewest in the net-structure web page among three web pages. Older participants spent less time to complete the tasks in the linear-structure web page than the other two web pages. The number of clicks and the accuracy of participants answered the questions in the tree-structure web page were the highest among three web pages. Second, older participants' performance of card sorting was positively correlated with the task completion time. And there was a positive correlation between spatial ability and the performance of older participants. Third, older participants showed the highest preference of the linear structure among three information structures. They always lost task targets in the tree-structure web page, especially when they needed to transfer from one branch of the tree structure to another branch. This indicated that a simple IS was better used and understood by older participants than a complicated one.

Keywords: Information structure · Older adults · Web pages · Navigation

1 Introduction

Older adults have some disadvantages in effectively utilizing the Internet as an information resource (e.g., shopping or reading news on the Internet) compared with young adults. For instance, older adults easily get lost in the deep hierarchical menus of mobile phones because of the declined spatial ability [1]. And other information structures such as the net structure and the linear structure are wildly used in the design of web pages or mobile devices. Previous studies have shown that users would have problems navigating the information in the website when the information structure did not match users' mental model [2]. To know which information structure(s) will be better used and understood by older adults is important for practitioners.

This study aims to investigate how information structure influences older adults' navigation performance on web pages. Specifically, older participants would use three

© Springer International Publishing Switzerland 2015
J. Zhou and G. Salvendy (Eds.): ITAP 2015, Part I, LNCS 9193, pp. 337–346, 2015.
DOI: 10.1007/978-3-319-20892-3_33

web pages built with the net structure, the tree structure, and the linear structure in an experiment. Results of this study help older adults have good user experience of technology products.

2 Literature Review

It is important to display the content according to how people access information when organizing the content of a website [3]. Since a meaningful information structure will promote efficient navigation, to ensure that information is organized in a way that is meaningful to its target users is essential when designing websites [4].

Compared with younger adults, it was difficult for older adults to find a function in a broad menu. Furthermore, it was also not a simple job for them to remember the interaction steps in a deep menu. Therefore, a mobile phone' menu which had fewer functions and was shallower than one which had broader functions and was deeper would be better used by older adults [5]. Zaphiris et al. (2003) had also found that shallow hierarchies were preferred to deep hierarchies by both young adults and older adults in a hierarchical online information system [6]. However, detailed information about the relationship of different branches in the tree structure is little known.

Previous studies indicated two solutions to reduce older adults' menu disorientation. One solution was to provide information about the position in the hierarchical menu. The "tree" aid with the parent categories and the "category" aid were tested. The results of the test showed that this solution was helpful for older adults [7]. The other solution was to use a circular menu in a smart phone for older adults' healthcare support. Older participants who evaluated the usability evaluation could rotate the wheel at the side of a smart phone to select menu items, and this circular menu was better used by them [8].

3 Methodology

An experiment was conducted to investigate which information structure(s) would be better used and understood by older adults. The net-structure web page, the tree-structure web page, and the linear-structure web page about Chinese history which were not widely known by older adults (e.g., those great poets in Tang dynasty such as Li Bai, Du Fu, and Bai Juyi were commonly known while Lu lun and Gu kuan were not) were utilized in this experiment. Older participants' performance among three web pages was observed.

3.1 Participants

A total of 12 older adults from Yuzui Citizen School in Jiangbei District of Chongqing, China were recruited as participants. Older adults who were literate and aged above 60 were eligible for this study. The age of the participants ranged from 60 to 75 years old (Mean = 64.3, SD = 5.46). In total, there were five male participants and seven female participants.

3.2   Task

In this experiment, three web pages about ancient invention, ancient books, and ancient historical character of different Chinese dynasties were presented to participants. There were eight tasks for each information structure. Each participant was required to read three web pages and complete the tasks separately. In each web page, participants firstly watched the task specification, secondly they found the target according to the task specification by touching the hyperlink in the web page, and finally they answered two questions according to the content which was shown in the web page (see Fig. 1).

Here is the explanation of the task specification provided by Morae Recorder which is shown in Fig. 1.

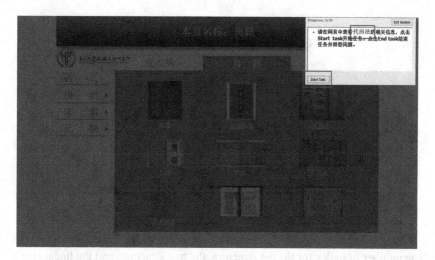

Fig. 1. Interface of the net-structure web page used in this experiment

Please find the message of **Daitian Method** *in this web page. Click the "Start Task" button to begin this task. Click the "End Task" button to finish this task and answer the question.*

*Only the Chinese characters were displayed in this experiment.

3.3   Dependent Variables

The dependent variable was participants' performance of using three web pages. It was measured through task completion time, the number of clicks, and task effectiveness. Both of the task completion time and the number of clicks were recorded by Morae Recorder. The number of errors of participants' answer was analyzed by Morae Manger.

3.4   Independent Variables

The independent variables were three information structures: the net structure, the tree structure, and the linear structure. Besides, demographic variables including age, spatial ability and computer experience were considered as covariates in this experiment. Age and computer experience of participants were measured through a questionnaire. Participants' spatial ability was tested through the spatial location-memory span tester. Under the display of the tester, red buttons would randomly appear, and participants were required to press the buttons in the sequence as they appeared. After that, the number of red buttons increased and participants would repeat this process. Participants' spatial ability was measured through the maximum number of digits, the highest scores, and the number of errors (see Fig. 2).

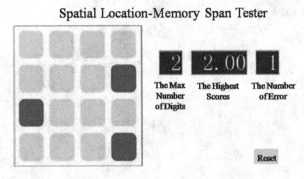

Fig. 2. Instruction of spatial location-memory span tester

The number of nodes for the net structure, the tree structure, and the linear structure is 40, 37, and 24 accordingly. Nodes of the vertical navigation bar and the horizontal navigation bar are connected by hyperlink. The depth of the tree structure is four, and the breadth of the tree structure is three. Figure 3 has shown one of the groups of the net structure, one of the branches of the tree structure and part of the linear structure.

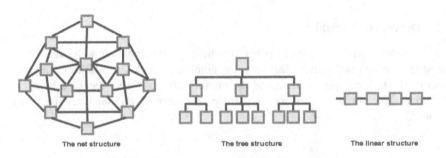

The net structure   The tree structure   The linear structure

Fig. 3. The information structure of three web pages

3.5 Experimental Design

Within-subjects design was used. Each participant read three web pages built with the net structure, the tree structure, and the linear structure (see Fig. 4) and completed the tasks. In order to prevent the "learning effect", the order of presentation of three web pages was counterbalanced.

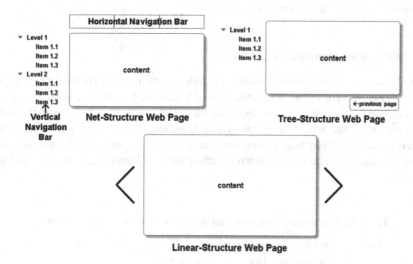

Fig. 4. Three web pages built with concept model

3.6 Equipment and Procedures

A notebook computer (ThinkPad S1 Yoga) with Microsoft's Windows 8.1 operating system and Google Chrome (version 37.0.2062.120m) Browser was used for the experiment. Since novice older adults have difficulty in using a mouse, a computer with a touch screen is a better choice than a mouse. The experiment was conducted in a separate room in the Yuzui Citizen School in Jiangbei District of Chongqing, China. Each participant was encouraged to complete the experiment individually. They could ask for help but it would be recorded.

The experiment took each participant about 60 min. Firstly, each participant began the experiment by filling out a consent form and a general questionnaire about his/her demographic information and experience with computers and mobile phones. Secondly, a spatial ability test was conducted by using a spatial location–memory span tester. Thirdly, a brief introduction and practice about the experiment was given to each participant. Fourthly, participants completed tasks of each web page and then went on with card sorting. The cards were the titles of each node in the information structure. Morae Recorder (version 3.3.3) was used to present the task specification for participants. At the end, the experimenter conducted a five-minute exploratory interview with the participants to know their thoughts and feelings about using three web pages. The question in the interview included "In three web pages, which was the most comfortable one and the worst one for you? And why?".

4 Results and Discussion

4.1 Descriptive Statistics

There were a total of 12 participants in this experiment (five males, seven females). 83.3 % of the participants earned 300–1200 RMB per month; 50 % of them had more than two-year experience of using smart phones; 34 % of the participants had more than two-year computer experience.

4.2 Effect of Information Structure

The influences of information structure on older participants' performance of using three web pages were tested. Repeated ANOVA was used to analyze data.

As to average completion time, the standard deviations were very large, making the interpretation of the results different. Table 1 indicated that there were significant differences among three information structures in task 2 and task 3. One possible reason was that participants accidently touched the end button immediately after the task began.

Table 1. The influences of information structure on task completion time

Task	Task completion time (s)						df	F	p
	Net structure		Tree structure		Linear structure				
	Mean	SD	Mean	SD	Mean	SD			
1	59.92	29.70	65.70	37.00	69.50	58.75	2	1.777	0.193
2	52.53	17.44	45.74	24.33	28.54	20.79	2	3.666	0.046*
3	64.12	30.93	55.99	22.73	29.89	21.51	2	4.528	0.026*
4	46.00	13.96	48.40	26.10	38.17	23.50	2	0.628	0.545
5	42.06	19.57	31.75	23.78	30.44	17.54	2	1.753	0.199
6	38.50	22.30	26.63	24.87	34.03	29.61	2	0.452	0.643
7	43.56	17.89	34.54	22.79	29.20	16.28	2	2.296	0.127
8	38.47	24.66	27.71	17.55	26.70	15.55	2	1.726	0.203
Average	48.14	22.06	42.06	24.89	35.81	25.44	2	2.322	0.114

Note: *Significant at 0.05 level

Table 2 indicated that information structure had significant influences on the number of clicks. Older participants clicked fewer to complete the tasks in the net structure than the tree structure and the linear structure, and this may because they could use the horizontal bar in the net structure to have an overview of the content in the web page. And the number of clicks to complete the tasks was the highest in the tree-structure web page among three web pages. One possible reason was that participants easily got lost when they found the target in the tree-structure web page.

Table 2. The influences of information structure on the number of clicks

Task	The number of clicks						df	F	p
	Net structure		Tree structure		Linear structure				
	Mean	SD	Mean	SD	Mean	SD			
1	6.83	3.81	9.67	6.86	12.75	12.82	2	1.777	0.193
2	6.70	3.23	6.60	5.40	5.20	3.65	2	0.330	0.721
3	7.20	4.80	11.20	5.07	6.40	6.90	2	1.598	0.230
4	4.90	2.38	12.20	10.86	11.50	10.66	2	2.793	0.087
5	7.27	6.52	9.55	7.42	5.18	2.63	2	2.055	0.154
6	4.90	2.72	8.50	6.29	6.50	3.97	2	1.211	0.321
7	5.82	2.31	10.00	7.52	7.00	3.71	2	3.629	0.045*
8	4.34	2.34	6.18	2.23	7.45	4.87	2	11.723	0.003*
Average	5.99	3.51	9.23	6.40	7.75	6.15	2	12.143	0.0008*

Note: *Significant at 0.05 level

As to the net-structure web page, older participants spent more time to complete tasks on the net structure than the tree structure and the linear structure. Meanwhile, it was easier for participants to find targets in the net-structure web page than the other two web pages. The number of clicks of the net structure was fewer than the tree structure and the linear structure.

As to the tree-structure web page, the number of clicks of the tree structure was higher than the net structure and the linear structure. Only one older participant preferred the tree structure to the net structure and the linear structure. Other older participants easily got lost in the tree structure. They stayed in a page for a long time or staying in a cycle of going and returning back of one page in the tree structure. Particularly it was difficult for them to cross one branch to another branch in the tree structure.

As to the linear-structure web page, older participants spent less time to complete the tasks than the other two web pages. 58 % of the older participants preferred the linear-structure web page to the net-structure web page and the tree-structure web page.

As to the task effectiveness, older participants completed the tasks with a higher accuracy in the linear structure than the net structure and the tree structure. The accuracy of participants answered the questions for the net structure, the tree structure, and the linear structure was 63 %, 67 %, and 87 % accordingly. And the total number of errors of participants' answer was 35 in the net structure (Mean = 2.92, SD = 1.505), 31 in the tree structure (Mean = 2.58, SD = 1.564), and 12 in the linear structure (Mean = 1.00, SD = 1.279). The results of repeated ANOVA indicated that information structure had significant influences on task effectiveness ($F = 7.654$, df = 2, $p = 0.003$).

4.3 Effect of Card Sorting

The total number of errors of participants' card sorting was 21 in the net structure (Mean = 1.75, SD = 1.423), 38 in the tree structure (Mean = 3.16, SD = 0.935), and 10 in the linear structure (Mean = 1.91, SD = 1.514).

As the results of correlation analysis between performance and the card sorting indicated, the performance of card sorting was positively correlated with the task completion time. However, it was not correlated with the number of clicks. The correlation coefficient between card sorting and performance are shown in Table 3.

Table 3. Correlation coefficient between performance and card sorting's result

	Task completion time	The number of clicks
Correlation coefficient	0.453*	0.302
p	0.006	0.074

Note: *Correlation is significant at the 0.05 level

4.4 Effect of Covariates

Three demographic variables (spatial ability, computer experience, age) were considered as covariates. The correlation between the demographic variables and older participants' performance are shown in Table 4. As to the spatial ability of participants, the maximum number of digits was ranged from five to seven (Mean = 6.16, SD = 0.572). The highest scores were ranged from 3.66 to 5.66 (Mean = 4.67, SD = 0.691). The number of errors of participants was ranged from three to nine (Mean = 6.00, SD = 1.852).

Table 4. Correlation coefficient between performance and demographic variables

	Task completion time			The number of clicks		
	Age	Computer experience	Spatial ability	Age	Computer experience	Spatial ability
Correlation Coefficient	0.481	−0.162	−0.758*	0.419	0.102	−0.585*
p	0.113	0.614	0.004	0.175	0.753	0.046

Note: *Correlation is significant at the 0.05 level

The results of this test showed that older participants would make more mistakes when the maximum number of digits was more than six. The number of errors of spatial ability was selected as the variable for the correlation between the performance and spatial ability. And participants who completed the spatial ability test with fewer errors may complete the tasks faster.

As to computer experience, four participants had more than two-year computer experience while eight participants had not used computer before. Older participants who had experience of using computer spent less time to complete the tasks than those who had not the experience.

4.5   Discussion

First, older participants completed tasks efficiently when finding targets in the net-structure web page. They clicked the web built with the net structure less frequently than the tree structure and the linear structure. However, older participants felt lost in the net structure. This was because the relationship between the vertical navigation bar and horizontal navigation bar in the net structure (see Fig. 4) was difficult for them to understand. Specifically, older participants could easily find the target with horizontal navigation bar while could not catch the detailed information of this target by the vertical navigation bar in the net structure. Therefore, they spent more time to complete the tasks in the net-structure web page than the tree-structure web page and the linear-structure web page.

Second, older participants felt confused at the second or third level of the tree structure in this experiment. They stayed in a page for a long time or staying in a cycle of going and returning back of one page in the tree structure. And it was difficult for older participants to transfer from one branch to another branch in the tree structure.

The experiment's results indicated that older participants could easily turn to the next page, but it was not a simple task for them to turn to the front page in the tree structure. Therefore, the design like the home button used in a smart phone may help older adults to understand technology products well.

Third, the linear structure was the easiest one to use for older participants among three information structures. Therefore, a design like a horizontal navigation bar continuing with a linear structure (e.g., the tree structure with eight items on each of two levels) may be accepted by older adults.

Fourth, older participants tended to focus on the content of the web page while always ignore the relationship between each page in this experiment. Therefore, a hint about the relationship between each page (level) in the web page may be better used by older adults.

5   Conclusion

This study investigated older adults' performance of using three web pages built with three information structures. To help older adults have good user experience of technology products, three web pages built with three information structures were tested. Based on the results, three main findings were derived:

First, the number of clicks was the fewest in the net-structure web page among three web pages. Meanwhile, older participants spent less time to complete the tasks in the linear-structure web page than the other two web pages. The number of clicks and the accuracy of older participants answered the questions were the highest in the tree-structure web page among three web pages.

Second, older participants' performance of card sorting was positively correlated with the task completion time. In addition, there was a positive correlation between spatial ability and the performance of older participants' usage of web pages.

Third, most of the older participants preferred the linear structure to the net structure and the tree structure. Meanwhile, most of the participants thought the tree structure was difficult to use, and they always lost task targets in the tree-structure web page, especially when they needed to transfer from one branch of the tree structure to another branch.

Acknowledgment. This work was supported with funding from a National Science Foundation China grant 71401018 and a Chongqing Scientific and Technological Project cstc2012gg-yyjs70009.

References

1. Ziefle, M., Bay, S.: How older adults meet complexity: aging effects on the usability of different mobile phones. Behav. Inf. Technol. **24**, 375–389 (2005)
2. Kurniawan, S.H., Zaphiris, P.: Web health information architecture for older users. It Soc. **1**, 42–63 (2003)
3. Bernard, M.: Constructing user-centered websites: design implications for content organization. Usability News **2** (2000)
4. Shneiderman, B.: Designing the User Interface-Strategies for Effective Human-Computer Interaction. Pearson Education India, New Delhi (1986)
5. Ziefle, M., Bay, S.: Mental models of a cellular phone menu. Comparing older and younger novice users. In: Brewster, S., Dunlop, M.D. (eds.) Mobile HCI 2004. LNCS, vol. 3160, pp. 25–37. Springer, Heidelberg (2004)
6. Zaphiris, P., Kurniawan, S.H., Ellis, R.: Age related differences and the depth vs. breadth tradeoff in hierarchical online information systems. In: Carbonell, N., Stephanidis, C. (eds.) UI4ALL 2002. LNCS, vol. 2615, pp. 23–42. Springer, Heidelberg (2003)
7. Ziefle, M., Bay, S.: How to overcome disorientation in mobile phone menus: a comparison of two different types of navigation aids. Hum.-Comput. Interact. **21**, 393–433 (2006)
8. John, K.Z., Shih-Chen, F., Ming-Hui, W., Chun-Tang, H., Chung-Hoo, H., Shang-Hwa, H., Ming-Chuen, C.: Activity-oriented design of Health Pal: A smart phone for elders' healthcare support. EURASIP J. Wirel. Commun. Netw. **27**, 1–27 (2008)

Perceived Barriers for Older Adults' Shopping Channel Selection Toward Online Shopping

Comparisons Between Different Business Models

Jiunn-Woei Lian[⊠]

Department of Information Management,
National Taichung University of Science and Technology, Taichung, Taiwan
jwlian@nutc.edu.tw

Abstract. The aim of this study is to understand perceived barriers for older adults to select novel shopping channel. Questionnaire survey was employed. Innovation resistance theory is served as the theoretical base for this study. Five innovativeness acceptance barriers (usage barrier, value barrier, risk barrier, traditional barrier, and image barrier) and three business models (online shopping oriented vs. TV shopping oriented vs. hybrid) were investigated. 108 valid respondents who are older than 50 years old and have online shopping experience participated in this study. The major results including: (1) The order of the barriers for older adults to adopt novel shopping business models is risk barrier, traditional barrier, image barrier, usage barrier, and value barrier. (2) There exist significant ($p < 0.01$) different in traditional barrier and image barrier among different business models. (3) Value barrier, risk barrier, and traditional barrier have significant ($p < 0.05$) impact on novel shopping business models acceptance.

Keywords: Older adults · Shopping channel · Perceived barriers · Business model

1 Introduction

Shopping behavior is an interesting topic in the marketing field. With the coming of EC (electronic commerce), issues related to shopping channel selection became more and more important, especially for online shopping. Scholars from difference fields paid more and more attention to the related issue. For example, many related researches from IS/IT perspective have been appear in EC related journal. International Journal of Electronic Commerce is a good example. However, most of the previous studies have been focused on younger customers (such as students), they serve younger as major potential market for online commerce. Indeed, with the coming of aging society, the role of older adults toward online commerce is becoming more and more critical. The percentage of older adults in Asia countries' population structure is listed in Table 1 [1]. From Table 1, we can see that older adult will becoming more and more important for consuming market. However, few study have been focused on the related topic. Therefore, this paper is focused on the barriers for the older adults' shopping channel

© Springer International Publishing Switzerland 2015
J. Zhou and G. Salvendy (Eds.): ITAP 2015, Part I, LNCS 9193, pp. 347–353, 2015.
DOI: 10.1007/978-3-319-20892-3_34

selection. Additionally, the difference between different business models (online shopping oriented vs. TV shopping oriented vs. hybrid) have also been investigated. The aim of this study is to understand perceived barriers for older adults to select novel shopping channel.

In addition to traditional in-store shopping, nowadays consumers always have other three shop channels in general. The first is pure online shopping which search, order, and

Table 1. Percentage of older adult in Asia countries

	2010	2015	2020	2025
Taiwan	10.9	12.5	15.7	19.4
Japan	22.8	26.6	29.2	30.7
China	8.6	10.1	12.4	14.3
Hong Kong	13.1	15.3	18.5	22.9
Korea	11.1	13.0	15.6	19.7
Singapore	7.2	8.9	10.9	13.2
Malaysia	4.8	5.6	6.9	8.5
Indonesia	6.2	6.6	7.8	9.4
Philippines	4.2	4.6	5.4	6.2
Thailand	8.5	9.9	11.8	14.6
Vietnam	5.5	5.8	6.9	8.9
India	5.3	6.0	6.7	7.7

pay are finishing online. The other one is buying through TV shopping channel, from TV platform consumer can understand the goods information and buying through telephone. The third one is that business (seller) who have bother online and TV shopping channel for consumers. This is defined as "hybrid" business model in present study.

The rest of the paper is organized as follows. Section 2 reviews related studies on older adults' shopping channel acceptance and innovation resistance theory. Section 3 introduces the research method and design. Section 4 describes the data analysis results. Section 5 is the discussions of the data analysis results. Finally, Sect. 6 presents our conclusions.

2   Literature Review

2.1   Related Studies

Little previous studies have paid attention to the issues which related to older adults, online shopping and perceived barrier. Focused on older adults' buying behaviors, Lim and Kim [5] indicated that in the context of TV shopping loneliness, parasocial interaction, and convenience are critical factors to understand older adults' satisfaction with TV shopping. Lin found that the TV and online shopping values will affect users' shopping channel selection [6]. In the study of Lian and Yen [4], based on UTAUT (Unified Theory of Acceptance and Use of Technology) and innovation resistance theory, they found that the major motivated factors affecting older adults toward online shopping are performance expectation and social influence which is the same with younger. On the other hand, the major barriers include value, risk, and tradition which is different from younger. Therefore, older adults have their own characteristics toward shopping channel selection.

2.2 Innovation Resistance Theory

Innovation resistance theory was proposed by Ram in 1987 [7] to understand why innovation is resisted by user. It has been applied in various research issues, including online shopping and IT adoption [3]. Besides, Ram and Sheth [8] also indicated that five critical barriers which belonging two categories will against users to adopt an innovation. The two categories are functional and psychological. The five barriers are usage barrier, value barrier, risk barrier, image barrier, and tradition barrier. The front three barriers are belonging to functional barrier; the last two barriers are belonging to psychological. Above five barriers are employed in the present study to understand the barriers for older adults buying online.

3 Methodology

Survey research method was employed in this study. Older adults who older than 50 years old and taking courses in "Evergreen University" in Taiwan participated in this study. Six variables are included in this study including: usage barrier, value barrier, risk barrier, traditional barrier, image barrier, and use intention. The measurement items have been adapted from previous literatures to insure their reliability and validity. Besides, items which related to shopping experience have been designed to understand their previous shopping experience. Famous and general online shopping and TV shopping businesses or platforms have been listed on the questionnaire to be selected. Additionally, questionnaire has been revised by researchers and practical experts. Questionnaires were collected during class. Finally, 108 valid respondents who have online or TV shopping experience were included in our analysis.

4 Data Analysis

Demographic data is illustrated in Table 2. More female than male and the major age level is between 56–65 years old. Besides, in Table 3 we can find that 54 % respondents only have online shopping experiences, 28 % only have TV shopping experiences. Finally, 20 % have both of the shopping experiences (hybrid).

Regarding the validity and reliability testing. Confirmation factor analysis and Cronbach's alpha were employed in this study. The results indicated that the data have acceptable validity and reliability (the alpha value is larger than 0.7) [2] except tradition barrier, but it still in accept level (>0.5) (Table 4). Following are data analysis results for the research questions.

Table 2. Demographic

		Number	Percentage
Gender	Male	46	43 %
	Female	62	57 %
	Total	108	100 %
Age	51–55	16	15 %
	56–60	37	34 %
	61–65	24	22 %
	66–70	18	17 %
	71–75	10	9 %
	Over 75	3	3 %
	Total	108	100 %

Table 3. Online or TV shopping experiences

Shopping channel	Number	Percentage
Online oriented	58	54 %
TV shopping oriented	28	26 %
Hybrid	22	20 %
Total	108	100 %

Table 4. Reliability testing

Variables	Usage barrier	Value barrier	Risk barrier	Tradition barrier	Image barrier	Intention
Cronbach's Alpha	0.90	0.76	0.75	0.56	0.80	0.95

4.1 Barriers for Older Adults Across Different Business Models

From Tables 5 and 6, we can see that the order (from high to low) of the five barriers for older adults buying online is risk barrier, traditional barrier, image barrier, usage barrier, and value barrier (the value is between 1 to 5, the lower the value is representing higher barrier). Besides, the orders of the barriers are various across different business models (Table 6).

4.2 Different Barriers Between Business Models

ANOVA analysis is employed to see the significant barrier difference between business models. From Table 7, we can see that there exist significant ($p < 0.01$) different in traditional barrier and image barrier among different business models. For tradition

Table 5. Barriers for older adults across different business models

Barrier	Business model	Mean	S.D.
Usage barrier (U)	Online shopping	3.63	0.63
	TV shopping	3.64	0.71
	Hybrid	3.68	0.39
	Total	3.64	0.61
Value barrier (V)	Online shopping	3.77	0.65
	TV shopping	3.63	0.70
	Hybrid	3.55	0.62
	Total	3.69	0.66
Risk barrier (R)	Online shopping	2.05	0.59
	TV shopping	2.12	0.70
	Hybrid	2.08	0.66
	Total	2.07	0.63
Tradition barrier (T)	Online shopping	2.58	0.63
	TV shopping	2.23	0.54
	Hybrid	2.89	0.63
	Total	2.55	0.64
Image barrier (I)	Online shopping	2.79	0.86
	TV shopping	2.52	0.76
	Hybrid	3.23	0.84
	Total	2.81	0.86

Table 6. Barrier comparison between different business models

Business model	The order of adoption barrier (From high to low)
Online shopping	R > T > I > U > V
TV shopping	R > T > I > V > U
Hybrid	R > T > I > V > U
Total	R > T > I > U > V

Table 7. Results of ANOVA analysis

	F-value	p-value	Post Hoc testing
Usage barrier	0.06	0.95	N/A
Value barrier	1.07	0.35	N/A
Risk barrier	0.11	0.90	N/A
Tradition barrier	7.29	0.00*	TV shopping vs. online shopping
			TV shopping vs. hybrid
Image barrier	4.51	0.01*	TV shopping vs. hybrid

* $p < 0.01$

barrier the difference were between TV shopping, online shopping and hybrid. However, the image barrier is between TV shopping and hybrid.

4.3   The Relationships Between the Barriers and Use Intention

Four multiple regressions were proposed to understand the relationships between the barriers and use intention toward different business models (online shopping, TV shopping, Hybrid, and total). The independent variables are the five barrier, and the dependent variable is the intention to adopt online shopping. Overall, the four models are significant and have acceptable explanatory power for user behavior (the adj-R^2 is between 0.55–0.61) (Table 8). Additionally, from Table 8, we can find that the critical barrier are various across different business model. Finally, value barrier, risk barrier, and traditional barrier have significant ($p < 0.05$) impact for older adults to shop on these novel shopping channels (all samples). Additionally, the explanatory power (Adj-R^2) is 57 %.

Table 8. Results of regressions analysis

	Adj-R^2	Critical barrier ($p < 0.05$)
Online shopping	0.55	Usage barrier, value barrier
TV shopping	0.61	Value barrier
Hybrid	0.59	Value barrier, risk barrier
Total	0.57	Value barrier, risk barrier, traditional barrier

5   Discussions

From the results, we can find that for older adults, the barrier for their acceptance of shopping channel are various across different business models. The major barriers for these novel shopping channels are risk barrier and tradition barrier (Table 5). This is because when people face new innovation, they will have uncertainty therefore their will have higher risk barrier (the highest risk barrier is online shopping, TV shopping have lowest risk barrier). Besides, most of people (especially for old adults) will familiar traditional physical shopping channel, therefore they will have higher tradition barrier.

Which business models have significant different? From the results of ANOVA analysis (Table 7), we can find that the major differences are tradition barrier and image barrier. The results meant that for older adults, psychological barriers have significant difference between different business models.

Finally, from the results of regression analysis (Table 8), we can find that innovation resistance theory is suitable for understanding older adults' acceptance of difference shopping channel (the R^2 are acceptable). Additionally, Table 8 indicates that functional barriers become critical for understand older adults' acceptance of difference shopping business model.

6 Conclusions

This study have three major findings which are listing below:

(1) The order (from high to low) of the five barriers for older adults adopting new shopping novel business models is risk barrier, traditional barrier, image barrier, usage barrier, and value barrier.
(2) There exist significant ($p < 0.01$) different in traditional barrier and image barrier among different business models for older users.
(3) Innovation resistance theory is suitable for understanding older adults' innovation acceptance. Besides, value barrier, risk barrier, and traditional barrier have significant ($p < 0.05$) impact on novel shopping business models acceptance. The explanatory powers (Adj-R^2) are between 0.55–0.61.

Regarding the limitations of this study, first of all, this study only focused on the older adults who take class in Evergreen University. Other general older adults are not included in our survey. Second, different countries have various shopping environment if the results from Taiwan can be applied to difference countries need to be investigated in the future.

Finally, this study provides advanced understandings regarding older adults to shop online. Findings can served as the references for academic area in conducting advanced research and practical area in providing better services for older adults to shop online.

Acknowledgements. The author would like to thank the Ministry of Science and Technology of Republic of China, Taiwan, for financially supporting this research under contract No. NSC 100-2410-H-025-003-.

References

1. United States Census Bureau. http://www.census.gov/
2. Hair, J.F., Black, W.C., Babin, B.J., Anderson, R.E.: Multivariate Data Analysis: A Global Perspective. Pearson, London (2010)
3. Lian, J.W., Yen, D.C.: To buy or not to buy experience goods online: perspective of innovation adoption barriers. Comput. Hum. Behav. **29**(3), 665–672 (2013)
4. Lian, J.W., Yen, D.C.: Online shopping drivers and barriers for older adults: age and gender differences. Comput. Hum. Behav. **37**, 133–143 (2014)
5. Lim, C.M., Kim, Y.K.: Older consumers' TV home shopping: loneliness, parasocial interaction, and perceived convenience. Psychol. Mark. **28**(8), 763–780 (2011)
6. Lin, H.H.: Gender differences in the linkage of online patronage behavior with TV-and-online shopping values. Serv. Bus. **5**(4), 295–312 (2011)
7. Ram, S.: A model of innovation resistance. Adv. Consum. Res. **14**(1), 208–212 (1987)
8. Ram, S., Sheth, J.N.: Consumer resistance to innovations: the marketing problems and its solutions. J. Consum. Mark. **6**(2), 5–14 (1989)

Processing Speed and Vocabulary are Related to Older Adults' Internet Experiences

Jennifer Romano Bergstrom[1]([✉]), Erica Olmsted-Hawala[2],
and Wendy A. Rogers[3]

[1] Facebook, 100 Hacker Way, Menlo Park, CA 94025, USA
JenRB@fb.com
[2] Center for Survey Measurement, U.S. Census Bureau, 4600 Silver Hill Road,
Washington, DC 20233, USA
Erica.L.Olmsted.Hawala@census.gov
[3] School of Psychology, Georgia Institute of Technology, 654 Cherry St.,
Atlanta, GA 30332, USA
Wendy@gatech.edu

Abstract. Some cognitive declines commonly occur with aging; yet they are seldom taken into account by Website designers and User Experience (UX) researchers. In this empirical study, we compared younger adults, middle-age adults, high-functioning older adults, and low-functioning older adults to examine whether there is a relationship between aspects of cognition and performance when using a Website. Performance was measured by accuracy (percent of tasks completed successfully), efficiency (mean time to complete tasks) and self-rated satisfaction, three commonly used usability metrics. Results suggest that processing speed and vocabulary may be related to Internet performance. Specifically, older adults with faster processing speed and/or high vocabulary may perform better than their lower-functioning counterparts. More importantly, these older adults perform similar to younger adults.

Keywords: Usability · Cognition · Aging · Computers · Internet · Technology

1 Introduction

The number of older adults who use the Internet is rapidly growing, and older adults are the fastest growing group of Internet users [1–5]. The Internet has the potential to help older adults (e.g., as a source of information, education, social support), yet at the same time, older adults may experience information overload and challenges when trying to find pertinent information. Some cognitive declines commonly occur with age, and various aspects of cognition are crucial to successfully navigating Websites. For example, spatial skills, short-term memory, processing speed, working memory,

J. Romano Bergstrom—This report is released to inform interested parties of research and to encourage discussion. Any views expressed on the methodological issues are those of the authors and not necessarily those of Facebook, the U.S. Census Bureau, or GA Tech.

J. Zhou and G. Salvendy (Eds.): ITAP 2015, Part I, LNCS 9193, pp. 354–364, 2015.
DOI: 10.1007/978-3-319-20892-3_35

and sustained attention, which are all well known to decline with age [6–11], are involved in navigating Websites [12]. Website designers often do not take into account the cognitive limitations of older users. Thus, many older Internet users end up frustrated and dissatisfied [1, 13–15]. Additionally, UX researchers often do not take into account the cognitive capabilities of research participants in general, which may lead to inaccurate assumptions about the usability of a product [16]. At present, there is little empirical evidence about the relationship between age-related cognitive differences and Internet performance.

The purpose of the present study was to examine the relationship between age-related decline in cognition and Internet performance. Younger, middle-age, and older adults completed a standard battery of cognitive tasks to assess processing speed and vocabulary (a backward counting task, the WAIS Digit Symbol Coding task, and the Shipley Vocabulary test), which represent fluid and crystallized ability, respectively, and have been shown to be predictive of computer use [17]. Participants also completed a computer and Internet experience questionnaire, five information-finding tasks on a US Census Bureau Website, and a satisfaction questionnaire. Performance on the Website was measured by accuracy (percent of tasks completed successfully), efficiency (mean time to complete tasks) and self-rated satisfaction, three commonly used usability metrics [18].

We hypothesized that: (1) There would be age-related differences in performance; (2) There would be a linear age-related difference such that middle-age adults would not differ in performance compared to younger and older adults; (3) Older adults with higher cognitive function would perform similar to younger adults, and older adults with lower cognitive function would perform worse than younger adults and their higher-functioning counterparts; (4) Older adults with lower cognitive function would report lower satisfaction with the Website.

2 Method

2.1 Participants

Twenty-one younger adults (6 males, 15 females), 19 middle-age adults (9 males, 10 females) and 21 older adults (9 males, 12 females) participated in the study. Participants were residents of the metropolitan Washington DC area and were recruited via advertisements in local newspapers or through a database that is maintained by the US Census Bureau's Human Factors and Usability Research Group. Participants were given a $40 honorarium. They completed a questionnaire about their computer use and Internet experience and completed tasks that measured processing speed and vocabulary. All participants reported being experienced with computers and the Internet but unfamiliar with the Website used in this study. There was no age-related difference in reported difficulty in using the Internet, but older adults reported greater difficulty in learning to use new Websites, compared to younger and middle-age adults. See Table 1 for participants' self-reported demographics and cognition scores.

Table 1. Mean (and range) demographics and cognition scores by age group

	Age group			Significance
	Younger	Middle-age	Older	
N	21	19	21	
Gender	15 F / 6 M	10 F / 9 M	12 F / 9 M	
Age	23 (18–28)	46 (40–51)	68 (65–76)	
	15 < BA/BS	11 < BA/BS	6 < BA/BS	
	3 BA/BS	8 BA/BS	4 BA/BS	
Education	3 > BA/BS	0 > BA/BS	11 > BA/BS	
Difficulty in learning to use new Websites[a]	1.5 (1–3)	1.4 (1–3)	2.3 (1–5)	$F(2,53) = 6.08$, $p < .01$
Difficulty in using the Internet[a]	1.1 (1–2)	1.2 (1–3)	1.4 (1–3)	$F(2,53) = 2.93$, $p = .06$
Backward counting (Processing speed)	51 (34–75)	57 (30–81)	66 (43–84)	$F(2,58) = 9.39$, $p < .001$
Digit Symbol Coding (Processing speed)[b]	79 (48–116)	73 (48–109)	55 (24–91)	$F(2,55) = 10.86$, $p = .0001$
Vocabulary (Verbal ability)[c]	31 (22–38)	30 (15– 40)	32 (22–40)	$F(2,58) = 0.86$, $p = .43$

[a] Scale: 1 (Not difficult at all) – 5 (Extremely difficult)

[b] WAIS-III, Wechsler Adult Intelligence Scale, 3rd Edition

[c] Shipley Institute of Living Scale (Shipley, 1986)

2.2   Procedure

Participants came to the Human Factors and Usability Research Group's laboratory at the US Census Bureau headquarters to participate in the study. Each participant sat individually in a 10′ × 12′ room, facing one-way glass and a wall camera.

The test administrator (TA) explained the study, and the participant read and signed a consent form. Participants completed a backward counting task, the WAIS Digit Symbol Coding task [19] and the Shipley Vocabulary test [20], each of which are detailed below. The TA left the room—the participant and the TA sat in separate rooms during the remainder of the session and communicated via microphones and speakers. The TA began video recording from the opposite side of the one-way glass.

Participants worked on five pre-determined information-seeking tasks on the American FaceFinder (AFF)[1] Website. AFF is the Census Bureau's primary data dissemination Website about the population, housing, and economy of the United States (see Fig. 1). Participants completed typical tasks for general users of the

---

[1] In 2012, a new American FactFinder (AFF) was released. The present study was conducted on the earlier AFF site, which is no longer available online and is referred to as the "legacy" version.

Website, and all completed tasks in the order of easiest to hardest to accomplish (determined by the complexity and number of steps needed to find the information). The first two tasks we categorized as easy; they required 2 and 3 steps, respectively, and the final three tasks we categorized as hard; they required 4, 4, and 6 steps, respectively. (For a list of tasks, see [21]. Participants read each task aloud then used the Website to locate the information (while working silently), and they stated their answer aloud when they felt they had found the correct answer. After the participant completed each task, the TA loaded the main page of the site, and the participant proceeded with the next task. At the conclusion of the study, participants completed a final satisfaction questionnaire and answered debriefing questions from the TA.

Fig. 1. AFF Website home page

Most participants attempted to complete all five tasks. After 7 min working on the task, the TA asked the participant if they felt they were close or far from the answer and if they wanted to move on. If the participant wanted to move on, the task ended, the TA loaded the main page, and the participant began the next task. These tasks, as well as tasks participants gave up on without the TA prompt, were classified as passes, and when calculating the accuracy, they were scored as 0. Seven percent of the tasks for younger adults, 18 % of the tasks for middle-age adults and 31 % of the tasks for older adults were passes.

2.3 Usability Metrics

We assessed accuracy, efficiency, and satisfaction. For our dependent measures, accuracy was calculated as the percent of users who successfully completed the task, efficiency was calculated as the time it took participants to complete each successfully completed task, and satisfaction was calculated as the participants' ratings for the 11 items on the satisfaction questionnaire (ratings of 1:low – 9:high). We then averaged the accuracy, efficiency and satisfaction scores across tasks for each participant (for accuracy and efficiency) and across participants in each age group (for accuracy, efficiency and satisfaction). We examined the relationship among age, cognition and Website performance (usability metrics).

2.4   Cognitive Metrics

We assessed processing speed with two tasks: a backward counting task and the Digit Symbol Coding task [19]. For the backward counting task, participants were given 30 s to count backward from 100, by ones, as quickly as possible. The score is the number that participants get to (i.e., lower number = higher score). For the Digit Symbol Coding task, participants were given a sheet of paper with seven lines of 20 number-box combinations (the first seven were practice trials). At the top of the paper, there was a key in which the numbers 1–9 were paired with a unique abstract symbol. Participants were required to fill in the boxes with the corresponding symbols, in order, as fast as they can, for two minutes. The score is the total number of correctly filled-in boxes.

We assessed verbal ability (i.e., vocabulary) with the Shipley's Institute of Living Scale [20]. The test was administered on paper and featured 40 items in which the first word was printed in capital letters, and four words were opposite it. Participants were instructed to circle the one word (of the four) "that means the same thing, or most nearly the same thing, as the first word," and an example was provided. The score is the sum of correctly identified words.

3   Results

We asked the following research questions:

1. Are there age-related differences in performance (accuracy, efficiency, satisfaction)?
2. Do middle-age adults differ in performance compared to younger and older adults?
3. Do older adults with higher cognitive function perform differently than older adults with lower cognitive function?
4. Do older adults with higher cognitive function perform similar to younger adults on the performance metrics?
5. Do older adults with lower cognitive abilities report lower satisfaction than older adults with higher cognitive abilities?

First we examined accuracy, efficiency and satisfaction across age groups, overall. We conducted one-way ANOVAs comparing age group and found an age-related difference for accuracy, $F(2,58) = 2.95$, $p = .06$. Planned two-tailed t-tests confirmed no difference in accuracy between middle-age and older adults ($p = 0.28$) and no difference between middle-age and younger adults ($p = 0.24$). However, there was a significant difference between younger and older adults ($p = 0.01$) such that younger adults had higher accuracy than older adults. For efficiency and satisfaction, there were no age-related differences ($p = 0.36$ and $p = 0.26$, respectively). See Table 2.

Table 2. Mean (and range) performance by age group

	Age group			Significance
	Younger	Middle-age	Older	
Accuracy	62% (20%–100%)	51% (0–100%)	41% (0–93%)	$F(2,58) = 2.95, p = .06$
Efficiency in seconds (successes only)	160 (60–325)	169 (59–391)	238 (47–915)	$F(2,54) = 1.03, p = .36$
Satisfaction	6.34 (3.75–8.45)	6.72 (3.00–8.64)	5.87 (2.82–8.70)	$F(2,58) = 1.38, p = .26$

Next we examined each cognitive measure and whether varying levels of cognitive function impact performance. For each cognitive measure, we split the data into three parts: upper, middle, and lower thirds. We then compared the "high-functioning" older adults, the "low-functioning" older adults and the younger adults.

Processing Speed. First we examined the ***backward counting task***. Seven older adults were classified as high-functioning (HF), with scores between 43 and 60 ($\bar{x} = 53$), and seven were classified as low-functioning (LF), with scores between 72 and 84 ($\bar{x} = 76$). Younger adults' scores were between 34 and 75 ($\bar{x} = 51$). A one-way ANOVA revealed a significant group difference, $F(2,32) = 20.39$, $p < 0.0001$. Tukey HSD post hoc test revealed a significant difference between HF and LF older adults ($p < 0.01$), a significant difference between LF older adults and younger adults ($p < 0.01$), and no significant difference between HF older adults and younger adults.

We compared accuracy by age group and found a significant difference between HF older adults, LF older adults and younger adults, $F(2,32) = 3.58$, $p < 0.05$. However, Tukey HSD post hoc test revealed no significant difference in accuracy between HF and LF older adults, between HF older adults ($\bar{x} = 50$ %) and younger adults ($\bar{x} = 62$ %), and between LF older adults ($\bar{x} = 32$ %) and younger adults. Thus, older adults with slower processing speed completed fewer tasks successfully compared to younger adults, and older adults with faster processing speed did not differ from younger adults. See Table 3.

We next compared efficiency and satisfaction by age group. For efficiency, we found no significant difference between HF older adults ($\bar{x} = 228$ s), LF older adults ($\bar{x} = 357$ s) and younger adults ($\bar{x} = 160$ s), $F(2,30) = 2.05$, $p = 0.15$. Similarly, for satisfaction, we found no significant difference between HF older adults ($\bar{x} = 5.79$), LF older adults ($\bar{x} = 5.34$) and younger adults ($\bar{x} = 6.34$), $F(2,32) = 1.34$, $p = 0.28$.

Next we examined the ***Digit Symbol Coding task***. Six older adults were classified as HF, with scores between 64 and 91 ($\bar{x} = 72$), and six were classified as LF, with scores

Table 3. Mean (and range) performance by age group: backward counting

	Age Group by Backward Counting Task			Significance
	Younger	HF Older	LF Older	
Accuracy	62%	50%	32%	$F(2,32) = 3.58, p < .05$
	(20%–100%)	(0–93%)	(0–60%)	
Efficiency	160	200	309	
	(60–325)	(47–351)	(72–915)	$F(2,30) = 2.05, p = .15$
Satisfaction	6.34	5.79	5.34	
	(3.75–8.45)	(2.82–8.27)	(2.91–7.00)	$F(2,32) = 1.34, p = .28$

between 24 and 38 ($\bar{x} = 34$). Younger adults' (N = 19) scores were between 48 and 116 ($\bar{x} = 79$). A one-way ANOVA revealed a significant group difference, $F(2,28) = 19.59$, $p < 0.0001$. Tukey HSD post hoc test revealed no difference between HF older adults and younger adults. However, there was a significant difference between LF older adults and younger adults ($p < 0.01$) and between HF and LF older adults ($p < 0.01$),

We next compared accuracy by age group and found a significant difference between HF older adults, LF older adults and younger adults, $F(2,30) = 5.08, p = 0.01$. Tukey HSD post hoc test revealed no significant difference in accuracy between HF older adults and younger adults and between LF older adults and younger adults. However, we found a significant difference between HF older adults and LF older adults ($p < 0.05$). Thus, for this measure, LF older adults completed fewer tasks successfully than HF older adults. See Table 4.

We next compared efficiency and satisfaction by age group. Consistent with the backward counting measure, we found no significant difference in efficiency between HF older adults, LF older adults, and younger adults, $F(2,28) = 1.63, p = 0.21$. Similarly, we found no significant difference in satisfaction between HF older adults, LF older adults and younger adults, $F(2,30) = 1.80, p = 0.18$.

Verbal Ability. Next we examined the **Shipley's Institute of Living Scale**. Seven older adults were classified as HF, with scores between 35 and 40 ($\bar{x} = 38$), and seven were

Table 4. Mean (and range) performance by age group: digit symbol coding

	Age Group by Digit Symbol Coding Task			Significance
	Younger	HF Older	LF Older	
Accuracy	62%	38%	28%	$F(2,32)=3.58, p<.05$
	(20%–100%)	(0–60%)	(0–73%)	
Efficiency	160	229	185	
	(60–325)	(47–339)	(90–351)	$F(2,28)=1.63, p=.21$
Satisfaction	6.34	5.06	6.39	
	(3.75–8.45)	(3.55–7.55)	(3.27–8.70)	$F(2,30)=1.80, p=.18$

classified as LF, with scores between 22 and 29 ($\bar{x} = 27$). Younger adults' scores were between 22 and 38 ($\bar{x} = 31$). A one-way ANOVA revealed a significant group difference, $F(2,32) = 16.55$, $p < 0.0001$. Tukey HSD post hoc test revealed a significant difference between HF and LF older adults ($p < 0.01$), a significant difference between HF older adults and younger adults ($p < 0.01$), and no significant difference between LF older adults and younger adults.

We next compared accuracy by age group and found a significant difference between HF older adults, LF older adults and younger adults, $F(2,32) = 3.57$, $p < 0.05$. However, Tukey HSD post hoc test revealed no significant difference in accuracy between HF and LF older adults, between HF older adults and younger adults, and between LF older adults and younger adults. See Table 5.

We next compared efficiency and satisfaction by age group. As with the processing speed measures, we found no significant difference in efficiency between HF older adults, LF older adults and younger adults, $F(2,30) = 0.78$, $p = 0.47$. For satisfaction however, we found a significant difference among the groups, $F(2,32) = 4.53$, $p < 0.05$. Tukey HSD post hoc test revealed a significant difference in satisfaction between HF and LF older adults ($p < 0.01$), and no significant difference between HF older adults and younger adults, and no significant difference between LF older adults and younger adults. Thus, older adults with higher vocabulary reported lower satisfaction than their lower vocabulary counterparts.

Table 5. Mean (and Range) Performance by Age Group: Vocabulary

	Age Group by Vocabulary Task			Significance
	Younger	HF Older	LF Older	
Accuracy	62%	44%	34%	
	(20%–100%)	(0–73%)	(0–73%)	$F (2,32) = 3.57, p < .05$
Efficiency	160	168	209	
	(60–325)	(47–339)	(90–439)	$F (2,30) = 0.78, p = .47$
Satisfaction	6.34	4.81	7.06	
	(3.75–8.45)	(2.91–6.91)	(3.18–8.70)	$F (2,32) = 4.53, p < .05$

4 Conclusion

In this empirical study, we observed age-related differences in Website performance. Consistent with other research [e.g., 22, 23 (study 3), 24] and with our first hypothesis, older adults had lower accuracy than younger and middle-age adults. Further, middle-age adults' performance did not differ from either younger adults or older adults, but older and younger adults differed. This may suggest an age-related linear decline that is consistent with previous literature on age-related decline in cognition, in general [11, 25] and is in-line with our second hypothesis. However, the difference may also be due to strategy and experience differences [24], as middle-age adults often have a wider range of both compared to younger and older adults – the "extreme" groups. We found this difference only for the accuracy measure and not for the efficiency and satisfaction measures.

When we split our older adults into "high-functioning" and "low functioning" based on the backward counting task performance (processing speed), we found an age-related difference. However, our post hoc analysis did not reveal significant differences among the groups, even though there was a trend for older adults with slower processing speed to complete fewer tasks successfully compared to younger adults (32 % and 62 % respectively), and for older adults with faster processing speed (50 %) to not differ from younger adults. We found a similar pattern for the Shipley's Vocabulary test: There was an overall age-related difference and a trend for older adults with lower vocabulary to complete fewer tasks successfully compared to younger adults, and older adults with high vocabulary to not differ from younger adults. We believe we did not find significance in the post hoc tests because we did not have sufficient power; the older adult groups were drastically reduced in size when we split them into three (high, middle, lower ability). For the Digit Symbol Coding task (processing speed), we also found a significant age-related difference. For this task, post hoc analysis revealed a significant difference between high-functioning and low-functioning older adults only, such that low-functioning older adults completed fewer tasks successfully than their high-functioning counterparts.

These findings suggest that cognitive abilities may play a role in older adults' ability to successfully complete tasks (our third hypothesis), consistent with research on technology use more generally [17]. Here, higher cognitive abilities appeared to mediate differences that are typically apparent with aging users. We did not find these differences in efficiency. For satisfaction, in contrast with our fourth hypothesis, we found that older adults with higher vocabulary reported lower satisfaction with the Website compared to their lower vocabulary counterparts. We speculate that HF adults may have higher expectations for the Website, and it may not have met their expectations whereas LF adults may have lower expectations for the Website and hence may be more satisfied with the site, as it may have exceeded their expectations. In addition, we speculate that LF adults may have a tendency to blame themselves rather than the Website for any issues they may have encountered with the site (based on anecdotal evidence from the lab). Future work should seek to understand what participants specifically consider when rating satisfaction and why this might differ by cognitive ability.

In this study, we assessed the mean performance across all tasks. However, previous research shows that older adults have greater difficulties with more difficult tasks, compared to younger adults [21, 26, 27]. Future research should couple cognitive measures with task difficulty to understand the multitude of factors that lead to successful user experiences for older users as well as other users with either reduced cognitive capabilities or limited Internet experience.

This study is the first to demonstrate that cognitive ability may play a role in older adults' ability to complete tasks successfully. User experience researchers should include such measures to understand participants' cognition and ensure that people with varying levels of processing speed and vocabulary are included in research. Otherwise, the assumptions we make about the usability of a product may be invalid.

In conclusion, the key findings from this study are that (a) a Website designed for a broad population of users posed problems for people of all ages, and participants could not always find what they were searching for; (b) the difficulties were more pronounced for older adults with lower levels of processing speed and verbal abilities. The design implications are clear – user experience testing must include users of all ages and the use of the site should not impose demands on processing speed and verbal ability.

References

1. O'Connell, T.A.: The why and how of senior-focused design. In: Lazar, J. (ed.) Universal Usability: Designing Computer Interfaces for Diverse Users, pp. 43–92. Wiley, West Sussex (2007)
2. Pew Internet & American Life Project (2009). http://pewinternet.org/Reports/2010/Generations-2010.aspx
3. US Census Bureau: Computer and Internet Use in the United States: 2003 (2005). http://www.census.gov/hhes/computer/publications/2003.html
4. US Census Bureau: Reported Internet Usage for Households, by Selected Householder Characteristics: 2009. Source: Current Population Survey, US Census Bureau (2010)
5. US Census Bureau: Computer and Internet Use in the United States: 2010 (2010). http://www.census.gov/population/www/socdemo/computer.html
6. Ball, K.K., Beard, B.L., Roenker, D.L., Miller, R.L., Griggs, D.S.: Age and visual search: expanding the useful field of view. J. Opt. Soc. Am. 5, 2210–2219 (1988)
7. Birren, J.E., Shaie, K.W.: Handbook of the Psychology of Aging. Elsevier, Burlington (2006)
8. Craik, F.I.M., Salthouse, T.A.: The Handbook of Aging and Cognition. Lawrence Erlbaum Associates, Mahwah (2000)
9. Fisk, A.D., Rogers, W.A.: Handbook of Human Factors and the Older Adult. Academic Press, San Diego (1997)
10. Fisk, A.D., Rogers, W.A., Charness, N., Czaja, S.J., Sharit, J.: Designing for Older Adults: Principles and Creative Human Factors Approaches, 2nd edn. CRC Press, Boca Raton (2009)
11. Park, D., Schwarz, N.: Cognitive Aging: A Primer, 2nd edn. Psychology Press, Philadelphia (2008)
12. Loos, E., Romano Bergstrom, J.C.: Older adults. In: Romano Bergstrom, J., Schall, A. (eds.) Eye Tracking in User Experience Design. Morgan Kaufmann, San Francisco (2014)
13. Pernice, K., Nielsen, J.: Web Usability for Senior Citizens. Design Guidelines Based on Usability Studies with People Age 65 and Older. Nielsen Norman Group, Fremont (2002)
14. Rogers, W.A., Badre, A.: The Web user: Older adults. In: Badre, A. (ed.) Shaping Web Usability: Interaction Design in Context, pp. 91–108. Addison-Wesley, Boston (2002)
15. Van Deursen, A., Van Dijk, J.: Measuring digital skills. Performance tests of operational, formal, information and strategic internet skills among the Dutch population. Presented at the ICA Conference, Montreal, Canada (2008)
16. Nichols, T.A., Rogers, W.A., Fisk, A.D.: Do you know how old your participants are? recognizing the importance of participant age classifications. Ergon. Des. 11, 22–26 (2003)

17. Czaja, S.J., Charness, N., Fisk, A.D., Hertzog, C., Nair, S.N., Rogers, W.A., Sharit, J.: Factors predicting the use of technology: findings from the Center for Research and Education on Aging and Technology Enhancement (CREATE). Psychol. Aging **21**, 333–352 (2006)
18. Frøkjaer, E., Herzum, M., Hornbaek, K.: Measuring usability: are effectiveness, efficiency, and satisfaction correlated? In: Proceedings of the SIGCHI Conference on Human Factors in Computing Systems, The Haag (2000)
19. Wechsler, D.: Wechsler Adult Intelligence Scale: (WAIS-III), 3rd edn. The Psychological Corporation, New York (1997)
20. Shipley, W.: Shipley Institute of Living Scale. Western Psychological Press, Los Angeles (1986)
21. Olmsted-Hawala, E., Romano Bergstrom, J.: Think-aloud protocols: does age make a difference? In: Proceedings of Society for Technical Communication (STC) Summit, Chicago, IL, May 2012
22. Grahame, M., Laberge, J., Sciafla, C.T.: Age differences in search of Web pages: The effects of link size, link number, and clutter. Hum. Factors J. Hum. Factors Ergon. Soc. **46**(3), 385–398 (2004)
23. Romano Bergstrom, J., Olmsted-Hawala, E., Jans, M.: Eye tracking and website usability in older adults: age-related differences in eye tracking and usability performance: website usability for older adults. Int. J. Hum.-Comput. Interact. **29**(8), 541–548 (2013)
24. Stronge, A.J., Rogers, W.A., Fisk, A.D.: Web-based information search and retrieval effects of strategy use and age on search success. Hum. Factors **48**, 443–446 (2006)
25. Salthouse, T.: When does age-related cognitive decline begin? Neurobiol. Aging **30**(4), 507–514 (2009)
26. Olmsted-Hawala, E., Romano Bergstrom, J.C., Rogers, W.A.: Age-related differences in search strategy and performance when using a data-rich web site. In: Stephanidis, C., Antona, M. (eds.) UAHCI 2013, Part II. LNCS, vol. 8010, pp. 201–210. Springer, Heidelberg (2013)
27. Olmsted-Hawala, E., Holland, T.: Age related differences when using smartphones for Census enumeration. In: Zhou, J., Salvendy, G. (eds.) HCII 2015. LNCS, vol. 9193, pp. 475–483. Springer, Heidelberg (2015)

Validation of the Computer Literacy Scale (CLS)

Michael Sengpiel[✉] and Nicole Jochems

Institut für Multimediale und Interaktive Systeme, Universität zu Lübeck,
23562 Lübeck, Germany
{sengpiel,jochems}@imis.uni-luebeck.de

Abstract. Successful use of ICT requires domain knowledge and interaction knowledge. It shapes and is shaped by the use of ICT and is less common among older adults. This paper focus on the validation of the computer literacy scale (CLS) introduced by [14]. The CLS is an objective knowledge test of ICT-related symbols and terms commonly used in the graphical user interface of interactive computer technology. It has been designed specifically for older adults with little computer knowledge and is based on the idea that knowing common symbols and terms is as necessary for using computers, as it is for reading and writing letters and books. In this paper the Computer literacy scale is described and compared with related measures for example computer expertise (CE), Computer Proficiency (CPQ) and computer anxiety (CATS). In addition criterion validity is described with predictions of successful ICT use exemplified with (1) the use of different data entry methods and (2) the use of different ticket vending machine (TVM) designs.

Keywords: Computer literacy · Computer experience · Computer proficiency · Measurement · Questionnaire · Validation

1 Introduction

Successful use of ICT requires domain knowledge and interaction knowledge. The basic interaction knowledge required for successful use of computers can be called "computer literacy". It shapes and is shaped by the use of ICT and is less common among older adults.

This paper describes the validation of the computer literacy scale (CLS) introduced by [14], following five steps. First, the CLS and related measures computer expertise (CE), Computer Proficiency (CPQ), control beliefs regarding technology use (KUT), attitude toward technology (ATT) and computer anxiety (CATS) are briefly described. Second, convergent and discriminant validity is described using correlations and a principal component analysis (PCA). Third, criterion validity is described with predictions of successful ICT use exemplified with (1) the use of different data entry methods and (2) the use of different ticket vending machine (TVM) designs. Fourth, since CLS is work in progress, the current developmental status and an outlook on upcoming procedural knowledge items and an adaptive CLS are provided. Finally, readers are encouraged to use the CLS in their own research involving human computer interaction and to contribute to the continuous validation and improvement of the CLS.

© Springer International Publishing Switzerland 2015
J. Zhou and G. Salvendy (Eds.): ITAP 2015, Part I, LNCS 9193, pp. 365–375, 2015.
DOI: 10.1007/978-3-319-20892-3_36

2   Method

This paper reports results of validation studies that used CLS and other measures of computer related user characteristics to predict successful use of diverse ICT applications for young and old age groups in two independent applications, namely the use of ticket vending machines (TVM, N = 124, [13]) and different data entry methods (mouse, touch screen, eye gaze [9]) and navigation in complex information spaces (N = 90, [8]). Convergent and discriminant validity of CLS will be reported along with psychometric properties and correlations with user characteristics such as computer expertise (CE), Computer Proficiency (CPQ), control beliefs regarding technology use (KUT), attitude toward technology (ATT) and computer anxiety (CATS).

2.1   The Computer Literacy Scale (CLS)

The CLS is an objective knowledge test of ICT-related symbols and terms commonly used in the graphical user interface of interactive computer technology. It has been designed specifically for older adults with little computer knowledge and is based on the idea that knowing common symbols and terms is as necessary for using computers, as it is for reading and writing letters and books.

The CLS focuses on a small but essential aspect of computer literacy and uses it as indicator for the broader construct: "If literacy can be considered the ability to read symbols and use them, then computer literacy could be considered the ability to understand and use computer related symbols, functional elements and interaction patterns" ([14], p. 8). These basic building blocks of computer literacy are tested in an objective knowledge test with 26 items (21 symbols and 5 terms) in a matching task, taking about 15 min to complete, depending on literacy level. The CLS can be downloaded for free as printable pdf. It is available in English, German and Spanish. Figure 1 shows sample items in the matching task.

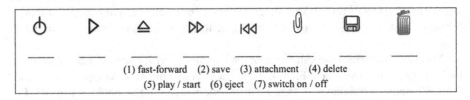

(1) fast-forward   (2) save   (3) attachment   (4) delete
(5) play / start   (6) eject   (7) switch on / off

Fig. 1. Sample items in the matching task of the CLS

2.2   The Computer Expertise Questionnaire (CE)

Based on the INCOBI computer expertise inventory by [11, 1] introduced the computer expertise (CE) questionnaire with 18 items assessing theoretical (9 items) and practical (9 items) computer knowledge by describing typical tasks or problems that occur using computers and asking participants to mark the optimal course of action in a multiple choice task with 4 alternatives [1].

2.3 The "Computer Proficiency Questionnaire" (CPQ)

Later, [2] developed the "Computer Proficiency Questionnaire" (CPQ) to assess the computer proficiency of seniors (from non-users to frequent computer and Internet users), arguing that the CE by [1] had been developed with data from older adults who had substantial computer experience and that the CLS by [14] had been designed for older adults, but focused largely on declarative knowledge rather than the ability to perform computer tasks. The CPQ consists of 33 items (there is also a short form with 12 items) that ask the respondent whether she can use technology divided in six categories: computer basics, printer, communication, Internet, calendar and entertainment. Thus, the CPQ is not a knowledge test but a self report measure.

2.4 Control Beliefs for Interaction with Technology (KUT)

The KUT (German akronym for "control beliefs for interaction with technology") was developed 1999 by [3] to extend the scope of observed user characteristics with a personality construct that guides user actions. Participants indicated on a Likert scale of 0 (not true at all) to 4 (absolutely true) their control beliefs regarding technology use, resulting in a maximum total score of $(8 \times 4 =)$ 32. A complete list of translated items, including polarity, mean, variance and discriminatory power can be found in [12].

2.5 Attitude Towards Technology (ATT)

Attitude determines motivation to use technology and thus will have a direct influence on successful use and an indirect influence through better experience and practice [6, 15]. Attitude towards ticket vending machines was measured using an eight item seven point semantic differential created for this study.

2.6 "Computer Anxiety Trait Scale" (CATS)

Computer anxiety and computer knowledge often show a strong negative correlation (e.g. [10], $r = -.83$, $p < .01$, $N = 222$). Anxiety towards ticket vending machines was measured using an adaptation of the "Computer Anxiety Trait Scale" (CATS) by [7], asking the participants to imagine being at the train station wanting to use a TVM and to rate their approval to 16 statements (e.g. "I sweat", "My heart beats faster") regarding this situation on a five-point Likert scale ranging from "not at all" to "absolutely".

3 Results

Unless marked otherwise, results regarding TVM use are from a study described by [13] $(N = 124)$ and those regarding different data entry methods (mouse, touch screen, eye gaze) and navigation in complex information spaces from a study described by [8] $(N = 90)$.

3.1 Reliability

When the CLS was introduced [14], the quality of the computer literacy scale was assessed with internal consistency, discrimination power and item difficulty measures. Internal consistency was high with a Cronbach's alpha between .93 and .96, indicating high homogeneity, with discrimination power ranging from r = .22 to r = .84. Item difficulty was low for the young group, but reasonably broad for the old group, ranging from P = .13 to .87. Kolmogorov-Smirnov-Tests revealed, that the CLS scores were normally distributed for the old group (D(39) = 0.10; p > .10) but not for the young group (D(81) = 0.12; p < .01), for whom most items were too easy. Table 1 shows reliability (Cronbach's alpha) and number of items for the scales CLS, KUT, ATT, CATS, CE and CPQ, indicating high reliability of the measures investigated.

3.2 Face Validity

Face validity of the CLS can be considered high, because the test directly asks for the meaning of terms and symbols associated with ICT use. Test participants did not doubt that knowing these would be relevant for successful ICT interaction. As with any objective knowledge test, there is little impact of personality traits when compared to subjective self report measures, which is generally perceived as an advantage.

Table 1. Scale reliability and number of items for the scales CLS, CE, CPQ, KUT, ATT and CATS.

Scale	CLS	CE	CPQ*	KUT	ATT	CATS
Cronbach's Alpha	.93		.98	.88	.90	.91
Number of items	26		33	8	8	16

* Data based on Boot et al. (2013)

3.3 Construct Validity

3.3.1 Computer Experience and Expertise (Convergent Validity)

Computer experience is necessary but not sufficient for high computer literacy. To capture different aspects of computer experience, it was operationalized using three measures added on the first page of the CLS: duration (measured in years), intensity (measured in hours per week) and diversity (measured in frequency of use for different computer applications).

In [14] older adults reported a mean duration of 7 years using computers and a mean intensity of 3 h per week, while younger adults reported to have used computers for a mean duration of 10 years, which was not significantly longer than the older group, and to spend an average of 27 h per week using computers, which was significantly more than the older group (t(18.49) = −7.06, p < .01, r = .85). For diversity of computer use, the older group scored $M = 4.14$ points while the younger group scored $M = 14.69$ points (max = 21), constituting again a significant difference t(28) = −6.70, p < .01, r = 0,78). As expected, computer experience and computer literacy were highly correlated. See Table 2 for an overview. In order to assess the unique contribution of computer literacy and computer experience on TVM-performance, a partial correlation analysis was conducted. The best predictor of performance was computer literacy R^2 = .37), followed by diversity of computer experience (R^2 = .25).

Table 2. Computer experience measured in duration, intensity and diversity in the older and younger participant group and their correlation with the CLS score.

Computer experience	Duration	Intensity	Diversity
Old group	7 years	3 h/week**	4.14**
Young group	10 years	27 h/week	14.69
Correlation with CLS	τ = .47*	τ = .51*	τ = .53*

Note: *p < .05, **p < .01

As another measure of convergent validity, the relationship of the CLS and the computer expertise questionnaire (CE, [1]) was investigated. A total of n = 90 adults (M = 47.5 years, SD = 16.8, 36 female, 54 male) participated in a study conducted and described in detail by [8]. Results show moderate correlations between CLS and CE (τ = .62, p < .01), indicating that they measure related constructs, even though they do so in very different ways.

In another study [8], a paper folding and a cube rotation test were administered additionally to measure mental rotation ability, which is considered relevant to navigate virtual spaces. Correlations of these measures can be seen in Table 5, indicating strong relations between them and even stronger relations between CLS and CE (Table 3).

Table 3. Correlations for the scales CLS, CE, paper folding and the cube rotation test

Scale	CLS	CE	Paper folding	Cube rotation test
age group	−.63**	−.69**	−.65**	−.55**
CLS		.77**	.63**	.48**
CE			.61**	.53**
Paper folding				.65**

**Correlation is significant at the 0.01 level

Table 4. Pearson correlations for usability measures and user characteristics in the control, videoand wizard conditions

Usability Measure	TVM	N	Age	CLS	KUT	ATT	CATS
Effectiveness	original	32	−.54**	.61***	.21	.48**	−.49**
	video	35	−.49**	.50**	.30*	.41**	−.20
	wizard	35	.05	.05	−.08	−.09	.09
Efficiency (time)	original	32	−.69***	.67***	.41*	.43**	−.46**
	video	35	−.78***	.70***	.35*	.52**	−.35*
	wizard	35	−.66***	.63***	.47**	.44**	−.45**
Efficiency (steps)	original	32	−.56***	.60***	.25	.50**	−.51**
	video	35	−.42**	.36*	.12	.29*	−.05
	wizard	35	−.01	.04	.05	.00	.07
Satisfaction	original	32	−.26	.49	.43**	.49**	−.47**
	video	35	−.27	−.01	.12	.15	−.26
	wizard	35	.15	.21	.29*	.15	−.36*

Correlation is significant at the ***0.001 / **0.01 / *0.05 level

3.3.2 Discriminant Validity

It was expected that besides computer literacy (CLS), interaction with computers would also be related to other user characteristics such as control beliefs regarding the use of technology (KUT), attitude toward technology (ATT) and computer anxiety (CATS). As Table 4 shows, these user characteristics were indeed highly correlated with Pearson correlations between .46** and −.73**.

To test whether the 58 items taken from these ICT use related scales actually measured distinct traits, a principal component analysis (PCA) with varimax rotation (with Kaiser normalization procedure) was conducted (total sample N = 124). The Kaiser-Meyer-Olkin measure confirmed sampling adequacy for the analysis with KMO = .82 and Bartlett's test of sphericity $\chi^2(1653) = 4643.59$, p < .001, indicated that correlations between items were sufficiently large for PCA. Four factors that explained 48.6 % of variance in all items were extracted. The rotated factor matrix in table A1 (appendix) shows that all items loaded on the appropriate latent constructs (indicated by bold values), confirming the factorial validity of the different scales.

Table 5. Pearson correlations (above the diagonal) and significance values (below the diagonal)for usability measures (N = 124, except for satisfaction N = 118) and user characteristics (N = 102,except for satisfaction N = 98)

	effect	e(time)	e(steps)	satisf	age	CLS	KUT	ATT	CATS
effectiveness	1	.56**	.75**	.43**	-.34**	.36**	.11	.24**	-.20*
eff (time)		1	.74**	.20*	-.62**	.63**	.38**	.44**	-.44**
eff (steps)			1	.26**	-.32**	.38**	.17*	.32**	-.30**
satisfaction		.028	.005	1	-.13	.23*	.27**	.26**	-.33**
age			.001	.099	1	-.76**	-.35**	-.54**	.43**
CLS				.012		1	.46**	.51**	-.51**
KUT	.138		.044	.004			1	.52**	-.53**
ATT	.007		.001	.005				1	-.73**
CATS	.024		.001	.001					1

Correlation is significant at the **0.01 / *0.05 level
To improve legibility, all fields with values of .000 have been left blank

3.4 Criterion Validity

A central question regarding the validity of the CLS is: How well does it predict actual success in ICT use? Success in TVM use was operationalized according to the usability criteria [5] effectiveness (in solving 11 tasks using the TVM to select tickets), efficiency (measured in the time and the steps needed to solve the tasks) and satisfaction (measured as the mean score of 13 items based on the Questionnaire for User Interface Satisfaction (QUIS) by [4]). ICT use was operationalized using three different TVM designs: (1) a simulation of the original TVM as used by the Berlin Public Transport System (2) the same TVM with a brief (2:37 min) instructional video before use and (3) a wizard redesign of the TVM that maintained the same functionality but was designed to require less computer literacy to be universally usable (see [13]) for details).

To estimate the impact of the user characteristics on usability measures in the original TVM, video and wizard conditions, first separate Pearson correlations are reported (see Table 4).

Using the original TVM, age was strongly related to effectiveness and efficiency but not to satisfaction. The same is true for the video condition, showing very similar if a little weaker negative correlations. The wizard redesign however shows no significant correlations between age and effectiveness, efficiency (steps) or satisfaction, indicating successful inclusive design - only the correlation to efficiency (time) persists. Interestingly, this pattern is largely replicated with the other user characteristics. Table 5 shows correlations between usability measures and user characteristics over all TVM designs, indicating that CLS has the strongest correlations with all usability measures.

Finally, a hierachical multiple regression with blockwise entry of (1) age (2) CLS and (3) KUT, ATT, CATS was conducted to estimate the degree to which these user characteristics predict effectiveness, efficiency and satisfaction, of which only effectiveness shall be reported here. As results presented in Table 6 show, age was a strong predictor of effective use of the original TVM with a $\beta = -.54**$. Yet if the CLS score was entered into the regression model, the impact of age was reduced to a non-significant $\beta = -.17$ and CLS was the best predictor (with $\beta = .48^m$). CLS remained the best predictor after KUT, ATT and CATS had been added in a third step. For the video and the wizard condition, the impact of these user characteristics was reduced, indicating that the design changes lowered some barriers to successful TVM use. Thus especially the wizard came close to the goal of universal usability. See Table 6 for an overview of the results of the hierarchical regression.

In another study [8] CLS and CE were administered before participants used a project planning software with four different layouts (control layout, Overview window, detail window and zoom function). In Table 7 the correlations between CLS, CE and the number of mistakes are presented. Table 8 described the correlations between CLS, CE and total execution time, participants needed to solve the tasks with the help of the different layouts. As you can see in Table 7, both, CLS and CE predict the number of mistakes. Regarding the execution time interesting results could be found (Table 8). In this case, only the CLS scale predicts total execution time.

4 Discussion

It is argued that ultimately, computer literacy could have an impact on any ICT-interaction and thus it should be measured as control variable in any study using ICT.

Table 6. Effects of age, CLS, KUT, ATT and CATS on effectiveness for original TVM, video andwizard re-design

Block	Condition model R^2	TVM, N=32 .481		Video, N=35 .332		Wizard, N=35 .043	
		β	sr^2	β	sr^2	β	sr^2
1	ΔR^2	.295**		.236**		.002	
	age	−.54**	.29	−.49**	.24	.05	<.01
2	ΔR^2	.088^m		.037		.015	
	age	−.17	.01	−.25	.02	.18	.01
	CLS	.48^m	.09	.31	.04	.18	.01
3	ΔR^2	.098		.059		.026	
	age	−.17	.01	−.18	.01	.23	.02
	CLS	.37	.04	.30	.04	.35	.03
	KUT	−.14	.01	.15	.02	−.15	.01
	ATT	.20	.02	.26	.02	.11	<.01
	CATS	−.20	.02	.30	.04	.15	.01

Note: ***p<.001, **p<.01, *p<.05, ^{m}p<.10

The CLS has shown to be a reliable and valid measure of computer literacy. It can be used to assess the computer literacy of a person as well as the computer literacy requirements of a user interface design.

Since symbols and terms used in human computer interaction change quickly, it remains a constant challenge to update and improve the CLS. From the beginning of the CLS development it was a central goal to improve computer literacy assessment with an objective knowledge test rather than subjective self report measure. With the ongoing development of the CLS, the test of declarative knowledge described above has been extended with a procedural knowledge test, in which users are asked to complete tasks online that require computer literacy [16]. Figure 2 shows screenshots of two of these tasks, booking a flight (left) and mixing colors (right).

Table 7. Correlations for the scales CLS and CE with the number of mistakes in the four investigated layouts.

Number of mistakes in	Control layout	Overview window	Detail window	Zoom function
Computer Expertise	−.36**	−.43**	−.37**	−.28**
Computer Literacy	−.33**	−.34**	−.21	−.19

**Correlation is significant at the 0.01 level

Table 8. Correlations for the scales CLS and CE with the total execution time in the four investigated layouts.

Total execution time in	Control layout	Overview window	Detail window	Zoom function
Computer Expertise	−.02	.03	−.01	.01
Computer Literacy	−.61**	−.45**	−.48**	−.34**

**Correlation is significant at the 0.01 level

Currently, efforts are directed at making an adaptive CLS available online, which will reduce testing time to about 3 min, without compromising reliability or validity of the results. The item base has been extended to over 120 items that have been tested and selected for conformity to the RASCH model, providing a solid base for adaptive testing. Figure 3 shows screenshots with sample items from the current prototype of the adaptive CLS. The adaptive CLS will be available shortly at www.computer-literacy.net. We invite everyone to use it in their own studies and would appreciate any feedback regarding the CLS that helps us to continually improve it.

Fig. 2. Screenshots of two tasks for the extended CLS, designed to test procedural computer interaction knowledge. The task on the left is to book a flight, on the right colors are to be chosen to mix a paint.

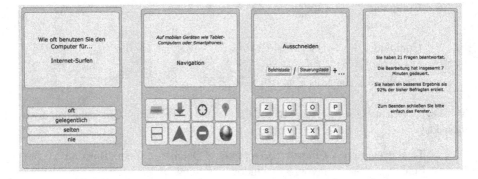

Fig. 3. Screenshots with sample items from the current prototype of the adaptive CLS

Acknowledgments. We thank all those involved in the development of the CLS, especially Diana Dittberner, Nadezda Arsenyeva, Susan Götzinger, Maria Spiering and Nico Zeissig.

References

1. Arning, K., Ziefle, M.: Development and validation of a computer expertise questionnaire for older adults. Behav. Inf. Technol. **27**(1), 89–93 (2008)
2. Boot, W.R., Charness, N., Czaja, S.J., Sharit, J., Rogers, W.A., Fisk, A.D., et al.: Computer Proficiency Questionnaire: Assessing Low and High Computer Proficient Seniors (2013). Gerontologist.Oxfordjournals.org
3. Beier, G.: Kontrollüberzeugung um Umgamg mit Technik. Rep. Psychol. **24**(9), 684–693 (1999)
4. Chin, J.P., Diehl, V.A., Norman, L.K.: Development of an Instrument Measuring User Satisfaction of the Human-Computer Interface. the sigchi conference, pp. 213–218. ACM Press, New York (1988)

5. DIN ISO: ISO 9241–2010:2010 – Ergonomics of human-computer interaction- Part 210: Human-centred design for interactive systems (2010). Iso.org
6. Fishbein, M., Ajzen, I.: Belief, Attitude, Intention, and Behaviour: An Introduction to Theory and Researcg. Addison-Wesley, Reading (1975)
7. Gaudron, J.-P., Vignoli, E.: Assessing computer anxiety with the interaction model of anxiety: development and validation of the computer anxiety trait subscale. Comput. Hum. Behav. **18**(3), 315–325 (2002)
8. Jochems, N.: Altersdifferenzierte Gestaltung der Mensch-Rechner-Interaktion am Beispiel von Projektmanagementaufgaben, In: Schlick, C. (Hrsg.) Schriftenreihe Industrial Engineering and Ergonomics, Dissertation RWTH Aachen. Shaker Verlag, Aachen (2010)
9. Jochems, N., Vetter, S., Schlick, C.: A comparative study of information input devices for aging computer users. Behav. Inf. Technol. **32**(9), 902–919 (2013)
10. Karavidas, M., Lim, N.K., Katsikas, S.L.: The effects of computers oon older adult users. Comput. Hum. Bahav. **21**, 697–711 (2005)
11. Richter, T., Naumann, J., Groeben, N.: Das Inventar zur Computerbildung (INCOBI): Ein Instrument zur Erfassung von Computer Literacy und computerbezogenen Einstellungen bei Studierenden der Geistes- und Sozialwissenschaften. [The computer literacy inventory: an instrument for the assessment of computer literacy and computer-related attitudes in students of humanities and social sciences]. Psychologie in Erziehung und Unterricht **48**, 1–13 (2001)
12. Sengpiel, M.: User characteristics and the effectiveness of inclusive design for older users of public access systems. Dissertation an der Humboldt-Universität zu Berlin (2015)
13. Sengpiel, M.: Teach or design? how older adults' use of ticket vending machines could be more effective. Trans. Accessible Comput. (in press)
14. Sengpiel, M., Dittberner, D.: The computer literacy scale (CLS) for older adults – development and validation. In: Herczeg, M., Kindsmüller, M.C. (eds.) Presented at Mensch & Computer 2008: Viel Mehr Interaktion, pp. 7–16. Oldenbourg Verlag, München (2008)
15. Wagner, N., Hassanein, K., Head, M.: Computer use by older adults: a multi-disciplinary review. Comput. Hum. Bahav. **26**(5), 870–882 (2010)
16. Zeissig, N.: Entwurf und Umsetzung einer webbasierten Diagnoseplattform zur Erhebung von deklarativem und prozeduralem Interaktionswissen. Unpublished mather's thesis, Humboldt-Universität zu Berlin (2009)

Age(ism) in Digital Information Provision: The Case of Online Public Services for Older Adults

Maria Sourbati[✉]

School of Art, Design and Media, College of Arts and Humanities,
University of Brighton, Brighton, UK
m.sourbati@brighton.ac.uk

Abstract. This paper draws on an empirical investigation of how older people are represented on the websites providing social care service information in the inner London Boroughs. My research questions follow the work of Loos [1, 2] on the relationship between representations of older age, information accessibility and access to digital services. Mirroring Loos and reflecting the specificities of the fieldwork my investigation found older people were largely invisible as a diverse group of citizens in the emerging cultures of digital public service. The images of older adults were few and lacked diversity. Inner London has an ethnically and culturally diverse population yet older adults were commonly represented though images of frail white women. The paper highlights representational politics of older age in digital public service information provision and their consequences for access and social inclusion; intra-generational diversity; ageism as a prevalent form of social discrimination.

Keywords: Age · Ageism · Access · Inclusion · Digital public service · Intragenerational diversity

1 Introduction

This paper draws on an empirical investigation of digital information provision in local government websites to discuss older age, diversity and inclusion in digital public service. Its broader context is the constant increase of ICT innovation, media use and ageing. As an ever increasing range of interpersonal, professional and civic communication activity is today digitally mediated, access to digital information services for a diverse population is essential to transact with government and market actors. In digital information services such as healthcare, mechanisms that control or facilitate our access to the media-technology interfaces (e.g., navigation systems, website design including the representation of their target users) have an impact on our access to services that support independent living, good life and life in the community etc. Media access and diversity are therefore gaining renewed currency. The 'digital turn' can be seen to increase the relevance of those legacy media policy values as well as the complexity and elusiveness that characterizes their implementation. The ageing turn, which is inscribed in the biological and social logic of ageing in our society [3, pp. 94, 102]

© Springer International Publishing Switzerland 2015
J. Zhou and G. Salvendy (Eds.): ITAP 2015, Part I, LNCS 9193, pp. 376–386, 2015.
DOI: 10.1007/978-3-319-20892-3_37

further accentuates them. This paper is a contribution to the policy discussion of digital media access for a diverse population of older people [1, 2, 4, 5] in our ageing and ageist societies.

The more specific context of the paper relates UK government's 'digital by default' strategy to deliver public service information online/digital only. According to the 2013 Government Digital Strategy [Executive Summary, 6] the UK public sector is now moving from multiple channels to delivery of public service information that is online/digital[1] only. Having committed to a target of digital by default public services by March 2015 [6] the strategy aimed to increase delivery of their services online by increasing the level of use of digital public services. According to government 'Digital by Default' wishes to encourage everyone who can use digital services independently to do so. For those who cannot use digital ICTs for themselves digital information provision will be implemented by assisted digital use, whereby individuals can access a service with help by proxy users. Government has declared assisted access ('assisted digital') will be the only 'non-digital' way to access services for the people who use government services but are not able to use digital services independently [6, 7]. Social health care information services are a core area of public service provision. The ideology of the government strategy of digital social policy can be summarized as 'fair access to services for those who are entitled to them.' [7]. Defined that way, 'fair' access is subject to availability of media-technological infrastructure, including internet connectivity, and digital information provision to a diversity of users. It will be determined by policy responses to understanding of who the users are, who can and who cannot use digital services – perceptions of accessibility, diversity, and information provision to a potential diversity of users.

The remainder of this paper discusses conceptualizations of older age in research and trends in internet use and the social demographics of the older adult population in the UK, and reports the findings of a study of older adults' representations in Local Authority social care service webpages. The final section discusses the findings and concludes the paper.

2 Media Technologies and the Perils of Abstracted, Temporally Bound Age

Older people are a large and growing group. We commonly refer to older adults as a single generational group, membership of which is defined by a shared chronological location. Frequently used to mean 'cohort' the term [older] generation defines people in terms of a specific chronological age range [8, pp. 31, 33]. Oddly, we take this common

---

[1] Information services are defined by government as covering the publishing of information to help citizens and businesses in their engagement with government (https://www.gov.uk/government/publications/government-digital-strategy/government-digital-strategy#introduction). 'Digital' is meant as a synonym to 'online'. The policy glossary reads: 'By 'digital', we mean internet-enabled; such as desktop, laptop, tablet, mobile or digital devices not yet invented' (Government Digital Strategy, 10/12/2013 https://www.gov.uk/government/publications/government-digital-strategy/government-digital-strategy#annex-1-glossary).

location to span five decades of birth dates, from 50+ to 100+ years. We then conceptualize age on the basis of assumptions of homogenous context. This politics is reproduced in media and ICT research though practical reasons that often inhibit research on the 70+ year-olds using popular research tools (e.g. limitations of telephone surveys: people living in retirement or residential homes without individual phone line are hard to get hold of) [9 p. 3]. When it comes to the use of new media technologies older people are treated as 'residual category' encompassing all ages above 50 or 60 years [9, p. 13]. Popular labels of digital natives and immigrants [10] can be seen to play upon exactly this abstraction and related socio-technical and life-world dichotomies, which are beyond the scope of this conference paper to discuss.

Society, research and policy communities are waking up to age. More recent empirical investigations of older/younger people and new ICTs have exposed substantial limitations in dominant conceptualizations of media-technological and age boundaries and the assumed clear-cut temporal-and spatial divisions in media use [1, 2, 4, 5, 9, 11, 12]. This new and growing body of research examines the contexts of the lived experience of age including the variability of media technology and internal diversity or intra-age variability [11]. Older people encompass an 'incredibly diverse' group of users of media technologies in terms of characteristics and functionality [13, p. 152], life events and experiences of education, jobs held, relational/familial networks and all forms of cultural capital. Differences tend to increase with age as a result of increased variability in cumulative life experiences [14, p. 68; 10, p. 265; 15, pp. 109–110] according to the concept of 'aged heterogeneity', originally used by Dannefer [16, pp. 360–362]. There is also a growing polarisation among people belonging in the same age group, particularly during the last part of the life course. Many older groups experience a restriction in social space and limited choice in access to adequate housing, leisure, health and communication infrastructure etc. [8, pp. 129–130]. Significant inequalities within the older population including functions of education, such as sex/gender can determine their place and location in the new technology landscape [3, pp. 101–102].

3   Intra-generational Variability: Sex, Ethnic Origin and the Internet

The body of older internet users grows constantly. Official internet use statistics reflect this increase in the ageing of media users. A majority of older people in the UK are using the internet today. In 2013 fifty nine per cent (59 %) of people aged over 65 were online (https://www.gov.uk/government/publications/digital-landscape-research/digital-landscape-research). According to the UK Office of National Statistics seven in ten of those aged 65 to 74 and four out of ten adults aged 75+ had used the internet in 2014 [17] http://www.ons.gov.uk/ons/rel/rdit2/internet-access-quarterly-update/q1-2014/stb-ia-q1 -2014.html#tab-Age. Seventy-one per cent of adults aged 65–74 had used the internet in Q1 2014 and thirty-seven per cent of adults aged 75 years and over, the latter category representing 1.8 million people. Socio-demographic data for older users reveal areas of inequality which are commonly understood as a thing of the past in countries with high internet diffusion. Sex is a notable one. Like race and ethnicity, sex it is no longer considered by the 'digital divide' research as a factor of social different in internet usage in the UK [18]. According to national statistics there is little difference in internet use between men and women in all groups under 65 years of age [17]. However, sex appears to determine access to the internet among older groups. Men over the age of 75 are twice as likely to use the internet compared to women of the same age [19] In 2014 five in ten men aged 75+ had used the internet against three in every ten women in the same age group [17].

These differences can be understood as functions of inequality in education and wealth/social position, which have been a constant backdrop in adults' engagement with digital media. Of about 18 % of the UK population who had never used the internet in 2013, blue collar non-users were more likely than other groups to identify age (78 %) as reasons not to use the Internet [20, p. 55]. By contrast 95 per cent of all adults with a higher educational qualification had used the internet in the UK [20, p. 19]. The relevance of education and social position and suggested correlations of age, sex and education in the UK mirror similar trends in international data [9].

Older adult cohorts are today becoming more ethnically diverse in the UK. According to the ONS [19] the 2011 census data show that between 2001 and 2011 the 65 and over age group became slightly more ethnically diverse. The older population identifying as White British increased in size from 7.8 million to 8.5 million but the proportion of the age group they accounted for decreased from 94 % in 2001 to 92 % in 2011. This compares with much larger changes in the under 65 age group, which saw the proportion of the population who were White British decrease from 86 % in 2001 to 72 % in 2011 (p. 9 in http://www.ons.gov.uk/ons/dcp171776_342117.pdf) Ethnic diversity is far greater in the city of London. Tables 1 and 2 present the ethnic breakdown (White/Black & Other Minority Ethnic, BAME) of adult populations aged over 65 years and of the total population of city residents in the twelve inner London Boroughs, based on data made available by the Greater London Authority in 2013 (http://data.london.gov.uk/datastore/applications/custom-age-range-creator-tool-gla-ethnic-group-population-projections-borough.

An increase in the ethnic diversity of the adult population is manifested online too, in the limited data made available by the ONS, which indicate the highest rates of internet use (over 90 %) among adults who indicated that their ethnic group was Mixed ethnic, Chinese, Black, or Other. The Pakistani ethnic group remained the group with the lowest rate of use (82 %) in Q1 2014. (ONS, Internet Access Quarterly update Q1 2014   http://www.ons.gov.uk/ons/rel/rdit2/internet-access-quarterly-update/q1-2014/stb-ia-q1-2014.html#tab-Ethnic-Group).

In short, according to national statistics older age cohorts become more heterogeneous across the UK. On the internet, sex ('gender') remains a manifestation of discrimination among the older adults who are 75+ and there is a strong correlation with sex, age, and education and internet use. Differences based on sex tend to be confounded with other factors determined by the respondents sex: 'Among this generation, the correlation of sex with education and income is stronger compared to later generations for which educational opportunities were more equal' [9, p. 13] Lastly the limited available data indicate a possibly divergent trend of higher levels of internet use among non-white, 'minority ethnic' adult groups.

Table 1. Inner London population by ethnic origin (White/BAME) data source GLA 2013

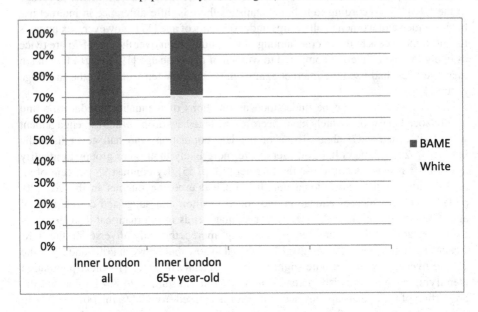

Table 2. Ethnic origin (white /BAME) 65+ year olds by Borough. Data source GLA 2013

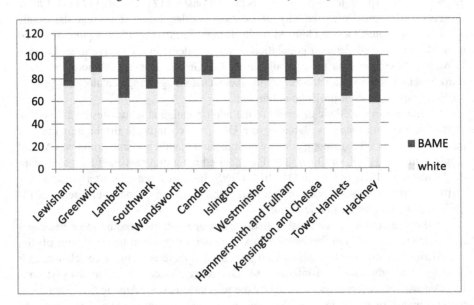

4   Older People in Digital Public Service Information Provision

The increase in the age, heterogeneity and diversity of adult internet users has been the backdrop to my examination of how older adults are represented visually on local government websites providing information about adult social care support services. Social care support services are provided at local authority level. Access to this kind of support services has been universal, with all UK residents able to use these services. This exploratory study was undertaken in December 2013, as the migration of public service information provision online was underway. The study examined how older adults are represented visually, though the use of pictures and photographs, in the adult social care portal/homepage of in the twelve inner city London Boroughs (Camden, Greenwich, Islington, Lambeth, Lewisham, Southwark, Kensington and Chelsea, Fulham, Tower Hamlets, Hackney, Wandsworth, Westminster) giving a snapshot of cultural attitudes to age in public policy. My research questions follow the work of Loos [1, 2] on older age, information accessibility and the relationship between representations and access to digital services.

A widespread practice in the Borough homepages was to show one or two images of mostly frail looking older people to illustrate their general ID/theme. This was the case of Tower Hamlets[2] (http://www.towerhamlets.gov.uk/lgnl/health_and_social_care.aspx), Greenwich (http://www.royalgreenwich.gov.uk/info/200050/help_for_adults) Ham mersmith and Fulham (http://www.lbhf.gov.uk/Directory/Health_and_Social_Care/ Services_for_the_elderly/homepage.asp), Lambeth[3] (http://www.Lambeth.gov.uk/ Services/HealthSocialCare/ServicesAdults/) (Figs. 1 and 2).

Two trends can be seen in these screenshots: One, there is a restricted visibility of older people in those websites. Images depicting older adults are limited in number. Two, when older people become visible, for example in the updated versions of Council websites, they are depicted as frail, white older women, not making visible potential differences based on sex, ethnic background and vitality. The webpages of Greenwich and Lambeth included some characteristically ageist representations (older lady and fruit assortment on the Greenwich page; a Polaroid picture of young adult woman and man doing craftwork in 1980 s' fashion fancy dress on the Lambeth page). The Greenwich social care services website is now redesigned and shows an image of two pairs of hands – the young ones holding the very old ones. In Islington older adults are not visible through images (no depiction of older adults) as all information is text-based (http://www.islington.gov.uk/services/social-care-health/older-people/Pag- es/default.aspx?extra=4). The websites of Wandsworth (http://www.wandsworth.gov. uk/homepage/146/adult_care_information_service) and Southwark (http://www.south- wark.gov.uk/info/200387/assessments_benefits_and_advice) were in the process of

---

[2] This website has now been redesigned and uses icon to represent services and users.

[3] The Lambeth pages (http://www.lambeth.gov.uk/Services/HealthSocialCare/ServicesAdults) were redesigned in summer 2014.

Fig. 1. Screenshot of Greenwich Adult Social Care Homepage December 2013

Fig. 2. Screenshot of Greenwich Adult Social Care Homepage January 2015

adopting a new, more visually oriented online information provision strategy. The Southwark social care home page shows eight older women and men, of which six are white and two are black or mixed race. The Wandsworth Borough page uses graphic icons as navigation buttons and there are no image depicting older people in the main menu of choices.

Two London Boroughs, Camden and Lewisham have implemented a new visual design with simplified, integrated one stop shop services: These Council services make *older people visible and recognizable* on their homepages. Power relationships of inclusion/exclusion and centring/marginalization can also be observed here. Camden (http://camdencarechoices.camden.gov.uk/) has implemented inclusive and experiential understandings of adult ageing. In the Camden site inclusive social demographics made visible though a lens of dynamic diversity.

Camden includes a spectrum of representations with adults of all ages, a range of ethnic groups and equally split sexes (eight women and eight men). By contrast the Lewisham homepage (http://www.lewishammylifemychoice.org.uk/) features a white elderly couple (woman and man). Westminster and Kensington and Chelsea provide both legacy websites and a new, common partnership service called *People First* http://www.peoplefirstinfo.org.uk/. This external website represents a flagship project which follows current priorities in the reorganization of social health and care services as formalized in the 2014 Care Act, which incorporates Digital by Default design requirements. Lambeth and Southwark are now running a joint social care services information provision and their newly designed website (http://directory.ageuklambeth.org.uk/) is visually inclusive: Images of a multi-ethnic groups of older adults are used, both vitality and frailness women and men (Figs. 3 and 4).

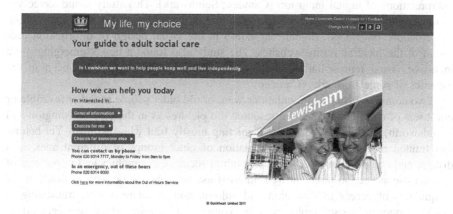

Fig. 3. Screenshot of Lewisham Guide to Social Care

Fig. 4. Screenshot of Camden Care Choices

5 Discussion and Conclusions: Digital Public Service and the Invisible Older Users

All twelve Inner London Boroughs provide online information about adult social care, most through dedicated pages. At the time of the research some Boroughs, and more generally local authorities across the country have been redesigning their web services, to meet digital by default targets and therefore the sample provided a good mix of what I'd call 'commonsense' age(ist) values (Greenwich; Lewisham) as well as some newer interpretations of digital inclusion (Camden; Southwark). This study found stereotypical understandings of older age being standing in the wrong end of a 'digital divide' (information 'have-nots', digital 'can-nots') in the visual design of information provision of the local authority websites. The study also found a newly emerging more inclusive visual representation of the age spectrum of adulthood has been in the websites of some Boroughs (Camden).

Two common visual representations were of old older people as either invisible or non-users of a digital information resource (no pictures as in the case of Islington and Wandsworth) or limited and partial, depicting mostly frail white women. Yet behind this limited and exclusionary representation of older groups of different ages, is a diverse and complex set of differences, both in social demographics and in patterns of internet use as section three showed. Internet use patterns can be seen as functions of inequalities of access to education and cultural and social resources, translating to unequal opportunities to employment for women and men, including 'first generation' immigrants, in the case of people over the age of 75. Translating this complex set of inequalities, and the diversity in the life-world experience of those people to homogenized representations of the old as frail non users of the internet can be seen as unhelpful to access a crude politics of ageism. Recently published studies [e.g. 9, 20] have demonstrated how social position and the social context appears to have a manifold influence on internet use among the older groups of people aged 70+ with the lower levels of internet use. In Friemel's study [9] gender differences in usage, which in the UK ONS data examined in the present study [16, 20] are the most pronounced among internet users aged 75+, were found to disappear if controlled for education, income, technical interest, pre-retirement computer use and marital status. Heatmaps in an eye-tracking study conducted by Loos [12] showed clearly that the navigation patterns of older participants with a high frequency of internet use were quite similar to those of younger ones (see also Hill et al. [21] Dutton et al. [20] demonstrate this for education: virtually all with a higher education degree are using the internet. Homogenous representations of the relationship of older age and new media use may mask, augment and further reinforce disadvantage experienced by older cohorts. Culturally entrenched ageist attitudes, institutionalized practice and research design bias can reinforce the marginalization of older people and reproduce patterns of inequality, including along lines of race and sex.

References

1. Loos, E.: Senior citizens: digital immigrants in their own country? Observatorio (OBS*) J. **6** (1), 1–23 (2012)
2. Loos, E.: Designing for dynamic diversity: representing various senior citizens in digital information sources. Observatorio (OBS*) J. **7**(1), 21–45 (2013)
3. Hagberg, J.-E.: Being the oldest old in a shifting technology landscape. In: Loos, E., Haddon, L., Mante-Maijer, E. (eds.) Generational Use of New Media, pp. 89–106. Ashgate, Farnham (2012)
4. Loos, E., Haddon, H., Mante-Meijer, E. (eds.): Generational Use of New Media. Ashgate, Farnham (2012)
5. Sourbati, M.: On older people, internet access and electronic service delivery: a study of sheltered homes. In: Loos, E.F., Haddon, L., Mante-Maijer, E.A. (eds.) The Social Dynamics of Information and Communication Technology, pp. 95–104. Ashgate, Aldershot (2008)
6. Government Digital Strategy, December 2013 Update, Executive Summary (2013). https://www.gov.uk/government/publications/government-digital-strategy/government-digital-strategy
7. Cabinet Office 'Government's approach to assisted digital' Policy Paper, 4 December 2013 (2013). http://publications.cabinetoffice.gov.uk/digital/assisted/
8. Vincent, J.A.: Old Age. Routledge/Taylor and Francis Group, London (2003)
9. Friemel, T.N.: The digital divide has grown old: determinants of a digital divide among seniors. In: New Media and Society (Online First), 12 June 2014
10. Prensky, M.: Digital natives digital immigrants. Horizon **9**(5), 1–6 (2001)
11. Loos, E.: Generational use of new media and the (ir)relevance of age. In: Colombo, F., Fortunati, L. (eds.) Broadband Society and Generational Change, pp. 259–273. Peter Lang, Berlin (2011)
12. Loos, E.: In search of information on websites: a question of age? In: Stephanidis, C. (ed.) Universal Access in HCI, Part II, HCII 2011. LNCS, vol. 6766, pp. 196–204. Springer, Heidelberg (2011)

13. Gregor, P., Newell, A.F., Zajicek, M.: Designing for dynamic diversity - interfaces for older people. In: Jacko, J.A. (eds.) ASSETS 2002 The Fifth International ACM Conference on Assistive Technologies, Edinburgh, Scotland, pp. 151–156, 8–10 July 2002. http://staff.computing.dundee.ac.uk//afn/pdf/2002%20Dynamic%20Diversity%20_with%20Mary%20-Z_pdf. Accessed Dec 2013

14. Bouma, H.: Document and interface design for older citizens. In: Westendorp, P., Jansen, C., Punselie, R. (eds.) Interface Design & Document Design, pp. 67–80. Rodopi, Amsterdam (2000)

15. Chisnell, D., Redish, J.: Modelling older adults for website design. In: Loos, E., Haddon, L., Mante-Meijer, E. (eds.) Generational Use of New Media. Ashgate, Farnham (2012)

16. Dannefer, D.: What's in a name? an account of the neglect of variability in the study of ageing. In: Birren, J.E., Bengtson, V.L. (eds.) Emergent Theories of Ageing, pp. 356–384. Springer, New York (1988)

17. Office of National Statistics (ONS) Internet Access Quarterly update Q1 2014 (2014). http://www.ons.gov.uk/ons/rel/rdit2/internet-access-quarterly-update/q1-2014/stb-ia-q1-20-14.html#tab-Ethnic-Group

18. Sparks, C.: What is the "digital divide" and why is it important. Javnost – Public 20(2), 27–46 (2013). http://javnost-thepublic.org/issue/2013/2/

19. Office of National Statistics (ONS) Internet Access Quarterly update, Q2 (2013). http://www.ons.gov.uk/ons/rel/rdit2/internet-access-quarterly-update/q2-2013/stb-ia-q2-20-13.html#tab-Age-and-sex

20. Dutton, W.H., Grant, B., Groselj, D.: Oxford Internet Survey 2013 Report: Cultures of the internet. Oxford Internet Survey, OxIS (2013). http://oxis.oii.ox.ac.uk/reports

21. Hill, R., Dickinson, A., Arnott, J., Gregor, P., McIver, L.: Older users' eye movements: experience counts. In: CHI 2011, Vancouver, BC, Canada 7–12 May 2011 (2011)

A Framework for Evaluating the Implementers' Experience in Making Existing Products Accessible: The Prosperity4all Approach

Katerina Touliou[1]([✉]), Maria Gemou[1], Till Riedel[2], Maria Panou[1], and Evangelos Bekiaris[1]

[1] Centre for Research and Technology/Hellenic Institute of Transport
(CERTH/HIT), Athens, Greece
{touliouk, mgemou, mpanou, abek}@certh.gr
[2] Karlsruhe Institute of Technology (KIT), Karlsruhe, Germany
riedel@teco.edu

Abstract. Prosperity4All is a continuous and dynamic paradigm shift towards an e-inclusion framework building on the architectural and technical foundations of other Global Public Inclusive Infrastructure (GPII) projects aiming to create a self-sustainable and growing ecosystem where developers, implementers, consumers, prosumers and other directly and indirectly actors (e.g. teachers, carers, clinicians) may play a role in its viability and diversity. An agile and dynamic approach is adopted in three evaluation phases, starting with formative evaluations with five internal implementers leading to more summative techniques towards the final evaluation phase where more (n = 25) and external professionals will use the tools and resources available in the project's repository (DeveloperSpace) to improve and enhance their own products and services. The evaluation approach for the implementers considers three dimensions: (a) the project's Key Performance Indicators (KPIs), (b) technical validation activities prior evaluation, and (c) three evaluation phases followed by a final impact assessment.

Keywords: Inclusive design · Implementers · Evaluation · Accessibility · Ecosystem

1 Introduction

Prosperity4All is a continuous and dynamic paradigm shift towards an e-inclusion framework building on the architectural and technical foundations of other Global Public Inclusive Infrastructure (GPII) projects by creating a self-sustainable and growing ecosystem, where developers, implementers, consumers, prosumers and other directly and indirectly actors (e.g. teachers, carers, clinicians) may interact with and play a role in its viability and diversity. The Global Public Inclusive Infrastructure (GPII) is a project of Raising the Floor, a consortium of academic, industry, and non-governmental organizations and individuals (http://gpii.net/). The GPII will

© Springer International Publishing Switzerland 2015
J. Zhou and G. Salvendy (Eds.): ITAP 2015, Part I, LNCS 9193, pp. 387–397, 2015.
DOI: 10.1007/978-3-319-20892-3_38

combine cloud computing, web, and platform services to make access simpler, more inclusive, available everywhere, and more affordable. When completed it will provide the infrastructure needed to make it possible for companies, organizations, and society to put the web within reach of all - by making it easier and less expensive for consumers with disabilities, ICT and AT companies, Public Access Points, employers, educators, government agencies and others to create, disseminate, and support accessibility across technologies.

In particular, the aim of Prosperity4All is to provide an infrastructure for the development of an ecosystem by employing modern and new techniques, like crowdsourcing and gamification, to enable new strategies for developing accessibility services and introduce a new approach to accessibility solution development. This ecosystem will allow seamless, efficient, cost-effective and unobtrusive communication between developers, implementers, consumers and prosumers. Consumers will be able to communicate with developers and implementers for ordering personalized and customized products and solutions (e.g. web-based business solutions customized for visual impaired users). However, with such diversity comes complexity that substantially affects the designing and planning process for the respective evaluation approach and framework.

The evaluation of the ecosystem will be achieved through impact estimations of its deployment. Before reaching the point to estimate small or large potential impacts, actuals evaluations will be carried out in three pilot sites in Europe; Austria, Germany, Greece, Spain with real users and implementers. The evaluations with implementers precede any testing with real end-users. The final evaluation phase with implementers will be the first evaluation phase with end-users. Evaluations with implementers will be performed with at least thirty users in different sites, including both internal to the project participants and externals for the second and third evaluation phase. The objectives and the Key Performance Indicators (KPIs) were the driving forces for drafting the evaluation questions to be considered and set.

1.1 The Overarching Evaluation Questions

Defining the questions to ask was a first step. The evaluation questions had to accommodate for the project's KPIs and the latter reflected the objectives. All three were mapped before overarching questions were prepared. Thus, a top-down approach was followed for the evaluation questions of the framework.

1. Are the tools/resources for Developers (DeveloperSpace and all of the frameworks, components, marketing tools, etc.) usable by and useful to developers/implementers (both internal developers and external developers, implementers)?
2. Do the tools/resources help implementers in their work or decrease cost to develop or increase market size/share? OR increase profits?

Evidently, the evaluation focusses not only on the utility and use of these tools and resources but also on their cost-efficiency in their everyday work. Therefore, implementer's previous experience with and involvement in accessibility work and projects is of importance. A bottom-up process is applied for preparing the actual evaluation materials were specific instruments are selected.

1.2   The Evaluation Framework for Implementers

Developing an inclusive and human-oriented framework that will adapt dynamic and agile methods and will be embedded in the development lifecycle, to the extent this is possible, is a challenging endeavor for planning the evaluation but as well as collecting data and draw inferences on the outcomes. Early evaluations are mostly formative leading later on to more summative efforts. The final evaluation phase will coincide with the first iteration with end-users and then their inter-play will be captured with pluralistic techniques.

There is keen interest in identified how cost-efficient and viable will be this eco-system for professionals working in diverse areas (e.g. web developers, hobbyists, etc.) in order to offer customized and personalized solutions to people with diverse and sometimes complex accessibility needs, aiming to address the tails-of-the-tails of populations of users they might be isolated by existing practices and offered market-place solutions. The evaluation framework addresses different users-actors based on their functional role which they may play in the ecosystem. The roles might as well be interchangeable when the ecosystem will be deployed, after all evaluations finish and optimization is achieved; wherever relevant and applicable.

Building up the evaluation framework requires knowledge in the areas of traditional usability and user experience testing and insight in customer perception and e-commerce marketing analytics. Most of the project's applications and services are already offered to consumers and therefore they will not be evaluated per se. On the contrary, the tools developed or improved during the project - tools and frameworks with Graphical User Interfaces for Development (IDEs), building blocks and frame-works (with no graphical interfaces) for developers (APIs), and web-based developer resources- will be available at a specially design repository, the DeveloperSpace.

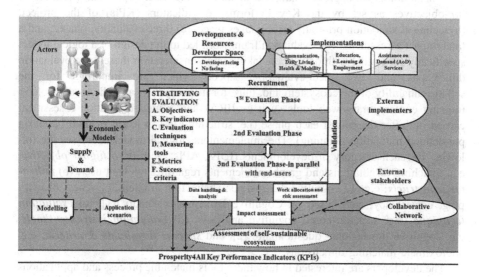

Fig. 1. The implementers' evaluation framework

The three evaluation activities will be harmonized with the enhancing development cycle. Firstly, the implementers will search the DeveloperSpace to find the appropriate tools and resources in order to add functionalities to their products and services for making them more accessible or adding functionalities that will make them even more accessible to users with other accessibility needs. The evaluation framework is "surrounded" by other activities (Fig. 1) as the inter-connections and inter-dependencies between the evaluations and the following project activities are necessary:

(a) the ecosystem's business cases defined by the demand and supply chains for the future actors in the alive ecosystem;
(b) the tools (e.g. developer-facing with interfaces like certain APIs) and resources chosen and used by implementers that reside in the DeveloperSpace; and
(c) the actual products that will be improved, representing different areas of interest and life activities (e.g. business, health, education).

The logical model prepared for the evaluation activities with implementers includes the *input* namely the actors and the developments, the *process* being the evaluation activities including recruitment and technical validation whenever and wherever relevant, and the *outcomes* being the collection of the indicators by using formative methods in the first iteration (i.e. pluralistic walkthroughs and workshops with emphasis on implementers' decision-making processes and utility of tools) and more summative in later stages (cost and time efficiency estimations and matching the expectations of developers with different levels of experience in accessibility with their post-responses).

2 Methodology

The methodological approach adopted includes three inter-dependent dimensions: (a) objectives as set by the Key Performance Indicators (KPIs) of the project, (b) technical validation prior any testing takes place, (c) three evaluation phases, and a final impact assessment. The evaluation framework led to the design of a logical model specifically for testing with developers taking into consideration these three evaluation dimensions and two meta-evaluation aspects which are important for the self-sustainability of the ecosystem and, thus, for its prosperity; an agile feedback loop utilizing contemporary web tools such as JIRAs and a meta-evaluation assessment carried out after the end of each phase (i.e. structured lesson learnt method based on pre-defined mitigation planning). The implementers' logical model addresses the following for each category of developments (IDEs, APIs, etc.): (a) *a higher objective*; e.g. matching of notations and graphical elements regarding relevant user, (b) *indicators/constructs*; e.g. 12 cognitive dimensions; abstraction gradient, closeness of mapping, consistency, etc., based on Cognitive Dimensions Theory [1], (c) *evaluation technique* (e.g. scenario-based cognitive analysis); (d) *evaluation instrument/tools*; e.g. cognitive dimensions' questionnaire [2], and *success thresholds & criteria*; e.g. approximate matching dimensions.

The developers are interested in how these tools match the process and applications (matchmaking) and how much they will save in money and time when using those tools (cost-effectiveness). These are also considered, as we want to understand how the developers will reach the decision to use the tools (i.e. revealing the decision making process) and which is the reference case (i.e. their professional preferences and decisions to use certain tools over others in their work environment). The evaluation focuses on measuring how usable and useful will be the DeveloperSpace and all of the frameworks, components, and tools for internal and external implementers, with consideration for how helpful they will be, how much they will decrease the cost to develop, and how much they will increase profits and market size. The last two aspects will be addressed by the impact assessment carried out after the deployment of Prosperity4All ecosystem. The professional experience of developers and implementers participating in the pilots in inclusive design and accessibility is taken into consideration. Three iteration phases will be carried out starting with a small group of internal implementers (N = 5) for the first iteration phase and gradually including external implementers in the last two (N = 25). Peer reviews and automatic documentation improvements are common qualitative methods for evaluating solution for developers. These methods have restricted transferability and therefore potential validity. Instead, heuristic walkthroughs and relevant formative techniques will be used in the first iteration. Summative evaluation will mostly take place in the iterations to follow; especially when the Prosperity4All platform will be deployed and analytics will be gathered from real life interaction with it.

2.1 Actors

Implementers are the Prosperity4All actors who will incorporate the tools and resources offered to them in the DeveloperSpace in order to make their applications and services more accessible or to improve the user experience of already accessible applications. Implementers are both the internal implementers and external professionals who might be freelancers or even companies, service providers, and other groups as identified in the list of actors (Table 1).

In these user groups, developers who will directly add outcomes to their applications and use existing resources during the improvement process (enhancement

Table 1. Primary categories of implementers

1. AT Developers	*4. Researchers*
• *Hardware AT*	• *University/College/Tech-Institute*
• *Software AT (install)*	• *Other technology-oriented education*
• *Web/Cloud AT*	*5. Community Developers*
2. Mainstream Developers	• *Micro Service Developers*
• *Desktop Applications*	• *Friends and Family*
• *Web/Cloud Applications*	• *Prosumers*
• *Cloud Service Providers*	*6. Service Delivery Professionals*
• *Hardware/Appliances*	• *Clinicians*
• *Mobile Applications*	• *Teachers*
3. System Integrators	

development lifecycle), their implementation will also evaluate this work and implementers will evaluate the utility –among other attributes-of the resources they will choose to "accessibilize" their products. The participants are sought to be representative of a bigger group of "implanters" that need to be considered in the wider scope (Table 1).

Other stakeholders may be influenced by the implementer's perspective of the DeveloperSPace; this particularly includes the government. Governmental agencies are setting the regulatory frame for many implementations as well as do procurement officers or decision makers. They highly influence what will be considered for implementation. The evaluation acknowledges that roles may be fluid, so that also consumers with decision making powers have influence on implementation decisions and that particularly prosumers are interesting stakeholders in the realm of accessibility. One underlying assumption of the evaluation framework is, however, that the implementers' perspective on Prosperity4All is common but very heterogeneous for all the stakeholders.

Examples of Generic Personas and Application Scenarios for Implementers. Based on the list of actors, application scenarios like short stories are created for three groups of actors which belong to the producer category (i.e. people who produce products, create applications, improve services, etc.) and have a direct impact to the Prosperity4All developments (i.e. belong to the family of Producer of Things (PoTs) scenarios). They were created for three different value propositions (i.e. reasons to join platform). At this stage, scenarios are characterized by the functional role of the stakeholder, the value proposition (broad), and the family of scenarios it belongs.

The value of these scenarios for the evaluation framework lies in the fact that they provide insight in the many types of actors that they could be involved as implementers, the way they can work and collaborate, and the variations in their expertise, knowledge and even the areas of interest within accessibility. They have a rather illustrative and communicative value between economic modelling and evaluation than a direct application and implementation to any measurable conditions and aspects.

The personas include functional elements (e.g. what the identified persona is doing with the system) accompanied by a short application scenario for testing purposes.

Three potential generic personas and application scenarios are based on initial ideas of the how main actors will interact with the system-in still a fragmented style- but focusing mainly on the story about who the user of a particular technology is, what they want, what they know.

Persona 1: Actor – Producer-Economics: GUI adaptation of route guidance system for visually impaired users (Support independent living).
    Simon is a developer (Actor -Producer – supply-end of chain) who has long been working in making accessible applications for many years. He has worked in a large company for many years and lately he is interested in navigation support systems for marginalized user groups such as people with visual impairments. He found out about the Prosperity4All multi-sided platform via blog for developers he often visits and receives the Newsletter. When he visits the developer part of the platform he is unsure about which component of the DeveloperSpace is more appropriate for what is looking

for to do. He checks the link and visits the Prosperity4All training platform. He selects the curriculum for external implementers and specifically the course on adapting GUIs for visually impaired users especially for navigation support software.

He then selects the component for changing the interface of the routing guidance system and makes it available to the platform for users to buy. There is also an option for the user to ask for a specific customization to be made and there is an opportunity to hold a discussion with the developer prior the purchase.

Application of scenario for testing: The implementer will adapt the GUI interface of the route guidance system for visually impaired users. Testing at early stages of development will be performed together with other low or medium fidelity prototypes.

Persona 2: Actor – Producer-Law: Making accessible learning materials (Support independent education and work).

Carla (Actor – Producer – supply end of chain) is a freelancer who is currently collaborating with a large public library aiming to make their digital resources accessible to blind and visually impaired users. She visits the Prosperity4All platform and accesses the part for developers and implementers in order to find relevant resources for her work. The training videos were very helpful and she found numerous resources about different screen readers and their implementation to the vast and diverse digital books and information available. The workload is huge but still the resources and tools available at the Prosperity4All platform will assist Carla by saving-time looking for methods and tools in the internet and increasing her potential and knowledge in the accessibility domain.

Application of scenario for testing: The implementer will select a tool to enhance the accessibility of digital documents to be accessible by blind and visually impaired users (e.g. either one or two screen readers). Testing at early stages of development will be performed together with other low or medium fidelity prototypes.

Persona 3: Actor – Producer-Ethics: Adaptation of Assistance on Demand (AoD) services for older people (Support inclusion of lower or no literacy computer users).

Nick (Actor-Producer-supply end of chain) is working as a developer and IT specialist in a national bank branch. He is also a volunteer at the regional Elderly Centre near his home. He is deeply concerned about older people and their lower digital literacy. He is helping them to learn how to use computers. He wants to find a way to help older visitors use the website of the elderly center. He is teaming up with a friend who is actually working as social worker at the center and is pretty aware of the problems older computer users might face and he is just an enthusiast (i.e. he is an amateur software designer). A friend informed him about the Prosperity4All platform and the availability of the AOD framework for enhancing the existing AOD set up of the service provided by the Elderly Centre in order to provide appropriate and adequate technical support to lower digital literacy older users. Their work aims to increase independent use of computers by the users.

Application of scenario for testing: The implementer will use the AoD infrastructure to enhance the AoD services and make them more accessible. Testing at early stages of development will be with other low or medium fidelity prototypes.

2.2   Tools, Resources and Products

The DeveloperSpace repository includes the tools and any relevant additional documentation (e.g. instructions, manuals, etc.). At the very early stages of the project, many of these tools and resources are available as prototypes, mock ups or even as a proof-of-concept. While most of the applications and services have been evaluated already within the scope of other projects, enhancing them is "another story to be told". These tools will be used to make accessible or improve the existing accessibility of different products and services, covering needs from many areas of daily activities (such as communication, education, health, and employment).

The tools and resources used by implementers fall in to the following three main categories and will be:

- Web-based Developer Resources and Assistance on Demand (AoD) services.
- Tools and Frameworks with Graphical User Interfaces for Development (IDEs).
- Building Blocks and Frameworks (with no graphical interfaces) for developers (API).

Those three categories are driven by both the categories of different outcomes (components, tools, services, and infrastructure) and practical considerations and needs for testing and evaluation. Both outcomes and implementations can belong to multiple categories. The implementers will use tools from these categories to improve, enhance and add new functionalities to more than ten existing products falling into the following three main types:

- Communication, Daily Living, Health, and Accessible Mobility.
- Education, eLearning, Business and Employment.
- Assistance on Demand (AoD) Services.

One important consideration was made within the evaluation framework and that was to evaluate the specific effect of Prosperity4Aall as much as possible. While most of the applications and services were evaluated already in the scope of other projects, enhancing them is "another story to be told". It is very important that human factor evaluation also focusses on the unique prosperity propositions that come through the project and the exposure of the tools within an ecosystem. Therefore it is important to understand that all interactions between developers and implementers are made through exactly that evolving ecosystem. Evaluation will be carried out for both the DeveloperSpace (where all tools will be available) and the use tools, resources and applications (internal and external) in the context of the DeveloperSpace.

Particularly for the infrastructure of the DeveloperSpace, the project will develop multiple developer-facing components that are exposed to implementers (there is also user facing components exposed to end-users that are not part of the testing methods). Many of those outcomes will be presented as web-based developer resources. Most prominent example is the component listing (repository) that will be a directly visible outcome. In those cases, proven user experience methodology can be applied. The user model of a developer is different from an end-user in the domain, however, particularly here transition between roles need to be considered for certain stakeholder classes (for user-programmers).

Particularly for the first and second category of tools, the matchmaking aspect is becoming of further importance. While many of the web-based resources will be an entry-point for many types of stakeholders, the picture differentiates quickly after that. Particularly there will be "no-one-fits-all" usability for components. The goal of Prosperity4All is to enable the selection of fitting components and furthermore the fitness of the components for relevant stakeholders, which differ for component to component.

Because often it is not easy to get a summative picture regarding components, services and tools and implementations there will be a two stage process. The first stage will be a match-making inside the project via the DeveloperSpace. This matchmaking already takes the usability of the web resources into account. After this initial match-making, the hypothesis is built that the selected implementation should be fitted to the implementer that selected it. In the second step we are particularly evaluating the usability based on this assumption and use the evaluation also as a formative tool to improve the tools to become better. For those evaluations, established human factor evaluation techniques can be partially applied; particularly if a tool exposes a graphical interface to the developer.

The following high level objectives will be measured:

- Strengths and weakness of used tools and resources.
- Cost-efficiency perceived measures (e.g. considering time and effort compared to current practices; consideration for experience in accessibility is important)
- Improved user experience.
- Utility, usefulness and learnability.
- Acceptance compared to current practice.
- Matching of notation and graphical elements regarding relevant user and development activities.
- Freeing of developer to concentrate on creative aspects of the process.
- Global developer experience with focus on perceived attractiveness (for developer-facing tools and efficiency of offered and available tools and resources).
- Matching of offered tools and resources to needs and requirements.
- Decision making process and changes to it.
- Knowledge and experience driven attitude and productivity.
- Willingness to use and apply in future.

They are high categories which are stratified further into simpler constructs and will be matched to further methods and indicators during the lifetime of the project.

2.3 Conditions and Techniques

Testing with implementers will be primarily carried out in three contexts: (a) in their own work environment with real use of components and tools (group assessment, i.e. peer heuristics), (b) remote testing (remote data gathering), and (c) face-to-face qualitative assessment. Considerable part of testing will be carried out in their own environment gathering mostly qualitative data. Focus groups will be carried out with implementers in small groups (5–8 participants) which could be organized in parallel with demo workshops. The focus groups will provide enriching data to the interviews held with participants and the rest of collected data. This is relevant to data triangulation and filling the "gaps" of other methods of data acquisition.

Conditions will vary between phases and among users. Each user might implement different outcomes for making an application or service accessible. During the first phase, implementation will be in some cases emulated as non-functional versions of tools might only be available (e.g. mock ups, paper prototypes). Another sample of implementers should be anticipated for the impact assessment. They will probably remotely assess the Prosperity4All ecosystem as part of impact assessment. These users will freely interact with the platform and evaluation will involve a real-life assessment of the ecosystem.

The conditions of testing are based on application scenarios which will serve the requirements of the evaluation framework.

Apart from traditional testing aspects, there are therefore two key features considered in the evaluation framework: (a) *matchmaking* – how tools fit the process and applications, (b) *cost-effectiveness* - of the use of specific tools in order to reveal how implementers are driven to choice of tool(s) (i.e. elaboration on decision process in relation to reference case). For the later multi-criteria analysis will be used for certain number of implementers. Tests with the applications and services will investigate the applicability and usefulness of the technology infrastructure. Most of the implementations are applications and services already offered to consumers and therefore they will not be evaluated per se. On the contrary, many of the tools and the DeveloperSpace will be developed within the project and therefore many of them will be offered as prototypes, mock ups or even proof-of-concept at the very early stages of the project.

3   Conclusion

The user model of a developer is different from an end-user in the domain, however, particularly in this case transition between roles needs to be considered for certain stakeholder classes (for user-programmers). This work will provide an understanding of implementer's experience. Developers and implementers usually are on the receiving end of the evaluation process (i.e. receiving feedback) but in this case they will be actively communicating their experience with certain tools and products.

In a world of increasing ICT expertise, and greater future overlap among professional disciplines, the boundaries between users and developers are expected to become difficult to draw and balanced knowledge of both ends is of core importance for valid and reliable inferences.

Acknowledgments. This paper presents work carried out in Prosperity4All project. This project has received funding from the European Union's Seventh Framework Programme for research, technological development and demonstration under grant agreement no. 610510. http://www. prosperity4all.eu/

References

1. Blackwell, A.F., Green, T.R.G.: A cognitive dimensions questionnaire optimised for users. In: Proceedings of the Twelfth Annual Meeting of the Psychology of Programming Interest Group (2000)
2. Green, T.R.G.: Cognitive dimensions of notations. In: Sutcliffe, A., Macaulay, L. (eds.) People and Computers V, pp. 443–460. Cambridge University Press, Cambridge (1989)

The Study of Using Facebook in Taiwan's Elderly Population—a Case Study in Learners of the Senior Citizens Academy in a City of Taiwan

Ming-Wei Wang[1(✉)] and Yu-Chin Lin[2(✉)]

[1] Senior Citizens Academy Lecturer in Chiayi, Chiayi, Taiwan, ROC
louis258306@gmail.com
[2] Director of Home-Service Management Center, Chiayi Christian Hospital,
Chiayi, Taiwan, ROC
cych03010@gmail.com

Abstract. Mark Zuckerberg founded Facebook site in 2004, and open to e-mail applications use in 2006. The global active users of the Facebook site surpassed one billion people on September 14th, 2012. It spent 13 years that the users of the Google site founded in 1998 surpassed one billion people in 2011. It spent 8 years that the Facebook site to do so. The official statistics of the Facebook site represented that there are about 15 million users visited the Facebook site monthly and there are about 12 million people visited the site by using the mobile Internet devices in the fourth quarter of 2013 in Taiwan. In the same time, there are about 11 million users visited the Facebook site daily and there are about 8.5 million people visited the site by using the mobile Internet devices in Taiwan. Taiwan is a mature market for the Facebook site, the website penetration is the highest in the world.

Taiwan in where the Facebook site utility rate is so high faces the rapidly aging population issue. According to the statistics from Ministry of the Interior, Republic of China, the ratio of the population over 65 years old has exceeded 7 % in 1993. It means that Taiwan is the aging society. The ratio of the population over 65 years old is 11.90 % in October, 2014. With the statistics from Council for Economic Planning and Development in the Republic of China Executive Yuan, the ratio of Taiwan elderly population will exceed 14 % in 2018, and Taiwan will be the aged society. The ratio of Taiwan elderly population will increase quickly from 2014 to 2025 because of the effect of the postwar baby boom.

This investigation using action research discusses the elderly people studying IT lessons in the Senior Citizens Academy of a city in Taiwan. How do they use the Facebook site? We found that the elderly people is not the main usage group of the Facebook site, but using the Facebook site impacts positively for their learning, social networking, and the interactions among their family members. There are two difficulties for elderly people to use the Facebook site, one reason is they are not used to share their thinking to others, and the other reason is the computer operation is difficult for them. We also found that some of the elderly people begin to use the mobile Internet devices what are new things for them, and they use the internet, the Facebook site, Line by making use of the mobile Internet devices.

© Springer International Publishing Switzerland 2015
J. Zhou and G. Salvendy (Eds.): ITAP 2015, Part I, LNCS 9193, pp. 398–404, 2015.
DOI: 10.1007/978-3-319-20892-3_39

1 Introduction

The author served as the Senior Citizens Academy lecturer since 2008, and the main teaching subject is computer and internet using. Most of the students are over 65 years old. According to the author's observation, they face the serious digital divide. The reason is the city they lived is a small city in Taiwan (The city area of 60.0256 square kilometers is the smallest city in the Taiwan Island.), most of the students' sons and daughters live and work in the other big cities such as Taipei, Taichung and Kaohsiung. The students don't have the opportunities to live with their sons and daughters, so they can't exchange of new knowledge with their families. They lack the opportunities to learn something new, their lifestyle cannot keep up with the Internet era, and their source of information is still television programs, newspapers or magazines.

In March 2008, the Senior Citizens Academy first ran computer courses in the city that the study refers to. When the senior citizens found that they have the opportunities to learn the computer technology and the internet, they found the focus of life, and the focus is to learn something new from the internet. They watch videos or listen music from YouTube, read news from Yahoo news, and contact others with emails. In recent years, Facebook users have a substantial increase. In order to catch up with the trend of the times, they started to learn how to use Facebook, to share their recent life with others and observe others' life. They found that they can see almost everything they want on the computer screen.

As the lecturer of trainees, we want to find how they use the Facebook? Do they have any difficult on using Facebook or computer? Is the interface of computer using or Facebook using friendly to the senior citizens? What teaching methods are suitable for the elderly to learn computer and internet using? This is the motivation for the study.

2 Literature Review

How can we define that people become to old? We will discuss the thing in four aspects (Huang 2007):

First, the point of real ages. Every country defines elderly people in different ages. In China, Russia and France, people over sixty years old are elderly. In America, England, Italy and Canada, people over sixty-five years old are elderly. In Taiwan, the government formulated the law of Senior Citizens Welfare Act. We define that people over sixty-five years old are elderly.

Second, the point of biological ages. When the individual organs reach maturity, they will begin to lose its proper function. There are four indicators:

1. The loss of reproductive capacity: The menopause occurrence is about fifty years old before or after for female. There are generally no obvious signs for male.
2. Grayed hair: What is the age for people's hair being gray? There is considerable variation between individuals, but the appearance is most likely to be considered to be an important feature of the elderly.

3. Physiological dysfunction: including audiovisual capabilities recession, shortness of breath, reduced lung capacity, decreased muscle elasticity, balance diminished capacity, inadequate stamina. The changes are the individual's self-perception and the impacting on the individual's self-identify. They will make individuals to define themselves becoming old.

4. Chronic generation: The chronic is the disease of unknown causes, no way to cure, controlling symptoms by drugs, such as hypertension, diabetes, arthritis, etc. When individuals suffer from the chronic diseases, and the diseases become a part of life, we think the individuals grow old.

Third, the point of psychology. This is the age of the individual at the psychologically subjective feelings. These feelings come from social and psychological factors. The social factors include that the children growing up and getting away from home, the birth of grandsons, the death of the spouse, the forgetfulness on the everyday life, the loss of the patience and so on. The psychological factors include that the loss of the thinking ability, memory loss, inability to concentrate, lack of capacity to solve problems and so on.

Fourth, the point of socialization. The social status of an individual or a particular behavior occurring will be treated as the individual development indicators. Individual aging indicators often consist of the following three:

1. Retirement: It means the individual don't work for full time or work for pay. His income is a pension. The retirement is generally considered an important of the elderly.

2. Becoming grandparents: The age to be grandparents was about fifty years old. Because of the change of social pattern, the general situation of late marriage, the age to be grandparents is older than before.

3. The parents loss: When the individual lose parents, he become the oldest generation in the family. The situation means the individual become old.

The most significant characteristics of the elderly are aging, followed by forgetting (Zhan 1991). The physical and psychological aging can be attributed to the natural laws, but how much time is the old age depends on the length of life. Some people live longer because they have a long old age, and some people die when they are not old because of various factors. Forgetfulness is another feature of the elderly. They often forget things around, but they remember for the last things very clearly. When a person regular wallows in the past things, maybe he is old.

The above references tell us that the meanings of old have different standards including age, physiology, psychology and social perception. The aspects of old contain subjective awareness more or less or the standards of old are different. Therefore, the definition of age as old is the most common definition and the definition is based on the laws.

The professionals for educating and serving the elderly adopt for four different thinking (Moody 1976).

1. Denial mode: The elderly population created limited economic value, so the elderly education is uneconomic. This idea does not meet the viewpoint of modern education, and the elderly population also has the right to continue learning. This idea is inconsistent with modern society.
2. Social serving mode: The problems caused by the increasing in the elderly population can be improved through changes in public policy. The observation emphasizes social justice and equality and does not research the problems that the elderly face and solve them. The elderly take the serves passively and do not face the life by enhancing their abilities. This viewpoint is derogatory (Long 1986).
3. Active mode: This viewpoint is certainly worth the elderly population because of their abilities, experience and living skills. The elderly can help our society to face some problems. Therefore, the elderly education can encourage and help them to participate in our society, to prepare reemployment, or to be volunteers.
4. Self-realization mode: This viewpoint extends from the active mode. It emphasizes that the educational activities enhance the spiritual growth. Moody said that the important feature of the elderly population is to seek the purpose of life from spirit level. Bramwell (1992) said that elderly education should focus on self-fulfillment, self-realization, self-growth and self-transcendence. Walker (1996) said that the final purpose of the elderly education is self-realization.

From the above literature, we find that helping the elderly to enhance their knowledge and ability to adapt to the ever-changing society is a part of the purpose of elderly education. The self-realization and the advancement of social status are important in the elderly education, too.

Until Dec. 2014, the population is 270,883 people in this small city in Taiwan, and the elderly (over 65 years old) is 33,336 people, over 12 % of the city population. The elderly is 2,808,690 people in Taiwan, accounting for 11.99 % of the country's total population. Establishment of ageing-friendly environment will be an important government policy.

For elderly computer users, unfriendly user interface (too much words, too small word, etc.) often causes trouble on the use of internet (Hui-Ming Guo et al. 2007). The scholars had pointed out that the reasons that the elderly refuse to learn new technology are the complex operation flow and unfriendly user interface (Zhao et al. 2009).

3 Research Methods

Action Research is a process of self-reflection inquiry in the social or educational context. Participants included teachers, students, principals and others. The research aims at rationality and justice of social or educational practices. It helps researchers to understand the practical work, and makes works more efficiently (Carr and Kemmis 1986).

On the teaching part, Action Research is a research method for educational environment. Its purpose is to understand the quality of teaching and looking for a better way to teach (Hensen 1996). It includes the observation of the teaching process, finding and solving the problems, and is a systematic and sequential method for research (Dinkelman 1997).

According to Johnson's book (A Short Guild to Action Research); he pointed out ten characteristics about Action Research:

- Action research is a systematic researching method.
- The researchers have no any presumptions.
- It is not necessary to get the way of research complex.
- It needs detailed plans to collect data.
- The research is no time limit.
- Regular observation is necessary, but it is not necessary to spend a lot of time on observation.
- The research process can be simple and informal, and it can be rigorous and formal, too.
- Action Research requires theoretical foundation.
- Action Research is not a quantitative research.
- When the research result is quantitated, the application of the result will be limited.

The object of the study is 89 elderly students attending the computer courses in the Senior Citizens Academy. The author is the course instructor, his jobs are teaching the elderly students to use the internet, to read the messages on the screen, to input the words (Traditional Chinese characters), etc.

4 Results

The computer courses are popular in the Senior Citizens Academy. We have to spend more than 8 weeks (3 h in a week) to teach the students the basic operations. The basic operations are turning on and off the computer, using the keyboard to input the words in Traditional Chinese Characters, using the mouse to click the desktop icon on the screen (to click the mouse left button twice quickly, this is the most hard operation process in the beginning of the courses), browsing the internet, learning to find something on the internet, etc.

When we start to teach the using of Facebook, it is difficult to teach the students to sign up a new username. It's too much data for them to input, and they have to write the username and password in their notebook, or they will forget the words (Some students' memory is not as strong as the young men). We understand that the point of the teaching is how to use Facebook, not to sign up, so we suggest that the instructor sign up for the elderly students before class, and give the username and password to the students in class. It will save o lot of time.

Taiwanese conservative personality makes the elderly students not used to share their motions to others. They don't understand why we share everything in Facebook. They will not share their thinking in Facebook. First of all, we suggest them to be the instructor's Facebook friend. They will understand what they can share in Facebook, just as the instructor share. And the next, we will suggest them to click the < Like > button. They will understand how to interact with others in Facebook. When they click the < Like > button, we will teach them how to leave a message in others' Facebook. They will input "Good!" or "Nice!".

To share photos is a good begin in the Facebook using. But the elderly students have to connect their camera and computer to download their photos to the computer's disk, and upload the photos to Facebook. The process is complex for them. We have to review the process for them several times and maybe 10 to 20 percent of the elderly will give up. It is necessary to encourage them to share their life in Facebook, and get more Facebook friends, just like their sons, daughters and grandchildren. It will make them be interested in using Facebook.

We will tell them how to share news or articles in Facebook. It is another way to use their Facebook. Maybe they would not share their feeling or thinking in their Facebook, but they like to share the articles to others, especially the content of the articles is about health. It is important for them to be healthy.

A handful of the elderly like to share their life experience in their Facebook, and this is our goal, to save their stories in Facebook. Typing is difficult for the elderly, and the handwriting input devices are not convenient for them. For our elderly students, to input words is always a trouble. How to improve the method of input is worthy of study.

After we finish the class, less than 25 % of the elderly students keep using their Facebook. To maintain the relationships with Facebook is maybe important for us, but not important for them. They maintain their relationships in a dinner party or regular meetings.

In the teaching process, we set up a bicycle team for the elderly students and set up a Facebook page for the team. At first the idea is to encourage the elderly to exercise for their healthy. We spent four days riding the bicycles to travel, and total distance is 220 km. We uploaded the photos taken in the activity to the Facebook page. The team members took the initiative to find ways to download their photos in Facebook page. It is the way to encourage the elderly to use Facebook.

In the observation, we found that when the elderly find something interesting or relate to them in the internet, they would take the initiative to learn the knowledge about the internet. Creating the goal is a good way to encourage the elderly to learn.

Due to the trend of the times, we set up the courses to teach the elderly students to use MID (mobile internet devices). The elderly students would set their personal data in their smartphone or tablet computer. When they use their MID, they don't need to input their username and password every time, and it is convenient for the elderly to maintain their Facebook running.

5 Future Research Directions

According to the survey about Taiwan wireless internet use, the proportion of people in Taiwan to use wireless internet access continue to increase. The internet applications people use most often with mobile internet are using the internet community websites, using instant messaging and visiting the websites (TWNIC 2015). We also found that Line (instant messaging) is popular in the elderly. The software makes a new way to communicate to others. The situation is suitable to be explained with Technology Acceptance Model. When the elderly students find an App (application) that is useful and using easily, they would like to learn the using and start to use it.

To keep one's Facebook running with desktop computer is maybe difficult for the elderly, but to do the same thing with MID is maybe easy for them. On the other hand, maybe Facebook is not their need. They are not used to share something in words. When they need to share some photos, they use the instant messaging just as Line. The interface of Line is simpler than Facebook.

On the point of Perceived ease of use, which one is easier to use for the elderly? Desktop computers or MID? When they don't need to type, the handwriting on MID is useful for them. To observe on their usage of MID is the next step for us to research. What kind of interface on MID is the elderly need? It is the future research directions.

References

Wikipedia: Facebook. 15 Dec 2014. http://zh.wikipedia.org/wiki/Facebook

Chiayi city government, Taiwan, ROC (2014). Demographics of Dec 2013. http://household.chiayi.gov.tw/population2/index-2.asp?m=99&m1=3&m2=150&gp=16

Ministry of the Interior, Taiwan, ROC. Statistical Yearbook of Interior. 15 Dec 2014. http://sowf.moi.gov.tw/stat/year/y02-01.xls

Huang, F.-S.: Various Senior Citizens' Education. Wu-Nan Book Inc, Taipei (2007)

Laws & Regulations Database of the Republic of China, Taiwan, ROC (2014). Senior Citizens Welfare Act. http://law.moj.gov.tw/Eng/LawClass/LawContent.aspx?PCODE=D0050037

Zhan, D.: The elderly psychology, ethics and education. Department of social education, Taiwan, ROC., The Elderly Education, Shta Book Inc Taipei (1991)

Moody, H.R.: Education and the life circle. In: Sherron, R.H., Lumsden, D.B., (eds.), Introduction to Educational Gerontology, Washington DC, Hemisphere (1976)

Long, H.B.: A brief history of education in the united stated with some implications for the public education of older adult. In: Peterson, D.A., Thornton, J.E., Brirren, J.E. (eds.) Education and Aging. Pretice-Hall Inc, Englewood Cliffs (1986)

Bramwell, R.D.: Beyond survival: curriculum model for senior adult education. Educ. Gerontol. **18**, 433–446 (1992)

Walker, A.: The new generational contract: intergenerational relation. In: Walker, A., (ed.), Old Age and Welfare, UCL Press, London (1996)

Guo, H.-M., Huai-Hui, F., Zhi-Hong, X.: The research of the difficult that the elderly internet consumer encountered. J. Ergonomic Study 9(2), 45–53 (2007)

Zhao, C., Popovic, V., Ferreira, L., Lu, X.: Understanding older vehicle user: an interpretative approach. In: Paper Presented at the 2008 Design Research Society Conference Sheffied, UK August 2009

Carr, W., Kemmis, S.: Becoming Critical: Education, knowledge and Action Research. Falmer, London (1986)

Hensen, K.T.: Teachers as researches. In: Sikula, J. (ed.) Handbook of Research on Teacher Education, 2nd edn. Macmillan, New York (1996)

Dinkelman, T.: The promise of action research for critically reflective teacher education. Teacher Educ. 32(4), 250–274 (1997)

TWNIC: The news release about Taiwan wireless internet use survey. 1 Feb 2015. http://www.twnic.net.tw/download/200307/20150202a.pdf

An Older Person and New Media in Public Discourses: Impossible Encounters?

Monika Wilińska[✉]

Sociology, Social Policy and Criminology,
University of Stirling, Stirling, Scotland, UK
Monika.wilinska@stir.ac.uk

Abstract. The aim of this paper is to consider the use and role of new media in the lives of older people. To this end, I focus on the social images of encounters between older people and new media. My focus is two-fold; on the one hand, I aim at opening the academic discussion on new media and older people to societal and structural considerations; on the other, I make an argument about the use of discourse, critical discourse analysis in particular, approaches to understand the main discourses that frame the experience of older people with new media. Thus, in this paper I question taken for granted assumptions regarding the inherent characteristics of older people that prevent them from entering the social media space. I draw on the concept of ageism to discuss the implications of this for an individual, older social media user.

Keywords: New media · Older person · Discourse · Social imaginaries

1 Introduction

The main argument of this paper is that the use of social media by older people needs to be understood in the context of societal discourses about the encounters between an older person and new media. The societal discourse of old age is understood to have overarching implications on both the personal and social experience of ageing [1–3]. The social dimension of ageing determines roles assigned to older people in a given society. Thus, age is regarded as one part of a social stratification system; it encompasses suppositions related to the appropriateness of certain social positions, which affect the behavior of a person or a group [4].

The socially constructed processes of ageing and old age are however materialized in the everyday choices and decisions made by, for, and on behalf of older people. In this, many activities and forms of behavior are coded [5] as either more or less appropriate for people who have entered the socially defined period of old age. The problem with these coding practices is that they often become naturalized and accepted as the expression of what is called 'the norm'. This is particularly visible at the level of language use. For example, a saying 'mutton dressed a lamb' is rarely questioned as inappropriate and derogatory to a person who is described in this way. Ageism is the main reason for this.

© Springer International Publishing Switzerland 2015
J. Zhou and G. Salvendy (Eds.): ITAP 2015, Part I, LNCS 9193, pp. 405–413, 2015.
DOI: 10.1007/978-3-319-20892-3_40

1.1 Ageism

The term 'ageism' refers to discrimination based on chronological age [6]. The term was coined in 1969 by Robert Butler, who stressed that this type of prejudice and discrimination refers to any age group, though old people are at the highest risk of being affected [7]. This "last form of discrimination" [7, p. 3], preceded by sexism and racism comprises the variety of negative attitudes towards old people. The ageing process is viewed as something that renders people unattractive, unintelligent, asexual, unemployable and mentally incompetent [4]. However, the phenomenon of ageism needs to be understood as much more than a set of attitudes because ageism "is also a complex tendency woven into the social fabric" [8, 9] that is built on age relations [10] and intersecting relationships of inequality [11].

Ageism operates at different levels, including the personal, interpersonal and structural domains of human life [12]. Its prevalence is so profound that some question even the possibility of thinking about non-ageist societies (see [13]). Ageism is a form of social oppression that produces a fear of the ageing process and uses age as a signifier of classes of people [6]. Ageism is manifested through a number of processes, including systematic stereotyping, discrimination and the reinforcement of divisions between 'us' (the young) and 'them' (the old) that are founded on the assumption of homogeneity among old people [6, 14].

Ageism is enacted in social relationships and attitudes, and it always has negative connotations, unlike age discrimination, which may have both positive and negative characteristics [7, 15, 16]. Ageism, as a form of social practice, always refers to the aged body, and there are many arenas in which ageism operates [17]. These include relationships in the labour market, welfare policies and culture [17]. Culture remains one of the major sites of ageist practices that sustain "decline ideologies" [18], which tend to reduce the experience of ageing and old age to the sense of loss, despair due to being 'defeated' by passing time.

A wide range of empirical investigations of ageism discusses its various enactments in popular culture. From birthday cards [19] to TV programs [20], newspapers and magazines [21, 22], marketing strategies [23–25], and the food and cosmetics industries [26, 27], we learn about various prejudices against ageing and old people. These studies tend to focus on linguistics practices in either talk or text to emphasize the extent to which ageist assumptions and practices find their way into everyday lives. Language remains one of the key mediators of ageism.

1.2 New Media and Ageing

According to the report published by Pew Internet Project (2013), the use of social networking sites (SNS) among 65+ Internet users increased from 13 % in 2005 to 43 % in 2013. These changes go hand in hand with increasing number of studies that examine the use of social networking sites among older people. Studies investigating older people's engagement with this type of media tend to look at reasons and experiences of using it (e.g. [28–30] as well as non-users views on why they prefer not to engage with social media (e.g. [31, 32] to recommend changes: (a) in design of social networking sites to make it more age friendly, and (b) in the perceptions of older people regarding SNS.

Those studies point at experiences of uneasiness, fear, and embarrassment about the use of SNS as common among older people. In an overview of literature that examines the interaction of older people with SNS [33] conclude that concerns regarding privacy and unsuitability of current SNS designs are found to be the key factors that prevent older people from engaging with this type of media. These findings need to be however seen in context.

This paper draws attention to the fact that how older people engage with SNS is not only related to their personal characteristics and technical features of SNS design. To understand these encounters and their lack, we need to understand how societal discourses envision such meetings and how the use of SNS is coded in relation to age. Further to that, debates regarding the use of new media in general and SNS in particular tend to be based on representations of older people as a specific group of users/non-users who require a special attention. Although the main reason for that is a genuine concern, the reality is that such representation may lead to static and essentialist understandings of old age that not only reduce old age to a disadvantageous condition but also propagate the image of older people as a homogenous group [14], preventing us in this way from seeing an individual with her/his unique life history.

2 Discourse

Discourse is understood as a symbolic system and social order [34] that is composed of "meaningful practices that form the identities of subjects and objects" [35, pp. 3–4]. Everything we do has some meaning that is relevant for our way of living. In other words, "discourses have implications for what we can do and what we should do" [36, p. 75], and whom we can become. For example, the discourse of ageism is created at the axes of many different practices, such as the use of discriminatory language, the production of anti-ageing face creams, and the building of age-segregated housing, to mention just a few examples. These are ready-to-go practices that show what to do to fit in and to be included. In addition, institutions and social relations take part in (re) producing certain discourses and are shaped by them. The discourse of ageism produces a divide between old-bad and young-good, which affects the ways in which old people and young people interact.

Discourses embody rules, principles, and values that, at a particular point in time and in a particular place, are crucial for the construction of social reality. These aspects of discourses are considered as normal, natural and standard. The concept of discourse allows us to understand, for example, not only why people spend money on anti-ageing treatments but also why elder abuse tends to be seen as less dangerous than other forms of abuse. The discourse of ageism constructs ageing as worthless and hazardous to people. It also explains the attempts to build segregated living areas for old people, and it sheds new light on active and positive ageing policies. These examples also highlight that discourses have *real*-life and material consequences.

2.1   Critical Discourse Analysis

The origin of critical discourse analysis (CDA) can be traced back to early 70s, when a group of British researchers initiated studies of relations existing between language, power and ideologies [37]. The concept of power and ideology lies at the core of CDA and their embodiment in discourse is used to explain life of societies, their members and cultures [38, 39]. Thus, CDA warrants the process of consciousness-raising, revealing, reflecting and transforming persistent in the societies inequalities and discriminations induced by the above [40]. Media discourse occupies the prime position within this tradition by the dint of its role in expressing, constructing and reconstructing power relations that are accustomed in the society. Its overarching scope encompasses assertions concerning representations, identities and relations among discussed groups of people and phenomena [41].

CDA emerges as a valuable framework when investigating the relationships between language, power and inequalities. Language is an indispensable part of society, in the sense that linguistic phenomena are social and vice versa [42]. The use of language is, hence, considered to be constitutive of social identities, social relations and systems of knowledge. CDA focuses on revealing how language-in-use constitutes unequal power relationships, contributes to injustice and perpetrates discrimination; at the same time, it offers insight into particularities of social change through language use. Importantly, CDA attends to the ways in which some people are given the vice while others are either silenced or neglected to discuss issues of social change.

3   An Older Person(s) and Social Networking Sites

In this section, I will consider several examples of cultural texts that touch upon the use of SNS by older people. Using the perspective of critical discourses analysis, I will discuss those examples within the context of ageist assumptions that pervade our societies. Ultimately, this section will demonstrate that even positively sounding messages, such as: "Social networking sites for older people are wonderful ways to meet and share information with like-minded people. Social networking isn't just for youngsters; there are many sites suitable for older people on a wide range of subjects" (http://socialnetworking.lovetoknow.com/Social_Networking_Site_for_Older_People) perpetuate ageism and contribute to the creation of an imaginary divide between different age groups.

3.1   'Groupism'

"Nearly two-thirds of people aged 50–64 are on Facebook, which could explain why many younger people are switching to Twitter. But many older people haven't grasped the lingo, misusing terms like LOL, believing it to mean 'lots of love' rather than 'laugh out loud.'"(Daily News, August 6, 2013).

"Although it [increasing number of older people using social media] may be bad news for younger people who don't want their parents snooping or uploading embarrassing baby photos, it's great news for marketers. (…) The key is to treat older media users just like any other consumer – though it might be worth teaching your mum what "lol" really means." (http://www.candidsky.com/blog/social-media-and-the-older-generation/).

Articles like the above are exemplary in demonstrating the way older people and their encounters with social media are presented in public sphere. The key appears to be the imaginary war between 'the young' and 'the old' that is presented as a natural feature of intergenerational relations. The ageist assumption that underlines such images leads the authors of the first quote to conclude that as older people increase their use of Facebook, younger people lost interest in it as the site becomes associated with old age. In this way, we are indirectly presented with an image of virtual space as 'naturally' age-segregated, which does not encourage relations across generations, but is rather bound by strictly defined rules regarding who is 'in' and who is 'out'. Once the outsiders manage to enter a given space, those who are 'naturally' found are quickly promoted to look for and to create a different space that will again stave off the presence of outsiders for some time.

In the second quote, the same assumption regarding the intergenerational war is expressed in the envisioned embarrassment of younger people over, what is considered, a typical behavior of older people. According to this image, older people are apparently motived to use social media for two reasons: either monitoring their children or extending their family life onto online spheres. Older people are therefore constructed as unusual users of social media, who are above all else, different than the 'natural' social media users-younger people. This quote goes however further than this; it uses a familiar family frame to strengthen the divide between different generations. By juxtaposing parents to their children who in our culture are always presented as two binary groups, the second quote applies a family frame to present relations between SNS users of different ages. Indirectly, the link between children and the future versus parents and the past is brought to the forefront. Therefore, older people using SNS are constructed as being out of space and having little if any understanding of the rules of the game. Interestingly, both quotes use the same phrase "lol" to illustrate the incompatibility of older people and new media. Language is used to both describe this unfit and to give evidence. In this, both examples reproduce the academic discourse on 'digital immigrants and natives' [43] who speak different languages.

The difference between two quotes is that although both are based on ageist assumptions, the second one finishes on a lightly more positive note. Clearly speaking from the perspective of adult children, the authors encourage their peers to teach older people (read: older parents) how to use and understand the language of SNS. This may appear as an anti-ageist gesture. However, as Hendricks [8, p. 5]warns, this form of "benign or compassionate ageism, sometimes labeled the "poor dear" syndrome, is no less dehumanizing than its negative counterpart - either way people are viewed through a stereotypic lens". In a similar vein, slogans, such as "Older adults warm up to social networking" (http://www.techhive.com/article/2045964/older-adults-warm-up-to-social-networking.html) and "Old School, Meet New School: Seniors Tackle Social Networks" (http://www.cnbc.com/id/100537483#) may at first appear as rather positive. However, they too are based on an image of older people as distinctive 'they' who are different from the regular, if not 'normal' users. Thus, the encounter between SNS and old age seem to result in a form of 'groupism' that characterizes all older people as the same, and portrays them as lacking knowledge and skills that are needed to effectively engage with this new type of media.

3.2   It is All in the Family

Mentioned above the family frame used to explain differences and relationships between various age groups of SNS users is commonly used to emphasize not only the specific characteristics of older people as SNS users but also to explain what motives older people to use SNS. The below quote from a blog post entitled: "Why Your Grandmother Should Use Social Media" is an example:

"Your grandkids will think you are the coolest grandma or grandpa around because you are Internet savvy!" (http://blogs.wsj.com/experts/2014/12/03/why-your-grand mother-should-use-social-media/).

Building on family relationships, this quote introduces older SNS users as grand-parents. This has far reaching consequences for creating images of how and why older people should use SNS. Contrary to earlier mentioned examples, the one discussed here implies even a bigger distance between two groups of users that are separated by one generation. The image of grandchildren and grandparents is often used to idealise the family relationships and intergenerational solidarity. Particularly, 'the perfect grandma' stereotype is effectively used to create an image of older women as entirely focused on family lives and devoted to their grandchildren [44]. This is a stereotype that combines ageist and sexist assumptions about the role of older women in societies to imply which activities and spheres of life are more natural to them and which are not [45]. Seen through the family lenses, older people as grandparents are thus imagined to live for their grandchildren and use their appreciation to build self-confidences and positive images of themselves. In this way, social media is presented as a natural habitat of younger people-grandchildren, and older people-grandparents are encouraged to enter that sphere to get closer to their family members. Importantly, the whole image is often built on the ideas of inherent incompatibility between older people and social media-this is further emphasized by pointing out that those who use it are exceptional and therefore, named as "coolest" by their grandchildren.

3.3   Social Problem

In October 2013, the British Health Secretary Jeremy Hunt in one of his speeches defined the problem of loneliness among older people as "national shame" [46]. This speech triggered many discussions in the UK particularly that families were to bear greater responsibility for ensuring that their older family members will not be lonely. In May 2014, a think-tank Policy Exchange announced a report which stated that increase in the use of internet among older people could reduce loneliness in old age [47].

Independent Age, a charity organization that offers advice and support to older people in the UK and Ireland aims to combat three forms of poverty among older people: financial, social and information. Within this context, defining its problem areas, it points to the figure of 5.3. mln people aged 65+ as those who "have never been online" (http://www.independentage.org/about-us/). In this, the use of online resources or rather lack of it appears to be as alarming as living below the poverty rate or suffering from fuel poverty.

The above helps to explain messages, such as "Get the Silver Surfers on Facebook: Experts say using social media can help prevent decline in elderly's health (http://www.dailymail.co.uk/news/article-2873604/Older-people-use-Facebook-social-media-prevent-decline-health-study-finds.html#ixzz3LxmkiAPN). Increasingly, the use of SNS among older people is presented as a health issue and a social problem. In her constructionist account of social problems, Loseke [46] discusses two concepts that aid our understanding of how social problems are constructed: (a) social problem work - an activity of categorizing something and/or someone as a problem; (b) social problems game – an activity focused on convincing everyone about the seriousness, severity of a given condition or groups of people. The rhetoric that begins to unfold in policy and media discourse is indicative of the process of constructing the problem of older people not using social media. In this, many actors are involved in categorizing the lack of use of social media by older people as something that we need to be concerned with. Consequently, we are convinced that poor use of social media among older people is directly linked to loneliness and ill-health. As with any other social problem, one of its key characteristics is the assumption that things can be changed [46]. In this case, it is older people who are to change to solve their problems. There is an underlying assumption that moving online will automatically make older people happy, healthy and it will enable them to live to their full potential.

4 Concluding Remarks

The main tenet of this paper is that to understand an older person and his/her ways of engagement with social media, we need to attend to societal discourses that frame and define these types of activities. Only upon understanding social and cultural context in which an older person may or may not interact with social media, can we discuss the role of social media in everyday lives of older people.

Drawing on the concept of discourse and critical discourse analysis, this paper identified several ageist practices that pervade our thinking about encounters between an older person and social media. Continually, older people are referred to as a homogenous group, they are often presented in their family roles and in general, and their low level of engagement with social media is represented as a social problem to deal with. Against this picture, the SNS activity in itself is coded as one most appropriate for young people; older people are seen as unusual if not say 'unnatural' users.

This study is neither disputing the usefulness of social media nor claiming that access to social media is easy and straightforward. Instead, the purpose of this paper is to draw attention to the way in which SNS and older people became appropriated as representing and belonging to opposing poles. This, as Loos [47] demonstrates, leads to a number of misconceptions and myths surrounding the use of social media by older people. In line with this, the paper at hand posits that discourses that remove an individual replacing him/her with a group identity tend to be inaccurate, discriminatory, and decontextualized. Thus, it becomes essential to question the images of older people (not) using SNS and invest in contextualizing the discussion. This however, as Loos [47] argues, requires not only shifting our thinking from 'digital gap' metaphors to those of 'digital landscapes', but recognizing that how and when we access new media is dependent on a variety of factors among which age is only one.

References

1. Feartherstone, M., Wernick, A. (eds.): Images of Aging. Routledge, London (1995)
2. Öberg, B.-M., Närvänen, A.-L., Näsman, E., Olsson, E. (eds.): Changing World and the Ageing Subject. Ashgate, Aldershot (2004)
3. Thorson, J.A.: Aging in a Changing Society. Brunner/Mazel, Philadelphia (2000)
4. Atchley, R.C.: Social Forces and Ageing: An Introduction to Social Gerontology. Wadsworth, Belmont (1997)
5. Krekula, C.: The intersection of age and gender: reworking gender theory and social gerontology. Curr. Sociol. **55**(2), 155–171 (2007)
6. Bytheway, B.: Ageism. Open University Press, Buckingham (1995)
7. Palmore, E.B.: Ageism: Negative and Positive. Springer, New York (1999)
8. Hendricks, J.: Societal ageism. In: Palmore, E.B., Branch, L., Harris, D.K. (eds.) Encyclopedia of Ageism, pp. 292–297. The Haworth Pastoral Press, New York (2005)
9. Hendricks, J.: Ageism: looking across the margin in the new millennium. Generations **29**, 5–7 (2005)
10. Calasanti, T.M.: Ageism, gravity, and gender: experiences of aging bodies. Generations **29**, 8–12 (2005)
11. Calasanti, T.M.: Bodacious berry, potency wood and the aging monster: gender and age relations in anti-aging ads. Soc. Forces **86**(1), 335–355 (2007)
12. Estes, C.L., Phillipson, C., Biggs, S.: Social Theory, Social Policy and Ageing: A Critical Introduction. Open University Press, Maidenhead (2003)
13. McHugh, K.E.: Three faces of ageism: society, image and place. Ageing Soc. **23**, 165–185 (2003)
14. Loos, E.: Designing for dynamic diversity: representing various senior citizens in digital information sources. Observatorio J. **7**(1), 21–45 (2013)
15. Macnicol, J.: Analysing age discrimination. In: Öberg, B.-M., Närvänen, A.-L., Näsman, E., Olsson, E. (eds.) Changing Worlds and the Ageing Subject, pp. 23–40. Ashgate, Aldershot (2004)
16. Macnicol, J.: Age discrimination : an historical and contemporary analysis. Cambridge University Press, Cambridge (2006)
17. Laws, G.: Understanding ageism: lessons from feminism and postmodernism. Gerontologist **35**(1), 112–118 (1995)
18. Gullette, M.M.: Aged by Culture. The University of Chicago Press, Chicago (2004)
19. Ellis, R.S., Morrison, T.G.: Stereotypes of ageing: messages promoted by age-specific paper birthday cards available in Canada. Int. J. Ageing Hum. Dev. **61**(1), 57–73 (2005)
20. Robinson, T., Callister, M., Magoffin, D., Moore, J.: The portrayal of older characters in Disney animated films. J. Aging Stud. **21**, 203–213 (2007)
21. Lewis, D.C., Medvedev, K., Seponski, D.M.: Awakening to the desires of older women: deconstructing ageism within fashion magazines. J. Aging Stud **25**(2), 101–109 (2011)
22. Wilińska, M., Cedersund, E.: "Classic ageism" or "brutal economy"? - old age and older people in the Polish media. J. Aging Stud. **24**(4), 335–343 (2010)
23. Carrigan, M., Szmigin, I.: Advertising in an ageing society. Ageing Soc. **20**, 217–233 (2000)

24. Coupland, J.: Gendered discourse on the problem of ageing: consumerised solutions. Discourse Commun. 1(1), 37–61 (2007)
25. Williams, A., Ylänne, V., Wadleigh, P.M.: Selling the 'elixir of life' images of the elderly in Olivio advertising campaign. J. Aging Stud. 21, 1–21 (2007)
26. Vincent, J.A.: Ageing contested: anti-ageing science and the cultural construction of old age. Sociology 40(4), 681–698 (2006)
27. Vincent, J.: Science and imaginary in the 'war on old age'. Ageing Soc. 27, 941–961 (2007)
28. Gatto, S.L., Tak, S.H.: Computer, internet, and e-mail use among older adults: benefits and barriers. Educ. Gerontol. 34(9), 800–811 (2008)
29. Lehtinen, V., Näsänen, J., Sarvas, R.: A little silly and empty-headed: older adults' understandings of social networking sites. In: Proceeding of the 2009 British Computer Society Conference on Human-Computer Interaction, BCS-HCI 2009, Cambridge, UK, pp. 45–54 (2009)
30. Sayago, S., Forbes, P., Blat, J.: Older people's social sharing practices in YouTube through an ethnographical lens. In: Proceedings of the 26th Annual BCS Interaction Specialist Group Conference on People and Computers, pp. 185–194. British Computer Society, September 2012
31. Lüders, M., Brandtzæg, P.B.: 'My children tell me it's so simple': A mixed-methods approach to understand older non-users' perceptions of Social Networking Sites. New Media Soc. First published online 9 October 2014
32. Xie, B., Watkins, I., Golbeck, J., Huang, M.: Understanding and changing older adults' perceptions and learning of social media. Educ. Gerontol. 38(4), 282–296 (2012)
33. Nef, T., Ganea, R.L., Müri, R.M., Mosimann, U.P.: Social networking sites and older users–a systematic review. Int. Psychogeriatr. 25(7), 1041–1053 (2013)
34. Howarth, D.: Discourse. Open University Press, Buckingham (2000)
35. Howarth, D., Stavrakakis, Y.: Introducing discourse theory and political analysis. In: Howarth, D., Norval, A.J., Stavrakakis, Y. (eds.) discourse theory and political analysis, pp. 1–23. Manchester University Press, Manchester (2004)
36. Burr, V.: Social Constructionism, 2nd edn. Routledge, London (2007[1995])
37. Blommaert, J.: Discourse. Cambridge University, Cambridge (2007[2005]
38. Fairclough, N.: Critical discourse analysis and the marketization of public discourse: the universities. Discourse Soc. 4(2), 133–168 (1993)
39. Wodak, R.: Disorders of Discourse. Longman, London (1996)
40. Locke, T.: Critical Discourse Analysis. Continuum, New York/London (2004)
41. Fairclough, N.: Critical discourse analysis and the marketization of public discourse: the universities. Discourse Soc. 4(2), 133–168 (1993)
42. Fairclough, N.: Language and Power. Longman, Harlow (2001[1989])
43. Prensky, M.: Digital natives, digital immigrants. Horizon 9(5), 1–6 (2001)
44. Williams, A., Ylänne, V., Wadleigh, P.M.: Selling the 'elixir of life': images of the elderly in Olivio advertising campaign. J. Aging Stud. 21, 1–21 (2009)
45. Wilińska, M.: Because women will always be women and men are just getting older: intersecting discourses of age and gender. Curr. Sociol. 58(6), 879–896 (2010)
46. BBC News. http://www.bbc.co.uk/news/uk-politics-24572231
47. Policy Exchange. http://www.policyexchange.org.uk/media-centre/press-releases/category/item/target-loneliness-by-encouraging-pensioners-online
48. Loseke, D.R.: Thinking About Social Problems. An Introduction to Constructionist Perspectives. Aldine de Gruyter, New York (2003)
49. Loos, E.: Senior citizens: digital immigrants in their own country? Observatorio J. 6(1), 1–23 (2012)

Technology Generation and Media Usage in B-2-B Communication: A Cross-Cultural View

Martina Ziefle[1]([⊠]), Vanessa Cabral[2], Judith Leckebusch[1],
and Toni Drescher[3]

[1] Human-Computer Interaction Center, Campus-Boulevard 57,
52074 Aachen, Germany
{ziefle,leckebusch}@comm.rwth-aachen.de
[2] KEX Knowledge Exchange AG, Campus Boulevard 55,
52074 Aachen, Germany
[3] Fraunhofer Institute for Production Technology, Steinbachstraße 17,
52074 Aachen, Germany

Abstract. In this work culture-specific and cross-cultural influences on frequency of use of media and trust in media for B-2-B communication purposes were explored, taking Brazil and Germany as exemplary countries. Using an online survey, 236 respondents from Brazil and Germany were examined regarding their professional media usage. Findings show both culture-specific as well as cultural insensitive media usage in B-2-B communication. Brazilians use new media more frequently than Germans. However, it was also revealed that cross-cultural variables as age, gender and technical self-efficacy influence even more significantly the frequency of use of media. Furthermore, trust in media for B-2-B communication showed to positively correlated with the frequency of use of media in both countries.

Keywords: Business-to-business · B-2-B · New media · Social media · Culture · Age

1 Introduction

Due to new technology developments, enterprises from all over the world have been facing the challenge of rebalancing between traditional and new media so as to effectively conduct local and global business-to-business (B-2-B) communication [1, 2]. From the perspective of Social, Media and Communication Sciences, this phenomenon is not only challenges regarding the question of which media and communication means might be appropriate and accepted for different professional areas and communication needs, more so, cultural identity and forms in social media usage in professional areas are not adequately considered so far.

The modern world is highly interconnected through information and communication technologies [3, 4]. New forms of electronic media keep constantly reshaping the ways of communicating all over the globe and in all areas of human interaction. In the

© Springer International Publishing Switzerland 2015
J. Zhou and G. Salvendy (Eds.): ITAP 2015, Part I, LNCS 9193, pp. 414–425, 2015.
DOI: 10.1007/978-3-319-20892-3_41

so-called global information society [5], the integration of new media in corporate settings is already a reality, following the enormous success of these new communication forms in the private sphere [6, 7]. For the business-to-business (B-2-B) communication field, which concerns enterprise communication to and among internal and external stakeholders, such changes have demanded a challenging process of rebalancing between traditional and new media [8]. Yet, there is still a considerable need for research in this area.

International B-2-B communication is on the rise, since cross-border transactions have become significantly more intense over the past 20 years [9, 10]. In spite of B-2-B's essential importance for the global economy, most of the actual reports and studies address primarily business-to-customer (B-2-C) communication issues, which are often not pertinent in B-2-B settings [11]. Besides, most trend studies and surveys on these topics provide findings that target mainly advertising and market aspects [12, 13], leaving aside the complexity of media usage or media effects patterns. Furthermore, there is not much investigation of the influence of cultures, cross-cultural individual determinants or even of the constantly changing media paradigms. Understanding and keeping pace with the changes in such a complex system that englobes media-based B-2-B communication reverberate in a positive way for marketing professionals or information system researchers [14].

B-2-B Communication. Opposite to business-to-customer (B-2-C), B-2-B-oriented companies do not target private consumers, but design and sell products and services mainly to organizations, [15]. The B-2-B sector is responsible for a very significant part of the total industry revenues worldwide. B-2-B communication regards all communicative activities performed by a company towards the human being as part of a procuring organization. With respect to the subject matter of communication, not only products and services can be promoted but also the company as a whole; hence, the term B-2-B is also regarded in marketing as 'corporate communication' [16]. Corporate communications aims not only to the formation and development of a strong and unique image of the company's personality, it also represents communication tools and activities that are used to represent the company and its services to the relevant internal and external target groups of communication [17]. More specifically, corporate communications can be divided into three branches: the market communication, the employee communication and public relations (Fig. 1).

'Public relations' ensure the company's fundamental sphere of influence [18], for constructing and keeping relationship and trust in social and political contexts [19, 20]. 'Market communication', in contrast, seeks the economic objective of advertisement, which means selling products and services to other companies. 'Employee communication' concerns internal necessities and processes, and it is oriented to organizational stakeholders so as to ensure their incorporation in internal decision-making processes that aim the corporate development [17]. The latter seeks for higher employee satisfaction and loyalty, as well as higher productivity and distribution of information and knowledge inside the organization. The present work refers to the communication activities of B-2-B-oriented organizations, which target external and internal stakeholder groups [21].

Corporate Communications		
Market communication	**Employee communication**	**Public relations**
Transaction-oriented	Task-oriented	Interaction-oriented
Stakeholders in market environment	Stakeholders inside the organization	Stakeholders in social and political contexts
Economic	PERSPECTIVE	Social-scientific

Fig. 1. Corporate communications regarding its functions [22]

Media Usage B-2-B Communication. In what concerns the typology of media, there is primarily the differentiation between individual and mass media [23]. The individual media can also be termed '1:1 media', since they enable a two-sided interpersonal (synchronous or asynchronous) commu-nication. Examples are mail, e-mail or telephone. Mass media (1:n media) allow to transmit content to many recipients. Typical mass media are TV, radio, newsletters, but also classical websites that are based on one-way communication [24].

With the further development of Internet as 'Web 2.0' and of technical devices, as well as due to the advent of social media tools, another type of media type has emerged: the so-called 'n:n media', which is characterized by the possibility of many senders communicate with many recipients on a global and public scale. Due to the intensification of use of n:n media, there is a switch from push to pull communication. Within push communication stimuli are sent unilaterally and the recipients respond to it or not. Pull communication, in contrast is based on dialogue. The users search actively for the information they need, recommend – or not – services and products (the 'word-of-mouth'), and step into dialogues with companies, not only for information but also in order to give feedback.

Due to the increasing development and successful diffusion of the already mentioned Web 2.0 technologies, companies were induced to gradually adopt the new tools for means of corporate communication. While B-2-C-oriented enterprises adapted more quickly to the new reality, B-2-B companies are still beginning to keep pace with the times [11]. Finally, since B-2-B communication is situated in the middle of a process of turnaround from push to pull communication strategies, it is still characterized by the broad use of both traditional and new media. Therefore, investigating the media usage in this context requires contemplating both kinds of media (Fig. 2).

Regarding the traditional 1:1 media, the present work focuses on some non-electronic media for interpersonal communication, which are face-to-face communication, telephone, FAX and mail. On the other hand, new – and hence electronic-based – 1:1 media is represented in this work by e-mail, videoconferencing, instant messenger (e.g. *WhatsApp*) and online chat (e.g. *Google Talk*).

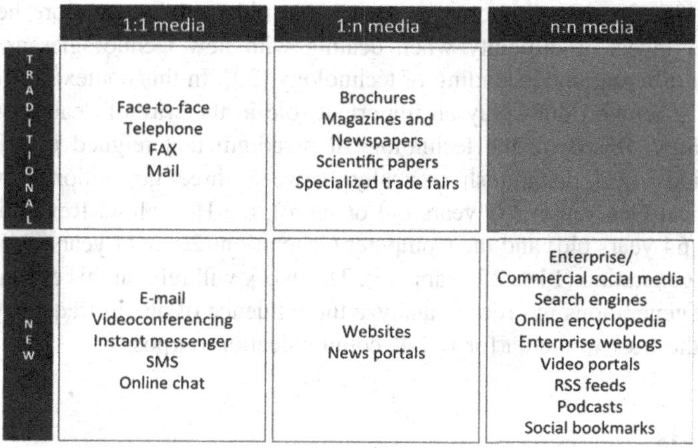

1:1 media	1:n media	n:n media
T R A D I T I O N A L Face-to-face Telephone FAX Mail	Brochures Magazines and Newspapers Scientific papers Specialized trade fairs	
N E W E-mail Videoconferencing Instant messenger SMS Online chat	Websites News portals	Enterprise/ Commercial social media Search engines Online encyclopedia Enterprise weblogs Video portals RSS feeds Podcasts Social bookmarks

Fig. 2. Chosen media for this research

The new 1:n media that are regarded here are websites (in its traditional, not dialog-based forms) and news portals. Since scientific papers can also be accessed online, they are also assigned to the category of new 1:n media. As new n:n media online encyclopedia, weblogs, social networks (both corporate and public), social bookmarking, RSS feeds, podcasts, video portals and search engines are explored.

Cultural Determinants in B-2-B Communication. In order to operationalize the concept of culture, the present work is based on the cultural dimensions used in the GLOBE study, that focuses on culture and leadership and comprises of 61 countries [25] and reports cultural values and practices across countries, identifying organizational practices and leadership attributes [26]. Overall, nine dimensions were developed: (1) *Uncertainty avoidance:* the extent to which members of a society or an organization strive to avoid uncertainty by reliance on norms and defined processes. (2) *Power distance:* the degree to which members of an organization expect and agree that power should be equally shared. (3) *Collectivism I (societal):* the degree to which social and organizational practices encourage and reward collective distribution of resources and collective action. (4) *Collectivism II (in-group):* the degree to which individuals express price, loyalty and cohesiveness in their groups. (5) *Gender Egalitarianism:* extent to which a society or an organization minimizes gender role differences and discrimination. (6) *Assertiveness:* degree to which individuals in organizations are assertive, confrontational and aggressive. (7) *Future Orientation:* degree to which individuals engage in future-oriented behaviors such as planning and investing in the future. (8) *Performance Orientation:* extent to which an organization encourages or rewards group member for performance improvement. *(9) Humane Orientation:* degree to which individuals encourage and reward others for being fair, altruistic, friendly, generous, caring and kind to others.

Age and Technical Generations. Historically, new technologies have caused visible changes in the way of living, of communicating and even of understanding the world. A huge body of knowledge is prevailing regarding the influence of age on technology acceptance [27, 28, 29]. Outcomes revealed that older adults are more hesitant and show higher levels of difficulty when dealing with new technologies as well as a significantly different understanding of technology [30]. In this context, the concept of technology generation does play an important role in the way of dealing with media and technology. Based on the technological paradigm that reigned in different formative periods [31] distinguish basically between three generational groups: the Early-technical Generation (65 years old or more), the Household Revolution Generation (49 to 64 years old) and the Computer Generation (26 to 44 years old) as well as the Internet generation (14 to 25 years old). This work will rely on this expanded model of technical generations in order to analyze the influence of age in frequency of use of media and the trust in media for B-2-B communication purposes.

2 Methods

In this paper we explore the Media Usage in B-2-B Communication and the questions if media usage is depending on the technology generation and in how far different cultures do use media differently.

Selection of Countries and Cultures: Brazil and Germany. In order to shed light on culture-specific and cross-cultural influences on media usage for B-2-B communication, we chose Brazil and Germany as two exemplary countries, which are comparably different, and have frequent business collaborations on a B-2-B communication basis. Although Brazil's cultural traits had large influence of European cultures – due to the mother country Portugal and the European immigration in the 19th century –, a first-time interaction of Brazilians with Germans reveal some clear differences between both countries.

The mixture of races and cultures, together with the tropical climate, are said to have produced in Brazil "people of easy-going disposition" [32], who also tend to have a close distance of comfort, to be tactile and informal. Germans are known worldwide for their effectiveness, straightforward communication and serious and formal approach [32]. Ultimately, such culture-related characteristics and tendencies may also influence specific recurrent patterns of media usage [33]. On the base of an interview, which was done prior to the questionnaire study, a Brazilian marketing specialist, who is also CEO at a big marketing agency in the country, affirmed that Brazilians "generally try to take the warmth of relationships into connections through new media, including for professional issues". Furthermore, he also claimed, that "Brazilians show a high level of acceptance and vivid interest for new technologies and media". In contrast, an interviewed German press and communications professional stated that the Germans "always look first for the fly in the ointment (…) when dealing with new technologies and new media", since they would tend to be very conservative, perfectionist and cautious.

Questionnaire. The questionnaire consisted of 30 questions and it was divided into six main parts: (a) culture and decision-making style; (b) self-efficacy when dealing with technology; (c) typification of the enterprise and working environment; (d) way of dealing with texts in the B-2-B context; (e) media usage in the B-2-B communication; and (f) demographic data. The survey was developed in German and translated into

Table 1. Item example of approval of information collection

Cultural dimensions:	Which item applies for your country?
Collectivism	• The system of seeks for individual interest
Power distance	• Heads have the full authority and need obedience
Humane orientation	• Most people have a clearly structured life with only few unexpected changes
Collectivism	• Group loyalty dominates individual interests
Collectivism	• Clerks are loyal towards the firm they are working for
Assertiveness	• Most people here avoid conflicts
Gender egalitarianism	• We have gender equality in professional careers is
Future orientation	• Most people live for the moment rather than the future
Performance orientation	• Students are encouraged to engage for high performance

Portuguese in order to be distributed both in Germany and in Brazil. The questionnaire was delivered online through personal and professional networks, social media and third-part indications. Its completion was estimated to take between 15 and 20 min. In the following we report those sections in greater detail, which will be reported later. Other parts remain uncovered due to space restrictions.

The first relevant section concerned culture and decision-making style. All culture-related items were adopted from a short version of the original GLOBE questionnaire.

The six-point scale ranged from 'fully applies' to 'does not apply at all' (Table 1).

The next section dealt with media usage for B-2-B communication and collected data about preferences and frequency of media usage in the working context. The items displayed both 1:1 and n:n traditional and new media. The seven and six-point scales (respectively) enabled the frequency range from 'never' to 'every day'.

Sample. A total of 236 people took part, 129 respondents from Brazil and 107 from Germany. Among the Brazilians, 69 % were male (21.3 % female). Among the Germans, 61.7 % were male (34.5 % are female). *Technology generation.* The majority (71 %) belongs to the computer generation (26–48). The second biggest group is represented by the Internet generation (14–25) with a total of 14 % of all respondents. The household revolution generation (49–64) is represented by 8 % of participants. *Education.* Overall, the sample was highly educated. 72 % of the Brazilians are or have been in college, or have a higher-level education, being a Master or a post-graduation qualification. Among the Germans, 62 % also have a Bachelor or Master degree. Around 8 % of the Brazilians and 5 % of the Germans have done a doctorate. *Professional experience.* Around 97 % of the Brazilian and 89 % of the German respondents have already been or are professionally active. 45 % of Brazilians have already worked abroad, most of them (13 %) for more than two years. 36 % of the Germans have worked or are currently working abroad, the majority (15 %) for less than six months. 57 % of Brazilian women against 47 % of men have been working outside Brazil, while 47 % of German men opposite to only 22 % of women have already worked elsewhere than in Germany. Most of respondents that are working abroad belong to the computer generation (26–48 years). 5 % of the Gameboy generation (14–25 years) from Brazil has already been working abroad.

3 Results

Technology Generation and Self-competence when Using Technology. In Fig. 3, outcomes in technical self-competence are depicted, assessed by a scale of [34]. This personality attitude is considerably related to technology generation. Putting nationality aside, the means for the technical generations are M = 76.8 (Gameboy), M = 75.7 (Computer) and M = 66.3 (Household Revolution). Concerning gender, men had significantly higher scores (M = 78.9) compared to women (M = 65.1). Nationality, in contrast, did not impact technical self-competence.

Cultural Dimensions in Brazil and Germany. When plotting the means of cultural dimensions on a radar z, the cultural differences become obvious (Fig. 4).

Mann-Whitney U tests show significant differences between both cultures for the following cultural dimensions 'Humane Orientation' (p = .000), 'Uncertainty

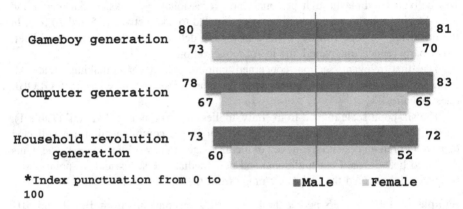

Fig. 3. Technical self-competence for gender and technology generations in both countries

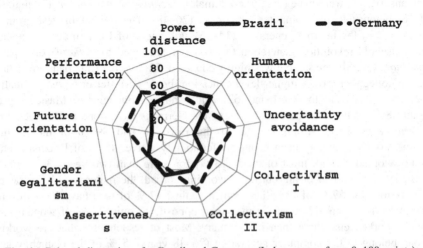

Fig. 4. Cultural dimensions for Brazil and Germany (Index ranges from 0–100 points)

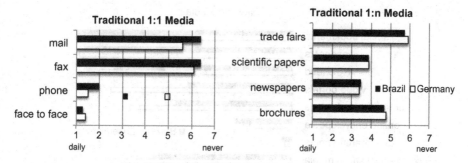

Fig. 5. Usage of traditional media in both countries

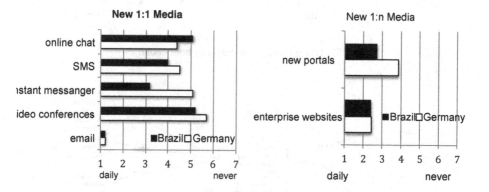

Fig. 6. Usage of new media in both countries

Avoidance' (p = .000), 'Collectivism I' (p = .000), 'Collectivism II' (p = .000), 'Performance Orientation' (p = .000) and 'Future Orientation' (p = .000).

Use of Media in Brazil and Germany. In the following the media usage in both countries is reported. Figure 5 shows outcomes in traditional media.

As can be seen, both countries show differences in traditional media usage. By means of non-parametric Mann-Whitney U tests, the frequency of use of telephone (p = .002), FAX (p = .005), and mail (p = .000) was more often used in Brazil in contrast to Germany, while the traditional 1: n media were used comparably often. The next analysis regarded the New Media (1:1, and 1:n, Fig. 6). Again significant differences between media usage in both countries showed up. In Germany, instant messenger (p = .000) and news portals (p = .002) are used less frequent in comparison to Brazil.

Finally we explored the usage frequency of new n:n Media (Fig. 7). Overall it could be revealed that new n:n Media are statistically significant more frequently used in Brazil in comparison to Germany (commercial social media tools (p = .014), enterprise web blogs (p = .000) and video portals (p = .000)).

In order to find out if media usage is impacted by technology generation, we run Spearman correlation analyses, revealing indeed effects of generational influences

422   M. Ziefle et al.

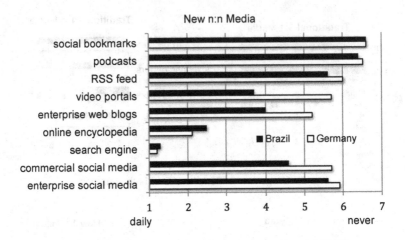

Fig. 7. Usage of new n:n media in both countries

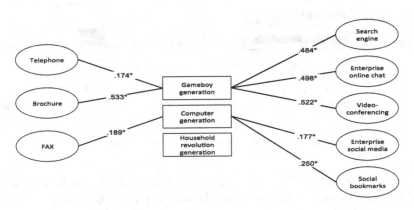

Fig. 8. Correlations between technology generation and media usage

(Fig. 8). All correlations are positive, which means that the higher the age, the more often the specific media are used for B-2-B communication purposes. However, the oldest technical generation does not correlate significantly with the frequency of use of any medium, which probably is due to the small sample. Moreover, concerning the use of social media for private purposes, the Gameboy generation presents the higher frequency levels: 78 % of the group said to use social media at home very frequently.

4   Discussion

This work showed that Brazil and Germany have significant differences in their cultural dimensions: while Brazilians tend to be more relationship-oriented and less meticulous about the future, Germans tend to avoid uncertainty and prize performance. At the same time, gender inequality seems to be an issue in both countries. Specific cultural values of both countries also proved to influence patterns of etiquette regarding formal addressing and texts for B-2-B purposes. Yet, there is a culture-independent consensus regarding general formal addressing and the proper use of language, which might be influenced mainly by the working context.

When it comes to the question if there are differences in media usage across both countries, at a first glimpse, the general patterns of frequency of use of media are quite similar. However, there were also differences: Germans tend to use traditional media more often than Brazilians, who tend to give preference to new media. This finding was confirmed by the fact that Germany had higher scores regarding the use of traditional media (telephone, FAX and mail), while Brazil's higher scores were for the use of new media (Instant Messenger, news portals, commercial social media tools, enterprise weblogs and video portals). In order to assess to what extent individual characteristics impact the use of media for B-2-B communication purposes, age and technology generations was focused. A construct that clearly bounds age and gender regarding the use of technology is technical self-efficacy. Findings showed that technical self-efficacy is closely related to age and gender, and independent from nationality. Both in Brazil and in Germany, men always report higher self-confidence than women, and younger people also higher scores than older persons. The cultural-insensitive pattern corroborates earlier findings according to which different technical generations experience technology in a different way [27, 29]. Whilst older persons prefer the use of telephone, fax or video portals, showing older people using traditional media more frequently than new medium, the technical generations correlated differently from 'age' when combined separately with specific new media – such as social bookmarks and enterprise social media. Finally, technical self-efficacy displayed greatest impact on the frequency of use especially of new n:n media. This shows that higher levels of confidence when dealing with technology also influence the acceptance and adoption of new communication technologies in a positive way.

Of course, this work represents only a first insight in the complex phenomenon "culture". Critically speaking, culture was treated like a "black box", which is related to political, geographic and historical frames. Yet, it is reasonably to assume that the use of a country as a proxy for culture may be misleading. Although this decision has helped to operationalize the concept of culture, relevant regional differences from each country were not taken into account. Also, individual cultural differences were also not considered. Thus, even though the results regarding cultural dimensions for both countries were similar to the GLOBE outcomes for both countries, conclusive assumptions may be premature and have to be replicated in future research.

References

1. Valdez, A.C., Schaar, A.K., Bender, J., Aghassi, S., Schuh, G., Ziefle, M.: Social media applications for knowledge exchange in organizations. In: Phillips-Wren, G., Razmerita, L., Jain, L.C. (eds.) Innovations in Knowledge Management. Springer, Heidelberg (2015)
2. Li, C.: Groundswell: winning in a world transformed by social technologies. Strateg. Dir. **26** (8) (2010)

3. Castells, M.: The Internet Galaxy: Reflections on the Internet, Business, and Society. Oxford University Press Inc, New York (2001)

4. McQuail, D.: Mass Communication Theory: An introduction. Sage Publications, New York (1987)

5. Teltscher, S., Gray, V., Magpantay, E., Olaya, D., Vallejo, I.: Measuring the Information Society. International Tele-communications Union, Geneva (2013). http://www.itu.int/en/ITUD/Statistics/Documents/publications/mis2013/MIS2013_withoutAnnex_4.pdf (2013)

6. Schaar, A.K., Calero Valdez, A., Ziefle, M., Eraßme, D., Löcker, A.-K., Jakobs, E.-M.: Reasons for using social networks professionally. In: Meiselwitz, G. (ed.) SCSM 2014. LNCS, vol. 8531, pp. 385–396. Springer, Heidelberg (2014)

7. Valdez, A.C., Schaar, A., Ziefle, M.: Personality influences on etiquette requirements for social media in the working context. In: Holzinger, A., et al. (eds.) Human Factors in Computing and Informatics, pp. 431–450. Springer, Berlin (2013)

8. Herbst, D.: Corporate Identity. Cornelsen, Berlin (2003)

9. Javidan, M., Stahl, G., Brodbeck, F., Wilderom, C.: Cross-border transfer of knowledge: cultural lessons from GLOBE. Acad. Manag. Executive 19(2), 59–76 (2005)

10. Croucher, S.: Social networking and cultural adaptation: a theoretical model. J. Int. Intercultural Commun. 4(4), 259–264 (2011)

11. Wiersema, F.: The B2B agenda: The current state of B2B marketing and a look ahead. Ind. Mark. Manag. 42, 470–488 (2013)

12. Ji, Y.G., Hwangbo, H., Yi, J.S., Rau, P.P., Fang, X., Ling, C.: The influence of cultural differences on the use of social network services and the formation of social capital. Int. J. Hum. Comput. Interact. 26(11–12), 1100–1121 (2010)

13. Holland, J., Gentry, J.W.: Ethnic consumer reaction to targeted marketing: a theory of intercultural accommodation. J. Advertising 28(1), 65–77 (1999)

14. McEwan, B., Sobre-Denton, M.: Virtual cosmopolitanism: constructing third cultures and transmitting social and cultural capital through social media. J. Int. Intercultural Commun. 4 (4), 252–258 (2011)

15. Fill, C.: Marketing Communications: Engagements, Strategies and Practice. Pearson Education, Harlow (2005)

16. Goldhaber, G.: Organizational communication. Brown & Benchmark, Madison (1993)

17. Smidts, A., Pruyn, A.T., Van Riel, C.B.: The impact of employee communication and perceived external prestige on organizational identification. Acad. Manag. J. 44(5), 1051–1062 (2001)

18. Daft, R., Huber, G.: How Organizations Learn: A Communication Framework (No. TR-ONR-DG-18). Texas Department Of Management, Texas (1986)

19. Zerfaß, A.: The corporate communications scorecard. In: van Ruler, B., Verčič, A.T., Verčič, D. (eds.) Public Relations Metrics Research and Evaluation, p. 139. Routledge, London (2008)

20. Ziefle, M., Röcker, C., Holzinger, A.: Medical Technology in Smart Homes: Exploring the User's Perspective on Privacy, Intimacy and Trust. In: 35th Annual IEEE Computer Software and Applications Conference, pp. 410–415 (2011)

21. Fink, S., Zerfaß, A.: Social Media Governance 2010–How companies, the public sector and NGOs handle the challenges of transparent communication on the Internet. University of Leipzig/Fink & Fuchs Public Relations AG, Leipzig/Wiesbaden (2010)

22. Mast, C., Huck, S., Güller, K.: Kundenkommunikation. UTB, Stuttgart (2005)

23. Schweiger, W.: Theorien der Mediennutzung: Eine Einführung. VS, Wiesbaden (2007)

24. Kärkkäinen, H., Jussila, J., Väisänen, J.: Social media use and potential in business-to-business companies' innovation. In: 14th International Academic Mindtrek Conference: Envisioning Future Media Environments, pp. 228–236. ACM (2010)

25. House, R., Javidan, M., Hanges, P., Dorfman, P.: Understanding cultures and implicit leadership theories across the globe: an introduction to project GLOBE. J. World Bus. **37**(1), 3–10 (2002)

26. House, R., Hanges, P., Javidan, M., Dorfman, P., Gupta, V.: Culture, Leadership, and Organizations: The GLOBE Study of 62 Societies. Sage, Beverly Hills (2004)

27. Gaul, S., Ziefle, M.: Smart home technologies: insights into generation-specific acceptance motives. In: Holzinger, A., Miesenberger, K. (eds.) USAB 2009. LNCS, vol. 5889, pp. 312–332. Springer, Heidelberg (2009)

28. Wilkowska, W., Alagöz, F., Ziefle, M.: How age and country of origin impact the readiness to adopt e-Health technologies: an intercultural comparison. J. Prev. Assess. Rehabil. **41**, 2072–2080 (2012)

29. Arning, K., Ziefle, M.: Different perspectives on technology acceptance: the role of technology type and age. In: Holzinger, A., Miesenberger, K. (eds.) Human – Computer Interaction for eInclusion, pp. 20–41. Springer, Heidelberg (2009)

30. Arning, K., Ziefle, M.: Ask and you will receive: training older adults to use a PDA in an active learning environment. Int. J. Mob. Hum. Comput. Interact. **2**(1), 21–47 (2010)

31. Sackmann, R., Winkler, O.: Technology generations revisited: the Internet generation. Gerontechnology **11**(4), 493–503 (2013)

32. Lewis, R.: When Cultures Collide: Leading Across Cultures. Nicholas Brealey, Boston (2006)

33. Inseong, L., Boreum, C., Jinwoo, K., Se-Joon, H.: Culture-technology fit: effects of cultural characteristics on the post-adoption beliefs of mobile Internet users. Int. J. Elect. Com. **11**, 11–51 (2007)

34. Beier, G.: Kontrollüberzeugungen im Umgang mit Technik. Report Psychologie **9**, 684–693 (1999)

Patterns for User Interface Adaptations

Towards Runtime Adaptations for Improving the Usability of Web Forms for Elderly Users

Gottfried Zimmermann[✉], Annkristin Stratmann, David Reeß, and Tobias Glaser

Responsive User Interface Experience Research Group, Stuttgart Media University, Stuttgart, Germany
gzimmermann@acm.org, {as198,dr044,tg049}@hdm-stuttgart.de

Abstract. Websites and web applications that require user input via web forms can be a usability barrier for elderly users if not designed carefully. This issue is even compounded by a broad diversity of needs and preferences as observed in this group of users. In this paper, we report about a current study in which we prototypically implemented and empirically evaluated four exemplary patterns of user interface adaptation. These patterns allow for dynamic substitution and/or augmentation of user interface parts at runtime, with the goal of improving the individual usability for an elderly user in a specific use context. This approach could eventually lead to highly personalized web forms within GPII and URC enabled infrastructures.

Keywords: User interface adaptation · Personalized user interface · Web forms · Supplemental user interface resources · GPII · URC

1 Introduction

User interaction with Web forms can be challenging for users, in particular for older users[1] who are unfamiliar with entering data on the Web [1]. Web forms that are not designed with elderly users in mind often result in low usability for those users, causing high error rates, poor efficiency and a low user satisfaction.

Many websites require form input from their users. This applies in particular to public Internet services (e.g. online government services, online banking, online shops, online travel agencies) which are becoming more and more essential for the citizens. With an increasing portion of people belonging to the group of "elderly people" due to the demographic change, it is important to allow for their full participation in a digital society.

---

[1] The term "older users" is often used for people of age 50 + , but this is not consistent throughout literature. In this paper, the terms "older users", "elderly users" and "seniors" are used as synonyms.

© Springer International Publishing Switzerland 2015
J. Zhou and G. Salvendy (Eds.): ITAP 2015, Part I, LNCS 9193, pp. 426–436, 2015.
DOI: 10.1007/978-3-319-20892-3_42

However, there are a vast number of websites that have not been designed with the needs of senior citizens in mind. Also, many web designers and developers are currently working on Internet services of the future, but do not have the knowledge and expertise to design them in a senior-friendly way. Is it possible to repair the existing online services with regard to their usability for elderly persons? Can we do so in a well-structured approach, driven by patterns of replacement and/or substitution, even at runtime?

Older adults are quite diverse in their digital interface preferences and needs [2]. The diversity is caused by factors such as their previous technical education and experiences, and their attitudes, but also by their abilities (in particular cognitive, motor, seeing, hearing) which may be affected by age [3]. Therefore, older users should not be understood as *one* coherent user group, as represented by one persona only.

A "one size fits all" approach would not be adequate for meeting the needs of elderly users. Therefore, the Global Public Inclusive Infrastructure (GPII) [4] promotes a "one size fits one" approach in which a user interface is adapted based on the needs and preferences of an individual user. Nevertheless, it is useful to investigate candidate patterns of user interface adaptation with regard to how many users could potentially benefit from them. In this paper, we focus on patterns that could be applied on Web forms at runtime to cater for "quick fixes" to improve the personal experience of a particular user.

The remainder of this paper is structured as follows: Sect. 2 provides an overview of existing guidelines on the design of web forms for older users. In Sect. 3, we briefly explain the concept of user interface adaptations at runtime for the purpose of improved usability. Section 4 proposes some exemplary patterns of user interface adaptations that could be applied on Web forms, and reports about empirical findings of a study on these patterns. Finally, we provide conclusions in Sect. 5, and relate the study's results to the future of user interface adaptations.

2   User Interface Guidance on Web Forms for Older Adults

The American Association of Retired Persons (AARP) published a literature review on designing web sites for older adults in 2004 [3]. This literature review and some follow-up empirical research [5] resulted finally in 20 high-level heuristics (broken down into checklist items) for "understanding older adults as web users" [6]. Among them, the heuristics on using task-relevant and familiar images for buttons (checklist items 2.5 and 2.6), and on avoiding scrolling lists (checklist item 4.3) relate to our pattern on using push-buttons vs. drop-down menus (see Sect. 4.1). The heuristic on descriptive error messages (checklist item 7.1) contributes to our pattern on validation on submit vs. validation on input field (see Sect. 4.2). Also, the advice on making pages look clean and well organized as opposed to being cluttered or busy (checklist item 13.1) is relevant for our pattern on the display of help text (see Sect. 4.4).

Kurniawan and Zaphiris structured existing guidelines on web design for older people in eleven categories containing a total of 38 guidelines [7]. Among them, the guidelines on simple and meaningful icons (H2.3) and on avoiding pull-down menus (H3.4) are a direct input for our pattern on using drop-down menus vs. push-buttons (with graphical symbols) (see Sect. 4.1). The advice on simple and easy-to-follow error messages is reflected in our pattern on validation on submit vs. validation on input field (see Sect. 4.2).

The National Institute on Aging in the United States has released their own set of guidelines for making websites "senior friendly" [8]. Among them, the guidance on using the same symbols and icons throughout a website (under the layout category) is relevant for our pattern on using drop-down menus vs. push-buttons (with graphical symbols) (see Sect. 4.1).

Pernice et al. [1] developed 106 design guidelines for "seniors citizens on the web", based on quantitative research. Their advice on presenting error messages clearly (guidelines 34) relates to our pattern on validation on submit vs. validation on input field (see Sect. 4.2). The guideline on showing only pictures that are clear or can be easily zoomed in is reflected in our pattern on making images available in enlarged format (see Sect. 4.2). The advice on being forgiving of errors in forms is a direct input for our pattern on validation on submit vs. validation on input field (see Sect. 4.2). While Pernice et al. do not completely discourage designers from using drop-down menus in general, they remind designers of the difficulties that could come with them for older users (guideline 92). Considering their guidance on ensuring that images are easy to see (guideline 53), our pattern on using drop-down menus vs. push-buttons (with graphical symbols) can be seen as a natural application of these guidelines (see Sect. 4.1).

Almost all guidelines emphasize that their application will make websites easier to use for all users, not only for older users. In particular, Chadwick-Dias et al. [9] report about a study in which performance improved significantly for both older and younger users when a website was redesigned to accommodate the usability issues that older users had.

3 Dynamic User Interface Adaptations

We postulate that it is possible to improve usability of Web forms for elderly users by applying dynamic adaptations on its presentation, structure and content. The adaptations could be performed at runtime, based on previously identified replacement and augmentation patterns. For example, one of the replacement patterns we investigated is to replace a drop-down menu with text entries by a set of push-buttons with graphical symbols. We assumed that elderly users prefer the set of graphical push-buttons because here they see their choices more plainly, without having to click on a small button to open a list of text entries. The result of the investigation on this and other patterns is presented in Sect. 4.

In [10], a framework for the development of fully adaptive user interfaces is presented, consisting of the following six steps:

1. *User Interface Modeling.* An abstract user interface is modeled (development time).
2. *Default User Interface Design.* A default user interface is designed, based on the abstract user interface model (development time).
3. *Supplemental User Interface Design.* Supplemental user interfaces for specific contexts of use are designed, based on the abstract user interface model (between development time and runtime).
4. *Context of Use Instantiation.* At runtime, a context of use is identified, including concrete values for a user model, a platform model and an environment model.

5. *User Interface Accommodation (System-Driven).* The system dynamically adapts its user interface to be tailored for the concrete context of use (at runtime). Dynamic adaptations can use the supplemental user interface components of step 3 (this is called *user interface integration*) or just "tweak" some aspects of the user interface, e.g. font size or mouse speed (this is called *user interface parameterization*).
6. *User Interface Customization (User-Driven).* The user requests the system to adapt its user interface along pre-defined options. This can happen through user interface integration and/or user interface parameterization at runtime.

In this 6-step framework, patterns for improving the usability would be prepared in step 3 (supplemental user interface design), and would be applied either automatically as part of step 5 or – on user request – as part of step 6. In case of automatic (system-driven) pattern application (step 5), the system would first check the given context of use (step 4) and whether the application of the pattern is likely to improve the usability. This could potentially involve a matchmaker [11] for finding best adaptation candidates for the concrete context of use, and potential user interface adaptation patterns. These patterns could be provided as a pool of supplemental user interface resources (step 3) and possible parameters for user interface parameterization. In case the user requests the adaptation along a pre-defined pattern (step 6), this would be stored in the user model part of the context of use, so that the system would remember the user's preferred pattern for the upcoming interaction sessions.

MyUI [12] is a pattern-based system for user interface adaptations. It automatically generates a user interface at runtime, based on an abstract user interface description borrowing elements from state machine diagrams (called *abstract application interaction model*). MyUI lacks a possibility for designers to hand-craft a user interface (step 2 of the 6-step framework) which is usually an important aspect for today's design processes. Also, designers and developers are usually not familiar with the development of abstract user interface models based on state machines, and prefer imperative approaches. Nevertheless, MyUI's adaptation patterns have influenced our thinking about dynamic adaptions for elderly Web users.

For other work related to user interface adaptations, refer to [10].

4 Exemplary Patterns of User Interface Adaptations

As described in Sect. 2, there are a large number of design guidelines available on how to make websites and web applications easy to use for older users. Many of these guidelines are supported by empirical data. However, we wanted to make the case for particular patterns of dynamic adaptations that could be run automatically to make web forms easier to use for an elderly individual. These should be applicable even when the author of the web form did not consider the needs and preferences of older users at all. Therefore, we decided to prototypically implement a selection of four substitution/augmentation patterns of which most are based on or related to existing guidelines (see Sect. 2). The prototype was implemented with Axure RP.[2]

---

[2] http://www.axure.com/.

In a study with desktop computers, we tested these patterns on acceptance for older adults. We had a total of 15 subjects (4 women, 11 men), aged between 64 and 84. We asked them for their experience with computers and the Internet. 10 subjects had already used computers in their workplace, 13 had used emails for communication, and 9 had already ordered a product in an online shop. During our observations, we noticed that 10 of the subjects used the tab key to navigate between input fields, which is an indication that they were quite familiar with the web and its forms.

Every subject got the same set of tasks:

1. Search for a specific product (sweater or t-shirt).
2. Put two pieces of the product in size "M" into the shopping cart.
3. Proceed with the payment process.
4. Enter name and address for delivery.
5. Pick a delivery method.
6. Pay with a credit card (a "faked" MasterCard was given to the user for this purpose).

In this set of tasks, we exposed the participants to four patterns of user interface adaptation, each coming in two versions (see subsections 4.1–4.4). For example, we had them order a sweater, whereby they had to choose the size from a drop-down menu (version A). After that, they had to order another sweater, this time selecting the size from a set of push-buttons with graphical symbols and letters for the different sizes (version B). We varied the order of version A and version B between subjects to counterbalance possible learning effects. At the end of the test, we collected feedback from the users on the different versions of the patterns.

The following subsections describe the patterns and the pertaining results of the empirical study.

4.1 Drop-Down Menu vs. Push-Buttons

In general, expandable menus that require a user action to open are often considered an issue for older users (see Sect. 2). This can be attributed to dexterity issues and cognitive difficulties. The menu choices are hidden and become only visible after clicking on a small button at the right of the drop-down menu field. Obviously, this is also an issue for users of touchscreen devices since it is hard to hit the "open menu" button with the finger. Also, if the user is not familiar with a drop-down menu, they may not know how to open it.

In our study, we contrasted drop-down menus with text items to sets of push-buttons, for selection of size and number of shopping items. In the choice of size, we also added the letter "S", "M" or "L" on top of the symbol to make their meanings more obvious (see Fig. 1).

The seniors' feedback was not completely uniform. Some commended the ease of recognizing and selecting the pictograms in version B, whereas others – being aware of their computer expertise – thought the pictograms were inappropriate and made them feel like analphabets or children. Also, some wanted to have a text input field for the number of items, so they would not be restricted to the values 1, 2 and 3.

Fig. 1. Version A (left) and version B (right) of the pattern "drop-down menu vs. push-buttons", implemented as part of a product page. In version A, size and number of items must be selected from a drop-down menu. In version B, push-buttons are shown for size and number.

4.2 Make Images Available in Enlarged Format

In many online shops it is already customary to have high-resolution versions of images available upon demand (often triggered by clicking on a magnifier glass icon in the upper left of the image). While the image file may only be available in low resolution – if the author of the web page did not bother to provide different versions of the image – a system could always add an "enlarge image" function at runtime. Once activated, this function would display the image on a larger area by stretching (e.g. in a popup window, see Fig. 2). For many users – in particular those with low vision – the fact that the large image version is not rendered in high resolution would be a minor problem, as long as the image is enlarged.

Most participants found that the possibility of enlarging the product images improves the website's ease of use. Many senior users were already familiar with this functionality due to its widespread use in online shops. Some even wanted to have multiple views on the items, e.g. from different perspectives, or have selected areas of the image magnified.

4.3 Validation on Submit vs. Validation on Input Field

Clear and descriptive error messages are an important aspect of senior-friendly websites (see Sect. 2). A related aspect is the timing of warnings in case of invalid form input. The user may be alerted to validation errors only after they have filled out and submitted the complete form (pattern version A), or they may get a message right away when they have left an input field with invalid content (version B). Figure 3 shows our prototypical implementation of this pattern, in both versions.

All participants were either pleased with the validation of input fields upon focus change (version B), or had a neutral opinion. One user appreciated the direct feedback – or better in this case the absence of a negative feedback – as a kind of reward for a doing a good job. The validation upon submit (version A) caused confusion for some elderly users since they did not immediately understand what the problem was and what they had to do to be able to move on.

Fig. 2. Version B of the pattern "make images available in enlarged format". On every product image, a magnifier class with a '+' sign is superimposed in the upper left corner. If the user clicks on it, a large image version is displayed in a popup. Note that version A (no screenshot included) has no magnifier glass on images, and the user cannot request an enlarged image version.

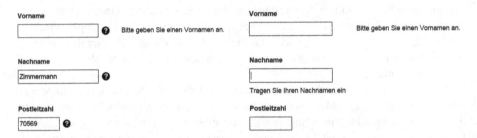

Fig. 3. Version A (left) and version B (right) of the pattern "Validation on submit vs. validation on input field". In both versions, the user did not enter their first name. In version A, the red validation message is only shown after the user has pressed the "submit" button (not included in the screen shot). In version B, the user is alerted to the error as soon as they set the focus to the next field.

4.4 Display of Help Text

Help texts for web forms can be presented to the user in various ways. Some websites display hints and help texts openly, others on the press of a button. Recently, some websites have provided hints as "placeholders" in input fields, but unfortunately a placeholder text disappears as soon as the user sets the focus in the field. On the other hand, hints and help texts may clutter the screen and distract the user (see Sect. 2).

In our fourth pattern, we implemented two versions of help text display for input fields. In version A, the help text appears below the input field when the user clicks on a button with a question mark ('?'). The button is placed to the right of the input field.

The help text disappears again when the user leaves the input field. In version B, the help text is shown automatically when the user sets focus to the input field, and disappears when the user leaves the input field (see Fig. 4).

Most users did not notice the help texts, neither for version A nor for version B. When asked for feedback, they deemed the input for name and address fields as trivial and not requiring any hints beyond the label. However, they appreciated help for more complex input fields such as the expiration date of the credit card. Here, they wished a permanent display of help text that would not disappear when moving away from the input field (as opposed to both versions implemented in our prototype), e.g. in the form of a long label.

4.5 General Observations

Aside from the assessment of the four patterns for user interface adaptation, the study brought about some other findings that could potentially be used in automatic user interface adaptations.

In general, participants had problems in recognizing that they needed to scroll vertically to get to the screen elements "below the fold". This problem is a common finding and reflected in various guidelines (see Sect. 2). An adaptation system could automatically break up one page into multiple pages to avoid the need for scrolling.

A related problem occurs when – upon a submit operation – error messages are displayed in a part of the screen that is currently not visible due to scrolling. This could be avoided by automatic scrolling or – even better – by validating upon leaving an input field rather than upon submit (cf. Sect. 4.3).

When filling out web forms, many participants used either all-capital characters or all-small characters in their typing. An adaptation system should be tolerant to this practice, and could further automatically correct the character case where appropriate.

The division of first name and surname into two input fields was unnatural for some participants. They entered their full name into the field for the first name, and noticed their mistake when they got to the next input field (requesting the surname). The same occurred with the input fields for street name and house number, and with the input fields for the expiration date of the credit card (month and year). An adaptation system could recognize these user input mistakes and automatically split the input and distribute its pieces into the appropriate fields.

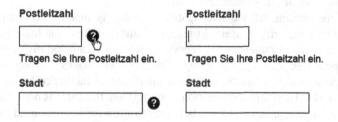

Fig. 4. Version A (left) and version B (right) of the pattern "display of help text". In both versions, input fields for the ZIP code and the city are displayed, and a hint is shown under the first input field: "Enter your ZIP code". In version A, the hint is shown upon pressing a '?' button. In version B, the hint is always shown when the focus is on the input field.

On typing their email address, many seniors typed a comma (',') instead of a dot ('.') due to vision and dexterity problems. This mistake could also be automatically corrected.

For the credit card, some participants entered its number in blocks of 4 digits, with spaces between the blocks. In fact, this allows for easier reading and double-checking of the number. An adaptation system could offer separate input fields for each block, and automatically jump to the next block when a block is full.

A frequent issue for the senior users was the entry of the 3-digit card validation code which they were not familiar with. An adaptation system could provide additional guidance for this input field on request, for example by a photo explaining where this code can be found on a real credit card.

Some participants did not have an email address. Therefore, an alternative contact for clients should be offered (e.g. a phone number), and the email address field should not be a mandatory field. While this problem cannot be easily fixed at runtime, it could be part of guidelines for web authors.

5   Conclusions and Outlook

The findings of this paper relate to the concepts of the Global Public Inclusive Infrastructure (GPII) [4], and the Universal Remote Console (URC) framework [13]. We have identified four exemplary patterns that can facilitate the dynamic personalization of Web forms at runtime. This approach fits well within the framework of fully context-sensitive user interfaces [10], in particular for the steps on "user interface accommodation (system-driven)" (step 5) and on "user interface customization (user-driven)" (step 6) (cf. Sect. 3). As always, the user should be in control over the adaptations performed, even though the system may anticipate and propose specific adaptation patterns.

It is important to note that for many adaptations at runtime, the author does not need to be involved. In fact, all exemplary adaptation patterns presented in this paper could be achieved in a fully automated fashion and facilitated by third-party authors providing supplemental user interface resources before runtime. Supplemental resources for personalization can be deployed through an online resource server [14] if the basic structure and abstract content of the user interface is known before runtime. Of course, the provision of supplemental user interface resources has significant security implications. Care needs to be taken for such a framework to prevent from malware sneaking in through the door of "supplemental resources".

None of the patterns that we investigated had a clearly superior version that would be preferred by a majority of users. Instead, this study confirms the findings of others that elderly users are a rather heterogeneous audience with a broad diversity of needs and preferences (see Sect. 2). The group of elderly users makes a strong case for the concept of personalized adaptations on user interfaces, as facilitated by the GPII and URC frameworks. Therefore, the question resulting from this study is not which version to implement for an adaptation pattern, but rather to allow for all versions to be available as possible adaptations for a user interface. That way a suitable version can be selected and instantiated at runtime, driven by the actual context of use, including the user's personal needs and preferences.

Acknowledgments. We thank Dr. Ulrich Schloz for his kind support in facilitating the user tests with seniors from the association "Senioren Online" in Reichenbach, and from the association "Arbeitsgemeinschaft Mikroprozessor und Minicomputer" in Stuttgart. We also thank the nursing home "Seniorenzentrum am Rosengarten" in Bondorf for their support and participation in the user tests.

The research leading to these results has received funding from the European Union Seventh Framework Programme (FP7/2007-2011) under the grants 289016 (Cloud4all) and 610510 (Prosperity4All). This publication reflects only the authors' views and the European Union is not liable for any use that may be made of the information contained herein.

References

1. Pernice, K., Estes, J., Nielsen, J.: Senior Citizens on the Web, 2nd edn., Research report by Nielsen Norman Group. http://www.nngroup.com/reports/senior-citizens-on-the-web/. Accessed 2013
2. Gregor, P., Newell, A.F., Zajicek, M.: Designing for dynamic diversity: interfaces for older people. In: Proceedings of the Fifth International ACM Conference on Assistive Technologies, pp. 151–156. ACM, New York. doi:10.1145/638249.638277 (2002)
3. Redish, J., Chisnell, D.: Designing web sites for older adults: a review of recent research, AARP. http://assets.aarp.org/www.aarp.org_/articles/research/oww/AARP-LitReview2004.pdf. Accessed 14 December 2004
4. Vanderheiden, G., Treviranus, J., Markus, K., Clark, C., Basman, A.: The global public inclusive infrastructure, Cloud4all and Prosperity4all. Assistive Technology: From Research to Practice, vol. 33, pp. 417–422. Presented at the AAATE 2013. IOS Press Ebooks, Villamoura, Portugal. doi:10.3233/978-1-61499-304-9-417 (2013)
5. Chisnell, D., Redish, J.: Designing web sites for older adults: expert review of usability for older adults at 50 web sites, AARP. http://www.redish.net/images/stories/PDF/AARP-50Sites.pdf. Accessed 1 February 2005
6. Chisnell, D., Redish, J., Lee, A.: New heuristics for understanding older adults as web users. Tech. Commun. **53**(1), 39–59 (2006)
7. Kurniawan, S., Zaphiris, P.: Research-derived web design guidelines for older people. In: Proceedings of the 7th International ACM SIGACCESS Conference on Computers and Accessibility, pp. 129–135. ACM, New York. doi:10.1145/1090785.1090810 (2005)
8. NIA:. Making your website senior friendly. National Institute on Aging, March 2009. http://www.nia.nih.gov/health/publication/making-your-website-senior-friendly. Accessed 15 August 2014
9. Chadwick-Dias, A., McNulty, M., Tullis, T.: Web usability and age: how design changes can improve performance. In: Proceedings of the 2003 Conference on Universal Usability, pp. 30–37. ACM, New York. doi:10.1145/957205.957212 (2003)
10. Zimmermann, G., Vanderheiden, G.C., Strobbe, C.: Towards deep adaptivity – a framework for the development of fully context-sensitive user interfaces. In: Stephanidis, C., Antona, M. (eds.) Universal Access in Human-Computer Interaction Design and Development Methods for Universal Access, pp. 299–310. Springer International Publishing, Heidelberg (2014)
11. Loitsch, C., Stiegler, A., Strobbe, C., Tzovaras, D., Votis, K., Weber, G., Zimmermann, G.: Improving Accessibility by Matching User Needs and Preferences. In: Assistive Technology From Research to Practice, pp. 1357–1365. IOS Press, Vilamoura. doi: 10.3233/978-1-61499-304-9-1357 (2013)

12. Peissner, M., Häbe, D., Schuller, A.: Adaptation concept and multimodal user interface patterns repository, FHG. http://myui.eu/deliverables/MyUI_D2-2_final.pdf. Accessed 2011
13. Zimmermann, G., Vanderheiden, G., Ma, M., Gandy, M., Trewin, S., Laskowski, S., Walker, M.: Universal remote console standard - toward natural user interaction in ambient intelligence. In: Extended Abstracts of the 2004 Conference on Human Factors and Computing Systems - CHI 2004, p. 1608. ACM Press, New York. doi:10.1145/985921.986169 (2004)
14. Zimmermann, G., Wassermann, B.: Why we need a user interface resource server for intelligent environments. In: Workshops Proceedings of the 5th International Conference on Intelligent Environments, vol. 4, pp. 209–216. IOS Press. doi:10.3233/978-1-60750-056-8-209 (2009)

The Elderly and Mobile Devices

Older People's Attitude Towards Mobile Communication in Everyday Life: Digital Literacy and Domestication Processes

Francesca Comunello[1,3(✉)], Simone Mulargia[2,3], Francesca Belotti[2], and Mireia Fernández-Ardèvol[3]

[1] Dipartimento Di Scienze Umane, Lumsa Università, Borgo Sant'Angelo 13, 00193 Rome, Italy
f.comunello@lumsa.it

[2] Dipartimento Di Comunicazione E Ricerca Sociale, Sapienza Università Di Roma, via Salaria 113, 00198 Rome, Italy
{simone.mulargia, francesca.belotti}@uniroma1.it

[3] Mobile Technologies and (G)Local Challenges Research Group IN3, Universitat Oberta de Catalunya, C/Roc Boronat 117, MediaTIC Building, 08018 Barcelona, Catalonia, Spain
mfernandezar@uoc.edu

Abstract. Older people's attitude towards mobile communication constitutes a privileged perspective for analyzing domestication processes of digital technologies. By means of a qualitative case study conducted in Italy, we study older users' motivations and usage practices. We focus on perceptions of mobile phones, adoption and domestication of mobile phones, as well as on usage skills. Participants, aged 60 to 95 years old, typically started to make use of mobile telephony in mid 1990 s and they mainly described a utilitarian approach to the mobile device even though there are cases of anthropomorphization. With a variety of profiles, from assisted to advanced users, those not having smartphones sometimes see touchscreen as challenging. They describe different learning strategies, which are shaped by personal interests. Finally, some participants adopt more sophisticated devices while others decide to slow down their relationship with mobile phones.

Keywords: Mobile telephony · Older people · Domestication · Learning strategies

1 Background

Mobile technology plays an increasing role in everyday interpersonal communication, representing a useful resource for different age cohorts. A wide number of publications deal with the usage of mobile phones by younger people: mobile phones re-place their personal interactions [1], are tools of emancipation from the family and facilitate social cohesion in the peer group [2]. Young people have created and implemented new communication practices [3], so that the appropriation of mobile telephony is commonly perceived as a juvenile phenomenon. Yet, the usage by older people is worthy to

© Springer International Publishing Switzerland 2015
J. Zhou and G. Salvendy (Eds.): ITAP 2015, Part I, LNCS 9193, pp. 439–450, 2015.
DOI: 10.1007/978-3-319-20892-3_43

be studied as well, firstly because in European societies older population is steadily growing [4]. The age structure of the population will change, with an increasing share of over 65 and a declining share of younger and working age persons [5]. Thus, focusing on the elderly and their use of the mobile phone means considering an increasingly growing section of the European population.

Furthermore, the relationship between the elderly and the mobile phone is interesting because it is the most popular information and communication technology (ICT) among older people, who show the lowest levels of ICT adoption. Thus, it is important to explore the relationship older people have with mobile telephony, considering that ageing shapes physical characteristics, basic abilities, communication habits and the choice of media. Several studies show that the elderly might face cognition and reading capacity challenges [6, 7], or problems in handling small devices and using messaging services [8, 9]. Nevertheless, mobile phone adoption keeps growing among the elder, while it is common for them to incorporate innovative communicative practices [10].

2 Theoretical Framework

All these aspects justify a special focus on seniors' relational and communication practices that show a relevant role of mobile phones both for personal safety and for social interaction. Age, thus, appears as a key factor affecting mobile phone's adoption and usage style [11]. Seniors are individuals who have been introduced to mobile communication late and mainly under the "pressure" coming from their closed social circle [12]. Nowadays, as society shifts towards networked individualism [13] and networked sociability [14], older people keep up and experience new patterns of sociability built on me-centered networks [15] that are growingly enabled by mobile technologies.

2.1 Domestication

In order to analyze older people's acquisition and consumption of mobile phone technology and their usage of mobile phone in everyday life we mainly rely on the domestication approach [16–18]. Paraphrasing Silverstone and Haddon [17] we can assume that mobile phones are more than merely machines. They can be considered cultural artifacts, whose meaning emerges at the intersection of technical features and ongoing processes of social understanding. The process which leads to mobile phone's incorporation into everyday life [19] is particularly evident considering older people experiences, because they have a precise memory of their first contact with this technology and can therefore offer a rich and detailed narration of their acquisition process.

According to the domestication approach, mobile phone (as other different information and communication technologies such as television and the Internet) undergoes a preliminary process of *appropriation* by users, characterized by the production of an analysis that (can) lead to the acquisition of the mobile phone. In this early phase users try to figure out how ICTs can play a role in everyday routines. Then we observe the *incorporation* process, related to the physical location of the mobile phone within the users' home and when they carry it with themselves, as this is a portable device. Spatial constraints (such as the lack of signal) contribute to influence users' choices; nevertheless, other elements must be taken into account in this process, such as aesthetic reasons or health concerns. The *objectification* is related to users' everyday practices as it considers how technology use takes its own place in users' daily routines. Objectification has therefore to be considered in relation to time structures and time constraints which constitutes limits in users' action. Everyday usage is not only connected with users' time budget, but also with time organization and users' perception of free time availability. The *conversion* process addresses how the presentation of technology produced by the users, and their reflections on ICTs' meanings contributes to the definition of users' identity. Users, for instance, tend to embed ICTs into their impression management strategies; this concern about the public image of the individual *as an ICT user* can even lead to non adoption phenomena in some cases [20, 21].

According to the domestication approach, mobile phone adoption and usage must be analyzed considering the role of users' relational networks. The lack of support from users' social networks is, for instance, a key element to understand nonadoption. Without that potential source of motivation and help for using ICTs, in fact, users in general (and older people in particular) can simply think that ICTs are not for them [21]. On the other hand, users' inclusion in dense social networks is a factor that can foster adoption processes.

Mobile phone usage in everyday life has been studied in relationship with, among others, two fundamental dimensions: safety and security issues and microcoordination [22, 23]. According to Ling [24] mobile phone everyday usage is often related to a sense of safety and security, especially for older people and for users affected by a chronic sickness. When coming to be integrated in everyday life, mobile phone offers a powerful tool to organize users communication and meetings on a real time basis, enabling a potential rearrangement of trips destination [22].

Even though both mobile phone usage in everyday life and domestication processes have a well-established tradition of studies, such theoretical perspectives should be considered as an evolving framework. When launched, mobile phone was considered a communication tool for businesspersons (among others, due to its high cost). However, nowadays it has reached almost all the population and the number of users is still growing. The domestication steps can be placed in a logical sequence, but we can not assume that all the stages are entered sequentially by all users [20, 24]. Differences among users belonging to specific age cohorts, gender, and living in different socio-cultural and country contexts also play a role in differentiating everyday usage practices.

2.2 Digital Literacy

Digital literacy is key in shaping adoption and practices of mobile phone use, which can constitute a factor both of inclusion and of exclusion from the mobile communication environment. In our analysis we refer to a broad understanding of digital literacy, that stresses multiple dimensions, including the social and relational aspects experienced by users in their everyday life [25–27]. More specifically, van Deursen and van Dijk [28] propose a framework for analyzing digital skills that includes: *operational skills* (the skills to operate digital media); *formal skills* (the skills needed to handle the specific structures of digital media); *information skills* (the skills to search, select and evaluate information in digital contexts); *strategic skills* (the skills to employ the information contained in digital media as a means to reach a specific goal). Even if his main focus is devoted to a computer-centric environment, Warschauer [29], on the other hand, underlines the role of interpersonal communication-related skills (*computer-mediated communication literacy*), as a central element for digital literacy.

Our understanding of digital literacy is also rooted in "second level" digital divide theories, that abandon any dichotomous vision (often refusing the very label of "digital divide"), and don't consider technology acquisition as a linear, unidimensional process [29, 30]. Following early research on technology adoption, we also recognize that technology adoption and usage are deeply related to motivation, on the one hand, and to literacy, on the other hand. In such a complex process, early research has underlined the role of so-called technology "want nots" [31], including technology "dropouts" (people who were using technology, but stopped to do so).

Following both the domestication perspective and the digital literacy framework, we also underline the role of personal networks in technology adoption and usage: a rich relational network does not only provide motivations for using digital technology (and, more specifically, mobile phones); it can also provide support in technology usage, both at an *operational* and at a *strategic* level.

3 The Research Project

The goal of this paper is to analyze the usage of mobile phones by the elderly in Italy. Why and how do older people use mobile phone? How do they adopt and domesticate the device in their everyday life? What is the level of competence and autonomy they have gained in handling the mobile phone? Due to such exploratory objectives and for considering the specific circumstances of the research context, we adopted a qualitative research strategy facilitating a flexible and interactive design [32, 33].

We conducted 51 semi-structured interviews in Rome and in a mid-sized town in Umbria (central Italy), between October 2013 and February 2014. Participants are both men and women from different sociocultural backgrounds. Their age varies between 60 and 95, thus considering elderly a non-homogenous group. We take into account different age segments, including individuals entering retirement and redefining their personal autonomy. All interviews have been recorded, transcribed and subjected to thematic analysis focusing on the following dimensions: personal characteristics; personal networks; adoption of mobile telephone; consumption patterns of mobile devices; used mobile services; location and mobility of mobile telephone; current mobile characteristics; attitude and opinions towards mobile technology.

4 Results and Discussion

The purchase of the first mobile phone happened, in most cases, about twenty years before the interview. It is the result of different trajectories of acquisition. Some participants, for instance, declared to have a precise idea about their special need for a mobile phone, perceived as a communication tool to be used for work or as a device able to foster a sense of safety and security. "The first [mobile phone]? I took a mobile phone thanks to a Coca Cola's commercial promotion about twenty years ago. I needed it, also to listen to ... I mean, while in the street ... something could happen. It was for security reasons" (M. Male, 60).

On the other hand, some respondents did not play an active role in choosing to purchase a mobile phone. In some cases, they received it as a gift, or a dismissed device from their relatives. "I think it was in June 2000. Very late, because mobile phones were already on the hype. It was a Philips; it was very heavy. So, in June 2000 I had my first mobile phone, they gave it to me as a gift, they literally imposed it on me" (E. Male, 60).

Apart from these utilitarian motivations, some participants claim they perceived a sort of social pressure on buying a mobile phone. Acquiring the mobile phone was, in participants' words, a way to connect them to a broader social trend. This sense of obligation played a role also in delaying the first purchase. "We decided not to buy a mobile phone; we decided not to yield to the temptation of modern times. [...] Then, technology went on [...] It seemed it was only a question of being fashionable, being "in" or "out". Twenty-five years ago, mobile phone was a real status symbol. I did not want to be among "those who"." (M. Male, 63) "Honestly, I would not say that we needed a mobile phone. Purchasing it, was a way to align ourselves to some evolutions. Then, once you have a mobile phone, the need to have it is created" (C. Male, 79).

Acquisition and appropriation processes described by older users tend to be not linear and, in some cases, even explicitly conflicting. "Because of our age, we had "a fight with" the advent of new technologies. But, slowly, if you have a little bit of common sense, you can learn to use them, and you can even learn to manage them" (T. Male, 70).

After an initial feeling of discomfort related to mobile phone use, a majority of participants show high levels of integration of the mobile phone in their everyday routines, even if they cannot be considered as high level users. "Among positive aspects [of having a mobile phone] I love receiving calls when, for instance, I am on the beach. That still seems to me a big novelty. Before, we cannot receive calls when on the beach" (I. Female, 84).

The more the mobile phone is integrated in everyday routines, the more it becomes a useful tool to manage everyday communications. "I usually use the mobile phone to manage contacts with artisans, for instance, the chimney sweeper. In the last months, we needed a lot of artisans to work on our house, and I called them with the mobile phone" (D. Female 62).

Some participants express a sort of emotional connection with the mobile phone. When talking about it, some users tend to ascribe human characteristics to the device. It emerges that mobile phone has undergone a process of anthropomorphization. This process signals a high level of intimacy with the mobile phone [34] and, in some occasions, it can be considered as a strategy the users employ in order to face the stress caused by mobile phone's adoption [35, 36]. "[Where should the mobile phone be switched off?] Where it can get under someone's skin. But, I mean, poor thing, if he is closed, he cannot do that." (N. Female, 87) "[Mobile phone] is very important, in my opinion. You feel relaxed because there is a mate, through which you can reach whatever" (B. Female, 67).

When considering mobile phone usage skills, participants can be positioned on a *continuum*, ranging from basic level usage skills (people using their device only for phone calls, sometimes without being able to access and use their phone book), to advanced skills (respondents showing high familiarity with mobile internet, Apps, geolocalization, etc.). Most respondents can be positioned between the two extremes.

A first level of access to mobile technology can be related to basic *operational skills* [28]. More specifically, several users report experiencing *physical* constraints when using mobile phones: their sight and their hearing are mostly mentioned as problematic, but they also report problems related to using their fingers on such small devices. "[Do you always check who is calling before answering the phone?] Yes. Well, if I don't wear my glasses, and I don't see the person [sic]... it happens to me that I answer even to people I don't wish to talk to." (T2. Female, 66) "[Do you always carry your mobile with you or do you sometimes leave it at home or somewhere else?]. I carry it on my neck, because, by the way, I'm a little deaf, so, if it's not on my neck I can't hear it " (P. Female, 70).

Constraints are not referred to as such: the participant does not complain about her limitations, but, instead, exposes the way in which she copes with them, adopting specific strategies in order to integrate the mobile phone in her everyday life, despite her physical handicap.

Some respondents, on the other side, explicitly mention "physical limits" referring them either to users themselves or to devices: "The mobile has the limit that displays are too small. It's our physical limits." (PS. Male, 67) "Yes, there are clearly some problems, because, as they have miniaturized everything [...] You shift to these [new mobile phones] where you have such small buttons... you push to write something, but with our big fingers, you write another thing. Even the LED: if you are in the sunlight, you can't see anything" (AB. Male, 62).

Such limitations are mentioned by the older-old as well as by some of the young-old in the study, particularly by those who have experienced a shift towards more advanced devices (and especially smartphones). Notably, participants tend to identify the smartphone with its interface: when talking about smartphones, they almost always use the English word touchscreen, often referring to it in a problematic way. User interfaces show their relevance not only in user experience, but also in user representation of technology. Moreover, while touchscreen is designed to be a "calm technology" [37], even young-old and well educated users appear to perceive them as a barrier for accessing more advanced services. "Well, my friends! When I see a friend who has a touch screen (sic)... how is it called? [...] well I admire them because, even if some of them are older than me, I see that they handle this screen, like that, with their fingers [...] I think it's not for me!" (DG. Female, 69).

Technology adoption and skill acquisition do not appear as linear processes. Some users refer to have *downgraded* their mobile phone use, having given up the most advanced features (or having stopped using more advanced devices). This is normally related both to the constant evolution of mobile devices and applications, and to vital trajectories (some users, for instance, refer to the time they retired as the moment in which they stopped acquiring new digital skills). Such phenomena are consistent with the literature on technology acquisition, and particularly with the concept of "want nots", as described by van Dijk [31]. "I've noticed that, since I retired, there has been somehow a regression: I used to use the PC in the office, and I'm stuck at that point... Well, there are many things I was able to do... I'm not able to do them anymore, I get angry and I give up."(DG. Female, 69) "Well, at some point the mobile started to show some flaws, it started losing incoming calls, I tried to call and it didn't work... So I bought a device that could only do phone calls." (G. Male, 77)"Earlier, some years ago, I did everything with my old mobile phone. Then, do you know what? At some point [...] I just forgot [how to do things], maybe on purpose. If I go and read the instruction book, I can maybe succeed, but I started focusing on other things and the phone just stays there"(PVT. Female, 79).

The mobile phone's usability may facilitate learning processes, by supporting the acquisition of new knowledge procedures that are useful to operate and interact with the device properly [38]. Motivational issues may play an important role as well, because older adults are stimulated to use mobile phones and learn new functions if they perceive the need, usefulness or interest in improving their knowledge and know-how [39, 40]. "[...] the phone calls and all things I need, well, I know how to use them; and the things I do not need... seeing the Internet on the phone [is not necessary] for me, what's more I am blind! [meaning that her sight is low]." (MG. Female, 67) "[...]the alarm clock, the calculator: no no, I do not use them! But I do not have a good relationship with the technical tools, so I learn just three things, the necessary ones, and those I make!" (PB. Female, 70).

One obvious problem for anyone using a mobile phone is approaching and handling a new device. If we consider that learning ability declines with age, while mobile phones rapidly evolve in their technological features and services, we can easily understand why the devices can be perceived as complex by elderly people, who might consider learning to use them as a difficult challenge [9]. "[...] considered my young age [ironic], when you switch from one phone to another, you might have some difficulty."(NI. Female, 84)"The problem is that, as I was used to a slightly simpler device, this one is a bit more complicated, more complete. It has more functions than the other one. [...] In writing messages, I felt better with the previous one" (PM. Male, 72).

Relevant differences in interviewees' responses have been observed in relation to what can be defined as mobile phone-related "learning style". Overall, the strategy to find out about new devices or functions seems to follow previous learning experiences, such as the scholastic one. "[...] in those rare occasions when you use it... "Why does it do so?", "I don't know"... I did not tolerate the answer "I don't know" as a logic setting and as a learning culture. When I was young, you could not say "I don't know" or "I don't understand": they were two banned phrases at school because, if you didn't know, you admitted not having studied, and if you didn't understand, you admitted being stupid. [...] But now you realize [you have] almost infinite learning opportunities with these tools" (PS. Male, 67).

Participants face the learning challenge either by adopting an exploratory or a didactic approach. Some of them seem to follow a constructivist model of experiential learning [41, 42]. By assimilating new experiences into an already existing framework and accommodating their mistakes or failures, older people autonomously learn to use the telephone set. This is like an artifact that they appropriate by discovering how to manage it [43, 44]. They attempt to face a difficulty within an interactive and complex media environment, such as the mobile phone, and information acquired in this experience become readily viable in future problem solving. "When I had problems, somehow I resolved them. It took me a bit more time, but I got out of them [...] Recently I had the problem that I had some photos, and I could not download them into the computer [...] I did it on my own: I downloaded [...] and I managed to put them on the computer [...] It was a bit difficult, but I succeed! "(TE. Male, 69) "My wife is who usually asks me [for help]; then, [...] I start trying until I find the solution, because these gadgets have their own logic; so just understand that!" (G. Male, 77).

Other respondents, on the contrary, seem to adopt an instructionist model, as they learn by means of an external transfer of knowledge. This approach is teacher-focused, skill-based, goal-oriented and not always interactive [45]. Users prefer to learn by consulting user's manual – though blaming instructions for being not so intelligible – or "teachers" who can bring them specific advice to use mobile phone. "I don't have the imagination to start reading the rules, I mean the [user's manual] [...] maybe you could use it more and have greater advantages. But compared to what I need, the game is not worth the candle! They should make [the instructions] a little bit more practical and synthetic, not [those] books!" (PG. Male, 67 "[Did you install the email on the phone by yourself?] No [...] At the store [...] I asked them to install all the things I needed [...]. I got them also to explain me how I had to do, I even wrote it on a little note book, at the beginning; then now I no longer need to read it" (B. Female, 67).

Nevertheless, this latter attitude is not necessarily passive as it can be based on the interaction between "pupils" and "teachers". In fact, many interviewees who adopt the instructionist approach usually turn into warm experts [46] for their peers. As personal social networks are a key element in adopting mobile phones and in acquiring the related usage skills, respondents mainly rely on younger family members who explain them how to use basic or advanced functions, thus transforming the teaching process in a socialization of subjec-tive knowledge [10]. "[Have you ever asked someone for help in using some function?] Yes, my grandson and my son. These are graduating in telephony as they go along!"(G. Male, 77)"[Have your grandchildren ever taught you to use the mobile phone?] Yes, in the early times. [...] They taught me: "Grandma, here you push, here you switch on, here you know when you have used up money"... I even know that! You can imagine how good I am! [...] After [they taught me], I do everything by myself."\(NS. Female, 87).

Asking for help is particularly frequent among assisted users, who are only able to answer calls and hang up, who dial numbers directly as they are not able to use the phonebook, who do not use any service beyond voice communication and who leave the handset permanently in a fixed place to keep it safe [47]. Nevertheless, in these cases there is not a real interactive and cooperative learning situation [48]: when the younger relative helps the senior and achieves the goal of solving the device's problem, the older user does not necessarily learn how to manage that situation, mainly because he or she is quite satisfied with the already acquired skills. "I have [the mobile phone] but it is at rest. [...] [I use it] Very little. [...] [At home], I keep it on this table [...], I leave it there. [...] Do you know when I do a call with the mobile phone? When I need to call my son-in-law, because I have all of his numbers: I just press a number, he has 2, 4 and 8. My daughter has 9 [...] [And with your mobile phone do you only call or use other services?] Nothing else! Only calls [...] It does not suit me!. [...] [For example, storing numbers that correspond to your contacts: did you do it by yourself or did you ask someone for help?] My son-in-law did it for me. I would not know ever do such a thing." (NN. Female, 86).

Overall, women tend to rely on their male spouse as they are influenced by gendered stereotypical (self)representation. In fact, participant women take for granted they are less likely to use digital technology and less competent, although they are actually building up intimate relationships with technology and are becoming advanced users [49]. Some men users refer to their partners as an example of lack of technological expertise; likewise, some women consider the male partner as a driver of innovation, even if their own level of usage skills and technological aptitude is not low. Consequently, women do not perceive any social expectation of competence and autonomy in the use of technology and, thus, are more inclined to ask men for help. "[Is there anyone else who uses you cell phone?] My husband [...] [If you must change the settings, do you ask someone?] I do not know how to do anything with the mobile phone." (I. Female, 84) "[Have you ever been asked to advise someone on how to use the mobile phone?] My wife, because she is more useless than me [...]. Sometimes she is in trouble, she asks the children for help; but the children are always evasive or show her electronically, ta-ta-ta-ta, so that she cannot follow them. Thus, sometimes she turns to me, especially when she needs to send a text message" (T. Male, 69).

An exception to the rule of relying on relatives can be traced, however, in those interviewees who report not to rely on relatives for privacy reasons, sometimes preferring to turn to professional figures, such as the shopkeepers. "It is handled only by me; but if for example I have to configure it for browsing the Internet or receiving emails - I have a Smart Phone - I go to a specialized store that set it for me. [For example, your wife or your children, friends, colleagues... does it happen that they handle your mobile phone?] No, it is always under my close supervision!" (MVT. Male, 61).

In any case, once participants become familiar with the device, they feel more comfortable with it; so that in some cases they prefer to buy a new device similar to the previous one, to avoid extra learning costs. "As the other [device] broke down, now I bought one like that because I tend to buy similar mobile phones, so I don't have to re-learn!" (T. Female, 66).

5 Conclusion

The mobile phone has already become an ordinary object among the 60 + years old participants of the study conducted in Italy. Interviews brought evidence of the four phases of the domestication process. Firstly, appropriation. We identified participants who bought their first mobile phone to avoid being out of the general adoption trend even though they did not feel the mobile as something needed in their lives. Yet, other participants did not make a decision on acquisition but received the handset (new or used) from a relative. Most of them had been using the mobile phone for twenty years. However, some of them, based in their peers' experience, expressed their concerns towards moving into a touchsecreen device (i.e., smartphone). This can be interpreted as one of the steps of the analysis that may, or may not, end in the acquisition of a new device.

Secondly, incorporation. Physical condition might shape the location of the mobile phone when we consider it a wearable. When usability issues appear in the first stages of adoption they may lead to rejection of the tool. However, if the device is already part of everyday routines, specific strategies might arise. We understand this is the case of a 70 years old woman who decided to wear the mobile on her neck because she was "slightly deaf".

Thirdly, objectification. Regardless of their skills, all the older participants report using mobile phones as a tool for managing everyday life activities. However, routines can change throughout time and individuals can decide either increasing use or reducing it, a decision that depends on personal interests and on the effort needed to operate the device. In addition, we found cases of anthropomorphization which denotes high degrees of intimacy with the device.

And fourthly, conversion. A particular result of this research is not only that women tended to define themselves as less skilled, but men also considered themselves more skilled than women, which denotes gendered stereotypical (self)representations.

Learning strategies in the case of mobile phones need to be permanently adapted, as ICTs are in constant evolution. Participants, in general, were attached to their previous learning experiences but described different learning strategies. Some took an exploratory approach, based on learning by doing; others preferred to rely on the users' manual and follow its instructions. In any case, the personal network was important as it shaped the expectations and pressures any individual would face for adopting, in this case, mobile communication. More importantly, close relatives could bring support, either to assisted or to more advanced users. Finally, older individuals who acquired enough skills can turn into supporters (teachers) of their peers.

In sum, stages of domestication and learning strategies are not homogeneous, which confirms the need to approach the study of the relationship older people have with mobile telephony by taking into account their heterogeneity.

References

1. Ito, M.: Mobile phones, Japanese youth, and the re-placement of social contact. In: Ling, R., Pedersen, P.E. (eds.) Mobile Communications: Re-negotiation of the Social Sphere, vol. 31, pp. 131–148. Springer, London (2005)
2. Ling, R.: Children, youth, and mobile communication. J. Child. Media 1(1), 60–67 (2007)
3. Oksman, V., Turtiainen, J.: Mobile communication as a social stage meanings of mobile communication in everyday life among teenagers in Finland. New Media Soc. 6(3), 319–339 (2004)
4. Eurostat. http://tinyurl.com/opv7b3y
5. European Commission - Directorate-General for Economic and Financial Affairs: The 2015 Ageing Report. Underlying Assumptions and Projection Methodologies. European Economy 8 (2014)
6. Park, D.C.: The basic mechanisms accounting for age-related decline in cognitive function. Cogn. aging: Primer 11, 3–15 (2000)
7. Charness, N., Parks, D.C., Sabel, B.A.: Communication, Technology and Aging: Opportunities and Challenges for the Future. Springer Publishing Company, New York (2001)
8. Oskman, V.: Young people and seniors in finnish 'mobile information society'. J. Interact. Media Educ. 02, 1–21 (2006)

9. Kurniawan, S.: Older people and mobile phones: a multi-method investigation. Int. J. Hum Comput Stud. **66**(12), 889–901 (2008)

10. Fernández-Ardèvol, M.: Deliberate missed calls: a meaningful communication practice for seniors? Mob. Media Commun. **1**(3), 285–298 (2013)

11. Karnowski, V., von Pape, T., Wirth, W.: After the digital divide? An appropriation-perspective on the generational mobile phone divide. In: Hartmann, M., Rössler, P., Höflich, J. (eds.) After the Mobile Phone? Social Changes and the Development of Mobile Communication, pp.185–202. Frank & Timme, Berlin (2008)

12. Ling, R.: Should we be concerned that the elderly don't text? Inf. Soc. **24**, 334–341 (2008)

13. Wellman, B.: Physical Place and Cyber-Place: Changing portals and the rise of networked individualism. Int. J. Urban Reg. Res. **25**(2), 227–252 (2001)

14. Hampton, K.: Networked sociability online, off-line. In: Castells, M. (ed.) The Network Society: A Cross-cultural perspective. Edward Elgar Publishing, Northampton (2004)

15. Rainie, L., Wellman, B.: Networked: The New Social Operating System. MIT Press, Cambridge (2012)

16. Silverstone, R., Hirsch, E., Morley, D.: Information and communication technologies and the moral economy of the household. In: Silverstone, R., Hirsch, E. (eds.) Consuming Technologies. Routledge, London (1992)

17. Silverstone, R., Haddon, L.: Design and the domestication of information and communication technologies: technical change and everyday life. In: Silverstone, R., Mansell, R. (eds.) Communication by Design: The Politics of Information and Communication Technologies, pp. 44–74. Oxford University Press, Oxford (1996)

18. Loos, E., Haddon, L., Mante-Meijer, E.: Generational Use of New Media. Ashgate, Franham (2012)

19. Silverstone, R.: Domesticating domestication. reflections on the life of a concept. In: Berker, T., Hartmann, M., Punie, Y., Ward, K.J. (eds.) Domestication of Media and Technology, pp. 229–248. McGraw-Hill International, Maidenhead (2006)

20. Haddon, L.: Domestication analysis, objects of study, and the centrality of technologies in everyday life. Can. J. Commun. **36**, 311–323 (2011)

21. Haddon, L.: The contribution of domestication research to in-home computing and media consumption. Inf. Soc. **22**, 195–203 (2006)

22. Ling, R., Haddon, L.: Mobile telephony, mobility and the coordination of everyday life. In: Katz, J.E. (ed.) Machines That Become Us: The Social Context of Personal Communication Technology, pp. 245–266. Transaction Publishers, New Brunswick (2003)

23. Ling, R., Yttri, B.: Hyper-coordination via mobile phones in Norway. In: Katz, J.E., Aakhus, M. (eds.) Perpetual Contact: Mobile Communications, Private Talk, Public Performance, pp. 139–169. Cambridge University Press, Cambridge (2002)

24. Ling, R.: The Mobile Connection: The Cell Phone's Impact on Society. Morgan Kaufmann Publishers, Elsevier, Oxford (2004)

25. Buckingham, D.: Media Education: Literacy, Learning and Contemporary Culture. Polity Press-Blackwell Publishing, London (2003)

26. Livingstone, S.: The Changing Nature and Uses of Media Literacy, Media@Ise Electronic Working Papers,4 (2003)

27. Kraut, R., Brynin, R. (eds.): Computers, Phones, and the Internet, Domesticating Information Technology. Oxford University Press, Oxford (2006)

28. Van Deursen, A., van Dijk, J.: Inequalities of digital skills and how to overcome them. In: Ferro, E., Dwivedi, Y.K., Gil-Garcia, R., Williams, M.D. (eds.) Overcoming Digital Divides: Constructing an Equitable and Competitive Information Society. IGI Global, Hershery (2010)

29. Warschauer, M.: Technology and Social Inclusion Rethinking the Digital Divide. MIT Press, Cambridge (2003)

30. Hargittai, E.: Second-Level Digital Divide: Differences in People's Online Skills. First Monday, 7 (4) (2002)

31. Van Dijk, J.: The deepening divide. Inequality in the information society. Sage, Thousand Oaks, CA (2005)

32. Maxwell, J.A.: Qualitative Research Design: An Interactive Approach, vol. 41, 2nd edn. Sage, Thousand Oaks (2005)

33. Miles, M.B., Huberman, M.A.: Qualitative Data Analysis. Sage, Thousand Oaks (1994)

34. Fortunati, L.: The human body: Natural and artificial technology. In: Katz, J.E. (ed.) Machines That Become Us: The Social Context of Personal Communication Technology, pp. 71–89. Transaction Publishers, New Brunswick (2003)

35. Luczak, H., Roetting, M., Schmidt, L.: Let's talk: anthropomorphization as means to cope with stress of interacting with technical devices. Ergonomics 46, 1361–1374 (2003)

36. Hepp, A., Krotz, F. (eds.): Mediatized Worlds: Culture and Society in a Media Age. Palgrave Macmillan, Basingstoke (2014)

37. Weiser, M., Brown, J.S.: The coming age of calm technology. In: Denning, P., Metcalfe, R. (eds.) Beyond Calculation, pp. 75–85. Springer Science Business Media, New York (1997)

38. Holzinger, A., Searle, G., Nischelwitzer, A.K.: On some aspects of improving mobile applications for the elderly. In: Stephanidis, C. (ed.) HCI 2007. LNCS, vol. 4554, pp. 923–932. Springer, Heidelberg (2007)

39. Mynatt, E.D., Melenhorst, A.S., Fisk, A.D., Rogers, W.A.: Aware technologies for aging in place: understanding user needs and attitudes. IEEE Pervasive Comput. 3(2), 36–41 (2004)

40. Melenhorst, A.S., Rogers, W.A., Bouwhuis, D.G.: Older adults' motivated choice for technological innovation: evidence for benefit-driven selectivity. Psychol. Aging 21(1), 190–195 (2006)

41. Piaget, J.: Development and learning. In: Ripple, R.E., Rockcastle, V.N. (eds.) Piaget Rediscovered: A Report on the Conference of Cognitive Studies and Curriculum Development, pp. 7–20. Cornell University, Ithaca (1964)

42. Kolb, D.A., Fry, R.: Toward an applied theory of experiential learning. In: Cooper, C. (ed.) Theories of Group Process, pp. 33–57. John Wiley, London (1975)

43. Papert, S., Harel, I.: Constructionism. Ablex Publishing Corporation, New York (1991)

44. Bruner, J.S.: The act of discovery. Harvard Educ. Rev. 31(1), 21–32 (1961)

45. Jonassen, D.H. (ed.): Handbook of Research for Educational Communications and Technology. Simon & Schuster, New York (1996)

46. Bakardjieva, M.: Internet society: The Internet in everyday life. Sage, London (2005)

47. Fernández-Ardèvol, M.: Older population and mobile communication in Los Angeles. Preliminary results of a case study, IN3 Working Paper Series (2012)

48. Johnson, D.W., Johnson, R.T.: Instructional goal structure: cooperative, competitive, or individualistic. Review of Educational Research 44(2), 213–240 (1974)

49. Ganito, C.: Women on the move: the mobile phone as a gender technology. Comunicação & Cultura 9, 77–88 (2010)

Differences in the Adoption of Smartphones Between Middle Aged Adults and Older Adults in China

Shang Gao[1(⊠)], John Krogstie[1], and Yuhao Yang[2]

[1] Department of Computer and Information Science,
Norwegian University of Science and Technology, Trondheim, Norway
{shanggao,krogstie}@idi.ntnu.no
[2] School of Business Administration,
Zhongnan University of Economics and Law, Wuhan, China
vincentyoo@foxmail.com

Abstract. This research aims to investigate the differences in the adoption of smartphones between middle aged adults and older adults in China. Based on a literature review from previous research, a research model with eight research hypotheses was developed by extending UTAUT with a consideration of observability and compatibility from IDT, and perceived enjoyment and price value. This research model was empirically examined using survey data from 196 middle aged adults and 146 older adults respectively from China. The findings indicated that the effects of perceived enjoyment, compatibility, and observability on users' intention to use smartphones were significant, but no age differences between middle aged adults and older age adults were found to exist. Furthermore, the findings also identified age-related differences in the use and adoption of smartphones. The effects of performance expectancy and social influence on users' intention to use smartphones were moderated by age, such that it was significant for older adults but insignificant for middle aged adults.

Keywords: Adoption of smartphones · UTAUT · Older adults · Middle aged adults

1 Introduction

Today, smartphones become increasingly important in peoples' daily life [7]. However, not everyone are using and adopting smartphones. For example, many older adults are still using basic mobile phones in China. The digital divide remains when it comes to new technologies [10]. The digital divide refers to the gap between those who do and those who do not have access to new forms of information technology [20]. Middle aged adults and older adults face challenges when they are using smartphones. A gap seems to exist in the adoption and use of smartphones by middle aged adults and older adults. We would like to examine the use and adoption of smartphones with both middle aged adults and older adults in China.

The objective of this research is to examine the adoption and usage of smartphones with both middle aged adults and older adults in China. This research aims to make

© Springer International Publishing Switzerland 2015
J. Zhou and G. Salvendy (Eds.): ITAP 2015, Part I, LNCS 9193, pp. 451–462, 2015.
DOI: 10.1007/978-3-319-20892-3_44

contributions to studies on ageing and the adoption of smartphones. We investigated how various factors impact middle aged adults' and older adults' intention to use smartphones in China by a research model based on previous technology diffusion and acceptance theories (e.g., [18, 22]). Since most previous research (e.g., [15, 24]) on the adoption of smartphones tended to focus on people below the age of 35 (e.g., students, young people), we wanted to examine the user group with people over the age of 35 in this study. We defined older adults as people over the age of 45 in this study and middle aged adults as people between the age of 35 and 45.

The remainder of this paper is organized as follows: Sect. 2 discusses the theoretical background of this study. The research model and hypotheses are presented in Sect. 3. The research method and results are described in Sect. 4. This is followed by a discussion of the findings in Sect. 5. Section 6 concludes this research.

2   Background

2.1   Digital Divide

Scholarly research on the digital divide has a long history back to the 1990s. There is well documented research (e.g., [3]) on digital divide connecting to Internet and computer penetration through the lens of technology diffusion theory (e.g., TAM [4], IDT [18], UTAUT [22]) in the past two decades. Digital divide is generally referred to as the 'uneven diffusion' or 'gap' or 'disparities' between different socio-economic levels or across countries or between developed and developing countries in terms of 'access' and 'use' in ICTs [12]. Research on digital divide often starts by looking at users' access to new technologies. Along with the popularity of computers and digital technologies, the digital divide in terms of physical access seems to be reduced in most developed countries. Van Dijk [20] found a shifted research attention on digital divide from physical access to skills and usage.

The uneven spread of the mobile applications on smartphones has contributed to the popularity of the concept of the 'digital divide' associated with smartphones. It highlights the emerging social gap between those individuals who use mobile applications on smartphones and those who do not. It is believed that a significant component of the digital divide is age. For example, some older adults may feel no need for smartphones because they are not aware of the benefits of smartphones. To reduce digital inequalities, we must understand the reasons for different age groups' resistance to the use of smartphones. Investigating this digital inequality is of help to understand the diffusion of smartphones with populations of different age.

2.2   Research on the Adoption of Smartphones

Research has been carried out in studying various aspects related to the adoption of smartphones [6, 8]. In [5], Gao et al. investigated the role of lifestyles on the adoption of smartphones. The findings indicated that users with different lifestyles had different preferences related to different services on smartphones. Based on a study on the performance of mobile applications, Huang et al. [11] indicated that smartphones could become a suitable substitute of the traditional computer. But, the performance of the applications on smartphones is poorly understood.

Although significant effort has been done to explore the adoption of smartphones, the samples used in previous research on the adoption of smartphones were relatively young. An examination of the current literature reveals that few studies have addressed the use and adoption of smartphones by middle aged adults and older adults. In [9], Gao et al. studied the adoption of smartphones among older adults in China. The results indicated that perceived enjoyment was the most important determinant for older adults to adopt smartphones. Pheeraphuttharangkoon et al. [16] investigated the adoption and use of smartphones with older adults in the UK. However, the sample size with people over 40 years old in their study is quite small.

This research was a continuing effort from our previous research on the adoption of smartphones with older adults in China [9]. The digital divide along the age dimension has become a major concern in China. Two different age groups were defined in this study. We examined how the role of age played in the explanation of variability in the intention to use smartphones.

3 Research Model and Hypotheses

A research model that identifies important factors that impact users' intention to use smartphones was developed in this research. The proposed research model (see Fig. 1) is an extension of UTAUT [22], with a consideration of observability and compatibility from IDT [18], and perceived enjoyment [19, 21] and price value [23] from other technology diffusion theories. We have developed the following eight research hypotheses (labeled in Fig. 1) based on the research model.

Hypotheses Developed from UTAUT. Four key factors from UTAUT, Social Influence, Facilitating Conditions, Performance Expectancy and Effort Expectancy,

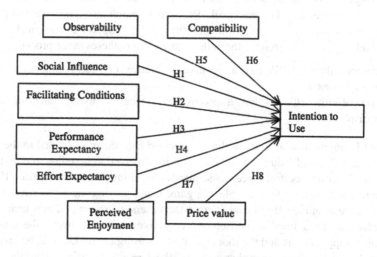

Fig. 1. Research model

were included in our research model. *Social Influence* is the extent to which users perceive that important others (e.g., family and friends) believe they should use a particular technology. Previous research also indicated that social influence is important for the adoption of smartphones [25]. *Facilitating Conditions* refer to users' perceptions of the resources and support available to perform a behavior. Users need to have digital skills to use smartphones. *Performance Expectancy* is defined as the degree to which using a technology will provide benefits to consumers in performing certain activities. Smartphones are able to provide potential benefits (e.g., always connected, healthcare information) for users. Once users have recognized these benefits, they are likely to use and adopt smartphones. *Effort Expectancy* is the degree of ease associated with users' use of technology. Learning a new technology often takes time and effort. If using smartphones is considered as an easy and straightforward process, users are likely to adopt smartphones. Thus, we proposed the following four hypotheses.

H1:   Social Influence (SI) has a positive influence on users' intention to use smartphones

H2:   Facilitating Conditions (FC) has a positive influence on users' intention to use smartphones

H3:   Performance Expectancy (PE) has a positive influence on users' intention to use smartphones

H4:   Effort Expectancy (EE) has a positive influence on users' intention to use smartphones

Hypotheses Developed from IDT. Rogers [18] indicated that innovation that are perceived by individuals as having greater relative advantage, compatibility, trialability, observability, and less complexity will be adopted more rapidly than other innovation. To further understand older adults' intention to use smartphones, two factors from IDT were included into our research model. As for the case of smartphones, *Observability* can be defined as the degree to which smartphones are visible to potential users. *Compatibility* can be seen as users' belief in the consistency of using smartphones with the way they live and work. Previous research also demonstrated that the importance of Observability and Compatibility to the adoption of new technologies (e.g., e-banking [13]). Therefore, the following two hypotheses were proposed.

H5:   Observability (OBS) has a positive influence on users' intention to use smartphones

H6:   Compatibility (COM) has a positive influence on users' intention to use smartphones

Perceived Enjoyment and Price Value. *Perceived Enjoyment* is defined as the extent to which the activity of using a specific system is perceived to be enjoyable in its own right, aside from any performance consequences resulting from system use [19, 21]. Users can have fun when they are playing games, and playing music on smartphones.

Price value is another significant factor affects users' adoption of a new technology. *Price value* can be defined as consumers' cognitive tradeoff between the perceived benefit of the applications and the monetary cost for using them [23]. It is believed that users are likely to adopt smartphones when the benefits of using smartphones are perceived to be greater than the monetary cost of smartphones. Hence, we proposed the following hypotheses.

H7:   Perceived Enjoyment (PEJ) has a positive influence on users' intention to use smartphones

H8:   Price Value (PV) has a positive influence on users' intention to use smartphones

4   An Empirical Study with the Research Model

To understand middle aged adults' and older adults' use and adoption of smartphones in China, the proposed research model and hypotheses were empirically tested using the structural equation modeling approach.

4.1   Instrument Development

The validated instrument measures from previous research [4, 18, 21–23] were used as the foundation to create the instrument for this study. In order to ensure that the instrument better fit this empirical study, some minor words changes were made to ensure easy interpretation and comprehension of the questions. For instance, wording was modified to fit the context of use of smartphones in China. A questionnaire was developed first in English and then translated into Chinese. Back-translation was conducted by bilingual third party to improve the translation accuracy. The final measurement questionnaire consisted of 24 items[1]. A seven point Likert scale was used to examine participants' responses to all items in this part.

4.2   Samples

The data for this study was collected through self-administered questionnaires in seven provinces in China. The survey was distributed as paper-based questionnaires to individuals from Dec 1st 2014 to Dec 30th, 2014. 359 completed questionnaires were collected, among which 341 of them were valid questionnaires (i.e., valid respondent rate 95 %). Among the participants, 186 of the participants were male, and 155 were female. Moreover, 85.3 % of participants had full-time jobs, 10.3 % of participants had part-time jobs, 4.4 % of participants had retired. In terms of age, 195 participants were from the age group of middle aged adults, while 146 participants were from the age group of older adults.

Further, the top three most used featured on smartphones for the age group of older adults were: making phone calls, text messaging and instant messaging services (e.g., QQ, Wechat). With regard to the age group of middle aged adults, instant messaging services, making phone calls, and websites browsing were rated as most frequently used features on smartphones. Moreover, using social media services is more popular

---

[1] The survey items are available at this link: http://www.idi.ntnu.no/~shanggao/maoadults.html.

in the age group of middle aged adults than the age group of older adults. Further, both the age groups have limited use of Emailing and mobile games on smartphones.

4.3   Measurement Model

The quality of the measurement model is determined by (1). Content validity, (2). Construct reliability and (3). Discriminant validity [1]. To ensure the content validity of our constructs, a pretest with 5 Chinese researchers in E-business was carried out. And we found that the questionnaire was well understood by all the researchers.

To further test the reliability and validity of each construct in the research model, the Internal Consistency of Reliability (ICR) of each construct was tested with Cronbach's Alpha coefficient. As a result, for the age group of middle aged adults, the Cronbach's Alpha values range from 0.71 to 0.93. With regard to the age group of older adults, the Cronbach's Alpha values range from 0.82 to 0.94. A score of 0.7 is marked as an acceptable reliability coefficient for Cronbach's Alpha [17]. All the constructs in the research model for both the age groups were above 0.70. Consequently, the scales were deemed acceptable to continue.

Convergent validity was assessed through composite reliability (CR) and the average variance extracted (AVE). Bagozzi and Yi [2] proposed the following three measurement criteria: factor loadings for all items should exceed 0.5, the CR should exceed 0.7, and the AVE of each construct should exceed 0.5. As shown in Tables 1 and 2, all constructs were in acceptable ranges for the age group of middle aged adults and the age group of older adults respectively.

The measurements of discriminant validity for both the age groups were presented in Tables 3 and 4. According to the results, the variances extracted by the constructs were more than the squared correlations among variables. The fact revealed that constructs were empirically distinct for both the age groups. As good results for convergent validity and discriminant validity were achieved, the test result of the measurement model was good.

4.4   Structural Model and Hypotheses Testing

The structural model was tested using SmartPLS. Table 5 presents the path coefficients, which are standardized regression coefficients. For the age group of middle aged adults, observability, compatibility and perceived enjoyment (H5, H6, H7) were found to have a statistically significant effect on users' intention to use smart phones, while the other hypotheses were not supported. For the age group of older adults, five (H1, H3, H5, H6, H7) of the proposed eight hypotheses were supported.

The R^2 (R square) denotes to coefficient of determination. It provides a measure of how well future outcomes are likely to be predicted by the model, the amount of variability of a given construct. In our analysis, the R^2 coefficient of determination is a statistical measure of how well the regression coefficients approximate the real data point. According to the result, for the middle aged adults, 58 % of the variance of behavior intention can be explained by the research model. With respect to the older adults, the research model manages to explain 78 % of the variable in the values of

Table 1. Factor loadings, composite reliability, and AVE for each construct (for the age group of middle aged adults).

Construct	Item	Factor loading	Composite reliability	AVE	Cronbach's Alpha
SI	SI1	0.90	0.87	0.78	0.71
	SI2	0.86			
FC	FC1	0.81	0.86	0.61	0.78
	FC2	0.78			
	FC4	0.81			
	FC4	0.71			
PE	PE1	0.78	0.88	0.70	0.79
	PE2	0.87			
	PE3	0.60			
EE	EE1	0.89	0.93	0.82	0.89
	EE2	0.93			
	EE3	0.89			
OBS	OBS1	0.92	0.91	0.84	0.81
	OBS2	0.92			
COM	COM1	0.93	0.95	0.86	0.92
	COM2	0.95			
	COM3	0.90			
PEJ	PEJ1	0.94	0.94	0.88	0.87
	PEJ2	0.94			
PV	PV1	0.91	0.95	0.88	0.93
	PV2	0.95			
	PV3	0.95			
IU	IU1	0.91	0.90	0.81	0.77
	IU2	0.90			

intention to use. The results revealed that the predicative strength of the research model for both the age groups was quite strong. Focusing on the two different age groups, the research model had a stronger predicative strength for the age group of older adults than the age group of middle aged adults.

5 Discussion

In this research, we studied the adoption of smartphones between middle aged adults and older adults in China. From an academic perspective, this research contributed to the literature on the adoption of smartphones with middle aged adults and older adults in China by building upon previous technology diffusion theories. From a practical perspective, it offered some insights for smartphones providers and mobile services providers to promote the use of smartphones to different age groups in China.

Table 2. Factor loadings, composite reliability, and AVE for each construct (for the age group of older adults).

Construct	Item	Factor loading	Composite reliability	AVE	Cronbach's Alpha
SI	SI1	0.93	0.92	0.85	0.82
	SI2	0.91			
FC	FC1	0.87	0.91	0.73	0.87
	FC2	0.83			
	FC4	0.90			
	FC4	0.81			
PE	PE1	0.89	0.91	0.77	0.85
	PE2	0.93			
	PE3	0.80			
EE	EE1	0.94	0.95	0.87	0.92
	EE2	0.94			
	EE3	0.91			
OBS	OBS1	0.93	0.93	0.88	0.86
	OBS2	0.94			
COM	COM1	0.93	0.94	0.85	0.91
	COM2	0.94			
	COM3	0.89			
PEJ	PEJ1	0.94	0.94	0.90	0.88
	PEJ2	0.95			
PV	PV1	0.83	0.93	0.81	0.89
	PV2	0.94			
	PV3	0.92			
IU	IU1	0.97	0.97	0.94	0.94
	IU2	0.97			

Table 3. Discriminant validity (for the age group of middle aged adults)

Variables	PEJ	PV	PE	FC	SI	EE	OBS	COM	IU
PEJ	**0.94**								
PV	0.50	**0.94**							
PE	0.63	0.48	**0.84**						
FC	0.57	0.59	0.71	**0.78**					
SI	0.62	0.58	0.60	0.60	**0.88**				
EE	0.47	0.51	0.38	0.56	0.38	**0.91**			
OBS	0.41	0.18	0.40	0.39	0.36	0.50	**0.92**		
COM	0.61	0.56	0.67	0.64	0.67	0.49	0.40	**0.93**	
IU	0.66	0.44	0.56	0.56	0.50	0.51	0.53	0.63	**0.90**

Table 4. Discriminant validity (for the age group of older adults)

Variables	PEJ	PV	PE	FC	SI	EE	OBS	COM	IU
PEJ	**0.95**								
PV	0.46	**0.90**							
PE	0.48	0.31	**0.88**						
FC	0.51	0.42	0.51	**0.85**					
SI	0.56	0.57	0.51	0.69	**0.92**				
EE	0.54	0.44	0.34	0.44	0.48	**0.93**			
OBS	0.49	0.25	0.33	0.34	0.32	0.37	**0.94**		
COM	0.62	0.47	0.59	0.55	0.70	0.57	0.30	**0.92**	
IU	0.82	0.42	0.60	0.56	0.64	0.45	0.52	0.68	**0.97**

Note: Diagonals represent the average variance extracted, while the other matrix entries represent the squared correlations.

Table 5. Test of hypotheses based on path coefficient for both the age groups

Hypothesis	Path coefficient and their significance	
	Middle aged adults	Older adults
H1	−0.090	0.161*
H2	0.093	0.008
H3	0.018	0.154*
H4	0.049	−0.106
H5	0.237*	0.135*
H6	0.248*	0.168*
H7	0.362***	0.561***
H8	0.047	−0.050

$*p < 0.05$; $**p < 0.01$; $*** p < 0.001$

The findings suggested that perceived enjoyment, observability, and compatibility proved to be important determinants for the adoption of smartphones with both middle aged adults and older adults. The most important determinant for both the age groups' intention to use smartphones was perceived enjoyment. If using smartphones is fun, both middle aged adults and older adults are more likely to accept smartphones. It highlighted the role that hedonic aspects play in the adoption of smartphones by both the age groups.

The findings also identified age-related differences in the use and adoption of smartphones. The effects of both performance expectancy and social influence on users' intention to use smartphones were significant for older adults, but insignificant for middle aged adults. Most middle aged adults tended to use features like voice phone calls, instant messaging services on their smartphones. They might use these features with basic mobile phones before. However, the advanced features (e.g., Emailing, document processing) on smartphones were less used by middle aged adults. They might be able to use email services on smartphones but chose not to because they did not want to change their habits. Consequently, they might not perceive the potential benefits provided by smartphones. For them, the costs of changing their habits may limit the adoption of smartphones. Therefore, the presence of the performance expectancy did not motivate older adults to use smartphones. In contrast, some older adults might not use basic mobile phones before. They found using basic features on their smartphones useful for their work and life. Thus, Performance expectancy had a significant positive impact on older adults' intention to use smartphones. Furthermore, middle aged adults appeared to have higher levels of self-recognition of new technologies than older adults. As a result, middle aged adults tended to decide for themselves whether to adopt smartphones without being influenced by those around them. Therefore, social influence did not have a significant positive impact on middle aged adults' intention to use smartphones.

There was no significant positive impact of facilitating conditions on the intention to use smartphones with both the age groups. One possible reason was that facilitating conditions might be considered as a limiting factor when the needed facilitating conditions are not perceived by them. Therefore, the presence of the facilitating conditions did not motivate them to use smartphones. Effort expectancy did not have a strong positive influence on both the age groups' intention to use smartphones. It seemed that they did not use smartphones just because it was easy to use, but rather because they found it fun to use. Another interesting finding was that price value had no significant positive impact on the intention to use smartphones with both the age groups. Since Chinese' economy is growing fast and smartphones has become inexpensive in China, most participants in this study can afford smartphones. It appeared that price value of smartphones became unimportant when it came to the adoption of smartphones with middle aged adults and older adults in China.

However, we were also aware of some limitations. Firstly, we only tested the research model and research hypotheses with samples from seven provinces in China. This sample might not be fully representative of the entire middle aged adults and older adults in China. Secondly, all the data were collected using self-reported scales in the research. This may lead to some caution because common method variance may account for some of the results that has been cited as one of the stronger criticisms of tests of theories with TAM and TAM-extended research [14]. However, our data analysis with convergent and discriminant validity does not support the presence of a strong common methods factor.

6   Conclusion and Future Research

This research was designed to study the differences in adoption of smartphones between middle aged adults and older adults in China. Since China is experiencing an increase in the average age of their population, the understanding on how middle aged adults and older adults use and adopt smartphones is important to increase their quality of life. The key contributions of this study are threefold. First, this study investigated middle aged adults' and older adults' adoption of smartphones by extending UTAUT with a consideration of observability and compatibility from IDT, and perceived enjoyment and price value. Second, the findings indicated that the effects of perceived enjoyment, compatibility, and observability on users' intention to use smartphones were significant, but no age differences between middle aged adults and older adults were found to exist. Third, the effects of performance expectancy and social influence on users' intention to use smartphones were moderated by age, such that it was significant for older adults but insignificant for middle aged adults. The results demonstrated that there was a difference between the two different age groups in China.

Continuing with this stream of research, we plan to further examine the applicability of the research model with other group of users in China (e.g., people below 35 years old). Future research is also needed to carry out a comparative study with middle aged adults and older adults in other countries.

References

1. Bagozzi, R.P.: The role of measurement in theory construction and hypothesis testing: toward a holistic model. In: Ferrell, O.C., Brown, S.W., Lamb, C.W. (eds.) Conceptual and Theoretical Developments in Marketing, pp. 15–32. American Marketing Association, Chicago (1979)
2. Bagozzi, R.P., Yi, Y.: Specification, evaluation, and interpretation of structural equation models. J. Acad. Mark. Sci. **40**(1), 8–34 (2012)
3. Chinn, M.D., Fairlie, R.W.: The Determinants of the Global Digital Divide: A Cross-Country Analysis of Computer and Internet Penetration. Oxford Economic Papers, Oxford (2006)
4. Davis, F.D.: Perceived usefulness, perceived ease of use and user acceptance of information technology. MIS Q. **13**(3), 319–340 (1989)
5. Gao, S., Krogstie, J., Chen, Z., et al.: Lifestyles and mobile services adoption in China. Int. J. E-Bus. Res. (IJEBR). **10**(3), 36–53 (2014)
6. Gao, S., Krogstie, J., Gransæther, P.A.: Mobile services acceptance model. In: Proceedings of International Conference on Convergence and Hybrid Information Technology. IEEE Computer Society (2008)
7. Gao, S., Krogstie, J., Siau, K.: Adoption of mobile information services: An empirical study. Mob. Inf. Syst. **10**(2), 147–171 (2014)
8. Gao, S., Krogstie, J., Siau, K.: Developing an instrument to measure the adoption of mobile services. Mob. Inf. Syst. **7**(1), 45–67 (2011)
9. Gao, S., Yang, Y., Krogstie, J.: The adoption of smartphones among older adults in China. In: Liu, K., Nakata, K., Li, W., Galarreta, D. (eds.) ICISO 2015. IFIP AICT, vol. 449, pp. 112–122. Springer, Heidelberg (2015)
10. Greengard, S.: Facing an age-old problem. Commun. ACM **52**(9), 20–22 (2009)
11. Huang, J., Xu, Q., Tiwana, B., et al.: Anatomizing application performance differences on smartphones. In: Proceedings of the 8th international conference on Mobile systems, applications, and services, pp. 165–178. ACM (2010)
12. Hwang, J.: Deconstructing the discourse of the global digital divide in the age of neo-liberal global economy. Ph.D. thesis, The Pennsylvania State University (2006)
13. Kolodinsky, J.M., Hogarth, J.M., Hilgert, M.A.: The adoption of electronic banking technologies by US consumers. Int. J. Bank Mark. **22**(4), 238–259 (2004)
14. Malhotra, N.K., Kim, S.S., Patil, A.: Common method variance in IS research: a comparison of alternative approaches and a reanalysis of past research. Manage. Sci. **52**(12), 1865–1883 (2006)

15. Payne, K.F.B., Wharrad, H., Watts, K.: Smartphone and medical related app use among medical students and junior doctors in the United Kingdom (UK): a regional survey. BMC Med. Inform. Decis. Mak. **12**(1), 121 (2012)

16. Pheeraphuttharangkoon, S., Choudrie, J., Zamani, E., et al.: Investigating the adoption and use of smartphones in the UK: a silver-surfers perspective. In: 22nd European Conference on Information Systems (ECIS2014) (2014)

17. Robinson, J.P., Shaver, P.R., Wrightsman, L.S.: Criteria for Scale Selections and Evaluation. Academic Press, San Diego (1991)

18. Rogers, E.M.: The Diffusion of Innovations. Free Press, New York (1995)

19. Van der Heijden, H.: Factors influencing the usage of websites: the case of a generic portal in The Netherlands. Inf. Manag. **40**(6), 541–549 (2003)

20. Van Dijk, J.A.: Digital divide research, achievements and shortcomings. Poetics. **34**(4), 221–235 (2006)

21. Venkatesh, V., Bala, H.: TAM 3: advancing the technology acceptance model with a focus on interventions. Manuscript in preparation. http://www.vvenkatesh.com/IT/organizations/Theoretical_Models.asp. Accessed 2013

22. Venkatesh, V., Morris, M.G., Davis, G.B., et al.: User acceptance of information technology: toward a unified view. MIS Q. **27**(3), 425–478 (2003)

23. Venkatesh, V., Thong, J.Y., Xu, X.: Consumer acceptance and use of information technology: extending the unified theory of acceptance and use of technology. MIS Q. **36**(1), 157–178 (2012)

24. Wee, S.Y., Hoe, L.S., Keat, T.K., et al.: Prediction of user acceptance and adoption of smart phone for learning with technology acceptance model. J. Appl. Sci. **10**(20), 2395–2402 (2011)

25. Zhou, T., Li, H., Liu, Y.: The effect of flow experience on mobile SNS users' loyalty. Ind. Manage. Data Syst. **110**(6), 930–946 (2010)

Ease-of-Use of Tactile Interaction for Novice Older Adults

Lilian Genaro Motti[1(✉)], Nadine Vigouroux[1], and Philippe Gorce[2]

[1] UPS, IRIT, University of Toulouse, 118 Route de Narbonne, 31062 Toulouse, France
{genaro,vigourou}@irit.fr
[2] HandiBio, University of Toulon, Avenue de l'université, 83957 Toulon, France
gorce@univ-tln.fr

Abstract. Usability, particularly ease-of-use, is a main factor affecting the acceptance of technologies by older adults. Mobile devices offer great possibilities for well-being applications, but they are often equipped with touchscreen. In order to evaluate the ease-of-use of tactile interaction, this study compares the performances of 16 novice (mean age 74) and 8 experienced older adults (mean 75) during the execution of drag-and-drop interaction for achieving tactile puzzle games on smartphone and tablet, with pen and fingers. Results show that novice users were able accomplish interaction accurately with longer times but no significant difference of errors of accuracy.

Keywords: Human-computer interaction · Interaction techniques · Older adults · Touchscreen · Drag-and-drop · Errors of accuracy · Ease-of-use · Usability

1 Introduction

Mobile devices offer great possibilities for well-being applications destined to older populations. Mobile technologies are also being developed to help older users to overcome age related declines in cognitive, motor and perceptual skills. Unfortunately, the adoption of technologies by this population is very limited [1]. In France, the availability of touchscreen mobile devices in the market and the reduction of the cost for devices and services (i.e. subscription for mobile connections) have a great impact on the number of elderly using mobile Internet: 16.4 % of people aged 60 to 74 years old and 3.1 % of people aged 75 years old or older in the end of 2012 according to a report of INSEE (National Institute of Statistics and Economics Studies) [2]. They are still a small part of the population when compared to the younger age groups: 75 % of 15 to 29 years old or 50.8 % of 30 to 44 years old people. In Europe, 42 % of people aged 55 to 74 years old declared a regular internet use (against 93 % of 16 to 24 or 78 % of 25 to 54 years old) but only 12 % of this population used mobile devices for internet access (against 58 % of 16 to 24 or 36 % of 25 to 54 years old) [3].

Barnard et al. (2013) [1] defined two stages for technology acceptance: first, the intention to use, referring to a behavior that is affected by performance expectancy, effort expectancy, social influence and facilitating conditions; second, the usability, i.e. "the effectiveness, efficiency and satisfaction with which specified users achieve specified goals in particular environments" (ISO 9241). According to Lee and Coughlin

© Springer International Publishing Switzerland 2015
J. Zhou and G. Salvendy (Eds.): ITAP 2015, Part I, LNCS 9193, pp. 463–474, 2015.
DOI: 10.1007/978-3-319-20892-3_45

(2014), enhancing usability means to meet older adults' needs, preventing errors and providing help to control [4]. They describe usability as "ease of learning and use" [4]. Renaud and van Bijon (2008) consider ease of use a determining factor for intention to use and consequently for technology acceptance among older adults [5].

Mobile devices are often equipped with touchscreen. But is tactile interaction easy to use by older adults? The aim of this study is to evaluate the ease-of-use of tactile interaction. Previous studies on human-computer interaction have discussed about the effects of prior experience on older adults performances [6]. So we compare the performances (time and error rate) of older adults with and without previous experience with touchscreen devices. Our main hypothesis is that tactile interaction is easy to use. Therefore, we expect that novices and experienced subjects would have similar performances during the drag-and-drop interaction for solving tactile puzzles on smartphone and tablet, with pen and fingers.

The remainder of this paper is organized as follows. Section 2 discuss usability as a determining factor for technology acceptance and the ease of use of tactile interaction for novice older adults, positioning this work in relation to the previous studies and justifying the need of studying and improving tactile interaction. Section 3 describes the experience. Section 4 shows the results of the statistical analysis. Results are discussed on Sect. 5 followed by conclusions on Sect. 6.

2   Related Work

2.1   Technology Acceptance for Older Adults

Acceptance has been defined as an attitude towards technologies, referring to early phase and essential step to an adoption process. Adoption is the process by which users embrace technologies, since the moment when potential users become interested to a technology until the moment the use of it has an impact in their daily lives [5].

Ease-of-use is one of the main factors of technology acceptance according to several authors. In a review of the literature, Peek et al. (2014) found that low ease of use is a key concern during pre-implementation acceptance factors of technologies for aging in place [7]. According to Lee and Coughlin (2014), "ease of learning and use" is one of the ten factors facilitating or determining the adoption of technology by this group of users [4]. Ease of learning and use has been considered a predictor for technology acceptance or rejection by Renaud and van Bijon (2008) [5].

Older adults are a heterogeneous population. Chronological age is not enough for describing the characteristics of adults aged 65 years old or more because aging is an individual process [8]. In addition to the physical and cognitive declines related to age, earlier experiences can affect older adults perception of their own ability to use new technologies [8]. Gudur et al. (2013) have demonstrated that previous experience with computers and technologies affects positively the self-confidence of older adults for interaction tasks [9]. By consequence, previous experience affects their attitudes and expectations towards technologies or even acceptance [1]. Older adults who did not learn how to use a computer during their professional carrier or education need more training to progress and feel confident compared to younger adults [1]. Technologies, interfaces and interaction techniques should be easy to learn and use in order to overcome lower technology literacy [4].

2.2 Ease-of-Use of Tactile Interaction for Novice Older Adults

Tactile interaction is considered easy to learn and use because direct interaction on the screen reduces the cognitive workload demanding less eye-control coordination than traditional input devices [10]. Direct interaction on touchscreen has been recommended for older adults as easier to use [10], reducing the gap of performances between adults and older adults when compared to traditional input devices [11].

When using new technologies, people might feel uncomfortable if they don't know how to control it [12]. Anxiety is related to lack of confidence and this feeling can affect the perceived benefit [4], disturbing the use of intuitive interaction. It also affects older user's performances because it causes distraction. The absence of physical keyboard and mouse diminishes the anxiety towards technologies, affecting positively user's attitudes [10]. Familiarity with the interaction and interfaces influences the attitudes towards technologies [4]. Systems and interaction techniques designed to prevent mistakes and support interaction help to increase confidence [9].

2.3 Difficulties Related to Tactile Interaction

8 % of French users, all age groups included, complained about difficulties for using tactile interaction [2]. Older users have reported several problems during touchscreen use as discouraging for the acceptance of technologies and disturbing for achieving interaction, such as lack of control, small targets, difficulties for error recovering among others.

The review of the literature of studies of tactile interaction of older adults describes problems related to the situations of use or users' abilities.

Concerning the situations of use, several factors have been reported. Small screen devices usually present small targets, difficult to acquire, especially during finger interaction [13]. Pen interaction has been indicated to improve accuracy, especially on small touchscreen devices [14]. Concerning the gestures of interaction that have been evaluated, tapping has been considered intuitive and faster than dragging [11, 15] but it requires bigger targets. Drag-and-drop allows accurate interaction on small devices [14] and performances increase rapidly with practice [15].

Concerning the abilities of older users, visually impaired users were able to accomplish drag-and-drop interaction during card games on mobile devices [6]. This gesture of interaction has been studied to improve text entry tasks for older users with tremor [16, 17]. During mouse interaction, dragging elements helps to track the cursor on the screen and it has been evaluated for cognitive impaired users [18]. The metaphor of drag interaction gesture is closer to the reality.

Familiar and ludic activities help novice users to discover the manipulation of devices and learning interaction [19]. When playing a game, an error is not supposed to be serious and discouraging because it doesn't have implications on real life. That is one of the reasons the present study evaluates tactile interaction during the execution of puzzle games.

3 Methods

Ease-of-use is one of the main factors of usability affecting technology acceptance [4, 7]. As mobile devices are often equipped with touchscreen, we want to investigate if tactile interaction is easy to use. As already presented in the Sect. 2, previous experience with technologies affects users' performances. So we will compare two groups of subjects: older adults with and without previous experience with touchscreen. Our hypothesis is that novice and experienced older adults will have similar performances.

HCI studies usually assess interaction performances through time and error rate. In order to reproduce different situations of use of mobile touchscreen, we will evaluate performances on smartphone and tablet, with pen and fingers and two levels of difficulty (corresponding to two accuracy requirements). The easier level requires 80 % of accuracy and the higher level requires 95 % of accuracy for the final positioning. These two levels will be treated indistinctly. As a complement, we will search for effects of screen size and interaction techniques. This study extends the analysis of a previous study about supplementary attempts for positioning the targets [14].

3.1 The Interactive System

The system "Puzzle Touch" is consisted of tactile puzzle games so older adults without previous experience with touchscreen would feel confident to participate of the experience by the familiarity with the proposed activity [19].

The main task is moving the puzzle pieces to place them on a grid (drag-and-drop). Targets sizes (the correct emplacement for a puzzle piece) were 19 × 19 mm on the smartphone (85 pixels width) and 35 × 35 mm (195 pixels width) on the tablet. 12 squared pieces are randomly placed on the mid bottom of the screen and a 3 × 4 grid with a watermark is displayed on the mid top. In order to compensate the lack of spacing between pieces, they are contoured by a 1 mm dark border. When the final position of a puzzle piece is validated, there is a visual feedback (a flash effect) and the piece is fixed on the grid.

3.2 Material

A 5.5 inches screen smartphone (Galaxy Note II with a WXGA 1280 × 720 Super AMOLED touchscreen) and a 10.1 inches screen tablet (Galaxy Note 10.1 with a WXGA 1280 × 800 LCD touchscreen) were used for this experiment. Both devices allow interaction with pen or fingers.

3.3 Procedure

Recruitment took place on associations, clubs and libraries frequented by older adults in Toulouse, France, where demonstration meetings were organized to explain the purposes of the study. Being aged 65 or older was the unique criteria of inclusion. Volunteers had an individual appointment for the experiment.

The individual session started by a familiarization phase with at least four complete interactions with both interaction techniques on the tablet and on the smartphone. After given their formal consent, they passed eyesight control tests and answered questionnaires about their motor abilities, previous experience with technologies and particularly frequency of use of touchscreen devices.

Subjects were told to install themselves comfortably, they were seated and the devices were horizontally placed on a table on portrait mode. Participants were told to complete the games accurately. Every subject played eight tactile puzzle games: with pen and finger interaction, on smartphone and tablet and two sets on different requirement levels (first the easier level, requiring 80 % accuracy, and then the difficult one, requiring 95 % of accuracy). The order of the use of devices and interaction techniques has been counter-balanced.

3.4 Measures

We assessed mean time of movement and number of errors of accuracy as evaluation criteria.

Time of movement refers to the time the subject spent moving the pieces before reaching their correspondent target (TM). It does not include reflection time.

The number of errors of accuracy was verified according to the position of the dropped piece on the game. One error of accuracy is counted once the puzzle piece is covering at least 50 % of its right emplacement but should be corrected positioned to meet the accuracy requirements of the game. The others movements of the puzzle pieces have been considered as a strategy to solve the puzzle. The number of errors of accuracy (EA) [14] counts the number of supplementary attempts for reaching a target.

4 Results

4.1 Participants

24 body-abled older users (range 65–86, mean 74.25, SD = 5.8) participated of the experience. User profiles were defined according to the information reported on the initial questionnaire: 8 of them had previous experience and regular use of touchscreen devices. Subjects have been divided into two groups:

- Group A includes 8 subjects who use touchscreen at least once a week (mean age 74.75, SD = 6.79), 4 of them use a smartphone and the other 4 use a tablet, all use finger interaction;
- Group B includes 16 novice subjects (mean 74, SD = 5.06) who had never or rarely use touchscreen devices before the experiment.

4.2 Statistical Analysis

Data is not normally distributed according to the results of Shapiro Wilk test (TM: W = 0.8788, p-value = 2.592e-11; EA: W = 0.7886, p-value = 2.202e-15). By consequence, Mann Whitney U test has been used to evaluate significant effects of user's profiles (Group A and Group B).

Data of each group of subjects is not normally distributed neither according to the results of Shapiro Wilk test: Group A (TM: W = 0.9518, p-value = 0.01409; EA: = 0.8462, p-value = 0.0003436) or Group B (TM: W = 0.8635, p-value = 1.68e-09; EA: W = 0.9189, p-value = 0.0004455).

Data distribution for TM and EA is skewed left. For this reason we detailed median for the tendencies and inter-quartiles (IQR) for the variability.

Friedman test has been used to search for significant differences between the four situations of the study (smartphone or tablet, pen or finger). For the post hoc analysis, the Wilcoxon signed rank test has been used to evaluate screen size or interaction techniques effects. In this case, a Bonferroni correction has been applied, setting the p-value to 0.0125.

4.3   Time of Movement

The statistical analysis show that there is a significant difference of experience of use of touchscreen on time of movement (TM) (Z = 10.51528, W = 5205.5, p-value = 0.002249). The mean time for Group A is 28.3 s (SD = 13, median = 27.2, IQR = 16.5) and for Group B it is 37.5 s (SD = 19.8, median = 30.9, IQR = 19.3). There is a bigger variability among novice users, as observed on Fig. 1.

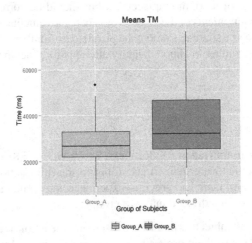

Fig. 1. Time of movement (TM) for experienced (Group A) and novices (Group B)

There is a significant effect of the different situations (screen sizes, interaction techniques) of the game on TM for all subjects (chi-squared = 75.8, df = 23, p-value = 1.499e-07), as well as for Group A (chi-squared = 21.5, df = 7, p-value = 0.003096) and for Group B (chi-squared = 50.3382, df = 15, p-value = 1.06e-05). Consequently, we search for effects of interaction techniques and screen sizes.

No significant effect of interaction techniques was found for Group A ($Z = 1.869894$, $V = 364$, p-value = 0.06222) neither for Group B ($Z = 1.123501$, $V = 1208$, p-value = 0.2626). There was no significant effect of the screen sizes for Group A ($Z = -2.262572$, $V = 143$, p-value = 0.02279). But there is a significant effect of screen sizes for Group B ($Z = -3.203315$, $V = 561$, p-value = 0.001374). On average, they spent 34.7 s (SD = 18.7, median = 29.6, IQR = 18.1) during inter-action on smartphone and 40.3 s (SD = 20.6, median = 31.6, IQR = 18.2) on tablet.

The shortest TMs for Group A and for Group B were executed during pen interaction on smartphone (Group A: mean 24.4, SD = 7.9, median = 23.8, IQR = 4.8 and Group B: mean 34.9, SD = 17.4, median = 27, IQR = 21.9). No significant difference between the two groups was found for any situation, details are presented on Fig. 2.

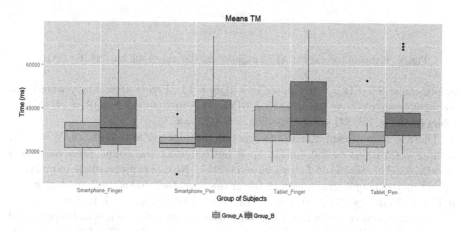

Fig. 2. Time of movement (TM) for experienced (Group A) and novices (Group B) during the different situations of the experience (Smartphone or Tablet with Finger or Pen).

4.4 Errors

There is no significant difference of experience of use of touchscreen on number of errors of accuracy (EA) ($Z = 7.595485$, $W = 4406.5$, p-value = 0.3922) as presented on Fig. 3. Mean EA for Group A is 10.5 (SD = 12.6, median = 5.5, IQR = 11.3) and for Group B is 12.4 (SD = 14.1, median = 6, IQR = 14.3).

There is a significant effect of the different situations of the game on EA for all subjects (chi-squared = 70.484, df = 23, p-value = 1.024e-06) as well as for Group A (chi-squared = 20.5945, df = 7, p-value = 0.004419) and for Group B (chi-squared = 44.9778, df = 15, p-value = 7.719e-05). Consequently, we search for effects of interaction techniques and screen sizes.

There are significant effects of interaction techniques ($Z = 0.5796671$, $V = 295$, p-value = 0.01105) and screen sizes ($Z = 1.76705$, $V = 358.5$, p-value = 0.009706) on EA for Group A. Experienced subjects made more errors of accuracy during interaction with finger (mean = 12.3, SD = 15, median = 6.5, IQR = 13) than with

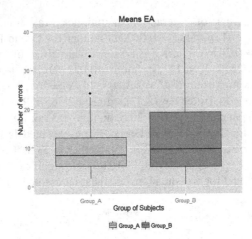

Fig. 3. Errors of accuracy (EA) for experienced (Group A) and novices (Group B)

pen (mean = 8.7, SD = 9.6, median = 5, IQR = 12). Errors of accuracy were more frequent on smartphone (mean = 13.2, SD = 14.3, median = 8.5, IQR = 19) than on tablet (mean = 7.8, SD = 10.2, median = 5, IQR = 6.3).

There is a significant effect of interaction technique (Z = 0.4748128, V = 1111, p-value = 0.01069) on EA for Group B but no effect was found for screen sizes (Z = 0.7055317, V = 1145.5, p-value = 0.04944). Novice subjects made more errors of accuracy during interaction with finger (mean = 14.1, SD = 14.7, median = 7.5, IQR = 15.3) than with pen (mean = 10.7, SD = 13.4, median = 5, IQR = 13.3).

Pen interaction on tablet was the most accurate situation for novices and experienced subjects. The number of EA for Group A was on average 6.25 (SD = 5.7, median = 5, IQR = 7.3) and for Group B it was 8.9 (SD12.4, median = 4.5, IQR = 9.3). The less accurate situation for both groups was finger interaction on smartphone, where average EA for Group A was 15.2 (SD = 16.3, median = 10, IQR = 18.8) and 15.4 for Group B (SD = 16.4, median = 7, IQR = 17.5). No significant effect of touchscreen experience was found for any situation, details are presented on Fig. 4.

5   Discussion

Novice and experienced subjects were able to complete the tactile puzzle games. Apparently, the familiarity with the task and the metaphor of drag-and-drop helped older adults with and without experience with touchscreen devices to accomplish the interaction on smartphone and tablet, with pen and finger.

The statistical analysis shows that there is a significant difference between the two groups of users on time of movement. Novice older adults spent longer times. There is a significant effect of screen sizes on time of movement only for novice users; they spent less time during interaction on smartphone, where the distances are smaller. The shortest time for both groups was executed during pen interaction on smartphone.

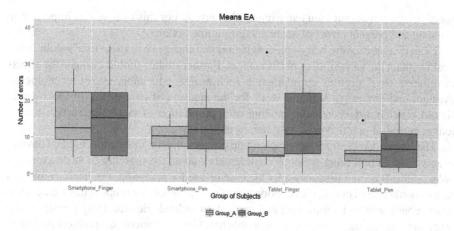

Fig. 4. Errors of accuracy (EA) for experienced (Group A) and novices (Group B) during the different situations of the experience (Smartphone or Tablet with Finger or Pen).

There is no significant difference of use of touchscreen on number of errors of accuracy. There is a bigger variability among novice subjects. A significant effect of interaction technique was found for both groups. They made fewer errors during pen interaction. Effects of screen size were found only for experienced subjects, who were more accurate during interaction on tablet.

Our main hypothesis is partially confirmed: novice spent longer movement times but novice and experienced older adults have similar number of errors on global results. However, some situations of the experience seem to facilitate the interaction for novice subjects. Pen interaction reduced time and error rates for this group. Other studies about tactile interaction of older adults demonstrated that older subjects take longer times but they are not less accurate than younger users [20], who have prior experience with technologies. Maybe using a pen is more natural for novice users. Generally subjects made more errors of placement during finger interaction but the difference is really small for experienced users. As already reported by previous studies about tactile interaction of older adults, the fingertip and the hand can occlude a part of the screen [11]. Experienced subjects would know how to adapt the gesture to avoid errors of accuracy during finger interaction since there are used to interact with fingers. Bigger screen sizes have also been recommended for older adults as bigger targets are easier to acquire [15], even if distances are bigger and so are the deviations [20].

Previous studies evaluating drag-and-drop have demonstrated higher accuracy for this interaction gesture, even if it takes longer times than tapping [11, 16]. Sliding the finger on the screen can increase the confidence of older users because they can better anticipate the acquisition of the targets. Errors of interaction increase considerably the cognitive workload for older users, especially novices who will need to create a strategy for recovering. Errors of accuracy as slipping or missing a target can have severe consequences. For example, missing a target during text entry tasks can cause insertion of characters and more interaction is necessary to correct the word [21]. In addition to that, supplementary manipulation can trigger other errors. For this reason, it is important to evaluate and prevent errors of accuracy during interaction.

Even if subjects were body-abled, aging related changes can affect user's skills, what could explain the variability of performances. Further studies should evaluate the effects of different user' profiles on interaction such as age, education, use of technologies, eyesight and dexterity. A future work for the analysis of ease-of-use of touchscreen should provide a deeper understanding of appropriation of tactile interaction after a longer period of practice or several iterations.

The results demonstrate that drag-and-drop interaction on mobile touchscreen devices is easy to use, confirming previous considerations about the usability of touchscreen for older adults. Potential users consider the ease-of-use for accepting a technology and this factor should persist during the adoption process [22]. Hence, we propose that tactile interaction continuous to be improved and applied on technologies for aging people. In the other hand, as touchscreen seems to be usable for older populations, the problem of limited acceptance and adoption of technologies need to be redressed through other factors. For example, the familiarity of the interfaces and interactions could reduce anxiety for novice users. Adaptive visual displays could also be used to improve the accessibility and reduce error rates. As younger populations have adopted mobile devices, we expect that tactile interaction will be adapted to respond to their needs for a longtime.

6   Conclusion

This study evaluated the ease-of-use of touchscreens by the comparison of novice and experienced older adults. Time of movement and the number of errors of accuracy were assessed during drag-and-drop interaction for achieving tactile puzzle games.

Results show that novice older adults were able to accomplish tactile interaction with longer movement times but not significant difference of error rates when compared to experienced older users. Tactile interaction can be considered ease to use but should be improved to allow older adults to adopt and use technologies for longer times. Familiar tasks and coherent metaphor for the gesture of interaction can help novice users to better understand and learn interaction. These factors could be used to redress the limitation of acceptance of technologies by older populations. Improving accessibility and usability is necessary to allow older populations to continuously access the benefits of mobile technologies and to prevent digital exclusion.

Acknowledgements. Phd Scholarship Ciência sem fronteiras, CNPQ, Brazil (#237079/2012-7). We kindly thank all the participants and the seniors associations in Toulouse, France, that helped us during the recruitment phase.

References

1. Barnard, Y., Bradley, M.D., Hodgson, F., Lloyd, A.D.: Learning to use new technologies by older adults: Perceived difficulties, experimentation behaviour and usability. Comput. Human Behav. **29**, 1715–1724 (2013)

2. Gombault, V.: L'internet de plus en plus prisé, l'internaute de plus en plus mobile. INSEE Première, 1452 (2013)
3. Seybert, H.: Internet use in households and by individuals in 2012. Eurostat Stat. Focus - Eurpoean Comm. **8** (2012)
4. Lee, C., Coughlin, J.F.: Older adults' adoption of technology: an integrated approach to identifying determinants and barriers. J. Prod. Innov. Manag (2014)
5. Renaud, K., Van Biljon, J.: Predicting technology acceptance and adoption by the elderly: a qualitative study. In: Proceedings of the ACM SAICSIT 2008, pp. 210–219. ACM, Wilderness (2008)
6. Leonard, V.K., Jacko, J.A., Pizzimenti, J.J.: An exploratory investigation of handheld computer interaction for older adults with visual impairments. In: Proceedings of the 7th International ACM SIGACCESS Conference on Computer and Accessibility – ASSETS2005, pp. 12–19 (2005)
7. Peek, S.T.M., Wouters, E.J.M., van Hoof, J., Luijkx, K.G., Boeije, H.R., Vrijhoef, H.J.M.: Factors influencing acceptance of technology for aging in place: a systematic review. Int. J. Med. Inform. **83**, 235–248 (2014)
8. Östlund, B.: The deconstruction of a targetgroup for IT-innovations: elderly users' technological needs and attitudes towards new IT. In: Avastson, G. (ed.) I-Users and Producers in an Evolving SocioculturalContext, International Workshop Report, pp. 84–100. Uppsala University, Norberg (2002)
9. Gudur, R.R., Blackler, A., Popovic, V., Mahar, D.: Ageing, technology anxiety and intuitive use of complex interfaces. In: Kotzé, P., Marsden, G., Lindgaard, G., Wesson, J., Winckler, M. (eds.) INTERACT 2013, Part III. LNCS, vol. 8119, pp. 564–581. Springer, Heidelberg (2013)
10. Caprani, N., O'Connor, N., Gurrin, C.: Touch screens for the older user. In: Fernando, A., Cheein, A. (eds.) Assistive Technologies, pp. 95–118. InTech, Rijeka (2012)
11. Findlater, L., Froehlich, J.E., Fattal, K., Wobbrock, J.O., Dastyar, T.: Age-related differences in performance with touchscreens compared to traditional mouse input. In: ACM CHI 2013, pp. 343–346 (2013)
12. Mallenius, S., Rossi, M., Tuunainen, V.: Factors affecting the adoption and use of mobile devices and services by elderly people–results from a pilot study. In: 6th Annual Global Mobility Roundtable (2007)
13. Hourcade, J.P., Berkel, T.: Tap or touch?: pen-based selection accuracy for the young and old. In: ACM CHI 2006, pp. 881–886 (2006)
14. Motti, L.G., Vigouroux, N., Gorce, P.: Drag-and-drop for older adults using touchscreen devices: effects of screen sizes and interaction techniques on accuracy. In: Proceedings of the 26th Conference on l'Interaction Homme-Machine, pp. 139–146, Lille, France (2014)
15. Kobayashi, M., Hiyama, A., Miura, T., Asakawa, C., Hirose, M., Ifukube, T.: Elderly user evaluation of mobile touchscreen interactions. In: Campos, P., Graham, N., Jorge, J., Nunes, N., Palanque, P., Winckler, M. (eds.) INTERACT 2011, Part I. LNCS, vol. 6946, pp. 83–99. Springer, Heidelberg (2011)
16. Wacharamanotham, C.: Evaluating swabbing: a touchscreen input method for elderly users with tremor. In: Proceedings ACM CHI 2011, pp. 623–626 (2011)
17. Mertens, A., Jochems, N.: Design pattern TRABING: touchscreen-based input technique for people affected by intention tremor. In: ACM SIGCHI EICS, pp. 267–272 (2010)
18. Vigouroux, N., Rumeau, P., Vella, F., Vellas, B.: Studying point-select-drag interaction techniques for older people with cognitive impairment. In: Stephanidis, C. (ed.) Universal Access in HCI, Part I, HCII 2009. LNCS, vol. 5614, pp. 422–428. Springer, Heidelberg (2009)

19. Genaro Motti, L., Vigouroux, N., Gorce, P.: Design of a social game for older users using touchscreen devices and observations from an exploratory study. In: Stephanidis, C., Antona, M. (eds.) UAHCI 2014, Part III. LNCS, vol. 8515, pp. 69–78. Springer, Heidelberg (2014)
20. Stößel, C., Wandke, H., Blessing, L.: Gestural interfaces for elderly users: help or hindrance? In: Kopp, S., Wachsmuth, I. (eds.) GW 2009. LNCS, vol. 5934, pp. 269–280. Springer, Heidelberg (2010)
21. Moffatt, K., McGrenere, J.: Slipping and drifting: using older users to uncover pen-based target acquisition difficulties. In: Proceedings of the 9th international ACM SIGACCESS conference on Computers and accessibility – ASSETS 2007, pp. 11–18, October 15–17. Tempe, Arizona (2007)
22. Conci, M., Pianesi, F., Zancanaro, M.: Useful, social and enjoyable: mobile phone adoption by older people. In: Gross, T., Gulliksen, J., Kotzé, P., Oestreicher, L., Palanque, P., Prates, R.O., Winckler, M. (eds.) INTERACT 2009. LNCS, vol. 5726, pp. 63–76. Springer, Heidelberg (2009)

Age-Related Differences in a Usability Study Measuring Accuracy, Efficiency, and User Satisfaction in Using Smartphones for Census Enumeration: Fiction or Reality?

Erica Olmsted-Hawala[✉] and Temika Holland

Center for Survey Measurement, U.S. Census Bureau, 4600 Silver Hill Road, Washington DC, WA 20233, USA
{Erica.L.Olmsted.Hawala,Temika.Holland}@census.gov

Abstract. Age-related differences were investigated in a usability study of an application developed for U.S. Census Bureau enumerators to collect survey data and automate their time and expenses. Accuracy, efficiency and satisfaction measures were collected as participants used a smartphone to answer typical tasks. Usability flaws were also identified with the application. Results indicate that in general there were no differences with task accuracy and efficiency when comparing all tasks, however when looking at individual tasks, the task that had the most usability flaws also revealed age-related differences for accuracy and efficiency – that is older adults were less accurate and took longer to complete. Surprisingly, there were age-related differences with the user satisfaction of the application such that older adults were less satisfied with the application than younger adults. Tying age-related differences to usability flaws highlights the importance of designing optimal applications for all users.

Keywords: Usability · Accuracy · Efficiency · Satisfaction · Age-related differences · NRFU · Census bureau

1 Introduction

Every ten years, the U.S. Census Bureau conducts a mandatory census of the population. Households are encouraged to self respond, either by answering survey questions on paper and mailing the survey back, or, for the 2020 Census, answering the survey online using the Internet. However, for the households that do not respond, the Census Bureau must send a census employee (enumerator) to their door so that the household has the opportunity to answer the survey questions in person. This operation is called the Non-Response Follow Up or NRFU. The NRFU operation is a massive undertaking and in preparation for the NRFU, the Census Bureau employs temporary workers as enumerators. The enumerators are diverse in age, ranging from recent college graduates to

---

Disclaimer: This report is released to inform interested parties of research and to encourage discussion. Any views expressed on the methodological issues are those of the authors and not necessarily those of the U.S. Census Bureau.

J. Zhou and G. Salvendy (Eds.): ITAP 2015, Part I, LNCS 9193, pp. 475–483, 2015.
DOI: 10.1007/978-3-319-20892-3_46

retirees. In fact, for the 2010 Census, 13 percent of all enumerators were over the age of 65. Forty-six percent were between the ages of 40 and 65 while 41 percent were 39 years old or younger [1]. All the enumerators for the 2010 Census conducted the NRFU on paper. However, for the 2020 Census, the business plan is to use small mobile devices (e.g., smartphones) to conduct census activities. Consequently, the software application that is created for mobile devices to aid the job of the enumerator must be suitable to enumerators of differing ages and with various levels of experience in use of smartphones.

One such prototype application under development for the 2020 Census is the Census Operations Mobile Platform for Adaptive Services and Solutions (COMPASS). COMPASS serves as an enumeration platform for conducting such activities as collecting survey data, case management, location aids, security services, and new modules that included automating time and expenses. The development team had not tested the new functionality with users and were interested in obtaining usability feedback on the new features of the COMPASS. In addition, the team was interested in identifying any usability issues that might exist in the application, including case management and icon usage on the screens.

This paper presents the results of a quantitative and qualitative usability study that investigated user behavior of effectiveness, efficiency, and satisfaction [2, 3] when using the COMPASS application.

The primary goal for the study was to identify usability issues of the application. We also wanted to get a better understanding of any performance differences among older and younger adult smartphone users. We hypothesized that (1) for the simple tasks, older adults and younger adults would be equally accurate in performance. The rationale for this was that when the task is simple, both age groups will perform with few difficulties. That is, on simple tasks, both younger and older adults will be able to complete the tasks effectively. For the complex tasks we hypothesized that (2) age and experience would come into play such that younger and older adults that were highly experienced with smartphones will perform with less difficulties, while, older adults with low to moderate experience on smartphones will have more difficulties. We further hypothesized that (3) older adults would take longer to complete the tasks. The rationale for this was twofold, older adults act slower due to, first, cognitive decline, e.g., Loos [4, 5] and Loos and Romano [6]; and second, the speed/accuracy trade off among older adults [7–10]. Finally we hypothesized that (4) there would be no age-related differences with respect to satisfaction. The rationale for this was that while intuitively it appears that satisfaction should be impacted by performance and efficiency, as we have seen in prior usability studies satisfaction rates have not been found to differ by age even when accuracy or efficiency scores did [11, 12].

2   Methods

2.1   Tasks

Participants in the usability study completed seven tasks using the COMPASS application. These tasks consisted of typical tasks that Census enumerators need to do to conduct census activities. Task difficulty was equivalent to what enumerators would do in the field

– and when initially constructing the tasks, they all appeared to be, in general, of simple cognitive complexity. These included activities such as listing the enumerators' weekly work availability, entering their hours worked, and expenses such as tolls, and completing sample enumeration cases that targeted use and understanding/use of icons within the application. The test assessed users' ability to perform tasks using the application and identified any problematic design features. See Appendix A for a list of the tasks.

2.2   Task Complexity

When initially planning the test, we intended tasks to be of the same complexity. While running participants through the usability study, however, it was clear that one task (e.g., Task 2) was proving more difficult for participants due to the usability flaws in the design of the application. Thus we categorized Task 2 as the most difficult and most cognitively challenging task.

2.3   Participants

Fourteen participants participated in the study: 7 younger (range 18–24) and 7 older adults (range 50–66). We divided the participants into two age groups purposely selecting age ranges that were far enough apart to detect age-related differences. The participants had at least one year experience using the Internet on a smartphone (e.g., iPhones or Androids) such as checking e-mail, getting mapping directions, reading the news, shopping online, using an app, etc. Nine of the participants were recruited from a database managed by the Center for Survey Measurement. These participants resided in the Washington DC metropolitan area and responded to a Craigslist online posting and/or flyers put up in local community centers. Five participants were former enumerators that lived in the Washington DC metropolitan area and had some prior experience in completing Census enumeration activities—however at the time of the study they were not federal employees. Participants were compensated $40.00 for their participation. Participant demographics are presented in Table 1.

2.4   Procedure

Usability testing was conducted at the U.S. Census Bureau's Human Factor's and Usability Laboratory in Suitland, MD. The participant sat in a room facing a one-way mirror in front of a table that had the TOBII mobile eye tracker stand with the X2-60 eye tracker mounted on it. The participant entered the testing room and was informed about the purpose of the study and the use of data to be collected. The participant then signed a consent form giving permission to be audio and video recorded. The participant completed an electronic initial questionnaire about his/her smartphone use, and demographic characteristics. After that, we calibrated the participants' eyes for eye-tracking purposes. The participant did a practice think-aloud task (e.g., the number of windows in their home) and then worked on the tasks. During the session, minimal concurrent think-aloud probing by the test administrator occurred, including such probes as "keep talking," and "um-hum?" After the tasks, the participant answered a

Table 1. Mean (and range) demographics by age group

	Age group	
	Younger	Older
N	7	7
Gender	2M / 5F	3M / 4F
Age	21 (18-24)	56 (50-66)
Education	2 BA/BS	4 BA/BS
	5 > BA/BS	3 > BA/BS
Hours per week using smartphone to access Internet?	17 (10-40)	12 (3-24)
Experience with your smartphone to use the Internet[a]	4.8 (4-5)	3.8 (3-5)

[a] Scale: 1 (None) – 5 (A great deal)

short satisfaction questionnaire to assess his/her experience using the application. Finally, we asked the participant debriefing questions about the screens and tasks that he/she had just worked on. During the session, the test administrator sat next to the participant. There were two reasons for this (1) due to the application still being in development, it could freeze up and the test administrator had to reset it. (2) The test administrator, when necessary, re-directed the participant when he/she required knowledge that he/she would learn in training, (e.g., during one task, participants needed to know that when conducting an interview with a neighbor, it was considered a "proxy visit").

2.5 Usability Metrics

We assessed three typical usability metrics: accuracy, efficiency, and satisfaction. Accuracy outcomes were assigned by the test administrator and were recorded as a success (1), a fail (0), or a partial correct (0.5).

Efficiency was calculated as the total duration of the task, starting after the participant read the task aloud and ending once the participant found the answer or said they were ready to move onto the next task.

Satisfaction was calculated by summing nine scores from the modified version of the QUIS [13] administered at the end of the session. Each score was on a Likert scale from 1 to 7; so the summed score for a participant ranged from 9 to 63. The higher the score, the more satisfied the user reported being with the site.

2.6 Analysis Methods

Due to our small sample size (N = 14) for accuracy we used the Fisher Exact Test with the Freeman-Halton extension in order to obtain a distribution of values in a 2 × 3 table (accuracy outcome was a categorical variable with three outcomes). Using this statistic, we can decide whether the population distributions are identical. To compare differences between the two age groups in both efficiency and satisfaction we used the Mann-Whitney Test because (a) small sample size and (b) we assumed the data to be continuous but not necessarily normally distributed.

3 Results

We examined the relationship between age and accuracy using the Fisher exact test. Across all tasks younger adults in general performed at a higher accuracy rate than older adults. By means of the Fisher Freeman-Halton test for our 2 × 3 table the relation between age and accuracy was significant $p = 0.01$. However when we tested each task individually, there appeared to be only one task that was making the significant difference. Task 1 $p = 0.71$, Task 2 $p = 0.01$, Task 3 $p = 0.56$, Task 4 $p = 1.0$, Task 5 $p = 0.23$, Task 6 $p = 0.71$, Task 7 $p = 1.0$. With Task 2 we see that younger adults were more accurate in task performance than older adults. This task was also the most difficult for participants to accomplish due to the usability flaws in the design. Consequently when we re-run the data removing Task 2, the results for all the other tasks were not significant, $p = 0.12$. This indicates that for tasks that are of low cognitive complexity, with fewer usability flaws, there appear to be no age-related differences, while for the task that required more cognitive fluency, and had more usability violations, age-related differences are apparent.

We examined efficiency and satisfaction using the Mann-Whitney Test. In the descriptions below *Med* stand for Median. For efficiency, across all tasks, again while younger adults generally performed faster (in seconds) (*Med* = 168), Range (47–240) than older adults (*Med* = 334) range (68-496), like in the accuracy scores, there appear to be significant differences when looking at average time spent on all tasks $Z = 1.85$, $p \leq 0.05$. However, as with the accuracy score, Task 2 was driving these results. When we look at the tasks individually, there were age-related differences only for Task 2, the task that was most difficult to accomplish such that younger adults were faster (*Med* = 168) range (99–224) at completing the task than older adults (*Med* = 496) range (381–660). The result is significant $Z = 3.10$, $p \leq 0.001$. If we look at all tasks together, but remove the results from Task 2, there were no statistically significant differences between the age groups with respect to efficiency, though the trend is leaning towards significance $Z = 1.60$, $p = 0.05$.

For satisfaction, young adult participants reported being more satisfied (*Med* = 40, range (36–45) with the application on the smart phone than their older adult counterparts (*Med* = 30), range (27–33). The result is significant $Z = 3.53$, $p = 0.0004$.

4 Discussion

The accuracy results support our first hypothesis, that for simple tasks, aside from Task 2, older and younger adults do not perform significantly different from each other. Simple tasks, such as syncing the device, work for all users. The sync task which requires users to press on a visible and somewhat universal refresh symbol is not complicated such that all users in our sample, even those who use the phones less frequently are familiar with such a symbol after even a brief exposure to smartphones, and consequently are able to accomplish this with ease. Finding no age-related differences on simple tasks is also seen elsewhere in the literature (see also Olmsted-Hawala, Romano Bergstrom, Rogers [14]).

As is the case with accuracy results, efficiency results are in parallel. That is for the simple tasks, there are no age-related differences among older and younger adults when working on simple tasks. It is only with the most difficult task (e.g., Task 2) that age-related differences emerge with respect to efficiency. This is in contrast to our third hypothesis that for *all* tasks, efficiency scores differ, such that older adults take longer. This is also in contrast to the literature (e.g., 4–10) and warrants more investigation on the correlation between age and task complexity on efficiency measures. However as the p-value for efficiency overall approaches significance, the trend in this direction indicates the possibility that with a higher sample size we would see differences. As has been described elsewhere in the literature (e.g., Fukuda and Bubb [15]) we too find that older adults are more vulnerable to usability flaws– such that on the most difficult task where the user interface didn't meet user expectations, older adults take longer and have more difficulties in progressing successfully on the task. This is not the case for younger adults who are able to recover when confronted with the less optimal design. The complexity of the cognitive demands, in the end influences the speed with which older adults are able to accomplish their task. This is consistent with the literature (Bashore, Ridderinkhof, Molen [16]).

The ability to self-correct – e.g., make a mistake, realize it, then back up and correct the mistake by going down the more optimal path – is crucial when working on more complex tasks. When this occurred, if the participant was a young adult, they were able to self-correct, while the older adult took longer to realize, or never realized that they were in the wrong place to accomplish the task.

The issues with usability flaws and the impact associated with one's age is important for the design team and developers to take into consideration as they decide what usability fixes to make and what will be postponed or put off until the next development cycle. This is particularly important for applications that need to be optimized for adults of varying ages.

With respect to the satisfaction results, we are surprised to find that age-related differences do emerge. This is in contrast to the literature on usability study satisfaction of participants' using websites (Romano Bergstrom, Olmsted-Hawala, Jans [11]) and is contrary to our fourth hypothesis. It is interesting that older adults reported less satisfaction with the use of the application when using it on a smartphone. We speculate that the use of a small screen compounded the frustration level such that satisfaction differences emerged. Subjective satisfaction measures with respect to age and small screens should be tested further.

4.1 Limitations

A caveat to these results is the small number of participants in each age group. While usability studies in general have smaller sample sizes, typically recruiting 5 to 8, users [17, 18] our small sample does limit the statistical analyses and generalizations we can make of the data.

In terms of experience, we were unable to recruit older adults that had equal experience with the younger adults on the use of smartphones. While we did have older adults that used smartphones, they did not use them to the same extent as their younger adult counterparts. Thus it is difficult to tease out whether older adults with the same amount of experience would also have performed well on the more complex task (see also Loos [4, 5] and Hill, Dickinson, Arnott, Gregor, McIver [19]). Hence in this study, we were unable to test our second hypothesis, due to insufficient data.

It will be interesting to continue the study with additional older and younger adults and see if the trends we find hold. In addition, it would be beneficial to have more tasks of greater complexity as well as additional older adults with greater expertise in use of smartphones.

Appendix A

Task 1: Your availability to work is as follows:
Wednesday (11/26) 8am to 4:30 pm for 6 h
Thursday (11/27) Unavailable
Friday (11/28) 8am to 12 pm for 3 h
Saturday (11/29) 8am to 12 pm for 3 h
Sunday (11/30) 8am to 12 pm for 3 h
Enter this information into the application.

Task 2: On last Tuesday 11/18 you ended up working from 9am to 12 pm. You travelled to an apartment in your assignment using your own car. You drove 13 miles to visit the apartment and 13 miles back home. You also crossed the Census Bridge, which has a toll of $3.50 each way. Enter this information into the application and submit when complete.

Task 3: You need to do a manual sync of the data. How would you manually synchronize the data in the application? Are there any clues as to how to do this? If the data had actually synchronized, how would you be able to verify that the sync completed successfully? Tell the test administrator how you would know.

Task 4: You arrive at the first address/home you've been assigned (first one on the list). The respondent reluctantly agrees to a quick interview.

Please begin interview and input the following responses for each screen that you encounter (in order): *Personal Visit*, *Attempting address*, *Yes*, *Yes*, *Yes*, *Bob Terry David*, *555-234-5678*, *No*, *No*).
You have arrived at the foster children screen and the respondent does not understand the purpose of this question. He asks you what the purpose is of this question. Find the answer to this question within the application.

Task 5: After you explain it to him, he suddenly grows agitated and abruptly ends the interview and refuses to answer any more questions. He goes on to say what a waste of taxpayer dollars the Census represents. No notice of visit is left as respondent orders you off his property. Exit the interview within the application and answer the questions that follow.

Task 6: You approach the second address/home of the day (second one on the list). When you arrive, you notice that the house is under construction. Based on this information, you are curious about the Contact History and Case Notes for this address. Find the Contact History and Case Notes for this house within the application.

Task 7: You are still at the same house as in Task #6 and you are growing more convinced that perhaps no one lives at this address but it's hard to tell. You then see a neighbor pull into her driveway next door. You walk over to this woman (Tammy Janice Hartmann, Phone number 202-555-5555, 345 ABC Road, Suitland, MD 20752) and ask her if she could answer a question or two about the house next door. She agrees to answer a few questions and says that no one has lived there in over 6 months (which includes July 1, 2014). She mentions that the owners abandoned the home after going way under water on their mortgage and that the bank is in the process of selling the property. She says she gets home from work around 5 pm each weekday and that it would be ok to call her if we have additional questions. Enter all of this information (including her name, phone number, address and availability) in the application.

References

1. US Census Bureau: Internal Census Report on Age Range of Enumerators. Field Division. (2010)
2. Frøkjaer, E., Herzum, M., Hornbaek, K.: Measuring usability: are effectiveness, efficiency, and satisfaction correlated? In: Proceedings of the SIGCHI Conference on Human Factors in Computing Systems, The Haag (2000)
3. Johnson, R., Kent, S.: Designing universal access: web application for the elderly and disabled. Cogn. Tech. Work **9**, 209–218 (2007)
4. Loos, E.F., Mante-Meijer, E.A.: Navigatie van ouderen en jongeren in beeld. Explorerend onderzoek naar de rol van leeftijd voor het informatiezoekgedrag van websitegebruikers [Older and younger adults' navigation: Explorative study on the role of age for website users' information search behaviour], Den Haag, Boom/Lemma (2009)
5. Loos, E.: In search of information on websites: a question of age? In: Stephanidis, C. (ed.) Universal Access in HCI, Part II, HCII 2011. LNCS, vol. 6766, pp. 196–204. Springer, Heidelberg (2011)

6. Loos, E.F., Bergstrom, J.R.: Older adults. In: Bergstrom, J.R., Schall, A.J. (eds.) Eye Tracking in User Experience Design, pp. 313–329. Elsevier, Amsterdam (2014)
7. Brébion, G.: Language processing, slowing, and speed/accuracy trade-off in the elderly. Exp. Aging Res. **27**(2), 137–150 (2001)
8. Howard, J.H., Howard, D.V., Dennis, N.A., Yankovich, H.: Event timing and age deficits in higher-order sequence learning. Aging, Neuropsychol. Cogn. **14**(6), 647–668 (2007)
9. Rabbitt, P.: How old and young subjects monitor and control responses for accuracy and speed. Br. J. Psychol. **70**, 305–311 (1979)
10. Salthouse, T.: Adult age and the speed–accuracy trade-off. Ergonomics **22**(7), 811–821 (1979)
11. Bergstrom, J.R., Olmsted-Hawala, E., Jans, M.: Eye tracking and Web site usability in older adults: age-related differences in eye tracking and usability performance: web site usability for older adults. Int. J. Hum. Comput. Interact. **29**(8), 541–548 (2013)
12. Olmsted-Hawala, E., Bergstrom, J.R.: Think-aloud protocols: does age make a difference? In: Proceedings of Society for Technical Communication (STC) Summit, Chicago, IL (2012)
13. Chin, J.P., Diehl, V.A., Norman, K.L.: Development of an instrument measuring user satisfaction of the human-computer interface. In: Proceedings of SIGCHI 1988, pp. 213–218 (1988)
14. Olmsted-Hawala, E., Bergstrom, J.R., Rogers, W.A.: Age-related differences in search strategy and performance when using a data-rich web site. In: Stephanidis, C., Antona, M. (eds.) UAHCI 2013, Part II. LNCS, vol. 8010, pp. 201–210. Springer, Heidelberg (2013)
15. Fukuda, R., Bubb, H.: Eye tracking study on web-use: comparison between younger and elderly users in case of search task with electronic timetable service. PsychNology J. **1**(3), 202–288 (2003)
16. Bashore, T.R., Ridderinkhof, K.R., Molen, M.W.V.D.: The decline of cognitive processing speed in old age. Curr. Dir. Psychol. Sci. **6**(6), 163–169 (1997)
17. Nielsen, J.: Estimating the number of subjects needed for a thinking aloud test. Int. J. Hum. Comput. Stud. **41**, 385–397 (1994)
18. Nielsen, J., Landauer, T.K.: A mathematical model of the finding of usability problems. In: Proceedings of ACM INTERCHI 1993, pp. 206–213 (1993)
19. Hill, R.L., Dickinson, A., Arnott, J.L., Gregor, P., McIver, L.: Older web users' eye movements: experience counts. In: Proceedings of the SIGCHI Conference on Human Factors in Computing Systems ACM, pp. 1151–1160 (2011)

Older Adults and the Appropriation and Disappropriation of Smartphones

Natalie Pang[1(✉)], Samantha Vu[2], Xue Zhang[2], and Schubert Foo[1]

[1] Wee Kim Wee School of Communication and Information, Nanyang Technological University, 50 Nanyang Avenue, 639798 Singapore, Singapore
{nlspang,sfoo}@ntu.edu.sg
[2] Centre of Social Media Innovations for Communities, Nanyang Technological University, 14 Nanyang Drive, HSS-06-15, 637332 Singapore, Singapore
{sgtvu,zhangxue}@ntu.edu.sg

Abstract. Research in recent years has focused on examining the acceptance as well as the appropriation of technologies amongst older adults, especially in how technologies alleviate issues of functional declines, loneliness, and financial difficulties brought about by ageing. Yet such studies have often overlooked meaningful appropriation or disappropriation of technologies amongst older adults. By drawing on a longitudinal study of ten older adults who were given a smartphone under a corporate social responsibility program by a telecommunications company, we followed the use of smartphones by ten older adult users using in-depth interviews lasting one to two hours each. Our findings revealed a mix of appropriation and disappropriation, which are linked to everyday technological use and routines, attitudes to technology, and social support.

Keywords: Non-use · Technology appropriation · Older adults · Smartphones

1 Introduction

Ageing brings with it related and interdependent issues such as functional declines, loneliness, isolation, and financial difficulties. With the loss of social contacts, older adults often find themselves facing social isolation and loneliness [1]. This may be further compounded by their exclusion from participating in today's technologically-oriented and driven society. Having access to technology as well as the ability to use it has been argued and thought to bring older adults out of isolation and ensure that they remain active in society. Such gaps have been recognized by various societies and non-profit organizations, which subsequently seek to provide access and train older adults in using technologies in their daily lives.

As potential technological interventions, smartphones provide many opportunities to meet the needs of older adults [2]. As handheld devices with advanced computing capabilities, smartphones provide applications that can assist older adults in various aspects of their lives, such as medicine adherence, lifelong learning, and assisted living [3]. Yet certain functional declines of older adults can result in specific needs and requirements, and many smartphones and computing devices are designed to handle these needs.

© Springer International Publishing Switzerland 2015
J. Zhou and G. Salvendy (Eds.): ITAP 2015, Part I, LNCS 9193, pp. 484–495, 2015.
DOI: 10.1007/978-3-319-20892-3_47

Yet despite the functionality, advances in the usability and usefulness of smartphones, some older adults do not use smartphones and computing devices. However, this may not always be a simple case of non-adoption, as the findings of this study would suggest.

2 Literature Review

Rogers [4] described technological adoption as a process "to make full use of an innovation as the best course of action available" (p.12). Beginning with awareness and access, it ends with the user embracing the technology and eventually using it for their functions and value. Acceptance, on the other hand, refers to attitudes towards technology. Acceptance is closely linked to adoption: acceptance is a precondition for adoption, and in cases where there is no acceptance, it is also unlikely for an individual to adopt the technology [5].

Whilst much has been written about the acceptance and adoption of technology by older adults, less has been written about their appropriation of technologies. Appropriation is a highly complex concept that is focused on the use of technology in a meaningful context. This is much harder to investigate compared to technological acceptance or adoption. As such, scholars, mostly guided by the postmodern traditions, have attempted to come up with frameworks to assist with their understanding and interpretation of technological appropriation by individuals in various sociological contexts.

2.1 ICT and Older Adults

Although there is much research and development done on technological innovations with the goal of assisting older adults and their specific needs, there is a lack of research exploring the needs of older adults in appropriating technology in the context of everyday tasks and life. This may be largely due to the following reasons: (a) older adults are hard-to-reach as research participants, (b) the goal of many studies is usually focused on the acceptance, adoption or use of technology, and older adults simply fall out of this scope if they do not use, adopt or have a negative attitude towards technology.

Scholars have tried to address the research gap in different ways. Some focus on the development of ICT innovations for older adults, and through such development argue for an increasing demand and usefulness of innovations that can help maintain current social ties or develop new ones [6, 7]. Communication devices such as mobile phones help older adults to maintain their ties, and smartphones, with potential connectivity and social networks available through games, apps, and social networking sites offer opportunities to forge new connections and social ties.

According to the Pew Research Center's Smartphone ownership report in 2013 [8], in the U.S., 14.6 % of people over the age of 55 own a smartphone, while in Europe, it is 18.9 % over the age 55. Research on the use of smartphones by older adults is largely focused on smartphones as new healthcare and assistive solutions for elderly [3, 9]. Apps to monitor falls [10], monitor and control food intake [11], advocate medication adherence [12] or improving cognitive ability [13] are some of the common solutions that have emerged on the smartphone.

Studies on older adults and smartphones can be broadly classified in two streams: one that focuses on acceptance and use; the other is oriented towards the adoption of technology. Studies belonging to the first tradition are interested in the effect and impacts of specific functions or characteristics of smartphones (touch screen or interface for instance), seeking to understand their usability, use and acceptance by older adults [14–16]. A consistent finding from many of the usability studies conducted suggest that older adults have difficulties using smartphones [16–19] and guidelines to design better interfaces for older adults have been developed in response [20, 21].

The second tradition which is oriented towards adoption is focused largely on the factors influencing adoption. For instance, Williams [22] did a study on how older adults perceive iPhones using the Socioemotional Selectivity Theory (SST) and the Technology Acceptance Model (TAM) by interviewing of 12 participants over the age of 60, 2 of which do not own an iPhone. Perceived usefulness, communication, information access, entertainment, and perceived ease of use were found to be motivational factors for older adults to adopt and use iPhones.

Rahmati and colleagues [23] conducted a longitudinal quasi-experiment on 34 iPhone 3 users (aged 19 on average) over six months to demonstrate the influence of Socioeconomic Status (SES) on how the iPhones were adopted. Their results show that lower SES groups spent more money on apps and installed more apps as compared to other SES groups; the lowest SES group did not find their iPhones as easy to use as compared to other SES groups.

A problem of many acceptance studies is that technology is usually viewed or assumed to be static and non-changing, whilst adoption studies tend not to acknowledge structural properties of technology or social structures in users' adoption of technology. As a result, scholars such as Orlikowski [24] and DeSanctis and Poole [25] developed the concept of appropriation to address the gap.

2.2   Smartphone Appropriation by Older Adults

Appropriation is a socio-cultural concept linking perspectives of technology acceptance and use, and adoption. It argues for recursive relationships between social structures, technology and human agency. Since the emergence of the concept, scholars such as DeSanctis and Poole [25], Orlikowski [24] and Carroll [26] have offered models to help guide research in understanding technology appropriation by various individuals and communities.

Structurational models of technology typically argue that the use of technology by human actors is done through their understanding of rules and norms: "…human agents build into technology certain interpretive schemes (rules reflecting knowledge of the work being automated), certain facilities (resources to accomplish that work), and certain norms (rules that define the organizationally sanctioned way of executing that work)" (p. 410) [27].

Building on the appropriation literature, Carroll [26] suggests that the evaluation of technology by users results in four outcomes: appropriation, disappropriation (abandonment), non-adoption, and simple adoption. It suggests that technology use result in outcomes that lie on a continuum, with simple adoption or non-adoption on the extreme end, and appropriation or disappropriation as outcomes that lie in between these extremes.

This model (Fig. 1) argues that a technology may be adopted or non-adopted at Level 1, and at Level 2, users start to explore and evaluate the technology even as they adapt to it. During this time, they may disappropriate and abandon, or appropriate and the technology becomes part of their everyday tasks and activities. All outcomes are conditional: many factors can trigger re-evaluation of the technology and result in changes in the outcomes.

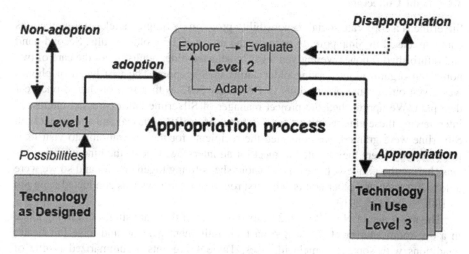

Fig. 1. Model of technology appropriation (Source: Carroll 2004, p. 3)

In our ongoing study of smartphone use by older adults, we have found instances of both non-adoption and disappropriation. Whilst confounding to our original research aims to evaluate smartphone appropriation, these have contributed to new research directions.

Research done on non-adoption and disappropriation is sparse with Selwyn being one of the most prolific in writing about non-use of ICT by older adults [28–30]. As he argued, little is known about the non-use phenomenon amongst older adults, especially in terms of the reasons and the outcomes of non-use [29]. Many of the conventional concepts of non-use are based on the technologically deterministic assumption that using ICTs is inherently beneficial for all including the older adults. Furthermore, most literature focused on use of ICTs rather than non-use and rendered non-use as a problem to be solved [28]. These resulted in a gap: the technological deterministic perspective has discounted the focus on the individual or the user who should be given, to a certain degree, a role to play in making the decision whether or not to use a technology. In other words, as Selwyn [28] advocated, it is important to understand how individuals use technologies. It is our intention to address this gap by examining the appropriation and disappropriation of smartphones by older adults.

3 Method

Using in-depth interviews, the study aimed to explore the use and non-use of the ten recipients of iPhones in a corporate social responsibility program by a telecommunications company in Singapore. The respondents received the phones in December 2012 and we conducted the first round of interviews in November 2013. The second round of interview was done with four participants six months later in May 2014. The remaining participants were either non-contactable or refused the second interview.

3.1 Data Collection

Silverline is a corporate social responsibility program by Singtel, a telecommunications company based in Singapore, to promote the use of ICT by older adults. Second-hand and refurbished iPhones were given away to selected older adults under the care of two non-profit organizations serving older adults in Singapore. The first batch of phones was given out to nine older adults in December 2013 with a free-of-charge one year data plan. We approached the project manager of Silverline and expressed interest in interviewing these nine recipients for the study. After IRB approval and agreement with Silverline were granted, we contacted the recipients for their permission to visit their homes or anywhere they wanted to meet for an interview. One of the nine interviewees was sharing the phone with her sister whom she is living together with and so we were able to interview ten older adults. The first round of interviews was conducted from 8th to 19th November 2013.

The mean age of $N = 10$ is 76.2 years old, most of them are single and living alone in a one-room apartment. Most live on their retirement pension and have fair health conditions with some chronicle illnesses. Table 1 presents a summarized profile of participants in our study.

A semi-structured in-depth interview approach was used, involving questions about the respondents' family background, health condition, employment (if any), and daily activities. Open ended questions revealed contexts of their use and non-use of the given iPhone, difficulties using the iPhone, reasons for non-use, their attitude towards older adults' using smartphones and the role that the iPhone plays in their lives, and their attitudes towards ageing.

Table 1. Overview of participants

Gender	Living arrangement	Marital status	Source of livelihood	Health condition[a]
Men (6) Women (4)	Alone (6) With a roommate (1) With family (3)	Married (3) Single (7)	Salary (part-time) (1) Retirement pension (7) Family/Relative members (2)	Excellent (2) Good (2) Fair (4) Poor (2)

[a] Simplified labeling based on health condition of participants as declared on their own. Excellent is without any illness or on-going medication. Good: with one illness or on medication with. Fair: with 2 illnesses and on medication. Poor: with more than 2 illnesses and on medication. Very poor: immobile.

A small audio recorder was used to record the interviews and transcribed each of them immediately after each visit. Observation notes were included in the transcripts as well and coded as memos in NVivo [31]. Photos were taken sporadically during the interview as the researchers felt the need to capture certain aspects such as photos taken in the iPhone. Some respondents could only speak Chinese so transcripts were translated into English. For the first phase of interviews in November 2013 with N = 10, a total of almost 9 h of recordings, 446 pages of transcripts and 156 photos were collected. For the second phase of interviews in May 2014 with N = 4, only observations and notes of differences in the usage or non-use as compared to the first phase were recorded.

3.2 Data Analysis

Using NVivo10, ten transcripts were coded in 3 stages: open coding, axial coding and selective coding [32]. Open coding was used to code each line of each transcript; responses associated with adoption, non-adoption, appropriation or non-appropriation were marked and labeled with codes. Next, similar concepts were grouped into categories and axial coding was used to explore the relations between the categories. The result of axial coding is a loose conceptual framework including casual conditions, context, and consequences of each kind of use or non-use. In the last stage of coding (selective coding), the categories were reexamined and synthesized into a series of grounded concepts of appropriation and disappropriation.

A code book was developed to include code definition and their hierarchies. Using the code book, 2 coders started coding separately and then the files were merged together in NViVo. The inter-coder reliability was satisfactory (Cohen's kappa = 0.75) for most of the codes in all transcripts. A total of 1,544 responses were coded (open codes) and categorized into categories.

4 Findings and Discussion

4.1 Appropriation

Unsurprisingly, positive perceptions of smartphones are associated with appropriation. Participants also felt that being given the iPhone implied that they had to use it otherwise it would be taken back. This provides many of them the motivation to appropriate the smartphone into their everyday routines, or adapt to the smartphone, introducing new routines into their lives. For instance, many participants use the device to forage for information such as winning lottery numbers and send short messages. But some participants have also shared how new activities are introduced into their lives as a result of appropriation: "...it eliminates my boredom...my life will be boring if I cannot play games [on his iPhone]." (Participant CS) (Fig. 2).

Another participant, Participant YH, talks about his discovery of new functions on the iPhone: "...the phone [the iPhone] contains a lot of interesting things. This one [pointing to his old mobile phone, a Nokia non-smartphone] doesn't. It [the iPhone] is fun...like the songs, I like the songs. This phone [is] like a friend".

Fig. 2. Some of the games played by participants (Source: Authors' own)

Games and getting onto social networking sites are the most common elements of the smartphone that appears to inject new routines and activities into their lives, whereas other functions such as making phone calls, messaging, camera, surfing the Web for information and music player are appropriated into the everyday lives of participants.

Social support from others in the appropriation of smartphones is crucial, with some participants relying on their neighbors for help. Participant CS described the importance of such social support in encouraging his persistent use: *"I will ask her [my neighbor] if it [the iPhone] is spoilt or when I want to install new games I will [also] ask her to help me".*

The result of smartphone appropriation is associated with feelings of empowerment and status amongst participants in our study. Participant KL, for instance, shared about her experience getting noticed holding the phone on a bus: *"...people will ask me, 'Aunty, you use this?'".* The smartphone is not simply a device, but something that is appropriated as part of ageing and being respected as an older person in society. Participant BM expressed his belief that the smartphone is a privilege accorded to him as an older adult: *"I think they respect this [pointing to his walking stick]...VIP treatment you know..."* and the iPhone is part of the package.

Such deep appropriation can be emotional, with one participant getting worked up by the hypothetical scenario of living without the iPhone again: *"I don't think I will give it back...if they take it back from me, I will ask them, "Why are you taking it away from me?" I will keep asking them, and discuss with them. I won't allow them to take it back from me easily. No way. You gave it to me!"* (Participant CC).

4.2   Disappropriation

Participants in our study reported substantial barriers to using the iPhones, resulting in disappropriation. 85.2 % of the data tagged with non-use are associated with barriers to using. These are further categorized into three main categories: (i) subjective barriers, (ii) technological barriers, and (iii) situational barriers. Subjective barriers are associated with individuals' attitudes and ability, such as the lack of knowledge on how to use, or about the smartphone. Participant YH said: *"I'm more familiar with others [Nokia phone], and they are easy to use… This [iPhone]… I see wrongly… press wrongly…"* Participant CS also pointed out: *"Most elderly… they only make and receive calls, they don't use the other functions."* In such cases, appropriation of the smartphone is not full and meaningful.

Social support was as important in the lack of appropriation as it was important in the appropriation of smartphones, as discussed earlier. All of the participants who reported disappropriation were living alone and had infrequent interactions with their neighbors, implying little external help from other smartphone users.

The lack of knowledge is compounded by declined mental and physical abilities due to old age (accounting for 25.8 % of non-use). Participant AT encountered the most difficulties with his iPhone because of his poor eyesight: *"the keyboard is too small for me to see. I can't see. Although this is small [pointing to the Nokia] but I suppose I'm used to it"*. Participant BM expressed that even though he would like to use the camera function, he could not use because of his shaky hands. Such disappropriation is contextual to the phase of ageing and condition of their wellbeing.

But disappropriation was not always related to physical or physiological barriers. Some participants were reluctant to use functions that they were just not keen on taking up. One example is the use of social networking sites such as Facebook, even for very competent smartphone users. Participant NW said: *"I know what it [Facebook] is, I just don't want to use it."* The fact that she uses certain elements of the smartphone but chooses not to use other elements reflects how in this case, disappropriation is an exercise of choice, a reflection of empowerment and strong internal locus of control over the smartphone.

Technological reasons for disappropriation are associated largely with interface issues. Participant GC relayed a story of how he once bought an Android smartphone for a friend: *"…and the next day she sold [the smart phone], saying [she] doesn't know how to use. Then I bought an old Nokia for her, and she said 'this was easy, the other [phone] I have to look at so many places to figure out how to call'".*

Cost is one of the greatest obstacles to persistent appropriation especially to this group of interviewees because they are considered the below average class (live mainly on retirement pension, one-room apartment on monthly rent). Participant KL, in talking about gaming on the smartphone, explained to us the barrier to her fully appropriating the smartphone: *"…although I want to play [the games], I don't dare to…I am afraid that I need to pay if I keep on playing."* Participant NW echoed this sentiment: *"…my friends do not use the iPhone even if they have one, they say [it is] expensive".* This fear of being charged is mainly because they do not have enough financial resources.

The eventual disappropriation is also associated with fear. Participant BM, for instance, always kept his iPhone in a pouch and then the pouch is further protected in a plastic bag. He explained that he does not want to drop it, and so he had to be very careful about using it.

5 Discussion

Our study showed that iPhones are used and appropriated/disappropriated in a variety of ways. Some respondents appropriate them meaningfully, in the fullest sense of what they are as smartphones, others do not. The concepts of appropriation and disappropriation are especially meaningful for the profile of older adults in our study. Appropriation and disappropriation emerged as concepts that can help to explain the ways participants interacted with their iPhones. For instance, Participant CS was so into playing games that he turned it into a gaming device to help him alleviate loneliness; he did not use other communication functions of the phone. But iPhones were not designed to only play games. Still, this was how Participant CS appropriated the iPhone into his daily life.

Our findings echo Chen et al.'s [33] study on elderly's use and non-use of gerontechnology which includes various technologies like ATM, computers, mobile phones, and smartphones. Respondents in Chen et al.'s study did not use certain gerontechnology due to social support, lack of knowledge and ability, cost, and interface which are similar reasons for how respondents in our study appropriated/disappropriated the iPhones they had. That older adults are unable to use smartphones due to ageing physical and mental ability also mediates the use of the iPhones is consistent with other studies' findings on ICTs' usage by older adults [34, 35]. Knowledge on how to use is especially important as one of the respondents repeated over and over again throughout the interview: "...I'm not familiar yet. I must learn slowly. Must learn...Once I am familiar with it I can use it." Other studies have found that knowledge plays a key role in technology usage too [36, 37].

Many studies have found that positive attitude towards using technology is the most influential factors to technological usage [33, 38, 39]. However, this factor did not seem to influence the appropriation/disappropriation of iPhones very much in our study, as participants with positive attitudes towards technology may not always appropriate meaningfully. Besides, the fact that these studies looked at gerontechnology [33] or technology in general [38] makes it difficult to grade the level of influence of the factors to specific technologies.

We found other factors associated with meaningful appropriation/disappropriation: fear of losing the iPhone, considering the iPhone as a social status, and using the iPhone to pass time and decrease loneliness. Our findings also reinforced Selwyn's argument [30] that non-use is mediated by conscious decision. For example, one of the participants knew about Facebook but does not use it at all because she insisted that she did not need it. Such individual and conscious choice to not use certain functions of smartphone reflects her human agency and her exercise of choice over the smartphone.

This notion applies to almost any technology, not only smartphone, as proven in Selwyn's earlier study on older adults' use of computers [29]: some of them just do not see a need in using computers and not tempted to use one either.

6 Conclusion

Our paper reports results on the appropriation and disappropriation of smartphones as part of an ongoing study about smartphones and older adults. Our in-depth interviews revealed insights on the factors behind both appropriation and disappropriation, and how appropriation or disappropriation of the smartphone is integrated into everyday routines and tasks. Some constraints exist, such as the limited number of participants. However, given that older adults are hard-to-reach as research participants and it is relatively hard to reach older adults who have had the opportunity to adopt a smartphone, our study provides rare insights on how older adults can appropriate or disappropriate a smartphone when given access.

Acknowledgements. This research is supported by the National Research Foundation, Prime Minister's Office, Singapore under its International Research Centers in Singapore Funding Initiative and administered by the Interactive Digital Media Program Office.

References

1. Chen, Y., Hicks, A., While, A.E.: Loneliness and social support of older people in China: a systematic literature review. Health Soc. Care Community **22**(2), 113–123 (2014)
2. Plaza, I., Martin, L., Martin, S., Medrano, C.: Mobile applications in an aging society: Society and trends. J. Syst. Softw. **84**(11), 1977–1988 (2011)
3. Boulos, M., Wheeler, S., Tavares, C., Jones, R.: How smartphones are changing the face of mobile and participatory healthcare: an overview, with example from eCAALYX. BioMed. Eng. Online **10**, 24 (2011)
4. Rogers, E.M.: Diffusion of Innovations, 5th edn. The Free Press, New York (2003)
5. Renaud, K., van Biljon, J.: Predicting technology acceptance and adoption by the elderly: a qualitative study. In: Annual Research Conference of the South African Institute of Computer Scientists and Information Technologists on IT Research in Developing Countries: Riding the wave of technology, pp. 210–219. ACM, New York (2008)
6. Greathead, D., Arief, B., Coventry, L., van Moorsel, A.: Deriving requirements for an online community interaction scheme: indications from older adults. In: CHI Conference on Human Factors in Computing Systems, CHI 2012, Extended Abstracts, pp.1541–1546. ACM, New York (2012)
7. Berkowsky, R.W.: Internet use and mental health/well-being in old age: exploring the roles of social integration and social support. Doctoral dissertation, The University of Alabama at Birmingham. ProQuest LLC, UMI No. 3618429 (2014)
8. Pew Research Center: Smartphone Ownership, http://www.pewinternet.org/~/media/Files/Reports/2013/PIP_Smartphone_adoption_2013.pdf
9. Gill, P.S., Kamath, A., Gill, T.S.: Distraction: an assessment of smartphone usage in health care work settings. Risk Manage. Healthc. Policy **5**, 105–114 (2012)

10. Mellone, S., Tacconi, C., Schwickert, L., Klenk, J., Becker, C., Chiari, L.: Smartphone-based solutions for fall detection and prevention: the FARSEEING approach. Z Gerontol Geriat. **45**(8), 722–727 (2012)

11. Martin, C.K., Correa, J.B., Han, H., Allen, H.R., Rood, J.C., Champagne, C.M., Gunturk, B. K., Bray, A.G.: Validity of the remote food photography method (RFPM) for estimating energy and nutrient intake in near real-time. Obesity **20**, 891–899 (2012)

12. Federico, B., Fernando, B., Joaquin, J.M.: Safer virtual pillbox: assuring medication adherence to elderly patients. In: 3rd ACM MobiHoc Workshop on Pervasive Wireless Healthcare, pp. 37–42. ACM, New York (2013)

13. Dufau, S., Dunabeitia, J.A., Moret-Tatay, C., McGonigal, A., Peeters, D., Alario, X.F., Balota, D.A., Brysbaert, M., Carreiras, M., Ferrand, L., Ktroi, M., Perea, M., Rastle, K., Sasburg, O., Yap, M.J., Ziegler, C.J., Grainger, J.: Smart phone, smart science: how the use of smartphones can revolutionize research in cognitive science. PLoS ONE **6**(9), e24974 (2011)

14. Zhou, J., Rau, P.P.L., Slvendy, G.: Older adults' use of smartphones: an investigation of the factors influencing the acceptance of new functions. J. Behav. Inf. Technol. **33**(6), 552–560 (2014)

15. Zhou, J., Rau, P.P.L., Slvendy, G.: Older adults' text entry on smartphones and tablets: investigating effects of display size and input method on acceptance and performance. Int. J. Hum. Comput. Interact. **30**(9), 727–739 (2014)

16. Kobayashi, M., Hiyama, A., Miura, T., Asakawa, C., Hirose, M., Ifukube, T.: Elderly user evaluation of mobile touchscreen interactions. In: Campos, P., Graham, N., Jorge, J., Nunes, N., Palanque, P., Winckler, M. (eds.) INTERACT 2011, Part I. LNCS, vol. 6946, pp. 83–99. Springer, Heidelberg (2011)

17. Dale, O., Schulz, T.: JusFone: A smartphone for everyone. http://publ.nr.no/5658

18. Judge, T., Neustaedter, C., Harrison, S., Blose, A.: Family portals: connecting families through a multi- family media space. In: Annual Conference on Human Factors in Computing Systems, pp. 1205–1214. ACM, New York (2011)

19. Lippincott, B., Morris, J., Mueller, J.: Keeping in touch: smartphone touchscreens and customers with disabilities. http://include11.kinetixevents.co.uk/4dcgi/prog?operation= author&id=1245

20. Fisk, A.D., Rogers, W.A., Charness, N., Czaja, S.J., Sharit, J.: Designing for Older Adults: Principles and Creative Human Factors Approaches. CRC Press, Boca Raton (2009)

21. Pak, R., McLaughlin, A.: Designing Displays for Older Adults. CRC Press, Boca Raton (2011)

22. Williams, L.E.: Perceptions of Older Adults toward iPhones. Master Dissertation, Purdue University, Indiana. ProQuest LLC, UMI No. 1529848 (2012)

23. Rahmati, A., Tossel, C., Shepard, C., Kortum, P., Zhong, L.: Exploring iPhone usage: the influence of socioeconomic differences on smartphone adoption, usage and usability. In: MobileHCI 2012 Proceedings of the 14th International Conference on Human-Computer Interaction with Mobile Devices and Services, pp. 11–20. ACM, New York (2012)

24. Orlikowski, W.J.: Using technology and constituting structures: a practice lens for studying technology in organizations. Organ. Sci. **11**(4), 404–428 (2000)

25. De Sanctis, G., Poole, M.S.: Capturing the complexity in advanced technology use: adaptive structuration theory. Organ. Sci. **5**(2), 121–147 (1994)

26. Carroll, J.: Completing design in use: closing the appropriation cycle. In: 12th European Conference on Information Systems (ECIS 2004), Turku, Finland, p. 11 (2004)

27. Orlikowski, W.: The duality of technology: rethinking the concept of technology in organisations. Organ. Sci. **3**(3), 398–427 (1992)

28. Selwyn, N.: Apart from technology: understanding people's non-use of information and communication technologies in everyday life. Technol. Soc. **25**, 99–116 (2003)
29. Selwyn, N.: The information aged: a qualitative study of older adults' use of information and communication technology. J. Aging Stud. **18**, 369–384 (2004)
30. Selwyn, N.: Digital division or digital decision? a study of non-users and low-users of computers. Poetics **34**, 273–292 (2006)
31. Strauss, A., Corbin, J.: Basics of Qualitative Research: Techniques and Procedures for Developing Grounded Theory. Sage Publications, Thousand oaks (1998)
32. Flick, U.: The Sage Qualitative Research Kit. Sage Publications, Los Angeles (2007)
33. Chen, K., Chan, A.H.: Use or non-use of gerontechnology - a qualitative study. Int. J. Environ. Res. Public Health. **10**, 4645–4666 (2013)
34. Johnson, R., Kent, S.: Designing universal access: web-applications for the elderly and disabled. Cogn. Technol. Work **9**(4), 209–218 (2007)
35. Werner, J.M., Carlson, M., Jordan-Marsh, M., Clark, F.: Predictors of computer use in community-dwelling, ethnically diverse older adults. J. Hum. Factors Ergon. Soc. **53**(5), 431–447 (2011)
36. Ham, D.H.: A model-based framework for classifying and diagnosing usability problems. Cogn. Technol. Work **16**(3), 373–388 (2014)
37. Broady, T., Chan, A., Caputi, P.: Comparison of older and younger adults' attitude towards and abilities with computers: Implications for training and learning. Br. J. Educ. Technol. **41** (3), 473–485 (2010)
38. Mitzner, T.L., Boron, J.B., Fausset, C.B., Adams, A.E., Charness, N., Czaja, S.J., Dijkstra, K., Fisk, A.D., Rogers, W.A., Sharit, J.: Older adults talk technology: technology usage and attitudes. Comput. Hum. Behav. **26**(6), 1710–1721 (2010)
39. Pillemer, K., Meador, R.H., Teresi, J.A., Chen, E.K., Henderson, C.R., Lachs, M.S., Boratgis, G., Silver, S., Eimicke, J.P.: Effects of electronic health information technology implementation on nursing home resident outcomes. J. Aging Health **24**(1), 92–112 (2012)

Abilities to Use Technological Communication Tools in Aging: Contribution of a Structured Performance-Based Evaluation

Lisa Quillion-Dupré[1(✉)], Emmanuel Monfort[2], and Vincent Rialle[1,3]

[1] AGIM, Université Grenoble Alpes, CNRS, 38000 Grenoble, France
{lisa.quilliondupre,vincent.rialle}@agim.eu
[2] LIPPC2S, Université Grenoble Alpes, 38000 Grenoble, France
emmanuel.monfort@upmf-grenoble.fr
[3] CHU de Grenoble, UF ATMISS - Pôle de Santé Publique/Dépt de Veille
Sanitaire, Grenoble, France

Abstract. New technologies remain little used by the elderly and their impact is not sufficiently evaluated. Our research aims to evaluate the potential benefits associated to the use of communication tools and specifically with digital applications on touch pad. The present research compared the ability to use a fixed or mobile phone and a touchpad, by 25 young adults and 25 older people, living in the community and without neurological or psychiatric history. Compared to younger adults, aging people produce more commission errors and need more assistance to correct themselves, especially for the most recent technologies. The data appear to validate a hierarchical assistance model to help aging people using technological communication tools. They should be better assisted in a strategic way, using reinsurance and specific cueing. The results also indicate that the combination of a specific observation grid for standardized daily living tasks is especially sensitive to evaluate autonomy loss in aging.

Keywords: Telephone · Performance-based assessment · Older person · Touchpad · Errors · Human assistance

1 Introduction

According to the World Health Organization (WHO) [1], the percentage of persons aged 60 years and over is expected to double between 2000 and 2050. Besides, the number of dependent people increases with age; Veber and Morel [2] reported 8 % of dependent people among adults of 60-year-old and over against more than 60 % beyond 95-year-old. At the same time, the number of cognitively impaired individuals is brought to grow [1]. As a consequence, the lengthening of life expectancy constraints society to face with a real challenge, specifically with the aim to support elderly dependent people, or at risk of loss of autonomy, at home. The wide scope of gerontechnology may provide innovative solutions both to promote assessments of daily living and to overcome the disability in activities of daily living (ADLs) [3].

© Springer International Publishing Switzerland 2015
J. Zhou and G. Salvendy (Eds.): ITAP 2015, Part I, LNCS 9193, pp. 496–508, 2015.
DOI: 10.1007/978-3-319-20892-3_48

Even if it's a common technology, the telephone is a communication tool essential to maintain independence and autonomy in aging people living in the community. Indeed, it enables to keep in contact with people living far away as well as to organize home-help services or call for help if needed, contributing to ensure personal safety [4], and keeping some control over his/her own life [5]. Furthermore, the ability to use the phone is identified as sensitive to early cognitive decline associated with dementia disorders [6]. More generally, the adaptation to new communication technologies becomes unavoidable to remain actively involved in our society. In addition, learning and using computers may develop the sense of well being, may stimulate the world understanding, and increase the sense of belonging of aging people [7]. Among these technologies, tablets offer both the opportunities of phone and computer, and then may be quite interesting. Indeed, for the elderly, the touch-sensitive screen seems to present the advantage of simplicity of use, compared with the computer [8, 9]. However, new technologies remain little used by the elderly, and their impact is not sufficiently evaluated, even in healthy individuals.

When developing easy-to-use technologies, adapted support to assist aging user in handling of the technology is an apparent need to encourage its adoption [10] and particularly to increase perceived sense of control, which strongly determines technology adoption [11]. Moreover, high quality training with a focus on establishing or restoring a person's confidence in technology but also in his/her own capacities would facilitate learning [12]. Thus, it is essential to promote education and learning, with seniors, their family, and professional caregivers. However, an adapted and effective support could not exist without a fine evaluation of the difficulties' nature and of the cues provided during the task.

A wide variety of tools can be used to assess ADLs: self- and proxy-reported, performance-based measures, as well as direct observation at home. Paper-and-pencil questionnaires allow easy and quick use but have been criticized for their lack of ecological validity: Items often rate a global functioning in an activity and can sometimes only be assumed to respond on a all-or-nothing basis, the measure do not then reflect the nature of the difficulty, the gradual nature of the disorder, or its heterogeneity [13]. Moreover, the activities are generally little or globally described, allowing the interpretation of respondent comprehension and appealing also to his/her memory or retrospection. Results obtained with self-reported measures may also suffer from bias, like over or underestimation of the abilities [14, 15]. In order to propose individually adapted readaptation activities, we need a more detailed ADLs measure, analyzing the task step by step and enabling to give the adapted cue at the right time. Direct observation tools enable to collect information on subject's performance by evaluating effective capacity, using real-world situations. They are considered to be less influenced by the education and cultural level, and could be more valid and objective measures than self-reports [15]. However, they have certain disadvantages: a major one is the time required, one hour and a half on average, for the observation [16]. In addition, data collection may require a suitable room with a more or less substantial specific material, a greater training of the observer, or video recording, making these assessment instruments barely usable in clinical practice [15]. Nonetheless, they provide accurate and relevant information on the patient's functioning, particularly useful in case where there is no family support.

Many researchers using performance-based measures have taken an interest on the type of errors occurring during the task execution. To allow for subtle ADLs analysis, Schwartz et al. [17–19] proposed two main errors categories: omission and commission (including objects substitution, action-addition, sequence errors like anticipation-omission, performance of a step in reverse order or perseveration). Several studies included this error taxonomy [20, 21]. Anselme et al. [22] did too and added initiation errors: when the participant does not start spontaneously the activity, for any reason. According to Giovannetti et al. [21], action-additions while linked to commissions or omissions will be conceptually different and have to be distinguished. Healthy people are likely to produce errors, although less than people with a neurocognitive disorder, and mostly of commission type [23], nonetheless omissions should be likely to be produced by healthy young participants in less familiar tasks [24]. Furthermore, Bettcher et al. [25] highlighted the significance of self-correcting ability as a relevant indicator of living alone at home. Indeed, the number of errors being never zero, detect and correct them is therefore of special importance. Different levels of hierarchical assistance can be provided to help people who do not correct themselves. Neistadt [26] proposed to make a distinction between general verbal (providing guidance with a series of questions) and physical assistance. This distinction has been reproduced in the analysis grid from the Profinteg tool [22, 27]. The authors added specific ("Would this not be written somewhere?") and total verbal assistances ("You have to..."). This enables to determine which assistance is adapted to the subject's difficulties, while exploiting his/her potential.

In that context, our research aims to precise the actual capacity of healthy aging persons to use fixed and mobile phones, and mobile tablet computers compared to young adults. We analyzed their performances in three usual tasks, considering the errors generated as well as the requested and provided cues.

2 Method

2.1 Participants

The study population consisted of two healthy groups, constituted by people living in the community and with no known cognitive impairment. For inclusion in the study, participants had to be between 18 and 40 old for the "younger" group and 64 or older for the "older" group, as well as having French as mother language. Visual and/or hearing impairments were exclusion criterion except if they could be compensated with technical aid(s). Other exclusion criteria were: reported history of psychiatric disorders or stroke, refusal to be filmed, or scoring less than 26 at the Mini Mental State Examination (MMSE) [28, 29]. We also considered the symptoms of depression with the 20-items French version of the Center for Epidemiological Studies Depression Scale (CES-D) [30], due to the possible impact of depressive symptoms on attention. Education status may reflect cohort effects. So, we administered a vocabulary questionnaire (Mill-Hill part B, French version) [31] as an indicator of the socio-educational level.

Fifty participants were met, 25 in each group. Three were excluded from the "older" group due to exclusion criteria: one because of a disabling visual condition and the two others because their MMSE score was 23 and 25.

Demographics of the samples are presented in Table 1. The cognitive level was significantly different (t(31.797) = 3.34, p < .01), which is not surprising if we consider that the aging process results in a slight decline of these performances. As expected, the "older" group had a statistically significant high vocabulary level (t(44.94) = −4.21, p < .001). No significant differences were found between groups in relation to years of education and level of depressive symptoms.

Table 1. Characteristics of the participants

	Age		Education (years)		MMSE		CES-D		Mill-Hill B	
	M SD	Range	M SD	Range	M SD	Range	M SD	Range	M SD	Range
"Younger" n = 25	31.8 6.8	18–40.4	14.5 3	9–20	29.2 0.8	28–30	11.1 5.6	5–25	35.6 3.0	28–41
"Older" n = 22	73.5 6.6	64.2–88.7	13.7 3.4	7–20	28.0 1.4	26–30	15.3 8.8	0–28	39.0 2.6	33–43

2.2 Procedure

A questionnaire was administered to collect demographic and technology habits information, including frequency of use. We also assessed global cognitive functions (MMSE), vocabulary level (Mill Hill part B) and depressive symptoms (CES-D). Finally, in order to meet the objectives of the research, we evaluated and compared the capacity of use in fixed phone, mobile, and tablet. The evaluation was individual and without time limitation. The analysis of the answers was based on verbal and non-verbal elements, and subjects were videotaped while they were using the three communication tools. Videos will next be analyzed by means of a specific scorecard.

The local ethic committee approved the research, and all participants signed the review board-approved consent form providing permission to videotape

2.3 Materials

To assess the capacity of use in the three communication tools, we adapted the hierarchical tasks of the telephone use domain from the Observed Tasks of Daily Living-R (OTDL-R) [32], a performance-based assessment tool of IADL. Participants had to perform three tasks of increasing difficulty and involving their ability to use the three technologies in a usual everyday activity: search for a phone number in a document before dialing it. For the third task, they also had to look for the date of a scheduled appointment in a medical letter then to check it in a diary. The evaluation tasks differed by the structuring level of material mentioning the phone number to dial and by the level of executive constraints linked to the organization and to the control of the steps required to complete the task. We focused on difficulties in using and understanding. We always assessed the technologies in the same order: from the simplest or more common (i.e. fixed) towards the more complex or less common (i.e. tablet). To analyze participants' performances, we used an adapted scorecard developed on the basis of the Profinteg grid [22]. To construct the analysis grid, we sequenced each task, establishing the nature, the number and the chronological order of the necessary steps required to carry out the activity, thus defining a reference script. We were also interested in the types of errors likely to be made (Table 2) and hierarchically listed the cues that might be provided during the task (Table 3). The order was pre-determined, based on a graduated set of responses: from the less informative to the most informative one. The participants were given no indication until they were stuck, asked for help, or made a mistake. According to Bettcher et al. [25], we decided to account the number of self-corrections as well as of external control strategies.

Table 2. Errors typology

Error type	Description
Initiation	The participant does not spontaneously start the activity after 15 s (for any reason) or says, "I don't know".
Omission	The participant does not execute a step (including forgetting of the contents) (e.g. He/she doesn't read the number). To be considered as an omission, an error must not be a consequence from any other error type.
Erroneous execution	Realization in an incorrect, inappropriate way, or not at the right time (e.g. He/she make a mistake in dialing the number or doesn't read the right number), including perseverations: A step is executed more than once (e.g. Read the number, look at the instructions and then read again the number)
Action-addition	Performing an action that cannot be considered like a necessary step to complete the task (e.g. write the appointment in the diary)

Table 3. Typology of the provided cues

Cue type	Description
General	Encouraging to continue or advising the participant of an error but without specified which one and where (e.g. "Be careful!"- "Hm hm")
Specific	Verbal indication on the nature of the error but without providing information about what needs to be done or how to do it (e.g. "You are forgetting something.")
Total	Detailed explanation of what the participant has to do (e.g. "Press the star * key")
Gestural	Showing the right key or number
Physical	Performing the step for the participant (e.g. Press the star key)

2.4 Statistical Analyses

To identify a difference in the use of communication technologies and age effect, we used a multivariate analysis of variance with repeated measures (MANOVA), under the assumption that there is a gradual progress of the technologies' complexity. First, we analyzed errors and assistance means. Then, we considered the performances more in details and compared the distributions of each type of errors and cues.

3 Results

3.1 General Results

We explored the capacities to use three communication technologies (fixed and mobile phones, and tablet computer) by "younger" and "older" people, considering the number of errors, cues, self-corrections, and control strategies. Repeated-measure MANOVA analyses confirmed that there were significant multivariate effects for age group (λ = .320, F(4,41) = 21.8, $p < .001$), technology (λ = .225, F(8,37) = 15.9, $p < .001$), and for the interaction between age and technology (λ = .270, F(8,37) = 12.5, $p < .001$). Univariate between-group analyses revealed that the "older" group significantly produced greater total error (F(1,44) = 64.93, $p < .001$), needed more cues (F(1,44) = 50.66, $p < .001$), and used more control strategies (F(1,44) = 21.78, $p < .001$). Within-group univariate analyses indicated significant differences between technologies for the sum of errors (F(1,1.65) = 58.87, $p < .001$) and cues (F(1,1.68) = 35.01, $p < .001$).

There were significant linear and quadratic effects of the technologies' complexity for the total number of self-corrections (respectively, F(1,44) = 24.00, $p < .001$; F(1,44) = 11.81, $p < .001$), errors (F(1,44) = 85.07, $p < .001$; F(1,44) = 12.47, $p < .001$), and cues (F(1,44) = 51.55, $p < .001$; F(1,44) = 4.00, $p = .05$). There was also a linear effect of the interaction with the age factor for errors (F(1,44) = 50.73, $p < .001$) and cues (F(1,44) = 62.97, $p < .001$): that is a significant major effect for aging people (Fig. 1).

Further analyses showed that, when using the tablet, "younger" produced significantly more errors (fixed: t(24) = −2.63, $p = .015$; mobile: t(24) = −3.24, $p < .01$) and self-corrections (fixed: t(24) = −2.91, $p = .008$; mobile: t(24) = −2.70, $p = .012$). They also needed more assistance with the fixed phone than with the mobile (t(24) = 3.26, $p < .01$). Other differences (Table 4) were not significant.

"older" needed significantly more cues with the tablet [mobile: (t(20) = −4.72, $p < .001$); fixed: (t(20) = −7.19, $p < .001$)], and with the mobile than with the fixed phone (t(20) = −4.28, $p < .001$). Similarly, they produced more errors with the tablet (mobile: t(20) = −600, $p < .001$; fixed: (t(20) = −8.31, $p < .001$) and with the mobile compared to the fixed phone (t(20) = −4.11, $p < .001$). The number of self-corrections was also significantly more important with the tablet (fixed: t(20) = −3.77, $p < .001$; mobile: t(20) = −3.65, $p < .01$). Other differences (Table 4) were not significant.

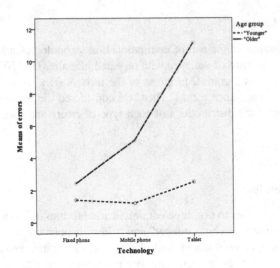

Fig. 1. Line graph – means of errors across technologies by age group

Table 4. Errors, cues, self-corrections, and control strategies scores by technology type and age group.

	"Young" mean (SD)	"Old" mean (SD)
Total number of errors		
Fixed phone	1.4 (1.6)	2.4 (2.0)
Mobile phone	1.2 (1.0)	5.1 (3.7)
Tablet computer	2.5 (1.9)	11.1 (4.4)
Total number of cues		
Fixed phone	4.4 (3.1)	8.9 (5.6)
Mobile Phone	2.3 (2.0)	18.7 (13.4)
Tablet computer	3.2 (2.9)	33.8 (20.2)
Total number of self-corrections		
Fixed phone	.2 (.5)	.2 (.4)
Mobile phone	.2 (.4)	.2 (.4)
Tablet computer	.7 (1.0)	1.3 (1.3)
Total number of control strategies		
Fixed phone	2.0 (1.4)	3.8 (2.7)
Mobile phone	1.8 (1.5)	4.5 (2.7)
Tablet computer	1.6 (1.6)	4.3 (2.5)

3.2 Errors and Cues Patterns

We explored in more details the errors produced (initiations, omissions, erroneous executions and action additions) and the assistance provided (general verbal, specific, total verbal, gestural and physical) across the three technologies for "younger" and "older". Repeated-measure MANOVA analyses highlighted significant multivariate effects for age group (λ = .35, F(4,41) = 19.33, p < .001), technology (λ = .27, F (8,37) = 12.66, p < .001), and for the interaction between age and technology (λ = .37, F(8,37) = 7.94, p < .001) for errors, as well as for assistance (respectively: λ = .40, F (5,40) = 12.17, p < .001; λ = .35, F(10,35) = 6.43, p < .001; λ = .314, F(10,35) = 7.66, p < .001). Univariate between-group analyses showed that "older" produced overall significantly more omissions (F(1,44) = 30.01, p < .001), erroneous executions (F(1,44) = 64.34, p < .001), and initiations (F(1,44 = 7.10, p = .011) than the "younger" group. They also needed more general (F(1,44) = 47.18, p < .001), specific (F(1,44) = 61.42, p < .001), total verbal (F(1,44) = 25.94, p < .001), and gestural assistance (F(1,44) = 5.63, p < .001).

Within-group univariate analyses indicated significant differences between technologies for the number of executions (F(2,88) = 69.91, p < .001) and action additions (F(2,88) = 6.38, p < .01) produced, as well as for general (F(2,88) = 30.44, p < .001), specific (F(2,88) = 32.99, p < .001), total verbal (F(2,88) = 13.92, p < .001), and gestural assistances (F(2,88) = 3.55, p = .042). Further analyses showed that the "younger" group produced only initiation errors with the fixed phone (m = 0.16, SD = 0.37, t(24) = 2.138, p = .043), and significantly more erroneous execution errors with the tablet (m = 1.84, SD = 1.40) than with the fixed (m = 0.76, SD = 1.23, t(24) = −3.36, p < .01) and mobile (m = 0.56, SD = 0.65, t(24) = −4.67, p < .001) phones. The "older" group produced significantly more omission (m = 2.05, SD = 1.02, t(20) = −3.02, p < .001), erroneous execution (m = 8.05, SD = 3.40, t(20) = −8.92, p < .001) and initiation errors (m = 0.71, SD = 1.19, t(20) = −2.55, p = .019) with the tablet than with the fixed phone (respectively, m = 1.14, SD = 1.08; m = 1.09, SD = 1.27; m = 0.14, SD = 0.35). The difference between erroneous execution errors scores was also significant between mobile phone (m = 3.10, SD = 2.45) and tablet (t(20) = −6.38, p < .001) as well as fixed phone (t(20) = −4.22, p < .001). Other differences were not significant. Figure 2 represents significant differences between groups.

"Older" group's scores of general and specific verbal assistance were significantly different between all the technologies (p < .001). Total verbal assistance also increased significantly with the technology [fixed phone (m = 0.14, SD = 0.35) compared to mobile phone (m = 0.67, SD = 1.20, t(20) = −2.25, p = .036) compared to tablet (m = 1.86, SD = 1.82, t(20) = −2.61, p = .017)]. By contrast, the "younger" group needed only more general verbal assistance with the fixed phone (m = 3.8, SD = 2.5) compared with the mobile (m = 1.76, SD = 1.33, t(24) = 3.89, p = .001). Finally, needs were also different between groups (Fig. 3).

4 Discussion

We compared the ability to use a phone (fixed and mobile) and a tablet computer considered across the total number of errors, cues, self-corrections and control strategies, by young and aging people, living in the community and without neuropsychological or psychiatric history. Every kind of errors occurs, even in young participants. Nevertheless, older participants produced more errors than younger adults and needed

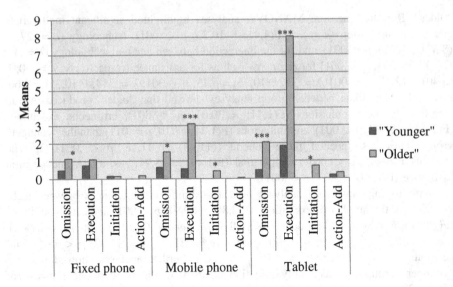

Fig. 2. Differences between the two groups in the distribution of error types for the three technologies (*$p < .05$; **$p < .01$; ***$p < .001$).

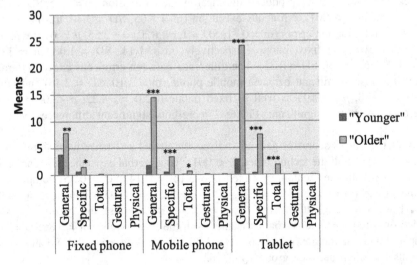

Fig. 3. Differences between the two groups in the distribution of assistance types for the three technologies (*$p < .05$; **$p < .01$; ***$p < .001$).

more assistance. In particular, the results highlighted that aging people produced more omission, execution and initiation errors than young adults. Errors are mostly erroneous execution ones, like reported in previous research in healthy aging population [22]. Nonetheless, we only considered the sum of errors, not the proportion of each error type which might be helpful to confirm patterns suggested by Fig. 2 and to verify if omission errors are more frequent in healthy adults when executing less familiar tasks [24]. Unexpectedly, we did not observe any differences concerning omissions for younger participants. According to our results, the distinction between omissions, commissions, initiations and action-additions, mainly used with impaired people, seems to be sensitive in healthy aging people. Nevertheless, we did not consider the commission error category in details. Yet, it includes several types of errors [17–19], like errors of quality. More explorations are needed considering the number of errors of quality identified, while they were relatively rare in previous research [20]. It may be related to the tablet handling, in particular the use of the touch screen may cause quality errors. It would then be insightful to explore if the nature and the number of errors produced are linked to the specific constraints of the situation (assessment context, documents to read, or technology to use).

Our findings confirm the increasing complexity of the three technologies. Nevertheless, the technology seemed to mainly impact aging people performances: They needed more assistance with the mobile phone than with the fixed phone, and with the tablet computer than with the two others. They also produced more errors with the tablet than with the cellphone, and with the cellphone than with the fixed phone. By comparison, younger participants only produced more errors when using the tablet computer. Moreover, there was a significant difference in the number and the type of human assistance provided: Aging people needed more help, and from higher level, to correct themselves and to learn to execute the task, especially for the most recent technologies. Despite this, all participants succeeded to use the three technologies, even when they had never had before the opportunity to use a computer tablet, confirming its potential simplicity of use [8, 9]. Nonetheless, the link between number of errors and cues with the experience of use deserves further study. Indeed, if 44 % of the younger participants had a tablet at home, they were only 13.6 % among the elderly. And even if the latter were 90.9 % to have a mobile phone, many of them pointed out that the model of the experiment was different from their own. Then, aging people could have more difficulties to adapt to a new technology, and not knowing the technology may increase the difficulty to anticipate the next step to execute. The helpfulness of the hierarchical assistance model seems also to be confirmed. However, more research are needed to confirm if it is more useful to start with general verbal cues in usual situations (increasing cues), while with unusual technologies or for new learning, it may be better to first propose a higher level of help (decreasing cues).

We did not notice any difference between groups for self-corrections; nonetheless, it is quite interesting that aging respondents produced more errors while using more control strategies. Furthermore, they seemed less confident, asking more frequently for help or seeking confirmation. The findings suggest that the main difficulty in the use of communication technologies concerns the decline of efficiency of control strategies and also support the recommendations of Berner [12] concerning the necessity to restore the confidence of the person. Aging people should thus be better assisted in a strategic way, using reinsurance and specific cueing while using the technology.

We acknowledge several limitations to this study. First the sample size was quite small therefore generalizations of the findings are limited. Secondly, we did not explore the inter-rater reliability to verify the objectivity of our analysis grid. Some others variables need also to be explored like, for example, the link with neurocognitive measures or with the frequency of use of each technology. Thus, more research is needed to confirm our results and to advance in the understanding of the data compiled. Nevertheless, favoring access to new information and communication technologies for the elderly give them the opportunity to be more involved in society and contribute to healthy aging. Training has a major role to limit the risk of foreclosure. Finally, the difficulties observed in aging people living at home alone indicate that the combination of a specific observation grid to analyze standardized daily living tasks may be especially sensitive to early neurocognitive disorders.

Acknowledgements. Funding for this project was provided by a grant from Région Rhône-Alpes.

References

1. World Health Organization (Ed.) Global Health and Ageing. World Health Organization (2011)
2. Veber, O., Morel, A.L.: Société et vieillissement. Rapport du groupe 1. Inspection générale des affaires sociales: (2011). http://www.ladocumentationfrancaise.fr/var/storage/rapports-publics/114000332/0000.pdf
3. Pigot, H., Giroux, S., Moktari, M.: La gérontechnologie, support au choix des personnes âgées. Premier Congrès de la Société Française des Technologies pour l'Autonomie et de Gérontechnologie (2009)
4. Mitzner, T.L., Boron, J.B., Fausset, C.B., Adams, A.E., Charness, N., Czaja, S.J., et al.: Older adults talk technology: technology usage and attitudes. Comput. Hum. Behav. **26**, 1710–1721 (2010)
5. Nygård, L., Starkhammar, S.: Telephone use among noninstitutionalized persons with dementia living alone: mapping out difficulties and response strategies. Scan. J. Caring Sci. **17**, 239–249 (2003)
6. Nygård, L., Pantzar, M., Uppgard, B., Kottorp, A.: Detection of disability in older adults with MCI or Alzheimer's disease through assessment of perceived difficulty in using everyday technology. Aging Mental Health (2011). doi:10.1080/13607863.2011.605055
7. Russell, H.: Later life ICT learners ageing well. Int. J. Ageing Later Life **6**(2), 103–127 (2011)
8. Findlater, L., Froehlich, J.E., Fattal, K., Wobbrock, J.O., Dastyar, T.: Age-related differences in performance with touchscreens compared to traditional mouse input. In: Proceedings of the SIGCHI Conference on Human Factors in Computing Systems, pp. 343–346. ACM (2013)
9. Werner, F., Werner, K., Oberzaucher, J.: Tablets for seniors – an evaluation of a current model (iPad). In: Wichert, R., Eberhardt, B. (eds.) Ambient Assisted Living. ATSC, vol. 2, pp. 177–184. Springer, Heidelberg (2012)
10. Alm, N., Dye, R., Gowans, G., Campbell, J., Astell, A.J., Ellis, M.: A communication support system for older people with dementia. IEEE Computer society, Washington (2007)
11. Heart, T., Kalderon, E.: Older adults: are they ready to adopt health-related ICT? Int. J. Med. Informatics **82**(11), e209–e231 (2013)
12. Berner, J.: Psychosocial, Socio-Demographic and Health Determinants in Information Communication Technology Use by Older-Adults (Thèse de doctorat). Blekinge Institute of Technology, Suède (2014)

13. Van der Linden, A.C.J.: Démence de type Alzheimer et évaluation des activités de la vie quotidienne. In: Dans, A.C., Van der Linden, J., Aubin, G., Gall, D.L., Van der Linden, M. (dir.) Neuropsychologie de la vie quotidienne, pp. 41–105. Marseille, Solal, France (2008)
14. Suchy, Y., Kraybill, M.L., Franchow, E.: Instrumental activities of daily living among community-dwelling older adults: discrepancies between self-report and performance are mediated by cognitive reserve. J. Clin. Exp. Neuropsychol. 33(1), 92–100 (2011)
15. Zanetti, O., Frisoni, G.N., Rozzini, L., Bianchetti, A., Trabucchi, M.: Validity of direct assessment of functional status as a tool for measuring Alzheimer's disease severity. Age Ageing 27, 615–622 (1998)
16. Sikkes, S.A.M., de Lange-de Klerk, E.S.M., Pijnenburg, Y.A.L., Scheltens, P., Uitdehaag, B.M.J.: A systematic review of instrumental activities of daily living scales in dementia: room for improvement. J. Neurol. Neurosurg. Psychiatry 80, 7–12 (2009)
17. Schwartz, M.F., Buxbaum, L.J., Montgomery, M.W., Fitzpatrick-DeSalme, E., Hart, T., Ferraro, M., Coslett, H.B.: Naturalistic action production following right hemisphere stroke. Neuropsychologia 37(1), 51–66 (1999)
18. Schwartz, M.F., Montgomery, M.W., Buxbaum, L.J., Lee, S.S., Carew, T.G., Coslett, H.B., Mayer, N.: Naturalistic action impairment in closed head injury. Neuropsychol. 12(1), 13–28 (1998)
19. Schwartz, M.F., Montgomery, M.W., Fitzpatrick-desalme, E.J., Ochipa, C., Coslett, H.B., Mayer, N.H.: Analysis of a disorder of everyday action. Cogn. Neuropsychol. 12(8), 863–892 (1995). doi:10.1080/02643299508251406
20. Cooper, R.P., Schwartz, M.F., Yule, P., Shallice, T.: The simulation of action disorganisation in complex activities of daily living. Cogn. Neuropsych 22(8), 959–1004 (2005). doi:10.1080/02643290442000419
21. Giovannetti, T., Libon, D.J., Buxbaum, L., Schwartz, M.F.: Naturalistic action impairments in dementia. Neuropsychologia 40, 1220–1232 (2002)
22. Anselme, P., Poncelet, M., Bouwens, S., Knips, S., Lekeu, F., Olivier, C., Majerus, S.: Profinteg: a tool for real-life assessment of activities of daily living in patients with cognitive impairment. Psychologica Belgia 53(1), 3–22 (2013)
23. Seligman, S.C., Giovannetti, T., Sestito, J., Libon, D.J.: A new approach to the characterization of subtle errors in everyday action: implications for mild cognitive impairment. Clin Neuropsychol. 28(1), 97–115 (2014)
24. Giovannetti, T., Schwartz, M.F., Buxbaum, L.J.: The coffee challenge: a new method for the study of everyday action errors. J. Clin. Exp. Neuropsychol. 29(7), 690–705 (2007). doi:10. 1080/13803390600932286
25. Bettcher, B.M., Giovannetti, T., Libon, D.J., Eppig, J., Wambach, D., Klobusicky, E.: Improving everyday error detection, one picture at a time: a performance-based study of everyday task training. Neuropsychol. 25(6), 771–783 (2011). doi:10.1037/a0024107
26. Neistadt, M.E.: A meal preparation treatment protocol for adults with brain injury. Am. J. Occup. Ther. 48(5), 431–438 (1994)
27. Wojtasik, V., Olivier, C., Lekeu, F., Quittre, A., Adam, S., Salmon, S.: A grid for a precise analysis of daily activities. Neuropsychol. Rehabil. 20(1), 120–136 (2010)
28. Folstein, M.F., Folstein, S.E., McHugh, P.R.: Mini-mental state. a practical method for grading the cognitive state of patients for the clinician. J. Psychiatr. Res. 12, 189–198 (1975)
29. Hugonot-Diener, L.: Mini-Mental-Status de Folstein (MMS) version GRECO consensuelle. In: Hugonot-Diener, D.L., Barbeau, E., Michel, B.F., Thomas-Antérion, C., Robert, P. (dir.) GRÉMOIRE: tests et échelles de la maladie d'Alzheimer et des syndromes apparentés, pp. 65–69. Marseille, Solal, France (2008)

30. Fuhrer, R., Rouillon, F.: La version française de l'échelle CES-D (Center for Epidemiologic Studies-Depression Scale): Description et traduction de l'échelle d'autoévaluation. Psychiatrie et Psychobiologie **4**, 163–166 (1989)
31. Deltour, J.J., Echelle de vocabulaire Mill Hill de Raven, J.C.: Adaptation française et normes comparées du Mill Hill et du Standard Progressive Matrices (PM38). Manuel et Annexes. Braine le Château, Belgique: Application des Techniques Modernes (1993)
32. Diehl, M., Marsiske, M., Horgas, A.L.: The revised observed tesks of daily living: a performance-based assessment of everyday problem solving in order adults. J. Appl. Gerontol. **24**(3), 211–230 (2005)

Elderly and Tablets: Considerations and Suggestions About the Design of Proper Applications

Eliseo Sciarretta[1], Andrea Ingrosso[1], Valentina Volpi[1,2],
Antonio Opromolla[1,2], and Roberta Grimaldi[1,2(✉)]

[1] Link Campus University, Via Nomentana 335, 00162 Rome, Italy
{e.sciarretta, a.ingrosso, v.volpi, a.opromolla}
@unilink.it, robertagrim@gmail.com
[2] ISIA Roma Design, Piazza della Maddalena 53, 00196 Rome, Italy

Abstract. In this paper, the authors support the idea that tablet is the ideal tool to assist and enhance the elderly living by providing them with value-added services. Currently the risk is that a poor design interface may exclude this substantial part of the population from using useful technologies because of their specific age category requirements. So, after an analysis of the related academic literature and an assessment both of elderly needs and tablet limits and potential, the authors select a set of considerations and suggestions for the design of tablet applications for elderly, in order to facilitate the interaction.

Keywords: Elderly · Tablet · Interaction design · Design considerations and suggestions

1 Introduction

Nowadays, the adoption and the usage of technologies are increased. Specifically, due to the size decreasing and computational power increasing of devices, technologies permeate people lives and enhance their abilities regardless of their level of technology confidence. At the same time, the economical affordability of the large part of devices has enlarged the ICT customers base. As a consequence, a large set of services is made available through these devices. However, a large share of the population is still on the fringes of this trend: the elderly. Several surveys, including one conducted by the United Nations [1], show that the world's population tends to aging. In addition, a study of the European Union [2], back in 2012, states that in 2030 30 % of the European population, a percentage that corresponds to more than 150 million people, will be over 65 years old.

Technologies can really assist and enhance the old people living by providing them with value-added services, but a poor design interface may impede it. Indeed, ignoring the requirements for this specific category of users usually regarded as fragile and in need of support may intensify the risk of excluding a substantial part of the population.

© Springer International Publishing Switzerland 2015
J. Zhou and G. Salvendy (Eds.): ITAP 2015, Part I, LNCS 9193, pp. 509–518, 2015.
DOI: 10.1007/978-3-319-20892-3_49

So, the challenge is to make this part of population able to fully and consciously use technologies for their own needs by designing apps and devices with the goal of creating systems that facilitate the interaction.

First of all, designing an interactive service for the elderly involves a choice on the device on which the service is delivered. The authors agree with the idea shared by the academic literature that tablet can be a particularly suitable device for get elderly close to the "digital services" and provide them with applications tailored on their age category requirements. This consideration further arises from a reflection about the comparison between two studies. In detail, altough the Audiweb statistics report that 25 % of 40 millions of Italian Internet users (age range: 11–74 years old) access through tablet, a study conducted by the authors of this paper on elderly healthcare shows more positive results. In effect, on a sample of 192 respondents with an average age of 71 years, 32 % access to the Internet through tablet. In consideration of this, it can be affirmed that elderly have a predisposition towards the use of the tablet.

Obviously, although tablet is not the panacea, the problems generally occurring in the interaction between the elderly and other type of devices decrease by using tablet. However, a proper design in user interfaces is needed, in order to assure high service usage. So, in this paper the authors aim to select a set of considerations and suggestions to design tablet applications for elderly.

In detail, in the following section, the authors investigate the proper design features for elderly-oriented tablet applications that emerged by the analysis of the related academic literature, while Sect. 3 focuses on elderly needs and tablet main strengths. Thus, in Sect. 4, the authors identify a selection of design considerations and suggestions in order to create applications actually usable by the elderly.

2 Overview on Elderly-Oriented Design in the Academic Literature

The evident difficulties of elderly in using general digital interfaces led user interface designers to find more inclusive solutions. One of the first challenges in the interface design for elderly is to engage old users who infrequently use technologies. Old people view themselves as being "too old" to use certain technologies. In detail, they believe technology offers no benefits or it is too difficult to learn, avoiding it as a consequence [3]. This attitude by the elderly population depends on the *level of technology understanding* that can directly and proportionally affect the *level of confidence* in the face of technology [4, 5]. In addition, old people may be reluctant to adopt technologies that do not meet their needs [6]. So, in order to promote the use of the device as a support rather than as a constraint, it is fundamental for designers to understand the common difficulties that elderly face when using new computing devices (e.g.: tablets), following a proper design method from the very beginning of the design process.

The academic literature has largely investigated the elderly user problems and needs in order to identify the most suitable kind of support that technology may offer. Williams et al. [4] identify several categories of impairments (cognition, auditory, haptic, visual, and motor-based troubles) that ideal and complete human-computer interface solutions for the elderly should take into account. Several studies focus on touch screen as the best interaction method for the elderly, considering pen or fingers interaction, one or two hands, single or multi-touch gestures. Still, according to Williams et al. [4], touch screen proves to be a more useful interaction method than keyboard and mouse in computer interaction (e.g.: because of possible problems caused by arthritis and swollen fingers). Favilla et al. [7] identify touch screen technologies as suited to be used by users affected by memory, cognitive, behavior and emotion diseases, since they are more portable technologies and easier to use than a computer. In addition, touch screen technologies have been continuously improved in touch resolution, multitouch interaction, luminance and high resolution screens, resistive and capacitive technologies, and gestures recognition, more and more meeting elderly requirements [8].

Some authors take into account the use of the tablet to overcome elderly impairments and support them in their activities. In detail, the use of a capacitive touch screen tablet is recommended as it causes less apprehension by avoiding the interaction with intermediary devices, such as pen [8]. So, the capacitive touch screen tablet can be considered a direct input device to interact with, since it only needs a direct contact on the display screen. According to Vasconcelos et al. [6], the tablet is better suited for novice users or those that do not want to memorize commands, as it demands less training and it is easier to use, since it requires little hand-eye coordination and minimal spatial (cognitive) demands. So, it is a suitable device for older people.

In other studies, some of the tablet features are considered in comparison with similar devices, such as smartphone. As the latter, the tablet is a mobile device. This allows old people to use it in a comfortable place and position, especially meeting the needs of users with physical impairments or who are bedridden [6]. But older users encounter great difficulties in using smartphone [9], e.g. because of the small size of buttons and display [5], while the tablet offers a larger display than a smartphone and the possibility to have labeled icons and larger fonts. However, the previous use of a smartphone make easier for the elder the use of the tablet, since she/he is already confident with settings that are similar [4].

The tablet could present even constraints. For example, Favilla et al. [7] report the difficulty encountered by elderly in making capacitive contact with the touch screen surfaces. Moreover, capacitive touch screen tablet does not offer any haptic response for users [4], while a traditional resistive panel is based on a logic of interaction closer to the interaction modes used in the physical world (e.g.: to push a switch button, or to lean a finger against a surface). Therefore, old people could be more used to exert pressure, rather than to swipe the fingertip, and even the difference can be hard to be understood by older adults, especially those affected from dementia [10]. Due also to elderly poor physical coordination [5] and slowed ability to combine motor and cognitive skills, multi-touch interaction, typical of capacitive touch screen, is not recommended for the elderly people (e.g.: rotate and zoom actions get diffculties for them) [11]. At the same time, resistive touch screen requires to exert and sustain a certain pressure that could represent a problem for older users [8]. Device inclination is another important element to consider, because of the glare on glossy screens. Since their dimension and weight, tablets are poor handling, so they may require the support of a table or a stand [10]. Regarding audio feedback, the sounds from the application or the device could be another hindrance for old people, startling or confusing them, or being unheard due to hearing loss [10], even if usually it is possible to adjust the levels of the sounds produced. Finally, one of the major risks with touch screen device is to accidentally give an input to the system in use. The risk may be higher for older people.

Otherwise, for a great part of the problems reported, a proper design methodology can offer an easy way out and create consistency. In this regard, tablet offers the possibility to give elderly applications with rich design interfaces. It is a very important feature, since a poor interface design may prevent elderly from using it. Several works proposed suggestions for designing mobile devices for older people, focusing on motivational and usability issues [6, 9, 12]. In addition, a participatory design involving the users in the ideation process represents an essential approach to create more useful and relevant services [13, 14].

In evaluating the suitability of the tablet for elderly, not only the technology, but also the social context they are used to has to be considered. Although mobile devices are generally designed for personal use, they can be usefully used in group activities, too (e.g. in collaborative music and game activities), to successfully engage the target audience [15].

In concluding, elderly could benefit from tablet (and technology in general) in order to be supported in a great number of application fields and everyday activities, achieving a more independent living [5, 15–17].

3   Framework

In this section, the authors intend to define the main characteristics about the subjects of this study: elders and tablets. The emerged elements will be useful in order to define the considerations and the suggestions for designing proper tablet applications for elderly in Sect. 4.

3.1   Users

United Nations define "older persons" as "people aged 60 years or over" [1] and predict that by 2050, the share of older people as portion of world population will reach 21,1 %. Among them, the share of persons aged 80 years old or over will reach 19 %. In this section the authors focus on the peculiarities and habits of this age group, considering its prevalent impairments, since they can affect the user interfaces of tablet applications.

Older people are a highly heterogeneous group regarding interests, preferences, skills, experiences and abilities, but they have in common the emergence of impairments affecting both physical and mental activities [4, 6, 7, 18].

The main impairments in physical activities concern *movements* (e.g.: difficulties in moving and controlling arms, hands, and legs; low coordination and flexibility; difficulties in maintaining movements; loss of tactile sensitivity; motor tremors), *vision* (e.g.: partial or poor vision; amplitude reduction of visual field; difficulties in visual perception of colours, contrasts, brightness, dark adaptations, etc.), and *hearing* (e.g.: reduced hearing, firstly of hear high-frequency sounds).

The main cognitive difficulties concern *memory* (i.e. working, spatial, and long-term memory), *attention* (e.g.: decrease of the selective attention and difficulties in managing information, causing confusion and disorientation), *response time* (to the stimuli), *executive functions* (e.g.: planning and executing tasks aimed at a purpose; problem solving; decision making), *motivation* (i.e. the older people need to be strongly motivated to do something), and *learning processes* (e.g.: difficulties in learning new information and in adapting himself/herself to new situations).

Physical and cognitive conditions not only affect the daily activities (e.g.: in mobility, shopping, personal care, etc.), but also the *emotional state* of older people, creating the needs of being encouraged and comforted, in order to do not let them give up their self-sufficiency.

Even the *relational* aspects of their lives are certainly compromised from being retired and having lost a more active social role. For these reasons, they need to build or strengthen their social networks, also as relief for loneliness and boredom.

However, elderly are usually considered wise, because of their gained experience and knowledge allowing them the identification of patterns and models: wisdom is here seen as the ability to improve problem solving and finding solutions.

The elements above discussed could be seen under different points of view: as needs (e.g.: social, security, and care need), as elements to be trained and improved (e.g.: the cognitive abilities can be kept constant with exercise, allowing continuous learning), and as elements to be considered in designing architecture, communication, and content aspects of interactive systems (e.g.: difficulties in color perception affect the use of colours in a mobile application user interface).

Older people are considered as "digital immigrant" [19], having a generalized difficulty in using new technologies and interactive systems. Indeed, in respect of "digital native", older people need to understand how an artefact works, before using it.

3.2   Tablets

Due to its own intrinsic features, the tablet is considered by the authors of this paper as the device better suited to enable the inclusion in the digital world of those categories of users who have little or no familiarity with technologies, such as the elderly.

In this section, the authors try to give evidence of what these features are, focusing on characteristics, potentialities, and limits of the technological devices usually known as "tablets".

First of all, a clarification on the terminology is needed. A tablet PC is commonly a laptop that allows a direct interface with its screen through fingers (or a pen). In other words, it is a Personal Computer with additional input modes than mouse and keyboard.

This definition lead to a form-based classification, which consists of at least three categories:

1. *Slates* are devoid of a physical keyboard, so for data entry a software keyboard or other forms of insertion (such as speech recognition) are required. Since 2010, when the Apple iPad was first marketed, the term "tablet" is commonly associated with

these devices, although improperly. Within this category, another distinction concerns the screen size: mini tablets are devices with a smaller screen (usually about 7 inches), while standard slates screen size is 9–10 inches. Mini tablets are the result of a hybridization process with smartphones. The same process has led more recently to the creation of the so-called Phablets (phone plus tablets), i.e. (mini) tablets that integrate telephone features.

2. *Convertibles* are real laptops with one main difference: thanks to a special swivel joint, their screen can be rotated and folded over the keyboard, so that it disappears. The keyboard, usually "hidden", can be extracted at any time, in order to make the data entry easier or to enable the interaction with applications not designed for touch screens. Due to its flexibility of use, convertible was the most popular type of tablet, until the advent of the iPad and similar devices.

3. *Hybrids* have a keyboard that can be attached or detached depending on the needs. This category had not a wide diffusion, since slates often have keyboards that can be connected via USB or Bluetooth.

The main differences among the categories of tablet are summarized in the Table 1.

Acknowledged this differentiation, hereafter with the word "tablets" the authors refer to the slate tablets.

The exclusive use at most of fingers or of a pen characterizes the tablet users' interfacing mode.

Unlike convertibles, tablets need to run an operating system specifically designed, in order to maximize the performance of the interaction. This makes tablets much more similar to smartphones in functioning and interaction mode. Moreover they run a similar operating system, usually based on iOS or Android, sometimes in customized versions.

In a second time, Microsoft has introduced a substantial innovation with the release of its Windows 8, an operating system designed to run both on traditional PCs and all types of tablets.

Despite the differencies in operating system or manufacturer, tablets share many features that make them recognizable:

1. High-definition display with a diagonal between 7 and 10 inches;
2. Wi-Fi or 3G/4G modules for Internet connection;
3. Applications (apps) supporting the performance of different activities (reading, writing, games, social networking, video conferencing, chat, music, eBooks), available (free or for a fee) on the related store;

Table 1. Comparison of the different tablet categories

	Categories of tablet PCs				
	Slates			Convertibles	Hybrids
	Tablets	Mini Tablets	Phablets		
Screen size	9"–13"	7"–8"	5"–7"	10"–13"	7"–9"
Keyboard	Via USB or BT	Via USB or BT	Via USB or BT	Built in	Detachable
Other			Phone		

4. GPS module for navigation and geo-referenced services;
5. Camera (usually less performing than smartphones ones);
6. Multi-touch screen that supports gestures;
7. Weight of about a kilogram or slightly less;
8. Variable battery life, still quantifiable in several hours (up to 12) of continuous use.

In order to understand why tablets could be the best device to encourage an audience of elderly to use apps, the authors compare tablet with other devices able to run similar applications: desktop PCs (or laptops), Smart TVs, smartphones.

In detail, tablets belong to the same family of smartphones, namely the mobile devices. Unlike Smart TVs and desktop PCs, the context of use of mobile devices is very variable, with environment and light conditions not always optimal. However, tablets are still seen by most people as small computers rather than large phones. As a consequence they are used to a great extent in domestic contexts. The possibility of being regarded as *technological knick-knacks*, makes tablet preferred over smartphones by elderly users. Indeed, smartphone devices are seen as *cold* and complicate, easily to be lost and forgotten because of their small size. Tablets, instead, have a larger screen that makes it easier to visualize information and to enjoy services, especially for an audience with significant vision problems, remaining transportable at the same time. The elderly can thus become inclined to the use of the tablet, even in a home environment.

Actually also Smart TV could be considered as the preferred device for accessing apps by elderly, since the latter makes large use of TV set. Moreover Smart TV offers a wide screen, a control device (remote control) and a context of use (at a distance of a couple of meters from the couch) familiar to the user. But Smart TV presents significant interaction constraints when passing from watching the broadcasted video contest to using apps, first of all due to the use of the remote control, familiar only for operations such as channel switch or volume change [20]. In addition, the big screen offers a non-optimal viewing distance for reading.

Focusing on the interaction mode, the touch screen interface typical of the tablet represent a strong point over the other devices. The user is able to directly manipulate the displayed objects of the interface, as it would happen in reality, by touching the screen and moving fingers according to pre-established gestures (e.g. swiping the finger on the display to change the page, as it occur on a paper book).

The interaction mode combined with the ease of use is the main strength of tablets compared to traditional desktop PCs or laptops, which require the user to input data via keyboard and mouse. In addition, because of their versatile nature, PCs run quite complex operating systems, which require a lot of experience to be controlled by users.

4 Considerations and Suggestions

On the basis of the elements emerged from the related research studies and the analysis of the framework (user needs and device features), the authors provide in this section some considerations and suggestions about the design of tablet applications for elderly. In detail, they identified 11 categories, providing different considerations for each of them. Such considerations and suggestions can represent a useful reference for inter-action designers during the design process for elderly-oriented tablet applications.

1. *Services/Applications* (the following is a not comprehensive list of possible application fields): gaming (e.g.: for learning, entertainment or training); information access; education; health care; working at home; community and social relations; safety; monitoring.
2. *Device:* use slate devices with a screen size greater than 9"; use a pillar in order to get users to arrange the tablet on a comfortable position to contain the glare glossy screen problem (the optimum angle is 30°); use added accessories (rubber cases with adjustable stands; screen protectors can help reduce glare).
3. *Text:* use a font size between 12 and 14 pt; use readable fonts, such as Sans Serif fonts (e.g.: Arial, Verdana); use a single line spacing; avoid bold, underlining or italics; avoid specific words (e.g. "nickname", "FAQ"); repeat contents, avoiding not key information; avoid capital letters, acronyms, and abbreviations; avoid scroll text; use calibration systems (e.g.: word prediction, swabbing and automatic correction).
4. *Graphic aspects:* use a sharp contrast between color background and text (in detail: use dark writing on clear background); use a uniform texture; adapt object and button size/dimension; use a border for pop-ups; use clear and concretes graphic elements, avoiding the ones far from reality; use metaphors close to everyday life; create coherent interfaces; design rich UI; offer an overview of the elements of the interface; avoid moving UI elements; use multi-layered interfaces; develop the applications in landscape (horizontal) view rather than portrait (vertical); maintain a stable landscape; use a combination of labelling and icons; adequately separate the different buttons; use explicit buttons rather than slider or cursor buttons.
5. *Colours:* prefer complementary colours in order to use a sharp contrast (e.g.: orange and blue, white and black); use few colours; avoid pastel colours; avoid blinding light.
6. *Sounds:* avoid sounds too quiet and blunted.
7. *Command input:* use single touch rather than multi-touch; use a voice interface; design the interaction process with a specific gesture-based method, establish a "hot area" around the buttons; use tactile input joined with haptic input.
8. *Output:* provide instant feedback (e.g.: after touching an icon, change colour); use multi-sensorial feedbacks (e.g.: tactile feedbacks joined with/rather than sounds or haptic output).
9. *Basic features:* combine touch-based and slide gesture interaction; use adaptable/customizable setting/interfaces (customizable fonts, icons, combination colours, button size, windows size, contrast level, sound level, on/off sounds, vibration/haptic effects); use social features; guide users with tutorials, frequent feedbacks, introductory videos on how use the application and the related technologies included into the device; use "help systems" (e.g.: frequently asked questions, send a message with a question); use a stable menu interface, with a not deep information architecture; focus application features and tasks; get user to set technologies into application (e.g.: GPS, etc.).

10. *Methodology:* exploit co-design and participatory design to build a service system/application; take data from users to determine the best method of grouping content categories; involve users in evaluation processes of services.
11. *Context of use:* the better context of use of tablet applications should be home, with the device on a desk and with the seated user.

5 Conclusions and Future Work

During the discussion of this paper, the authors investigated the issues concerning possible interaction between the elderly and the tablets, aiming to understand whether these devices can actually be, as many claim, the drivers that allow older adults to enjoy interactive applications, at last.

The result of this study lead to the conclusion that by following a proper design method it is possible to develop tablets applications that provide added value to users of the target audience. So, she authors identify some suggestions in order to make the design of tablet applications suitable for the elderly.

The next steps will be oriented to field test the effectiveness of the set out considerations, which will be challenged in the implementation of specific projects and applications. Moreover, will be taken into account and evaluated additional variables connected to the context that affect the way users interact, such as public contexts.

References

1. United Nations-Department of Economic and Social Affairs Population Division: World Population Ageing 2013. United Nations (2013)
2. European Commission: The 2012 Ageing Report. Economic and budgetary projections for the 27 EU Member States (2010–2060). European Union (2012)
3. Durick, J., Robertson, T., Brereton, M., Vetere, F., Nansen, B.: Dispelling ageing myths in technology design. In: 25th Australian Computer-Human Interaction Conference on Augmentation, Application, Innovation, Collaboration, pp. 467–476. ACM, New York (2013)
4. Williams, D., Ul Alam, M.A., Ahamed, S.I., Chu, W.: Considerations in designing human-computer interfaces for elderly people. In: 13th International Conference on Quality Software, pp. 372–377. IEEE (2013)
5. Malik, S.A., Abdullah, L.M., Mahmud, M., Azuddin, M.: Mobile applications using augmented reality to support older people. In: International Conference on Research and Innovation in Information Systems, pp. 374–379. IEEE (2013)
6. Vasconcelos, A., Silva, P.A., Caseiro, J., Nunes, F., Teixeira, L.F.: Designing tablet-based games for seniors: the example of CogniPlay, a cognitive gaming platform. In: 4th International Conference on Fun and Games, pp. 1–10. ACM, New York (2012)
7. Favilla, S., Pedell, S.: Touch screen ensemble music: collaborative interaction for older people with dementia. In: 25th Australian Computer-Human Interaction Conference on Augmentation, Application, Innovation, Collaboration, pp. 481–484. ACM, New York (2013)

8. Motti, L.G., Vigouroux, N., Gorce, P.: Interaction techniques for older adults using touchscreen devices: a literature review. In: 25ième Conférence Francophone on l'Interaction Homme-Machine, pp. 125–135. ACM, New York (2013)
9. Qiuhui, W.: The effects of interface design about mobile phones on older adults' usage. In: 4th International Conference on Wireless Communications, Networking and Mobile Computing, pp. 1–4. IEEE (2008)
10. Yamagata, C., Kowtko, M., Coppola, J.F., Joyce, S.: Mobile app development and usability research to help dementia and Alzheimer patients. In: IEEE Long Island Systems, Applications and Technology Conference, pp. 1–6. IEEE (2013)
11. Lepicard, G., Vigouroux, N.: Comparison between single-touch and multi-touch interaction for older people. In: Miesenberger, K., Karshmer, A., Penaz, P., Zagler, W. (eds.) ICCHP 2012, Part I. LNCS, vol. 7382, pp. 658–665. Springer, Heidelberg (2012)
12. Massimi, M., Baecker R.M., Wu, M.: Using participatory activities with seniors to critique, build, and evaluate mobile phones. In: 9th International ACM SIGACCESS Conference on Computers and Accessibility, pp. 155–162. ACM, New York (2007)
13. Davidson, J.L., Jensen, C.: Participatory design with older adults: an analysis of creativity in the design of mobile healthcare applications. In: 9th ACM Conference on Creativity & Cognition, pp. 114–123. ACM, New York (2013)
14. Waycott, J., Pedell, S., Vetere, F., Ozanne, E., Kulik, L., Gruner, A., Downs, H.: Actively engaging older adults in the development and evaluation of tablet technology. In: Farrell, V., Farrell, G., Chua, C., Huang, W., Vasa, R., Woodward, C. (eds.) Proceedings of the 24th Australian Computer-Human Interaction Conference (OzCHI 2012), pp. 643–652. ACM, New York (2012)
15. Pedell, S., Beh, J., Mozuna, K., Duong, S.: Engaging older adults in activity group settings playing games on touch tablets. In: 25th Australian Computer-Human Interaction Conference on Augmentation, Application, Innovation, Collaboration, pp. 477–480. ACM, New York (2013)
16. Grosinger, J., Vetere, F., Fitzpatrick, G.: Agile life: addressing knowledge and social motivations for active aging. In: 24th Australian Computer-Human Interaction Conference, pp. 162–165. ACM, New York (2012)
17. Benoit, O., Marc, K., Fernand, F., Dieter, F., Martine, H.: User-centered activity management system for elderly people empowering older people with interactive technologies to manage their activities at the retirement home. In: 3rd International Conference on Pervasive Computing Technologies for Healthcare, pp. 1–4. IEEE (2009)
18. Mann, W.C.: The aging population and its needs. J. Pervasive Comput. IEEE 3(2), 12–14 (2004)
19. Prensky, M.: Digital natives, digital immigrants. Horizon 9(5), 1–6 (2001)
20. Jose, C., Tiago, G., Duarte, C., Biswas, P., Aslan, G., Langdon, P.: TV applications for the elderly: assessing the acceptance of adaptation and multimodality. In: 6th International Conference on Advances in Computer-Human Interactions, pp. 234–242 (2013)

Developing New Gesture Design Mode
in Smartphone Use for Elders

Ming-Hong Wang[⊠], Yu-Chi Chang, Shuo-Fang Liu,
and Hsin-Hsi Lai

Department of Industrial Design, National Cheng-Kung University, Tainan,
Taiwan, ROC
{wming0403, hsinhsi6699}@gmail.com,
{liusf, hsinhsi}@mail.ncku.edu.tw

Abstract. This article is aimed to design new hand gesture mode of smart-phone for better used by the elderly. The method first use focus grouping to find out the most difficult use hand gestures for the elderly. Secondly, we develop new gesture mode with one-finger gesture. Finally, we compare the traditional gesture with new design gesture mode. Results show that (1) use two fingers as gesture are the most difficult for the elderly; (2) new design mode are better than traditional mode statistically significant in usability evaluation. Accordingly, we suggest the new design gesture mode may be as one solution to substitute the traditional gesture mode for the elderly.

Keywords: Hand gesture mode · Smartphone design · Focus grouping · Usability evaluation · The elderly people

1 Introduction

With the rising in smartphone use in recent years, there have been many academic studies on mobile phone use.

Nowadays, smartphone use is one of the study areas that should be explored and invested. Many studies have shown that it is a big challenge for elderly people to use smartphones, especially touch-screens. Because of factors related to aging in visual acuity, aging of tactile perception, aging of cognitive ability and aging in motor ability.

Many studies mentioned that touch-screen user interface. Such as Guenther et al. (2010) [1] compared with gesture inputting and traditional inputting, gesture inputting interface is more efficiency; Kine et al. (2009) indicated that in selection task "one finger direct-touch is faster than using a mouse and bimanual interactions are faster than using one finger"; Park and Han (2010) [2] indicated that in regard to reaction time, icon size design 10 mm is better than 7 mm and 7 mm is better than 4 mm [2]; And Piper et al. (2010) [3] compared with multi-touch inputting device and traditional inputting device by interview survey, they indicated "multi-touch inputting device is less intimidating, less frustrating, and less oppressive than a traditional computer".

Gestures for human to human interaction are a natural and powerful tool of com-munication. And it has instead speech communication in many situations (Seow et al. 2010) [4]. Charness et al. (2004) [5] and Rogers et al. (2005) [6] compared with direct

© Springer International Publishing Switzerland 2015
J. Zhou and G. Salvendy (Eds.): ITAP 2015, Part I, LNCS 9193, pp. 519–527, 2015.
DOI: 10.1007/978-3-319-20892-3_50

input devices and indirect input devices (e.g. mouse or trackball), with respect to older users have shown a general benefit of direct input devices over indirect ones. The direct nature of gesture input thus might facilitate interaction for elderly. Therefore, it's necessary to avoid excessive wrist joint flexion and extension, continuous and rapid movements, high coordination movements and to attention tactile perception feedback.

Gestural input interfaces are applying on many technical systems and it can be classified roughly into 2D gestures, using finger or hand movement on touch-screens to operate. And 3D gestures, using free-form movements in space to operate (Saffer, 2008) [7]. This study is focus on 2D gestures to explore better Smartphone operating gesture for elderly.

However, the literature on elderly motor ability aging has documented a couple of observations which might put the suitability of finger gesture input for elderly into question, shown as Chaparro et al. (2000) [5] indicated that compared with two age groups: the younger (aged 25 to 30) and the elderly (aged 60 to 69), the elderly wrist joint flexion is decreased 12–14 %. Therefore, if included gesture input wrist activity should be considered elderly wrist flexibility, judgment whether the gesture of the elderly is a gracious gesture input. Walker et al. (1997) [8] indicated that the elderly have less efficiency tactile perceptual feedback systems and lack the force to produce very rapid movements. And Microsoft (2009) [9] indicated that the elderly are difficult to conduct continuous moving task or the coordination of moving task.

The smartphone use is not conductive for the elderly. As of now, there still have few studies on smartphone operating gesture designs for the elderly. Thus this study takes an attempt to develop a new gesture mode of operating smartphone for elders.

To reach the aim of this research, three stages are adopted. In the first stage we use focus grouping to find out the most difficult use hand gestures for the elderly. In second stage, we develop new gesture mode with one finger gesture. In Final stage, we compare the traditional gesture with new design gesture mode.

2 Method

2.1 Focus Grouping

- *Sample products.* The most sail products are used as samples in Taiwan market. These include five brands smartphone, which are brand SS, A, H SN, and A. Please see Fig. 1.
- *Subjects.* Five individuals older than 60 (Mean = 63.2; female = 2, male = 3) with at least one year previous smartphone use experience were found to explore and discuss smartphone operating gestures of five brand sample products that might be suitable for the elderly.
- *Process.* Initially, a host provides subjects with five brand sample products and shows them how to do gestures of different sample (with 30 min.). Then let each subject to operate them (with 30 min.) in order to determine which smartphone operating gesture is the most difficult for the elderly, and the top three most difficult gestures become the main research core (with 60 min.).

Brand	Brand SS	Brand A	Brand H	Brand SN	Brand AU
Gesture					

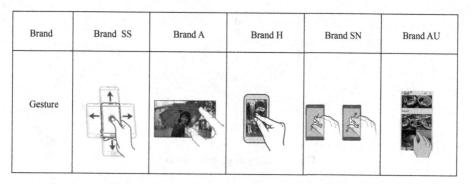

Fig. 1. Five brands are used as sample products

2.2 Developing New Gesture Mode

First, a team consisted of five designers with at least 6-year product design experience are organized to find feasible solutions (with 2D sketch drawing) to solve operational difficulty of two-finger gesture for the elderly using smartphone. Then 10 elders are invited to evaluate feasible solutions and choose best new solution for the designer team to develop computer simulation.

2.3 Usability Evaluation of New Design Gesture Mode

This research uses usability evaluation to compare traditional gesture with new designs. Usability evaluation include five sector indexes as the following:

1. Learnability-ease to learn and learning quickly.
2. Efficiency-efficient to use and after learning, then quickly to reach high efficiency.
3. Memorability-easy to memorize and casual user can operate immediately, no need to learn again.
4. Errors-lower error rate.
5. Satisfaction-total feeling of usability to satisfy the operation.

Experimental procedure follows three steps. First, three experimenters teach subjects how to operate traditional smartphone and new gesture design mode. Second, all subjects practice till they familiarly to use traditional smartphone and new design mode. Finally, all subjects answer the questions of usability evaluation.

3 Result

3.1 Result of Focus Grouping

The final summary of focus grouping is the top three most difficult gestures for elders are rotate gesture, zoom in gesture and zoom out gesture (refer to Figs. 2, 3 and 4). The reason is two-handed gesture is too messy and that multi-finger gestures are sometimes not so easy for elders.

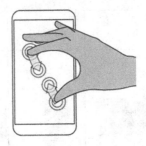

Fig. 2. Zoom in gesture (shrink)

Fig. 3. Zoom out gesture (enlarge)

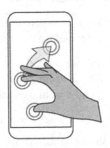

Fig. 4. Rotate gesture

3.2 Result of Developing New Design Gesture Mode

Two new design gesture mode are built (please see Figs. 5 and 6). The character of new designs is singer-finger gesture that is easier to operate than multi-finger gesture for elders, according to the result of focus grouping (Figs. 7, 8 and 9).

3.3 Result of Usability Evaluation to New Design Gesture Mode

Tables 1 and 2 show that ND 1(New Design Gesture 1) is the best gesture mode and reach to statistical significant ($P < 0.05$) in usability evaluation which includes 5 items

Fig. 5. Zoom in (slide down gesture new design 1)

Fig. 6. Zoom out (slide up gesture new design 1)

Fig. 7. Zoom in (reverse clock circle gesture new design 2)

Fig. 8. Zoom out (clock circle gesture new design 2)

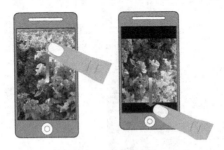

Fig. 9. Rotation (slide up and rotation gesture new design 3)

Table 1. Mean and S.D. in different gesture mode

			Evaluation items				
			Learnability	Efficiency	Memorability	Errors	Satisfaction
Gesture mode	TR	number	30	30	30	30	30
		Mean	3.80	3.43	3.40	3.37	3.13
		S.D.	0.407	0.626	0.498	0.669	0.730
	ND1	number	30	30	30	30	30
		Mean	4.40	4.30	4.00	4.30	4.70
		S.D.	0.675	0.651	0.643	0.466	0.466
	ND2	number	30	30	30	30	30
		Mean	3.30	3.50	3.80	3.20	3.80
		S.D.	0.651	0.509	0.761	0.407	0.761

(learnability, efficiency, memorability, errors and satisfaction). However, ND 2 (New Design Gesture 2) is only better than traditional gesture mode in regard to usability evaluation in 3 items (efficiency, memorability and satisfaction).

Table 2. Comparisons in usability evaluation Font sizes

Variable	(I) gesture	(J) gesture	Standard error	Significance	Comparison result
Learnability	ND 1	ND2	0.152	0.000	ND1>TR>ND2
		TR	0.152	0.001	
	ND2	ND1	0.152	0.000	
		TR	0.152	0.006	
	TR	ND1	0.152	0.001	
		ND2	0.152	0.006	
Efficiency	ND1	ND2	0.155	0.000	ND1>ND2> TR
		TR	0.155	0.000	
	ND2	ND1	0.155	0.000	
		TR	0.155	0.911	
	TR	ND1	0.155	0.000	
		ND2	0.155	0.911	
Memorability	ND1	ND2	0.166	0.487	ND1>ND2> TR
		TR	0.166	0.002	
	ND2	ND1	0.166	0.487	
		TR	0.166	0.060	
	TR	ND1	0.166	0.002	
		ND2	0.166	0.060	
Errors	ND1	ND2	0.136	0.000	ND1>TR> ND2
		TR	0.136	0.000	
	ND2	ND1	0.136	0.000	
		TR	0.136	0.474	
	TR	ND1	0.136	0.000	
		ND2	0.136	0.474	

3.4   Result of Rotation New Design in Usability Evaluation

Table 3 shows that rotation design gesture (RN1) is better than traditional gesture (TR) in all aspects of usability evaluation and all reach statistical significance.

Table 3. statistical result of rotation new design gesture in usability evaluation

			Effecttive evaluation items				
			Leanabity	Efficiency	Memor ability	Errors	Satisfaction
Rotation gesture mode	TR	Number	30	30	30	30	30
		Mean	2.6	2.3	3.0	3.2	2.7
		S.D.	0.81	0.65	0.45	0.61	0.91
	RN 1	Number	30	30	30	30	30
		Mean	4.4	4.6	4.0	4.6	4.6
		S.D.	0.93	0.93	0.78	0.67	0.93
F value			63.5	122.7	36.3	71.1	63.4
P value (significance)			0.00	0.00	0.00	0.00	0.00
Compare result			RN1>TR	RN1>TR	RN1>TR	RN1>TR	RN1>TR

4   Conclusion and Further Study

Given the analysis results, this study suggests that the elderly aged 55 up may use new design mode (ND 1) with single-finger operating gesture as a smartphone operating gesture mode. These results also contribute to further study intended to develop an elderly touch-screen user interface. Finally, this study expects to be an entry point by which to explore more suitable way to make smartphone use more accessible for the elderly.

Further study will focus on motion analysis on muscle fatigue and joint anger vary of finger gesture and tracking eye movement of finger gesture to new design mode. These study will scientifically prove that the new design gesture mode is really better than traditional one.

Acknowledgements. The authors would like to appreciate that this research is financially supported by MOST (Ministry of Science and Technology) at Taiwan, R.O.C, under the project number: MOST 103-2221-E-006 -214 -. All invited subjects and designers are also appreciated very much.

References

1. Guenther, M.J., Volk, F., Shaneck: Proposing a multi-touch interface for intrusion detection environments. In: Proceedings of the Seventh International Symposium on Visualization for Cyber Security VizSec, Ottawa, Ontario, Canada, pp. 13–21. ACM (2010)
2. Park, T.S., Han, S.H.: Touch key for one –hand thumb interaction with a mobile phone: effects of touch key size and touch key location. Int. J. Ind. Ergon. **40**(1), 68–76 (2010)
3. Piper, A.M., Campbell, R., Hollan, J.D.: Exploring the accessibility and appeal of surface computing for older adult health care support. In: Proceedings of the 28th International Conference on Human Factors in Computing Systems, CHI 2010, pp. 907–916. ACM Press (2010)
4. Seow, S.C., Wixon, D., MacKenzie, S., Jacucci, G., Morrison, A., Wilson, A.: Multi-touch and surface computing. In: Proceedings of the 27th International Conference Extended Abstracts on Human Factors in Computing Systems, CHI EA 2009, pp. 4767–4770. ACM Press (2009)
5. Chaparro, A., Rogers, M., Fernandez, J., Bohan, M., Choi, S.D., Stumpfhauser, L.: Range of motion of the wrist: implications for designing computer input devices for the elderly. Disabil. Rehabil. **22**(13), 633–637 (2000)
6. Rogers, W.A., Fisk, A.D., McLaughlin, C., Park, R.: Touch a screen or turn a knob: choosing the best device for the job. Hum. Factors **47**(2), 271–288 (2000)
7. Saffer, D.: Designing Gestural Interfaces, 1st edn. O'Reilly Media, Sebastopol (2008)
8. Walker, N., Philbin, D.A., Fisk, A.D.: Age-related differences in movement control: adjusting sub movement structure to optimize performance. J. Gerontol. B Psychol. Sci. Soc. Sci. **52**(1), 40–52 (1997)
9. Microsoft Corporation: Application gestures and semantic behavior (2009). http://msdn.microsoft.com/en-us/library/ms704830VS.85.aspx

Research on Interaction Design of Intelligent Mobile Phone for the Elderly Based on the User Experience

Minggang Yang[✉] and He Huang[✉]

School of Art, Design and Media,
East China University of Science and Technology, M. BOX 286,
NO. 130 Meilong Road, Xuhui District, Shanghai 200237, China
{yangminggang,1983222hh}@163.com

Abstract. Whether in the developed or developing countries, aging of population has been a common global trend. With the development of the communication technology and the Internet era of prosperity, the elderly people also inevitably need to use modern communication products such as mobile phone so that they could keep contact with their family, children, the outside world, including quick call in case of an emergency etc. But the physiology and psychology of the elderly are very different from the young people, which mainly is reflected in the degradation of vision, hearing, touch, reaction ability, hand strength, text and graphics memory ability and so on. Thus when the elderly people are using the mobile phone there are a lot of inconvenience and special requirements by them and the user experience is also far different form the other age groups. Therefore, in the design of the mobile phone for the older age groups whether the appearance design or the interaction design should reflect on our care for this special group, to improve the usability of the product, to bring convenience for them. This paper firstly studies the physiological and psychological characteristics of the elderly. Then it analyses the behavior characteristics of the elderly in the use of mobile phone and the user experience. Moreover some principles and methods of interaction design for the elderly mo-bile phone are presented in this essay; Additionally through several practical cases of the mobile phone design for the elderly in China and by using the research method such as the user behavior analysis, user survey, Analysis of the availability of products, product evaluation, this paper will analyze and summarize the shortcomings of the current mo-bile phone for the elderly in interaction design. Finally this paper will not only point out the direction of improvement for the elderly mobile interaction design but also provide some useful suggestions and enlightenment for the elderly mobile phone design in the future.

Keywords: Interaction design · The elderly mobile phone · User experience

1 Introduction

The application and development of digitizing have made new demands to mobile phone interaction design and other fields constantly. Mobile phone has become a smart media tool which help people communicate with others release news and express

© Springer International Publishing Switzerland 2015
J. Zhou and G. Salvendy (Eds.): ITAP 2015, Part I, LNCS 9193, pp. 528–536, 2015.
DOI: 10.1007/978-3-319-20892-3_51

personal views in 21th century when it was a kind of ordinary communication tool in the late 20th century. In one hand, Phone as a new media into our lives, it has both information dissemination functions, but also has editing functions of information, its function determines the phone has a very wide range of user groups. In the other hand, with the advent of the era of Chinese society aging, older products, particularly growing demand for mobile phones. How to use information technology to improve the quality of life of older persons to researchers, developers, community managers, market players are needed to solve a problem, it has both a large market potential and economic significance, but also has great social significance and cultural value.

2012 is the Chinese smart-phone outbreak, the use of smart phones have entered the vast majority of Chinese families. Smart-phone is the use of touch-screen technology, the technology is applied to a type of mobile phone handset screen above. The greatest feature is its large screen that you can make to bring visual enjoyment, whether text or images from aspects reflect the characteristics of the big screen. There are currently a lot of smart phones on the market, but it is not suitable for the elderly, through surveys and studies have found that older user experience research has been at a relatively low level. Currently, there are many shortcomings for older smart-phones. Relatively small, such as font, icon is relatively small, there is a complex operation, for main-stream IOS and Android operating systems, elderly or inconvenient to use. Therefore, upgrading older smart-phone interaction design is very important.

This paper focuses on the interaction design of smart phones for the elderly, based on a sense of how to improve the experience of interacting with older smart-phones. To sum up, the paper work and the main results obtained are as follows: 1. based on the relevant literature to define the user experience, interaction design, older smart-phone concept. 2. through research and analysis in the form of user interviews and questionnaires, the results of the interaction of many factors that affect the elderly smart phone design, and described from four users, behavior, technology and scenes. 3. the older design of the smart-phone user experience is divided into three layers, namely, the experience level of human caring, emotional care experience level, transcendent experience level, and targeted research on the characteristics of these three experiences. 4. finally, discusses the strategies and recommendations to enhance the older smart-phone interaction design.

In this paper, the elderly smart-phone for the study, theoretically designed to enrich the user experience as the core of the interaction de-sign study for the integration of technology and art filled with more possibilities bridge erected in practice to businesses and designers to provide a reference.

2 Research Background

With the improvement of people's health and life expectancy of the population, the elderly account for a growing proportion of the population in China in recent years, the concept of healthy aging in-creasing attention from the international community. The United Nations, the healthy aging as a global goal to address aging issues.

International definition of the elderly are not uniform, usually 60 or 65 years of age or older citizens regarded. By the end of 2011, the Chinese elderly population aged 60 and above has reached 185 million people, 13.7 percent of the total population. A longer period of time in the future, the proportion of the elderly population will average 3.2 % growth rate in 2020, the elderly population will reach 248 million, the level of aging will reach 17.17 %, of which, 80 years old and older population will reach 3067 million, accounting for 12.37 % of the elderly population.

At present, China's number of mobile subscribers has more than 960 million, of which smart mobile terminal growth trend showing violent. Chinese smart phone users accounted for 33.9 % share of the global smart phone, smart phone users in China the proportion of people over the age of 45 and gradually increased, as of the end of March 2013, this group accounted for 7.1 %, up 3.5 percentage points higher than the end of 2011. The absolute number of elderly Chinese smart-phones are weak, although in all age groups, but its growth rate is impressive.

According to the middle-aged group of professional survey results reflect, in which the middle-aged group, 60-year-old former people, 85.59 % have a mobile phone, but 62.38 % over a two-year service life; parents of children with a cell phone from 52.25 %, which a large part of the children out of product, 45.38 % of respondents intend to replace parents/buy mobile phones; nearly 69 percent of people think that there is little old mobile phones on the market, so the 67.8 % of the elderly welcomed the phone; the main product information Get through the Internet, 48.48 %, 43.94 % is searching through the store; 70.37 per-cent choose to purchase traditional stores, selected by the network to buy 19.75 %, 9.26 % choose phone orders only.

Looking at the current mobile phone market, although many varieties, but the use of smart phones for the elderly, but very few. At pre-sent, the smart phone market also belong to the elderly incubation period, the low-end market is mainly dominated by older machines, old ordinary phone call can solve the basic needs of the elderly, but can not meet the fashion of the elderly for health, recreation and social demand, smart-phones complex operation, is still the biggest obstacles to the elderly to use.

Due to the aging of bodily functions and the consequent changes in mental aging makes use of smart phones for the elderly constitute a significant obstacle. Due to the aging of the body, slowing the elderly brain reaction speed, sensory organs and organ function decline movement, so they fall on the ability to learn new things, reduced ability to coordinate action, seeing and hearing decline. Overall, the obstacles Chinese elderly smart-phone include: physical, mental, skills, services and economic barriers. Mainly in the following areas: Content smart-phone display text, especially for the elderly seem difficult; smart phone operating mode for the elderly is not very applicable; realize the functions of the smart phone is not intuitive, but to go through learning. In summary, the barriers older people use smart phones mainly on smart-phones and human interaction, to overcome these obstacles, we must take into account the common characteristics of older users, starting from the interactive mode, based on user experience design ideas applied to interaction design for smart phones in. Therefore, from the perspective of the user experience, based on the behavior of the elderly and psychological research, as well as the basis for understanding the context of the elderly to use, to explore the experience of older smart-phone design factors conducive to design a truly meet the elderly are particularly smart-phones important.

3 Literature Review

User experience is the user in the use of a product or a service in an interview, with their own experience built up a feeling both physical and psychological, including.

Field of study abroad in the elderly mobile phone user experience interaction design focused on appearance, function, development and usability, and more and more attention and depth. For example, Sanches Lam (2009) used a variety of methods to confirm the elderly have to use smart phones for learning needs and interests. British Sri Kurniawan (2006) study found that mobile phone design through face problems in the elderly, as well as suitable for the elderly phone "good interface" with the characteristics. Malaysia Hazrina Hassan, Mohd Hairul Nizam Md Nasir (2008) study in the elderly mobile phones mainly in older handsets look and functional design. Wonkyu Park (2011) propose a systematic methodology to derive broad design guidelines for mobile user interfaces, and verified through a case study of the method are summarized in three key factors derived using the method that the general usability criteria, the user interface components and the development of principles and guidelines attributes, user interface designers this method can be used to develop and improve the standard and standard phone interface. Karen Renaud and Judy made in the elderly mobile phone handset design, attention should shortcuts design, streamline operations, user-centric. Hartmut Wandke and Lucienne Blessing designed a set of experiments designed the 42 non-contact interaction actions were a certain number of elderly and young people compared comparison found complete accuracy of these actions elderly and young people and there is not much difference, which is slower than on the completion of young people.

Chinese elderly mobile phone interaction design is still in its infancy. Yang Jingjing (2008) to the elderly mobile phone design, for example, a mobile phone for the elderly and attitude survey of existing multi-function mobile phones is reasonable analysis. Wu Xia, Wu Chao (2009) using the ergonomic and cognitive psychology theory, a design approach to the elderly as the center of the man-machine interface, and make the phone better services for the elderly, people and machines real match. Zhou Yu, Dong Jixian (2009), Yang Yakun (2013) for the multi-functional mobile phones currently on the market phenomenon, the modular design method is introduced to solve the elderly handset design capabilities waste, pointing out the necessity of product function properly designed. User research Peng Jia (2013) to the elderly smart-phone APP interaction design interface for the study, health aides APP interface design, for example, confirmed that the interface design process should always carry out the user experience-oriented, not only have a thorough preliminary design profound insight into the needs of users, the latter should also be repeated user testing. Sun since Tudor (2014) believes that the smart-phone complex operation, is still the biggest factor impeding the elderly to use in intelligence, we should be simplified for the physiological characteristics of the elderly, operating practices, so that the elderly will be able to learn to use short, manufacturers need to overcome the problem.

In summary, the present study abroad interaction design more mature, smart phones for the study of interaction design practice focused, practice and technology development, but there are still problems, interaction design research for the theory to a third-party application design guide books still less. There are currently no systematic a good way to help the elderly mobile phone designers to design development and evaluation, theoretical and applied research on older mobile phones to interact intelligently designed room for improvement there.

4 Research Methods

4.1 The Main Research Methods of this Paper

The first one is the multidisciplinary research method. The content framework of this paper uses interdisciplinary knowledge system interaction design to construct the elderly intelligent mobile phone, enriches the connotation and direction for the traditional interface design. First of all, by using the knowledge of user psychology analysis of hierarchy of needs, the application needs to try to satisfy higher level of the hierarchy of needs to make the user to generate sustained and strong point of application; secondly, try to concept study of the elderly interaction design in intelligent mobile phone using psychology, aesthetics, art design.

The second one is the research method of literature. This paper studies the translation and collected books related to mobile internet interaction design and old product design and design aesthetics, psychology and information, research for the elderly intelligent mobile phone interaction design content, method, characteristic, sorted out and analyzed; the contents of each part system adopts the inductive method for the elderly intelligent mobile phone interaction design re organization; at the same time, through the comparison and analysis of literature, obtains the product user centered design methods, should be closely combined with the analysis of market environment and competitive factors, choose more paths and methods suitable for the elderly intelligent mobile phone interaction design.

The third is to study the method of model. Through analyzing the user needs of the elderly level relationship between the induction intelligent mobile phone applications, the research proposes the user cognition, behavior and emotion model, and emphasizes the designer models need to be as much as possible match the user model, so as to make the application in accordance with the user's psychological expectations.

4.2 The Specific Research Method in this Paper

The first is the user observation and interview method. According to the basic information of the user and a mobile phone with health related topics, user interview, observation method combined with observation of user behavior, to existing products operation, confusion and problems encountered in the process of using record, analyze user cognitive model, behavior habit and other elements.

The second is the qualitative and quantitative research method. Qualitative research is mainly user interview, quantitative research is mainly a questionnaire survey method.

The third is the personas method. According to the interview and questionnaire survey results, user goal definition, including the target task, mental model and behavior pattern.

The fourth is the objective oriented method. In determining the older users put forward the promotion strategy and suggestions on the basis of intelligent mobile phone demand, interaction design, information including hardware and software interaction design and interactive experience design.

5 Result

5.1 Research on the Influence Factors of the Elderly in Intelligent Mobile Phone Interaction Design

The elderly is the target user of the study, they are exactly different from the young in physical, mental health and behavior. So in order to design intelligent mobile phone conforms to the characteristics of the elderly, we must understand the differences between them and the young people first. This difference is one of the key to solve the elder's difficulty in learning using intelligent mobile phone.

The main effect of design of the intelligent mobile phone interaction is the user, behavior, technology, environment and other factors.

User impact factors. Changes in physiology of the elderly is mainly reflected in its perception system. For example, physiological changes in the elderly in the visual aspects mainly: presbyopia, color change, physiological Ming and dark vision changes, the decrease of contrast sensitivity, glare sensitivity of vision and depth perception, smaller weakened etc.

The behavior influence factor. The old man's hand is the most important part for the operation of the mobile phone, but the hand of each joint with age aging gradually become rigid, inflexible, maybe even a trembling.

Technical factors. The elder people is lack of knowledge of science and technology, they do not quite understand some of the application and proper nouns in the language to describe the function, in the process of using intelligent mobile phone will usually appear confusion, frustration.

Scene influence factors. When the aged used interactive scene changes, elder people may feel unable to adapt to the changes, and even affect the use of mobile phone.

5.2 The Elderly Intelligent Mobile Phone Interaction Design User Experience Level Model Construction

Interaction design of mobile phone is mainly to solve the interaction process and information architecture and design, including menu design, hardware interface definitions and interactive design documentation. The author will be elderly intelligent mobile phone interactive user experience design experience, emotion experience, care for humanity transcending experience level model.

The first human caring experience level. On the basic of interaction design principles, intelligent mobile phone for the elderly to humanity is: simplicity, respect, friendly user feedback, consistency. One is simple. Interactive design of the elderly a smart phone interface: no need to learn, one will see two seconds of wait time, operating within step three. The two is to respect the user. In the real life of common element applied to the elderly the Smart phone application interface design. Three is the friendly feedback. To provide the elderly immediate and positive feedback, according to different circumstances difference design. Four is the consistency. Consistent visual, elderly intelligent mobile phone function, information architecture, operation mode. For example: the expression of interface function should also try to match the elderly cultural knowledge, so that the elderly can quickly understand and operate.

Beyond the experience level again. After investigation and analysis, the characteristics of intelligent mobile phone that older users is one of the most critical is the personification of remote interactive, intelligent, caring. The first one is personification. For natural interaction through language, gestures, facial expressions, gaze and body language. The second one is the remote interaction. With the intelligent mobile phone based mobile intelligent terminal, in a whole new way to interact. The third one is the smart care. Through the intelligent mobile phone positioning real-time understanding of the position of the elderly and health.

5.3 Elderly Smart-Phone Interaction Design and Recommend Strategies to Enhance

Elderly smart-phone interaction design is to allow the elderly more quickly, simply and efficiently operate the phone. On the one hand we realize the function; on the other hand we must also get pleasure visual, auditory, tactile and psychological. For example ITT Easy 5, Jitterbug Touch, Life Plus, Doro HandleEasy 330GSM, Emporia Connect, Raku Raku (F-12D), NOKIA X (RM-980), Hisense E360M, obooy EA508 elderly and other smart phones. It includes hardware and software interaction design, information design and interaction design interactive experience. Its promotion strategy and recommendations are as follows:

The interaction design of hardware is the need to pay attention to the following aspects. The first is handset size. In determining the scale of older phones, designer ergonomic reference to the definition of the best features of size: the size of the best features of the human dimension percentile = + + psychological correction function to correct the amount of volume. The sizes of the phone within $110 \times 84 \times 18$ mm, the elderly in order to meet the requirements of scale. The Second is the key size. The size of the older phone keys, thumb finger widest, ac-cording to this size, the higher the accuracy of the size of the phone keys, take fifty percentile: 21 mm. Hand of freedom has a certain range of factors in this regard attention should be designed in older phones. The last is volume. According to the previous analysis and the elderly affect the physical and psychological characteristics, when designing the sound, not only to consider whether to listen carefully to the elderly, but also need to consider the impact of the size of the sound on vision. Set the size of the sound into an adjustable mode, the maximum volume can be designed to 70 db, 70 db above may cause damage to hearing on the elderly. While ensuring clear sound clear, gentle not harsh, especially voice prompts operation, should bring clear message reminders and feedback to the elderly.

About software interaction design should pay attention to the following aspects one simple smart-phone. Have the following functions: First Call functions: designed to loud and clear, the best talk in a noisy environment also affected the pattern. Second Ring features: ringing loud and in accordance with the elderly hobby, it is best oldies and classic drama. Third, the text input function: the key input method based, voice or handwriting supplement. Pinyin input method selection or stroke input method. Fourth Display: Screen color soft and easy to identify, soft interface font larger. The second is in the end smart-phones. In addition to these functions, but also includes the following four functions: First radio function: can receive more channels, the effect is more clear and better. Second alarm: Tone big, it is best voice broadcast to remind time and content. Third, the memo: Voice memo reminding content, such as rationing medi-cation such matters. Fourth Call Alert: voice reminder, speed to slow, soft and clear voice. Set caller photo display. The third is about the high-end intelligent mo-bile phone. This phone addition to the above features, but also includes the following three functions: First, the entertainment features: Set chess and mahjong games, MP3, for old people listen to music, theater and entertainment purposes. Second, the calculator function: designed to be simple model suggested by way of handwriting input, and can deliver results fast, easy and convenient to use when computing for the elderly. Third, GPRS positioning function: to determine the location of the elderly, in time to help families find lost, lost in the elderly. Other features: health care software, physical exercise software, flashlight function.

Several aspects of information interaction design, one reasonable arrangement density information of the project. Need to design a suitable way to highlight the key information that is adjustable font and icon arrangement. Second, should use the user's language to convey information, rather than the language technology. Third, make the font size, color, icon design focus on symbolic. Fourth boot animation, consistent detail and intangible elements of the framework. Fifth avoid the same element that contains too much information.

On improving the experience of interaction design has the following strategies and suggestions. First let older users control interactive process, "Next", "Finish" button. Secondly, Interactive experience de-signs to have a certain commonality and intelli-gence, to help or hints for older users operating role. Third icons, multimedia design, detail design and additional features designed for older users to experience the value, effectively enhance the experience degrees. Fourth visual design, for example, switch machine animation, interface display effects. Fifth older users consider the privacy of information, providing effective protection mechanisms, such as a fingerprint to unlock, unlock graphics, digital unlocking.

6 Conclusions and Discussion

Elderly smart-phone user experience based on interaction design is to design user-desired goal, to meet user demand for the product of emotional experience.

Elderly smart-phone interaction design focuses on simplicity, simple interface, easy to identify with buttons to ensure older people can be spotted in any case to see stability.

Emotional experience of the elderly should be based on its function, given the emotional content of products, and through the "form of love," allowing users to feel a certain emotional satisfaction. "Emotion-ally moving" is the key to emotional expe-rience, the taste of the appearance, intimate functions, is the key to enhance the emotional experience of older smart-phone design.

Elderly smart-phone is necessary to meet the child needs for care and love their parents, but also realize the emotional communication between parents and children, especially in the strong emotional appeal when parents participate in patency between the old and the phone, the phone with their children, is very important.

Elderly smart-phone design study investigated sensory effects not only the elderly, but also to fully relate to a specific mobile application interaction processes, and other aspects of experience, complete mobile Internet ecosystem is intelligent hardware, operating systems and third-party applications the composition, of a portion of the adverse experience will affect the user experience across the elderly.

In short, the elderly smart-phone user experience, interaction de-sign, based on the requirements in the design is closely integrated with the elderly, the elderly needed attention, understanding the elderly emotion. For the elderly in order to meet the basic requirements on product functionality, interactivity and focus on the emotional expe-rience of the elderly to the technical support, the closer to the man-machine from design better and more humane interaction works.

References

China mobile internet user behavior research report 2014 - iresearch. http://report.iresearch.cn/2163.HTML

Sanches, l., Chung, W.: Understanding the need of mobile ICT learning as an elderly learning tool. Int. Emerg. Technol. Learn. 435–440 (2009)

Mohd H.N.M. Nasir, Hazrina Hassan., Jomhari, N.: The use of mobile phones by elderly: a study in Malaysia perspectives. ACM SIGACCESS Accessibility and computing. Issue 92, pp. 77–86. September 2008

Park, W.: A factor combination approach to developing style guides for mobile phone user interface. Int. J. Ind. Ergon. **41**, 192–199 (2011)

Jingjing, Y.: Discussion on the design of multi function of product – talking the old people's mobile phone design an example. Des. Art **100**(8), 211–213 (2008)

Xia, W., Chao, W.: Function matchiong analysis and prospect of the human computert system for the old people's mobile phone. In: China Occupational Safety and Health Association in 2009 academic annual meeting, pp. 67–68 (2009)

Yu, Z., Jixian, D.: Further study on the mobile phone with the old man mobile phone an example. Des. Art **112**(6), 134–135 (2009)

Jia, P.: Research on interactive design of the APP interface of the old smart phone based on the user experience. East China University of Science and technology (2013)

Ziduo, S.: Thinking about the design of the old people's smart phone. J. Hefei Univ. (Social Science Edition), 67–69 (2014)

Author Index